TEMPUS
SPEEDWAY
YEARBOOK
2005

TEMPUS
SPEEDWAY
YEARBOOK
2005

edited by

ROBERT BAMFORD

TEMPUS

Dedicated to the memory of Colin Hill

First published 2005

Tempus Publishing Limited
The Mill, Brimscombe Port,
Stroud, Gloucestershire, GL5 2QG
www.tempus-publishing.com

British Library Cataloguing in Publication Data.
A catalogue record for this book is available from the British Library.

ISBN 0 7524 3396 2

Typesetting by Liz Rudderham
Origination by Tempus Publishing Limited
Printed in Great Britain

CONTENTS

ACKNOWLEDGEMENTS **6**
INTRODUCTION **7**
ABBREVIATIONS **12**

SKY BET ELITE LEAGUE 2004 **13**

Racing Diary of the Season 15
Sky Bet Elite League Table 28
Play-Offs 28
Knock-Out Cup 28

Arena-Essex AF Stocktaking Hammers 30
Belle Vue Aces 34
Coventry Buildbase Bees 39
Eastbourne Eagles 43
Ipswich Evening Star Witches 48
Oxford Silver Machine 52
Peterborough ASL Freight Panthers 57
Poole RIAS Pirates 61
Pebley Beach Swindon Robins 66
Wolverhampton Parrys International Wolves 73

PREMIER LEAGUE 2004 **79**

Racing Diary of the Season 81
Premier League Table 100
Young Shield 100
Premier Trophy (South) Table 101
Premier Trophy (North) Table 101
Knock-Out Cup 102

Berwick Elm Bank Bandits 103
Edinburgh Fulfilment Factory Monarchs 108
Exeter Falcons 114
Glasgow Travel Inn Tigers 120
Hull BHK Vikings 126
Isle of Wight Wightlink Islanders 132
King's Lynn Money Centre Stars 137
Newcastle Tap & Spile North Shields Diamonds 142
Newport Wasps 147
Reading Euphony Racers 153
Rye House Silver Ski Rockets 159
Sheffield Pirtek Tigers 164
Somerset Orchard FM Rebels 170
Stoke Easy-Rider Potters 174
Workington Thomas Armstrong Comets 180

CONFERENCE LEAGUE 2004 **185**

Racing Diary of the Season 187
Conference League Table 201
Conference Trophy Table 201
Knock-Out Cup 201

Armadale AWG Dale Devils 203
Boston N.C. Williams & Son Insurance Barracuda-Braves 207
Buxton Hitmen 211
Carmarthen Dragons 216
Coventry DLG Cougars 220
King's Lynn Starlets 223
Mildenhall Superior Exteriors Fen Tigers 227
Newcastle Ultrafast Gems 233
Newport GMB Mavericks 236
Oxford Silver Machine Academy 240
Rye House Elmside Raiders 243
Sheffield Pirtek Prowlers 247
Sittingbourne Set Lighting Crusaders 250
Stoke Easy-Rider Spitfires 253
Team Artdeans Swindon Sprockets 257
Weymouth Haven Wildcats 260
Wimbledon GMB Dons 267

MAJOR BRITISH MEETINGS 2004 **273**

GRAND PRIX 2004 **303**

MAJOR INTERNATIONAL MEETINGS 2004 **333**

RIDER INDEX 2004 **357**

ACKNOWLEDGEMENTS

Following the success of the 2004 Yearbook, I was encouraged to produce another volume by Holly Bennion and James Howarth at Tempus Publishing. As ever, this would not be at all possible without the great network of enthusiasts scattered around the country and, in particular, I would like to thank the following people who have helped in various way throughout the season: Ian Adam, Nick Barber, Richard Crowley, Jeff Davies, Gordon Day, Chris Durno, Frank Ebdon, Neil Evans, Matt Ford, Colin Goddard, Mike Golding, Mike Hinves, Roger Hulbert, Mike Hunter, Tracy Irwin, Jeremy Jackson, Tony Jackson, Dick Jarvis, Pam Johnson, Roger Last, Tony Lethbridge, Dennis McCleary, Charles McKay, Nigel Meakins, Jayne Moss, Peter Oakes, Robert Peasley, Robbie Perks, Lee Poole, Andy Povey, Geoff Ridsdale, Laurence Rogers, Alun Rossiter, John Sampford, Chezza Satchell, Martin Satchell, Glynn Shailes, George Sheridan, Jan Staechmann, Dave Stallworthy, Barry Stephenson, Norrie Tait, Kev Tew, Steve Thorn, Peter Toogood, Malcolm Vasey, Barry Wallace, Bob Wayte, Bryn Williams and Richard Williams. I am particularly grateful to Matt Jackson for help with numerous dates of birth and indeed, to all the riders who were more than helpful with similar information when asked. Statistical genius Mike Moseley has kept me on the straight and narrow as far as the accuracy of averages is concerned and I am deeply indebted for his time and trouble in the cross-checking of my figures.

I am also grateful for the assistance of various photographers, so many thanks indeed to the following for expertly producing all the images contained herein: main photographic content by Mike Patrick (www.mike-patrick.com) but special thanks to the following photographers for their help with supplying team photographs: Ian Adam (Glasgow), Les Aubrey (Carmarthen and Swindon Sprockets), Steve Brock (Newcastle Gems), Ken Carpenter (Sheffield Tigers and Prowlers), Ian Charles (Buxton, Coventry Cougars and King's Lynn Starlets), Jeff Davies (Coventry Bees), Dave Fairbrother (Wimbledon), Eddie Garvey (Stoke Potters), Phil Hilton (Boston Barracuda-Braves), Tony Jackson (Workington), Hywel Lloyd (Newport Wasps) and Graham Platten (Berwick). The internet has also proved invaluable in helping to keep up with everything in the speedway world, so grateful thanks to all the webmasters for doing such a marvellous job. I also wish to pay tribute to *Speedway Star* magazine, which has been an excellent and invaluable reference point. Finally, for guidance purposes, please note that in the calculation of rider averages, any tactical ride or tactical substitute points are recorded as those normally given for the relevant finishing position, e.g. 1st = 3 points, 2nd = 2 points and 3rd = 1 point.

I trust this publication will provide a useful reference, as well as rekindling many happy memories of the 2004 season.

Robert Bamford
31 October 2004

INTRODUCTION

A winter of change began with Terry Russell buying out Peter Toogood at Swindon and immediately taking the Robins back into the Sky Bet Elite League. The top flight was soon swelled further when his brother Ronnie Russell took the opportunity of elevating his Arena-Essex outfit, thereby giving the league a more acceptable ten-team line-up. A new grading system was introduced to help the two new sides make the jump into the Elite League and, although this was average-based, it certainly had the effect of levelling out the team strengths. There were casualties, however, with riders like Billy Hamill, Piotr Protasiewicz, Peter Karlsson and Jaroslaw Hampel missing out on a British berth. The promoters had to start somewhere though, and with hopes that more sides can be brought into the higher echelon, there is every chance that some of the missing stars can make a return to these shores.

The traditional-style tactical substitute was done away with, being replaced by the formerly called golden double from a fifteen-metre handicap. Each team was permitted one such ride per meeting should they be 8 points in arrears after the fourth heat. All teams were also allowed to have two so-called tactical rides (formerly the tactical joker), whereby a nominated rider could gain double points from the gate. Again, this only came into play if a side was 8 points down and certainly made for some interesting scorelines: there weren't too many normal-sounding 50-40 or 46-44 results to be seen. Another change saw the abandonment of the unsatisfactory British League Cup after just one season. The competition had been a good idea inasmuch as it allowed Elite and Premier League teams to race against each other. However, in practice it was regarded as something of a joke on the terraces, with the rules regarding the make-up of teams being too 'flexible'.

One innovation was that every Elite League track had an air safety barrier installed to help with rider safety. All the riders at each club happily agreed to race one home and one away match at no cost in order to defray the expense associated with this project and, as such, a series of Air-Tek Challenge matches took place. The scheme was a real step forward and hopefully the Premier League will implement it in due course.

The 2004 season will, there is no doubt whatsoever, be remembered for being one of the worst weather-wise for many a long year, with Belle Vue being particularly unlucky. Seemingly, week in, week out, the Aces' promotion battled with the elements and many of their scheduled fixtures were postponed, with one Elite League match never actually ridden. It was quite understandable that promoter John Perrin felt enough was enough and put the club up for sale. As the final drafts of this publication were completed, it was announced that Kidderminster businessman Tony Mole, who already owned both Workington and Mildenhall, had concluded a deal to purchase the Manchester outfit and that Ian Thomas would leave the Cumbrian club to manage Belle Vue's fortunes. However, it wasn't all doom and gloom with the Aces during 2004, as their number-one rider, Australian Jason Crump, finally captured the World Championship. 'Crumpie' had been there or thereabouts for some time, but his luck finally held and the crown was his. It is hard to believe that his triumph was the first by an Australian since the great Jack Young rode to his second title way back in 1952. Getting the first one is always the toughest and there is now no reason why 'Crumpie' shouldn't add further successes to his record.

Poole, the 2003 Elite League Champions, again went to the top of the standings early on and parked themselves there for the duration. The new grading system robbed the Pirates of Leigh Adams and the Dryml brothers, but the go-ahead promotional team at Wimborne Road are not people who let the grass grow under their feet. Having appeared mainly in the British League Cup the previous season, the sensational Brazilian-Swede Antonio Lindback came into the line-up on a full-time basis and, in the early weeks of the campaign while riding at reserve, he was simply sensational. When he moved up to the main body of the team, he remained a solid scorer. Such is his ability and rate of progress that he is World Championship material if ever one saw it. However, it wasn't just Lindback that made Poole the place to be on speedway evenings. Jason Lyons joined the 'Pirate Ship' at the start of the season on loan from Belle Vue, but struggled to find form and was eventually released to Premier League Newcastle, where he immediately got back to his very best. To fill the gap, Poole signed Matej Ferjan and from day one the Slovenian proved to be an outstanding success. The Pirates went on to retain the League Championship, beating Wolverhampton in the Play-Off final and they also again won the Knock-Out Cup, with an aggregate victory over a gallant Ipswich side. For good measure, Bjarne Pedersen scooped the Elite League Riders' Championship on his home track, with teammate Ryan Sullivan finishing as runner-up.

Having mentioned Sullivan, the Australian was another Poole signing when Tony Rickardsson quit the British racing scene. Such a loss could have finished most sides, but not the Pirates. Sullivan had initially missed out on a team spot due to the grading system, but he quickly agreed to join the South Coast club and proved to be an excellent acquisition. True, he didn't record the sort of scores that Rickardsson did, but he was a more-than-useful heat leader and gave the Pirates strength in depth. Speedway supporters, and those at Poole especially, must now wait and see what the rules will do to their side in 2005. After all, it is quite an achievement to take back-to-back league and cup titles with an almost completely rebuilt side for the second attempt.

At the other end of the league table were Coventry, who lost Billy Hamill, Lee Richardson and Ryan Fisher under the new system. Richardson and Fisher got themselves fixed up with Peterborough and Oxford respectively, but Hamill found himself out in the cold and was unable to find a berth within the rules. It was a great pity that such a rider, who has given much entertainment over the years, should find himself in this position, but then again, there always seems to be someone who misses out. There was at least one bright spot at Brandon, however, since the Bees gave an opportunity to sixteen-year-old Dane Morten Risager and the boy turned out to be pure stardust. Sure enough, he had meetings where points were hard to come by, and riding on away tracks for the first time was difficult. Nevertheless, he was always professionally equipped and was a quick learner. He must have a real future in the sport and his warming-up routine was well worth seeing prior to every meeting. Coventry also signed Chris Harris from defunct Premier League side Trelawny and although the 'Bomber' was expected to fill a heat-leader role, in reality it was asking a bit too much. Bees' boss Colin Pratt thought the grading given to Harris was high, but nothing could be done by officialdom and the Cornishman had to do things the hard way. There can be no doubt that what he learned should stand him in good stead for 2005.

Bryan Yarrow, the young American, was another pre-season signing for Coventry, but unfortunately he was out of his depth and returned home when the side was rebuilt at the lower end midway through the year. Initially, Pole Tomasz Piszcz (who had begun the campaign with Peterborough) was brought in, with Russian Sergei Darkin and German Martin Smolinski following. Darkin was very much a success and had he been in from the start, he would surely have helped the side to enjoy a much better time of it. Piszcz tried hard meanwhile, probably too hard in reality, and suffered some nasty injuries. Based with a team where he could take his time and learn the ropes, he could doubtless develop into a more than useful scorer. When it comes to sheer professionalism, few youngsters are better than Smolinksi, who arrived with superb equipment and his own publicity officer. If the Bees can retain his services and strengthen the heat-leader berths, Smolinski, like Morten Risager, could be a real winner.

The addition of Swindon and Arena-Essex made the Elite League far more interesting. Leigh Adams returned to the Robins' nest after a long time away and was a monumental compiler of points, both at home and away. Former rider Alun Rossiter was installed as promoter and did a good job, while still learning about life on the other side of the fence. Cheery Dane Charlie Gjedde would have been even better but for a broken right ankle which kept him out of the saddle for a ten-week period. Peter Ljung scored much better after he left Eastbourne, but prior to that, there was great sadness at the club when promising young Pole Rafal Kurmanski took his own life in a hotel room in his native land. As was to be expected, this hit the Robins very hard indeed. Swindon also had to cope with almost as many rained-off meetings as Belle Vue, but despite all their problems, they soldiered on and sixth place in the final table could be regarded as an achievement; and of course, they did pocket the Elite League Pairs Championship, held on their own Blunsdon raceway.

Ipswich, Oxford and Eastbourne all played a real part in making the Elite League a success and all enjoyed the highs that the sport can provide. At Eastbourne for instance, the fans of the Eagles thrilled to the 'new' David Norris. 'Floppy' was honest enough to admit his old lifestyle wasn't compatible with speedway and he firmly put the sport first. The result was amazing, for he fulfilled all the promise he'd shown in seasons past and, as well as proving to be an outstanding club captain, he became a regular choice for England team manager Neil Middleditch.

Wolverhampton chased Poole all the way for the League Championship and their semi-final fixture against Ipswich for the right to meet the Pirates in the Play-Off final was an absolute cracker. So too were the subsequent matches against Poole, when the Dorseteers raised their game to beat the Wolves in both legs. Sam Ermolenko had an excellent final fling, if indeed it was his last year of domestic racing, while young Swede Fredrik Lindgren pointed the way forward. Following an early injury to Daniel Nermark, the Wolverhampton management decided to stick with the rider-replacement facility to cover his absence and while this perhaps put added pressure on the remaining teamsters, it certainly didn't show in their season-long efforts to catch Poole. With a rebuilt line-up, Peterborough endured a year of difficulty, mainly due to injuries. Problems were also reported with the availability of their circuit at the East of England Showground, with the result that their match versus Oxford was actually raced at Arena-Essex in order to complete their 'home' fixtures before the cut-off point for the Play-Offs.

In the Premier League, there was no doubting that the success story of the year were Hull, who, like their Elite League cousins Poole, won everything there was to win. What a rags-to-riches story the Vikings enjoyed! At the end of 2003, they were bottom of the league and faced possible closure. Things happily turned around when a new promoter, Paul Hodder, was prepared to take on the club and he signed Eric Boocock to manage affairs. What a truly magnificent appointment this turned out to be. 'Booey' made some good acquisitions and although they wouldn't have generally been described as top stars, they were solid scorers who had a will to win. With him also came his special brand of Boocock magic: the ability to create a good team spirit, while convincing his charges that they could go out and beat anyone, anywhere, anytime. An excellent motivator, Booey must be one of the finest managers in the sport and Hull's winning of the League Championship, Knock-Out Cup and Young Shield must have given him tremendous satisfaction. It must have been a very great shock to all those connected with Hull Speedway, when, after the season had finished, Boocock resigned his post. He appeared to want a good rest, claiming he'd often worked nearly a twenty-four-hour day and travelled thousands of miles in the cause of the team. No-one doubts that he deserves a break, but it is hoped that he isn't lost to the sport, since he still has much to offer.

There were other excellent teams in the Premier League and Reading boasted a very attractive side, as did both Workington and the Isle of Wight. Matej Zagar and Danny Bird formed a powerful spearhead for the Racers, while the signing of Craig Boyce gave the Islanders some real punch. Up in Cumbria, the Comets boasted the very best rider in the entire league in Simon Stead, who unfortunately had a period on the sidelines through a broken heel. However, upon recovery, he showed that he'd lost none of his dash or skill and surely the next stage in his career must be a full-time move into the higher echelons of Elite League racing. Who knows, but with the boss of Workington also now being in charge at Belle Vue, maybe his future has been mapped out? Only time will tell. Sheffield would certainly have fared better had they not lost skipper Sean Wilson to a serious neck injury in Joe Screen's Testimonial at Belle Vue on 2 May. That put the popular York-born racer out of action for the rest of the year and, as the season moved into its final lap, Somerset's Matt Read suffered very serious injuries in a World Long-track Championship round at Morizes, France. Only towards the end of October was he able to return to the UK and everyone looks forward to seeing him make a full recovery in due course.

It was just an average season 'up north', with neither Scottish side experiencing much success, although Edinburgh did possess a most exciting rider in Australian teenager Rory Schlein, who also doubled-up with Belle Vue. The 'Roo Boy' was one of those rare riders who could hold down a heat-leader berth in either sphere of the British scene and his ability really showed in the Elite League Riders' Championship at Poole on 17 October. Revealing outstanding track-craft as the Belle Vue representative, he amassed 12 points and qualified direct to the final. Although he was unable to improve on fourth place in that final, he had clearly proved that the Elite League held no fears for him. As this publication went to print, several of the top-flight clubs were in the bidding for his services. Who can blame them? It begs the question 'what would have been said had the talented Aussie won the prestigious meeting at Poole?' With Schlein moving on to pastures new, it does look as though Edinburgh will have a major team-building exercise to complete in 2005, if, as has been reported, Peter Carr and Frede Schott retire.

Newcastle took the unwanted wooden spoon and only the move of Jason Lyons saved them from even more defeats than they suffered. Many times after his arrival, it was a case of the Australian versus the opposition. It is to be hoped that with his confidence restored, he can return to the Elite League, where he still has much to offer.

As the season drew to its close, there was great sadness when Exeter promoter Colin Hill passed away after a two-year battle with cancer. He had been in charge of the Falcons for twenty years, keeping the club going through thick and thin in the best possible way of always working to a budget. He is a hard act to follow and will be very much missed, not just by everyone connected with Exeter, but by speedway folk the length and breadth of Britain.

Mildenhall cleaned up in the Conference League sector of racing, in much the same way as Poole had dominated in the Elite and Hull in the Premier. Graham Drury, the Fen Tigers' boss, always tried to ensure that a winning combination was assembled and his side seldom failed to come up with the goods. Drury and his wife, Denise, were named as the new promotional team at Workington at the season's close, in place of the Belle Vue-bound Ian Thomas, so it seems there will be a new face in charge at West Row in 2005.

In general, it is good to report that the Conference League has continued to grow in stature and new names, hoping to make good in the sport, are always cropping up. That is proof that the league is doing its job and it is important that is does so too. Other countries, notably Sweden and Denmark, have always encouraged young talent from an early age and with Peter Oakes organizing the British Under-15 Championship, as well as managing the Great Britain Under-21s, the future is looking brighter for our home-grown youth.

In addition to the league, there was also the Conference Trophy, which comprised seven teams. Thirteen sides competed in the league, with Buxton, Mildenhall, Weymouth and Wimbledon taking part in both competitions. Of the other teams, Armadale, Coventry, King's Lynn, Newcastle, Newport, Oxford, Rye House, Sheffield, Stoke and Swindon all staged racing at either Premier or Elite League level as well. All of this means that the future is being taken on board by the various promoters, which can only be for the good of speedway in the years to come.

While on the subject of the Conference League, spare a thought for Mark Burrows of Wimbledon. 'Buzz' has been around for a few years now and his experience is a big help to the Dons in many ways. He was awarded a Testimonial in 2004, but unfortunately the dreadful weather that lashed these shores throughout the year meant that three attempts to hold his special meeting ended in postponement. Let's hope the mega-popular Buzz has better luck in 2005.

Glynn Shailes and Robert Bamford
31 October 2004

ABBREVIATIONS

GENERAL

AL	Amateur League
BSPA	British Speedway Promoters Association
CL	Conference League
CLKOC	Conference League Knock-Out Cup
CT	Conference Trophy
DNA	Did Not Arrive
DNR	Did Not Ride
EL	Elite League
ELKOC	Elite League Knock-Out Cup
FIM	Fédération Internationale de Motorcyclisme
KOC	Knock-Out Cup
PL	Premier League
PLKOC	Premier League Knock-Out Cup
R/R	Rider Replacement
YS	Young Shield

AVERAGES TABLES

Mts	Matches
Rds	Rides
Pts	Points
Bon	Bonus Points
Tot	Total Points
Avge	Average
Max	Maximums

SCORE TABLES

DNA	Did Not Arrive
DNR	Did Not Ride
(R)	Replay
R/R	Rider Replacement
<u>15 (5)</u>	Maximum (applies to any underlined total)

LEAGUE TABLES

Mts	Matches
Won	Won
Drn	Drawn
Lst	Lost
For	For
Agn	Against
Pts	Points
Bon	Bonus Points
Tot	Total Points

RACE POSITIONS

ex	Excluded
f	Fell
n.s.	Non-starter
rem	Remounted
ret	Retired

RACE SCORES TABLES

F	Fell
M	Excluded, 2 minutes
n	Non-starter
R	Retired
X	Excluded
T	Excluded, tapes

SKY BET ELITE LEAGUE
2004

RACING DIARY OF THE SEASON

MARCH

10 On a bitterly cold night, Poole make an early start to the campaign, defeating elevated Swindon 51-39 in the first leg of the Champagne Stakes.

11 Swindon's much-publicized opener is curtailed after just two heats due to heavy snowfall, with the Robins holding an 8-4 lead over Poole in the return Champagne Stakes encounter at the time.

12 Oxford's attractive challenge match versus Coventry is called off early in the morning, due to the effects of snow. The day's other meeting between Peterborough and Ipswich in the Air-Tek Challenge also falls victim to a waterlogged track.

15 Heavy rainfall washes out Belle Vue's Air-Tek Challenge against Swindon minutes before the scheduled start time. Wolverhampton gain a hard-fought 49-44 success over Coventry in the Air-Tek Challenge, with Mikael Max netting a faultless full house (15).

17 Poole defeat Oxford 51-44 in a tense Air-Tek Challenge fixture at Wimborne Road; the win clinched by a penultimate heat 5-1 from Antonio Lindback and Daniel Davidsson. Belle Vue's swiftly rearranged Air-Tek Challenge versus Swindon provides plenty of thrills, as the Aces just edge home 48-47.

18 Ipswich come from behind to post a 49-44 Air-Tek Challenge success over Peterborough in the season's opener at Foxhall Heath. A 52-42 second-leg Air-Tek Challenge victory gives Coventry an aggregate win against Midlands rivals Wolverhampton, with Billy Janniro bagging a fine 15-point maximum for the Bees. Swindon play host to Belle Vue in the return Air-Tek Challenge match and, despite heavy afternoon rain, the Blunsdon raceway serves up a marvellous meeting, with the Robins impressively racing to a 54-40 victory.

19 A waterlogged track ensures Oxford again fail to start their home programme, with their Air-Tek Challenge versus Poole called off at lunchtime.

20 Eastbourne's eagerly awaited first home meeting against Arena-Essex in the Air-Tek Challenge is washed out by heavy rain in mid-afternoon.

22 Terrific Knock-Out Cup action at Monmore Green sees Wolverhampton edge to a 50-43 first-leg win over a dogged Swindon septet. The day's other Knock-Out Cup tie between Belle Vue and Coventry is lost to a waterlogged circuit following heavy Manchester rain.

24 Arena-Essex edge a thrilling encounter 48-47 against Eastbourne in the Air-Tek Challenge, as they celebrate their return to top-flight speedway. Poole begin their defence of the Knock-Out Cup, comfortably defeating Peterborough 58-37 in a first-leg tie at Wimborne Road.

25 Adverse weather again plays havoc as Swindon's Knock-Out Cup second-leg tie versus Wolverhampton is postponed shortly after 5 p.m., due to a saturated track. Greg Hancock's 15-point maximum against his former club Coventry paves the way for Oxford's 49-43 challenge match success at Brandon. Ipswich gain a first-leg 51-42 victory over Eastbourne in a hard-fought Knock-Out Cup match at Foxhall Heath.

26 Oxford overcome an early deficit to beat Arena-Essex 47-46 in the Knock-Out Cup at Cowley.

27 Eastbourne suffer a 46-44 reverse at the hands of visiting Arena-Essex, with Kelvin Tatum bagging an unbeaten 12 points for the Hammers. The win gives the Purfleet side an aggregate 94-91 victory in the Air-Tek Challenge.

28 Ipswich complete an aggregate Air-Tek Challenge win over Peterborough, thanks to a 50-46 success at the East of England Showground.

29 The Elite League campaign gets underway, with the Sky Sports cameras at Arena-Essex to witness visiting reigning Champions Poole triumph 47-43, with Tony Rickardsson posting a full 15-pointer. Further league action sees Belle Vue lose 49-41 at home to Ipswich, while Wolverhampton claim a 53-40 success against Oxford, despite Greg Hancock's tactical-ride-enhanced 18-point maximum for the Silver Machine outfit.

31 Poole end the month in style by gaining a 52-40 league victory over Arena-Essex, with Tony Rickardsson bagging a paid maximum (14+1).

APRIL

1 Swindon's appalling luck with the weather continues, as their opening Elite League match versus Eastbourne is terminated amid pouring rain after nine heats, with the Robins holding a 33-22 advantage. Coventry suffer a 54-42 reverse to visiting Belle Vue in the Knock-Out Cup, as Jason Crump bags a five-ride maximum for the Aces. Ipswich defeat Poole 50-43 in a thrilling league encounter at Foxhall Heath.

2 Oxford lead all the way to register a 52-43 victory over Wolverhampton in super league fare at Cowley. Tony Rickardsson equals the East of England Showground track record, as Peterborough lose 46-44 to visiting Poole in the Knock-Out Cup, with the holders comfortably going through on aggregate.

3 The return league match between Eastbourne and Swindon is depressingly curtailed due to heavy rainfall after seven heats, with the Eagles leading 25-17 at the time.

5 For a third time in four weeks, Belle Vue's Monday night fixture is washed away by rain, this time with the eagerly awaited league clash versus Poole halted by the elements. Before the Sky cameras, Oxford claim a narrow 50-45 success against Ipswich in a no-holds-barred League confrontation. Mikael Max remains undefeated (15), as Wolverhampton net a 53-39 league win over Peterborough.

7 Thanks to a final shared heat, Arena-Essex edge home 48-46 against a spirited Oxford side in the Knock-Out Cup, in the process progressing through on aggregate by a single point.

8 Swindon finally complete their first Elite League fixture, defeating old rivals Oxford 54-42 at Blunsdon, with Leigh Adams ripping to a superb 15-point maximum. On-song Ipswich are always ahead at Coventry and eventually emerge with a 49-45 league success.

9 It's a noon start at Poole for a Bank Holiday league fixture versus Eastbourne, with the Pirates always in command as they win 52-44. Early afternoon fare sees Ipswich complete a quick-fire double over Coventry, as their 54-41 victory takes them to the top of the Elite League standings. Thanks to astute use of the tactical rules, Peterborough overcome a 10-point deficit to snatch a dramatic 47-46 success in a hugely entertaining Elite League match against Arena-Essex. Poole repeat their earlier triumph over Eastbourne, winning 50-40 in the return league match at Arlington to leapfrog Ipswich at the head of the table. Further league activity sees Jason Crump scorch to a 15-point maximum, as Belle Vue grab a 50-42 success against Wolverhampton. Leigh Adams romps to another full house (15) for Swindon, but his efforts can't prevent Oxford from gaining a 49-44 league victory in a full-blooded local derby at Cowley.

11 Swindon host the Suzuki-sponsored Elite League Pairs Championship in front of a huge attendance. The Blunsdon raceway produces twenty-four heats of super-quick racing, with the Robins duo of Leigh Adams and Charlie Gjedde eventually triumphing ahead of Belle Vue's Jason Crump and Joe Screen.

12 Midday Easter Monday league action at the East of England Showground results in a 51-42 triumph for Peterborough against Coventry. The return fixture at Brandon sees Coventry gain revenge courtesy of a 53-42 scoreline. Ipswich jump back into pole position in the Elite League thanks to a hard-fought 48-42 victory at Wolverhampton.

14 Mark Loram grabs a maximum (15), as Arena-Essex only just hold off a spirited Peterborough side to win a pulsating league match 47-46. Poole overcome Wolverhampton 53-43, regaining top spot in the Elite League table as a result.

15 Leigh Adams' sensational form continues, as he plunders another full 15-pointer and leads Swindon to a 52-40 Elite League success over high-flying Ipswich.

16 Oxford beat Poole 48-45 in the second leg of the Air-Tek Challenge, but it's the Pirates who succeed on aggregate. Belle Vue are never headed as they record a 48-42 victory at Peterborough in the Sky Bet Elite League.

17 With unbeaten tallies from Adam Shields (15), Joonas Kylmakorpi (12+3) and David Norris (11+1), Eastbourne thunder to a 62-29 league win versus Coventry.

19 Tony Rickardsson dramatically announces he is quitting British racing at the end of the month in order to spend more time in Sweden with his family. The five-times World Champion is quoted as saying: 'It's the toughest decision I have made in my professional career, but I'm sure Poole's great supporters will understand that my wife and children must come first.' Belle Vue's scheduled return league fixture with Peterborough is called off at 9 a.m., due to a waterlogged racing strip. Inspired by a full house from Mikael Max (15), Wolverhampton notch a 50-40 victory over Poole, with the brilliant Swede also winning the subsequent run-off for the aggregate league bonus point.

21 Leigh Adams amazingly records his fourth maximum (18) in four league matches for Swindon, but his superhuman efforts can't prevent home side Arena-Essex from winning 49-43. Poole's home league encounter versus Coventry is postponed due to a waterlogged Wimborne Road circuit.

22 Coventry slump to their fourth home loss in six matches, as league leaders Poole coast to a 55-40 triumph, aided by an unbeaten tally from the soon-to-be-departing Tony Rickardsson (13+2). Ipswich surprisingly lose 51-41 to a hungry Wolverhampton outfit in the league at Foxhall Heath. Despite a fifth straight maximum from Leigh Adams (18), Swindon lose 47-46 to a determined Belle Vue in a thrilling league tussle at Blunsdon.

23 Oxford work hard to overcome Belle Vue 48-45 in the league, with the brilliant Jason Crump netting maximum points (15) for the battling Aces.

24 Wolverhampton come from 10 points down to win a gripping league encounter 46-45 at Eastbourne. A packed house witnesses Ipswich overpower Swindon to win 56-40 in the league.

26 Coventry's problems continue as their league match against Eastbourne is abandoned after nine heats, with the Eagles holding a 29-25 advantage. Wolverhampton's match versus Arena-Essex is also abandoned, but not before the vital twelfth heat. The 44-33 success for the homesters takes them to the head of the Elite League table above Poole and Ipswich. Rounding off the day's league fixtures at a seemingly unusually dry Kirkmanshulme Lane, Belle Vue defeat Swindon 48-42 in an enthralling fixture.

28 Due to a saturated track, Arena-Essex are forced to postpone their mouth-watering league fixture against table-topping Wolverhampton. The day's other match sees Poole take advantage and jump to the head of the league standings, courtesy of a 49-42 win over Belle Vue. The meeting marks Tony Rickardsson's departure from British racing, although he is somewhat upstaged by Jason Crump's superb maximum (18) for the Aces.

29 Swindon's Knock-Out Cup fixture with Wolverhampton unfortunately falls victim to inclement weather for a second time.

MAY

2 Joe Screen celebrates his Testimonial at Belle Vue, but an action-packed meeting is marred by a dreadful semi-final crash which leaves Sheffield's Sean Wilson with a crushed vertebrae. The meeting is immediately abandoned and Jason Crump is awarded first place, having scored maximum points (15) in the qualifying heats.

3 Following persistent rainfall, the scheduled afternoon league match between Ipswich and Arena-Essex is put back until 6 p.m., only for the elements to prevail. Wolverhampton regain first position in the Elite League by posting their fifth straight victory, defeating Swindon 51-44 in an exciting encounter at Monmore Green.

5 Arena-Essex suffer a 48-42 league reverse to in-form visitors Ipswich. Antonio Lindback celebrates his nineteenth birthday with a paid maximum (16+2) as Poole defeat Oxford 54-37 to regain first place in the league table. The match also marks Ryan Sullivan's return to British racing.

6 Coventry's league clash with Belle Vue is called off over twenty-four hours beforehand, with the Brandon circuit in a waterlogged state after three days of almost continual rain. With Charlie Gjedde missing after suffering a broken right ankle in Sweden, the remaining Swindon riders produce a spirited showing to defeat Wolverhampton 56-38 and claim an aggregate Knock-Out Cup success.

7 With the car park flooded, Peterborough's eagerly awaited league match versus Ipswich is postponed following abysmal weather conditions in and around the area. Oxford gain some revenge for their Knock-Out Cup defeat, as they beat their conquerors, Arena-Essex, 52-43 in the league.

8 Eastbourne grab a narrow 47-43 success over Peterborough in the league at Arlington.

10 Belle Vue's league encounter with Poole is rained off for the second time in five weeks. Jesper B. Jensen nets a paid full house (14+1), as Ipswich beat Coventry 54-41 to keep the pressure on Poole at the top of the Elite League table.

12 Powerful Poole have little difficulty in staying on top of the pile courtesy of a 56-38 victory over Swindon in the Elite League. Arena-Essex trounce beleaguered Coventry 62-34 in a one-sided league match at the Purfleet raceway. Peterborough narrowly beat Eastbourne 50-46 in a pulsating league contest at the East of England Showground.

13 Leigh Adams rips to a new Blunsdon track record of 64.46 seconds and a full 18-pointer, as Swindon gain revenge over Poole, winning the return league fixture 53-39. Coventry suffer their fifth successive league defeat, as Arena-Essex steal away from Brandon with a 51-44 victory under their belts.

14 Peterborough stage their second home league match in three days and it's another thriller as they pip Wolverhampton 48-45, with guest Joe Screen scorching to a fabulous 18-point full house for the visitors.

17 Jason Crump bags his fourth league maximum (15) of the season as Belle Vue register a

53-40 win against Arena-Essex. At Arlington, Eastbourne dig deep to defeat high-flying Ipswich 50-40 in a gripping league encounter. Wolverhampton move to within a point of Poole at the head of the league standings by virtue of a 50-39 success over basement club Coventry.

19 Paul Hurry returns to the sport following an arm operation and plays a key role in helping Arena-Essex to defeat Belle Vue 51-42 in the league. League leaders Poole are made to graft before narrowly coming out on top by a 48-45 scoreline against Peterborough in a thriller at Wimborne Road.

20 Rain continues to create fixture chaos for Swindon as their Elite League match against Oxford is called off following late-afternoon rain. Coventry lose their seventh consecutive league match as Wolverhampton come away from Brandon with a 52-41 victory in the bag. The win takes Wolves level with top club Poole on 23 points, although the Pirates retain first place on race points difference. There's almost a shock at Foxhall Heath and it goes right to the last heat before Ipswich grab a 47-46 league win against a lively Eastbourne septet.

21 Solid scoring down the line carries Oxford to a 53-43 league success over Eastbourne, despite guest Mark Loram's superb 18-point maximum for the visitors.

22 After league defeats on the previous two evenings, Eastbourne return to winning ways in defeating Belle Vue 57-38, with club skipper David Norris remaining unbeaten by an opponent (14+1). A bumper crowd turns out at Monmore Green as Mikael Max enjoys a successful Testimonial meeting. Run under sunny skies, the honours end even as Wolverhampton and the Mikael Max Select play out a 45-45 draw. Belle Vue come out on top in a tight league tussle at Kirky Lane, beating Eastbourne 48-45. The match is marred by a ninth-heat crash, however, which rules Toni Svab out for the rest of the season with a broken right femur. Meanwhile, the evening's other league match features thrills and spills galore as Oxford comfortably see off Peterborough 54-38.

26 Mark Loram plunders a maximum (15), as Arena-Essex claim a 53–41 Elite League win against Oxford. It's David versus Goliath at Wimborne Road and league leaders Poole are pushed all the way before finally beating Coventry 47-45.

27 Bottom-of-the-table Coventry end their sequence of eight successive defeats by posting a 58-36 success over an Oxford side reduced to just four fit riders after the same number of heats. Ipswich secure a 52-41 success against Belle Vue, despite Jason Crump's fifth league maximum for the Aces. Swindon make it two league wins on the trot, beating Eastbourne 48-42 at Blunsdon.

28 An absorbing league contest sees Peterborough come from behind to salvage a 46-46 draw with Poole.

30 Swindon are rocked by the news that recently recruited Rafal Kurmanski has taken his own life in his Polish homeland.

31 Peterborough overcome an early deficit to beat Ipswich 55-40 in the first part of a live double-bill of league action on Sky Sports. The second match sees Leigh Adams brilliantly scoop his seventh full house in eleven league matches as Swindon determinedly win 47-43 at Coventry, with the victory dedicated to the memory of the late Rafal Kurmanski. Further league activity at Monmore Green results in a 51-42 success for Wolverhampton against Belle Vue.

JUNE

2 With solid scoring all the way down the line, Poole ease to a 58-34 victory over third-in-the-table Ipswich.

3 Steady drizzle finally comes out on top, causing Ipswich's league clash with Peterborough to be postponed at 8.15 p.m. Exciting league fare at Blunsdon results in a hard-fought 48-45 win for Swindon against Wolverhampton.

4 Arena-Essex claim the scalp of Poole, winning a pulsating league encounter 53-40 at their Purfleet home. Oxford hammer a depleted Coventry outfit 71-21 in the league, with paid maximums coming from Travis McGowan (17+1), guest David Norris (16+2) and skipper Greg Hancock (11+4). Top-class Elite League fare serves up passing in every race at Peterborough, with the homesters holding on to triumph 47-46 against battling Swindon.

5 Eastbourne repel a late comeback to beat Poole 51-44 in a dramatic league encounter at Arlington.

7 Third-from-bottom Belle Vue suffer a 46-44 reverse at the hands of visiting Oxford. Poole are stretched at home for the second successive week, eventually winning 47-43 against Arena-Essex. Wolverhampton remain second from top, despite slipping to a 45-44 reverse at the hands of visiting Eastbourne.

9 Mark Loram plunders his third league full house (15) of the campaign as Arena-Essex comfortably beat Peterborough 59-36.

10 Coventry gain only their third league victory of a difficult season, coming from behind to win 46-44 against table-topping Poole. League action at Ipswich sees Greg Hancock land maximum points (15) as the American ace inspires Oxford to a 46-44 success. Leigh Adams lands yet another league maximum (15) as depleted Swindon battle out a 45-45 draw with Eastbourne.

14 Jason Crump nets his sixth maximum (15) of the league campaign as Belle Vue wallop Peterborough 63-32 at Kirky Lane. After trailing for much of the match, Eastbourne's battling efforts are rewarded as they finally win 47-46 against Oxford. Second-placed Wolverhampton suffer their third successive defeat, going down 49-41 to visiting Poole as the Pirates further extend their advantage at the head of the table.

16 Solid-scoring Arena-Essex claim the league points courtesy of a 47-43 success over Eastbourne. Ryan Sullivan lowers the Poole track record to 57.06 seconds as the Pirates race to a 54-40 league victory against Wolverhampton.

17 Basement club Coventry grab their second successive home league win, beating Ipswich 45-44 thanks to a last heat 5-1 from Andreas Jonsson and Billy Janniro. Leigh Adams bags his ninth unbeaten league tally of the season (14+1), as Swindon beat Arena-Essex 47-42.

18 Wolverhampton run riot to claim a surprisingly easy 54-40 victory in the league at Oxford.

19 League action at Arlington results in a 53-40 win for Eastbourne against Arena-Essex.

21 Due to England's participation in the Euro 2004 Championship, two Elite League matches are understandably postponed: Wolverhampton *v.* Oxford and Belle Vue *v.* Coventry. The televised match at Ipswich goes ahead, however, with Ipswich defeating Swindon 49-46, despite Leigh Adams' tenth league maximum (18) for the battling Robins.

23 Rain is the day's only winner as both scheduled league matches fall victim to waterlogged circuits, namely Arena-Essex *v.* Wolverhampton and Poole *v.* Oxford.

24 Due to England's continuation in the Euro 2004 Championship two further league matches are postponed: Swindon *v.* Belle Vue and Coventry *v.* Arena-Essex.

25 Making full use of their tactical rides, Peterborough come from behind to force a 48-48 draw in thrilling Elite League fare at Alwalton.

26 With rain sweeping across much of the country, Eastbourne's league encounter against Swindon is called off at 10.30 a.m.

28 Led by yet another unbeaten tally from Leigh Adams (11+1), Swindon roar to 63-31 victory over Peterborough in a televised league match at Blunsdon. Domestic fare at Monmore Green sees Mikael Max surge to a full house (15), as Wolverhampton ease to a 58-35 success over Oxford.

30 Belle Vue's league fixture versus Wolverhampton is called off at 7.40 p.m., with referee David Peet declaring the circuit 'unraceable', following intermittent rain during the morning and afternoon. Arena-Essex bag the league points with a hard-fought 48-42 victory over Ipswich. The match also sees home man Mark Loram equal the track record of 57.4 seconds in the tenth heat. League leaders Poole go down 49-46 to inspired visitors Eastbourne in a thriller at Wimborne Road.

JULY

1 The scheduled league encounter between Coventry and Eastbourne unfortunately falls victim to a waterlogged track. Swindon overpower Ipswich 56-37 in the league, led by another unbeaten tally from Leigh Adams (17+1) and a first in British racing for David Ruud (13+2).

2 Despite lengthy work on the track, Peterborough's league match against Arena-Essex is called off due to the effects of heavy rain. Oxford lose 47-46 to a determined Poole side in a tight league tussle at Cowley.

3 Eastbourne jump to third spot in the league table, courtesy of a 50-40 victory over Peterborough.

5 Despite missing several regular teamsters, Belle Vue come from behind to defeat league leaders Poole 47-43. Exciting league action at Oxford results in a hard-earned 51-43 success for the homesters against Eastbourne. At Monmore Green, a late Swindon revival restricts Wolverhampton to a 52-44 league win.

7 Poole's league match against Belle Vue falls victim to heavy afternoon rainfall. The wet stuff also unfortunately washes out the league clash between Arena-Essex and Coventry shortly after 4.00 p.m. There's rain at Peterborough too, but the meeting goes ahead with visiting Swindon showing a keen appetite for racing. Although conditions deteriorate, twelve heats are completed before the league match is abandoned, with the Robins holding a winning 46-30 advantage.

8 A heavy downpour results in Swindon's attractive league match-up with Wolverhampton being postponed at 6.30 p.m. The league's bottom two clubs meet at Coventry and it's the homesters who post their third success in a row, defeating Peterborough 61-31, with unbeaten tallies from Andreas Jonsson (15) and Billy Janniro (12+3). Ipswich jump to third spot in the league standings, courtesy of a hard-earned 50-43 victory over first-placed Poole.

9 After scoring a maximum (15) in the qualifying heats, mechanical gremlins put paid to Scott Nicholls' chances in the final showdown of the Championship of Great Britain at Oxford. Bizarrely, Mark Loram also retires, while David Norris falls, leaving Joe Screen to claim his second British title.

10 Wolverhampton gain their fourth league win on the trot, triumphing 49-43 at injury-hit Eastbourne.

11 At Coventry, Stuart Robson's Testimonial Best Pairs results in victory for Steve Johnston and Chris Harris, with Craig Boyce and Tomas Topinka finishing as runners-up.

12 Due to major work on the Kirkmanshulme Lane greyhound circuit, Belle Vue's league match versus Coventry has to be rescheduled. Peterborough produce a gallant effort, but they can't prevent visiting Poole from winning 51-42 in a televised league encounter. Second-in-the-table Wolverhampton make it five successive league victories as they defeat Eastbourne 54-42. Top Eagle David Norris at least has the consolation of setting a new track record of 55.87 seconds in the opening race.

14 Arena-Essex beat Coventry 53-41 in an entertaining league contest at their Purfleet home. Peterborough claim a hard-fought 47-43 league victory over Oxford. At Wimborne Road, quicker-starting Poole plunder the league points as they race to a 57-38 success against Swindon.

15 Coventry defeat Arena-Essex 52-41 in a rain-affected league encounter at Brandon. Ipswich pull away in the latter stages to post a 55-38 win over Oxford, thereby consolidating third spot in the league standings. A last-heat 4-2 sees Swindon salvage a 45-45 draw against league leaders Poole in a thriller at Blunsdon.

16 An early afternoon downpour puts paid to the return league clash between Oxford and Ipswich.

17 Banishing three successive league defeats to the memory banks, Eastbourne ease to a 55-39 victory against Coventry.

19 Team Great Britain lock horns with Denmark in Test match action at Wolverhampton, with the Danes collecting a narrow 50-44 success.

21 Despite several injuries, battle-scarred Arena-Essex dig deep to beat second-placed Wolverhampton 51-44. It's a thriller at Belle Vue, with a last-heat 5-1 giving victory and the all-important league points to visiting Eastbourne courtesy of a 45-44 scoreline. The day's other match sees Poole beat Peterborough 53-40 to comfortably stay top of the league standings.

22 A thunderstorm leaves Coventry's circuit underwater, with the scheduled league fixture against Wolverhampton inevitably called off as a result. With the riders warming-up in the pits, torrential rain hits Swindon and literally floods the track within minutes, causing the league encounter versus Peterborough to be postponed. Ipswich escape the wet stuff and ease to a 57-38 league success over Arena-Essex, aided by unbeaten tallies from Hans N. Andersen (14+1), Scott Nicholls (14+1) and Chris Louis (11+1).

23 Oxford get the better of the league derby against Swindon, winning 53-41 at Cowley.

24 Leigh Adams scorches through the card, netting maximum points (12) to head the qualifiers in Scott Nicholls' Testimonial at Ipswich. The brilliant Aussie then takes victory in the grand final, defeating Ryan Sullivan, Scott Nicholls and Billy Janniro. Eastbourne beat Belle Vue 51-39 to leapfrog Ipswich and go third in the league standings.

26 Scott Robson bags a first-ever paid maximum (13+2) in Elite League racing, as Belle Vue triumph 57-38 over Arena-Essex. The league's basement sides engage in pulsating fare at the East of England Showground, with Gary Havelock paid for a maximum (10+2), as Peterborough narrowly beat Coventry 47-43. Second-in-the-table Wolverhampton are pushed hard, before posting a 49-44 success against an inspired Ipswich outfit.

28 Leigh Adams hits another full house (15), as Swindon step up their hopes of a place in the

Elite League Play-Offs with a well-earned 48-45 success at Arena-Essex. League leaders Poole ease to a 55-39 success over Coventry at Wimborne Road.

29 Coventry suffer their fourth league loss in a row, going down 46-44 to visiting Belle Vue following a last-heat decider. Scott Nicholls is paid for a maximum (14+1), as Ipswich leapfrog Eastbourne and go third in the standings, courtesy of a 51-39 victory against Wolverhampton. Led by Leigh Adams' 15-point maximum, Swindon beat Peterborough 52-44 and jump to fifth spot in the league table.

30 Greg Hancock's unbeaten tally (16+2) leads Oxford to a 49-41 win over Peterborough, as the Silver Machine displace local rivals Swindon in fifth position.

AUGUST

4 Belle Vue are forced to call off their league match versus Peterborough, due to the non-availability of riders competing in the Speedway World Cup.

9 Eastbourne claim a hard-earned 52-45 success against Ipswich in a televised league fixture at Arlington. The win sees the Eagles exchange places with the Witches and take up third spot in the table. The day's other two scheduled league matches fall victim to waterlogged tracks: Peterborough *v.* Oxford and Wolverhampton *v.* Belle Vue.

11 Following a serious spill for Scott Robson on the first lap of heat two, a lack of medical cover forces the abandonment of Belle Vue's league fixture against Oxford with the score standing at 3-3. Rain curtails Poole's league match against Ipswich, but with thirteen heats completed, the result stands as a 48-33 win for the reigning Champions. An absorbing league encounter at Purfleet finally results in a 47-46 victory for Arena-Essex against Eastbourne. Meanwhile, at the East of England Showground, there's two league points for second-from-bottom Peterborough, as they beat Wolverhampton 54-41.

12 Coventry's scheduled league match versus Oxford is postponed due to a waterlogged racing strip. Scott Nicholls plunders his fourth unbeaten tally in six league matches (17+1), as Ipswich chalk up a 63-31 success over Eastbourne. At Blunsdon, Swindon claim a hard-earned 47-42 win against Belle Vue to go fifth in the league standings.

13 Oxford again displace local rivals Swindon in the table, courtesy of beating Arena-Essex 53-42.

14 Eastbourne come from behind to clinch a 50-43 win against Arena-Essex in an elongated and crash-strewn Elite League fixture. The match marks the end of Kelvin Tatum's speedway career, with the two-times British Champion suffering severe pain from a long-standing hip injury.

16 A Manchester monsoon at around 6.00 p.m. quickly washes away Belle Vue's league encounter with Swindon. At Cowley, Oxford collect their fourth league win on the trot, beating Coventry 53-41. The day's one remaining league fixture sees Wolverhampton wallop a depleted Arena-Essex outfit 62-30.

18 Wet weather causes the postponement of the day's two scheduled league fixtures: Arena-Essex *v.* Oxford and Belle Vue *v.* Ipswich.

18 Challenge-match action at Wimborne Road sees Swindon snatch a surprise last-heat 47-46 success over Poole.

19 Swindon's league match against Wolverhampton only reaches the sixth heat, before rain curtails the action with the Robins leading 21-15. Further Elite League activity at Brandon results in a 50-45 reverse for Coventry at the hands of Eastbourne. Meanwhile, at Foxhall Heath, Ipswich race to a 55-39 victory over Belle Vue in the league.

21 Both David Norris (18) and Adam Shields (14+4) go through the card unbeaten as Eastbourne cruise to a 60-32 win against a depleted Swindon side. The Eagles' success takes them back to third position in the league table.

23 Belle Vue's league encounter with Poole is postponed following heavy overnight rain. Remarkably, for one reason or another, it's the thirteenth scheduled race night of the season to be wrecked at Kirkmanshulme Lane. The league match between Wolverhampton and Coventry is called off early in the afternoon due to torrential rainfall. Unfortunately, with the first bend under two feet of water following a mid-afternoon cloudburst, it's the same story at Swindon as the eagerly awaited league clash against local rivals Oxford is called off at 6.00 p.m.

25 Belle Vue suffer yet another rain-off, their scheduled league fixture versus Coventry being a mid-morning casualty to the elements. Injury-hit Arena-Essex dig deep to beat second-in-the-league Wolverhampton 48-42. Meanwhile, at Wimborne Road, Poole comfortably beat Oxford 58-37 in an Elite League encounter.

26 A double dose of league action at Blunsdon sees basement side Coventry push Swindon all the way, before a last-heat 5-1 gives the Robins a 47-46 success in the first match. In the second fixture, also against the Bees, Swindon again register a heat-fifteen maximum to win with just a tad more breathing space, 50-44. Ipswich collect two more points in their quest for a Play-Off place, comfortably defeating Peterborough 54-40.

27 With their tails up on a track described as heavy and grippy, Oxford run riot to thrash league pacesetters Poole 65-29. Despite the scoreline, only Greg Hancock records an unbeaten tally (13+2).

28 Nicki Pedersen registers only his second full house of the league campaign (15), as the Eagles of Eastbourne swoop from behind to beat Oxford 47-43.

29 The remarkable Leigh Adams notches his fifteenth league maximum of the season (18), as Swindon secure a 49-47 win over Wolverhampton, thanks to another of their final-race 5-1 specials.

30 Oxford race to a 52-43 win against Belle Vue in lunchtime Bank Holiday league fare at Cowley. Following eight successive league defeats, Coventry claim a 52-38 victory over Play-Off chasing Swindon. The day's other meeting sees Belle Vue suffer their second league defeat in little over nine hours, going down 55-36 at Wolverhampton.

SEPTEMBER

1 Having missed a couple of league matches through injury, Josh Larsen makes a fabulous return to land a paid maximum (14+1), as Arena-Essex beat Oxford 57-38. Belle Vue just come out on top in a thriller at Kirky Lane, winning 47-46 in their league encounter with Wolverhampton.

2 Maximums from Chris Louis (15) and Danny Bird (9+3) help Ipswich to a 60-33 success over Rye House in a challenge match at Foxhall Heath.

3 The East of England Showground serves up an Elite League classic, with Peterborough finally winning 48-45 against Arena-Essex.

6 Jason Crump bags his seventh league maximum of the season (12), as Belle Vue beat Coventry 50-45 in the first match of a double-header. The second fixture, also versus Coventry, results in a narrower 48-45 victory for the Aces. At Eastbourne, a dramatic televised league encounter ends in a 45-45 draw against Swindon, with Nicki Pedersen subsequently taking the flag from Leigh Adams in a vital bonus-point run-off. The

meeting includes a couple of horrific accidents, the worst of which leaves inspirational Eagles skipper David Norris with a double break to his right leg after being catapulted over the back-straight safety fence. Persistent rain fails to prevent Peterborough from winning 53-44 against Ipswich in the day's other league fixture.

8 Belle Vue continue to catch up with their Elite League fixture backlog, easily beating Oxford 57-38, with Jason Crump racing through the card (18). Wolverhampton overcome an early deficit to triumph 49-41 against Coventry; the win consolidating second position in the league standings.

9 It's a busy day on the league front, as basement side Coventry prevail from a ding-dong battle, winning 49-41 versus third-in-the-table Eastbourne. Meanwhile, Ipswich grit their teeth to emerge victorious from a rip-roaring tussle against Arena-Essex. The final scoreline of 49-41 keeps the Witches on track for a place in the Play-Offs. With first position in the table assured and as such, a direct seeding to the Play-Off final, Poole cruise to a 54-40 success over a Belle Vue side containing three guests and also using rider replacement for Kenneth Bjerre. Billed as the match of the season, local rivals Swindon and Oxford lock horns at Blunsdon, with the Robins' 52-44 victory lifting them to fifth place in the table.

10 As the charge for the Play-Offs hots up, Oxford slump to their fourth successive loss, going down 45-44 at home to a lively Ipswich septet. Before a large and appreciative audience, Arena-Essex wrap-up their home league programme with an untroubled 57-40 win against Belle Vue.

11 In the Knock-Out Cup, Ipswich lead throughout to post a 48-46 victory at Eastbourne and move through to meet Arena-Essex in the semi-finals.

12 At Poole, the prestigious Elite League Riders' Championship is called off half an hour after the scheduled 4.00 p.m. start time, following heavy showers.

13 Coventry are unable to prevent Oxford from winning 48-42 at Brandon, as the Silver Machine boys reclaim the all-important fifth spot in the league table. Jason Crump canters to maximum points (12), as Belle Vue virtually end Swindon's hopes of a Play-Off place, crushing the Wiltshire team 60-30. Wolverhampton make light work of defeating Peterborough 57-36 to more or less guarantee second place in the final Elite League standings.

14 With just three days to the cut-off point for Play-Offs qualification, Peterborough get the better of top-five hopefuls Belle Vue to win 49-41.

15 Jason Crump bags a maximum (15), as Belle Vue defeat Ipswich 50-41 in the first part of a league double-header at Kirkmanshulme Lane. The second match sees Crump again go through the card (15), while Joe Screen (11+1) and Kenneth Bjerre (10+2) are also unbeaten, as the Aces destroy table-toppers Poole 68-25. In order to cram in the league fixtures, Peterborough's 'home' match against Oxford is held at Arena-Essex and it's the Silver Machine who win 46-44 to clinch their place in the Play-Offs. Leading Oxford to victory is guest Mark Loram, who uses his considerable knowledge of the Purfleet circuit to good effect, scoring a full 15-pointer.

16 Belle Vue race their thirteenth league match in a hectic eighteen-day schedule, losing 45-44 at bottom-of-the-table Coventry. At Foxhall Heath, Ipswich beat Peterborough 52-42 to finish third in the league table and ensure a home tie in the quarter-final of the Play-Offs. Swindon complete their league programme, comfortably winning 51-43 against Arena-Essex in an entertaining encounter.

20 Wolverhampton are never extended as they brush Oxford aside in the Elite League Play-Offs, handsomely winning 61-33, with Mikael Max registering a stunning maximum (15). The other Play-Off quarter-final results in a 55-39 success for Ipswich over Eastbourne, with the Witches progressing forward to an away meeting versus Wolverhampton in the semi-final.

22 Due to inclement weather, Belle Vue are unable to stage the second leg of their Knock-Out Cup tie versus Coventry, however, with a 12-point lead from the first match at Brandon, the BSPA decide that the Aces should progress through.

23 Following a delayed start at Brandon, basement club Coventry narrowly lose 45-44 to Wolverhampton in their final league match of a frustrating campaign. Poole defeat Eastbourne 67-46 in an eighteen-heat challenge match at Wimborne Road. Swindon claim a hard-fought 48-42 victory over Belle Vue in the first leg of the Knock-Out Cup quarter-final.

24 With a combined total of 23 points, Adam Shields and Adam Pietraszko scoop the first prize of £1,000 in the Super 2s Best Pairs contest at Peterborough.

25 Due to the effects of rain, the scheduled second leg of the challenge between Eastbourne and Poole is postponed in mid-afternoon.

27 There are dramatic events in the Play-Off semi-final, as Ipswich force a 45-45 draw at Wolverhampton, before Mikael Max steers the homesters through to a two-legged final showdown against Poole, courtesy of a run-off victory from Hans N. Andersen. Belle Vue's Knock-Out Cup encounter with Swindon becomes yet another victim of a rain-affected season at Kirkmanshulme Lane.

29 For the second time in three days, Belle Vue's Knock-Out Cup clash versus Swindon is called off and the BSPA decree that the Robins should progress to the semi-final stage, having won their home leg by 6 points. This follows the same precedent that saw Coventry eliminated from the previous round when their away match against Belle Vue was called off on 22 September, with the Aces going through by virtue of holding the advantage from the first leg at Brandon. There was on-track action at Arena-Essex, however, with the homesters easily sweeping aside a Polish Select 62-33 in a challenge match.

30 Ryan Sullivan's maximum (15), helps Poole to a 58-35 success over the Polish Select in a one-sided challenge.

OCTOBER

3 Swindon's scheduled challenge match versus the Polish Select falls victim to inclement weather at lunchtime.

4 Wolverhampton are unable to stop double-chasing Poole from winning 49-41 in the first leg of the Play-Off final at Monmore Green.

6 Belle Vue's final league match of the campaign, versus Peterborough, becomes another unwanted cancellation statistic of a desperately difficult campaign for the Manchester club. Ipswich take a firm grip on their Knock-Out Cup semi-final tie with Arena-Essex, winning the first leg 46-43 at the Purfleet raceway. Capping a fine night for the Witches, skipper Scott Nicholls equals the track record of 57.4 seconds. Maximum points from Ryan Sullivan (12) help powerful Poole crush Swindon 61-30 in the other semi-final at Wimborne Road.

7 Ipswich move safely through to the Knock-Out Cup final, defeating a fighting Arena-Essex side 51-42 for a 12-point aggregate success. The other semi-final results in a 53-40

victory for Swindon over Poole, but it's the Pirates who win through by 18 points on aggregate.

11 Super Dane Bjarne Pedersen goes through the card (12), as Poole overwhelm Wolverhampton 63-30 in the return leg of the Play-Off final to retain the League Championship by 112 points to 71 on aggregate.

13 Following afternoon rain, Belle Vue's outstanding league meeting versus Peterborough is again called off, just prior to the scheduled start time.

15 Heavy morning rainfall unfortunately puts paid to Leigh Lanham's Testimonial at Arena-Essex. Meanwhile, just twelve heats are completed in the Todd Wiltshire Farewell at Oxford before Jupiter Pluvius intervenes. With 9 points from three starts, Mikael Max is deemed victorious, ahead of Wiltshire himself (8) and Sam Ermolenko (7).

17 At Poole, the restaging of the Elite League Riders' Championship results in a home one-two, as Bjarne Pedersen wins the final ahead of Ryan Sullivan, with Hans N. Andersen and surprise package Rory Schlein finishing third and fourth respectively.

18 The saga of Belle Vue's final league match against Peterborough continues, with overnight rain leading to a morning call-off. Amazingly, it is the twentieth postponement of the season at the Manchester venue.

20 The scheduled first leg of the Knock-Out Cup final between Poole and Ipswich becomes yet another casualty of wet weather.

21 Tony Mole is unveiled as the new owner of Belle Vue, after concluding a deal to take over from long-serving Aces promoter John Perrin. The incoming boss takes over the reigns on 1 November, with his son, Redvers, and Ian Thomas joining the Manchester outfit as co-promoters. Mr Mole, who also owns Premier League side Workington, along with Mildenhall in the Conference League, commented: 'This is a terrific opportunity for me and I'm delighted to be involved with the most famous club in the world. I can confirm we will remain in the Elite League.' Meanwhile, at Foxhall Heath, Ipswich claim a 48-42 victory over League Champions Poole in the first leg of the Knock-Out Cup final.

22 The Leigh Lanham Testimonial is rained off for a second time at Arena-Essex and it is subsequently decided to hold the meeting over to 2005.

25 At Wolverhampton, the prestigious Ladbroke Olympique sees David Howe triumph on 13 points, with Peter Karlsson (12) and Scott Nicholls (11) occupying the other podium positions.

28 The annual 16-Lap Classic at Ipswich, first held in 1979, goes the way of Adam Shields, with David Howe and Jesper B. Jensen finishing second and third respectively.

31 Antonio Lindback's paid maximum (13+2) helps Poole bring the curtain down in glorious fashion, as a 57-39 victory over Ipswich wraps up the Knock-Out Cup and also completes back-to-back doubles for the Dorset wonders.

SKY BET ELITE LEAGUE TABLE

	Mts	Won	Drn	Lst	For	Agn	Pts	Bon	Tot
Poole	36	23	2	11	1721	1603	48	13	61
Wolverhampton	36	21	0	15	1729	1586	42	16	58
Ipswich	36	21	0	15	1701	1626	42	11	53
Eastbourne	36	18	3	15	1699	1632	39	11	50
Oxford	36	19	0	17	1679	1672	38	10	48
Swindon	36	18	3	15	1657	1667	39	6	45
Belle Vue	35	17	0	18	1630	1597	34	9	43
Arena-Essex	36	16	0	20	1651	1679	32	8	40
Peterborough	35	12	2	21	1514	1722	26	2	28
Coventry	36	9	0	27	1565	1762	18	3	21

NOTE: One match was not ridden: Belle Vue *v.* Peterborough.

PLAY-OFFS

QUARTER-FINALS

Wolverhampton	61	Oxford	33	
Ipswich	55	Eastbourne	39	

SEMI-FINAL

Wolverhampton	45	Ipswich	45

(Wolverhampton's Mikael Max subsequently defeated Scott Nicholls in a run-off to take his side through to the final.)

FINAL

Wolverhampton	41	Poole	49	
Poole	63	Wolverhampton	30	(Poole won 112-71 on aggregate)

KNOCK-OUT CUP

ROUND ONE

Wolverhampton	50	Swindon	43	
Swindon	56	Wolverhampton	38	(Swindon won 99-88 on aggregate)
Coventry	42	Belle Vue	54	
Belle Vue	–	Coventry	–	

(Due to inclement weather, Belle Vue were unable to stage the second leg. However, with a 12-point lead from the first match at Brandon, the BSPA decreed that the Aces should progress through.)

QUARTER-FINALS

Poole	58	Peterborough	37	
Peterborough	44	Poole	46	(Poole won 104-81 on aggregate)
Ipswich	51	Eastbourne	42	
Eastbourne	46	Ipswich	48	(Ipswich won 99-88 on aggregate)
Oxford	47	Arena-Essex	46	
Arena-Essex	48	Oxford	46	(Arena-Essex won 94-93 on aggregate)
Swindon	48	Belle Vue	42	
Belle Vue	-	Swindon	-	

(Due to inclement weather, Belle Vue were unable to stage the second leg. However, with Swindon holding a 6-point lead from the first leg at Blunsdon, the BSPA decreed that the Robins should progress through.)

SEMI-FINALS

Poole	61	Swindon	30	
Swindon	53	Poole	40	(Poole won 101-83 on aggregate)
Arena-Essex	43	Ipswich	46	
Ipswich	51	Arena-Essex	42	(Ipswich won 97-85 on aggregate)

FINAL

Ipswich	48	Poole	42	
Poole	57	Ipswich	39	(Poole won 99-87 on aggregate)

ARENA-ESSEX AF STOCKTAKING HAMMERS

ADDRESS: Arena-Essex Raceway, A1306 Arterial Road, Thurrock, Essex, RM19 1AE.
PROMOTER: Ronnie Russell.
TRACK LENGTH: 252 metres.
TRACK RECORD: 57.4 seconds – Joonas Kylmakorpi (23/08/03), Mark Loram (30/06/04) & Scott Nicholls (6/10/04).
FIRST MEETING: 5 April 1984.
YEARS OF OPERATION: 1984-90 National League; 1991 British League Division Two; 1992-94 British League Division One; 1995 Premier League; 1996 Conference League; 1997-03 Premier League; 2004 Elite League.

CLUB HONOURS

LEAGUE CHAMPIONS: 1991.
KNOCK-OUT CUP WINNERS: 1991.
FOUR-TEAM CHAMPIONS: 1991.

RIDER ROSTER 2004

Dean BARKER; Paul HURRY; Leigh LANHAM; Josh LARSEN; Mark LORAM; Roman POVAZHNY; Kelvin TATUM; Grzegorz WALASEK.

OTHER APPEARANCES/GUESTS (official matches only):
Henning BAGER; Gary HAVELOCK; Steve MASTERS; Ray MORTON; David NORRIS; Ulrich OSTERGAARD; Shane PARKER; Ronni PEDERSEN; Adam SHIELDS; George STANCL; Tomas TOPINKA.

SKY BET ELITE LEAGUE

No	DATE	OPPONENTS	H/A	RESULT	BARKER	PEDERSEN	WALASEK	LARSEN	LORAM	LANHAM	TATUM	HURRY	POVAZHNY	MORTON	OTHERS
1	29/3	Poole	H	L43-47	8+2 (5)	2+1 (4)	7+1 (4)	6+2 (4)	11+1 (5)	7 (4)	2 (4)	–	–	–	–
2	31/3	Poole	A	L40-52	4 (4)	3 (4)	6 (5)	6+2 (4)	11+2 (5)	2 (4)	8+1 (4)	–	–	–	–
3	9/4	Peterborough	A	L46-47	8 (4)	7+3 (4)	9 (5)	3+2 (4)	13 (5)	3 (4)	3+2 (4)	–	–	–	–
4	14/4	Peterborough	H	W47-46*	7+1 (4)	3 (4)	7 (5)	5 (4)	15 (5)	6+2 (4)	4 (4)	–	–	–	–
5	21/4	Swindon	H	W49-43	5+1 (4)	6 (4)	8+2 (5)	5+2 (4)	9+2 (5)	5 (4)	11 (4)	–	–	–	–
6	26/4	Wolverhampton†	A	L33-44	8 (3)	R/R	1 (4)	4 (4)	12 (3)	6+1 (6)	2 (4)	–	–	–	–
7	5/5	Ipswich	H	L42-48	4 (4)	R/R	6+1 (5)	1 (3)	7+1 (5)	9+1 (6)	15+1 (7)	–	–	–	–
8	7/5	Oxford	A	L43-52	7+1 (4)	R/R	8+1 (5)	2 (5)	17 (5)	2 (5)	7 (6)	–	–	–	–
9	12/5	Coventry	H	W62-34	7+3 (4)	R/R	8+1 (4)	12+2 (6)	14 (5)	13+4 (7)	8+1 (4)	–	–	–	–
10	13/5	Coventry	A	W51-44*	5+1 (4)	R/R	5 (4)	5 (5)	11 (5)	14+1 (7)	11+2 (5)	–	–	–	–
11	17/5	Belle Vue	A	L40-53	5 (4)	R/R	0 (4)	9 (6)	14 (5)	4+1 (6)	8 (6)	–	–	–	–
12	19/5	Belle Vue	H	W51-42	6+1 (4)	–	6+2 (4)	11+1 (5)	13 (5)	4+1 (4)	4+1 (4)	7+1 (4)	–	–	–
13	26/5	Oxford	H	W53-41*	8+2 (5)	–	5 (4)	10+1 (4)	15 (5)	5+1 (4)	3 (4)	7+2 (4)	–	–	–
14	4/6	Poole	H	W53-40	6 (4)	–	13+1 (5)	10+2 (5)	12+1 (5)	1 (3)	0 (3)	11+2 (5)	–	–	–

No	DATE	OPPONENTS	H/A	RESULT	BARKER	PEDERSEN	WALASEK	LARSEN	LORAM	LANHAM	TATUM	HURRY	POVAZHNY	MORTON	OTHERS
15	7/6	Poole	A	L43-47*	6+2 (4)	–	12 (5)	0 (4)	12 (5)	3 (4)	5+1 (4)	5+1 (4)	–	–	–
16	9/6	Peterborough	H	W59-36	3+2 (4)	–	5 (4)	11+4 (5)	15 (5)	8+1 (4)	8 (4)	9 (4)	–	–	–
17	16/6	Eastbourne	H	W47-43	8+1 (5)	–	4+1 (4)	7+1 (4)	12 (5)	6 (4)	4 (4)	6+2 (4)	–	–	–
18	17/6	Swindon	A	L42-47*	3+2 (4)	–	9 (5)	3+2 (4)	11 (5)	1 (3)	6 (4)	9+2 (5)	–	–	–
19	19/6	Eastbourne	A	L40-53	8 (6)	–	R/R	6+3 (7)	16 (5)	4+1 (5)	2 (3)	4+2 (4)	–	–	–
20	30/6	Ipswich	H	W48-42	6+1 (5)	–	–	11+1 (7)	15+1 (6)	1+1 (2)	R/R	6+2 (5)	–	–	9 (5)
21	14/7	Coventry	H	W53-41	9+1 (5)	–	5+1 (4)	7 (5)	13 (5)	6+1 (5)	R/R	13+1 (6)	–	–	–
22	15/7	Coventry	A	L41-52*	6+1 (4)	–	3 (4)	1 (2)	16+1 (5)	3 (3)	10 (5)	2 (4)	–	–	–
23	21/7	Wolverhampton	H	W51-44	11+3 (5)	–	3+1 (4)	R/R	11 (5)	13+2 (6)	10 (5)	3 (4)	–	–	–
24	22/7	Ipswich	A	L38-57	2 (1)	–	R/R	–	2 (1)	13 (7)	–	–	–	–	21+6 (19)
25	26/7	Belle Vue	A	L38-57	9 (6)	–	2 (4)	–	13 (5)	5+2 (5)	R/R	5 (5)	–	–	4+4 (5)
26	28/7	Swindon	H	L45-48	12+2 (5)	–	5+3 (4)	R/R	11 (5)	6 (5)	5 (5)	6+1 (5)	–	–	–
27	11/8	Eastbourne	H	W47-46	3 (4)	–	R/R	8+2 (6)	12 (5)	10+3 (5)	5+1 (4)	9 (6)	–	–	–
28	13/8	Oxford	A	L42-53	12+2 (6)	–	R/R	3+1 (5)	17 (5)	3+1 (4)	–	1 (5)	–	–	6 (5)
29	14/8	Eastbourne	A	L43-50	10+1 (6)	–	R/R	3+1 (5)	13 (5)	11+1 (7)	1 (2)	5 (5)	–	–	–
30	16/8	Wolverhampton	A	L30-62	3 (3)	–	R/R	–	13 (5)	2 (6)	–	5 (6)	–	–	7 (10)
31	25/8	Wolverhampton	H	W48-42	–	–	1+1 (4)	–	14 (6)	8 (5)	–	R/R	8+1 (5)	5 (4)	12+2 (6)
32	1/9	Oxford	H	W57-38*	6+1 (4)	–	1 (3)	14+1 (5)	14 (5)	11+2 (5)	–	6+2 (4)	5+1 (4)	–	–
33	3/9	Peterborough	A	L45-48*	5+1 (4)	–	12 (5)	0 (3)	–	9 (5)	–	2 (4)	7+1 (4)	–	10 (5)
34	9/9	Ipswich	A	L41-49	4+3 (4)	–	4 (4)	4+1 (4)	13 (5)	4 (4)	–	5+2 (4)	7 (5)	–	–
35	10/9	Belle Vue	H	W57-40	8+1 (4)	–	1+1 (3)	11+3 (5)	14 (5)	11 (4)	–	6+3 (4)	6+2 (5)	–	–
36	16/9	Swindon	A	L43-51	3+1 (4)	–	R/R	6+2 (6)	14 (5)	6+1 (5)	–	5+1 (5)	9+1 (5)	–	–

*Denotes bonus-point victory

†Meeting abandoned after heat twelve, with the result permitted to stand.

DETAILS OF OTHER RIDERS:

Match No. 20: Henning Bager 9 (5); Match No. 24: Shane Parker 10+1 (6); George Stancl 5+3 (6); Ulrich Ostergaard 6+2 (7); Match No. 25: Shane Parker 4+4 (5); Match No. 28: Tomas Topinka 6 (5); Match No. 30: Tomas Topinka 7 (7); Steve Masters 0 (3); Match No. 31: Gary Havelock 12+2 (6); Match No. 33: David Norris 10 (5).

TACTICAL SUBSTITUTE AND TACTICAL RIDES, AS INCLUDED IN THE SCORES GRID:

Match No. 2: Loram 4 points (TR); Lanham 0 points (TR); Match No. 6: Loram 6 points (TR); Barker 4 points (TR); Match No. 8: Loram 6 points (TR); Barker 4 points (TR); Match No. 11: Loram 6 points (TR); Match No. 19: Loram 6 points (TR); Match No. 22: Loram 6 points (TR); Barker 0 points (TR); Match No. 24: Lanham 4 points (TR); Parker 4 points (TR); Ostergaard 2 points (TS); Match No. 25: Barker 6 points (TR); Loram 4 points (TR); Match No. 26: Barker 6 points (TR); Match No. 28: Loram 6 points (TR); Barker 4 points (TR); Match No. 29: Barker 6 points (TR); Loram 6 points (TR); Match No. 30: Loram 4 points (TR); Hurry 0 points (TR); Match No. 33: Walasek 6 points (TR); Match No. 36: Povazhny 4 points (TR); Loram 4 points (TR).

ARENA-ESSEX: back row, left to right: Paul Hurry, Ray Morton, Leigh Lanham, Ronnie Russell (Team Manager), Grzegorz Walasek, Mark Loram. Front, kneeling: Dean Barker, Billy Gander (Mascot), Josh Larsen. On bike: Kelvin Tatum.

ELITE LEAGUE AVERAGES

Rider	Mts	Rds	Pts	Bon	Tot	Avge	Max
Mark Loram	35	171	416	9	425	9.94	3 full
Dean Barker	35	150	210	37	247	6.59	–
Roman Povazhny	6	28	40	6	46	6.57	–
Josh Larsen	30	140	184	36	220	6.29	2 paid
Paul Hurry	23	106	137	24	161	6.08	–
Kelvin Tatum	24	103	142	10	152	5.90	–
Leigh Lanham	36	171	223	28	251	5.87	–
Grzegorz Walasek	28	120	153	17	170	5.67	–
Ray Morton	1	4	5	0	5	5.00	–
Ronni Pedersen	5	20	21	4	25	5.00	–
Guests	10	55	66	12	78	5.67	–

KNOCK-OUT CUP

No	DATE	OPPONENTS	H/A	RESULT	BARKER	PEDERSEN	LARSEN	WALASEK	LORAM	LANHAM	TATUM	HURRY	POVAZHNY	OTHERS
1	26/3	Oxford	A	L46-47	13+1 (5)	1+1 (4)	3 (4)	5 (4)	11 (5)	7 (4)	6 (4)	–	–	–
2	7/4	Oxford	H	W48-46*	9+1 (5)	2+1 (3)	6 (4)	3+2 (4)	13 (5)	2+1 (4)	13+2 (5)	–	–	–
3	6/10	Ipswich	H	L43-46	2+2 (3)	–	5+2 (5)	4+1 (4)	11+1 (6)	12 (6)	–	9+1 (6)	R/R	–
4	7/10	Ipswich	A	L42-51	–	–	2 (4)	7+2 (5)	18 (6)	2 (4)	–	4+1 (5)	R/R	9+1 (6)

*Denotes aggregate victory

DETAILS OF OTHER RIDERS:

Match No. 4: Adam Shields 9+1 (6).

TACTICAL RIDES, AS INCLUDED IN THE SCORES GRID:

Match No. 1: Barker 6 points (TR); Match No. 4: Loram 6 points (TR).

OTHER MEETINGS

24 March: Air-Tek Challenge (first leg)

Arena-Essex 48 (Mark Loram 11+1; Dean Barker 9+1; Kelvin Tatum 7+1; Josh Larsen 7; Leigh Lanham 6+2; Ronni Pedersen 4+1; Grzegorz Walasek 4) Eastbourne 47.

27 March: Air-Tek Challenge (second leg)

Eastbourne 44 Arena-Essex 46 (Kelvin Tatum 12; Dean Barker 10+1; Ronni Pedersen 7; Mark Loram 6+2; Grzegorz Walasek 5; Josh Larsen 3+2; Leigh Lanham 3+1) – Arena-Essex won 94-91 on aggregate.

29 September: Challenge

Arena-Essex 62 (Paul Hurry 13+1; Mark Loram 12; Leigh Lanham 10+1; Dean Barker 8; Henning Bager 7+2; Josh Larsen 6+3; Ray Morton 6+2) Polish Select 33 (Tomasz Chrzanowski 12; Adam Skornicki 9+1; Krzysztof Kasprzak 7+1; Jacek Rempala 3; Adam Pawliczek 2+1; Robert Kasprzak 0; Roman Chromik 0).

BELLE VUE ACES

ADDRESS: Greyhound Stadium, Kirkmanshulme Lane, Gorton, Manchester, M18 7BA.
PROMOTERS: John Perrin & Jim Lynch.
CLUB SPONSOR: Li-Lo Leisure Products Ltd.
TRACK LENGTH: 285 metres.
TRACK RECORD: 57.9 seconds – Jason Crump (01/09/03).
FIRST MEETING: 28 July 1928.
YEARS OF OPERATION: 1928 Open; 1988-90 British League; 1991-94 British League Division One; 1995-96 Premier League; 1997 Elite League & Amateur League; 1998-04 Elite League.

PREVIOUS VENUE: Zoological Gardens, Hyde Road, Manchester.
YEARS OF OPERATION: 1929 English Dirt-track League; 1930 Northern League; 1931 Northern League & Southern League; 1932-33 National League; 1934 National League & Reserve League; 1935-36 National League; 1937 National League & Provincial League; 1938 National League Division One; 1939 National League Division One & National League Division Two; 1940-45 Open; 1946 National League; 1947-56 National League Division One; 1957-64 National League; 1965-67 British League; 1968-69 British League Division One & British League Division Two; 1970-74 British League Division One; 1975-87 British League.

CLUB HONOURS

LEAGUE CHAMPIONS: 1930, 1931, 1933, 1934, 1935, 1936, 1963, 1970, 1971, 1972, 1982, 1993.
NOTE: The Division Two side were also crowned League Champions in 1968 and 1969.
KNOCK-OUT CUP WINNERS: 1931, 1972, 1973, 1975.
NOTE: The Division Two side also won their Knock-Out Cup competition in 1969.
NATIONAL TROPHY WINNERS: 1933, 1934, 1935, 1936, 1937, 1946, 1947, 1949, 1958.
ACU CUP WINNERS: 1934, 1935, 1936, 1937, 1946.
BRITISH SPEEDWAY CUP WINNERS: 1939.
BRITANNIA SHIELD WINNERS: 1957, 1958, 1960.
INTER-LEAGUE KNOCK-OUT CUP WINNERS: 1975.
PREMIERSHIP WINNERS: 1983.
LEAGUE CUP WINNERS: 1983.
PAIRS CHAMPIONS: 1984.
FOUR-TEAM CHAMPIONS: 1992.

RIDER ROSTER 2004

Kenneth BJERRE; Andre COMPTON; Ronnie CORREY; Jason CRUMP; Jan JAROS; Tomasz JEDRZEJAK; Tobias JOHANSSON; Scott ROBSON; Rory SCHLEIN; Joe SCREEN; Toni SVAB.

OTHER APPEARANCES/GUESTS (official matches only):

Adam ALLOTT; Jon ARMSTRONG; Henning BAGER; Craig BOYCE; Jason BUNYAN; Neil COLLINS; Sergei DARKIN; Paul FRY; Graeme GORDON; Gary HAVELOCK; Kaj LAUKKANEN; Antonio LINDBACK; Morten RISAGER; Chris SCHRAMM; George STANCL; Carl STONEHEWER; Paul THORP; Craig WATSON; Brent WERNER; Brett WOODIFIELD.

SKY BET ELITE LEAGUE

No	DATE	OPPONENTS	H/A	RESULT	SCREEN	JEDRZEJAK	SVAB	BJERRE	CRUMP	SCHLEIN	ARMSTRONG	ROBSON	JOHANSSON	LAUKKANEN	CORREY	OTHERS
1	29/3	Ipswich	H	L41-49	8 (5)	7 (4)	1+1 (4)	7 (4)	11 (5)	5 (5)	2 (3)	–	–	–	–	–
2	9/4	Wolverhampton	H	W50-42	10 (5)	R/R	7+3 (4)	8+1 (5)	15 (5)	–	1+1 (4)	9+1 (7)	–	–	–	–
3	16/4	Peterborough	A	W48-42	11+3 (5)	8+1 (4)	1 (4)	8 (4)	13 (5)	–	–	–	–	–	–	7+1 (8)
4	22/4	Swindon	A	W47-46	10 (5)	13+1 (6)	1 (3)	11+1 (5)	6 (4)	6+3 (4)	–	–	0 (2)	–	–	–
5	23/4	Oxford	A	L45-48	6 (5)	17 (7)	1 (3)	R/R	15 (5)	–	–	5 (7)	1 (3)	–	–	–
6	26/4	Swindon	H	W48-42*	4 (3)	13+1 (7)	6+2 (5)	9+1 (4)	14 (5)	2+1 (2)	–	–	0 (3)	–	–	–
7	28/4	Poole	A	L42-49	R/R	1 (4)	6+1 (5)	8+1 (6)	18 (6)	–	–	–	1 (3)	–	–	8+1 (6)
8	17/5	Arena-Essex	H	W53-40	9 (5)	8+2 (6)	R/R	14+1 (6)	15 (5)	7+1 (5)	–	–	0 (3)	–	–	–
9	19/5	Arena-Essex	A	L42-51*	5 (4)	4+1 (5)	2+2 (3)	8 (5)	14 (5)	9+1 (5)	–	–	0 (3)	–	–	–
10	22/5	Eastbourne	A	L38-57	11+1 (6)	2 (5)	R/R	6+1 (5)	14 (5)	–	–	–	–	–	–	5+1 (9)
11	24/5	Eastbourne	H	W48-45	8 (5)	3+2 (6)	2+1 (3)	14 (6)	11 (4)	10+2 (6)	–	–	R/R	–	–	–
12	27/5	Ipswich	A	L41-52	3 (2)	–	R/R	1 (1)	18 (5)	10+1 (6)	–	6+2 (7)	–	–	–	3 (6)
13	31/5	Wolverhampton	H	L42-51	4+2 (5)	–	R/R	11 (6)	12+1 (5)	–	–	3 (5)	–	–	–	12 (9)
14	7/6	Oxford	H	L44-46	7 (4)	3 (4)	–	6+1 (4)	11 (5)	12+3 (6)	–	–	–	3+2 (4)	–	2 (3)
15	14/6	Peterborough	H	W63-32*	8+1 (4)	7+4 (4)	–	9+1 (5)	15 (5)	9+1 (4)	4+1 (4)	–	–	11 (4)	–	–
16	5/7	Poole	H	W47-43	14+1 (6)	R/R	–	8 (4)	13+1 (5)	–	–	–	–	–	–	12+3 (15)
17	21/7	Eastbourne	H	L44-45	5+1 (5)	–	–	6+1 (4)	13 (5)	5+2 (4)	–	5 (5)	–	7 (4)	–	3 (3)
18	24/7	Eastbourne	A	L39-51	10+1 (6)	–	–	R/R	13 (6)	–	0 (3)	–	–	–	–	16+4 (15)
19	26/7	Arena-Essex	H	W57-38	12 (4)	–	–	8+1 (5)	14 (5)	6+2 (4)	0 (3)	13+2 (5)	–	4+2 (4)	–	–
20	29/7	Coventry	A	W46-44	11 (5)	–	–	4+1 (4)	11 (5)	12+1 (5)	–	8+2 (7)	–	R/R	–	0 (4)
21	12/8	Swindon	A	L42-47	8 (4)	–	–	9+1 (5)	10 (5)	7+2 (4)	–	–	–	–	2+1 (4)	6+1 (8)
22	19/8	Ipswich	A	L39-55	8 (5)	–	–	3+2 (5)	16 (5)	7 (6)	–	–	–	–	R/R	5+1 (9)
23	30/8	Oxford	A	L43-52	7 (5)	–	–	4+1 (4)	16 (5)	10+2 (5)	–	–	–	–	3+1 (4)	3+1 (7)
24	30/8	Wolverhampton	A	L36-55	5 (4)	–	–	5 (4)	14+1 (5)	2+1 (4)	–	2 (5)	–	–	8+1 (5)	0 (3)
25	1/9	Wolverhampton	H	W47-46	11+2 (6)	–	–	R/R	11+1 (5)	11+1 (5)	–	–	–	–	4+1 (4)	10+1 (10)
26	6/9	Coventry	H	W50-45*	5 (4)	–	–	11 (5)	12 (4)	3+1 (4)	–	–	–	–	9 (5)	10+1 (8)
27	6/9	Coventry	H	W48-45	9+2 (4)	–	–	11+1 (5)	14 (5)	2+1 (4)	–	–	–	–	6 (4)	6 (8)
28	8/9	Oxford	H	W57-38*	12+3 (5)	–	–	–	18 (6)	7+3 (5)	–	5+1 (4)	–	–	R/R	15 (10)
29	9/9	Poole	A	L40-54	7+1 (5)	–	–	R/R	17 (5)	–	–	–	–	–	1+1 (4)	15+3 (17)
30	10/9	Arena-Essex	A	L40-57*	2 (3)	–	–	R/R	15 (5)	–	–	DNA	–	–	9+1 (5)	14 (11)
31	13/9	Swindon	H	W60-30*	9 (4)	R/R	–	10 (5)	12 (4)	10+3 (6)	–	–	–	–	12+3 (6)	7+2 (5)
32	14/9	Peterborough	A	L41-49	6+1 (5)	–	–	R/R	13 (5)	9+1 (6)	–	–	–	–	1+1 (3)	12 (11)
33	15/9	Ipswich	H	W50-41	4 (4)	R/R	–	5+1 (4)	15 (5)	5+1 (5)	–	–	–	–	9+1 (5)	12+2 (7)
34	15/9	Poole	H	W68-25*	11+1 (4)	R/R	–	10+2 (4)	15 (5)	7+3 (5)	–	–	–	–	12+2 (6)	13+3 (6)
35	16/9	Coventry	A	L44-45*	12 (5)	R/R	–	3 (4)	–	14 (6)	–	–	–	–	5+1 (5)	10+2 (10)

*Denotes bonus-point victory

NOTE: One match was not ridden: Belle Vue *v.* Peterborough ('B' fixture).

DETAILS OF OTHER RIDERS:

Match No. 3: Brett Woodifield 4 (4); Paul Thorp 3+1 (4); Match No. 7: Brent Werner 8+1 (6); Match No. 10: Leigh Lanham 5+1 (5); Paul Fry 0 (4); Match No. 12: Antonio Lindback 3 (6); Match No. 13: Brent Werner 10 (5); Adam Allott 2 (4); Match No. 14: Neil Collins 2 (3); Match No. 16: Craig Watson 6+2 (5); Neil Collins 4 (5); George Stancl 2+1 (5); Match No. 17: Neil Collins 3 (3); Match No. 18: Gary Havelock 8+2 (5); Henning Bager 4+1 (4); Brent Werner 4+1 (6); Match No. 20: Jan Jaros 0 (4); Match No. 21: Brent Werner 3+1 (5); Jan Jaros 3 (3); Match No. 22: Jan Jaros 3 (4); Adam Allott 2+1 (5); Match No. 23: Neil Collins 3+1 (4); Jan Jaros 0 (3); Match No. 24: Jan Jaros 0 (3); Match No. 25: Neil Collins 7 (6); Jan Jaros 3+1 (4); Match No. 26: Andre Compton 9+1 (4); Jan Jaros 1 (4); Match No. 27: Andre Compton 6 (5); Jan Jaros 0 (3); Match No. 28: Carl Stonehewer 12 (6); Neil Collins 3 (4); Match No. 29: Craig Boyce 8+1 (6); Graeme Gordon 5 (5); Jason Bunyan 2+2 (6); Match No. 30: Sergei Darkin 11 (6); Chris Schramm 3 (5); Match No. 31: Andre Compton 7+2 (5); Match No. 32: Morten Risager 7 (5); Andre Compton 5 (6); Match No. 34: Andre Compton 12+2 (7); Match No. 34: Andre Compton 13+3 (6); Match No. 35: Carl Stonehewer 6 (4); Brett Woodifield 4+2 (6).

TACTICAL SUBSTITUTE AND TACTICAL RIDES, AS INCLUDED IN THE SCORES GRID:

Match No. 5: Jedrzejak 6 points (TR); Match No. 7: Svab 2 points (TR); Match No. 9: Schlein 6 points (TR); Match No. 10: Crump 6 points (TR); Screen 4 points (TR); Match No. 12: Crump 6 points (TR); Schlein 0 points (TR; two-minute exclusion); Match No. 13: Bjerre 4 points (TR); Werner 2 points (TR); Match No. 22: Crump 6 points (TR); Screen 2 points (TR); Match No. 23: Crump 6 points (TR); Schlein 4 points (TR); Screen 0 points (TS); Match No. 24: Crump 4 points (TR); Screen 0 points (TR); Match No. 27: Bjerre 6 points (TR); Match No. 29: Crump 6 points (TR); Screen 2 points (TR); Match No. 30: Crump 6 points (TR); Correy 6 points (TR); Darkin 2 points (TS).

ELITE LEAGUE AVERAGES

Rider	Mts	Rds	Pts	Bon	Tot	Avge	Max
Jason Crump	34	169	444	4	448	10.60	11 Full
Joe Screen	34	156	268	20	288	7.38	1 Full; 2 Paid
Andre Compton	6	33	52	8	60	7.27	–
Kaj Laukkanen	4	16	25	4	29	7.25	–
Rory Schlein	25	121	182	37	219	7.24	–
Kenneth Bjerre	28	128	212	19	231	7.22	1 Paid
Ronnie Correy	13	60	78	14	92	6.13	–
Tomasz Jedrzejak	12	62	83	12	95	6.13	–
Scott Robson	9	52	56	8	64	4.92	1 Paid
Toni Svab	9	34	26	10	36	4.24	–
Paul Thorp	1	4	3	1	4	4.00	–
Jon Armstrong	5	17	7	2	9	2.12	–
Jan Jaros	8	28	10	1	11	1.57	–
Tobias Johansson	6	17	2	0	2	0.47	–
Paul Fry	1	4	0	0	0	0.00	–
Guests	28	139	139	17	156	4.49	–

BELLE VUE: back row, left to right: Kenneth Bjerre, Ronnie Correy, Rory Schlein, Jim Lynch (Team Manager). Front, kneeling: Joe Screen, Jan Jaros. On bike: Jason Crump.

KNOCK-OUT CUP

No	DATE	OPPONENTS	H/A	RESULT	SCREEN	JEDRZEJAK	SVAB	BJERRE	CRUMP	SCHLEIN	ROBSON	CORREY	OTHERS
1	1/4	Coventry	A	W54-42+	8 (4)	R/R	8 (5)	9+1 (5)	15 (5)	10+4 (7)	4+1 (5)	–	–
2	23/9	Swindon	A	L42-48†	R/R	–	–	5 (5)	17 (6)	3 (5)	2 (3)	5+1 (5)	10 (6)

+ The second leg of the tie versus Coventry was twice rained off and by virtue of their first-leg success, Belle Vue progressed to the next round.

† The second leg of the tie versus Swindon was twice rained off and by virtue of their first-leg success, the Robins progressed to the next round.

DETAILS OF OTHER RIDERS:

Match No. 2: Craig Boyce 10 (6).

OTHER MEETINGS

17 March: Air-Tek Challenge (first leg)

Belle Vue 48 (Kenneth Bjerre 11; Jason Crump 11; Joe Screen 8+1; Tomasz Jedrzejak 8+1; Rory Schlein 6+1; Jon Armstrong 3; Toni Svab 1+1) Swindon 47

18 March: Air-Tek Challenge (second leg)

Swindon 54 Belle Vue 40 (Kenneth Bjerre 13; Jason Crump 13; Joe Screen 4; Rory Schlein 3+2; Tomasz Jedrzejak 3; Toni Svab 2; Paul Fry 2) – Swindon won 101-88 on aggregate.

11 August: Elite League

Belle Vue 3 (Kenneth Bjerre 3; Rory Schlein 0; Scott Robson 0; Jan Jaros 0; Joe Screen DNR; Jason Crump DNR; Ronnie Correy R/R) Oxford 3 – meeting abandoned after heat one.

INDIVIDUAL MEETING

2 May: The Super Joe Show (Joe Screen Testimonial)

QUALIFYING SCORES: Jason Crump 15; Leigh Adams 14; Billy Janniro 10; Jason Lyons 9; Stuart Robson 9; Sean Wilson 9; Steve Johnston 8; Chris Harris 8; Jan Staechmann 8; Craig Boyce 7; Gary Havelock 6; Ricky Ashworth 4; Edward Kennett 4; Dean Barker 4; Mark Loram 3; Paul Sharples (Res) 2; Joe Screen 0; Benji Compton (Res) 0. Meeting abandoned following a crash in the first semi-final. Jason Crump was awarded first place, with Leigh Adams as the runner-up, while Chris Harris was placed third as he was leading the semi-final at the time the race was prematurely halted.

COVENTRY BUILDBASE BEES

NOTE: The information below relates only to the main Coventry team. For details of the second side, please refer to the Conference League section.

ADDRESS: Coventry International Motor Speedway, Rugby Road, Brandon, nr. Coventry, Warwickshire, CV8 3GJ.
PROMOTERS: Colin Pratt & Jeremy Heaver; the latter becoming co-promoter in September 2004.
TRACK LENGTH: 303 metres.
TRACK RECORD: 57.4 seconds – Lee Richardson (15/09/03).
FIRST MEETING: 29 September 1928.
YEARS OF OPERATION: 1928 Open; 1929-31 Southern League; 1932-33 National League; 1934 Open; 1936 Open; 1948 National League Division Three; 1949-56 National League Division Two; 1957-64 National League; 1965-67 British League; 1968-74 British League Division One; 1975-90 British League; 1991-94 British League Division One; 1995-96 Premier League; 1997-04 Elite League.

CLUB HONOURS

LEAGUE CHAMPIONS: 1953, 1968, 1978, 1979, 1987, 1988.
KNOCK-OUT CUP WINNERS: 1967.
PAIRS CHAMPIONS: 1978 (Shared with Cradley Heath).
LEAGUE CUP WINNERS: 1981, 1985, 1987.
PREMIERSHIP WINNERS: 1986.
CRAVEN SHIELD WINNERS: 1997, 2000.

RIDER ROSTER 2004

Jason BUNYAN; Sergei DARKIN; Chris HARRIS; Billy JANNIRO; Andreas JONSSON; John JORGENSEN; Tomasz PISZCZ; Morten RISAGER; Stuart ROBSON; Bryan YARROW.

OTHER APPEARANCES/GUESTS (official matches only):

Michael COLES; Matej FERJAN; Ritchie HAWKINS; Jamie SMITH; Martin SMOLINSKI; Seemond STEPHENS; Shaun TACEY.

SKY BET ELITE LEAGUE

No	DATE	OPPONENTS	H/A	RESULT	JANNIRO	RISAGER	HARRIS	ROBSON	JONSSON	YARROW	BUNYAN	JORGENSEN	SMITH	PISZCZ	DARKIN	OTHERS
1	8/4	Ipswich	H	L45-49	7+3 (5)	7 (4)	3+1 (4)	7 (4)	14 (5)	2 (3)	5+3 (5)	–	–	–	–	–
2	9/4	Ipswich	A	L41-54	5 (4)	2+1 (4)	3 (4)	10+1 (5)	17 (5)	0 (3)	4+1 (5)	–	–	–	–	–
3	12/4	Peterborough	A	L42-51	7 (4)	2+1 (4)	8 (5)	10+1 (4)	9 (5)	1+1 (3)	5+2 (5)	–	–	–	–	–
4	12/4	Peterborough	H	W53-42*	10+2 (5)	6 (4)	9 (4)	7+2 (4)	13 (5)	0 (2)	–	8+2 (6)	–	–	–	–
5	17/4	Eastbourne	A	L29-62	4 (6)	R/R	4 (4)	9+1 (6)	6 (4)	1 (4)	–	5+2 (6)	–	–	–	–
6	22/4	Poole	H	L40-55	11 (5)	1+1 (4)	8+1 (4)	4+1 (4)	12+1 (5)	1 (3)	3 (5)	–	–	–	–	–

SKY BET ELITE LEAGUE continued

No	DATE	OPPONENTS	H/A	RESULT	JANNIRO	RISAGER	HARRIS	ROBSON	JONSSON	YARROW	BUNYAN	JORGENSEN	SMITH	PISZCZ	DARKIN	OTHERS
7	10/5	Ipswich	A	L41-54	R/R	0 (4)	7+2 (5)	8+1 (6)	16 (6)	0 (3)	10+1 (6)	–	–	–	–	–
8	12/5	Arena-Essex	A	L34-62	0 (1)	3 (4)	1 (4)	10+1 (5)	15 (5)	2 (5)	–	–	3 (6)	–	–	–
9	13/5	Arena-Essex	H	L44-51	R/R	3 (5)	7+1 (6)	9 (5)	20 (6)	1 (3)	4 (5)	–	–	–	–	–
10	17/5	Wolverhampton	A	L39-50	R/R	4 (5)	8+2 (5)	11 (6)	9 (6)	0 (3)	7+2 (6)	–	–	–	–	–
11	20/5	Wolverhampton	H	L41-52	4 (3)	3+2 (4)	6+1 (4)	16 (5)	8+1 (6)	2 (3)	2 (5)	–	–	–	–	–
12	26/5	Poole	A	L45-47	R/R	8+2 (5)	6+1 (5)	11+2 (6)	17 (6)	–	3+1 (5)	–	–	–	–	0 (3)
13	27/5	Oxford	H	W58-36	R/R	12+1 (5)	9+6 (6)	13+1 (6)	14 (5)	–	–	8+1 (4)	2+1 (4)	–	–	–
14	31/5	Swindon	H	L43-47	R/R	4 (4)	7+3 (5)	9 (6)	14 (6)	–	3 (3)	6+1 (6)	–	–	–	–
15	4/6	Oxford	A	L21-71	R/R	–	4 (5)	7 (6)	8 (5)	0 (4)	–	–	–	–	–	2 (10)
16	10/6	Poole	H	W46-44	R/R	15+1 (7)	7+2 (6)	6 (3)	12 (5)	–	3+2 (4)	–	–	3+1 (5)	–	–
17	17/6	Ipswich	H	W45-44	12+1 (5)	11+2 (7)	2 (4)	2 (4)	14 (5)	–	4+1 (4)	–	–	0 (1)	–	–
18	8/7	Peterborough	H	W61-31	<u>12+3 (5)</u>	11+2 (5)	2 (3)	7+1 (4)	<u>15 (5)</u>	–	9+2 (4)	5 (4)	–	–	–	–
19	14/7	Arena-Essex	A	L41-53	11 (5)	1+1 (4)	9 (4)	5 (4)	11 (5)	–	1 (4)	3 (4)	–	–	–	–
20	15/7	Arena-Essex	H	W52-41	10+1 (5)	6+1 (4)	6+1 (4)	7+2 (4)	7+2 (5)	–	9+1 (4)	7+2 (4)	–	–	–	–
21	17/7	Eastbourne	A	L39-55	9 (5)	2+1 (4)	4+1 (4)	5 (4)	13+1 (5)	–	4 (4)	–	–	–	–	2+2 (4)
22	26/7	Peterborough	A	L43-47*	7+2 (5)	5+3 (4)	8 (4)	5 (4)	7+1 (5)	–	–	4+3 (4)	–	–	7+1 (4)	–
23	28/7	Poole	A	L39-55	6+1 (4)	3+1 (4)	4+1 (5)	5 (4)	15 (5)	–	–	–	–	–	3+1 (4)	3+1 (4)
24	29/7	Belle Vue	H	L44-46	9+1 (5)	5+1 (4)	1 (4)	6+1 (4)	14 (5)	–	–	5+2 (4)	–	–	4+1 (4)	–
25	16/8	Oxford	A	L41-53	14 (6)	1 (3)	2 (4)	5+1 (4)	12 (5)	–	–	3+2 (4)	–	–	4 (4)	–
26	19/8	Eastbourne	H	L45-50	10 (4)	3 (4)	5+1 (4)	10+1 (5)	14 (5)	–	–	–	–	–	2 (4)	1+1 (4)
27	26/8	Swindon	A	L46-47	2 (3)	8+1 (4)	6 (4)	7+1 (5)	12 (5)	–	–	–	–	–	7+1 (4)	4+1 (5)
28	26/8	Swindon	A	L44-50	R/R	6+2 (5)	2 (5)	9 (6)	15 (6)	–	–	–	–	–	8 (4)	4+2 (4)
29	30/8	Swindon	H	W52-38*	11 (5)	7+1 (4)	5+2 (4)	6+2 (4)	11+2 (5)	–	–	–	–	–	11+2 (5)	1 (3)
30	6/9	Belle Vue	A	L45-50	12+1 (6)	3+1 (3)	6+1 (4)	7+1 (4)	14+1 (5)	–	–	–	–	0 (3)	3+1 (5)	–
31	6/9	Belle Vue	A	L45-48	7+1 (5)	R/R	8+2 (5)	6+1 (4)	9 (5)	–	–	–	–	1 (3)	14+1 (7)	–
32	8/9	Wolverhampton	A	L41-49	5 (5)	3 (3)	5+1 (4)	3+1 (4)	11+1 (5)	–	–	–	–	1 (3)	13+1 (6)	–
33	9/9	Eastbourne	H	W49-41	10+2 (5)	7+1 (4)	6+1 (4)	5+1 (4)	13 (5)	–	–	–	–	1+1 (3)	7+1 (5)	–
34	13/9	Oxford	H	L42-48	0 (1)	6 (4)	2+2 (4)	8+1 (5)	12 (5)	–	–	–	–	3+1 (4)	11 (7)	–
35	16/9	Belle Vue	H	W45-44	R/R	13+1 (6)	12+2 (6)	3 (5)	–	–	–	–	–	2 (3)	9 (5)	6 (5)
36	23/9	Wolverhampton	H	L44-45	R/R	13+1 (6)	4+1 (5)	3+3 (5)	14 (6)	–	–	–	–	2 (3)	8+1 (5)	–

*Denotes bonus-point victory

DETAILS OF OTHER RIDERS:

Match No. 12: Seemond Stephens 0 (3); Match No. 15: Shaun Tacey 1 (5); Ritchie Hawkins 1 (5); Match No. 21: Michael Coles 2+2 (4); Match No. 23: Shaun Tacey 3+1 (4); Match No. 26: Shaun Tacey 1+1 (4); Match No. 27: Martin Smolinski 4+1 (5); Match No. 28: Martin Smolinski 4+2 (4); Match No. 29: Martin Smolinski 1 (3); Match No. 35: Matej Ferjan 6 (5).

TACTICAL SUBSTITUTE AND TACTICAL RIDES, AS INCLUDED IN THE SCORES GRID:

Match No. 1: Jonsson 6 points (TR); Risager 2 points (TR); Match No. 2: Jonsson 6 points (TR); Janniro 4 points (TR); Match No. 3: Robson 6 points (TR); Match No. 5: Jonsson 2 points (TR); Janniro 0 points (TS); Match No. 6: Jonsson 6 points (TR); Janniro 4 points (TR); Match No. 7: Jonsson 6 points (TR); Harris 4 points (TR); Match No. 8: Jonsson 6 points (TR); Robson 6 points (TR); Match No. 9: Jonsson 6 points (TR); Robson 4 points (TR); Match No. 11: Robson 6 points (TR); Jonsson 2 points (TS); Match No. 15: Jonsson 2 points (TR); Robson 2 points (TR); Match No. 19: Harris 4 points (TR); Janniro 4 points (TR); Match No. 21: Jonsson 4 points (TR); Janniro 4 points (TR); Match No. 23: Jonsson 6 points (TR); Janniro 2 points (TR); Match No. 25: Jonsson 6 points (TR); Janniro 4 points (TR); Match No. 26: Janniro 6 points (TR); Jonsson 4 points (TR); Match No. 28: Robson 4 points (TR); Jonsson 4 points (TR); Match No. 30: Jonsson 4 points (TR); Janniro 4 points (TS); Robson 2 points (TR).

COVENTRY: back row, left to right: Bryan Yarrow, Morten Risager, Chris Harris, Jason Bunyan, Stuart Robson. Front, on bikes: Andreas Jonsson, Billy Janniro.

ELITE LEAGUE AVERAGES

Rider	Mts	Rds	Pts	Bon	Tot	Avge	Max
Andreas Jonsson	35	182	402	10	412	9.05	1 full
Billy Janniro	25	112	179	18	197	7.04	1 paid
Sergei Darkin	15	73	111	11	122	6.68	–
Stuart Robson	36	168	246	28	274	6.52	–
John Jorgensen	10	46	54	15	69	6.00	–
Morten Risager	33	145	183	29	212	5.85	–
Chris Harris	36	161	192	36	228	5.66	–
Jason Bunyan	16	74	76	16	92	4.97	–
Martin Smolinksi	3	12	9	3	12	4.00	–
Jamie Smith	2	10	5	1	6	2.40	–
Tomasz Piszcz	9	28	13	3	16	2.29	–
Bryan Yarrow	12	39	10	1	11	1.13	–
Ritchie Hawkins	1	5	1	0	1	0.80	–
Guests	6	25	13	4	17	2.72	–

KNOCK-OUT CUP

No	DATE	OPPONENTS	H/A	RESULT	JANNIRO	RISAGER	HARRIS	ROBSON	JONSSON	YARROW	BUNYAN
1	1/4	Belle Vue	H	L42-54+	11+3 (5)	5+1 (4)	4+2 (4)	5 (4)	15 (5)	0 (3)	2 (5)

+The second leg of the tie versus Belle Vue was twice rained-off and by virtue of their first leg success, the Aces progressed to the next round.

TACTICAL RIDES, AS INCLUDED IN THE SCORES GRID:

Match No. 1: Jonsson 6 points (TR); Janniro 6 points (TR).

OTHER MEETINGS

15 March: Air-Tek Challenge (first leg)

Wolverhampton 49 Coventry 44 (Andreas Jonsson 12; Chris Harris 10+1; Stuart Robson 9+2; Billy Janniro 8; Bryan Yarrow 2; Jason Bunyan 2; Morten Risager 1+1).

18 March: Air-Tek Challenge (second leg)

Coventry 52 (Billy Janniro 15; Andreas Jonsson 10+1; Jason Bunyan 9; Stuart Robson 7; Chris Harris 6; Morten Risager 4+2; Brian Yarrow 1) Wolverhampton 42 – Coventry won 96-91 on aggregate.

25 March: Challenge

Coventry 43 (Andreas Jonsson 10; Jason Bunyan 9+2; Stuart Robson 9+1; Chris Harris 8+1; Morten Risager 5; Billy Janniro 2+1; Brian Yarrow 0) Oxford 49.

26 April: Elite League

Coventry 25 (Stuart Robson 7+1; Lee Richardson 6; Morten Risager 4; Chris Harris 3; Jason Bunyan 3; Billy Janniro 2; Brian Yarrow 0) Eastbourne 29 – meeting abandoned after heat nine.

11 July: Stuart Robson Testimonial Best Pairs

GROUP A: Billy Janniro (12) & Jason Bunyan (7+1) = 19; Stuart Robson (8) & Scott Robson (8+2) = 16; Joe Screen (9) & David Meldrum (2) = 11; Josh Larsen (8) & Nick Simmons (0) = 8.

GROUP B: Steve Johnston (11+1) & Chris Harris (9+1) = 20; Craig Boyce (6+1) & Tomas Topinka

(6) = 12; Ryan Fisher (4+1) & Travis McGowan (6) = 10; Paul Clews (0) & Morten Risager (10) = 10. FIRST SEMI-FINAL: 1st Topinka; 2nd Janniro; 3rd Boyce; 4th Bunyan. SECOND SEMI-FINAL: 1st Johnston; 2nd Harris; 3rd Scott Robson; 4th Stuart Robson. FINAL: 1st Boyce; 2nd Johnston; 3rd Harris; 4th Topinka. WINNERS: Johnston & Harris. TOP SCORERS RACE: 1st Janniro; 2nd Johnston; 3rd Harris; 4th Risager.

EASTBOURNE EAGLES

ADDRESS: Arlington Stadium, Arlington Road West, Hailsham, East Sussex, BH27 3RE.
PROMOTERS: Terry Russell & Jon Cook.
CLUB SPONSOR: Cinque Ports Holidays.
TRACK LENGTH: 275 metres.
TRACK RECORD: 55.1 seconds – Tony Rickardsson (10/05/03).
FIRST MEETING: September 1928.
YEARS OF OPERATION: 1928-37 Open; 1938 Sunday Dirt-track League; 1939 Open; 1946 Open; 1947 National League Division Three; 1948-53 Open; 1954-57 Southern Area League; 1958 Open; 1959 Southern Area League; 1960-63 Open; 1964 Metropolitan League; 1965 Training; 1969-74 British League Division Two; 1975-78 National League; 1979-84 British League; 1985-90 National League; 1991-94 British League Division One; 1995 Premier League; 1996 Premier League & Conference League; 1997-04 Elite League.

CLUB HONOURS

LEAGUE CHAMPIONS: 1938, 1947, 1959, 1971, 1977, 1986, 1987, 1995, 2000.
KNOCK-OUT CUP WINNERS: 1975, 1977, 1978, 1985, 1986, 1987, 1994, 1997, 2002.
PREMIERSHIP WINNERS: 1995, 1996.

RIDER ROSTER 2004

Steen JENSEN; Edward KENNETT; Joonas KYLMAKORPI; Peter LJUNG; Adrian MIEDZINSKI; Andrew MOORE; David NORRIS; Ulrich OSTERGAARD; Nicki PEDERSEN; Adam SHIELDS; Davey WATT.

OTHER APPEARANCES/GUESTS (official matches only):
Adam ALLOTT; Dean BARKER; Michael COLES; Sergei DARKIN; Rusty HARRISON; Gary HAVELOCK; Mads KORNELIUSSEN; Mark LORAM; Jason LYONS; Paul PICKERING; Roman POVAZHNY; Matt READ; Chris SCHRAMM; Joe SCREEN; Seemond STEPHENS; Tomas TOPINKA; Sebastian TRESARRIEU; Brent WERNER; Brett WOODIFIELD.

SKY BET ELITE LEAGUE

No	DATE	OPPONENTS	H/A	RESULT	PEDERSEN	OSTERGAARD	NORRIS	KYLMAKORPI	SHIELDS	LJUNG	KENNETT	READ	MOORE	JENSEN	MIEDZINSKI	OTHERS
1	9/4	Poole	A	L44-52	13 (5)	2 (3)	13 (5)	4+1 (4)	2 (4)	10+2 (6)	0 (3)	–	–	–	–	–
2	9/4	Poole	H	L40-50	7 (5)	2+1 (4)	7+1 (4)	16+2 (6)	3 (4)	3 (4)	2 (3)	–	–	–	–	–
3	17/4	Coventry	H	W62-29	10+1 (4)	4+1 (4)	11+1 (4)	12+3 (5)	15 (5)	3+1 (4)	7 (4)	–	–	–	–	–
4	24/4	Wolverhampton	H	L45-46	12 (5)	4+1 (4)	13+1 (5)	7+3 (4)	5 (4)	–	3 (5)	1 (3)	–	–	–	–
5	8/5	Peterborough	H	W47-43	12 (5)	6+2 (5)	R/R	9 (5)	14 (6)	–	6 (6)	–	–	–	–	0 (3)
6	12/5	Peterborough	A	L46-50	15+1 (5)	0 (3)	13 (4)	2+1 (4)	10+1 (5)	–	–	–	–	–	–	6+1 (9)
7	17/5	Ipswich	H	W50-40	10+1 (5)	1+1 (3)	14 (5)	5+1 (4)	7 (4)	–	5 (3)	–	–	–	–	8+3 (6)
8	20/5	Ipswich	A	L46-47*	–	1 (3)	16 (5)	4+2 (4)	8 (5)	8 (6)	–	–	–	–	–	9+2 (7)
9	21/5	Oxford	A	L43-53	–	0 (3)	15 (5)	1+1 (4)	6 (4)	0 (5)	–	–	3 (4)	–	–	18 (6)
10	22/5	Belle Vue	H	W57-38	–	6+1 (4)	14+1 (5)	8+2 (4)	6+1 (4)	5 (4)	–	–	4+1 (4)	–	–	14 (5)
11	24/5	Belle Vue	A	L45-48*	–	2+1 (4)	12+1 (5)	4+1 (4)	12 (5)	3 (4)	–	–	2+1 (4)	–	–	10+1 (4)
12	27/5	Swindon	A	L42-48	11 (5)	R/R	8+1 (4)	7+1 (5)	10 (5)	4+3 (7)	–	2 (4)	–	–	–	–
13	5/6	Poole	H	W51-44	15 (5)	2+1 (3)	13+2 (5)	10+1 (4)	6 (4)	0 (3)	–	–	5 (6)	–	–	–
14	7/6	Wolverhampton	A	W45-44	10+1 (4)	1+1 (4)	12+1 (5)	11 (5)	7+1 (4)	3+1 (4)	–	–	1 (4)	–	–	–
15	10/6	Swindon	A	D45-45	12 (5)	2+1 (5)	9+2 (5)	5+1 (4)	7+2 (4)	9 (4)	–	–	–	–	–	1 (3)
16	14/6	Oxford	H	W47-46	11+1 (5)	0 (4)	16 (5)	5 (4)	8+3 (4)	6 (4)	1 (4)	–	–	–	–	–
17	16/6	Arena-Essex	A	L43-47	8 (4)	4+1 (5)	14 (5)	6 (3)	8+2 (5)	1 (4)	2+1 (4)	–	–	–	–	–
18	19/6	Arena-Essex	H	W53-40*	13 (5)	1 (3)	14+1 (6)	R/R	15+2 (6)	9+2 (6)	–	–	–	1 (4)	–	–
19	25/6	Peterborough	A	D48-48	–	–	15 (6)	R/R	3 (2)	7+2 (6)	–	–	10+2 (6)	3 (4)	–	10+1 (6)
20	30/6	Poole	A	W49-46*	9 (5)	–	12+4 (6)	R/R	–	12+1 (5)	–	–	0 (3)	–	3+1 (5)	13+1 (6)
21	3/7	Peterborough	H	W50-40*	14 (5)	–	12+2 (5)	R/R	11 (5)	–	–	–	8+3 (6)	–	4+1 (5)	1+1 (4)
22	5/7	Oxford	A	L43-51	12+1 (5)	0 (3)	6 (4)	R/R	16 (6)	–	–	–	8 (7)	–	1 (5)	–
23	10/7	Wolverhampton	H	L43-49	9+1 (5)	–	12 (5)	0 (2)	13 (5)	–	6+1 (7)	–	–	–	R/R	3 (6)
24	12/7	Wolverhampton	A	L42-54	11+1 (5)	–	16+2 (6)	R/R	9+1 (5)	–	3 (5)	–	1 (4)	–	–	2 (5)
25	17/7	Coventry	H	W55-39	12 (5)	–	13+1 (5)	R/R	13+1 (5)	–	9+1 (5)	–	8+1 (7)	0 (3)	–	–
26	21/7	Belle Vue	A	W45-44	11 (5)	–	11+2 (5)	–	6+1 (4)	–	9 (5)	–	–	–	1+1 (3)	7 (8)
27	24/7	Belle Vue	H	W51-39*	14 (5)	–	9 (4)	–	13+1 (5)	–	–	–	4+1 (6)	–	R/R	11 (10)
28	9/8	Ipswich	H	W52-45	10+1 (5)	–	14 (5)	8+2 (4)	8+1 (4)	–	4+1 (4)	–	7+1 (5)	–	1 (3)	–
29	11/8	Arena-Essex	A	L46-47	12+2 (5)	–	15 (6)	3+1 (4)	11 (4)	–	3+1 (4)	–	–	–	–	2+1 (7)
30	12/8	Ipswich	A	L31-63	11 (5)	0 (3)	6 (4)	2+1 (4)	9 (6)	–	1 (4)	–	–	–	2+1 (4)	–
31	14/8	Arena-Essex	H	W50-43*	10+1 (4)	–	–	10+3 (5)	8 (4)	–	0 (0)	–	6+1 (3)	–	3+1 (4)	13 (5)
32	19/8	Coventry	A	W50-45*	8 (4)	–	10+1 (4)	5+2 (4)	10 (5)	–	5+1 (4)	–	–	5+1 (4)	–	7+2 (5)
33	21/8	Swindon	H	W60-32*	R/R	–	18 (6)	13 (5)	14+4 (6)	–	10+1 (5)	–	–	0 (4)	–	5 (4)
34	28/8	Oxford	H	W47-43	15 (5)	–	11+1 (5)	5+2 (4)	10+1 (4)	–	5 (6)	–	–	1 (3)	–	0 (3)
35	6/9	Swindon	H	D45-45*	14 (5)	–	4+1 (3)	8+1 (4)	10 (5)	–	6 (4)	–	–	3 (5)	0 (4)	–
36	9/9	Coventry	A	L41-49*	13 (5)	–	–	6+2 (5)	7 (4)	–	4+1 (4)	–	–	–	–	11+1 (12)

*Denotes bonus-point victory

DETAILS OF OTHER RIDERS:

Match No. 5: Seemond Stephens 0 (3); Match No. 6: Brett Woodifield 4+1 (6); Paul Pickering 2 (3); Match No. 7: Brent Werner 8+3 (6); Match No. 8: Gary Havelock 7+2 (4); Brent Werner 2 (3); Match No. 9: Mark Loram 18 (5); Match No. 10: Mark Loram 14 (5); Match No. 11: Jason Lyons 10+1 (4); Match No. 15: Michael Coles 1 (3); Match No. 19: Joe Screen 10+1 (6); Match No. 20: Gary Havelock 13+1 (6); Match No. 21: Rusty Harrison 1+1 (4); Match No. 23: Mads Korneliussen 3 (6); Match No. 24: Davey Watt 2 (5); Match No. 26: Roman Povazhny 6 (4); Davey Watt 1 (4); Match No. 27: Roman Povazhny 7 (5); Davey Watt 4 (5); Match No. 29: Chris Schramm 1+1 (4); Davey Watt 1 (3); Match No. 31: Joe Screen 13 (5); Match No. 32: Tomas Topinka 7+2 (5); Match No. 33: Sebastian Tresarrieu 5 (4); Match No. 34: Sebastian Tresarrieu 0 (3); Match No. 36: Gary Havelock 6 (4); Davey Watt 5+1 (5); Sebastian Tresarrieu 0 (3).

TACTICAL SUBSTITUTE AND TACTICAL RIDES, AS INCLUDED IN THE SCORES GRID:

Match No. 1: Pedersen 6 points (TR); Norris 6 points (TR); Match No. 2: Kylmakorpi 2 points (TS); Ljung 0 points (TR); Match No. 6: Pedersen 6 points (TR); Norris 6 points (TR); Match No. 8: Norris 6 points (TR); Match No. 9: Loram 6 points (TR); Norris 6 points (TR); Match No. 11: Lyons 6 points (TR); Match No. 16: David Norris 6 points (TR); Match No. 22: Shields 6 points (TR); Pedersen 2 points (TR); Match No. 23: Shields 4 points (TS); Norris 0 points (TR); Pedersen 0 points (TR); Match No. 24: Norris 6 points (TS); Pedersen 4 points (TR); Shields 2 points (TR); Match No. 29: Norris 6 points (TR); Match No. 30: Pedersen 6 points (TR); Norris 2 points (TR); Shields 0 points (TS).

ELITE LEAGUE AVERAGES

Rider	Mts	Rds	Pts	Bon	Tot	Avge	Max
David Norris	33	161	376	26	402	9.99	1 full; 3 paid
Nicki Pedersen	30	145	332	12	344	9.49	2 full
Adam Shields	35	161	314	22	336	8.35	1 full
Joonas Kylmakorpi	27	114	175	34	209	7.33	1 paid
Roman Povazhny	2	9	13	0	13	5.78	–
Peter Ljung	16	76	83	12	95	5.00	–
Andrew Moore	14	69	67	11	78	4.52	–
Edward Kennett	21	89	91	8	99	4.45	–
Ulrich Ostergaard	19	70	38	12	50	2.86	–
Davey Watt	5	22	13	1	14	2.55	–
Adrian Miedzinski	8	33	15	5	20	2.42	–
Steen Jensen	7	27	13	1	14	2.07	–
Sebastian Tresarrieu	3	10	5	0	5	2.00	–
Matt Read	2	7	3	0	3	1.71	–
Guests	18	82	114	13	127	6.20	1 full

KNOCK-OUT CUP

No	DATE	OPPONENTS	H/A	RESULT	PEDERSEN	OSTERGAARD	KYLMAKORPI	NORRIS	SHIELDS	LJUNG	KENNETT	OTHERS
1	25/3	Ipswich	A	L42-51	9 (5)	4 (4)	7+1 (5)	13 (5)	5 (4)	4+1 (4)	0 (3)	–
2	11/9	Ipswich	H	L46-48	17 (5)	–	2+1 (4)	–	10 (5)	–	3+1 (4)	14 (13)

DETAILS OF OTHER RIDERS:

Match No. 2: Tomas Topinka 7 (5); Dean Barker 5 (4); Adam Allott 2 (4).

EASTBOURNE: back row, left to right: David Norris, Edward Kennett, Joonas Kylmakorpi, Nicki Pedersen. Front row: Peter Ljung, Ulrich Ostergaard, Adam Shields.

TACTICAL SUBSTITUTE AND TACTICAL RIDES, AS INCLUDED IN THE SCORES GRID:

Match No. 1: Norris 4 points (TR); Kylmakorpi 2 points (TS); Pedersen 0 points (TR); Match No. 2: Pedersen 6 points (TR); Barker 2 points (TR).

OTHER MEETINGS

24 March: Air-Tek Challenge (first leg)

Arena-Essex 48 Eastbourne 47 (David Norris 16; Adam Shields 10; Joonas Kylmakorpi 9+2; Nicki Pedersen 7+1; Ulrich Ostergaard 2+1; Edward Kennett 2; Peter Ljung 1).

27 March: Air-Tek Challenge (second leg)

Eastbourne 44 (David Norris 13+1; Nicki Pedersen 12+1; Joonas Kylmakorpi 8+1; Edward Kennett 4; Peter Ljung 3+2; Adam Shields 3; Ulrich Ostergaard 1+1) Arena-Essex 46 – Arena-Essex won 94-91 on aggregate.

1 April: Elite League

Swindon 33 Eastbourne 22 (Nicki Pedersen 6; Adam Shields 6; David Norris 5; Peter Ljung 3; Ulrich Ostergaard 1+1; Joonas Kylmakorpi 1+1; Edward Kennett 0) – meeting abandoned after heat nine.

3 April: Elite League

Eastbourne 25 (David Norris 6; Nicki Pedersen 5; Adam Shields 5; Joonas Kylmakorpi 4+2; Peter Ljung 4+1; Edward Kennett 1+1; Ulrich Ostergaard 0) Swindon 17 – meeting abandoned after heat seven.

26 April: Elite League

Coventry 25 Eastbourne 29 (Peter Ljung 7+1; Joonas Kylmakorpi 7; Nicki Pedersen 6; Adam Shields 5+1; David Norris 2+2; Edward Kennett 2; Ulrich Ostergaard R/R) – Meeting abandoned after heat nine.

31 May: Inter-League Challenge

Rye House 46 Eastbourne 45 (David Norris 12; Steen Jensen 9+2; Andrew Moore 8+2; Adam Shields 7+1; Sebastian Tresarrieu 7; Daniel Giffard 2; Ulrich Ostergaard R/R).

20 September: Elite League Play-Off quarter-final

Ipswich 55 Eastbourne 39 (Nicki Pedersen 15; Davey Watt 9+2; Adam Shields 5+1; Sergei Darkin 4+1; Joonas Kylmakorpi 4; Edward Kennett 1+1; Sebastian Tresarrieu 1).

23 September: Challenge

Poole 67 Eastbourne 46 (Nicki Pedersen 17; Adam Shields 13; Paul Hurry 6; Davey Watt 3+2; Dean Barker 3; Leigh Lanham 2; Sebastian Tresarrieu 1+1; Edward Kennett 1+1).

IPSWICH EVENING STAR WITCHES

ADDRESS: Foxhall Heath Stadium, Foxhall Road, Ipswich, Suffolk, IP4 5TL.
PROMOTER: John Louis.
TRACK LENGTH: 300 metres.
TRACK RECORD: 57.5 seconds – Jaroslaw Hampel (12/09/02).
FIRST MEETING: 25 October 1950.
YEARS OF OPERATION: 1950-51 Open; 1952-53 Southern League; 1954-56 National League Division Two; 1957-58 National League; 1959 Southern Area League; 1960-62 National League; 1964 Metropolitan League; 1965 Open; 1969-71 British League Division Two; 1972-74 British League Division One; 1975-88 British League; 1989-90 National League; 1991-94 British League Division One; 1995-96 Premier League; 1997-04 Elite League.

NOTE: Ipswich also competed in the 1997 Amateur League, sharing their fixtures with King's Lynn and riding under the banner of 'Anglian Angels'.

CLUB HONOURS

KNOCK-OUT CUP WINNERS: 1970, 1971, 1976, 1978, 1981, 1984, 1998.
LEAGUE CHAMPIONS: 1975, 1976, 1984, 1998.
PAIRS CHAMPIONS: 1976, 1977.
INTER-LEAGUE KNOCK-OUT CUP WINNERS: 1977.
FOUR-TEAM CHAMPIONS: 1991.
CRAVEN SHIELD WINNERS: 1998.

RIDER ROSTER 2004

Hans N. ANDERSEN; Danny BIRD; Trevor HARDING; Kim JANSSON; Jesper B. JENSEN; Daniel KING; Chris LOUIS; Scott NICHOLLS; Paul PICKERING.

OTHER APPEARANCES/GUESTS (official matches only):

Leigh ADAMS; Tom BROWN; Jason BUNYAN; Kevin DOOLAN; Mark LORAM; Lee RICHARDSON; Davey WATT.

SKY BET ELITE LEAGUE

No	DATE	OPPONENTS	H/A	RESULT	ANDERSEN	BIRD	JENSEN	LOUIS	NICHOLLS	KING	JANSSON	HARDING	PICKERING	OTHERS
1	29/3	Belle Vue	A	W49-41	11 (5)	5+2 (4)	5+2 (4)	8+1 (4)	10+1 (5)	0 (3)	10+2 (5)	–	–	–
2	1/4	Poole	H	W50-43	11 (5)	9+2 (4)	4+2 (4)	8 (4)	11+2 (5)	1 (3)	6+2 (5)	–	–	–
3	5/4	Oxford	A	L45-50	12 (5)	–	6 (4)	6+1 (4)	12 (5)	3+1 (5)	5+1 (4)	1 (3)	–	–
4	8/4	Coventry	A	W49-45	8 (4)	6+1 (4)	8+2 (5)	8 (4)	13 (5)	0 (3)	6+1 (5)	–	–	–
5	9/4	Coventry	H	W54-41*	9+1 (5)	8+1 (4)	12+1 (5)	9+1 (4)	8+1 (4)	1 (4)	7+2 (4)	–	–	–
6	12/4	Wolverhampton	A	W48-42	10 (4)	–	12 (5)	4 (4)	12+1 (5)	4 (4)	4+1 (4)	2+1 (4)	–	–

No	DATE	OPPONENTS	H/A	RESULT	ANDERSEN	BIRD	JENSEN	LOUIS	NICHOLLS	KING	JANSSON	HARDING	PICKERING	OTHERS
7	15/4	Swindon	A	L40-52	9+1 (5)	9+1 (4)	6 (4)	4+1 (4)	9 (5)	1 (3)	2+1 (5)	–	–	–
8	22/4	Wolverhampton	H	L41-51	8+2 (5)	9 (5)	R/R	7 (5)	11 (5)	2+2 (3)	4+1 (7)	–	–	–
9	24/4	Swindon	H	W56-40*	13 (5)	10+2 (6)	R/R	12+1 (5)	9+2 (4)	5 (4)	7+4 (6)	–	–	–
10	5/5	Arena-Essex	A	W48-42	14 (5)	–	11+1 (5)	6+1 (4)	–	3 (5)	3 (4)	1 (3)	–	10 (4)
11	10/5	Coventry	H	W54-41	12+1 (5)	–	14+1 (5)	9+1 (4)	–	5 (4)	7+2 (4)	3 (4)	–	4+1 (4)
12	17/5	Eastbourne	A	L40-50	11 (6)	–	11 (6)	8 (5)	R/R	3+1 (5)	7+1 (5)	0 (3)	–	–
13	20/5	Eastbourne	H	W47-46	12 (5)	6+1 (4)	7 (4)	3+2 (4)	–	2+1 (3)	6+1 (5)	–	–	11 (5)
14	27/5	Belle Vue	H	W52-41*	8+2 (5)	11+1 (6)	10+2 (6)	12+1 (5)	R/R	4 (4)	7+1 (4)	–	–	–
15	31/5	Peterborough	A	L40-55	14 (5)	–	0 (4)	9 (5)	9 (4)	7+1 (5)	1 (4)	0 (3)	–	–
16	2/6	Poole	A	L34-58	8 (4)	–	6 (5)	4 (4)	12 (5)	1 (4)	2 (4)	1 (4)	–	–
17	10/6	Oxford	H	L44-46	5+2 (4)	9+1 (4)	7+1 (5)	12+1 (5)	5 (4)	5 (3)	1+1 (1)	–	–	–
18	17/6	Coventry	A	L44-45*	9+1 (5)	5 (4)	10+1 (5)	7 (4)	8+1 (4)	0 (4)	5 (4)	–	–	–
19	21/6	Swindon	H	W49-46	8 (4)	6+1 (4)	8+1 (4)	8 (5)	12 (5)	4+1 (4)	3+1 (4)	–	–	–
20	30/6	Arena-Essex	A	L42-48	7 (4)	1 (4)	7 (4)	7+2 (5)	14 (5)	0 (3)	6 (5)	–	–	–
21	1/7	Swindon	A	L37-56	5 (4)	8+1 (5)	7+1 (5)	7+1 (4)	3+1 (4)	0 (3)	7+2 (5)	–	–	–
22	8/7	Poole	H	W50-43	10+2 (5)	6+1 (4)	4+2 (4)	11 (4)	12+1 (5)	3 (3)	4+1 (5)	–	–	–
23	15/7	Oxford	H	W55-38	8 (4)	5+2 (4)	5+3 (4)	11 (4)	14 (5)	1 (3)	11+1 (6)	–	–	–
24	22/7	Arena-Essex	H	W57-38*	14+1 (5)	2+1 (4)	5+1 (3)	11+1 (4)	14+1 (5)	1 (4)	10+2 (5)	–	–	–
25	26/7	Wolverhampton	A	L44-49	4 (4)	–	R/R	18+1 (6)	11 (5)	4+2 (7)	5+1 (5)	–	–	2 (3)
26	29/7	Wolverhampton	H	W51-39*	12+1 (5)	–	R/R	12+1 (5)	14+1 (5)	4 (7)	9+3 (5)	–	–	0 (3)
27	9/8	Eastbourne	A	L45-52	R/R	–	8+1 (5)	16 (6)	14 (7)	4+2 (4)	2+1 (5)	–	1 (3)	–
28	11/8	Poole†	A	L33-48	R/R	–	–	5 (4)	18 (5)	3 (4)	5+1 (5)	–	2+1 (5)	0 (3)
29	12/8	Eastbourne	H	W63-31*	R/R	–	15+2 (6)	13+1 (5)	17+1 (6)	5 (4)	6+2 (5)	–	7+3 (4)	–
30	19/8	Belle Vue	H	W55-39	12+1 (5)	–	8+3 (4)	11+2 (5)	9 (4)	2+1 (4)	5+2 (4)	–	8 (5)	–
31	26/8	Peterborough	H	W54-40	8 (4)	–	6+2 (4)	10+1 (5)	13+1 (5)	7+1 (4)	7+3 (4)	–	3 (4)	–
32	6/9	Peterborough	A	L44-53	9 (5)	–	2+1 (4)	13 (5)	15+1 (5)	3 (4)	2+2 (4)	0 (3)	–	–
33	9/9	Arena-Essex	H	W49-41*	10+1 (5)	5+1 (4)	5 (4)	7 (4)	14 (5)	2 (3)	6+3 (5)	–	–	–
34	10/9	Oxford	A	W45-44*	7+1 (5)	7+1 (4)	6+1 (4)	8+1 (4)	12 (5)	1 (3)	4+1 (5)	–	–	–
35	15/9	Belle Vue	A	L41-50*	6 (4)	2+1 (4)	12 (5)	7+2 (4)	10 (5)	0 (3)	4 (5)	–	–	–
36	16/9	Peterborough	H	W52-42*	11 (5)	6+1 (4)	3 (3)	6+1 (4)	10 (4)	4+1 (4)	12+2 (6)	–	–	–

*Denotes bonus-point victory

†Meeting abandoned after heat thirteen, with the result permitted to stand.

DETAILS OF OTHER RIDERS:

Match No. 10: Leigh Adams 10 (4); Match No. 11: Lee Richardson 4+1 (4); Match No. 13: Mark Loram 11 (5); Match No. 25: Kevin Doolan 2 (3); Match No. 26: Jason Bunyan 0 (3); Match No. 28: Tom Brown 0 (3).

TACTICAL SUBSTITUTE AND TACTICAL RIDES, AS INCLUDED IN THE SCORES GRID:

Match No. 3: Nicholls 6 points (TR); Andersen 6 points (TR); Match No. 7: Bird 6 points (TR); Match No 8: Nicholls 4 points (TR); Match No. 15: Andersen 6 points (TR); Nicholls 4 points (TR); Match No. 16: Andersen 2 points (TR); Nicholls 2 points (TR); Match No. 21: Bird 4 points (TR); Louis 4 points (TR); Match No. 25: Louis 6 points (TR); Match No. 27: Louis 6 points (TR); Nicholls 4 points (TS), Jensen 4 points (TR); Match No. 28: Nicholls 6 points (TR); Match No. 32: Nicholls 6 points (TR); Louis 6 points (TR); Andersen 2 points (TS); Match No. 35: Jensen 6 points (TR).

IPSWICH: back row, left to right: Hans N. Andersen, Daniel King, Danny Bird, Mike Smillie (Team Manager), Kim Jansson, Chris Louis, Jesper B. Jensen. Front, on bike: Scott Nicholls.

ELITE LEAGUE AVERAGES

Rider	Mts	Rds	Pts	Bon	Tot	Avge	Max
Scott Nicholls	31	150	339	15	354	9.44	1 full; 3 paid
Hans N. Andersen	33	155	307	17	324	8.36	1 paid
Chris Louis	36	161	306	25	331	8.22	1 paid
Jesper B. Jensen	31	139	225	31	256	7.37	1 paid
Danny Bird	21	90	130	22	152	6.76	–
Kim Jansson	36	168	198	49	247	5.88	–
Paul Pickering	5	21	21	4	25	4.76	–
Daniel King	36	140	95	14	109	3.11	–
Trevor Harding	8	27	8	1	9	1.33	–
Tom Brown	1	3	0	0	0	0.00	–
Guests	5	19	27	1	28	5.89	–

KNOCK-OUT CUP

No	DATE	OPPONENTS	H/A	RESULT	ANDERSEN	BIRD	JENSEN	LOUIS	NICHOLLS	KING	JANSSON	HARDING	OTHERS
1	25/3	Eastbourne	H	W51-42	11+1 (5)	4+1 (4)	7+1 (4)	9+1 (4)	11 (5)	1 (3)	8+1 (5)	–	–
2	11/9	Eastbourne	A	W48-46*	9 (5)	-	4+1 (4)	8+1 (4)	13 (5)	4 (4)	8+3 (4)	2+1 (4)	–
3	6/10	Arena-Essex	A	W46-43	13 (5)	3 (4)	6+1 (4)	7+1 (4)	10 (5)	1 (4)	6+2 (4)	–	–
4	7/10	Arena-Essex	H	W51-42*	14 (5)	5 (4)	9 (5)	9+2 (4)	7 (4)	5+2 (4)	2+1 (4)	–	–
5	21/10	Poole	H	W48-42	11+1 (5)	6+1 (4)	6 (4)	8+2 (4)	9+2 (5)	3 (3)	5+2 (5)	–	–
6	31/10	Poole	A	L39-57	14 (5)	–	3+1 (4)	4 (4)	11+3 (5)	0 (3)	7+1 (6)	–	0 (3)

*Denotes aggregate victory

DETAILS OF OTHER RIDERS:

Match No. 6: Davey Watt 0 (3).

TACTICAL RIDES, AS INCLUDED IN THE SCORES GRID:

Match No. 6: Nicholls 6 points (TR); Andersen 6 points (TR).

OTHER MEETINGS

18 March: Air-Tek Challenge (first leg)

Ipswich 49 (Scott Nicholls 13+1; Jesper B. Jensen 13; Hans N. Andersen 9+1; Danny Bird 7+1; Chris Louis 4+1; Daniel King 2; Kim Jansson 1) Peterborough 44.

28 March: Air-Tek Challenge (second-leg)

Peterborough 46 Ipswich 50 (Hans N. Andersen 14; Scott Nicholls 14; Jesper B. Jensen 11; Chris Louis 5+2; Kim Jansson 5+1; Daniel King 1; Matthew Wright 0) – Ipswich won 99-90 on aggregate.

2 September: Challenge

Ipswich 60 (Chris Louis 15; Danny Bird 9+3; Leigh Lanham 9+2; Daniel King 9+1; Tom P. Madsen 9; Shane Parker 7+2; Matthew Wright 2) Rye House 33.

20 September: Elite League Play-Off quarter-final

Ipswich 55 (Scott Nicholls 13+1; Chris Louis 10+1; Daniel King 9+2; Hans N. Andersen 9+1; Jesper B. Jensen 8+1; Kim Jansson 6+2: Trevor Harding 0) Eastbourne 39.

27 September: Elite League Play-Off semi-final

Wolverhampton 45 Ipswich 45 (Hans N. Andersen 14; Jesper B. Jensen 9+1; Scott Nicholls 9+1; Chris Louis 5+1; Daniel King 5; Kim Jansson 3; Paul Pickering 0). Mikael Max subsequently defeated Hans N. Andersen in a run-off to give Wolverhampton a place in the final.

INDIVIDUAL MEETINGS

24 July: Scott Nicholls' Testimonial

QUALIFYING SCORES: Leigh Adams 12; Ryan Sullivan 11; Scott Nicholls 11; Billy Janniro 9; Shane Parker 9; Sam Ermolenko 7; Mark Loram 7; Chris Louis 6; Kevin Doolan 6; Dean Barker 5; Tom P. Madsen 4; Leigh Lanham 4; Jeremy Doncaster 2; Magnus Zetterstrom 1; Ryan Fisher 1; David Howe 0; Olly Allen 0. SEMI-FINAL: 1st Nicholls; 2nd Janniro; 3rd Ermolenko; 4th Parker. FINAL: 1st Adams; 2nd Sullivan; 3rd Nicholls; 4th Janniro.

28 October: 16-Lap Classic

QUALIFYING SCORES: Scott Nicholls 8; Chris Louis 8; Fredrik Lindgren 8; Sam Ermolenko 7; David Howe 6; Maciej Kuciapa 6; Daniel King 6; Adam Shields 6; Jesper B. Jensen 5; Karol Baron 5; Kim Jansson 5; Chris Harris 2. FINAL: 1st Shields (14); 2nd Jensen (12); 3rd Howe (10+2); 4th King (8); 5th Lindgren (6+2); 6th Nicholls (4+2); 7th Kuciapa (2); 8th Ermolenko (0+2). OVERALL RESULT: 1st Shields 20; 2nd Howe 18; 3rd Jensen 17; Lindgren 16; Nicholls 14; King 14; Ermolenko 9; Kuciapa 8. CONSOLATION FINAL: 1st Harris; 2nd Baron; 3rd Jansson; 4th Wright.

OXFORD SILVER MACHINE

NOTE: The information below relates only to the main Oxford team. For details of the second side, please refer to the Conference League section.

ADDRESS: Oxford Stadium, Sandy Lane, Cowley, Oxford, OX4 6LJ.

PROMOTER: Nigel Wagstaff.

TRACK LENGTH: 297 metres.

TRACK RECORD: 56.2 seconds – Hans Nielsen (13/10/88).

FIRST MEETING: 8 April 1939.

YEARS OF OPERATION: 1939-41 Open; 1949-50 National League Division Three; 1951-52 National League Division Two; 1953 Southern League; 1954-56 National League Division Two; 1957-64 National League; 1965-67 British League; 1968-74 British League Division One; 1975 British League; 1976-83 National League; 1984-90 British League; 1991-92 British League Division One; 1993-94 British League Division Two; 1995-97 Premier League; 1998-04 Elite League.

CLUB HONOURS

LEAGUE CHAMPIONS: 1950, 1964, 1985, 1986, 1989, 2001.
NATIONAL TROPHY (DIVISION THREE) WINNERS: 1950.
NATIONAL TROPHY WINNERS: 1964.
BRITANNIA SHIELD WINNERS: 1964.
PAIRS CHAMPIONS: 1985, 1986, 1987.
KNOCK-OUT CUP WINNERS: 1985, 1986 (Shared with Cradley Heath).
LEAGUE CUP WINNERS: 1986 (Shared with Cradley Heath).
PREMIERSHIP WINNERS: 1987.
GOLD CUP WINNERS: 1989.
FOUR-TEAM CHAMPIONS: 1994, 1996.

RIDER ROSTER 2004

Jonas DAVIDSSON; Rafal DOBRUCKI; Ryan FISHER; Greg HANCOCK; Niels-Kr stian IVERSEN; Travis McGOWAN; Tom P. MADSEN; Sebastian ULAMEK.

OTHER APPEARANCES/GUESTS (official matches only):

Leigh ADAMS; Craig BOYCE; Lukas DRYML; Emil KRAMER; Josh LARSEN; Mark LORAM; Andrew MOORE; David NORRIS; Brent WERNER.

SKY BET ELITE LEAGUE

No	DATE	OPPONENTS	H/A	RESULT	HANCOCK	McGOWAN	FISHER	IVERSEN	ULAMEK	DAVIDSSON	KRAMER	DOBRUCKI	MADSEN	OTHERS
1	29/3	Wolverhampton	A	L40-53	18 (5)	<u>5+1 (5)</u>	2 (4)	3 (4)	6 (4)	1+1 (3)	5+1 (5)	–	–	–
2	2/4	Wolverhampton	H	W52-43	10+1 (5)	8 (4)	6+1 (4)	7+1 (4)	13+1 (5)	4 (4)	4+1 (4)	–	–	–
3	5/4	Ipswich	H	W50-45	9+2 (4)	6+1 (4)	3+1 (4)	5+1 (4)	9+1 (5)	10 (5)	–	8+1 (4)	–	–
4	8/4	Swindon	A	L42-54	–	5+2 (5)	2+1 (5)	14 (6)	R/R	1 (3)	–	5+2 (5)	–	15 (6)
5	9/4	Swindon	H	W49-44	–	6+4 (5)	5+1 (4)	3+1 (3)	5 (4)	6+2 (3)	–	14+1 (6)	–	10 (5)
6	23/4	Belle Vue	H	W48-45	9+3 (5)	12+1 (5)	5+1 (4)	R/R	6 (4)	5+1 (5)	–	11+2 (7)	–	–
7	5/5	Poole	A	L37-54	13+1 (5)	1 (4)	2+1 (3)	3 (4)	8 (5)	3 (4)	–	7+1 (6)	–	–
8	7/5	Arena-Essex	H	W52-43	11+1 (5)	9+2 (5)	R/R	–	8+2 (5)	7+3 (5)	–	16 (7)	–	1 (3)
9	21/5	Eastbourne	H	W53-43	9+2 (5)	7+1 (5)	7+1 (4)	7+2 (4)	8+2 (4)	7+2 (4)	–	8+2 (4)	–	–
10	24/5	Peterborough	H	W54-38	8+2 (4)	8+1 (5)	9+1 (5)	R/R	11 (5)	13+2 (7)	–	5+1 (3)	–	–
11	26/5	Arena-Essex	A	L41-53	9 (5)	1+1 (4)	7 (4)	4+2 (4)	11+2 (5)	1 (3)	–	–	–	8 (5)
12	27/5	Coventry	A	L36-58	12 (5)	5+1 (5)	9 (4)	7+2 (5)	0 (1)	0 (0)	–	–	3 (2)	–
13	4/6	Coventry	H	W71-21*	<u>11+4 (5)</u>	<u>17+1 (6)</u>	11+1 (5)	–	–	9+2 (4)	–	F/R	–	23+5 (10)
14	7/6	Belle Vue	A	W46-44*	13 (5)	7+1 (5)	9+1 (6)	8+2 (5)	R/R	0 (3)	–	9 (6)	–	–
15	10/6	Ipswich	A	W46-44*	<u>15 (5)</u>	4+1 (5)	3+1 (4)	11+1 (5)	R/R	6+3 (5)	–	7 (6)	–	–
16	14/6	Eastbourne	A	L46-47*	13+1 (5)	7 (5)	11+1 (7)	7+1 (5)	R/R	3+2 (3)	–	5+1 (5)	–	–
17	18/6	Wolverhampton	H	L40-54	13+1 (4)	9 (6)	4 (5)	3 (5)	R/R	3 (4)	–	8 (6)	–	–
18	28/6	Wolverhampton	A	L35-58	13+1 (5)	2+1 (3)	11 (7)	4 (4)	1 (4)	1 (3)	–	3+1 (4)	–	–
19	2/7	Poole	H	L46-47	12 (5)	5+3 (4)	15+2 (7)	8 (4)	4+1 (4)	–	1+1 (3)	1 (3)	–	–
20	5/7	Eastbourne	H	W51-43	12+1 (5)	6+1 (4)	5+3 (5)	7+2 (4)	9 (5)	–	–	9+1 (4)	3+1 (3)	–

SKY BET ELITE LEAGUE continued

No	DATE	OPPONENTS	H/A	RESULT	HANCOCK	McGOWAN	FISHER	IVERSEN	ULAMEK	DAVIDSSON	KRAMER	DOBRUCKI	MADSEN	OTHERS
21	14/7	Peterborough	A	L43-47*	–	8+2 (5)	9+2 (6)	5 (4)	7+1 (4)	0 (3)	–	5 (4)	–	9 (4)
22	15/7	Ipswich	A	L38-55	–	4+1 (4)	3 (3)	5 (5)	6 (4)	5+1 (4)	–	4+1 (4)	–	11 (6)
23	23/7	Swindon	H	W53-41	11+1 (5)	13+2 (6)	9+2 (5)	7+1 (5)	R/R	–	–	11+1 (6)	2+1 (3)	–
24	30/7	Peterborough	H	W49-41	<u>16+2 (6)</u>	14 (6)	5+3 (5)	8 (5)	R/R	4 (4)	–	–	–	2+1 (4)
25	13/8	Arena-Essex	H	W53-42	14+2 (6)	12+1 (6)	11+1 (5)	–	R/R	3+1 (4)	–	7+1 (5)	6+1 (4)	–
26	16/8	Coventry	H	W53-41	16+1 (6)	11+2 (6)	6 (5)	8+1 (5)	R/R	6 (3)	–	6 (5)	–	–
27	25/8	Poole	A	L37-58	18 (6)	1 (3)	3+2 (5)	10 (7)	R/R	0 (3)	–	5+1 (6)	–	–
28	27/8	Poole	H	W65-29*	<u>13+2 (5)</u>	15+2 (6)	10+3 (5)	9+3 (5)	R/R	9 (4)	–	9+1 (5)	–	–
29	28/8	Eastbourne	A	L43-47*	11 (6)	7 (5)	7+2 (5)	–	R/R	7+3 (5)	–	8+2 (6)	3 (3)	–
30	30/8	Belle Vue	H	W52-43	15+1 (6)	5+2 (5)	7+2 (5)	–	R/R	12 (6)	–	10+1 (5)	3+1 (4)	–
31	1/9	Arena-Essex	A	L38-57	16 (6)	9+1 (6)	2 (4)	5+1 (6)	R/R	1 (3)	–	5 (5)	–	–
32	8/9	Belle Vue	A	L38-57	14 (6)	10+3 (6)	7 (5)	5 (6)	R/R	0 (3)	–	2+1 (4)	–	–
33	9/9	Swindon	A	L44-52*	17 (6)	0 (3)	6+2 (5)	11 (7)	R/R	0 (3)	–	10 (6)	–	–
34	10/9	Ipswich	H	L44-45	15+1 (6)	9+2 (6)	6 (4)	10 (7)	R/R	–	–	2 (4)	2+1 (3)	–
35	13/9	Coventry	A	W48-42*	12+1 (6)	7+3 (5)	10+1 (5)	12+1 (7)	R/R	4 (3)	–	3 (4)	–	–
36	15/9	Peterborough	A®	W46-44*	–	5+2 (6)	7 (6)	14+1 (7)	R/R	1 (3)	–	4 (3)	–	<u>15 (5)</u>

*Denotes bonus-point victory

®Match raced at Arena-Essex.

DETAILS OF OTHER RIDERS:

Match No. 4: Lukas Dryml 15 (6); Match No. 5: Lukas Dryml 10 (5); Match No. 9: Brent Werner 1 (3); Match No. 11: Brent Werner 8 (5); Match No. 14: David Norris <u>16+2 (6)</u>; Andrew Moore 7+3 (4); Match No. 22: David Norris 9 (4); Match No. 23: David Norris 11 (6); Match No. 25: Craig Boyce 2+1 (4); Match No. 36: Mark Loram <u>15 (5)</u>.

TACTICAL SUBSTITUTE AND TACTICAL RIDES, AS INCLUDED IN THE SCORES GRID:

Match No. 1: Hancock 6 points (TR); Match No. 4: L. Dryml 6 points (TR); Iversen 6 points (TR); Match No. 8: Hancock 2 points (TR); Dobrucki 0 points (TR); Match No. 12: Ulamek 6 points (TR); Iversen 2 points (TR); Match No. 13: Hancock 6 points (TR); Fisher 4 points (TR); Iversen 2 points (TS); Match No. 18: Hancock 6 points (TR); Dobrucki 2 points (TR); McGowan 2 points (TS); Match No. 19: Hancock 6 points (TR); McGowan 0 points (TR); Match No. 23: Ulamek 4 points (TR); Dobrucki 2 points (TR); Norris 0 points (TS); Match No. 28: Hancock 6 points (TR); Iversen 4 points (TR); Match No. 32: Hancock 6 points (TR); McGowan 4 points (TR); Match No. 33: McGowan 6 points (TR); Hancock 4 points (TR); Match No. 34: Dobrucki 6 points (TR); Hancock 6 points (TR).

ELITE LEAGUE AVERAGES

Rider	Mts	Rds	Pts	Bon	Tot	Avge	Max
Greg Hancock	31	163	374	31	405	9.94	2 full; 3 paid
Sebastian Ulamek	16	68	107	10	117	6.88	–
Travis McGowan	36	178	254	46	300	6.74	1 paid
Ryan Fisher	35	169	232	37	269	6.37	–
Niels-Kristian Iversen	29	146	203	23	226	6.19	–
Rafal Dobrucki	30	148	202	22	224	6.05	–
Jonas Davidsson	32	119	132	23	155	5.21	–
Tom P. Madsen	7	22	22	5	27	4.91	–
Emil Kramer	3	12	10	3	13	4.33	–
Guests	10	48	91	6	97	8.08	1 full; 1 paid

OXFORD: back row, left to right: Travis McGowan, Niels-Kristian Iversen, Sebastian Ulamek, Ryan Fisher. Front row: Rafal Dobrucki, Jonas Davidsson, Greg Hancock.

KNOCK-OUT CUP

No	DATE	OPPONENTS	H/A	RESULT	HANCOCK	McGOWAN	FISHER	IVERSEN	ULAMEK	DAVIDSSON	KRAMER	DOBRUCKI	OTHERS
1	26/3	Arena-Essex	H	W47-46	8 (5)	9+1 (5)	6 (4)	7 (4)	6 (4)	6+2 (4)	5 (4)	–	–
2	7/4	Arena-Essex	A	L46-48	–	3+1 (4)	1 (3)	12 (5)	5 (4)	4+1 (4)	–	6+1 (5)	15 (5)

DETAILS OF OTHER RIDERS:

Match No. 2: Leigh Adams 15 (5).

TACTICAL SUBSTITUTE AND TACTICAL RIDES, AS INCLUDED IN THE SCORES GRID:

Match No. 2: Iversen 6 points (TR); Adams 4 points (TR).

OTHER MEETINGS

17 March: Air-Tek Challenge (first leg)

Poole 51 Oxford 44 (Sebastian Ulamek 11+1; Greg Hancock 11; Niels-Kristian Iversen 9+1; Rafal Dobrucki 9+1; Ryan Fisher 3+1; Travis McGowan 1; Jonas Davidsson 0).

21 March: Staechmann Slideshow (Jan Staechmann Testimonial)

Stoke Select 22, Long Eaton Select 14, Oxford Select 10 (Jason Crump 4; Ronni Pedersen 3; Craig Boyce 3; Lee Derbyshire 0), Wolverhampton Select 8 – meeting abandoned after heat nine.

25 March: Challenge

Coventry 43 Oxford 49 (Greg Hancock 15; Niels-Kristian Iversen 10+2; Sebastian Ulamek 8+1; Ryan Fisher 7+1; Jonas Davidsson 5; Travis McGowan 4+1; Craig Branney 0; Rafal Dobrucki R/R).

16 April: Air-Tek Challenge (second leg)

Oxford 48 (Rafal Dobrucki 15+1; Greg Hancock 13+1; Sebastian Ulamek 8+2; Jonas Davidsson 6+2; Niels-Kristian Iversen 5; Ryan Fisher 1; Travis McGowan 0) Poole 45 – Poole won 96-92 on aggregate.

11 August: Elite League

Belle Vue 3 Oxford 3 (Greg Hancock 2; Travis McGowan 1+1; Jonas Davidsson 0; Niels-Kristian Iversen 0; Ryan Fisher DNR; Rafal Dobrucki DNR; Greg Hancock DNR) – meeting abandoned after heat one.

20 September: Elite League Play-Off quarter-final

Wolverhampton 61 Oxford 33 (Niels-Kristian Iversen 13+1; Rafal Dobrucki 8; Ryan Fisher 5+2; Josh Larsen 4; Travis McGowan 2+1; Jonas Davidsson 1; Sebastian Ulamek R/R).

INDIVIDUAL MEETING

15 October: Todd Wiltshire Farewell

1st Mikael Max 9; 2nd Todd Wiltshire 8; = 3rd Sam Ermolenko, Nicki Pedersen 7; Adam Shields 6; Craig Watson 6; Craig Boyce 6; David Howe 5; Billy Hamill 5; Mark Lemon 4; Steve Johnston 3; Steve Masters 2; Adam Skornicki 1; Thomas Stange 1; Davey Watt 1; Michael Hertrich 1 – meeting abandoned after heat twelve, with the result permitted to stand.

PETERBOROUGH ASL FREIGHT PANTHERS

ADDRESS: East of England Showground, Alwalton, Peterborough, PE2 0XE.
PROMOTER: Mick Horton.
TRACK LENGTH: 336 metres.
TRACK RECORD: 59.6 seconds – Ryan Sullivan (12/10/01 and 25/06/03), Leigh Adams (20/06/03) & Tony Rickardsson (2/04/04).
FIRST MEETING: 12 June 1970.
YEARS OF OPERATION: 1970-74 British League Division Two; 1975-90 National League; 1991-94 British League Division Two; 1995-96 British Premier League; 1997 Elite League; 1998 Premier League; 1999-04 Elite League.

CLUB HONOURS

FOUR-TEAM CHAMPIONS: 1977, 1978, 1988, 1989, 1992, 1997, 1998.
LEAGUE CHAMPIONS: 1992, 1998, 1999.
KNOCK-OUT CUP WINNERS: 1992, 1999, 2001.
PREMIERSHIP WINNERS: 1993.
PAIRS CHAMPIONS: 1998.
CRAVEN SHIELD WINNERS: 1999.

RIDER ROSTER 2004

Ricky ASHWORTH; Henning BAGER; Ales DRYML; Lukas DRYML; Gary HAVELOCK; Norbert MAGOSI; Tomasz PISZCZ; Lee RICHARDSON; Dariusz SLEDZ.

OTHER APPEARANCES/GUESTS (official matches only):

Adam ALLOTT; Hans N. ANDERSEN; Andrew APPLETON; Sam ERMOLENKO; Chris HARRIS; Ritchie HAWKINS; Robbie KESSLER; Jason KING; Claus KRISTENSEN; Josh LARSEN; Henrik MOLLER; Adam PIETRASZKO; Roman POVAZHNY; Adrian RYMEL; Emiliano SANCHEZ; Joe SCREEN; Andy SMITH; Kelvin TATUM; Brent WERNER.

SKY BET ELITE LEAGUE

No	DATE	OPPONENTS	H/A	RESULT	RICHARDSON	PISZCZ	HAVELOCK	A. DRYML	L. DRYML	BAGER	ASHWORTH	APPLETON	KESSLER	SLEDZ	MAGOSI	OTHERS
1	5/4	Wolverhampton	A	L39-53	8 (5)	1 (3)	7 (4)	4+1 (4)	6+1 (5)	1+1 (3)	12+1 (6)	–	–	–	–	–
2	9/4	Arena-Essex	H	W47-46	8 (5)	5+1 (4)	9+1 (5)	12 (4)	5+1 (4)	3+1 (4)	5+1 (4)	–	–	–	–	–
3	12/4	Coventry	H	W51-42	11+1 (5)	R/R	9+2 (5)	8+3 (5)	13+1 (5)	8+1 (6)	–	2 (4)	–	–	–	–
4	12/4	Coventry	A	L42-53	4 (2)	R/R	8+3 (6)	13+1 (6)	6 (3)	5+3 (7)	–	–	–	–	–	6 (6)
5	14/4	Arena-Essex	A	L46-47	–	R/R	16 (6)	2+1 (4)	2+1 (2)	16+2 (7)	0 (4)	–	–	–	–	8+2 (5)
6	16/4	Belle Vue	H	L42-48	–	R/R	11+2 (6)	12 (6)	5 (4)	3+1 (5)	–	3+2 (5)	–	–	–	8 (4)
7	8/5	Eastbourne	A	L43-47	15 (6)	4+1 (5)	9 (5)	–	R/R	–	3+1 (4)	3 (4)	–	–	–	9+1 (6)
8	12/5	Eastbourne	H	W50-46*	10 (5)	4+2 (4)	14 (5)	6+2 (4)	3 (4)	3 (3)	10+2 (5)	–	–	–	–	–
9	14/5	Wolverhampton	H	W48-45	–	2+1 (4)	14+1 (6)	–	R/R	4+1 (4)	7+1 (5)	–	–	–	–	21+2 (11)

SKY BET ELITE LEAGUE continued

No	DATE	OPPONENTS	H/A	RESULT	RICHARDSON	PISZCZ	HAVELOCK	A. DRYML	L. DRYML	BAGER	ASHWORTH	APPLETON	KESSLER	SLEDZ	MAGOSI	OTHERS
10	19/5	Poole	A	L45-48	11 (5)	1 (3)	6+3 (4)	5 (4)	13+1 (5)	5+1 (5)	–	–	–	–	–	4 (4)
11	24/5	Oxford	A	L38-54	5 (4)	2+2 (3)	12 (6)	3+1 (4)	6 (2)	9 (7)	1 (4)	–	–	–	–	–
12	28/5	Poole	H	D46-46	–	4+3 (4)	15+1 (6)	–	R/R	8+1 (6)	3 (4)	–	–	–	–	16+2 (10)
13	31/5	Ipswich	H	W55-40	12+1 (5)	1 (3)	12+2 (5)	10 (4)	6+2 (4)	7+4 (5)	7+1 (4)	–	–	–	–	–
14	4/6	Swindon	H	W47-46	11+1 (5)	–	10+1 (5)	9 (4)	5+1 (4)	5+2 (4)	6+2 (5)	–	–	–	–	1 (3)
15	9/6	Arena-Essex	A	L36-59	10 (5)	–	10 (5)	2 (4)	1 (4)	10 (7)	2 (3)	–	–	–	–	1 (3)
16	14/6	Belle Vue	A	L32-63	15 (5)	–	5 (4)	5 (5)	3+1 (4)	4 (5)	–	–	0 (2)	–	–	0 (4)
17	25/6	Eastbourne	H	D48-48	–	–	16+2 (6)	R/R	–	7+1 (5)	–	–	–	4 (5)	–	21+4 (14)
18	28/6	Swindon	A	L31-63	3+1 (4)	–	1 (4)	6 (5)	14 (5)	5 (4)	–	–	–	1+1 (4)	–	1 (4)
19	3/7	Eastbourne	A	L40-50	9 (5)	–	4+3 (4)	9 (4)	10 (5)	3+2 (4)	2 (5)	–	–	3 (3)	–	–
20	7/7	Swindon†	H	L30-46	10 (3)	–	8 (3)	4+1 (3)	2+1 (4)	5 (4)	0 (4)	–	–	1 (4)	–	–
21	8/7	Coventry	A	L31-61	5 (2)	–	8+1 (4)	1 (5)	0 (1)	5 (4)	–	12+1 (7)	–	0 (1)	–	–
22	12/7	Poole	H	L42-51	13+1 (5)	–	6+1 (4)	11 (6)	R/R	4+1 (5)	6+1 (6)	–	2+2 (4)	–	–	–
23	14/7	Oxford	H	W47-43	13+1 (5)	–	8+1 (4)	12+1 (6)	R/R	8 (5)	–	–	4+2 (6)	–	–	2+1 (4)
24	21/7	Poole	A	L40-53	–	–	8+1 (5)	5 (4)	12+2 (5)	3+1 (4)	0 (4)	–	–	0 (3)	–	12 (5)
25	26/7	Coventry	H	W47-43	11 (5)	–	10+2 (4)	13+1 (5)	6 (4)	4 (4)	–	–	3 (5)	–	0 (3)	–
26	29/7	Swindon	A	L44-52	15 (5)	–	4+2 (4)	6 (4)	13 (5)	3+1 (4)	–	–	0 (3)	–	–	3+1 (5)
27	30/7	Oxford	A	L41-49	7 (4)	–	6+2 (4)	7 (5)	10+1 (5)	5+1 (4)	5+1 (5)	1 (3)	–	–	–	–
28	11/8	Wolverhampton	H	W54-41	14 (5)	–	10+2 (5)	6+1 (4)	9+1 (4)	8 (4)	3+2 (4)	–	–	–	4+1 (4)	–
29	26/8	Ipswich	A	L40-54*	16 (5)	–	4 (4)	8 (5)	4+1 (4)	4 (4)	–	–	–	–	1 (3)	3+1 (5)
30	3/9	Arena-Essex	H	W48-45	–	–	12 (6)	–	R/R	9+1 (5)	–	–	–	–	4 (4)	23+3 (16)
31	6/9	Ipswich	H	W53-44	14 (5)	–	6+1 (4)	11+1 (5)	6+1 (4)	7+2 (4)	8+3 (5)	–	–	–	1+1 (3)	–
32	13/9	Wolverhampton	A	L36-57	16 (5)	–	7 (4)	4 (4)	1+1 (4)	3+1 (4)	5 (6)	–	–	–	0 (3)	–
33	14/9	Belle Vue	H	W49-41	–	–	6+2 (4)	R/R	16 (6)	9+2 (6)	10+1 (7)	–	–	–	1 (3)	7+1 (4)
34	15/9	Oxford	H®	L44-46	–	–	8+1 (6)	–	R/R	5+1 (5)	–	–	–	–	2 (3)	29+5 (16)
35	16/9	Ipswich	A	L42-52	15 (5)	–	8+1 (4)	8+1 (4)	0 (1)	5 (6)	–	–	–	–	1 (3)	5+1 (7)

*Denotes bonus-point victory

†Meeting abandoned after heat twelve, with the result permitted to stand.

®Match raced at Arena-Essex.

NOTE: One match was not ridden: Belle Vue *v.* Peterborough ('B' fixture).

DETAILS OF OTHER RIDERS:

Match No. 4: Emiliano Sanchez 6 (6); Match No. 5: Hans N. Andersen 8+2 (5); Jason King 2 (2); Match No. 6: Hans N. Andersen 8 (4); Match No. 7: Kelvin Tatum 9+1 (6); Match No. 9: Chris Harris 11+1 (6); Andy Smith 10+1 (5); Match No. 10: Brent Werner 4 (4); Match No. 12: Chris Harris 11+1 (6); Andy Smith 5+1 (4); Match No. 14: Adam Allott 1 (3); Match No. 15: Ritchie Hawkins 1 (3); Match No. 16: Henrik Moller 0 (4); Match No. 17: Sam Ermolenko 12+1 (5); Andy Smith 7+2 (5); Emiliano Sanchez 2+1 (4); Match No. 18: Claus Kristensen 1 (4); Match No. 23: Adrian Rymel 2+1 (4); Match No. 24: Hans N. Andersen 12 (5); Match No. 26: Adrian Rymel 3+1 (5); Match No. 29: Adrian Rymel 3+1 (5); Match No. 30: Joe Screen 10 (5); Andy Smith 7+1 (5); Adam Pietraszko 6+2 (6); Match No. 33: Sam Ermolenko 7+1 (4); Match No. 34: Josh Larsen 13+3 (6); Brent Werner 10+1 (6); Roman Povazhny 6+1 (4); Match No. 35: Adrian Rymel 5+1 (7).

PETERBOROUGH: back row, left to right: Emiliano Sanchez, Ricky Ashworth, Robbie Kessler, Henrik Moller, Henning Bager, Andrew Appleton, Lukas Dryml. Front, kneeling: Tomasz Piszcz, Ales Dryml. On bikes: Gary Havelock, Lee Richardson.

TACTICAL SUBSTITUTE AND TACTICAL RIDES, AS INCLUDED IN THE SCORES GRID:

Match No. 1: Ashworth 6 points (TR); Match No.2: A. Dryml 6 points (TR); Match No. 4: A. Dryml 6 points (TR); L. Dryml 4 points (TR); Match No. 5: Havelock 6 points (TR); Match No. 10: Richardson 6 points (TR); Match No. 11: L. Dryml 4 points (TR); Havelock 2 points (TS); Richardson 0 points (TR); Match No. 12: Havelock 4 points (TR); Match No. 15: Richardson 6 points (TR); Havelock 4 points (TR); Match No. 16: Richardson 6 points (TR); A. Dryml 2 points (TR); L. Dryml 2 points (TS); Match No. 17: Havelock 6 points (TR); Ermolenko 6 points (TR); Match No. 18: L. Dryml 6 points (TR); Richardson 2 points (TR); Match No. 20: Havelock 4 points (TR); Richardson 4 points (TR); Match No. 21: Appleton 2 points (TS); Bager 2 points (TR); Havelock 2 points (TR); Match No. 22: Richardson 6 points (TR); Match No. 24: L. Dryml 4 points (TR); Havelock 2 points (TR); Andersen 2 points (TS); Match No. 26: Richardson 6 points (TR); L. Dryml 6 points (TR); Match No. 29: Richardson 6 points (TR); Havelock 2 points (TR); Match No 32: Richardson 6 points (TR); L. Dryml 0 points (TR); Match No. 35: Havelock 4 points (TR); Richardson 4 points (TR); Bager 0 points (TS).

ELITE LEAGUE AVERAGES

Rider	Mts	Rds	Pts	Bon	Tot	Avge	Max
Lee Richardson	26	120	255	6	261	8.70	–
Gary Havelock	35	166	289	38	327	7.88	1 paid
Lukas Dryml	27	107	164	17	181	6.77	–
Ales Dryml	28	127	195	15	210	6.61	–
Henning Bager	34	163	192	32	224	5.50	–
Adam Pietraszko	1	6	6	2	8	5.33	–
Ricky Ashworth	20	94	92	17	109	4.64	–
Tomasz Piszcz	9	33	24	10	34	4.12	–
Andrew Appleton	5	23	20	3	23	4.00	–
Jason King	1	2	2	0	2	4.00	–
Emiliano Sanchez	2	10	8	1	9	3.60	–
Adrian Rymel	4	21	13	4	17	3.24	–
Robbie Kessler	5	20	9	4	13	2.60	–
Norbert Magosi	9	29	14	2	16	2.21	–
Dariusz Sledz	6	20	9	1	10	2.00	–
Henrik Moller	1	4	0	0	0	0.00	–
Guests	20	95	149	17	166	6.99	–

KNOCK-OUT CUP

No	DATE	OPPONENTS	H/A	RESULT	RICHARDSON	PISZCZ	HAVELOCK	A. DRYML	L. DRYML	BAGER	ASHWORTH
1	24/3	Poole	A	L37-58	4 (4)	1 (3)	9 (5)	3+1 (4)	14 (5)	3+1 (5)	3+1 (4)
2	2/4	Poole	H	L44-46	12+1 (5)	5 (4)	9+3 (5)	6+1 (4)	6+1 (4)	4 (4)	2+1 (4)

TACTICAL RIDES, AS INCLUDED IN THE SCORES GRID:

Match No. 1: L. Dryml 6 points (TR); Havelock 4 points (TR).

OTHER MEETINGS

18 March: Air-Tek Challenge (first leg)

Ipswich 49 Peterborough 44 (Gary Havelock 9+1; Lee Richardson 9; Lukas Dryml 7; Henning Bager 5+2; Ales Dryml 5; Andrew Appleton 5; Tomasz Piszcz 4+1).

28 March: Air-Tek Challenge (second leg)

Peterborough 46 (Lee Richardson 11+1; Gary Havelock 9; Matej Zagar 8+1; Henning Bager 6; Ricky Ashworth 5+3; Lukas Dryml 5; Emiliano Sanchez 2+2) Ipswich 50 – Ipswich won 99-90 on aggregate.

PAIRS MEETING

24 September: Super 2s Best Pairs

1st Adam Shields (12+3) & Adam Pietraszko (11+2) = 23; 2nd Henning Bager (16) & Tom P. Madsen (4+2) = 20; 3rd Lee Richardson (17) & Jason King (2) = 19; Ricky Ashworth (10) & Brett Woodifield (8+2) = 18; Ales Dryml (13) & Jordan Jurczynski (4+2) = 17; Daniel King (10+1) & Henrik Moller (6+3) = 16; David Howe (12) & James Mann (1) = 13.

POOLE RIAS PIRATES

ADDRESS: Poole Stadium, Wimborne Road, Poole, Dorset, BH15 2BP.
PROMOTERS: Pete Ansell, Matt Ford & Mike Golding.
TRACK LENGTH: 299.1 metres.
TRACK RECORD: 57.06 seconds – Ryan Sullivan (16/06/04).
FIRST MEETING: 26 April 1948.
YEARS OF OPERATION: 1948-51 National League Division Three; 1952-55 National League Division Two; 1956 National League Division One; 1957 Open; 1958-59 National League; 1960-63 Provincial League; 1964 Provincial League & Metropolitan League; 1965-67 British League; 1968-74 British League Division One; 1975-84 British League; 1985-90 National League; 1991-94 British League Division One; 1995-96 Premier League; 1997-04 Elite League.

CLUB HONOURS

LEAGUE CHAMPIONS: 1951, 1952, 1955, 1961, 1962, 1969, 1989, 1990, 1994, 2003, 2004.
NATIONAL TROPHY (DIVISION TWO) WINNERS: 1952, 1955.
KNOCK-OUT CUP WINNERS: 1990, 2003, 2004.
FOUR-TEAM CHAMPIONS: 1994.
CRAVEN SHIELD WINNERS: 2001, 2002.
BRITISH LEAGUE CUP WINNERS: 2003.

RIDER ROSTER 2004

Daniel DAVIDSSON; Matej FERJAN; Krzysztof KASPRZAK; Antonio LINDBACK; Jason LYONS; Bjarne PEDERSEN; Tony RICKARDSSON; Ryan SULLIVAN; Davey WATT; Magnus ZETTERSTROM.

OTHER APPEARANCES/GUESTS (official matches only):

Leigh ADAMS; Andre COMPTON; Graeme GORDON; Mark LEMON; Phil MORRIS; David NORRIS; George STANCL; Brent WERNER.

SKY BET ELITE LEAGUE

No	DATE	OPPONENTS	H/A	RESULT	LYONS	PEDERSEN	ZETTERSTROM	WATT	RICKARDSSON	DAVIDSSON	LINDBACK	SULLIVAN	COMPTON	FERJAN	KASPRZAK	OTHERS
1	29/3	Arena-Essex	A	W47-43	4 (4)	7+3 (4)	8+1 (4)	0 (3)	15 (5)	1+1 (3)	12+1 (7)	–	–	–	–	–
2	31/3	Arena-Essex	H	W52-40*	6+2 (4)	10 (5)	6+1 (4)	7 (4)	14+1 (5)	1 (4)	8+1 (4)	–	–	–	–	–
3	1/4	Ipswich	A	L43-50	1 (4)	6 (4)	10+1 (5)	3 (4)	11+1 (5)	10+1 (5)	2+1 (3)	–	–	–	–	–
4	9/4	Eastbourne	H	W52-44	7+2 (4)	12+1 (5)	7 (4)	5+1 (4)	13+1 (5)	3 (4)	5 (4)	–	–	–	–	–
5	9/4	Eastbourne	A	W50-40*	7+2 (5)	9+2 (5)	2 (4)	5+2 (4)	11 (4)	2+1 (3)	14+1 (6)	–	–	–	–	–
6	14/4	Wolverhampton	H	W53-43	7 (4)	9+1 (5)	6+1 (4)	1+1 (2)	11+2 (5)	5+1 (4)	14+2 (6)	–	–	–	–	–
7	19/4	Wolverhampton	A	L40-50	5+3 (4)	13 (5)	4 (3)	1 (3)	11+1 (5)	2 (4)	4+1 (6)	–	–	–	–	–
8	22/4	Coventry	A	W55-40	9 (5)	4+2 (4)	3+1 (4)	3+1 (3)	13+2 (5)	10+1 (4)	13 (5)	–	–	–	–	–
9	28/4	Belle Vue	H	W49-42	5 (4)	7+3 (5)	8 (4)	4+2 (4)	10+2 (5)	7 (5)	8+1 (4)	–	–	–	–	–
10	5/5	Oxford	H	W54-37	6+3 (4)	11 (5)	6+2 (4)	5+1 (3)	–	1 (3)	16+2 (6)	9+1 (5)	–	–	–	–
11	12/5	Swindon	H	W56-38	5+1 (4)	6+2 (4)	10 (4)	3+1 (3)	–	9 (4)	11+4 (6)	12+1 (5)	–	–	–	–
12	13/5	Swindon	A	L39-53*	3 (4)	9 (5)	1 (4)	4 (4)	–	1 (3)	8+2 (5)	13+1 (5)	–	–	–	–
13	19/5	Peterborough	H	W48-45	3 (4)	12+1 (5)	3 (3)	0 (3)	–	8+2 (4)	13+2 (7)	9 (4)	–	–	–	–
14	26/5	Coventry	H	W47-45*	1 (5)	6 (3)	3+1 (3)	3 (3)	–	5+3 (4)	16+3 (7)	13 (5)	–	–	–	–
15	28/5	Peterborough	A	D46-46*	8 (5)	R/R	7+1 (4)	–	–	0 (3)	15+2 (7)	–	–	–	–	16+4 (11)
16	2/6	Ipswich	H	W58-34*	9 (4)	11+2 (5)	8+2 (4)	–	–	7+1 (4)	8+2 (5)	10+1 (4)	–	–	–	5+2 (4)
17	4/6	Arena-Essex	A	L40-53	5+2 (5)	18 (6)	1 (5)	–	–	5 (5)	R/R	9 (6)	2+1 (3)	–	–	–
18	5/6	Eastbourne	A	L44-51	5 (5)	14+1 (6)	8+1 (5)	–	–	5 (4)	R/R	9 (6)	3+3 (4)	–	–	–
19	7/6	Arena-Essex	H	W47-43	3+2 (4)	11+1 (5)	1+1 (3)	–	–	10+1 (6)	8 (4)	13 (5)	1 (3)	–	–	–
20	10/6	Coventry	A	L44-46	1+1 (4)	8 (4)	6+2 (4)	–	–	4 (4)	10+1 (5)	12 (5)	–	–	–	3 (4)
21	14/6	Wolverhampton	A	W49-41	3+3 (4)	13 (5)	6 (4)	–	–	5 (5)	7+1 (4)	13+1 (5)	–	–	–	2+1 (3)
22	16/6	Wolverhampton	H	W54-40*	–	7+1 (4)	7+2 (4)	–	–	2 (4)	13 (5)	13 (5)	–	6+1 (4)	6+2 (4)	–
23	30/6	Eastbourne	H	L46-49	–	7 (4)	4 (4)	–	–	–	11+1 (5)	13 (5)	–	6 (4)	3 (4)	2+1 (4)
24	2/7	Oxford	A	W47-46*	–	6 (4)	6+2 (5)	–	–	–	R/R	16 (5)	–	6+2 (6)	12+1 (7)	1 (3)
25	5/7	Belle Vue	A	L43-47*	–	12 (5)	5+2 (4)	–	–	2+1 (3)	8 (4)	8 (5)	–	2+1 (4)	6 (5)	–
26	8/7	Ipswich	A	L43-50	–	5 (4)	4+3 (4)	–	–	1 (3)	4 (4)	15 (5)	–	9+1 (5)	–	5+1 (5)
27	12/7	Peterborough	A	W51-42	–	11 (5)	4+1 (4)	–	–	4 (4)	4+1 (4)	8+1 (4)	–	11 (5)	9 (5)	–
28	14/7	Swindon	H	W57-38	–	9+1 (5)	1 (3)	–	–	11+1 (5)	7+3 (4)	13+1 (5)	–	9 (4)	7+2 (4)	–
29	15/7	Swindon	A	D45-45*	–	13 (5)	3 (4)	–	–	2 (4)	10+1 (5)	9 (4)	–	7 (4)	1+1 (4)	–
30	21/7	Peterborough	H	W53-40*	–	14 (5)	5+1 (4)	–	–	7+1 (4)	6 (4)	7+1 (4)	–	6+2 (4)	8+2 (5)	–
31	28/7	Coventry	H	W55-39*	–	13+1 (5)	5+2 (4)	–	–	0 (2)	8+3 (4)	8 (4)	–	14 (5)	7 (6)	–
32	11/8	Ipswich†	H	W48-33*	–	10 (4)	13+1 (5)	–	–	–	6+2 (3)	6+1 (4)	–	9+2 (4)	0 (3)	4+2 (3)
33	25/8	Oxford	H	W58-37	–	14 (5)	4 (4)	–	–	8+1 (4)	10 (4)	7 (5)	–	7+3 (4)	8+3 (4)	–

No	DATE	OPPONENTS	H/A	RESULT	LYONS	PEDERSEN	ZETTERSTROM	WATT	RICKARDSSON	DAVIDSSON	LINDBACK	SULLIVAN	COMPTON	FERJAN	KASPRZAK	OTHERS
34	27/8	Oxford	A	L29-65	–	0 (1)	6+2 (7)	–	–	5 (7)	R/R	13 (5)	–	4 (5)	1 (5)	–
35	9/9	Belle Vue	H	W54-40	–	11+1 (5)	3+2 (4)	–	–	4 (4)	7+1 (4)	9+1 (4)	–	14 (5)	–	6+2 (4)
36	15/9	Belle Vue	A	L25-68	–	8 (6)	6 (7)	–	–	0 (3)	R/R	3 (4)	–	0 (4)	8+1 (6)	–

*Denotes bonus-point victory

†Meeting abandoned after heat thirteen, with the result permitted to stand.

DETAILS OF OTHER RIDERS:

Match No. 15: David Norris 8+2 (5); Graeme Gordon 8+2 (6); Match No. 16: Brent Werner 5+2 (4); Match No. 20: Phil Morris 3 (4); Match No. 21: Brent Werner 2+1 (3); Match No. 23: Phil Morris 2+1 (4); Match No. 24: Phil Morris 1 (3); Match No. 26: George Stancl 5+1 (5); Match No. 32: Mark Lemon 4+2 (3); Match No. 35: Mark Lemon 6+2 (4).

TACTICAL SUBSTITUTE AND TACTICAL RIDES, AS INCLUDED IN THE SCORES GRID:

Match No. 3: Zetterstrom 6 points (TR); Match No. 12: Sullivan 4 points (TR); Lindback 0 points (TR); Match No. 14: Sullivan 4 points (TR); Pedersen 0 points (TR; 2 minute exclusion); Match No. 17: Pedersen 4 points (TR); Sullivan 2 points (TR); Match No. 18: Zetterstrom 6 points (TR); Pedersen 6 points (TR); Match No. 23: Sullivan 6 points (TR); Zetterstrom 4 points (TR); Match No. 24: Sullivan 6 points (TR); Match No. 26: Sullivan 6 points (TR); Match No. 34: Sullivan 6 points (TR); Ferjan 4 points (TR); Match No. 36: Pedersen 2 points (TR); Sullivan 2 points (TR); Zetterstrom 2 points (TS).

ELITE LEAGUE AVERAGES

Rider	Mts	Rds	Pts	Bon	Tot	Avge	Max
Tony Rickardsson	9	44	109	10	119	10.82	1 ful ; 2 paid
Bjarne Pedersen	35	162	330	23	353	8.72	–
Antonio Lindback	31	151	286	39	325	8.61	1 paid
Ryan Sullivan	26	123	252	10	262	8.52	–
Mark Lemon	2	7	10	4	14	8.00	–
Matej Ferjan	15	67	108	12	120	7.16	–
Magnus Zetterstrom	36	150	181	33	214	5.71	–
Krzysztof Kasprzak	13	62	76	12	88	5.68	–
Jason Lyons	21	90	103	21	124	5.51	–
Daniel Davidsson	33	132	147	16	163	4.94	–
Davey Watt	14	47	44	9	53	4.51	–
Andre Compton	3	10	6	4	10	4.00	–
Phil Morris	3	11	6	1	7	2.55	–
Guests	5	23	28	8	36	6.26	–

KNOCK-OUT CUP

No	DATE	OPPONENTS	H/A	RESULT	LYONS	PEDERSEN	ZETTERSTROM	WATT	RICKARDSSON	LINDBACK	DAVIDSSON	KASPRZAK	FERJAN	SULLIVAN
1	24/3	Peterborough	H	W58-37	5+2 (4)	9+1 (4)	10+2 (5)	7+1 (4)	14 (5)	12+1 (5)	1 (3)	–	–	–
2	2/4	Peterborough	A	W46-44*	2 (4)	9 (5)	9 (4)	3+2 (4)	13+1 (5)	7+2 (4)	3 (4)	–	–	–
3	6/10	Swindon	H	W61-30	–	7+3 (4)	6 (4)	–	–	6+3 (4)	5+1 (4)	11+2 (5)	14 (5)	12 (4)
4	7/10	Swindon	A	L40-53*	–	5+1 (5)	0 (4)	–	–	3 (4)	3 (4)	9+1 (5)	6+1 (4)	14 (4)
5	21/10	Ipswich	A	L42-48	–	5+1 (4)	4+1 (5)	–	–	8+1 (4)	1+1 (3)	8 (5)	8 (4)	8 (5)
6	31/10	Ipswich	H	W57-39*	–	6+1 (4)	7+2 (4)	–	–	13+2 (5)	3 (4)	7+3 (4)	10 (4)	11 (5)

*Denotes aggregate victory

POOLE: back row, left to right: Bjarne Pedersen, Ryan Sullivan, Krzysztof Kasprzak, Neil Middleditch (Team Manager), Antonio Lindback, Matej Ferjan, Daniel Davidsson. On bike: Magnus Zetterstrom.

TACTICAL RIDE, AS INCLUDED IN THE SCORES GRID:

Match No. 4: Sullivan 6 points (TR).

OTHER MEETINGS

10 March: Champagne Stakes (first leg)

Poole 51 (Tony Rickardsson 12+1; Antonio Lindback 10; Jason Lyons 9+3; Magnus Zetterstrom 7+2; Bjarne Pedersen 6; Davey Watt 4+1; Daniel Davidsson 3) Swindon 39

11 March: Champagne Stakes (second leg)

Swindon 8 Poole 4 (Bjarne Pedersen 3; Antonio Lindback 1; Jason Lyons 0; Daniel Davidsson 0; Magnus Zetterstrom DNR; Davey Watt DNR; Tony Rickardsson DNR) – meeting abandoned after heat two.

14 March: Inter-League Challenge

Newcastle 41 Poole 49 (Magnus Zetterstrom 14; Bjarne Pedersen 12+1; Daniel Davidsson 11; Jason Lyons 8+2; Antonio Lindback 4; Davey Watt 0; John Branney 0).

17 March: Air-Tek Challenge (first leg)

Poole 51 (Tony Rickardsson 11; Antonio Lindback 10+1; Bjarne Pedersen 10 Daniel Davidsson 8+1; Jason Lyons 5+1; Magnus Zetterstrom 5+1; Phil Morris 2+1) Oxford 44.

16 April: Air-Tek Challenge (second leg)

Oxford 48 Poole 45 (Tony Rickardsson 15; Bjarne Pedersen 11+2; Mark Lemon 5+1; Antonio Lindback 5+1; Jason Lyons 4+1; Magnus Zetterstrom 4; Daniel Davidsson 1) – Poole won 96-92 on aggregate.

12 August: Inter-League Challenge

Isle of Wight 42 Poole 50 (Magnus Zetterstrom 12+2; Krzysztof Kasprzak 11; Bjarne Pedersen 10+1; Ryan Sullivan 10+1; Matej Ferjan 6+1; Danny Warwick 1; Robert Mikolajczak 0).

18 August: Challenge

Poole 46 (Bjarne Pedersen 11; Matej Ferjan 11; Krzysztof Kasprzak 7; Magnus Zetterstrom 6+1; Antonio Lindback 5+1; Ryan Sullivan 4; Daniel Davidsson 2+1) Swindon 47.

23 September: Challenge

Poole 67 (Ryan Sullivan 14; Matej Ferjan 10+2; Bjarne Pedersen 10+1; Daniel Davidsson 10+1; Krzysztof Kasprzak 8+1; Antonio Lindback 6+2; Tomasz Chrzanowski 5; Magnus Zetterstrom 4+2) Eastbourne 46.

30 September: Challenge

Poole 58 (Ryan Sullivan 15; Matej Ferjan 12; Bjarne Pedersen 9+2; Daniel Davidsson 9+1; Magnus Zetterstrom 7+1; Mark Lemon 4; Danny Warwick 2) Polish Select 35 (Krzysztof Kasprzak 12; Tomasz Chrzanowski 8; Roman Chromik 7+1; Andy Smith 5+1; Adam Pawliczek 3; Robert Kasprzak 0; Jacek Rempala 0; Karol Malecha 0).

4 October: Elite League Play-Off final (first leg)

Wolverhampton 41 Poole 49 (Antonio Lindback 12+2; Leigh Adams 11; Bjarne Pedersen 9+1; Matej Ferjan 6+1; Magnus Zetterstrom 6+1; Krzysztof Kasprzak 4; Daniel Davidsson 1).

11 October: Elite League Play-Off final (second-leg)

Poole 63 (Bjarne Pedersen 12; Antonio Lindback 11+2; Ryan Sullivan 11+1 Matej Ferjan 8+2; Daniel Davidsson 8; Magnus Zetterstrom 7+2; Krzysztof Kasprzak 6+1) Wolverhampton 30 – Poole won 112-71 on aggregate.

PEBLEY BEACH SWINDON ROBINS

NOTE: The information below relates only to the main Swindon team. For details of the second side, please refer to the Conference League section.

ADDRESS: Swindon Stadium, Blunsdon, nr. Swindon, Wiltshire, SN25 4DN.
PROMOTER: Alun Rossiter.
TRACK LENGTH: 361.2 metres.
TRACK RECORD: 64.46 seconds – Leigh Adams (13/05/04).
FIRST MEETING: 23 July 1949.
YEARS OF OPERATION: 1949 Open & National League Division Three; 1950-51 National League Division Three; 1952-53 Southern League; 1954-56 National League Division Two; 1957-64 National League; 1965-67 British League; 1968-74 British League Division One; 1975-90 British League; 1991-92 British League Division One; 1993-94 British League Division Two; 1995-96 Premier League; 1997-98 Elite League; 1999-03 Premier League; 2004 Elite League.

CLUB HONOURS

LEAGUE CHAMPIONS: 1956, 1957, 1967.
PAIRS CHAMPIONS: 1994, 2004.
KNOCK-OUT CUP WINNERS: 2000.
YOUNG SHIELD WINNERS: 2000.
FOUR-TEAM CHAMPIONS: 2003.

RIDER ROSTER 2004

Leigh ADAMS; Olly ALLEN; Glenn CUNNINGHAM; Charlie GJEDDE; Steve JOHNSTON; Peter LJUNG; Steve MASTERS; David RUUD; Andy SMITH.

OTHER APPEARANCES/GUESTS (official matches only):
Ross BRADY; Eric CARRILLO; Michael COLES; Billy JANNIRO; Claus KRISTENSEN; Rafal KURMANSKI; Leigh LANHAM; Andrew MOORE; David NORRIS; Simon STEAD; Tomas TOPINKA.

SKY BET ELITE LEAGUE

No	DATE	OPPONENTS	H/A	RESULT	GJEDDE	SMITH	JOHNSTON	RUUD	ADAMS	MOORE	ALLEN	KRISTENSEN	CUNNINGHAM	KURMANSKI	LJUNG	OTHERS
1	8/4	Oxford	H	W54-42	5+2 (4)	10+1 (5)	8+1 (4)	5+1 (4)	15 (5)	8+2 (6)	3 (2)	–	–	–	–	–
2	9/4	Oxford	A	L44-49*	14+1 (5)	5+1 (4)	7 (4)	2 (4)	15 (5)	–	–	1 (4)	–	–	–	0 (4)
3	15/4	Ipswich	H	W52-40	10+1 (5)	5+1 (4)	6 (4)	9+1 (4)	15 (5)	–	5 (5)	2+1 (3)	–	–	–	–
4	21/4	Arena-Essex	A	L43-49	1 (4)	2 (4)	9 (5)	0 (3)	18 (5)	5 (4)	8 (5)	–	–	–	–	–
5	22/4	Belle Vue	H	L46-47	8 (5)	6+2 (4)	7 (4)	5+2 (4)	18 (5)	–	1 (5)	1 (3)	–	–	–	–
6	24/4	Ipswich	A	L40-56	4 (4)	4 (5)	10 (5)	R/R	16 (5)	–	4+1 (7)	–	2 (4)	–	–	–
7	26/4	Belle Vue	A	L42-48	12+1 (5)	5+1 (4)	5+1 (4)	3+1 (3)	11+1 (5)	2 (4)	4 (5)	–	–	–	–	–

No	DATE	OPPONENTS	H/A	RESULT	GJEDDE	SMITH	JOHNSTON	RUUD	ADAMS	MOORE	ALLEN	KRISTENSEN	CUNNINGHAM	KURMANSKI	LJUNG	OTHERS
8	3/5	Wolverhampton	A	L44-51	7 (4)	R/R	14+1 (6)	3 (5)	–	2+1 (4)	5+1 (6)	–	–	–	–	13 (5)
9	12/5	Poole	A	L38-56	R/R	3 (5)	11 (6)	5+1 (5)	18 (6)	–	0 (4)	–	–	1 (4)	–	–
10	13/5	Poole	H	W53-39	R/R	10+3 (5)	11+1 (6)	4 (5)	18 (6)	–	5+1 (4)	–	–	5+1 (4)	–	–
11	27/5	Eastbourne	H	W48-42	R/R	7+2 (5)	5+1 (5)	9 (6)	15+2 (6)	–	–	–	5+2 (4)	7 (4)	–	–
12	31/5	Coventry	A	W47-43	R/R	8 (5)	9 (6)	5 (5)	18 (6)	–	1 (3)	–	6+1 (5)	–	–	–
13	3/6	Wolverhampton	H	W48-45	R/R	6+1 (5)	5+2 (5)	13+1 (7)	14 (5)	–	7+1 (4)	–	–	–	–	3 (4)
14	4/6	Peterborough	A	L46-47	R/R	10+1 (5)	16 (6)	–	11 (5)	–	1 (4)	–	–	–	–	8+1 (10)
15	10/6	Eastbourne	H	D45-45	R/R	7+1 (5)	8 (6)	6 (3)	15 (5)	–	7+3 (7)	–	2+1 (4)	–	–	–
16	17/6	Arena-Essex	H	W47-42	R/R	4+1 (5)	13+1 (6)	–	14+1 (5)	–	3 (3)	–	3+1 (3)	–	–	10 (5)
17	21/6	Ipswich	A	L46-49	R/R	4+2 (5)	12 (6)	6+1 (6)	18 (5)	–	0 (3)	–	–	–	–	6 (5)
18	28/6	Peterborough	H	W63-31*	R/R	8+3 (5)	13+3 (6)	16+1 (6)	11+1 (4)	–	3+1 (4)	–	–	–	12+2 (5)	–
19	1/7	Ipswich	H	W56-37*	R/R	6+2 (5)	14+1 (6)	13+2 (5)	17+1 (6)	–	6 (7)	–	0 (0	–	–	–
20	5/7	Wolverhampton	A	L44-52	R/R	4 (5)	11 (6)	9 (5)	16+2 (6)	–	2 (4)	–	–	–	2 (4)	–
21	7/7	Peterborough†	A	W46-30	R/R	0 (0)	8 (4)	9+3 (5)	9+1 (4)	–	6+1 (5)	–	–	–	14+3 (6)	–
22	14/7	Poole	A	L38-57	3 (4)	1 (3)	5 (4)	5+3 (5)	16 (5)	–	4+1 (4)	–	–	–	4+1 (5)	–
23	15/7	Poole	H	D45-45	8 (4)	4+2 (4)	9 (5)	2+2 (4)	12 (5)	–	1 (3)	–	–	–	9+3 (5)	–
24	23/7	Oxford	A	L41-53	10 (5)	5 (4)	4+1 (4)	0 (3)	14 (5)	–	3 (4)	–	–	–	5 (5)	–
25	28/7	Arena-Essex	A	W48-45	7 (5)	6+1 (4)	6+1 (4)	7+2 (4)	15 (5)	–	2+1 (4)	–	–	–	5+1 (4)	–
26	29/7	Peterborough	H	W52-44*	6+1 (4)	4+2 (4)	8 (5)	6+1 (4)	15 (5)	–	5+1 (4)	–	–	–	8+1 (4)	–
27	12/8	Belle Vue	H	W47-42	9+1 (5)	4+1 (4)	4+1 (4)	4 (4)	12 (5)	–	5+1 (3)	–	–	–	9+1 (5)	–
28	21/8	Eastbourne	A	L32-60	6 (5)	6 (5)	8 (5)	R/R	–	–	4+1 (5)	–	–	–	–	8+4 (10)
29	26/8	Coventry	H	W47-46*	13 (5)	1 (5)	10+1 (5)	R/R	17 (5)	–	4+1 (7)	–	–	–	2 (1)	–
30	26/8	Coventry	H	W50-44	9 (5)	9+1 (5)	12+1 (5)	R/R	13+1 (5)	–	4 (4)	–	–	–	–	3+1 (6)
31	29/8	Wolverhampton	H	W49-47	18+1 (6)	7+2 (5)	5+1 (4)	R/R	18 (5)	–	0 (5)	–	1 (5)	–	–	–
32	30/8	Coventry	A	L38-52	4 (4)	2+1 (4)	9 (5)	7+2 (4)	12 (5)	–	4 (5)	–	0 (3)	–	–	–
33	6/9	Eastbourne	A	D45-45	8 (4)	6+2 (4)	5+1 (5)	5 (4)	12 (5)	–	5+1 (4)	–	–	–	4+1 (4)	–
34	9/9	Oxford	H	W52-44	10+1 (5)	8+2 (5)	6 (4)	8 (4)	12+2 (5)	–	–	–	–	–	7 (4)	1+1 (3)
35	13/9	Belle Vue	A	L30-60	8+1 (5)	2 (4)	2 (4)	1 (5)	11 (5)	–	–	–	–	–	R/R	–
36	16/9	Arena-Essex	H	W51-43*	13 (5)	7 (4)	7 (4)	9+1 (5)	9 (4)	–	–	–	–	–	3+1 (4)	3+1 (4)

*Denotes bonus-point victory

†Meeting abandoned after heat twelve, with the result permitted to stand.

DETAILS OF OTHER RIDERS:

Match No. 2: Steve Masters 0 (4); Match No. 8: David Norris 13 (5); Match No. 13: Leigh Lanham 3 (4); Match No. 14: Michael Coles 5+1 (6); Ross Brady 3 (4); Match No. 16: Simon Stead 10 (5); Match No. 17: Tomas Topinka 6 (5); Match No. 28: Billy Janniro 5+1 (5); Michael Coles 3+3 (5); Match No. 30: Steve Masters 3+1 (6); Match No. 34: Steve Masters 1+1 (3); Match No. 35: Eric Carrillo 6 (6); Match No. 36: Steve Masters 3+1 (4).

TACTICAL RIDES, AS INCLUDED IN THE SCORES GRID:

Match No. 2: Gjedde 6 points (TR); Match No. 4: Adams 6 points (TR); Johnston 0 points (TR); Match No. 5: Adams 6 points (TR); Match No. 6: Adams 6 points (TR); Johnston 6 points (TR); Match No. 8: Norris 6 points (TR); Johnston 4 points (TR); Match No. 9: Adams 4 points (TR); Johnston 4 points (TR); Match No. 14: Johnston 6 points (TR); Match No. 17: Adams 6 points (TR); Johnston 4 points (TR); Match No. 20: Adams 6 points (TR); Ruud 6 points (TR); Match No. 22: Adams 6 points (TR); Johnston 4 points (TR); Match No. 24: Adams 6 points (TR); Gjedde 2 points (TR); Match No. 28: Gjedde 4 points (TR); Janniro 0 points (TR); Match No. 29: Adams 6 points (TR); Match No. 31: Adams 6 points (TR); Gjedde 6 points (TR); Match No. 35: Gjedde 2 points (TR).

SWINDON: back row, left to right: Alun Rossiter (Team Manager), Glenn Cunningham, Steve Johnston, Krzysztof Kasprzak, Claus Kristensen, Olly Allen, Charlie Gjedde. Front, kneeling: Andrew Moore, David Ruud. On bike: Leigh Adams.

ELITE LEAGUE AVERAGES

Rider	Mts	Rds	Pts	Bon	Tot	Avge	Max
Leigh Adams	34	173	461	12	473	10.94	12 Full; 3 Paid
Charlie Gjedde	23	107	183	10	193	7.21	–
Peter Ljung	13	56	84	14	98	7.00	–
Steve Johnston	36	177	288	19	307	6.94	–
David Ruud	29	131	173	25	198	6.05	1 Paid
Andy Smith	35	154	186	36	222	5.77	–
Rafal Kurmanski	3	12	13	1	14	4.67	–
Andrew Moore	4	18	17	3	20	4.44	–
Olly Allen	31	139	112	16	128	3.68	–
Glenn Cunningham	8	31	19	5	24	3.10	–
Steve Masters	4	17	7	3	10	2.35	–
Claus Kristensen	3	10	4	1	5	2.00	–
Guests	9	45	51	5	56	4.98	–

NOTE: Figures for Peter Ljung include one match as a guest.

KNOCK-OUT CUP

No	DATE	OPPONENTS	H/A	RESULT	GJEDDE	RUUD	JOHNSTON	ALLEN	ADAMS	MOORE	CUNNINGHAM	SMITH	MASTERS	LJUNG	OTHERS
1	22/3	Wolverhampton	A	L43-50	7 (4)	4+1 (4)	10+1 (5)	5+1 (4)	13 (5)	4 (4)	0 (4)	–	–	–	–
2	6/5	Wolverhampton	H	W56-38*	R/R	10+2 (6)	12+1 (6)	8+1 (4)	12+1 (5)	–	–	8+2 (5)	6+1 (1)	–	–
3	23/9	Belle Vue	H	W48-42+	10 (5)	4+2 (4)	7 (4)	-	12+1 (5)	–	–	7+3 (6)	1 (3	7+1 (4)	–
4	6/10	Poole	A	L30-61	3 (4)	5+2 (5)	3+1 (4)	–	11 (5)	–	–	4+1 (5)	–	4 (4)	0 (3)
5	7/10	Poole	H	W53-40	13 (5)	4 (4)	10 (4)	–	12+2 (5)	–	–	4+2 (4)	–	4+1 (4)	6+3 (4)

*Denotes aggregate victory

+The second leg of the tie versus Belle Vue was twice rained-off and by virtue of their first leg success, Swindon progressed to the next round.

DETAILS OF OTHER RIDERS:

Match No. 4: Tomas Topinka 0 (3); Match No. 5: Tomas Topinka 6+3 (4).

TACTICAL RIDES, AS INCLUDED IN THE SCORES GRID:

Match No. 1: Johnston 6 points (TR); Match No. 4: Adams 2 points (TR); Gjedde 0 points (TR).

OTHER MEETINGS

10 March: Champagne Stakes (first leg)

Poole 51 Swindon 39 (Leigh Adams 12; Charlie Gjedde 8+1; Steve Johnston 7; Krzysztof Kasprzak 6+1; David Ruud 4; Claus Kristensen 2; Olly Allen 0).

11 March: Champagne Stakes (second leg)

Swindon 8 (Krzysztof Kasprzak 3; Claus Kristensen 2+1; David Ruud 2; Charlie Gjedde 1+1; Steve Johnston DNR; Olly Allen DNR; Leigh Adams DNR) Poole 4 – meeting abandoned after heat two.

17 March: Air-Tek Challenge (first leg)

Belle Vue 48 Swindon 47 (Leigh Adams 11+1; Charlie Gjedde 11; Olly Allen 11; Krzysztof Kasprzak 6; Andrew Moore 3+1; David Ruud 3; Glenn Cunningham 2+2).

18 March: Air-Tek Challenge (second leg)

Swindon 54 (Leigh Adams 11; Olly Allen 10+2; Charlie Gjedde 10+1; Steve Johnston 7+2; David Ruud 7+1; Krzysztof Kasprzak 5+2; Claus Kristensen 4) Belle Vue 40 – Swindon won 101-88 on aggregate.

1 April: Elite League

Swindon 33 (Steve Johnston 6+1; Olly Allen 6+1; Leigh Adams 6; David Ruud 5+2; Charlie Gjedde 5; Claus Kristensen 3; Andy Smith 2+1) Eastbourne 22 – meeting abandoned after heat nine.

3 April: Elite League

Eastbourne 25 Swindon 17 (Leigh Adams 6; Olly Allen 4; Andy Smith 3; Charlie Gjedde 1+1; Steve Johnston 1; David Ruud 1; Andrew Moore 1) – meeting abandoned after heat seven.

6 April: Inter-League Challenge

Isle of Wight 48 Swindon 42 (Olly Allen 11; Andy Smith 8+1; Steve Johnston 6; Steve Masters 5+1; Glenn Cunningham 5; David Ruud 4; Malcolm Holloway 3).

18 August: Challenge

Poole 46 Swindon 47 (Leigh Adams 17; Charlie Gjedde 9; Peter Ljung 7; Steve Johnston 6+1; Craig Boyce 5; Andy Smith 2; Olly Allen 1).

19 August: Elite League

Swindon 21 (Leigh Adams 6; Charlie Gjedde 6; Andy Smith 4+1; Peter Ljung 4; Olly Allen 1; Steve Johnston 0; David Ruud R/R) Wolverhampton 15 – meeting abandoned after heat six.

RAFAL KURMANSKI – A TRIBUTE

The 2004 season was barely a couple of months old when Swindon Speedway were pleased to announce the signing of the much-sought-after Rafal Kurmanski to add some pep in a reserve berth. Indeed, to emphasize how highly rated the twenty-one-year-old was, club owner Terry Russell had actually first tried to sign the Pole two seasons beforehand. Clearly delighted at the acquisition, promoter Alun Rossiter stated at the time: 'Rafal is very highly rated and I'm so pleased to have got him on board. Showing his undoubted pedigree, he finished seventh in last year's World Under-21 final in Kumla, Sweden and that was against a very good field, including another of our Robins in Olly Allen, of course. Rafal becomes a full club asset and will slot in nicely at reserve to give us a boost in that department. This is no disrespect to the boys who have been 'doubling-up' – they have been doing well in the Premier League, but by and large not carrying that kind of form into the Elite League; hence we have decided to bring in a permanent rider.'

The youngster duly arrived on these shores to make his club debut in an Elite League match at Poole on 12 May. He spoke very little English, but was evidently happy to be part of the Robins' side. He went on to score 1 point from four starts on the night and his efforts in heat six particularly emphasized his promise, when three times he nearly squeezed past the Pirates' number one Jason Lyons exiting the fourth turn, only to be blocked on each occasion. The following evening saw the return fixture at Swindon and while Rafal prepared his machine for action, he sported a cheery smile and greeted members of the track staff with a warm handshake. He started the meeting quietly, running two lasts while he weighed up the 361.2-metre raceway. Then, in heat eleven, the crowd was treated to something really special, as Swindon's out-and-out number one, Leigh Adams, took a rider replacement outing alongside his new teammate. Showing lightning reactions, it was Adams to the fore and with him on the first corner went Rafal. Four laps of superb team-riding followed, as the Aussie demonstrated all his skills in slowing the race down, while keeping a constant eye on his partner. The Poole representatives, Davey Watt and Jason Lyons, simply had no answer to the tactics, as the Robins duo raced to a full house. The Blunsdon regulars were naturally delighted, but the reaction of Rafal's fellow Robins spoke volumes as they ventured over to him and offered hearty congratulations upon his return to the pits. There was more for those present to drool over in the penultimate race, when the Pole made the start, with colleague Andy Smith darting past Bjarne Pedersen to link with him up front on the back straight. Known as 'Smudger' to all at Blunsdon, the popular speedster then called upon his vast experience to hold up the opposition and guide Rafal home; their combined efforts brought well-deserved applause from an appreciative audience and another round of praise for Rafal from his teammates.

With the following week's home match versus Oxford postponed due to rain, Rafal wasn't seen on the Blunsdon circuit again until 27 May, when Swindon faced Eastbourne on Elite League business. Regrettably, it was to be the last on-track appearance of his short life. He started with a third-bend fall in heat two, but recovered brilliantly to take victory five races later, when shepherded home by Leigh Adams. The youngster was then on the receiving end of a 5-1 in heat eleven, but finished in style by leading partner Andy Smith across the line for a match-winning 5-1 in the penultimate race. The joy was there for all to see as he punched the air and when he returned to the pits, there was an infectious grin from ear-to-ear.

Having grazed his leg in the heat-two tumble, Alun Rossiter helped bandage Rafal's leg on the Friday morning, before he left for his homeland. In the early afternoon of Sunday 30 May came the tragic news that Rafal had taken his own life. Clearly devastated, Rossiter commented: 'I just cannot believe what has happened, as Rafal was so happy when he departed for home on Friday morning. He had a ready smile and came across as a really nice lad in the short space of time that I had known him. We have already had a number of problems to overcome this season, but this sad news really puts everything into perspective. Everyone connected with the club sends their heartfelt condolences to Rafal's family and friends back home in Poland.'

Ironically, BBC Radio Swindon presenter Richard Crowley had interviewed Rafal for an upcoming race-day programme article, with fellow Polish rider Grzegorz Walasek on hand to help out as an interpreter. Rafal's words were poignant and are worth recalling, since he was clearly happy to be with the Pebley Beach Robins. He said: 'I was keen to come to England to further my career. At one stage I though it would be with Coventry, but at the same time Swindon came in and now I'm here. I've been riding well in Poland for Zielona Gora and I think it's the right time for me to come to England. I'm happy with my form so far, but it will take a few weeks to get used to the track and get everything fully set up for speedway in England.' Obviously ambitious, Rafal continued: 'Although I've only ridden a few meetings here, I hope that I can get up to a seven-point average by the end of the year. I knew Leigh Adams before I signed for Swindon and it's great to be in the same team as him. Hopefully, racing alongside Leigh in England will help me become a better rider.'

He left a lot of happy memories with those lucky enough to have met him or seen him in action during his all-too-brief time with the club. May he rest in peace.

CAREER SUMMARY

POLISH LEAGUE: Zielona Gora, 1999-04.
EUROPEAN UNDER-19 CHAMPIONSHIP: 3rd, 2001.
POLISH JUNIOR PAIRS CHAMPIONSHIP: 1st, 2001 – accompanied by Zielona Gora teammate Dawid Kujawa.
WORLD UNDER-21 CHAMPIONSHIP: 6th, 2002; 7th, 2003.
EUROPEAN GRAND PRIX: 19th, 2003 – wildcard entrant.

By Robert Bamford

WOLVERHAMPTON PARRYS INTERNATIONAL WOLVES

ADDRESS: Ladbroke Stadium, Sutherland Avenue, Wolverhampton, West Midlands, WV2 2JJ.
PROMOTERS: Chris Van Straaten, John Woolridge & Terry Gough.
TRACK LENGTH: 264 metres.
TRACK RECORD: 55.87 seconds – David Norris (12/07/04).
FIRST MEETING: 30 May 1928.
YEARS OF OPERATION: 1928-30 Open; 1950 Open; 1951 National League Division Three; 1952 Southern League; 1953-54 National League Division Two; 1961-64 Provincial League; 1965-67 British League; 1968-74 British League Division One; 1975-80 British League; 1981 National League; 1984-90 British League; 1991-94 British League Division One; 1995-96 Premier League; 1997-04 Elite League.

CLUB HONOURS

LEAGUE CHAMPIONS: 1963, 1991, 1996, 2002.
PREMIERSHIP WINNERS: 1992, 1997.
GOLD CUP WINNERS: 1992.
KNOCK-OUT CUP WINNERS: 1996.

RIDER ROSTER 2004

Eric CARRILLO; Sam ERMOLENKO; David HOWE; Fredrik LINDGREN; Mikael MAX; Chris NEATH; Daniel NERMARK; Adam SKORNICKI.

OTHER APPEARANCES/GUESTS (official matches only):

James BIRKINSHAW; James GRIEVES; Richard JUUL; Magnus KARLSSON; Joe SCREEN; Andy SMITH; Simon STEAD.

SKY BET ELITE LEAGUE

No	DATE	OPPONENTS	H/A	RESULT	HOWE	ERMOLENKO	SKORNICKI	NERMARK	MAX	NEATH	CARRILLO	KARLSSON	GRIEVES	LINDGREN	STEAD	OTHERS
1	29/3	Oxford	H	W53-40	7+3 (5)	8+1 (4)	10 (4)	6+4 (4)	12 (5)	10+2 (5)	0 (3)	–	–	–	–	–
2	2/4	Oxford	A	L43-52*	9+2 (5)	6 (4)	8+1 (4)	6 (4)	10 (5)	4+2 (5)	0 (3)	–	–	–	–	–
3	5/4	Peterborough	H	W53-39	6 (4)	5+1 (4)	7+1 (4)	7+2 (4)	15 (5)	13+3 (6)	0 (3)	–	–	–	–	–
4	9/4	Belle Vue	A	L42-50	11 (5)	5+2 (4)	2+1 (4)	5+1 (4)	8+1 (5)	10+1 (4)	1 (4)	–	–	–	–	–
5	12/4	Ipswich	H	L42-48	6 (5)	2+2 (4)	0 (1)	9 (4)	14 (5)	–	2+1 (5)	9 (6)	–	–	–	–
6	14/4	Poole	A	L43-53	3+1 (4)	12 (5)	5 (4)	2 (4)	16 (5)	4+1 (5)	1+1 (3)	–	–	–	–	–
7	19/4	Poole	H	W50-40*	5+1 (5)	6+4 (5)	5 (4)	R/R	15 (5)	11 (6)	–	–	8+2 (5)	–	–	–
8	22/4	Ipswich	A	W51-41*	7 (4)	14+1 (6)	4+1 (4)	R/R	12+2 (5)	13+2 (7)	1 (4)	–	–	–	–	–
9	24/4	Eastbourne	A	W46-45	5+1 (4)	13 (6)	6+2 (4)	R/R	12+2 (6)	–	2+1 (3)	–	–	–	–	8+1 (7)
10	26/4	Arena-Essex†	H	W44-33	6+2 (3)	7+2 (4)	9 (4)	R/R	8 (3)	–	1 (4)	–	13+1 (6)	–	–	–
11	3/5	Swindon	H	W51-44	9+1 (4)	13 (6)	6+3 (4)	R/R	13 (5)	7+2 (7)	3 (4)	–	–	–	–	–
12	14/5	Peterborough	A	L45-48*	4 (4)	14 (6)	1+1 (4)	R/R	–	8+1 (7)	0 (4)	–	–	–	–	18 (5)

SKY BET ELITE LEAGUE continued

No	DATE	OPPONENTS	H/A	RESULT	HOWE	ERMOLENKO	SKORNICKI	NERMARK	MAX	NEATH	CARRILLO	KARLSSON	GRIEVES	LINDGREN	STEAD	OTHERS
13	17/5	Coventry	H	W50-39	11 (5)	16+1 (6)	4+1 (4)	R/R	9 (4)	8+2 (7)	2+1 (4)	–	–	–	–	–
14	20/5	Coventry	A	W52-41*	12+2 (5)	12 (5)	4+1 (4)	R/R	12 (5)	8+1 (6)	4+1 (5)	–	–	–	–	–
15	31/5	Belle Vue	H	W51-42*	R/R	13 (6)	–	–	17 (6)	11+1 (7)	3+1 (3)	7+3 (5)	–	–	–	0 (3)
16	3/6	Swindon	A	L45-48*	6+1 (5)	13+1 (5)	3 (4)	R/R	9+1 (5)	2 (4)	–	–	–	12+2 (7)	–	–
17	7/6	Eastbourne	H	L44-45*	9 (5)	2+1 (5)	6+1 (5)	R/R	10 (5)	–	–	12+1 (5)	–	5+3 (5)	–	–
18	14/6	Poole	H	L41-49	13+1 (6)	3 (4)	10+1 (7)	R/R	11 (5)	3+1 (4)	–	–	–	1 (2)	–	–
19	16/6	Poole	A	L40-54	15 (6)	4 (4)	0 (4)	R/R	9 (6)	–	2+1 (3)	–	–	10+1 (7)	–	–
20	18/6	Oxford	A	W54-40	11 (5)	6 (5)	10+2 (5)	R/R	13+1 (5)	–	–	–	9+2 (6)	5+3 (4)	–	–
21	28/6	Oxford	H	W58-35*	14 (5)	8+1 (5)	9+4 (6)	R/R	<u>15 (5)</u>	3 (4)	–	–	–	9+2 (6)	–	–
22	5/7	Swindon	H	W52-44	8+2 (5)	9 (5)	7+1 (5)	R/R	11 (5)	–	–	–	–	9+2 (6)	8+1 (4)	–
23	10/7	Eastbourne	A	W49-43	10+1 (5)	9+1 (5)	9+2 (6)	R/R	7 (5)	–	–	–	–	12+2 (5)	–	2+1 (4)
24	12/7	Eastbourne	H	W54-42*	11+1 (5)	7+1 (4)	13+1 (6)	R/R	13+1 (5)	4+2 (5)	–	–	–	6 (5)	–	–
25	21/7	Arena-Essex	A	L44-51*	6+2 (4)	4+1 (4)	0 (3)	R/R	14 (6)	8+2 (6)	–	–	–	12 (7)	–	–
26	26/7	Ipswich	H	W49-44	7+2 (5)	9+1 (5)	7+1 (5)	R/R	11+1 (5)	–	–	–	–	5+1 (5)	10+1 (5)	–
27	29/7	Ipswich	A	L39-51	7+1 (5)	4+1 (5)	10+2 (6)	R/R	10 (5)	0 (3)	–	–	–	8+1 (6)	–	–
28	11/8	Peterborough	A	L41-54	4 (4)	13 (5)	6+2 (6)	R/R	–	3 (5)	–	–	–	10+1 (6)	–	5 (4)
29	16/8	Arena-Essex	H	W62-30	11+1 (5)	10+1 (5)	12+1 (6)	R/R	10+1 (4)	–	–	–	–	9+1 (5)	10+3 (5)	–
30	25/8	Arena-Essex	A	L42-48*	5+1 (5)	7 (4)	9 (6)	R/R	14 (5)	5+2 (6)	–	–	–	2+1 (4)	–	–
31	29/8	Swindon	A	L47-49*	3+2 (4)	8+1 (5)	7+2 (5)	R/R	6 (4)	–	–	–	–	10+2 (6)	13+2 (6)	–
32	30/8	Belle Vue	H	W55-36	7+1 (4)	12+1 (5)	10+3 (6)	R/R	13 (5)	5+1 (5)	–	–	–	8+2 (5)	–	–
33	1/9	Belle Vue	A	L46-47*	9+1 (4)	7 (5)	6+2 (6)	R/R	15 (5)	–	2 (4)	–	–	7+2 (6)	–	–
34	8/9	Coventry	H	W49-41	9+1 (4)	14 (6)	8+2 (5)	R/R	13 (5)	2+1 (5)	–	–	3+1 (5)	–	–	–
35	13/9	Peterborough	H	W57-36*	11+1 (5)	8+3 (5)	16+3 (7)	R/R	11 (5)	–	–	–	–	3+1 (3)	8+1 (5)	–
36	23/9	Coventry	A	W45-44*	11 (5)	5+1 (5)	5 (4)	R/R	5+1 (4)	6+2 (6)	–	–	–	13+1 (6)	–	–

*Denotes bonus-point victory

† Meeting abandoned after heat twelve, with the result permitted to stand.

DETAILS OF OTHER RIDERS:

Match No. 9: Richard Juul 8+1 (7); Match No. 12: Joe Screen <u>18 (5)</u>; Match No. 15: James Birkinshaw 0 (3); Match No. 23: Richard Juul 2+1 (4); Match No. 28: Andy Smith 5 (4).

TACTICAL SUBSTITUTE AND TACTICAL RIDES, AS INCLUDED IN THE SCORES GRID:

Match No. 2: Max 6 points (TR); Nermark 4 points (TR); Match No. 4: Howe 4 points (TR); Skornicki 0 points (TR); Match No. 6: Ermolenko 6 points (TR); Max 6 points (TR); Match No. 9: Max 4 points (TS); Match No. 12: Screen 6 points (TR); Match No. 16: Ermolenko 6 points (TR); Match No. 19: Howe 6 points (TR); Lindgren 2 points (TR); Max 0 points (TS); Match No. 25: Lindgren 6 points (TR); Howe 4 points (TR); Max 2 points (TS); Match No. 28: Ermolenko 6 points (TR); Lindgren 4 points (TR); Match No. 33: Max 6 points (TR).

WOLVERHAMPTON: back row, left to right: Sam Ermolenko, Adam Skornicki, Daniel Nermark, Eric Carrillo. Front row: David Howe, Mikael Max, Chris Neath.

ELITE LEAGUE AVERAGES

Rider	Mts	Rds	Pts	Bon	Tot	Avge	Max
Mikael Max	34	168	381	11	392	9.33	3 Full
Simon Stead	5	25	49	8	57	9.12	–
James Grieves	3	17	30	5	35	8.24	–
Magnus Karlsson	3	16	28	4	32	8.00	–
David Howe	35	163	281	32	313	7.68	–
Sam Ermolenko	36	176	299	29	328	7.45	–
Daniel Nermark	6	24	33	7	40	6.67	–
Adam Skornicki	35	166	234	42	276	6.65	–
Fredrik Lindgren	21	111	153	29	182	6.56	–
Chris Neath	23	125	148	29	177	5.66	–
Eric Carrillo	16	59	24	7	31	2.10	–
Guests	5	23	30	2	32	5.57	1 full

KNOCK-OUT CUP

No	DATE	OPPONENTS	H/A	RESULT	HOWE	ERMOLENKO	SKORNICKI	NERMARK	MAX	CARRILLO	GRIEVES
1	22/3	Swindon	H	W50-43	5+3 (4)	12 (5)	2+2 (4)	8 (4)	14 (5)	4 (4)	5 (4)
2	6/5	Swindon	A	L38-56	2 (4)	15 (6)	3+1 (4)	R/R	14+1 (5)	1 (5)	3 (6)

TACTICAL RIDES, AS INCLUDED IN THE SCORES GRID:

Match No. 2: Max 6 points (TR); Ermolenko 2 points (TR).

OTHER MEETINGS

15 March: Air-Tek Challenge (first leg)

Wolverhampton 49 (Mikael Max 15; Sam Ermolenko 10+2; Chris Neath 9+1; Daniel Nermark 8+1; David Howe 6+2; Eric Carrillo 1; Adam Skornicki R/R) Coventry 44.

18 March: Air-Tek Challenge (second leg)

Coventry 52 Wolverhampton 42 (David Howe 11; Mikael Max 10+1; Sam Ermolenko 9+1; Eric Carrillo 6+3; Daniel Nermark 6; Darren Andrews 0; Adam Skornicki R/R) – Coventry won 96-91 on aggregate.

21 March: Staechmann Slideshow (Jan Staechmann Testimonial)

Stoke Select 22, Long Eaton Select 14, Oxford Select 10, Wolverhampton Select 8 (Mikael Max 3; Chris Collins 3; Sam Ermolenko 1; Josh Larsen 1; Ryan Fisher 0) – meeting abandoned after heat nine.

28 March: Richard Juul Testimonial

Newcastle Select 44 Wolverhampton 45 (Sam Ermolenko 11+2; Mikael Max 11+1; David Howe 9; Adam Skornicki 8; Daniel Nermark 2+1; Eric Carrillo 2+1; Wayne Carter 2).

23 May: Mikael Max Testimonial

Wolverhampton 45 (Mikael Max 14; Fredrik Lindgren 8+3; Adam Skornicki 8; Magnus Karlsson 7; Sam Ermolenko 6+1; David Howe 1+1; Kevin Little 1) Mikael Max Select 45 (Peter Karlsson 11+1; Steve Johnston 10+1; Ryan Fisher 10; Billy Hamill 7+2; Jason Lyons 5+1; Richard Juul 2+1; Peter Nahlin 0).

19 July: Test Match

Team Great Britain 44 (Scott Nicholls 12+2; David Norris 9+1; David Howe 9; Gary Havelock 6; Chris Neath 4+4; Stuart Robson 4; Lee Richardson 0) Denmark 50 (Nicki Pedersen 11; Hans N. Andersen 10; Kenneth Bjerre 9; Bjarne Pedersen 7+1; Niels-Kristian Iversen 7+1; Charlie Gjedde 6+1; Morten Risager 0).

19 August: Elite League

Swindon 21 Wolverhampton 15 (Simon Stead 7; David Howe 3+2; Mikael Max 3; Sam Ermolenko 2; Fredrik Lindgren 0; Adam Skornicki 0; Daniel Nermark R/R) – meeting abandoned after heat six.

20 September: Elite League Play-Off quarter-final

Wolverhampton 61 (Sam Ermolenko 15+2; Mikael Max 15; Adam Skornicki 9+1; David Howe 9; Chris Neath 8+3; Fredrik Lindgren 5+3; Daniel Nermark R/R) Oxford 33.

27 September: Elite League Play-Off semi-final

Wolverhampton 45 (Mikael Max 12+1; Adam Skornicki 10+3; David Howe 8+1; Fredrik Lindgren 6+1; Sam Ermolenko 5; Chris Neath 4; Daniel Nermark R/R) Ipswich 45. Mikael Max subsequently defeated Hans N. Andersen in a run-off to give Wolverhampton a place in the final.

4 October: Elite League Play-Off final (first leg)

Wolverhampton 41 (Mikael Max 13; Fredrik Lindgren 9+1; David Howe 7; Sam Ermolenko 6; Adam Skornicki 5+1; Chris Neath 1; Daniel Nermark R/R) Poole 49.

11 October: Elite League Play-Off final (second leg)

Poole 63 Wolverhampton 30 (Fredrik Lindgren 12; Mikael Max 7; Sam Ermolenko 7; Adam Skornicki 2+1; David Howe 2; Magnus Karlsson 0; Daniel Nermark R/R) – Poole won 112-71 on aggregate.

INDIVIDUAL MEETINGS

18 October: British Under-18 Championship

1st Daniel King 15; 2nd James Wright 14; 3rd Edward Kennett 12; James Cockle 11; William Lawson 11; Jamie Robertson 10; Ben Wilson 9; Jack Hargreaves 7; Jamie Courtney 7; Karl Mason 5; James Brundle 5; Lee Smart 4; Jamie Westacott 3; Josh Auty 3; Darren Mallett 2; Shane Waldron 1; Barry Burchatt (Res) 1.

25 October: Ladbroke Olympique

1st David Howe 13; 2nd Peter Karlsson 12; 3rd Scott Nicholls 11; Charlie Gjedde 10; Mikael Max 10; Jesper B. Jensen 9; Sam Ermolenko 9; Fredrik Lindgren 9; Josh Larsen 8; Chris Neath 8; Adam Skornicki 8; Ricky Ashworth 6; Robin Tornqvist 3; Marius Rokeberg 3; Karol Malecha 1; Shaun Harmatiuk 0.

PREMIER LEAGUE
2004

RACING DIARY OF THE SEASON

MARCH

6 The season begins very early as Berwick host the Carlos Villar Benefit meeting to aid the Argentinian racer, who was left paralysed after a nasty spill at Shielfield Park on 18 October the previous year. Before a crowd of some 2,000, a combined Edinburgh/Workington side net 32 points to take victory from Berwick (28), Glasgow (19) and Newcastle (17). Following the main meeting, Michal Makovsky wins the Carlos Villar Trophy, beating Paul Cooper, David Meldrum and Simon Cartwright in the final.

10 Hull narrowly defeat Yorkshire rivals Sheffield 46-44 in the first leg of their opening challenge.

11 Sheffield quickly gain revenge to beat Hull 52-43, claiming an aggregate success in the process.

12 Somerset's encounter with Newport in the Severn Bridge Trophy falls victim to inclement weather.

13 Edinburgh's Rory Schlein shows his paces to lift the Karl Friar Memorial at Berwick, ahead of home trio Michal Makovsky, Adrian Rymel and Claus Kristensen. Power-packed Rye House comfortably beat King's Lynn 55-40 in the A10 Trophy, with solid scoring throughout. Jan Staechmann bags a paid maximum (14+1), as Stoke claim a 53-44 victory over a composite side entitled Stoke Guests. Workington open up with a huge 66-27 success against Swedish tourists Valsarna, with both Brett Woodifield (14+1) and Rusty Harrison (13+2) hitting paid maximums. The match is marred by a heat four smash which leaves triple British Under-21 Champion Simon Stead nursing a broken heel.

14 Heavy rain washes out Glasgow's challenge match versus Valsarna an hour before the start time. Newport come from behind to post a 46-44 win over Somerset in the Severn Bridge Trophy, with Craig Watson recording the lot (15). After failing to score, Polish recruit Dawid Kujawa subsequently loses his place in the Wasps side. Newcastle produce a battling show before finally going down 49-41 to reigning Elite League Champions Poole in an exciting challenge.

15 Reading get off to an impressive start, overcoming King's Lynn 56-38 in a challenge match at Smallmead, as both new signing Danny Bird (13+2) and long-serving skipper Phil Morris remain unbeaten (11+1).

17 Despite a full 21-pointer from star visitor Carl Stonehewer, Hull claim a 49-44 victory over Workington in the Premier Trophy. King's Lynn have no answer as Rye House win 51-42 at Saddlebow Road to post an aggregate success in the A10 Trophy.

18 Sheffield gain a hard-fought 52-42 win over a battling Workington side in the Premier Trophy at Owlerton.

19 Edinburgh's attractive Spring Trophy match against arch rivals Glasgow is called off due to a waterlogged track. Somerset complete an aggregate victory over Newport in the Severn Bridge Trophy, courtesy of a 53-43 scoreline at the Oak Tree Arena.

20 Berwick's Premier Trophy clash with Sheffield is postponed following heavy rainfall. Rye House surge to a 56-37 Premier Trophy victory against Reading, the Rockets packing the score chart with solid scoring all the way down the line. A thriller at Derwent Park results in a 50-46 win for Workington over Edinburgh in the Premier Trophy.

21 Understrength Newport suffer a 50-43 reverse to visiting Exeter in the Premier Trophy. The cleverly titled Staechmann Slideshow only lasts nine heats before the articulate Dane's Testimonial is abandoned due to a deluge of hailstones and rain. At the time, a Stoke Select (22) are leading the Four-Team Tournament ahead of Long Eaton Select (14), Oxford Select (10) and Wolverhampton Select (8). Full-blooded Scottish derby action sees Glasgow claim a narrow 46-44 victory against Edinburgh in the Spring Trophy on a heavy Ashfield raceway. Czech ace Tomas Topinka celebrates his Testimonial at King's Lynn, with Mark Loram eventually taking victory from Nicki Pedersen, Hans N. Andersen and Chris Louis in the grand final of a star-studded individual event. Newcastle go down to a heavy 56-40 defeat at the hands of visiting Berwick, for whom Claus Kristensen plunders an unbeaten 15-point return.

22 Exeter complete a quick-fire Premier Trophy double over Newport, easily winning 63-29 at the County Ground. Reading overcome an early deficit to defeat Rye House 48-45 in an exciting Premier Trophy tussle at Smallmead, with Danny Bird's 18-point full house including a maximum return from a tactical outing.

24 Hull have no answers, as visiting Glasgow collect a 54-39 Premier Trophy success at Craven Park. Somerset overcome an eight-point deficit to triumph 49-43 in an exciting Premier Trophy tussle at King's Lynn.

25 Sheffield scorch to a 65-30 victory against Newcastle, with Ricky Ashworth (14+1), Sean Wilson (12) and Andre Compton (11+1) remaining unbeaten for the rampant Tigers.

26 Fully committed action at Armadale sees Edinburgh beat Glasgow 48-45 to lift the Spring Trophy by a single point on aggregate. Somerset romp to a 60-34 Premier Trophy win over King's Lynn, despite trailing for the opening couple of heats.

27 Berwick dig deep to defeat Edinburgh 48-45 in the Premier Trophy at Shielfield Park. Rye House overcome stern resistance to register a 51-42 success against Exeter in the Premier Trophy at Hoddesdon. Carl Stonehewer grabs a paid maximum (17+1), as Workington power to a 59-35 win against Glasgow in the Premier Trophy. Completing the day's activity, Stoke race to a commanding 54-38 victory over Sheffield in the Premier Trophy at Loomer Road.

28 Newport beat King's Lynn 52-42 in the Premier Trophy, with Mads Korneliussen storming to a paid full house (14+1). Glasgow overwhelm Berwick 63-28 in a Premier Trophy encounter at Ashfield, with Paul Bentley (12+3), Shane Parker (12) and George Stancl (10+2) remaining unbeaten. Richard Juul celebrates his Testimonial at Brough Park, with visiting Wolverhampton narrowly winning 45-44 over a Newcastle Select side. After the match, Mikael Max takes the chequered flag to triumph in the Testimonial Trophy and Kenny Carter Remembrance Cup, ahead of Bjarne Pedersen, Juul himself and Sam Ermolenko.

29 Following a day of glorious Devon sunshine, Exeter cruise to a 60-35 win against Somerset in the Premier Trophy.

31 Hull post an easy 58-35 victory over Newcastle in the Premier Trophy. Thrilling stuff at Saddlebow Road sees King's Lynn narrowly defeat Reading 49-45 in the Premier Trophy.

APRIL

1 Premier Trophy fare at Owlerton results in a comfortable 59-35 success for Sheffield over visiting Stoke.

2 Rory Schlein bags the lot (15), as Edinburgh cruise to a 59-31 win against Berwick in the

Premier Trophy. Somerset and the Isle of Wight play out an exciting 45-45 draw in the Premier Trophy, with Craig Boyce hitting a paid maximum (14+1) for the Islanders.

3 Berwick thrash Newcastle 66-27 in a one-sided Premier Trophy match, with three riders unbeaten: Claus Kristensen (15), Josef Franc (12) and Michal Makovsky (10+2). Workington are comfortable 58-35 victors against Hull in the Premier Trophy, with number one Carl Stonehewer going through the card (15). The day's other two Premier Trophy matches are rained off, namely Rye House *v.* Newport and Stoke *v.* Edinburgh.

4 Newport crash 58-38 to visiting Reading in the Premier Trophy. Thanks to rain, Glasgow's Premier Trophy fixture against Stoke is abandoned after four heats, with the Tigers leading 16-8. Newcastle go down 51-42 to visiting Sheffield in the Premier Trophy, with Sean Wilson remaining unbeaten for the triumphant Tigers (14+1).

5 Exeter race to a 59-33 Premier Trophy victory over the Isle of Wight, with both Mark Simmonds (12) and Seemond Stephens (9+3) unbeaten. Due to heavy rain, Reading's Premier Trophy clash with Somerset is postponed two hours before the scheduled start time.

6 With new banking on the third and fourth turns, the Isle of Wight open their home programme by beating Elite League Swindon 48-42 in a challenge fixture.

7 Hull overcome an opening heat deficit to beat Edinburgh 52-43 in the Premier Trophy. The day's other Premier Trophy fixture between King's Lynn and the Isle of Wight is postponed at 1 p.m., due to a waterlogged Saddlebow Road circuit.

9 Seventy-five years of super track action are celebrated at Owlerton, with Andre Compton netting a paid full house (13+2), as Sheffield defeat 'The Stars' 57-35. Following a successful hernia operation, Frede Schott makes his first appearance of the season and the Dane is straight back in the groove with a 12-point maximum, as Edinburgh defeat Workington 54-40 in the Premier Trophy. Rory Schlein (14+1) and Peter Carr (11+1) also remain unbeaten for the victorious Monarchs. 2003 Somerset teamster Mark Lemon returns to his former home to land a five-ride maximum, as Exeter claim a 45-44 victory in a ding-dong Premier Trophy encounter.

10 Berwick ease to a 58-36 victory over Workington in the Premier Trophy at Shielfield Park. Rye House romp to a massive 66-27 Premier Trophy win against Newport, with three men going through the card unbeaten by an opponent, namely Davey Watt (15), Chris Neath (13+2) and Scott Robson (9+3). Stoke are made to fight all the way before narrowly beating Hull 50-45 in an entertaining Premier Trophy tussle at Loomer Road.

11 Newport reveal great determination, coming from ten-points down to post a 48-45 win against the Isle of Wight in the Premier Trophy. Glasgow show no mercy to beleaguered Newcastle, as they storm to a 60-35 success in the Premier Trophy, with four team members undefeated: Shane Parker (15), George Stancl (12+3), James Grieves (11+1) and Graham Jones (10+2).

12 Premier Trophy action sees Exeter kick-off at 11 a.m. and the Falcons comfortably rack up a 65-29 victory against King's Lynn, with Mark Lemon (14+1), Roger Lobb (12) and Seemond Stephens (11+1) notching unbeaten totals. The first Premier League fixture of the season takes place at Rye House and it's the Rockets who overcome Sheffield to win 52-42. Glasgow complete an Easter weekend Premier Trophy double over struggling Newcastle, winning 56-38 at Brough Park, with James Grieves recording a paid maximum (13+2). Further Premier Trophy action sees Workington cruise to a 60-32 success against Berwick. Rain prematurely halts the Premier Trophy clash between Reading and the Isle

of Wight, but not before a conclusive result has been achieved, with the Racers 38-34 ahead after the magical heat twelve mark.

13 The Isle of Wight swamp King's Lynn 65-28 in the Premier Trophy, with both Sebastian Tresarrieu (14+1) and Glen Phillips (13+2) bagging paid maximums.

14 Rare Wednesday evening action at Shielfield Park sees Berwick narrowly defeat Stoke 49-44 in the Premier Trophy. The scores are even closer in a gripping Premier League match at Craven Park, as Hull win 46-44 against visiting Reading. At Saddlebow Road, King's Lynn triumph 51-40 over Exeter in the Premier Trophy.

15 Both Sean Wilson (14+1) and Andre Compton (14+1) remain unbeaten as Sheffield have little difficulty in claiming a comprehensive 63-32 Premier Trophy victory over Edinburgh.

16 Edinburgh quickly gain revenge over Sheffield, narrowly winning 47-42 in the return Premier Trophy match at Armadale. The day's other Premier Trophy fixture between Somerset and Rye House is postponed due to rain.

17 A superb Premier Trophy meeting at Hoddesdon results in a 47-42 victory for Rye House against the Isle of Wight. Still in the Premier Trophy, Stoke easily beat Berwick 54-36 at Loomer Road. Workington's Premier Trophy clash with Newcastle is called off following late-afternoon rainfall.

18 Newport suffer a 47-43 reverse to Rye House in the Premier Trophy at a wet Queensway Meadows. Two other scheduled Premier Trophy matches are regrettably postponed: Glasgow *v.* Workington and Newcastle *v.* Edinburgh.

19 Exeter's Mark Lemon tallies 14 points to triumph in the Westernapolis at his home track, with Chris Harris and Craig Watson finishing second and third respectively. Premier Trophy fare sees Reading ease to a 58-38 success against King's Lynn.

20 The Isle of Wight's Premier Trophy match versus Newport is abandoned after six heats, with the homesters leading 24-15.

21 The day's two scheduled Premier Trophy fixtures are washed out: Hull *v.* Berwick and King's Lynn *v.* Rye House.

22 Sean Wilson remains unbeaten (14+1), as Sheffield defeat a gritty Glasgow side 53-40 in the Premier Trophy.

23 Edinburgh post a 59-34 success over Stoke in the Premier Trophy, with their powerful spearhead of Rory Schlein (15), Frede Schott (14+1) and Peter Carr (11+1) tallying full houses. Somerset record a 48-41 victory against Reading in the Premier Trophy.

24 Berwick make it five home wins out of five by defeating Hull 52-42 in the Premier Trophy. Staying with the Premier Trophy, Rye House comfortably triumph 58-37 against King's Lynn. At Derwent Park, it's a comfortable 55-40 victory for Workington against Sheffield in the Premier Trophy. Stoke and Glasgow battle out a 45-45 draw in a thrilling Premier Trophy tussle at Loomer Road.

25 Craig Watson's full 15-pointer can't prevent Newport from losing 46-44 at home to Somerset in the Premier Trophy. Shane Parker bags a maximum (15), as Glasgow defeat Northern group leaders Sheffield 49-41 in the Premier Trophy. At Saddlebow Road, King's Lynn post a 52-43 Premier Trophy success over the Isle of Wight. Still in the Premier Trophy, underfire Newcastle suffer a 55-37 home reverse at the hands of a workmanlike Hull septet, for whom Emil Kramer hits maximum points (12).

26 Exeter retain top spot in the Southern section of the Premier Trophy by scorching to a 67-26 success over Rye House. At Smallmead, an incident-packed Premier Trophy clash results in a 52-38 win for Reading versus Somerset.

27 The Isle of Wight's Premier Trophy encounter with Somerset is lost to a waterlogged track.

28 Hull defeat Yorkshire rivals and Northern group leaders Sheffield 57-37 in the Premier Trophy at Craven Park. The day's other Premier Trophy encounter between King's Lynn and Newport falls victim to the vagaries of the British climate.

29 The wet stuff wins again, as Sheffield's return Premier Trophy match against Hull is a mid-morning call-off.

30 Edinburgh make it nine Premier Trophy losses on the trot for Newcastle, as they comfortably win 63-29 at Armadale, with both Frede Schott (15) and Peter Carr (11+1) carding unbeaten tallies. The Premier Trophy match between Somerset and Rye House is called off at 2 p.m., due to a waterlogged circuit.

MAY

1 After weaving his way through the qualifying heats, Ritchie Hawkins dashes to victory in the final of the British Under-21 Championship at Rye House, with Steve Boxall and Edward Kennett filling the other two podium positions respectively. Glasgow leap up to second spot in the Northern group of the Premier Trophy, thanks to a 48-42 victory at Berwick. Meanwhile, at Loomer Road, Stoke repel a Workington comeback to win 48-44 in an exciting Premier Trophy encounter.

2 Led by a paid full house from Aussie flyer Shane Parker (14+1), Glasgow beat old rivals Edinburgh 53-42 and move into pole position in their Premier Trophy group. King's Lynn and Rye House end all-square at 45-45 in a cracking Premier Trophy meeting at Saddlebow Road. Newcastle win at last, but only just, as they claim a 49-47 success over Workington in the Premier Trophy. In defeat, Carl Stonehewer is majestic for the Comets, recording a 21-point maximum. Reading surge to a 58-36 win against Southern group leaders Exeter in the Premier Trophy, with Matej Zagar paid for the lot (14+1).

3 Morning activity sees Exeter narrowly beat a spirited Reading outfit 48-45 in the return Premier Trophy match, with Matej Zagar netting a magnificent six-ride maximum (18) for the Racers. The afternoon league meeting between Rye House and Hull is postponed due to the effects of rain. Carl Stonehewer maintains his electric form to hit an 18-point maximum, as Workington race to a 54-41 victory against Stoke in the Premier Trophy.

4 The Isle of Wight suffer another postponement due to inclement weather, with their Premier Trophy match against Exeter a lunchtime casualty.

5 At King's Lynn, the much-anticipated Championship of Great Britain semi-final is postponed due to the effects of heavy rainfall. Hull beat Stoke 50-44 in an entertaining Premier Trophy fixture at Craven Park.

6 Sheffield wallop Berwick 67-25 to take over top spot in the Northern group of the Premier Trophy, with their scoring led by maximum-men Andre Compton (15), Ricky Ashworth (13+2), guest Shane Parker (10+2) and James Birkinshaw (9+3).

7 Pulsating Premier Trophy fare sees Edinburgh defeat Glasgow 52-40 in front of a large Armadale audience. Headed by maximum points from Glenn Cunningham (12), Somerset narrowly win 46-44 against Newport in the Premier Trophy.

8 Rye House are made to dig deep before overcoming Somerset 49-44 in a thrilling Premier Trophy clash. Workington thrash Newport 65-28 in their opening league match of the season. Meanwhile, persistent rain causes two washouts, namely Berwick *v.* Hull (Knock-Out Cup) and Stoke *v.* Newcastle (Premier Trophy).

9 Tony Atkin suffers a serious arm injury as Newport go down to a 47-42 loss at the hands

of Rye House in a closely fought League tussle. Shane Parker records another maximum (15) as Glasgow win 47-43 against Reading in the Knock-Out Cup, with the visitors' Matej Zagar clocking a new Ashfield track record of 57.9 seconds. In the Northern section of the Premier Trophy, bottom club Newcastle lose 51-40 to visiting Stoke.

10 Exeter's Knock-Out Cup tie versus Newport is postponed following an early evening thunderstorm. Also in the Knock-Out Cup, Reading beat Glasgow 52-43 and safely move into the next round on aggregate.

11 The Isle of Wight simply outclass King's Lynn as they romp to a 63-29 Knock-Out Cup success.

12 Knock-Out Cup fare sees Hull comfortably defeat Berwick 59-36. Staying with the Knock-Out Cup, King's Lynn gain the consolation of a 56-39 second-leg success over the Isle of Wight, but it's the visitors who progress through by a 17-point margin on aggregate.

13 Led by Andre Compton's superb 18-point full house, Sheffield race to a 57-38 victory against Exeter in their first home league match of the campaign.

14 Edinburgh gain a hard-fought 50-43 win over Workington in the first leg of their Knock-Out Cup tie. Also in the Knock-Out Cup, Somerset defeat Stoke 48-42 on the occasion of the 100th meeting at the Oak Tree Arena since the venue opened in June 2000.

15 Rye House defeat Newcastle 55-39 in the Knock-Out Cup at Hoddesdon. Meanwhile, Workington progress through to the next round, courtesy of a 57-35 second-leg success over Edinburgh. Also safely on to the next stage go Somerset, thanks to a gritty 46-44 victory in the second leg of their tie at Stoke. In the Premier Trophy, Berwick narrowly beat Northern group leaders Sheffield 47-43 in tight tussle at Shielfield Park.

16 Newport narrowly lose 50-46 to visiting Exeter in the Knock-Out Cup. Newcastle go out of the Knock-Out Cup, as both Chris Neath (12) and former Diamond Davey Watt (15) notch maximums in Rye House's 49-41 second-leg success. A thrilling ding-dong Premier Trophy match at Ashfield finally results in a 47-46 victory for Glasgow against Workington.

17 Mark Lemon cards a paid maximum (14+1) as Exeter kick-off their home league programme with a big 62-31 win over Somerset. Brilliant Slovenian Matej Zagar nets his fourth Premier Trophy maximum (12) on the trot as Reading defeat Newport 54-41. Danny Bird also remains undefeated for the Racers in notching a tally of 14+1 points.

18 Tuesday evening action at Ashfield sees Shane Parker net another full house (15), as Glasgow defeat Hull 49-41 to retake pole position in their Premier Trophy group. Meanwhile, in the other section of the Premier Trophy, the Isle of Wight and second-in-the-table Reading play out a 45-45 draw at Smallbrook Stadium.

19 Hull edge ahead in the latter stages to defeat a spirited Berwick 51-42 in the Premier Trophy. At King's Lynn, the Championship of Great Britain semi-final sees Chris Neath defeat Andrew Moore in a first-place run-off after both had tallied 13 points.

20 Ricky Ashworth stars with a six-ride paid maximum (17+1), as Sheffield post a 54-42 league win against Somerset.

21 Edinburgh crash to a 47-43 loss to visiting Hull in the Premier Trophy. The reverse brings to an end a run of thirty-three successive home wins for the Monarchs at Premier League level stretching back to 6 September 2002. Somerset win 51-41 against Berwick in a competitive league encounter, with John Jorgensen carding a super maximum (15). Workington easily overpower Newcastle 58-33 to take over second position in their Premier Trophy group. With Sheffield and Hull just a point behind, a place in the semi-final remains finely balanced.

22 League activity results in a 56-39 victory for Rye House against Workington, with Steve Masters recording a paid full house (9+3). At Loomer Road, Jan Staechmann's scintillating 18-point maximum paves the way for Stoke's 55-39 league victory over Berwick.

23 By defeating Stoke 50-43 at Ashfield, Glasgow clinch top spot in the Northern section of the Premier Trophy and a much-deserved semi-final slot.

24 Fast-starting Seemond Stephens is paid for the lot (14+1), as Exeter crush Newcastle 64-32 in the league. Matej Zagar (15) and Danny Bird (13+2) plunder maximums as Reading begin their home league campaign with a 51-39 success against Hull.

25 The Isle of Wight overcome stern resistance before posting a 53-38 league victory over a battling Newcastle outfit.

26 Hull register a comfortable 55-38 league win against Somerset. Turning to the Premier Trophy, King's Lynn suffer all manner of mechanical problems before defeating Newport 50-45.

27 Catching up with their fixtures, the Isle of Wight eke out a narrow 45-44 success over Exeter in the Premier Trophy.

28 Edinburgh suffer a second successive home loss, going down 46-44 to high-flying Rye House in a Premier League fixture. Further domestic activity sees Somerset come from behind to beat Workington 54-41 in a pulsating match.

29 After claiming victories in their first four league matches, Rye House go down to a 53-42 loss at Berwick. Jan Staechmann's paid maximum (13+2) helps guide Stoke to a 56-37 league success over Workington.

30 Newport have no answers as Hull run riot to win 58-38 in a league encounter at Queensway Meadows. Riding their second home match in two days, Stoke lose 48-47 to a determined Edinburgh side in the Premier Trophy.

31 Rain curtails the second leg of Exeter's Bank Holiday Knock-Out Cup tie against Newport, but with the Falcons 53-19 ahead after twelve heats, they comfortably progress to the next round. Frede Schott's maximum (12) helps Edinburgh to a 51-39 victory in the Premier Trophy at Newcastle. The result leaves the Monarchs sweating on the outcome of the Sheffield *v.* Hull match for the outstanding semi-final place. Reading race to 53-44 success against Glasgow in the league at Smallmead. Further league action sees Simon Stead return to action as Workington beat Stoke 52-42. An inter-league challenge results in a narrow 46-45 victory for Rye House against top-flight Eastbourne.

JUNE

1 The Isle of Wight lead right from the opening heat, before running out 53-42 winners in a Premier League fixture versus Glasgow.

2 League fare at Hull results in the homesters beating Edinburgh 49-46, as the Vikings take up top spot in the table. At Saddlebow Road, King's Lynn claim a hard-fought 49-47 league victory over Reading.

3 Sheffield race into the semi-finals of the Premier Trophy, courtesy of a comfortable 55-40 success against Hull.

4 'Roo Boy' Rory Schlein nets maximum points (15), as Edinburgh return to winning ways at their Armadale home, thumping the Isle of Wight 62-32 in a league encounter. Somerset overcome a mid-match deficit and eventually run-out comfortable 56-37 victors over Rye House in the Premier Trophy.

5 It's close throughout, but Berwick claim the league points with a 48-45 win versus a

battling Isle of Wight outfit. League leaders Hull continue their excellent start to the domestic campaign, registering a tremendous 51-44 success at Rye House. There's more league activity at Loomer Road, and after losing the first heat 5-1, Stoke step up the pace to beat Exeter 57-36. Reading have no answers as Carl Stonehewer's paid full house (13+2) guides Workington to a convincing 57-39 league victory at Derwent Park.

6 Stoke become the latest team to win at Newport and their 54-41 success takes them to the head of the league table, above Hull on race points difference. A storming finish at Brough Park sees Newcastle go down fighting, 48-47, at the hands of Reading in a gripping league fixture. Shane Parker again shows brilliant form at Ashfield, netting an unbeaten 14+1 points as Glasgow get their home league programme off to a flying start, defeating the Isle of Wight 58-34.

7 Stoke consolidate their position at the head of the league standings with a 50-43 win at Exeter. Further league action at Smallmead results in a hard-earned 49-43 victory for Reading against Rye House.

8 The Isle of Wight defeat Rye House 54-42 in the Premier Trophy, thereby dashing any lingering hopes of the Hertfordshire side reaching the semi-final of the competition. The Rockets' loss is Reading's gain and it's the Berkshire side who are assured of a place in the last four.

9 Emiliano Sanchez hits a paid full house (13+2), as Hull jump to the top of the Premier League table, courtesy of easily defeating Newport 61-35. Tomas Topinka (14+1), Tom P. Madsen (12) and new signing Paul Lee (9+3) all remain unbeaten as King's Lynn comfortably win 61-33 against Somerset in the league.

10 Sheffield overcome Glasgow 55-41 in Premier League action at Owlerton.

11 Edinburgh suffer another home defeat at the hands of Hull, as the East Yorkshire side win an exciting league encounter 47-43. Craig Watson thunders to a maximum (15) as Newport claim their first league win of the season, narrowly beating Newcastle 46-44. There's more hard-fought league action at Somerset, with John Jorgensen's super 15-point maximum helping the homesters to pip Glasgow 46-44.

13 Before a packed Newport audience, home favourite Craig Watson takes victory in the Welsh Open Championship after defeating Chris Harris, Adam Shields and Jesper B. Jensen in the final. Exciting league action sees Rye House defeat Berwick 48-42. In the final group match of the Premier Trophy (North), both Jan Staechmann (18) and Alan Mogridge (13+2) plunder unbeaten tallies as Stoke crush basement club Newcastle 61-31.

14 In the league, Exeter come from behind to post a 49-41 success over a plucky Berwick outfit. Newcastle's match versus Newport is abruptly curtailed after William Lawson receives back injuries in a horror smash on the first bend of heat fourteen. With the Diamonds holding a 49-32 lead after thirteen races, the result stands and gives the homesters their first league points of the season. Reading repel a late fightback to beat Sheffield 50-45 in a thrilling league encounter at Smallmead.

15 The Isle of Wight convincingly beat Sheffield 57-35 in the league at Smallbrook Stadium.

16 Both Ross Brady (15) and Garry Stead (14+1) card unbeaten tallies as table-topping Hull extend their lead in the standings with a huge 65-27 victory over Exeter. At the Norfolk Arena, King's Lynn post their third straight league success, hammering Stoke 67-27, with Tomas Topinka (13+2), Adam Allott (12) and Paul Lee (10+2) remaining undefeated by an opponent.

17 Thursday evening action at Ashfield results in a 56-38 league win for Glasgow against

King's Lynn. Further league activity at Owlerton results in a whopping 67-26 success for Sheffield over beleaguered Newcastle, with Richard Hall (13+2), James Birkinshaw (12+3) and Andrew Moore (12+3) paid for the lot.

18 Aided by Peter Carr's maximum (12), Edinburgh return to winning ways in the league, beating King's Lynn 55-38. Hull continue their merry march with a 53-44 win at Somerset, it being their eighth league victory on the trot.

19 Berwick's league encounter with King's Lynn is postponed following overnight rain. Rye House snatch a last-heat 45-44 victory over Exeter in a pulsating league match, with Falcons' guest Chris Harris establishing a new track record of 55.8 seconds. Simon Stead stylishly accrues maximum points (15), as Workington collect a 51-44 success over Sheffield in the league. A controversial league encounter at Loomer Road eventually ends in a 52-40 win for Stoke against Glasgow.

20 Riding at home proves advantageous for Reading as Danny Bird and Phil Morris take the Racers to victory from Stoke in the Premier League Pairs Championship.

21 In the first leg of the Premier Trophy semi-final, Exeter romp to a big 64-30 win against Sheffield, with unbeaten totals from guest Chris Harris (15) and flying reserve Graeme Gordon (12+3).

22 Rain unfortunately scuppers the Isle of Wight's scheduled Knock-Out Cup tie versus Rye House.

23 Both scheduled league matches are called off due to persistent rainfall: Hull *v.* Workington and King's Lynn *v.* Sheffield.

24 Led by a paid maximum from Andre Compton (16+2), Sheffield win 56-38 against Exeter in the second leg of the Premier Trophy semi-final, but it's the Falcons who progress to the final by a 16-point margin on aggregate.

25 Both Frede Schott (15) and Peter Carr (12) bag maximums as Edinburgh romp to a 65-27 victory over Newcastle in the league. In the Knock-Out Cup, Somerset win 48-44 against Workington in their first-leg tie.

26 Rain washes out two Knock-Out Cup matches: Berwick *v.* Hull and Rye House *v.* Isle of Wight. The day's other KOC tie goes ahead, however, with Carl Stonehewer posting an unbeaten tally (17+1), as Workington defeat Somerset 54-40 to reach the semi-final stage.

27 Craig Watson's third successive league maximum (15) paves the way for Newport's narrow 46-44 win against Exeter. After dropping down from the top flight, Jason Lyons registers a classy full house (15) as Newcastle beat Edinburgh 49-43 in the league at Brough Park. Shane Parker hits a full 15 points as Glasgow comfortably post a 54-39 win against Stoke in the league.

28 After three league defeats on the road, Exeter return to winning ways by beating top-of-the-table Hull 50-45 at their sweeping County Ground home. Reading comfortably beat Newcastle 57-38 in the day's other league fixture, with Danny Bird (14+1) and Andrew Appleton (12+3) notching paid maximums.

29 League leaders Hull rack up their fifth away success of the campaign, courtesy of a 49-44 scoreline at the Isle of Wight.

30 Hull further extend their advantage at the head of the table, defeating Stoke 50-46, as Magnus Karlsson establishes a new track record for Craven Park of 64.4 seconds. Rain forces the abandonment of the league match between King's Lynn and Exeter after nine heats, with the Stars holding a 35-22 lead at the time.

JULY

1 Identical paid maximums (14+1) from Andre Compton and guest Simon Stead help Sheffield to a 55-38 victory over Berwick in the league. The match sees Stead lower the track record to 59.9 seconds in heat four, only for Andrew Moore to go even faster in heat nine, when clocking 59.6 seconds.

2 Frede Schott's paid maximum (14+1) leads Edinburgh to a 49-41 league success over Exeter on a track made heavy by rain. Somerset overcome an early deficit to defeat the Isle of Wight 49-44 in a thrilling league fixture. Friday night action at Derwent Park sees Workington net their fourth straight league success in defeating Rye House 58-34, aided by an unbeaten score from the stylish Simon Stead (13+2).

3 Berwick beat Exeter 55-41 in lively league activity at Shielfield Park. Brent Werner's paid full house (13+2) paves the way as Rye House claim a 49-41 league win over Somerset. The day's third league match sees Paul Pickering go through the card (15), as Stoke triumph 56-38 against the Isle of Wight.

4 Newport record their second league win on the trot, beating King's Lynn 50-44 in a rain-affected meeting. Glasgow wallop Exeter 61-34 in a one-sided league contest, with both George Stancl (14+1) and James Grieves (13+2) remaining unbeaten by an opponent.

5 Racing their fourth league match in as many days, Exeter cruise to a 61-33 success over Edinburgh. Jason Lyons romps to his second maximum (18) in four league matches for Newcastle, as the Diamonds win 50-43 against second-in-the-table Stoke.

6 Knock-Out Cup action results in a 59-36 victory for the Isle of Wight over Rye House, with Craig Boyce bagging maximum points (15).

7 A sudden downpour washes out Somerset's league match against Edinburgh at 6.30 p.m. League leaders Hull are made to sweat, but eventually come out on top, narrowly beating Workington 46-44. Amid worsening storms, King's Lynn's league fixture against Glasgow is halted after twelve heats, with the homesters in command by a 41-28 scoreline.

8 Overnight rain leaves the Owlerton circuit under water, causing the postponement of Sheffield's league encounter with Edinburgh.

10 Workington provide all fifteen race winners as they crush Glasgow 68-25 in the league, with the rout including unbeaten returns from Carl Stonehewer (13+2), Rusty Harrison (12+3) and Simon Stead (12). Berwick cruise to a 57-37 success over Sheffield in a league encounter at Shielfield Park. Rare Saturday evening Premier League racing at Armadale sees Edinburgh come from behind to beat Reading 47-42. The day's other two scheduled matches are postponed due to the effects of rain: King's Lynn *v.* Hull (PL) and Rye House *v.* Isle of Wight (KOC).

11 At Queensway Meadows, a thriller sees Workington narrowly pip Newport 46-44 to take up second position in the league. A late rally earns Glasgow a 50-40 victory against Reading in the first leg of the Premier Trophy semi-final, with Shane Parker scorching to his latest maximum (15). Newcastle capitulate as visiting Hull storm to a 60-34 win at Brough Park, with guest Shaun Tacey carding a paid maximum (10+2) for the rampant Vikings. The victory is Hull's sixth on the road and leaves them a massive fourteen points clear at the top of the league table.

12 Led by unbeaten tallies from Matej Zagar (15) and Andrew Appleton (10+2), Reading beat Glasgow 57-36 to book a place against Exeter in the Premier Trophy final. Meanwhile, at Exeter, the Falcons race to a 56-39 success over Workington in domestic league fare.

13 Terrific league action at Smallbrook Stadium results in a 45-45 draw between the Isle of Wight and Workington.

14 Runaway league leaders Hull notch their fifth win in a row, beating Yorkshire rivals Sheffield 54-40. King's Lynn romp to a mammoth 66-26 success over Newcastle in a the league at Saddlebow Road.

15 Glasgow maintain their 100 per cent home league record, comfortably beating Newport 54-40 in Thursday evening action at Ashfield. The day's other scheduled league fixture between Sheffield and Hull is postponed due to the effects of heavy rain.

16 On a night of entertaining Premier League racing, Edinburgh record a 55-41 win over on-tour Newport. Meanwhile, Somerset overcome a mid-match deficit to defeat Rye House 52-40.

17 Berwick inflict a third tour defeat on Newport, winning the league encounter 54-40. Courtesy of a 50-40 scoreline, Rye House complete a league double over Edinburgh. Both Carl Stonehewer and Simon Stead plunder paid maximums (14+1), as second-in-the-table Workington triumph 58-35 versus Somerset. The match sees Stead burn-up the Derwent Park circuit to shave 0.7 of a second off the track record as he establishes a new best time of 64.1. Stylish Dane Jan Staechmann nets maximum points (15), as third-placed Stoke consolidate their position with a 55-38 success against King's Lynn.

18 Newport grab only their fourth league win of the season, beating Edinburgh 50-43 in an exciting encounter. Jason Lyons notches another full house for Newcastle as the Diamonds defeat Somerset 47-43 for what is also their fourth league success of the campaign. The victories for Newport and Newcastle leave the Isle of Wight propping up the league table. After falling behind early on, Glasgow rally to defeat Sheffield 51-42 in Ashfield's second league fixture of the week.

19 Exeter overcome early resistance to beat bottom-of-the-table Isle of Wight 54-40. Andrew Appleton remains unbeaten (13+2) at home for the second successive league match as Reading ease to a 55-39 win against Edinburgh.

20 Craig Boyce's paid maximum (14+1) helps the Isle of Wight to defeat Berwick 56-37 – the victory lifting the Islanders off the foot of the league standings.

21 Hull make it six league wins in a row as they crush Glasgow 62-31. King's Lynn comfortably collect the league points from Berwick, their 61-35 success aided by identical unbeaten returns from Tomas Topinka and Shaun Tacey (13+2).

22 Both Andrew Moore (14+1) and Andre Compton (14+1) are paid for a full quota of points as Sheffield post a 57-37 victory over Exeter in the Knock-Out Cup.

23 Edinburgh host the Hampton Hotel Summer Special Pairs, with Theo Pijper and Blair Scott (29) narrowly claiming first place from Peter Carr and Trent Leverington (28). Exciting league action at the Oak Tree Arena results in a 51-39 win for Somerset against Sheffield.

24 A double-header at Berwick firstly sees the Bandits grab a hard-earned 48-45 success over Reading in the Premier League. Knock-Out Cup action follows, with the match against Hull abandoned after fourteen heats due to the time curfew. However, the 42-42 scoreline stands and it's the Vikings who progress through on aggregate. Carl Stonehewer (14+1) and Simon Stead (12) are unbeaten as Workington stay second in the league, thanks to a 49-41 victory over the Isle of Wight. At Loomer Road, third-in-the-table Stoke eventually come out on top 51-39 against a dogged Edinburgh side.

25 Glasgow grab the league points at their fabulous Ashfield raceway, beating a determined Reading outfit 51-45. Jason Lyons scorches to his fourth maximum (18) in five home

league matches, but his efforts can't prevent Newcastle from going down 49-46 at the hands of the Isle of Wight.

26 Mark Lemon returns to action after a long injury lay-off and lands a paid full-house (11+1), as Exeter power to a 62-29 success over Sheffield in the Knock-Out Cup, thereby progressing to the quarter-final stage. Despite injury problems, Reading come from behind to defeat the league's basement club, Newport, by a 48-42 scoreline.

27 The Isle of Wight move further up the league standings, thanks to a 50-44 success against Stoke.

28 With the cream of the Premier League on show, Craig Watson comes out on top in the Champions Chase at King's Lynn, winning the final ahead of John Jorgensen, Matej Zagar and Jason Lyons.

29 Sheffield have to dig deep, before finally defeating Reading 51-46 in an exciting league encounter at Owlerton.

30 'Roo Boy' Rory Schlein gets the better of David Howe, Shane Parker and Theo Pijper to win the prestigious Scottish Open Championship at Edinburgh. Meanwhile, at the Oak Tree Arena, Somerset ease to a 55-39 success over Exeter in entertaining Premier League fare.

31 Berwick narrowly beat Glasgow 45-44 in a thrilling league fixture at Shielfield Park. Knock-Out Cup action at Hoddesdon sees Rye House defeat the Isle of Wight 52-42, but it's the visitors who safely go through on aggregate. Having gone on the rampage to hammer Glasgow three weeks previously, Workington let rip again, thrashing beleaguered Newcastle 69-25 in the league. Both Simon Stead (15) and Brett Woodifield (10+2) register unbeaten tallies in the rout. Saturday night racing at Craven Park sees league leaders Hull triumph 62-33 against King's Lynn, with Magnus Karlsson (15) and Paul Thorp (11+4) remaining unbeaten by an opponent. Alan Mogridge's paid maximum (14+1) helps Stoke cruise to a 62-32 success over Somerset, as the Potters retain third spot in the standings.

AUGUST

1 A cracker of a league match ends in a 45-45 draw between Newport and the Isle of Wight at Queensway Meadows, with Craig Watson scoring the lot (15) for the Wasps. That result, coupled with Newcastle losing 51-43 at home to Berwick, sees the Welsh side relegate the Diamonds to the foot of the table. Hull remarkably net their seventh away league success of the season, winning 47-43 at Glasgow. Reading can only post a 46-43 victory over a determined Exeter outfit in the first leg of the Premier Trophy final.

2 Fired-up Exeter complete their task, defeating Reading 59-35 to lift the Premier Trophy, with their success dedicated to unwell promoter Colin Hill.

3 Craig Boyce breaks the track record on his way to a paid maximum (14+1), as the Isle of Wight comfortably beat Edinburgh 65-31 in the league at Smallbrook Stadium.

4 Hull make it nine league wins in a row, romping to a 62-32 success over Rye House. Meanwhile, at Saddlebow Road, King's Lynn have little difficulty in notching a 63-32 league victory against Edinburgh.

5 Having gone through the motions of the parade, torrential rain prior to heat one forces the postponement of Sheffield's attractive league match versus Stoke.

6 After six straight league defeats on the road, Edinburgh return to winnings ways, beating Somerset 55-39. Skipper Frede Schott leads the way for the Monarchs, bagging an exquisite full-house (15). Rare Friday evening action at Hoddesdon sees Davey Watt

remain unbeaten (14+1), as Rye House post a 49-44 victory against Reading in exciting league fare.

7 League activity at Shielfield Park sees Berwick ease to a 53-42 success over Somerset. Simon Stead amazingly hits his seventh home league maximum on the bounce (14+1), as Workington comfortably defeat Edinburgh 65-30. Stoke crush Sheffield 62-30 in the league, with Robbie Kessler registering a paid maximum (11+1).

8 Heavy rain causes the abandonment of Newport's league clash against Reading, with the Wasps leading 17-13 after five heats. Rye House come from behind to win 48-45 in a thrilling league encounter at Newcastle. At Ashfield, unbeaten tallies from George Stancl (14+1), James Grieves (12+3) and Shane Parker (12) help Glasgow to a 54-42 victory against Somerset in PL action. Guest Simon Stead lowers the Owlerton track record and scores maximum points (15), as Sheffield defeat Yorkshire rivals Hull 52-38 in an entertaining league battle.

9 Reading's league clash with Workington is postponed following heavy early evening rainfall. League action at the County Ground results in a 55-38 success for Exeter over King's Lynn.

11 Runaway league leaders Hull are given a real fright, before narrowly overcoming the Isle of Wight 48-46. Tomas Topinka cards a classy maximum as King's Lynn win 52-42 against second-in-the-table Workington.

12 Continuous rain forces the postponement of Glasgow's league match against Berwick. A bumper holiday crowd witness the Isle of Wight go down fighting against top-flight opposition, with visiting Poole finally clinching a 50-42 challenge-match success. Ricky Ashworth bags a maximum (15), as Sheffield thump depleted Newport 65-26 in the league.

13 Edinburgh cruise to a morale-boosting 57-37 league success over arch-rivals Glasgow, with both Rory Schlein (15) and Peter Carr (11+1) remaining unbeaten. Somerset ease to a 51-43 victory against PL cellar position occupiers Newcastle.

14 Hull notch their eighth league win on the road, beating Berwick 47-45 at Shielfield Park. Rye House run out comfortable 56-36 victors against Newcastle in entertaining league fare at Hoddesdon. Simon Stead bags his eighth unbeaten home tally in a row (15), as Workington dispatch King's Lynn 54-36. Stoke are beaten for pace as Andrew Appleton's paid full house inspires Reading to a 49-41 success at Loomer Road. The result lifts the Racers above the Potters to third position in the league standings.

15 Newport's scheduled league match against Berwick is cancelled due to the effects of heavy rainfall. Another Jason Lyons maximum (15) leads Newcastle to their first league success in seven attempts, as they defeat Sheffield 52-44. The Diamonds' win takes them off the foot of the table, with Newport taking over as the basement club. Glasgow gain some revenge for their heavy loss two nights earlier, defeating Edinburgh 50-45 in the return league fixture at Ashfield.

16 Exeter triumph 65-27 against Newport, with Michael Coles going through the card unbeaten (10+2) from the reserve berth. The day's other league match results in a comfortable 59-32 win for Reading against Berwick, as both Matej Zagar (17+1) and Phil Morris (15) post maximums.

17 Rain forces the abandonment of the Isle of Wight's Premier League clash aginst Newport after six heats, with the homesters holding a 25-11 advantage.

18 The league encounter between King's Lynn and Sheffield is washed out following early

evening storms. Knock-Out Cup action sees Hull defeat Reading 53-39 in the first leg of their second-round tie.

19 Shane Parker is paid for the lot (13+2), as Glasgow triumph 57-37 against Berwick in the league. There's a paid maximum for Jason Bunyan (14+1), as the Isle of Wight comfortably collect the league points, courtesy of a 63-31 victory over Exeter. Meanwhile, Andre Compton also cards an unbeaten league tally (14+1) in Sheffield's huge 69-25 success against Rye House.

20 Edinburgh easily beat Berwick 60-36 in domestic fare at Armadale, with both Frede Schott (13+2) and Theo Pijper (13+2) in the maximum mood. Run under grey skies, Rye House quickly regain their winning touch, beating King's Lynn 58-35 in league activity. Somerset fail to halt Reading from claiming their third league win on the bounce, the Berkshire side triumphing 52-42 at the Oak Tree Arena.

21 At Derwent Park, home track knowledge proves fruitful as Workington plunder their sixth trophy in six years, scoring 29 points to win the Premier League Four-Team Championship final from Stoke (20), Glasgow (12) and Rye House (11). Simon Stead goes through the whole event unbeaten, recording a 6-point tally in the semi-final and a further 9 in the final.

22 The day serves up four high-quality Premier League matches, with Newport and Somerset playing out a thrilling 45-45 draw in the first at Queensway Meadows. Jesper Olsen dramatically returns to the saddle, but the Dane's presence can't prevent Newcastle from losing 51-43 to visiting Workington. It's a close call at Ashfield, as a last heat 4-2 gives Glasgow a 48-47 victory over Rye House in a sparkling encounter. Finally, Champions-elect Hull continue their charge as they amazingly notch a ninth away success, winning 52-42 at Stoke.

23 Phil Morris records a wonderful 21-point maximum as Reading beat Hull 51-42 in the Knock-Out Cup, but it's the Vikings who progress to the semi-finals on aggregate.

24 The Isle of Wight steam to a 62-31 win against Somerset in a rain affected PL encounter.

25 The league match between King's Lynn and the Isle of Wight is postponed at lunchtime due to rain. With the Shielfield Park circuit in a tricky condition following heavy rainfall, Berwick's league match with Stoke is also eventually called off half an hour after the scheduled 7.30 p.m. start time. There is racing at Hull, however, where Emiliano Sanchez canters to maximum points (12), as the Vikings thrash Newcastle 60-31. John Jorgensen's five-ride full house (15) paves the way, as Somerset triumph 61-33 over 2003 Champions Edinburgh.

26 It's tight at the County Ground, but Exeter hold on to win 48½-47½ against Reading in a thrilling league encounter. The Isle of Wight temporarily jump to fourth spot in the league table courtesy of a 63-29 demolition job on basement-dwellers Newport. The Islanders boast a number of high scorers in the match, but it's only Krister Marsh (9+3) who remains unbeaten by an opponent. Meanwhile at Sheffield, Andre Compton (14+1) and guest Simon Stead (11+1) are paid for full tallies, as the Tigers easily beat Edinburgh 65-27 in a league fixture.

27 Edinburgh get back to that winning feeling, with a dogged 53-43 success over second-in-the-league Workington.

28 The destiny of the league title is decided, as Berwick's hard-earned 49-44 win against Workington means the Comets can no longer catch Hull at the head of the standings. Meanwhile, the Vikings suffer a rare defeat, going down 50-42 at King's Lynn. Although

Hull grab the bonus point, the result is academic and they have deservedly landed their first-ever League Championship. Unbeaten tallies from Paul Pickering (15) and Alan Mogridge (13+2) lead Stoke to a 56-40 success against Rye House in the day's other PL match.

29 Sheffield notch their first away league victory of the season, winning 46-43 in a dramatic finale at Newport. Meanwhile, at their super Ashfield raceway, Glasgow cruise to a fourth league success on the trot, beating Newcastle 59-35.

30 A busy Bank Holiday Monday of league activity begins with Mark Lemon recording a paid maximum (12+3), as Exeter beat Sheffield 59-36. At Hoddesdon, Rye House eke out a 50-45 success over a battling Stoke septet. Jesper Olsen suffers severe facial injuries as Newcastle collect only their sixth win of the campaign, narrowly beating Glasgow 49-47. The amazing Simon Stead notches his ninth successive unbeaten tally (12) at Derwent Park, as Workington overwhelm Berwick 60-33. Long-serving Comet Carl Stonehewer also gets in on the act, remaining unbeaten from five starts (13+2). Reading defeat King's Lynn 56-39, with Danny Bird making a sensational return to score a paid maximum (14+1), having missed seven matches through a shoulder injury.

31 The Isle of Wight notch their fourth Premier League victory in a row, thumping King's Lynn 66-29.

SEPTEMBER

1 The first of two league matches features Adam Allott sizzling to a six-ride paid maximum (17+1), as King's Lynn return to winning ways, beating Rye House 57-38. Meanwhile, Wednesday night action at Smallmead sees Reading race to a 58-36 win over Exeter, with Phil Morris (14+1) and Danny Bird (12) going through the card unbeaten.

2 Jason Bunyan storms to a paid full house (13+2), as the Isle of Wight beat Workington 56-38 in the first leg of the Knock-Out Cup semi-final. In the league, Sheffield win 56-38 against King's Lynn, with both Andre Compton (14+1) and guest Paul Thorp (11+1) remaining unbeaten.

3 Edinburgh are never headed, as they ease to a 54-39 league victory over Sheffield. The day's only other league match sees Somerset triumph 50-43 against Stoke, with 'Bristol Bomber' Glenn Cunningham scorching to a paid maximum (14+1).

4 A terrific league encounter at Shielfield Park sees Berwick lose 49-48 to visiting Stoke. The three other league matches result in home wins, beginning with Workington's 66-26 hammering of Exeter. Carl Stonehewer (14+1) and Rusty Harrison (10+2) card paid maximums for the Comets, while a last place in heat fifteen sees Simon Stead's wonderful run come to an end – after going fifty-three consecutive races in official competition without being beaten by an opposing rider at Derwent Park. Rye House finally come out on top in a ding-dong match, beating a determined Glasgow 51-41. At Saddlebow Road, Adam Allott records his second home maximum in four days (17+1), with Tomas Topinka joining him on the same total as King's Lynn overpower Sheffield 56-36.

5 Super Aussie Craig Watson scores the lot (15), as bottom-of-the-table Newport gain only their fifth win of the campaign, beating Glasgow 53-39. Jason Lyons' unbeaten return (14+1) helps Newcastle to a 49-45 success against Exeter in a highly entertaining league tussle.

6 At the County Ground, Exeter comfortably beat Glasgow 54-39 in the league. Reading maintain their unbeaten home league record, winning 57-38 against Somerset, with both Andrew Appleton (12+3) and Matej Zagar (12) helping themselves to maximums.

7 The Isle of Wight go on another points spree to overwhelm Rye House 63-32 and again jump to fourth place in the league, with both Jason Bunyan (15) and Craig Boyce (14+1) remaining unbeaten.

8 Edinburgh boss Alex Harkess hands the League Championship to Hull, with the Vikings subsequently racing to a 54-40 success over Berwick in their final home match of the domestic programme. Long-serving Paul Thorp marks the occasion with a paid full house (11+1). King's Lynn romp to a 62-33 victory over Newport at their super-fast Saddlebow Road raceway.

9 Sheffield's remarkable sequence of home wins, stretching right back to 29 April 1999, is finally ended as Simon Stead's maximum (15) leads Workington to a narrow 46-44 success and the league points.

10 Amid increasing rainfall and with the 64-20 scoreline somewhat conclusive, Edinburgh's league match against Stoke is abandoned after fourteen heats. No fewer than four of the Monarchs are credited with maximums, namely Peter Carr (15), Frede Schott (14+1), Theo Pijper (10+2) and Cameron Woodward (9+3). King's Lynn race to their thirteenth consecutive home league win of the campaign, comfortably beating the Isle of Wight 57-39. Paul Fry pockets his first unbeaten league score of the season (13+2) and helps Somerset to a 59-34 victory against Newport.

11 Four league matches are scheduled, although one fails to last the course, as rain causes the abandonment of Stoke's fixture versus Newport after eight heat, the Potters holding a 25-23 advantage at the time. Berwick quickly overturn a first-heat reverse to beat old rivals Edinburgh 57-38. Tommy Allen registers a first-ever Premier League paid maximum (10+2), as Rye House beat the Isle of Wight 52-41. Workington finish their home league programme with a 53-43 victory over recently crowned Champions Hull. Both Simon Stead (15) and Carl Stonehewer (12+3) record maximums, as the Comets complete a 100 per cent domestic record at Derwent Park for the first time in their history.

12 Jason Lyons' latest maximum (18) helps Newcastle to their third successive league win, as they triumph 57-39 against King's Lynn. A double dose of league activity at Queensway Meadows firstly sees Newport claim an excellent 50-43 success over Reading. The Wasps then leapfrog Newcastle at the foot of the league table, courtesy of a 51-44 victory against Berwick, with Craig Watson hitting his seventh full maximum of the term (15). Glasgow suffer their fifth straight league defeat, losing 46-44 to visiting Workington. At Owlerton, rain curtails the day's other league match between Sheffield and Stoke after twelve heats, although the result stands as a 44-33 win for the Tigers.

13 Exeter riders finish first and second in every race as the Falcons romp to a 75-18 whitewash over Rye House in the league. Six of the victorious homesters are paid for double-figure maximums: Seemond Stephens (15+3), Mark Simmonds (14+1), Mark Lemon (10+2), Michael Coles (10+2), Roger Lobb (10+2) and Graeme Gordon (10+2). Reading are pushed hard, but manage to defeat the Isle of Wight 48-42 in entertaining league fare at Smallmead.

14 Krister Marsh's paid maximum (10+2) helps the Isle of Wight to a 55-40 success over Reading in the return league match at Smallbrook Stadium.

15 Wednesday evening action at Shielfield Park results in a comfortable 59-35 victory for Berwick over Newcastle as the Bandits approach the end of their league campaign. King's Lynn ensure themselves a place in the Young Shield by hammering Exeter 64-29 in their

final home league match. Leading the scoring for the Stars are maximum men Shaun Tacey (17+1), Tomas Topinka (15) and James Brundle (13+5). At Hull, an Inter-Continental Best Pairs event results in a triumph for England (28), courtesy of Paul Thorp and Garry Stead. Swedish duo Emil Kramer and Magnus Karlsson finish second (27), while Shane Parker and Joel Parsons' efforts give Australia third spot (21).

16 Sheffield book their place in the Young Shield with a hard-fought 55-39 victory over the Isle of Wight.

17 An unusual Friday race-night at Smallmead sees third-in-the-table Reading defeat second-placed Workington 56-37. Somerset finish their league schedule by easing to a 49-41 success against King's Lynn. At Loomer Road, Stoke comfortably defeat Newport 57-37 in the day's third league match. Meanwhile, in the first leg of the Scottish Cup, Edinburgh pull away in the latter stages to defeat Glasgow 51-40.

18 Simon Cartwright (18), Adam Pietraszko (15) and Adrian Rymel (14+4) all remain unbeaten as Berwick close their league campaign with a comprehensive 65-29 victory over King's Lynn. A 51-39 win over Newport gives Rye House sixth place in the final league table and, with it, a place in the Young Shield. Stoke beat Newcastle 58-37 to finish fourth in the standings, while the unfortunate Diamonds are condemned to the cellar position on race points difference behind Newport. In the Knock-Out Cup, the Isle of Wight produce a solid display to win 46½-43½ at Workington, thereby clinching a place in the final.

19 At Sheffield, the Premier League Riders' Championship ends dramatically, with home-track rider Andre Compton awarded the title following an horrific coming together with Workington's Simon Stead in the final. Exeter's Mark Lemon ends the meeting as runner-up, with Stead having to settle for third position ahead of Craig Boyce, who suffered a two-minute exclusion prior to the race.

20 The first leg of the other Knock-Out Cup semi-final sees Mark Lemon scorch to maximum points (15), as Exeter gain a 57-34 victory over Championship-winning Hull. The last Premier League match of the season is staged at Smallmead and it's Reading who race to a big 61-33 win against Stoke.

22 Although curtailed by rain after fourteen heats, Paul Thorp's Testimonial results in a 45-39 success for the interestingly-titled Tape Toucher's against the Ref's Rebels at Hull, with Garry Stead plundering a maximum (12) for the defeated combination.

24 Frede Schott's Wha Hae Testimonial sees the Bacon Heids beat the Hot Schotts 40-38 in front of a packed Armadale audience. Meanwhile, at Somerset, the final of Glenn Cunningham's Testimonial goes the way of Jason Crump ahead of Magnus Zetterstrom and Craig Boyce.

25 Sam Ermolenko takes victory in the final of Berwick's showpiece, Bordernapolis, as Paul Bentley and Simon Cartwright fill the other podium positions. Continuing with the individual theme, Jason Lyons (13) emerges victorious ahead of Rory Schlein (12) and James Wright (11) in the Cumberland Classic at Workington. In the Young Shield, Rye House claim a hard-fought 47-44 victory against League Champions Hull in the first leg of their quarter-final clash. Staying with the Young Shield, Alan Mogridge's five-ride full house paves the way as Stoke beat the Isle of Wight 52-40.

26 Jesper Olsen makes a surprise return to finish third in the final of the George English Memorial Trophy at Newcastle. Up front, Jason Lyons collects his second individual success in two days, while George Stancl occupies the runner-up spot.

27 By virtue of his earlier win when they met, Nick Simmons takes victory over Simon Walker in the Young Guns Championship at Exeter, both having totalled 11 points. Matej Zagar hits a brilliant maximum (15), as Reading beat Sheffield 58-34 in the Young Shield.

28 Ray Morton nets a paid maximum (13+2), as the Isle of Wight beat Stoke 59-32 to reach the last four in the Young Shield.

29 The first of two Young Shield matches sees Hull continue on their merry way, defeating Rye House 52-42 to reach the semi-finals. Meanwhile, in the first leg of their quarter-final tie, Czech ace Tomas Topinka nets a maximum (15), as King's Lynn post a 52-41 victory against Workington.

30 Sheffield beat Reading 56-41 in the Young Shield, but it's the Racers who progress to the semi-final stage on aggregate.

OCTOBER

2 In the Young Shield, Workington's return match against King's Lynn is abandoned after five heats, with the Comets holding a 20-10 advantage.

3 Rain curtails the Scottish Cup encounter at Glasgow, but as twelve heats are completed, the result stands as a 38-37 victory for visiting Edinburgh, with the Monarchs also retaining the trophy on aggregate.

5 The Isle of Wight have to work hard to beat a tactically aware Reading 53-45 in the first leg of the Young Shield semi-final.

6 In defeating Exeter 62-35, Hull overcome their first-leg deficit to reach the Knock-Out Cup final.

9 At Rye House, Scott Robson's Testimonial results in a 53-33 win for his Red Devils side against brother Stuart's Blue Angels. Making a rare British appearance, Billy Hamill jets to a paid maximum (11+1) for the victorious septet. Workington move through to the semi-finals of the Young Shield, courtesy of a 55-41 success over King's Lynn.

10 Carl Stonehewer lands the £1,000 first prize in the City of Glasgow Ashfield Classic, beating Josh Larsen, Rory Schlein and Magnus Karlsson in the final. Matej Zagar's paid maximum (14+1) leads the way as Reading defeat the Isle of Wight 51-42 to reach the Young Shield final.

13 Rain curtails the Young Shield semi-final clash between Hull and Workington after eight heats, with the Vikings holding a 33-15 lead at the time.

16 Simon Stead goes through the card, as Workington beat Hull 52-44 in the Young Shield.

17 Super Simon Stead scorches to victory in the Northern Classic at Sheffield, with Magnus Karlsson and Sam Ermolenko following him across the line in the final.

20 Rain wipes out any chance of staging the Pride of the East at King's Lynn. The initial part of an exciting double-header at Hull sees the Vikings defeat the Isle of Wight 56-39 in the first leg of the Knock-Out Cup final. In the second installment of a bumper night, Hull win 52-42 versus Workington to reach the Young Shield final by a margin of just two points on aggregate.

21 A determined Davey Watt cards 14 points to win the quickly rescheduled Pride of the East at King's Lynn, with Tomas Topinka defeating Craig Boyce in a second-place run-off after both had recorded tallies of 13.

23 Rain is the only victor as Rye House cancel their attractive three-team tournament against Elite League opposition from Ipswich and Peterborough. The wet stuff also sees off the annual Pride of the Potteries at Stoke.

24 The hastily rearranged Pride of the Potteries results in a final victory for Mark Lemon ahead of Adam Allott and Adam Skornicki after early leader Paul Pickering had unluckily shed a chain.

25 Emil Kramer bags a fabulous paid maximum (16+2), as treble-chasing Hull win 52-41 at Reading in the first leg of the Young Shield final.

26 The Isle of Wight beat Hull 52-43, but it's the Vikings who add the Knock-Out Cup to their League Championship success by an eight-point margin on aggregate.

27 Hull complete a wonderful treble, as a 52-44 victory over Reading lands them the Young Shield by 104 points to 85 on aggregate.

30 Long-serving Exeter promoter Colin Hill unfortunately loses his brave battle with cancer in the early hours of the morning. Falcons official Tony Lethbridge commented: 'This is a very sad day for everyone who knows Colin; he was a very close friend of mine. Even though I was aware of Colin's illness, this still comes as a massive shock. I am told his passing was very peaceful in the Exeter Hospice. Colin kept speedway alive in Exeter for the last twenty years and he deserves a tremendous amount of credit for that. I think it's fair to say he was always regarded as one of the sport's nice guys.' At Rye House, Stuart Robson nets 14 points to take the Ace of Herts Championship, with Edward Kennett beating Adam Shields in a run-off for second spot after both had tied on a total of 12.

31 Adam Shields defeats Danny Bird in a run-off to lift the Euphony Classic at Reading, both riders having tallied 14 points. Third place is also decided via a match race, with Davey Watt getting the better of Matej Zagar after each had totalled 11 points.

PREMIER LEAGUE TABLE

	Mts	Won	Drn	Lst	For	Agn	Pts	Bon	Tot
Hull	28	23	0	5	1445	1166	46	12	58
Workington	28	18	1	9	1425	1179	37	12	49
Reading	28	17	0	11	1389½	1228½	34	12	46
Stoke	28	15	0	13	1328	1268	30	9	39
Isle of Wight	28	13	2	13	1370	1240	28	10	38
Rye House	28	16	0	12	1243	1353	32	5	37
King's Lynn	28	14	0	14	1321	1281	28	7	35
Sheffield	28	14	0	14	1344	1252	28	6	34
Berwick	28	13	0	15	1282	1337	26	7	33
Exeter	28	13	0	15	1306½	1306½	26	6	32
Glasgow	28	12	0	16	1282	1310	24	8	32
Edinburgh	28	12	0	16	1282	1319	24	5	29
Somerset	28	12	1	15	1246	1361	25	4	29
Newport	28	7	2	19	1127	1450	16	1	17
Newcastle	28	8	0	20	1133	1473	16	1	17

YOUNG SHIELD

QUARTER-FINALS

Rye House	47	Hull	44	
Hull	52	Rye House	42	(Hull won 96-89 on aggregate)
Stoke	52	Isle of Wight	40	
Isle of Wight	59	Stoke	32	(Isle of Wight won 99-84 on aggregate)
Reading	58	Sheffield	34	
Sheffield	56	Reading	41	(Reading won 99-90 on aggregate)
King's Lynn	52	Workington	41	
Workington	55	King's Lynn	41	(Workington won 96-93 on aggregate)

SEMI-FINALS

Isle of Wight	53	Reading	45	
Reading	51	Isle of Wight	42	(Reading won 96-95 on aggregate)
Workington	52	Hull	44	
Hull	52	Workington	42	(Hull won 96-94 on aggregate)

FINAL

Reading	41	Hull	52	
Hull	52	Reading	44	(Hull won 104-85 on aggregate)

PREMIER TROPHY (SOUTH) TABLE

	Mts	Won	Drn	Lst	For	Agn	Pts	Bon	Tot
Exeter	12	8	0	4	619	489	16	5	21
Reading	12	7	1	4	579	516	15	5	20
Rye House	12	7	1	4	569	542	15	3	18
Somerset	11	6	1	4	511	494	13	3	16
Isle of Wight	10	3	2	5	451	448	8	2	10
King's Lynn	12	4	1	7	498	625	9	0	9
Newport	11	2	0	9	454	567	4	1	5

NOTE: Two matches were not ridden: Isle of Wight *v.* Somerset; Isle of Wight *v.* Newport.

PREMIER TROPHY (NORTH) TABLE

	Mts	Won	Drn	Lst	For	Agn	Pts	Bon	Tot
Glasgow	14	10	1	3	689	604	21	4	25
Sheffield	14	8	0	6	706	595	16	5	21
Edinburgh	14	8	0	6	684	615	16	5	21
Workington	14	7	0	7	693	619	14	6	20
Hull	14	8	0	6	661	643	16	4	20
Berwick	14	7	0	7	612	679	14	2	16
Stoke	14	6	1	7	651	648	13	2	15
Newcastle	14	1	0	13	505	798	2	0	2

SEMI-FINALS

Exeter	64	Sheffield	30	
Sheffield	56	Exeter	38	(Exeter won 102-86 on aggregate)
Glasgow	50	Reading	40	
Reading	57	Glasgow	36	(Reading won 97-86 on aggregate)

FINAL

Reading	46	Exeter	43	
Exeter	59	Reading	35	(Exeter won 102-31 on aggregate)

KNOCK-OUT CUP

ROUND ONE

Glasgow	47	Reading	43	
Reading	52	Glasgow	43	(Reading won 95-90 on aggregate)
Isle of Wight	63	King's Lynn	29	
King's Lynn	56	Isle of Wight	39	(Isle of Wight won 102-85 on aggregate)
Hull	59	Berwick	36	
Berwick	42	Hull	42	(Hull won 101-78 on aggregate)
Edinburgh	50	Workington	43	
Workington	57	Edinburgh	35	(Workington won 100-85 on aggregate)
Somerset	48	Stoke	42	
Stoke	44	Somerset	46	(Somerset won 94-86 on aggregate)
Rye House	55	Newcastle	39	
Newcastle	41	Rye House	49	(Rye House won 104-80 on aggregate)
Newport	46	Exeter	50	
Exeter	53	Newport	19	(Exeter won 103-65 on aggregate)

QUARTER-FINALS

Somerset	48	Workington	44	
Workington	54	Somerset	40	(Workington won 98-88 on aggregate)
Isle of Wight	59	Rye House	36	
Rye House	52	Isle of Wight	42	(Isle of Wight won 101-88 on aggregate)
Sheffield	57	Exeter	37	
Exeter	62	Sheffield	29	(Exeter won 99-86 on aggregate)
Hull	53	Reading	39	
Reading	51	Hull	42	(Hull won 95-90 on aggregate)

SEMI-FINALS

Isle of Wight	56	Workington	38	
Workington	43½	Isle of Wight	46½	(Isle of Wight won 102½-81½ on aggregate)
Exeter	57	Hull	34	
Hull	62	Exeter	35	(Hull won 96-92 on aggregate)

FINAL

Hull	56	Isle of Wight	39	
Isle of Wight	52	Hull	43	(Hull won 99-91 on aggregate)

BERWICK ELM BANK BANDITS

ADDRESS: Shielfield Park, Tweedmouth, Berwick-upon-Tweed, Northumberland, TD15 2EF.
PROMOTER: Peter Waite.
TRACK LENGTH: 368 metres.
TRACK RECORD: 64.2 seconds – Sean Wilson (21/08/99).
FIRST MEETING: 18 May 1968.
YEARS OF OPERATION: 1968-74 British League Division Two; 1975-80 National League; 1995 Demonstration; 1996 Conference League; 1997 Premier League & Amateur League; 1998-04 Premier League.

PREVIOUS VENUE: Berrington Lough Stadium, nr. Ancroft, Northumberland.
YEARS OF OPERATION: 1982-90 National League; 1991 British League Division One; 1992 British League Division Two; 1993 Open; 1994 British League Division Three; 1995 Academy League.

CLUB HONOURS

KNOCK-OUT CUP WINNERS: 1980, 1989, 1995.
GOLD CUP WINNERS: 1991.
LEAGUE CHAMPIONS: 1994, 1995.
FOUR-TEAM CHAMPIONS: 2002.

RIDER ROSTER 2004

Tom BROWN; Simon CARTWRIGHT; Josef FRANC; Ritchie HAWKINS; Claus KRISTENSEN; Michal MAKOVSKY; David MELDRUM; Adam PIETRASZKO; Adrian RYMEL; Blair SCOTT; Lee SMETHILLS.

OTHER APPEARANCES/GUESTS (official matches only):
Craig BRANNEY; Paul COOPER; Tom P. MADSEN; Krister MARSH; John MORRISON; Michael PICKERING; Carl SHIELD; Scott SMITH.

PREMIER LEAGUE

No	DATE	OPPONENTS	H/A	RESULT	FRANC	MELDRUM	RYMEL	KRISTENSEN	MAKOVSKY	SCOTT	HAWKINS	PIETRASZKO	SMETHILLS	CARTWRIGHT	MADSEN	OTHERS
1	21/5	Somerset	A	L41-51	8 (5)	1+1 (3)	4+2 (4)	7+1 (5)	7 (4)	1 (3)	13+2 (6)	–	–	–	–	–
2	22/5	Stoke	A	L39-55	R/R	2 (4)	9+2 (6)	10 (5)	10 (6)	0 (3)	8+2 (6)	–	–	–	–	–
3	29/5	Rye House	H	W53-42	12+1 (5)	2+1 (2)	11+3 (5)	10+1 (4)	4 (2)	5+2 (6)	9+3 (7)	–	–	–	–	–
4	5/6	Isle of Wight	H	W48-45	R/R	–	10 (6)	14 (6)	–	6+2 (6)	11+3 (6)	6+2 (4)	–	–	–	1 (3)
5	13/6	Rye House	A	L42-48*	3+2 (4)	–	3 (4)	7 (5)	–	3 (3)	7+3 (5)	14 (5)	5 (4)	–	–	–
6	14/6	Exeter	A	L41-49	7 (4)	–	13+1 (5)	2 (3)	–	8 (7)	2+1 (2)	2 (4)	7+2 (5)	–	–	–
7	1/7	Sheffield	A	L38-55	8+1 (4)	–	10+1 (5)	0 (1)	–	–	5+1 (7)	8 (5)	1+1 (3)	6+1 (5)	–	–
8	3/7	Exeter	H	W55-41*	–	–	14+1 (6)	R/R	–	–	9+2 (6)	14+2 (6)	8+1 (4)	10+2 (5)	–	0 (3)
9	10/7	Sheffield	H	W57-37*	9+1 (5)	–	R/R	13 (6)	–	–	7+2 (5)	13 (5)	11–1 (5)	4+2 (5)	–	–
10	17/7	Newport	H	W54-40	8 (4)	–	3 (3)	9 (5)	–	–	8+4 (4)	11 (5)	8+3 (4)	7+1 (5)	–	–

PREMIER LEAGUE continued

No	DATE	OPPONENTS	H/A	RESULT	FRANC	MELDRUM	RYMEL	KRISTENSEN	MAKOVSKY	SCOTT	HAWKINS	PIETRASZKO	SMETHILLS	CARTWRIGHT	MADSEN	OTHERS
11	20/7	Isle of Wight	A	L37-56	6 (4)	–	6 (4)	10+1 (5)	–	–	5 (5)	9+1 (5)	0 (3)	1 (4)	–	–
12	21/7	King's Lynn	A	L35-61	11 (5)	–	3+1 (4)	2 (4)	–	–	6+1 (5)	12 (5)	0 (3)	1 (4)	–	–
13	24/7	Reading	H	W48-45	R/R	–	15 (6)	6 (4)	–	–	–	4 (5)	11+2 (5)	8 (6)	–	4+2 (5)
14	31/7	Glasgow	H	W45-44	3 (5)	–	9 (6)	11 (5)	–	–	–	R/R	6+1 (4)	11+1 (6)	–	5+2 (4)
15	1/8	Newcastle	A	W51-43	13+2 (6)	–	10+1 (6)	7 (5)	–	–	–	R/R	10+1 (5)	9+1 (5)	–	2 (3)
16	7/8	Somerset	H	W53-42*	8+1 (5)	–	7 (4)	9+2 (4)	–	–	3+2 (4)	6 (4)	8+2 (4)	12+1 (5)	–	–
17	14/8	Hull	H	L45-47	6 (4)	–	7+2 (4)	10+1 (5)	–	–	5+1 (3)	8 (5)	6 (5)	3 (4)	–	–
18	16/8	Reading	A	L32-59	6+2 (5)	–	2 (4)	4 (4)	–	–	6 (4)	2 (4)	5+1 (4)	7 (5)	–	–
19	19/8	Glasgow	A	L37-57	9 (5)	–	11 (5)	1+1 (4)	–	–	2 (4)	4 (4)	10 (5)	0 (3)	–	–
20	20/8	Edinburgh	A	L36-60	2 (4)	–	5+2 (4)	9+1 (5)	–	–	4 (4)	0 (3)	15 (6)	1 (4)	–	–
21	28/8	Workington	H	W49-44	9+2 (5)	–	9+1 (5)	8 (4)	–	–	–	6 (4)	11+2 (6)	5+1 (4)	–	1+1 (3)
22	30/8	Workington	A	L33-60	4+1 (4)	–	10 (5)	1 (4)	–	–	3+1 (4)	8 (5)	5 (4)	2+1 (4)	–	–
23	4/9	Stoke	H	L48-49	5 (4)	–	16+1 (6)	4 (4)	–	–	1+1 (3)	10+1 (5)	10+1 (5)	2+1 (3)	–	–
24	8/9	Hull	A	L40-54	R/R	–	14 (6)	–	–	–	7+1 (6)	2+2 (4)	4+1 (6)	0 (4)	13+1 (5)	–
25	11/9	Edinburgh	H	W57-38	8+3 (5)	–	12 (5)	–	–	–	R/R	7+1 (4)	11+2 (6)	–	14+2 (6)	5+3 (4)
26	12/9	Newport	A	L44-51*	5+1 (4)	–	12 (5)	–	–	–	4 (4)	2 (4)	6+2 (4)	–	1 (3)	14+2 (6)
27	15/9	Newcastle	H	W59-35*	–	–	10+1 (4)	–	–	–	8+2 (4)	5+1 (4)	10+1 (4)	9+3 (5)	8 (4)	9+3 (5)
28	18/9	King's Lynn	H	W65-29*	R/R	–	14+4 (6)	–	–	–	7+2 (5)	15 (5)	4+2 (4)	18 (6)	7+2 (4)	–

*Denotes bonus-point victory

DETAILS OF OTHER RIDERS:

Match No. 4: Michael Pickering 1 (3); Match No. 8: Scott Smith 0 (3); Match No. 13: Paul Cooper 4+2 (5); Match No. 14: Paul Cooper 5+2 (4); Match No. 15: Craig Branney 2 (3); Match No. 21: Craig Branney 1+1 (3); Match No. 25: Craig Branney 5+3 (4); Match No. 26: Krister Marsh 14+2 (6); Match No. 27: Craig Branney 9+3 (5).

TACTICAL SUBSTITUTE AND TACTICAL RIDES, AS INCLUDED IN THE SCORES GRID:

Match No. 1: Hawkins 4 points (TR); Match No. 2: Kristensen 6 points (TR); Rymel 2 points (TR); Match No. 7: Franc 4 points (TR); Rymel 4 points (TR); Match No. 11: Rymel 4 points (TR); Pietraszko 2 points (TR); Match No. 12: Pietraszko 6 points (TR); Franc 6 points (TR); Match No. 18: Franc 2 points (TR); Pietraszko 0 points (TR); Match No. 19: Rymel 4 points (TR); Franc 4 points (TR); Match No. 20: Smethills 6 points (TR); Kristensen 6 points (TR); Match No. 22: Pietraszko 4 points (TR); Franc 2 points (TR); Match No. 23: Smethills 6 points (TR); Rymel 6 points (TS); Franc 2 points (TR); Match No. 24: Madsen 4 points (TR); Rymel 4 points (TR); Match No. 26: Marsh 6 points (TR); Rymel 4 points (TR).

PREMIER LEAGUE AVERAGES

Rider	Mts	Rds	Pts	Bon	Tot	Avge	Max
Tom P. Madsen	5	22	41	5	46	8.36	–
Adrian Rymel	27	133	235	23	258	7.76	1 paid
Lee Smethills	24	108	166	26	192	7.11	–
Michal Makovsky	3	12	21	0	21	7.00	–
Adam Pietraszko	23	104	162	10	172	6.62	1 full
Josef Franc	21	96	140	17	157	6.54	–
Claus Kristensen	22	97	148	8	156	6.43	–
Craig Branney	4	15	17	7	24	6.40	–

BERWICK: back row, left to right: Lee Smethills, Ritchie Hawkins, Simon Cartwright, Tom Graham (Team Manager), Adrian Rymel, Adam Pietraszko, Peter Waite (Promoter). Front: Claus Kristensen (on bike), Josef Franc (kneeling).

Rider	Mts	Rds	Pts	Bon	Tot	Avge	Max
Ritchie Hawkins	23	109	138	34	172	6.31	1 paid
Paul Cooper	2	9	9	4	13	5.78	–
Simon Cartwright	20	92	116	15	131	5.70	1 full
Blair Scott	6	28	23	4	27	3.86	–
David Meldrum	3	9	5	2	7	3.11	–
Michael Pickering	1	3	1	0	1	1.33	–
Guests	2	9	11	2	13	5.78	–

PREMIER TROPHY

No	DATE	OPPONENTS	H/A	RESULT	FRANC	MELDRUM	RYMEL	KRISTENSEN	MAKOVSKY	CARTWRIGHT	BROWN	SHIELD	HAWKINS	MORRISON	SCOTT	OTHERS
1	21/3	Newcastle	A	W56-40	7+1 (4)	7+1 (4)	4+1 (4)	15 (5)	9+1 (4)	13+2 (6)	1+1 (3)	–	–	–	–	–
2	27/3	Edinburgh	H	W48-45	8+1 (4)	10+2 (5)	4+1 (4)	8 (4)	8+2 (5)	9 (5)	1 (3)	–	–	–	–	–
3	28/3	Glasgow	A	L28-63	4+2 (4)	4 (3)	5+1 (4)	4 (4)	7 (5)	3 (5)	1+1 (5)	–	–	–	–	–
4	2/4	Edinburgh	A	L31-59	10 (5)	0 (4)	5 (4)	5+1 (5)	3+1 (4)	8 (5)	–	0 (3)	–	–	–	–
5	3/4	Newcastle	H	W66-27*	12 (4)	6+1 (4)	7+3 (4)	15 (5)	10+2 (4)	14+2 (6)	–	2+1 (3)	–	–	–	–
6	10/4	Workington	H	W58-36	11+2 (5)	8+1 (4)	11+2 (5)	10+1 (4)	8+1 (4)	8+1 (4)	2 (4)	–	–	–	–	–
7	12/4	Workington	A	L32-60	6 (5)	2 (4)	8+2 (6)	9 (4)	6+1 (4)	0 (4)	1 (3)	–	–	–	–	–
8	14/4	Stoke	H	W49-44	4+3 (4)	9 (5)	6+4 (4)	14 (5)	8 (4)	7+2 (5)	1+1 (3)	–	–	–	–	–
9	17/4	Stoke	A	L36-54	3+1 (4)	7 (5)	4 (4)	6+1 (4)	8 (5)	6+1 (5)	2 (3)	–	–	–	–	–
10	24/4	Hull	H	W52-42	6+1 (4)	8+1 (4)	12 (5)	4+1 (4)	12 (5)	4 (4)	–	–	–	–	–	6+2 (4)
11	1/5	Glasgow	H	L42-48	5+1 (4)	8+1 (5)	10 (6)	R/R	11 (5)	3 (1)	5+4 (7)	0 (1)	–	–	–	–
12	6/5	Sheffield	A	L25-67	3+1 (4)	6+1 (5)	7 (6)	R/R	6 (5)	–	0 (3)	–	3+1 (6)	0 (1)	–	–
13	15/5	Sheffield	H	W47-43	6+1 (4)	6+1 (4)	10+1 (5)	9 (5)	6+1 (4)	–	–	–	8+4 (5)	–	2 (3)	–
14	19/5	Hull	A	L42-51*	9 (5)	R/R	11 (5)	0 (3)	5+1 (4)	–	–	–	12 (7)	–	5 (6)	–

*Denotes bonus-point victory

DETAILS OF OTHER RIDER:

Match No. 10: Paul Cooper 6+2 (4).

TACTICAL SUBSTITUTE AND TACTICAL RIDES, AS INCLUDED IN THE SCORES GRID:

Match No. 3: Meldrum 2 points (TR); Match No. 4: Franc 2 points (TR); Meldrum 0 points (TR); Match No. 7: Kristensen 4 points (TR); Franc 0 points (TR); Rymel 0 points (TS); Match No. 9: Meldrum 0 points (TR); Kristensen 0 points (TR); Match No. 12: Meldrum 2 points (TR); Rymel 2 points (TR); Match No. 14: Hawkins 6 points (TR).

PREMIER TROPHY AVERAGES

Rider	Mts	Rds	Pts	Bon	Tot	Avge	Max
Paul Cooper	1	4	6	2	8	8.00	–
Claus Kristensen	12	52	97	4	101	7.77	2 full
Michal Makovsky	14	62	107	10	117	7.55	1 paid
Adrian Rymel	14	66	103	15	118	7.15	–
Josef Franc	14	60	93	14	107	7.13	1 full
Simon Cartwright	11	50	75	8	83	6.64	–

Rider	Mts	Rds	Pts	Bon	Tot	Avge	Max
David Meldrum	13	56	79	9	88	6.29	–
Ritchie Hawkins	3	18	20	5	25	5.56	–
Blair Scott	2	9	7	0	7	3.11	–
Tom Brown	9	34	14	7	21	2.47	–
Carl Shield	3	7	2	1	3	1.71	–
John Morrison	1	1	0	0	0	0.00	–

KNOCK-OUT CUP

No	DATE	OPPONENTS	H/A	RESULT	FRANC	MELDRUM	RYMEL	KRISTENSEN	MAKOVSKY	COOPER	SCOTT	PIETRASZKO	SMETHILLS	CARTWRIGHT
1	12/5	Hull	A	L36-59	6 (5)	3+2 (4)	13+1 (5)	5 (4)	3 (4)	1 (3)	5 (5)	–	–	–
2	24/7	Hull†	H	D42-42	R/R	–	11 (5)	5 (4)	–	2+2 (5)	–	8+1 4)	9+2 (5)	7 (5)

†Meeting abandoned after heat fourteen, with the result permitted to stand.

TACTICAL RIDES, AS INCLUDED IN THE SCORES GRID:

Match No. 1: Rymel 6 points (TR); Franc 4 points (TR).

OTHER MEETINGS

6 March: Carlos Villar Benefit

Edinburgh/Workington 32, Berwick 28 (Sam Ermolenko 11; David Meldrum 9; Claus Kristensen 4; Michal Makovsky 3; John Morrison 1), Glasgow 19, Newcastle 17. Carlos Villar Trophy: FIRST SEMI-FINAL: 1st Paul Cooper; 2nd Simon Cartwright; 3rd John Morrison; 4th John Branney. SECOND SEMI-FINAL: 1st Michal Makovsky; 2nd David Meldrum; 3rd Adrian Rymel; 4th Steven McAllister. FINAL: 1st Makovsky; 2nd Cooper; 3rd Meldrum; 4th Cartwright – staged at Berwick.

INDIVIDUAL MEETINGS

13 March: Karl Friar Memorial

QUALIFYING SCORES: Shane Parker 11; Kevin Little 9; Michal Makovsky 8; Rory Schlein 7; David Meldrum 7; Claus Kristensen 7; Adrian Rymel 6; Chris Harris 4; Emiliano Sanchez 4; Ross Brady 4; Simon Cartwright 3; Josef Franc 2. FIRST SEMI-FINAL: 1st Rymel; 2nd Makovsky; 3rd Parker; 4th Meldrum. SECOND SEMI-FINAL: 1st Schlein; 2nd Kristensen; 3rd Harris; 4th Little. FINAL: 1st Schlein; 2nd Makovsky; 3rd Rymel; 4th Kristensen.

25 September: Bordernapolis

QUALIFYING SCORES: Lee Smethills 11; Adam Pietraszko 10; Paul Bentley 9; Sam Ermolenko 8; Ritchie Hawkins 8; Josh Larsen 8; Simon Cartwright 6; Jordan Jurczynski 3; Niklas Fridell 3; Karol Malecha 3; Adrian Rymel 2; John MacPhail (Res) 1; Andreas Lekander 0; Alan Ferrow (Res) 0. FIRST SEMI-FINAL: 1st Bentley; 2nd Cartwright; 3rd Smethills; 4th Hawkins. SECOND SEMI-FINAL: 1st Ermolenko; 2nd Jurczynski; 3rd Pietraszko; 4th Larsen. FINAL: 1st Ermolenko; 2nd Bentley; 3rd Cartwright; 4th Jurczynski.

EDINBURGH FULFILMENT FACTORY MONARCHS

NOTE: The information below relates only to the main Edinburgh team. For details of the second side, please refer to the Conference League section.

ADDRESS: Armadale Stadium, 2 Bathgate Road, Armadale, West Lothian, EH48 2PD.
PROMOTERS: John Campbell & Alex Harkess.
TRACK LENGTH: 260 metres.
TRACK RECORD: 55.4 seconds – Charlie Gjedde (24/09/04).
FIRST MEETING: 4 April 1997.
YEARS OF OPERATION: 1997-04 Premier League.

PREVIOUS VENUES AS 'MONARCHS':
(1) Old Meadowbank Stadium, Clockmill Road, Edinburgh.
YEARS OF OPERATION: 1948-54 National League Division Two; 1957 Training; 1959 Open; 1960-64 Provincial League; 1965-67 British League; 1998 Demonstration.
(2) Cliftonhill Stadium, Main Street, Coatbridge, Lanarkshire.
YEARS OF OPERATION: 1968-69 British League Division One (Team rode as 'Coatbridge Monarchs').
(3) Powderhall Stadium, Beaverhall Road, Edinburgh.
YEARS OF OPERATION: 1977-90 National League; 1991-94 British League Division Two; 1995 Premier League.
(4) Shawfield Stadium, Glasgow Road, Rutherglen, Glasgow.
YEARS OF OPERATION: 1996 Premier League (Team rode under the name of 'Scottish Monarchs').

CLUB HONOURS

QUEEN'S CUP WINNERS: 1953.
FOUR-TEAM CHAMPIONS: 1981, 1993.
KNOCK-OUT CUP WINNERS: 1981, 1997, 1999.
PAIRS CHAMPIONS: 1986.
PREMIERSHIP WINNERS: 1998.
LEAGUE CHAMPIONS: 2003.

RIDER ROSTER 2004

Peter CARR; Gary PHELPS; Theo PIJPER; Rory SCHLEIN; Frede SCHOTT; Sean STODDART; Matthew WETHERS; Cameron WOODWARD.

OTHER APPEARANCES/GUESTS (official matches only):
Ben BARKER; Gary BEATON; Craig BOYCE; Barry CAMPBELL; James COCKLE; Benji COMPTON; Barrie EVANS; James GRIEVES; Tobias JOHANSSON; Michael PICKERING; Luke PRIEST; Carl SHIELD; Carl STONEHEWER; Andrew TULLY; Craig WATSON.

EDINBURGH: back row, left to right: Cameron Woodward, Peter Carr, Theo Pijper, Rory Schlein. Front row: Matthew Wethers, Frede Schott, Gary Phelps.

PREMIER LEAGUE

No	DATE	OPPONENTS	H/A	RESULT	SCHOTT	PIJPER	CARR	WOODWARD	SCHLEIN	WETHERS	PHELPS	JOHANSSON	STODDART	OTHERS
1	28/5	Rye House	H	L44-46	11 (5)	8+3 (4)	6 (3)	0 (3)	11 (5)	7+1 (7)	1 (3)	–	–	–
2	2/6	Hull	A	L46-49	15+1 (5)	3+1 (4)	16 (5)	2 (4)	8 (4)	2 (5)	–	–	–	0 (3)
3	4/6	Isle of Wight	H	W62-32	10 (4)	8+2 (4)	13+1 (5)	7+3 (4)	15 (5)	7+2 (5)	–	–	2 (3)	–
4	11/6	Hull	H	L43-47	13 (5)	4 (4)	10 (4)	3+1 (4)	11+1 (5)	1 (4)	–	1 (4)	–	–
5	18/6	King's Lynn	H	W55-38	12+1 (5)	5 (4)	12 (4)	1 (4)	13+1 (5)	8+3 (4)	–	4 (3)	–	–
6	25/6	Newcastle	H	W65-27	15 (5)	8+2 (4)	12 (4)	7+3 (4)	7 (4)	13+3 (6)	–	–	3 (3)	–
7	27/6	Newcastle	A	L43-49*	10 (5)	5+1 (4)	9 (4)	1+1 (3)	13+1 (6)	5+1 (6)	–	–	0 (2)	–
8	2/7	Exeter	H	W49-41	14+1 (5)	7+2 (4)	6 (4)	1+1 (4)	13 (5)	6 (4)	–	–	–	2 (4)
9	5/7	Exeter	A	L33-61	13 (5)	R/R	6 (4)	1+1 (5)	10 (5)	2 (5)	1 (6)	–	–	–
10	10/7	Reading	H	W47-42	13 (5)	6+2 (4)	10 (4)	6 (5)	8 (5)	4+2 (4)	–	–	0 (3)	–
11	16/7	Newport	H	W55-41	14 (5)	9+3 (4)	11 (4)	5+2 (5)	10+1 (5)	6+1 (4)	–	–	0 (3)	–
12	17/7	Rye House	A	L40-50	12 (5)	6+2 (4)	5 (5)	12+1 (7)	2 (2)	3 (4)	–	–	–	0 (3)
13	18/7	Newport	A	L43-50*	15+1 (5)	6+1 (4)	2 (3)	7+2 (6)	7+1 (5)	4+1 (4)	–	–	–	2 (3)
14	19/7	Reading	A	L39-55	11 (5)	3 (4)	7 (4)	5+2 (7)	9 (4)	4+1 (4)	–	–	–	0 (3)
15	24/7	Stoke	A	L39-51	13 (6)	5+2 (5)	11 (6)	7 (7)	R/R	2+1 (4)	–	–	–	1 (3)
16	3/8	Isle of Wight	A	L31-65	8 (5)	1 (5)	7 (5)	2 (6)	13 (5)	R/R	–	–	–	0 (4)
17	4/8	King's Lynn	A	L32-63	10+1 (5)	4 (6)	3 (4)	1 (2)	14 (5)	R/R	–	–	–	0 (7)
18	6/8	Somerset	H	W55-39	15 (5)	10+2 (5)	10 (4)	–	13 (5)	R/R	–	–	0 (4)	7+1 (7)
19	7/8	Workington	A	L30-65	7 (4)	3 (5)	5 (4)	–	14 (5)	R/R	–	–	0 (6)	1 (7)
20	13/8	Glasgow	H	W57-37	11+1 (5)	6+1 (4)	11+1 (4)	6 (5)	15 (5)	6 (4)	–	–	2 (3)	–
21	15/8	Glasgow	A	L45-50*	7+1 (4)	9+2 (5)	6 (4)	6 (5)	14 (5)	3 (4)	–	–	0 (3)	–
22	20/8	Berwick	H	W60-36	13+2 (5)	13+2 (5)	0 (0)	14+1 (7)	9 (4)	8+3 (4)	–	–	3+1 (5)	–
23	25/8	Somerset	A	L33-61	7+1 (4)	0 (4)	7 (5)	4 (5)	13+1 (5)	2 (4)	–	–	0 (3)	–
24	26/8	Sheffield	A	L27-65	3 (4)	4 (5)	0 (1)	11 (7)	6 (4)	2 (4)	–	–	1 (5)	–
25	27/8	Workington	H	W53-43	16 (6)	8+1 (5)	R/R	10+3 (6)	14+2 (6)	5+1 (4)	–	–	0 (3)	–
26	3/9	Sheffield	H	W54-39	12+1 (5)	8+2 (4)	8 (4)	9+3 (5)	12+1 (5)	5 (4)	–	–	0 (3)	–
27	10/9	Stoke†	H	W64-20*	14+1 (5)	10+2 (4)	15 (5)	9+3 (4)	R/R	11+3 (5)	–	–	4+2 (4)	1 (1)
28	11/9	Berwick	A	L38-57*	17+1 (6)	9 (6)	8 (5)	2+1 (5)	R/R	2 (5)	–	–	0 (3)	–

*Denotes bonus-point victory

†Meeting abandoned after heat fourteen, with the result permitted to stand.

DETAILS OF OTHER RIDERS:

Match No. 2: Benji Compton 0 (3); Match No. 8: Barry Campbell 2 (4); Match No. 12: Ben Barker 0 (3); Match No. 13: James Cockle 2 (3); Match No. 14: Ben Barker 0 (3); Match No. 15: Luke Priest 1 (3); Match No. 16: James Cockle 0 (4); Match No. 17: Michael Pickering 0 (7); Match No. 18: Barry Campbell 7+1 (7); Match No. 19: Barrie Evans 1 (7); Match No. 27: Andrew Tully 1 (1).

TACTICAL SUBSTITUTE AND TACTICAL RIDES, AS INCLUDED IN THE SCORES GRID:

Match No. 2: Carr 6 points (TR); Schott 4 points (TR); Match No. 7: Schlein 4 points (TS); Match No. 9: Schott 6 points (TR); Schlein 2 points (TR); Match No. 13: Schott 6 points (TR); Schlein 0 points (TR); Match No. 14: Schott 6 points (TR); Match No. 15: Wethers 0 points (TR); Match No. 16: Schlein 6 points (TR); Schott 4 points (TR); Carr 2 points (TS); Match No. 17: Schlein 6 points (TR); Schott 2 points (TR); Pijper 2 points (TS); Match No. 18: Schlein 6 points (TR); Schott 4 points (TR); Match No. 21: Schlein 6 points (TR); Carr 4 points (TR); Match No. 23: Schott 4 points (TR); Schlein 4 points (TR); Match No. 24: Schlein 2 points (TR); Woodward 2 points (TR); Match No. 28: Schott 6 points (TR); Pijper 4 points (TR).

PREMIER LEAGUE AVERAGES

Rider	Mts	Rds	Pts	Bon	Tot	Avge	Max
Frede Schott	28	138	310	13	323	9.36	2 full; 3 paid
Rory Schlein	25	119	256	9	265	8.91	2 full
Peter Carr	27	108	210	2	212	7.85	3 full; 1 paid
Theo Pijper	27	120	165	33	198	6.60	3 paid
Matthew Wethers	24	108	118	23	141	5.22	–
Cameron Woodward	26	129	138	28	166	5.15	1 paid
Andrew Tully	1	1	1	0	1	4.00	–
Barry Campbell	2	11	9	1	10	3.64	–
Tobias Johansson	2	7	5	0	5	2.86	–
Luke Priest	1	3	1	0	1	1.33	–
Sean Stoddart	16	56	15	3	18	1.29	–
James Cockle	2	7	2	0	2	1.14	–
Gary Phelps	2	9	2	0	2	0.89	–
Barrie Evans	1	7	1	0	1	0.57	–
Ben Barker	2	6	0	0	0	0.00	–
Benji Compton	1	3	0	0	0	0.00	–
Michael Pickering	1	7	0	0	0	0.00	–

PREMIER TROPHY

No	DATE	OPPONENTS	H/A	RESULT	SCHOTT	PIJPER	SCHLEIN	PHELPS	CARR	WOODWARD	WETHERS	OTHERS
1	20/3	Workington	A	L46-50	–	3+2 (4)	14+1 (5)	0 (3)	6 (4)	3 (5)	4+1 (4)	16 (5)
2	27/3	Berwick	A	L45-48	–	5 (4)	10 (5)	0 (3)	9 (4)	3+1 (5)	5 (4)	13+1 (5)
3	2/4	Berwick	H	W59-31*	–	8+4 (5)	15 (5)	3+1 (4)	10+1 (4)	6+1 (4)	6+1 (4)	11 (4)
4	7/4	Hull	A	L43-52	–	4+1 (4)	7 (5)	2+1 (3)	9 (4)	2 (4)	3+1 (5)	16 (5)
5	9/4	Workington	H	W54-40*	12 (4)	9+1 (4)	14+1 (5)	2 (3)	11+1 (4)	6 (7)	–	0 (3)
6	15/4	Sheffield	A	L32-63	4 (4)	4 (4)	9 (5)	0 (3)	12 (5)	3 (5)	0 (4)	–
7	16/4	Sheffield	H	W47-42	13+1 (5)	3+3 (4)	12 (5)	0 (3)	5 (4)	5+1 (4)	9 (5)	–
8	23/4	Stoke	H	W59-34	14+1 (5)	8+2 (4)	15 (5)	3+1 (4)	11+1 (4)	4 (4)	4 (4)	–
9	30/4	Newcastle	H	W63-29	15 (5)	8 (4)	10+1 (4)	1 (3)	11+1 (4)	12+3 (6)	6+2 (4)	–
10	2/5	Glasgow	A	L42-53	8 (4)	4+1 (4)	13 (5)	0 (3)	7+1 (5)	2+1 (4)	8+1 (6)	–
11	7/5	Glasgow	H	W52-40*	14 (5)	8 (4)	11 (5)	1 (3)	9+1 (4)	3 (4)	6+2 (5)	–
12	21/5	Hull	H	L43-47	12 (5)	4+2 (4)	8 (5)	0 (3)	9 (4)	0 (3)	10+1 (6)	–
13	30/5	Stoke	A	W48-47*	17 (5)	4 (4)	8+1 (5)	–	12 (4)	1+1 (4)	6+1 (5)	0 (3)
14	31/5	Newcastle	A	W51-39*	12 (4)	3 (4)	13+1 (5)	–	11+1 (5)	3 (4)	9 (5)	0 (3)

*Denotes bonus-point victory

DETAILS OF OTHER RIDERS:

Match No. 1: Craig Boyce 16 (5); Match No. 2: Craig Watson 13+1 (5); Match No. 3: James Grieves 11 (4); Match No. 4: Carl Stonehewer 16 (5); Match No. 5: Carl Shield 0 (3); Match No. 13: Sean Stoddart 0 (3); Match No. 14: Gary Beaton 0 (3).

TACTICAL SUBSTITUTE AND TACTICAL RIDES, AS INCLUDED IN THE SCORES GRID:

Match No. 1: Schlein 6 points (TR); Boyce 6 points (TR); Match No. 2: Carr 6 points (TR); Match No. 4: Carr 6 points (TR); Stonehewer 4 points (TS); Match No. 6: Carr 6 points (TR); Schlein 4 points (TR); Match No. 10: Schlein 6 points (TR); Schott 4 points (TR); Match No. 13: Schott 6 points (TR); Carr 4 points (TR).

PREMIER TROPHY AVERAGES

Rider	Mts	Rds	Pts	Bon	Tot	Avge	Max
Frede Schott	10	46	116	2	118	10.26	3 full; 1 paid
Rory Schlein	14	69	151	5	156	9.04	2 full; 1 paid
Peter Carr	14	59	121	7	128	8.68	3 paid
Theo Pijper	14	57	75	16	91	6.39	–
Matthew Wethers	13	61	76	10	86	5.64	–
Cameron Woodward	14	63	53	8	61	3.87	–
Gary Phelps	12	38	12	3	15	1.58	–
Gary Beaton	1	3	0	0	0	0.00	–
Carl Shield	1	3	0	0	0	0.00	–
Sean Stoddart	1	3	0	0	0	0.00	–
Guests	4	19	51	1	52	10.95	–

KNOCK-OUT CUP

No	DATE	OPPONENTS	H/A	RESULT	SCHOTT	PHELPS	SCHLEIN	PIJPER	CARR	WETHERS	WOODWARD
1	14/5	Workington	H	W50-43	12+1 (5)	R/R	12+1 (5)	6+1 (5)	10 (4)	8 (7)	2+1 (4)
2	15/5	Workington	A	L35-57	8 (5)	R/R	10+1 (6)	7+1 (5)	4 (4)	3 (5)	3 (5)

TACTICAL SUBSTITUTE AND TACTICAL RIDES, AS INCLUDED IN THE SCORES GRID:

Match No. 2: Pijper 2 points (TR); Carr 2 points (TR); Schlein 0 points (TS).

OTHER MEETINGS

6 March: Carlos Villar Benefit

Edinburgh/Workington 32 (Simon Stead 12; Carl Stonehewer 9; Paul Cooper 7; Simon Cartwright 4; Steven McAllister DNR), Berwick 28, Glasgow 19, Newcastle 17 – staged at Berwick.

21 March: Spring Trophy (first leg)

Glasgow 46 Edinburgh 44 (Sean Wilson 12; Rory Schlein 10+1; Cameron Woodward 6+2; Theo Pijper 6+1; Matthew Wethers 5+2; Peter Carr 5+1; Gary Phelps 0).

26 March: Spring Trophy (second leg)

Edinburgh 48 (Carl Stonehewer 13+1; Peter Carr 11; Cameron Woodward 8+1; Theo Pijper 6+1; Rory Schlein 5; Matthew Wethers 4+2; Gary Phelps 1) Glasgow 45 – Edinburgh won 92-91 on aggregate.

17 September: Scottish Cup (first leg)

Edinburgh 51 (Rory Schlein 12; Cameron Woodward 10+1; Frede Schott 9; Peter Carr 7; Matthew Wethers 6+3; Theo Pijper 6+1; Sean Stoddart 1) Glasgow 40.

24 September: Schott's Wha Hae! (Frede Schott Testimonial)

Bacon Heids 40 (Frede Schott 10+1; Charlie Gjedde 9+2; Kristian Lund 6+1; Niels-Kristian Iversen 6; Mads Korneliussen 5; Niklas Fridell 3; Andreas Lekander 1+1) Hot Schotts 38 (Carl Stonehewer 9+1; Peter Carr 7+1; Rory Schlein 7+1; Theo Pijper 7+1; Jason Lyons 3; Ross Brady 3; Wayne Carter 2+1). PEUGEOT KNOCK-OUT FINAL: 1st Gjedde; 2nd Iversen; 3rd Carr; 4th Schott.

3 October: Scottish Cup (second leg)

Glasgow 37 Edinburgh 38 (Rory Schlein 11; Peter Carr 8+2; Frede Schott 7; Cameron Woodward 6+2; Theo Pijper 5; Matthew Wethers 1+1; Sean Stoddart 0) – meeting abandoned after heat twelve, with the result permitted to stand. Edinburgh won 89-77 on aggregate.

PAIRS MEETING

23 July: Hampton Hotel Summer Special Pairs

1st Theo Pijper (19) & Blair Scott (10+1) = 29; 2nd Peter Carr (19) & Trent Leverington (9+1) = 28; 3rd Frede Schott (19) & James Cockle (4) = 23; David Meldrum (13+1) & Jamie Robertson (7+2) = 20; Cameron Woodward (13), Matthew Wethers (3) & Gary Beaton (Res; 2+1) = 18; Ross Brady (17), Derek Sneddon (0) & Keith Maben (Res; 0) = 17.

INDIVIDUAL MEETING

30 July: Fulfilment Factory Scottish Open Championship

QUALIFYING SCORES: Shane Parker 14; Rory Schlein 13; David Howe 12; Frede Schott 12; Theo Pijper 11; George Stancl 10; Carl Stonehewer 10; Peter Carr 10; Mads Korneliussen 6; Cameron Woodward 5; Robert Mikolajczak 4; Matthew Wethers 4; Kristian Lund 3; Adam Pietraszko 3; Lubos Tomicek 2; Gary Beaton (Res) 1; Ross Brady 0; Andrew Tully (Res) 0.
SEMI-FINAL: 1st Pijper; 2nd Howe; 3rd Stancl; 4th Schott. FINAL: 1st Schlein; 2nd Howe; 3rd Parker; 4th Pijper.

EXETER FALCONS

ADDRESS: County Ground Stadium, Cowick Street, St Thomas, Exeter, Devon, EX2 9BQ.
PROMOTERS: Colin Hill & David Short – the latter becoming co-promoter in July 2004.
TRACK LENGTH: 396 metres.
TRACK RECORD: 64.3 seconds – Mark Loram (29/04/96).
FIRST MEETING: 9 March 1929.
YEARS OF OPERATION: 1929-31 Open; 1934 Open; 1947-51 National League Division Three; 1952-53 Southern League; 1954-55 National League Division Two; 1957-58 Open; 1960 Open; 1961-64 Provincial League; 1965-67 British League; 1968-74 British League Division One; 1975-79 British League; 1980-83 National League; 1984 British League; 1985-90 National League; 1991-94 British League Division Two; 1995-04 Premier League.

NOTE: Exeter also ran a second team in the 1995 Academy League, the 1996 Conference League and the 1997 Amateur League. The team of 1995-96 rode as 'Devon Demons', whereas in 1997, the fixtures were shared with Newport, under the banner of 'Western Warriors'.

CLUB HONOURS

LEAGUE CHAMPIONS: 1948, 1974, 2000.
NATIONAL TROPHY (DIVISION THREE) WINNERS: 1951.
KNOCK-OUT CUP WINNERS: 1962, 1983.
YOUNG SHIELD WINNERS: 1997.
PREMIER TROPHY WINNERS: 2004.

RIDER ROSTER 2004

Michael COLES; Graeme GORDON; Mark LEMON; Roger LOBB; Mark SIMMONDS, Nick SIMMONS, Seemond STEPHENS.

OTHER APPEARANCES/GUESTS (official matches only):

Adam ALLOTT; Craig BOYCE; Ross BRADY; Tom BROWN; Jason BUNYAN; Paul CANDY; Benji COMPTON; Chris COURAGE; Paul FRY; Chris HARRIS; Gary PHELPS; Paul PICKERING; Jamie SMITH; David SPEIGHT; George STANCL; Craig WATSON; Brent WERNER.

PREMIER LEAGUE

No	DATE	OPPONENTS	H/A	RESULT	LEMON	GORDON	STEPHENS	SIMMONDS	COLES	LOBB	SIMMONS	OTHERS
1	13/5	Sheffield	A	L38-57	8 (4)	6+3 (5)	11+1 (5)	1 (4)	2 (4)	10 (7)	0 (1)	–
2	17/5	Somerset	H	W62-31	14+1 (5)	8+2 (4)	9+2 (4)	7+2 (4)	11+2 (5)	13+1 (5)	–	0 (3)
3	24/5	Newcastle	H	W64-32	5+1 (2)	14+2 (6)	14+1 (5)	8+2 (4)	12+2 (5)	10+1 (4)	–	1+1 (4)
4	5/6	Stoke	A	L36-57	–	–	0 (2)	R/R	12+2 (6)	6 (5)	2 (7)	16+2 (10)
5	7/6	Stoke	H	L43-50	–	–	5+1 (4)	R/R	6+3 (5)	14 (5)	0 (4)	18+2 (12)
6	14/6	Berwick	H	W49-41	R/R	12+2 (7)	4 (5)	7+2 (5)	13+1 (6)	13 (6)	0 (1)	–

No	DATE	OPPONENTS	H/A	RESULT	LEMON	GORDON	STEPHENS	SIMMONDS	COLES	LOBB	SIMMONS	OTHERS
7	16/6	Hull	A	L27-65	–	4 (4)	4 (4)	7+1 (5)	4+1 (5)	2 (4)	–	6 (8)
8	19/6	Rye House	A	L44-45	–	7 (5)	4 (4)	6 (4)	6+1 (4)	7+3 (5)	–	14 (8)
9	27/6	Newport	A	L44-46	–	11+1 (7)	5 (4)	5+2 (4)	6+1 (4)	10+1 (5)	4+3 (4)	3+1 (3)
10	28/6	Hull	H	W50-45	–	6+1 (4)	9 (5)	7 (4)	8+1 (4)	7+2 (4)	3+1 (4)	10 (5)
11	2/7	Edinburgh	A	L41-49	–	9+2 (5)	6 (4)	5+1 (5)	4 (4)	8+1 (5)	3+2 (3)	6+1 (4)
12	3/7	Berwick	A	L41-55	–	9 (4)	3 (4)	6 (5)	6+2 (5)	3 (4)	0 (3)	14 (5)
13	4/7	Glasgow	A	L34-61	–	9 (5)	1 (3)	10+1 (6)	0 (4)	2+2 (4)	0 (3)	12 (5)
14	5/7	Edinburgh	H	W61-33*	–	9+2 (4)	6+3 (4)	13+1 (5)	8+1 (4)	11+1 (5)	5+2 (4)	9 (4)
15	12/7	Workington	H	W56-39	–	10+1 (5)	6+1 (4)	12+2 (5)	8+1 (4)	7+2 (4)	0 (3)	13+1 (5)
16	19/7	Isle of Wight	H	W54-40	–	12+1 (5)	6+1 (4)	11+1 (5)	7+2 (4)	7+2 (4)	0 (3)	11 (5)
17	30/7	Somerset	A	L39-55*	13 (4)	11 (5)	2 (4)	9+1 (6)	3 (4)	0 (3)	1+1 (4)	–
18	9/8	King's Lynn	H	W55-38	8+1 (4)	9+1 (5)	6 (4)	11+1 (5)	11+3 (5)	8+2 (4)	2+1 (3)	–
19	16/8	Newport	H	W65-27*	8+1 (4)	9+2 (4)	11+3 (5)	10+1 (4)	10+2 (4)	13+1 (5)	4+2 (4)	–
20	19/8	Isle of Wight	A	L31-63	12 (5)	6 (4)	2 (4)	3 (4)	2+1 (4)	2 (4)	4+1 (5)	–
21	26/8	Reading	H	W48½-47½	7+1 (5)	6 (4)	8+1 (4)	5+1 (4)	9+1 (4)	9½+1 (5)	4+1 (4)	–
22	30/8	Sheffield	H	W59-36*	12+3 (5)	9 (4)	9+1 (4)	12 (5)	9+1 (5)	8+1 (4)	0 (3)	–
23	1/9	Reading	A	L36-58	6+1 (5)	2+1 (4)	10+1 (6)	6+2 (5)	11+1 (6)	R/R	1+1 (4)	–
24	4/9	Workington	A	L26-66	10 (5)	4 (4)	7+1 (7)	3 (5)	2+1 (5)	R/R	0 (4)	–
25	5/9	Newcastle	A	L45-49*	10+1 (5)	10+1 (5)	12+2 (6)	7 (5)	6+1 (5)	R/R	0 (4)	–
26	6/9	Glasgow	H	W54-39	13+1 (5)	5 (3)	8+1 (5)	9+1 (4)	8+2 (5)	7+2 (4)	4+2 (4)	–
27	13/9	Rye House	H	W75-18*	10+2 (4)	10+2 (4)	15+3 (6)	14+1 (5)	10+2 (4)	10+2 (4)	6+3 (3)	–
28	15/9	King's Lynn	A	L29-64	9 (5)	5 (4)	3 (5)	8 (6)	3+1 (5)	R/R	1 (5)	–

*Denotes bonus-point victory

DETAILS OF OTHER RIDERS:

Match No. 2: Paul Candy 0 (3); Match No. 3: Paul Candy 1+1 (4); Match No. 4: Craig Watson 11 (4); Jamie Smith 5+2 (6); Match No. 5: Craig Watson 10 (5); Jason Bunyan 8+2 (7); Match No. 7: Brent Werner 6 (4); Gary Phelps 0 (4); Match No. 8: Chris Harris 14 (5); Gary Phelps 0 (3); Match No. 9: Chris Harris 3+1 (3); Match No. 10: Paul Fry 10 (5); Match No. 11: Ross Brady 6+1 (4); Match No. 12: George Stancl 14 (5); Match No. 13: Ross Brady 12 (5); Match No. 14: Chris Harris 9 (4); Match No. 15: Paul Fry 13+1 (5); Match No. 16: Chris Harris 11 (5).

TACTICAL RIDES, AS INCLUDED IN THE SCORES GRID:

Match No. 1: Stephens 6 points (TR); Lemon 4 points (TR); Match No. 4: Watson 6 points (TR); Coles 0 points (TR); Match No. 5: Lobb 6 points (TR); Match No. 7: Coles 2 points (TR); Werner 2 points (TR); Match No. 12: Stancl 6 points (TR); Gordon 6 points (TR); Match No. 13: Brady 6 points (TR); Gordon 4 points (TR); Match No. 17: Lemon 6 points (TR); Gordon 2 points (TR); Match No. 20: Lemon 4 points (TR); Gordon 4 points (TR); Match No. 23: Coles 4 points (TR); Stephens 4 points (TR); Match No. 24: Lemon 4 points (TR); Simmonds 0 points (TR); Match No. 25: Gordon 4 points (TR); Lemon 4 points (TR); Match No. 28: Lemon 4 points (TR); Gordon 2 points (TR).

PREMIER LEAGUE AVERAGES

Rider	Mts	Rds	Pts	Bon	Tot	Avge	Max
Mark Lemon	15	67	132	13	145	8.66	3 paid
Roger Lobb	24	109	184½	25	209½	7.69	1 paid
Graeme Gordon	26	120	201	24	225	7.50	1 paid
Mark Simmonds	26	123	202	23	225	7.32	1 paid

EXETER: back row, left to right: Tony Lethbridge (Press Officer), Michael Coles, Seemond Stephens, Nick Simmons, The Late Colin Hill (Promoter). Front row: Mark Lemon, Graeme Gordon, Mark Simmonds, Roger Lobb.

Rider	Mts	Rds	Pts	Bon	Tot	Avge	Max
Michael Coles	28	129	194	36	230	7.13	2 paid
Seemond Stephens	28	125	181	23	204	6.53	2 paid
Nick Simmons	24	87	44	20	64	2.94	–
Paul Candy	2	7	1	1	2	1.14	–
Gary Phelps	2	7	0	0	0	0.00	–
Guests	14	67	122	7	129	7.70	–

PREMIER TROPHY

No	DATE	OPPONENTS	H/A	RESULT	LEMON	GORDON	STEPHENS	SIMMONDS	COLES	LOBB	SIMMONS	OTHERS
1	21/3	Newport	A	W50-43	12+1 (5)	4+3 (4)	7+2 (4)	4 (4)	9+1 (5)	9+1 (4)	5+2 (4)	–
2	22/3	Newport	H	W63-29*	13+1 (5)	9+1 (4)	7+1 (3)	10+1 (4)	10+3 (5)	9+2 (5)	5+1 (4)	–
3	27/3	Rye House	A	L42-51	14+1 (5)	3+1 (4)	5+1 (4)	5 (4)	9 (5)	0 (3)	6+3 (5)	–
4	29/3	Somerset	H	W60-35	12+1 (5)	8+1 (4)	9+2 (4)	11+2 (5)	4+2 (4)	10+1 (4)	6+2 (4)	–
5	5/4	Isle of Wight	H	W59-33	13 (5)	4+1 (4)	9+3 (4)	12 (4)	10+3 (5)	10 (5)	1 (3)	–
6	9/4	Somerset	A	W45-44*	15 (5)	7+1 (5)	7 (4)	6+1 (4)	3 (4)	7+2 (7)	0 (0)	–
7	12/4	King's Lynn	H	W65-29	14+1 (5)	7+1 (4)	11+1 (4)	8+2 (4)	10+1 (5)	12 (4)	3+1 (4)	–
8	14/4	King's Lynn	A	L40-51*	6+2 (4)	9+1 (5)	8 (4)	4+1 (4)	11 (5)	1 (4)	1+1 (4)	–
9	26/4	Rye House	H	W67-26*	9+2 (4)	12+2 (5)	13+1 (5)	7+1 (4)	9+2 (4)	10+2 (4)	7+2 (4)	–
10	2/5	Reading	A	L36-58	11 (5)	R/R	5+1 (4)	9 (6)	4 (4)	6+2 (6)	1+1 (5)	–
11	3/5	Reading	H	W48-45	11 (5)	R/R	11 (5)	8+2 (5)	3+1 (4)	11+1 (6)	4+2 (5)	–
12	27/5	Isle of Wight	A	L44-45*	–	12+1 (6)	5+1 (4)	6 (4)	1+1 (4)	5 (4)	–	15+1 (8)
13	21/6	Sheffield	H	W64-30	–	12+3 (5)	10 (4)	6+2 (4)	8+2 (4)	10+1 (5)	–	18+1 (8)
14	24/6	Sheffield	A	L38-56*	–	14+1 (5)	6 (4)	4+2 (4)	4 (4)	7 (5)	–	3+1 (8)
15	1/8	Reading	A	L43-46	13+1 (5)	6+1 (5)	6 (4)	6+3 (4)	8 (5)	3+1 (4)	1+1 (3)	–
16	2/8	Reading	H	W59-35*	11+2 (5)	10+1 (4)	7+1 (4)	8+2 (4)	10+1 (5)	8+1 (4)	5+2 (4)	–

*Denotes bonus-point/aggregate victory

DETAILS OF OTHER RIDERS:

Match No. 12: Craig Watson 14 (5); Chris Courage 1+1 (3); Match No. 13: Chris Harris 15 (5); Gary Phelps 3+1 (3); Match No. 14: Paul Pickering 2+1 (4); Tom Brown 1 (4).

TACTICAL RIDES, AS INCLUDED IN THE SCORES GRID:

Match No. 3: Lemon 4 points (TR); Stephens 2 points (TR); Match No. 8: Lemon 2 points (TR); Stephens 0 points (TR); Match No. 10: Lemon 4 points (TR); Simmonds 4 points (TR); Match No. 14: Gordon 6 points (TR); Simmonds 2 points (TR).

PREMIER TROPHY AVERAGES

Rider	Mts	Rds	Pts	Bon	Tot	Avge	Max
Mark Lemon	13	63	149	12	161	10.22	1 full; 1 paid
Seemond Stephens	16	65	125	14	139	8.55	2 paid
Graeme Gordon	14	64	114	19	133	8.31	1 paid
Mark Simmonds	16	68	111	19	130	7.65	1 full
Michael Coles	16	72	113	17	130	7.22	–

Rider	Mts	Rds	Pts	Bon	Tot	Avge	Max
Roger Lobb	16	74	118	14	132	7.14	1 full; 1 paid
Gary Phelps	1	3	3	1	4	5.33	–
Nick Simmons	13	49	45	18	63	5.14	–
Chris Courage	1	3	1	1	2	2.67	–
Tom Brown	1	4	1	0	1	1.00	–
Guests	3	14	31	1	32	9.14	1 full

KNOCK-OUT CUP

No	DATE	OPPONENTS	H/A	RESULT	LEMON	GORDON	STEPHENS	SIMMONDS	COLES	LOBB	CANDY	SIMMONS	OTHERS
1	16/5	Newport	A	W50-46	11+1 (5)	6+1 (4)	10+1 (5)	8+1 (4)	5 (4)	9+1 (5)	1 (3)	–	–
2	31/5	Newport†	H	W53-19*	R/R	–	12 (4)	10+1 (4)	10+2 (4)	11+3 (5)	–	8+2 (4)	2+1 (3)
3	22/7	Sheffield	A	L37-57	–	11 (5)	4+1 (4)	–	3+1 (4)	4+1 (4)	–	–	15+2 (13)
4	26/7	Sheffield	H	W62-29*	11+1 (4)	10+4 (5)	9 (4)	7+1 (4)	9+1 (4)	13 (5)	–	3 (4)	–
5	20/9	Hull	H	W57-34	15 (5)	3 (4)	12+1 (5)	9+2 (4)	6+1 (4)	11+3 (5)	–	1+1 (3)	–
6	6/10	Hull	A	L35-62	10 (6)	R/R	13+1 (6)	2 (5)	7+1 (6)	1 (4)	–	2 (4)	–

*Denotes aggregate victory

†Meeting abandoned after heat twelve, with the result permitted to stand.

DETAILS OF OTHER RIDERS:

Match No. 2: Adam Allott 2+1 (3); Match No. 3: Craig Boyce 10 (5); Benji Compton 3 (4); David Speight 2+2 (4).

TACTICAL SUBSTITUTE AND TACTICAL RIDES, AS INCLUDED IN THE SCORES GRID:

Match No. 3: Gordon 4 points (TR); Boyce 4 points (TR); Match No. 6: Lemon 6 points (TR); Stephens 6 points (TR); Coles 2 points (TS).

OTHER MEETINGS

30 June: Premier League

King's Lynn 35 Exeter 22 (Craig Watson 9; Graeme Gordon 5; Michael Coles 3+1; Seemond Stephens 2+1; Roger Lobb 1; Mark Simmonds 1; Nick Simmons 1) – meeting abandoned after heat nine.

INDIVIDUAL MEETINGS

19 April: Westernapolis

1st Mark Lemon 14; 2nd Chris Harris 13; 3rd Craig Watson 13; Leigh Lanham 12; Seemond Stephens 11; Michael Coles 10; Shane Parker 7; Graeme Gordon 7; Paul Fry 7; Roger Lobb 7; Jason Bunyan 6; Krister Marsh 4; Mark Simmonds 4; Tony Atkin 3; Nick Simmons 1; Pavel Ondrasik 1; Paul Candy (Res) 0.

27 September: Young Guns Championship

1st Nick Simmons (on countback) 11; 2nd Simon Walker 11; 3rd James Cockle (on countback) 9; Karlis Ezergailis 9; Benji Compton 7; Jordan Frampton 7; Lee Smart 6; Danny Warwick 4; Matt Cambridge 2; Andrew Jackson 2; Sam Martin 2; David Hooper 1.

COLIN HILL – A TRIBUTE

Exeter promoter Colin Hill died in the early hours of Saturday 30 October. He was fifty-nine and had been fighting cancer for almost two years. Hill was one of the longest-serving promoters in speedway and had just fulfilled his ambition of completing twenty years in charge at the County Ground. He first became involved in 1984 as a shareholder with then-promoter Peter Oakes, as the Falcons made an ill-fated bid to return to First Division racing. In November of that year, Hill bought out Oakes and once again established the Falcons as a Second Division outfit. Although Exeter became part of one big league in 1995 and 1996, tracking world-class stars such as Mark Loram and Simon Wigg, the venture lost in excess of £40,000, which confirmed Hill's belief that the West Country could not support top-flight speedway. It was with the Premier League that Hill felt at home and enjoyed his greatest successes. The Falcons were crowned League Champions in 2000 and in 2004 won the Premier Trophy final. Colin himself admitted privately that his team's victory in the 1997 Jack Young Shield gave him the most pleasure because, as he said: 'That was the first major trophy we ever won.'

Loram went on to win the World Championship in 2000. Although since 1997 he has ridden in the Elite League, he remains an Exeter asset. Hill had a brief spell in charge at Milton Keynes in 1992 and also served for a short time on the BSPA Management Committee. Hill was the epitome of the self-made man. Although of Devon stock, he was actually born in Rugby, close to the BSPA offices, on Christmas Day 1944, but returned to his parents' home village of Dunsford within a few weeks. After leaving school, he worked as a carpenter, but by the age of nineteen owned his own milk round, which he later extended. In 1981, he was diagnosed with cancer for the first time. As a result, he sold the milk business and moved into property that, up until his death, Hill maintained alongside his speedway interests. Outwardly a quiet and modest man, Colin enjoyed life to the full and boasted a wicked sense of humour. He loved music, particularly country and western and, although never a connoisseur, relished a big steak and a glass of sweet white wine.

Hill's shrewd financial abilities enabled the Falcons to survive when more illustrious teams and promoters fell by the wayside. It was these skills that earned him the unqualified respect of his fellow promoters. Colin was also held in high esteem by his riders, who knew that once a deal had been agreed, he stuck by it and they were always paid – usually in the legendary Bonus Print film envelope! Known with great affection as 'Hilly', it was this quality, which earned the loyalty of many of his riders. His hope was to see a new venue for Exeter Speedway materialize, and he once commented: 'I may not live to see it, but would rather like the bar to be called Hillbillies!' Those left with the task of fulfilling his dream long ago agreed that the venue, wherever it may be, will be called the Colin Hill Stadium. *Speedway Star* editor Richard Clark said of Hill: 'Colin was both a gentleman and a gentle man.'

By Tony Lethbridge and Bob Radford, with grateful thanks to Speedway Star.

GLASGOW TRAVEL INN TIGERS

ADDRESS: Ashfield Stadium, Saracen Park, 404 Hawthorn Street, Possilpark, Glasgow.
PROMOTERS: Alan Dick, Stewart Dickson & Gordon Pairman.
TRACK LENGTH: 302 metres.
TRACK RECORD: 57.6 seconds – Shane Parker (18/05/04).
FIRST MEETING: 19 April 1949.
YEARS OF OPERATION: 1949-52 National League Division Two; 1953 Open; 1999-04 Premier League.

NOTES: (1) Between 1949-53, the track was home to 'Ashfield Giants'; (2) Ashfield Stadium also played host to a second team in the 2000 Conference League, under the banner of 'Lightning Ashfield Giants'.

PREVIOUS VENUES AS 'TIGERS':

(1) White City Stadium, Paisley Road West, Ibrox, Glasgow.
YEARS OF OPERATION: 1928-29 Open; 1930-31 Northern League; 1939 Union Cup; 1940 Open; 1945 Open; 1946 Northern League; 1947-53 National League Division Two; 1954 Northern Shield; 1956 Open; 1964 Provincial League; 1965-67 British League; 1968 British League Division One.
NOTE: Glasgow first acquired the 'Tigers' moniker in 1946.

(2) Hampden Park, Mount Florida, Glasgow.
YEARS OF OPERATION: 1969-72 British League Division One.

(3) Cliftonhill Stadium, Main Street, Coatbridge, Lanarkshire.
YEARS OF OPERATION: 1973 British League Division One; 1974 British League Division Two; 1975-77 National League (Team rode as 'Coatbridge Tigers' throughout their stay at this venue).

(4) Blantyre Sports Stadium, Glasgow Road, Blantyre, nr. Glasgow.
YEARS OF OPERATION: 1977-81 National League (Coatbridge moved to Blantyre midway through the 1977 season, reverting back to the name of 'Glasgow Tigers').

(5) Craighead Park, Forrest Street, Blantyre, nr. Glasgow.
YEARS OF OPERATION: 1982-86 National League.

(6) Derwent Park, Workington, Cumbria.
YEAR OF OPERATION: 1987 National League (Began year as 'Glasgow Tigers', before becoming 'Workington Tigers').

(7) Shawfield Stadium, Glasgow Road, Rutherglen, Glasgow.
YEARS OF OPERATION: 1988-90 National League; 1991-94 British League Division Two; 1995 Premier League; 1997-98 Premier League.

NOTE: In 1996, Shawfield Stadium was used by the 'Scottish Monarchs', who competed in the Premier League.

CLUB HONOURS

NATIONAL SERIES WINNERS: 1990.
LEAGUE CHAMPIONS: 1993, 1994.
KNOCK-OUT CUP WINNERS: 1993, 1994.

RIDER ROSTER 2004

Paul BENTLEY; Corey BLACKMAN; Barry CAMPBELL; Eric CARRILLO; James COCKLE; James GRIEVES; Graham JONES, David McALLAN; Shane PARKER; George STANCL.

OTHER APPEARANCES/GUESTS (official matches only):

Gary BEATON; Tom BROWN; Lee DICKEN; Trent LEVERINGTON; Darren ROLPH; Mark THOMPSON; Cameron WOODWARD.

PREMIER LEAGUE

No	DATE	OPPONENTS	H/A	RESULT	STANCL	JONES	BENTLEY	GRIEVES	PARKER	BLACKMAN	CARRILLO	DICKEN	COCKLE	McALLAN	OTHERS
1	31/5	Reading	A	L44-53	14+1 (5)	3+1 (4)	7+2 (4)	4 (4)	14+1 (6)	2 (4)	–	–	–	–	0 (3)
2	1/6	Isle of Wight	A	L42-53	4+1 (4)	8+1 (5)	8+1 (5)	6 (4)	15 (5)	1 (4)	–	–	–	–	0 (3)
3	6/6	Isle of Wight	H	W58-34*	5 (4)	9 (4)	6+1 (4)	13+1 (5)	14+1 (5)	1 (3)	10+1 (5)	–	–	–	–
4	10/6	Sheffield	A	L41-55	5+1 (4)	9+1 (5)	6 (4)	0 (4)	17 (5)	0 (3)	4 (5)	–	–	–	–
5	11/6	Somerset	A	L44-46	5+2 (4)	8 (5)	8+1 (4)	5+1 (4)	8 (5)	1 (3)	9+1 (5)	–	–	–	–
6	17/6	King's Lynn	H	W56-38	14 (5)	1+1 (3)	7+3 (4)	10 (4)	12+2 (5)	2+1 (4)	10+1 (5)	–	–	–	–
7	19/6	Stoke	A	L40-52	12 (5)	5 (4)	7+1 (4)	5+2 (4)	8 (5)	0 (3)	3+1 (5)	–	–	–	–
8	27/6	Stoke	H	W54-39*	3+1 (4)	4+1 (4)	11 (4)	11+1 (5)	15 (5)	6+1 (4)	4+1 (4)	–	–	–	–
9	4/7	Exeter	H	W61-34	14+1 (5)	8 (4)	7+1 (4)	13+2 (5)	11 (4)	2+1 (4)	6+1 (4)	–	–	–	–
10	7/7	King's Lynn†	A	L28-41*	5 (3)	0 (1)	3 (3)	5 (4)	9 (3)	2+1 (4)	4+1 (4)	–	–	–	–
11	10/7	Workington	A	L25-68	7+1 (5)	0 (3)	8 (5)	3 (4)	5 (5)	1 (4)	1 (4)	–	–	–	–
12	15/7	Newport	H	W54-40	14+1 (6)	–	R/R	13 (5)	13+1 (5)	1 (3)	11+2 (6)	2+2 (4)	–	–	–
13	18/7	Sheffield	H	W51-42	9 (4)	–	5 (4)	14 (6)	12 (5)	–	10+3 (7)	R/R	–	–	1+1 (4)
14	21/7	Hull	A	L31-62	9 (5)	–	8 (5)	2+2 (4)	6+1 (4)	–	5 (5)	0 (4)	–	–	1 (3)
15	25/7	Reading	H	W51-45	9+1 (4)	–	8+3 (5)	9+1 (5)	10+1 (5)	–	14+1 (7)	R/R	–	–	1 (3)
16	31/7	Berwick	A	L44-45	12+1 (5)	–	11+1 (5)	R/R	9+1 (5)	–	6 (5)	–	2 (4)	–	4+2 (5)
17	1/8	Hull	H	L43-47	4 (4)	–	4+1 (5)	R/R	13 (5)	–	14+2 (7)	–	0 (3)	–	8+2 (6)
18	8/8	Somerset	H	W54-42*	14+1 (5)	–	6 (4)	12+3 (5)	12 (4)	–	–	–	2 (4)	3+1 (4)	5 (4)
19	13/8	Edinburgh	A	L37-57	5+1 (4)	–	1+1 (3)	10 (5)	10 (5)	–	6+1 (5)	–	0 (4)	5+1 (4)	–
20	15/8	Edinburgh	H	W50-45	6 (4)	–	12+1 (5)	8+3 (5)	11 (4)	–	10+1 (5)	–	1 (3)	2 (4)	–
21	19/8	Berwick	H	W57-37*	14 (5)	–	7+1 (4)	9+1 (4)	13+2 (5)	–	6+2 (4)	–	2 (4)	6+2 (4)	–
22	22/8	Rye House	H	W48-47	8 (4)	–	9+1 (5)	7+1 (4)	12 (5)	–	6+1 (5)	–	3 (3)	3+2 (4)	–
23	29/8	Newcastle	H	W59-35	12 (5)	–	12+1 (5)	9+2 (4)	9+2 (4)	–	7+1 (4)	–	5+[illegible] (4)	5+2 (4)	–
24	30/8	Newcastle	A	L47-49*	15+1 (6)	–	12+1 (4)	0 (0)	16 (5)	–	2 (6)	–	1 (5)	1+1 (4)	–
25	4/9	Rye House	A	L41-51	13 (5)	–	11+1 (6)	R/R	8+1 (5)	–	5 (5)	–	1+[illegible] (5)	3 (4)	–
26	5/9	Newport	A	L39-53*	10 (5)	–	13 (6)	R/R	10+1 (5)	–	1 (4)	–	0 (3)	5+2 (7)	–
27	6/9	Exeter	A	L39-54*	17 (6)	–	8+1 (5)	R/R	9+1 (5)	–	1 (5)	–	3+[illegible] (6)	1 (3)	–
28	12/9	Workington	H	L44-46	16 (6)	–	9+2 (5)	R/R	9+1 (5)	–	5 (5)	–	3+[illegible] (4)	2+1 (5)	–

*Denotes bonus-point victory

†Meeting abandoned after heat twelve, with the result permitted to stand.

DETAILS OF OTHER RIDERS:

Match No. 1: Darren Rolph 0 (3); Match No. 2: Tom Brown 0 (3); Match No. 13: Barry Campbell 1+1 (4); Match No. 14: Mark Thompson 1 (3); Match No. 15: Gary Beaton 1 (2); Mark Thompson 0 (1); Match No. 16: Cameron Woodward 4+2 (5); Match No. 17: Trent Leverington 8+2 (6); Match No. 18: Barry Campbell 5 (4).

TACTICAL SUBSTITUTE AND TACTICAL RIDES, AS INCLUDED IN THE SCORES GRID:

Match No. 1: Stancl 6 points (TR); Parker 6 points (TS); Bentley 2 points (TR); Match No. 2: Parker 6 points (TR); Jones 2 points (TR); Bentley 2 points (TS); Match No. 4: Parker 6 points (TR); Jones 6 points (TR); Carrillo 0 points (TS); Match No. 7: Stancl 6 points (TR); Match No. 10: Stancl 0 points (TR); Match No. 11: Stancl 4 points (TR); Bentley 2 points (TS); Parker 0 points (TR); Match No. 14: Stancl 4 points (TR); Parker 2 points (TR); Match No. 19: Parker 4 points (TR); Grieves 4 points (TR); Match No. 24: Bentley 6 points (TR); Parker 4 points (TR); Stancl 4 points (TS); Match No. 25: Bentley 4 points (TR); Match No. 26: Parker 2 points (TR); Stancl 2 points (TR); Match No. 27: Stancl 4 points (TR); Parker 2 points (TR).

PREMIER LEAGUE AVERAGES

Rider	Mts	Rds	Pts	Bon	Tot	Avge	Max
Shane Parker	28	134	294	16	310	9.25	2 full; 2 paid
George Stancl	28	131	260	14	274	8.37	2 paid
James Grieves	22	94	166	20	186	7.91	2 paid
Paul Bentley	27	121	206	25	231	7.64	–
Eric Carrillo	25	126	160	21	181	5.75	–
Graham Jones	11	42	51	5	56	5.33	–
David McAllan	11	47	36	12	48	4.09	–
Barry Campbell	2	8	6	1	7	3.50	–
Corey Blackman	12	43	19	4	23	2.14	–
James Cockle	13	52	23	4	27	2.08	–
Gary Beaton	1	2	1	0	1	2.00	–
Lee Dicken	2	8	2	2	4	2.00	–
Mark Thompson	2	4	1	0	1	1.00	–
Tom Brown	1	3	0	0	0	0.00	–
Darren Rolph	1	3	0	0	0	0.00	–
Guests	2	11	12	4	16	5.82	–

PREMIER TROPHY

No	DATE	OPPONENTS	H/A	RESULT	STANCL	JONES	BENTLEY	GRIEVES	PARKER	BLACKMAN	CAMPBELL	CARRILLO	DICKEN
1	24/3	Hull	A	W54-39	9+5 (5)	14 (5)	8+1 (4)	6+2 (4)	10 (4)	3+1 (4)	4+2 (4)	–	–
2	27/3	Workington	A	L35-59	5+1 (4)	10+2 (6)	11 (5)	0 (4)	8 (4)	1 (4)	0 (3)	–	–
3	28/3	Berwick	H	W63-28	10+2 (4)	8+1 (4)	12+3 (5)	12 (5)	12 (4)	5 (4)	4+1 (4)	–	–
4	11/4	Newcastle	H	W60-35	12+3 (5)	10+2 (4)	9+2 (4)	11+1 (4)	15 (5)	2 (4)	1 (4)	–	–
5	12/4	Newcastle	A	W56-38*	9+1 (4)	6+1 (4)	9+1 (4)	13+2 (5)	13 (5)	5+1 (5)	1+1 (3)	–	–
6	22/4	Sheffield	A	L40-53	6 (4)	6+1 (4)	5+2 (4)	7+1 (5)	13 (6)	3 (4)	0 (3)	–	–
7	24/4	Stoke	A	D45-45	9+1 (5)	7+1 (4)	10 (4)	4+2 (4)	12 (5)	1 (4)	2 (4)	–	–
8	25/4	Sheffield	H	W49-41	9+2 (5)	6 (4)	8+1 (4)	8+1 (4)	15 (5)	1+1 (4)	2 (4)	–	–
9	1/5	Berwick	A	W48-42*	13+1 (5)	3 (4)	10+1 (5)	8+1 (4)	9 (4)	5+1 (5)	0 (3)	–	–

No	DATE	OPPONENTS	H/A	RESULT	STANCL	JONES	BENTLEY	GRIEVES	PARKER	BLACKMAN	CAMPBELL	CARRILLO	DICKEN
10	2/5	Edinburgh	H	W53-42	12+1 (5)	8 (4)	6 (4)	9 (4)	14+1 (5)	3+1 (5)	1 (3)	–	–
11	7/5	Edinburgh	A	L40-52	5 (5)	5 (4)	4+2 (4)	6 (4)	15 (6)	4+1 (4)	1 (3)	–	–
12	16/5	Workington	H	W47-46	11+3 (5)	4 (3)	7+1 (4)	8+2 (4)	14 (5)	0 (3)	3 (6)	–	–
13	18/5	Hull	H	W49-41*	9+1 (4)	2+1 (3)	8+1 (4)	11+2 (5)	15 (5)	3 (5)	1 (4)	–	–
14	23/5	Stoke	H	W50-43*	9+1 (4)	R/R	10+1 (4)	15+2 (6)	13+1 (5)	3 (6)	0 (5)	–	–
15	11/7	Reading	H	W50-40	10+1 (5)	–	0 (2)	10 (4)	15 (5)	2+1 (4)	–	10+2 (6)	3 (4)
16	12/7	Reading	A	L36-57	11 (6)	–	R/R	3+2 (6)	8+1 (5)	1+1 (4)	–	13 (7)	0 (2)

*Denotes bonus-point victory

TACTICAL SUBSTITUTE AND TACTICAL RIDES, AS INCLUDED IN THE SCORES GRID:

Match No. 2: Parker 6 points (TR); Jones 2 points (TS); Stancl 0 points (TR); Match No. 6: Parker 4 points (TS); Stancl 2 points (TR); Match No. 11: Parker 4 points (TS); Match No. 16: Parker 4 points (TR); Stancl 4 points (TR).

PREMIER TROPHY AVERAGES

Rider	Mts	Rds	Pts	Bon	Tot	Avge	Max
Shane Parker	16	78	192	3	195	10.00	5 full; 1 paid
George Stancl	16	75	146	23	169	9.01	2 paid
Paul Bentley	15	61	117	16	133	8.72	1 paid
James Grieves	16	72	131	18	149	8.28	2 paid
Eric Carrillo	2	13	23	2	25	7.69	–
Graham Jones	13	53	88	9	97	7.32	1 paid
Corey Blackman	16	69	42	8	50	2.90	–
Lee Dicken	2	6	3	0	3	2.00	–
Barry Campbell	14	53	20	4	24	1.81	–

KNOCK-OUT CUP

No	DATE	OPPONENTS	H/A	RESULT	STANCL	JONES	BENTLEY	GRIEVES	PARKER	BLACKMAN	CAMPBELL
1	9/5	Reading	H	W47-43	9+1 (4)	0 (2)	6+2 (4)	11 (5)	15 (5)	4 (5)	2 (5)
2	10/5	Reading	A	L43-52	7 (4)	R/R	8+1 (5)	9+2 (5)	17 (6)	1+1 (6)	1 (4)

TACTICAL SUBSTITUTE AND TACTICAL RIDES, AS INCLUDED IN THE SCORES GRID:

Match No. 2: Parker 6 points (TS); Stancl 4 points (TR); Bentley 0 points (TR).

OTHER MEETINGS

6 March: Carlos Villar Benefit

Edinburgh/Workington 32, Berwick 28, Glasgow 19 (Paul Bentley 9; Emiliano Sanchez 8; James Grieves 1; Barry Campbell 1; Gary Beaton 0), Newcastle 17 – staged at Berwick.

21 March: Spring Trophy (first leg)

Glasgow 46 (Shane Parker 14; James Grieves 11; George Stancl 9; Barry Campbell 6+1; Paul Bentley 3+1; Graham Jones 2+1; Corey Blackman 1) Edinburgh 44.

GLASGOW: back row, left to right: Graham Jones, Shane Parker, Paul Bentley, James Grieves. Front, kneeling: Corey Blackman, Barry Campbell. On bike: George Stancl.

26 March: Spring Trophy (second leg)

Edinburgh 48 Glasgow 45 (Shane Parker 16; George Stancl 9+1; James Grieves 8+1; Graham Jones 6+1; Paul Bentley 4+2; Corey Blackman 1; Barry Campbell 1) – Edinburgh won 92-91 on aggregate.

4 April: Premier Trophy

Glasgow 16 (Graham Jones 3; James Grieves 3; Shane Parker 3; Barry Campbell 3; George Stancl 2+1; Paul Bentley 1; Corey Blackman 1) Stoke 8 – meeting abandoned after heat four.

17 September: Scottish Cup (first leg)

Edinburgh 51 Glasgow 40 (George Stancl 14; Shane Parker 11+1; Ross Brady 7; Richard Juul 3+1; David McAllan 3; Paul Bentley 1; James Cockle 1).

3 October: Scottish Cup (second leg)

Glasgow 37 (Paul Bentley 8+1; Shane Parker 8; George Stancl 6; Trent Leverington 5; David McAllan 4+1; Phil Morris 3+1; James Cockle 3+1) Edinburgh 38 – meeting abandoned after heat twelve, with the result permitted to stand. Edinburgh won 89-77 on aggregate.

INDIVIDUAL MEETINGS

26 September: Heathersfield Golden Helmet

1st Sean Stoddart 14; 2nd Gary Flint 13; 3rd Gary Beaton 12; Kriss Irving 10; Andrew Tully 10; Luke Priest 10; David Speight 10; Adam McKinna 9; James McBain 8; David Haigh 6; Colin McDonald 4; John MacPhail 4; Kieran Morris 4; Cal McDade 3; Keith Maben 2.

10 October: City of Glasgow Ashfield Classic

QUALIFYING SCORES: Josh Larsen 13; Magnus Karlsson 12; George Stancl 11; Paul Bentley 10; Rory Schlein 10; Carl Stonehewer 9; Rusty Harrison 8; Shane Parker 7; Josef Franc 7; Mark Lemon 7; David McAllan 7; Jesper Olsen 6; Kevin Doolan 4; Paul Thorp 4; William Lawson 2; Tomas Topinka 2; Gary Beaton (Res) 1. SEMI-FINAL: 1st Stonehewer; 2nd Schlein; 3rd Harrison; 4th Bentley. FINAL: 1st Stonehewer; 2nd Larsen; 3rd Schlein; 4th Karlsson.

HULL BHK VIKINGS

ADDRESS: Craven Park Stadium, Poorhouse Lane, Preston Road, Kingston-upon-Hull, East Yorkshire, HU9 5HE.
PROMOTERS: Paul Hodder & Eric Boocock.
TRACK LENGTH: 346 metres.
TRACK RECORD: 64.4 seconds – Magnus Karlsson (30/06/04).
FIRST MEETING: 5 April 1995.
YEARS OF OPERATION: 1995-98 Premier League; 1999 Elite League; 2000-04 Premier League.

PREVIOUS VENUE AS 'VIKINGS': The Boulevard Stadium, Airlie Street, Kingston-upon-Hull, East Yorkshire.
YEARS OF OPERATION: 1971-73 British League Division Two; 1974 British League; 1975-81 British League.

CLUB HONOURS

INTER-LEAGUE KNOCK-OUT CUP WINNERS: 1976.
PREMIER TROPHY WINNERS: 2000.
KNOCK-OUT CUP WINNERS: 2001, 2004.
PREMIERSHIP WINNERS: 2002.
LEAGUE CHAMPIONS: 2004.
YOUNG SHIELD WINNERS: 2004.

RIDER ROSTER 2004

Ross BRADY; Magnus KARLSSON; Emil KRAMER; Danny NORTON; Joel PARSONS; Emiliano SANCHEZ; Garry STEAD; Paul THORP.

OTHER APPEARANCES/GUESTS (official matches only):
Ricky ASHWORTH; Gary BEATON; Paul BENTLEY; Jason BUNYAN; Neil COLLINS; Chris NEATH; Michael PICKERING; Jamie SMITH; Shaun TACEY; Mark THOMPSON.

PREMIER LEAGUE

No	DATE	OPPONENTS	H/A	RESULT	THORP	KRAMER	STEAD	SANCHEZ	KARLSSON	BRADY	PARSONS	OTHERS
1	14/4	Reading	H	W46-44	9 (5)	7+1 (4)	7+1 (4)	7 (4)	8 (5)	7+1 (5)	–	1 (3)
2	24/5	Reading	A	L39-51	7 (4)	7+2 (5)	7 (5)	4+1 (4)	5 (4)	8+2 (6)	1 (3)	–
3	26/5	Somerset	H	W55-38	11+2 (5)	4+1 (4)	6+2 (4)	6+2 (4)	12 (5)	10+1 (4)	6+1 (4)	–
4	30/5	Newport	A	W58-38	7+1 (4)	12+1 (5)	7+1 (4)	8 (4)	12+2 (5)	7+2 (4)	5+3 (4)	–
5	2/6	Edinburgh	H	W49-46	7 (5)	7+1 (4)	5+1 (4)	7+1 (4)	10+1 (5)	8+2 (4)	5+3 (4)	–
6	5/6	Rye House	A	W51-44	9 (5)	3+1 (3)	2+1 (4)	9+1 (4)	9+2 (5)	8+1 (4)	11+1 (5)	–
7	9/6	Newport	H	W61-35*	16+1 (6)	R/R	4+1 (4)	12+3 (5)	–	12+2 (6)	8+2 (5)	9 (4)

No	DATE	OPPONENTS	H/A	RESULT	THORP	KRAMER	STEAD	SANCHEZ	KARLSSON	BRADY	PARSONS	OTHERS
8	11/6	Edinburgh	A	W47-43*	1+1 (4)	5+3 (4)	3 (4)	8+1 (4)	11+1 (5)	13 (5)	6+1 (4)	–
9	16/6	Exeter	H	W65-27	7+3 (4)	8+1 (4)	14+1 (5)	5+1 (4)	9 (4)	15 (5)	7+1 (4)	–
10	18/6	Somerset	A	W53-44*	11 (5)	9+1 (4)	7 (4)	7+1 (5)	11+1 (5)	7+2 (4)	1 (3)	–
11	28/6	Exeter	A	L45-50*	5+1 (4)	5 (4)	13+1 (5)	6+1 (5)	9 (5)	7 (4)	0 (4)	–
12	29/6	Isle of Wight	A	W49-44	2+1 (4)	7+2 (4)	10+1 (5)	7+1 (5)	13 (5)	9 (4)	1 (3)	–
13	30/6	Stoke	H	W50-46	7+1 (4)	6+2 (4)	8 (4)	7+3 (5)	10 (5)	11 (5)	1+1 (3)	–
14	7/7	Workington	H	W46-44	3+2 (4)	8 (4)	6+2 (4)	10+2 (6)	6 (3)	10+1 (5)	3 (4)	–
15	11/7	Newcastle	A	W60-34	10+4 (5)	3+1 (4)	10 (4)	10+1 (4)	4+2 (4)	13 (5)	–	10+2 (4)
16	14/7	Sheffield	H	W54-40	7+1 (4)	10 (4)	7+1 (4)	15+1 (6)	5+1 (4)	9 (5)	–	1 (3)
17	21/7	Glasgow	H	W62-31	14 (5)	13+1 (5)	7+2 (4)	9+1 (4)	7 (4)	8+3 (4)	4+2 (4)	–
18	31/7	King's Lynn	H	W62-33	11+4 (5)	5+1 (4)	7+1 (4)	7+1 (4)	15 (5)	10 (4)	7+1 (4)	–
19	1/8	Glasgow	A	W47-43*	13+1 (5)	5+2 (4)	7+1 (4)	6+1 (5)	9 (5)	4+1 (3)	3 (4)	–
20	4/8	Rye House	H	W62-32*	9+2 (4)	14 (5)	8+3 (5)	6+3 (3)	10+1 (4)	8+1 (4)	7 (5)	–
21	8/8	Sheffield	A	L38-52*	8+2 (5)	6+1 (4)	4+1 (4)	6+1 (5)	9 (5)	5 (4)	0 (4)	–
22	11/8	Isle of Wight	H	W48-46*	10+2 (5)	2+1 (4)	11+1 (5)	7 (4)	9+1 (4)	6+1 (4)	3 (4)	–
23	14/8	Berwick	A	W47-45	3+1 (4)	8+1 (4)	6+4 (5)	12+1 (6)	10+1 (5)	7+1 (4)	1 (3)	–
24	22/8	Stoke	A	W52-42*	6+2 (4)	13 (5)	6+3 (4)	11+3 (6)	10 (5)	6 (4)	0 (2)	–
25	25/8	Newcastle	H	W60-31*	10+1 (4)	9+1 (4)	8+1 (4)	12 (4)	8+2 (4)	6+3 (5)	7+3 (5)	–
26	28/8	King's Lynn	A	L42-50*	11 (5)	6+1 (4)	6+1 (4)	7+1 (6)	10+1 (5)	0 (1)	–	2+1 (5)
27	8/9	Berwick	H	W54-40*	11+1 (4)	3+1 (4)	11+1 (5)	10+1 (4)	10+1 (5)	6+1 (4)	3+1 (4)	–
28	11/9	Workington	A	L43-53	11+2 (4)	1 (4)	10 (4)	11+2 (6)	6 (5)	4 (4)	0 (3)	–

*Denotes bonus-point victory

DETAILS OF OTHER RIDERS:

Match No. 1: Danny Norton 1 (3); Match No. 7: Chris Neath 9 (4); Match No. 15: Shaun Tacey 10+2 (4); Match No. 16: Neil Collins 1 (3); Match No. 26: Danny Norton 2+1 (5).

TACTICAL RIDES, AS INCLUDED IN THE SCORES GRID:

Match No. 11: Stead 6 points (TR); Brady 4 points (TR); Match No. 23: Kramer 4 points (TR); Thorp 0 points (TR); Match No. 26: Thorp 4 points (TR); Match No. 28: Thorp 6 points (TR); Stead 6 points (TR).

PREMIER LEAGUE AVERAGES

Rider	Mts	Rds	Pts	Bon	Tot	Avge	Max
Paul Thorp	28	126	231	36	267	8.48	2 paid
Magnus Karlsson	27	125	247	17	264	8.45	1 full
Ross Brady	28	120	222	25	247	8.23	1 full
Emiliano Sanchez	28	130	232	35	267	8.22	1 full; 1 paid
Garry Stead	28	120	201	32	233	7.77	1 paid
Emil Kramer	27	112	184	27	211	7.54	–
Joel Parsons	24	92	90	20	110	4.78	–
Danny Norton	2	8	3	1	4	2.00	–
Guests	3	11	20	2	22	8.00	1 paid

PREMIER TROPHY

No	DATE	OPPONENTS	H/A	RESULT	THORP	KRAMER	STEAD	SANCHEZ	KARLSSON	BRADY	NORTON	PARSONS	OTHERS
1	17/3	Workington	H	W49-44	5 (4)	9+2 (5)	10+2 (5)	4+2 (4)	7+1 (4)	13 (5)	1 (3)	–	–
2	24/3	Glasgow	H	L39-54	4 (4)	12 (5)	9 (5)	4+1 (4)	3 (4)	6+1 (5)	1+1 (3)	–	–
3	31/3	Newcastle	H	W58-35	5+1 (4)	8 (4)	12+1 (5)	6+1 (4)	13+1 (5)	12 (5)	2+1 (4)	–	–
4	3/4	Workington	A	L35-58	6 (4)	3+2 (4)	12 (5)	3+1 (4)	10 (5)	1 (3)	0 (4)	–	–
5	7/4	Edinburgh	H	W52-43	–	8 (4)	11+1 (5)	7+3 (4)	10+1 (5)	7 (5)	2 (3)	–	7+2 (4)
6	10/4	Stoke	A	L45-50	13 (5)	6+1 (4)	8 (4)	2 (4)	13 (5)	3+1 (5)	0 (3)	–	–
7	24/4	Berwick	A	L42-52	15+1 (6)	4 (5)	14 (6)	3 (5)	R/R	6 (4)	–	–	0 (4)
8	25/4	Newcastle	A	W55-37*	10+1 (5)	<u>12 (4)</u>	11+2 (5)	4+1 (4)	8 (4)	7 (4)	–	3+1 (4)	–
9	28/4	Sheffield	H	W57-37	2+1 (4)	8 (4)	11+1 (5)	8+3 (4)	11+1 (5)	9 (4)	–	8+1 (5)	–
10	5/5	Stoke	H	W50-44*	6+2 (5)	7+1 (4)	7 (4)	5 (4)	13 (5)	10 (4)	–	2 (4)	–
11	18/5	Glasgow	A	L41-49	6 (5)	10+2 (5)	7 (4)	0 (3)	–	12+3 (6)	–	6+1 (5)	0 (3)
12	19/5	Berwick	H	W51-42	12+1 (5)	6+1 (4)	6+1 (4)	6+3 (4)	13+1 (5)	0 (3)	–	8+3 (5)	–
13	21/5	Edinburgh	A	W47-43*	6+1 (5)	7 (4)	6 (4)	5+2 (4)	10+1 (5)	8+1 (4)	–	5+1 (4)	–
14	3/6	Sheffield	A	L40-55*	5+1 (4)	–	9+1 (5)	1 (4)	15 (5)	5 (4)	–	5+2 (6)	0 (3)

*Denotes bonus-point victory

DETAILS OF OTHER RIDERS:

Match No. 5: Paul Bentley 7+2 (4); Match No. 7: Michael Pickering 0 (4); Match No. 11: Gary Beaton 0 (3); Match No. 14: Mark Thompson 0 (3).

TACTICAL RIDES, AS INCLUDED IN THE SCORES GRID:

Match No. 2: Kramer 6 points (TR); Thorp 0 points (TR); Match No. 4: Stead 4 points (TR); Karlsson 2 points (TR); Match No. 6: Thorp 6 points (TR); Stead 4 points (TR); Match No. 7: Thorp 4 points (TR); Stead 4 points (TR); Match No. 14: Karlsson 6 points (TR); Stead 4 points (TR).

PREMIER TROPHY AVERAGES

Rider	Mts	Rds	Pts	Bon	Tot	Avge	Max
Magnus Karlsson	12	57	122	6	128	8.98	–
Garry Stead	14	66	125	9	134	8.12	–
Emil Kramer	13	56	97	9	106	7.57	1 full
Ross Brady	14	61	99	6	105	6.89	–
Paul Thorp	13	60	90	9	99	6.60	–
Joel Parsons	7	33	37	9	46	5.58	–
Emiliano Sanchez	14	56	58	17	75	5.36	–
Danny Norton	6	20	6	2	8	1.60	–
Gary Beaton	1	3	0	0	0	0.00	–
Michael Pickering	1	4	0	0	0	0.00	–
Mark Thompson	1	3	0	0	0	0.00	–
Guest	1	4	7	2	9	9.00	–

HULL: back row, left to right: Eric Boocock (Team Manager), Emiliano Sanchez, Ross Brady, Emil Kramer, Magnus Karlsson, Paul Hodder (Promoter). Front, kneeling: Garry Stead, Joel Parsons. On bike: Paul Thorp.

KNOCK-OUT CUP

No	DATE	OPPONENTS	H/A	RESULT	THORP	SANCHEZ	KRAMER	STEAD	KARLSSON	PARSONS	BRADY	OTHERS
1	12/5	Berwick	H	W59-36	10+2 (5)	4 (3)	10+1 (4)	9+2 (4)	11+1 (5)	7+1 (5)	8+1 (5)	–
2	24/7	Berwick†	A	D42-42*	8 (4)	7+2 (4)	6 (4)	6 (4)	8+1 (4)	2 (4)	5+2 (4)	–
3	18/8	Reading	H	W53-39	12+2 (5)	7+3 (5)	8 (4)	5 (3)	7 (5)	6+3 (4)	8+1 (4)	–
4	23/8	Reading	A	L42-51*	3+3 (4)	12+1 (5)	3+1 (4)	7+2 (4)	5 (4)	4+2 (4)	8 (5)	–
5	20/9	Exeter	A	L34-57	13+1 (6)	6+1 (5)	4 (4)	3+1 (5)	–	0 (4)	R/R	8+2 (6)
6	6/10	Exeter	H	W62-35*	11+1 (5)	16+2 (7)	8+2 (5)	11+1 (5)	8+3 (4)	8+1 (4)	R/R	–
7	20/10	Isle of Wight	H	W56-39	8+2 (4)	11 (7)	11+1 (5)	15+2 (6)	10 (5)	1 (4)	R/R	–
8	26/10	Isle of Wight	A	L43-52*	9 (5)	4+2 (5)	6+2 (5)	11+1 (5)	12 (5)	1 (5)	R/R	–

*Denotes aggregate victory

† Meeting abandoned after heat fourteen, with the result permitted to stand.

DETAILS OF OTHER RIDERS:

Match No. 5: Jason Bunyan 8+2 (6).

TACTICAL RIDES, AS INCLUDED IN THE SCORES GRID:

Match No. 5: Thorp 4 points (TR); Sanchez 0 points (TR); Match No. 8: Thorp 6 points (TR); Stead 4 points (TR).

YOUNG SHIELD

No	DATE	OPPONENTS	H/A	RESULT	BRADY	THORP	STEAD	KRAMER	KARLSSON	SANCHEZ	PARSONS	OTHERS
1	25/9	Rye House	A	L44-47	3 (3)	4+1 (4)	6 (5)	8+1 (4)	–	17+1 (7)	3+1 (4)	3 (4)
2	29/9	Rye House	H	W52-42*	R/R	10+2 (6)	9+1 (6)	9+1 (5)	–	12+1 (5)	3+1 (3)	9 (5)
3	16/10	Workington	A	L44-52	R/R	7 (4)	14+2 (6)	4+1 (5)	8 (5)	9 (5)	2 (5)	–
4	20/10	Workington	H	W52-42*	R/R	9+1 (4)	13+1 (6)	9+2 (5)	8+1 (5)	10+2 (6)	3+1 (4)	–
5	25/10	Reading	A	W52-41	R/R	10+2 (5)	8 (5)	16+2 (6)	9+1 (4)	1+1 (4)	8+1 (6)	–
6	27/10	Reading	H	W52-44*	R/R	9 (5)	13 (5)	4+2 (3)	9+1 (5)	10+2 (7)	7+2 (6)	–

*Denotes aggregate victory

DETAILS OF OTHER RIDERS:

Match No. 1: Jamie Smith 3 (4); Match No. 2: Ricky Ashworth 9 (5).

TACTICAL RIDES, AS INCLUDED IN THE SCORES GRID:

Match No. 1: Kramer 6 points (TR); Match No. 3: Thorp 6 points (TR); Stead 6 points (TR).

OTHER MEETINGS

10 March: Challenge (first leg)

Hull 46 (Emiliano Sanchez 12+1; Paul Thorp 10+1; Emil Kramer 8+2; Garry Stead 6+1; Magnus Karlsson 5; Danny Norton 3; Ross Brady 2+1) Sheffield 44.

11 March: Challenge (second leg)

Sheffield 52 Hull 43 (Ross Brady 14+1; Paul Thorp 14; Garry Stead 6; Magnus Karlsson 4+1; Emiliano Sanchez 3+2; Emil Kramer 2; Danny Norton 0) – Sheffield won 96-89 on aggregate.

22 September: Paul Thorp Testimonial

Tape Touchers 45 (Paul Thorp 9; Emil Kramer 9; Ross Brady 8+2; Ray Morton 6+2; Jamie Smith 5+1; Shane Parker 4+2; Ricky Ashworth 4) Ref's Rebels 39 (Garry Stead 12; Steve Johnston 8; George Stancl 5+2; Paul Bentley 4; Les Collins 4; Robbie Kessler 3+1; Emiliano Sanchez 3+1) – meeting abandoned after heat fourteen, with the result permitted to stand.

13 October: Young Shield semi-final (first leg)

Hull 33 (Emiliano Sanchez 8; Emil Kramer 7+1; Paul Thorp 6; Joel Parsons 4+2; Garry Stead 4+1; Magnus Karlsson 4+1; Ross Brady R/R) Workington 15 – meeting abandoned after heat eight.

PAIRS MEETING

15 September: Inter-Continental Best Pairs

1st England 28 (Paul Thorp 14+3; Garry Stead 14+1); 2nd Sweden 27 (Emil Kramer 19; Magnus Karlsson 8+2); 3rd Australia 21 (Shane Parker 12+1; Joel Parsons 9+2); Denmark 21 (Kristian Lund 11; Mads Korneliussen 10+1); Italy 20 (Emiliano Sanchez 18; Simone Terenzani 2+1); Scotland 18 (Ross Brady 15+1; Blair Scott 3).

INDIVIDUAL MEETING

1 September: Yorkshire Junior Open Championship

1st Jon Armstrong (after run-off) 14; 2nd Joel Parsons 14; 3rd Paul Cooper 13; Benji Compton 11; Harland Cook 11; Tony Dart 11; Byron Bekker 8; James Mann 8; Michael Pickering 7; John Branney 6; David Speight 5; Paul Burnett 3; Phil Downes 3; Carl Belfield 3; Carl Downs 2; David Baker (Res) 1; Barry Burchatt 0.

ISLE OF WIGHT WIGHTLINK ISLANDERS

ADDRESS: Smallbrook Stadium, Ashey Road, Ryde, Isle of Wight, PO33 4BH.
PROMOTERS: Dave Pavitt & Martin Newnham.
TRACK LENGTH: 385 metres.
TRACK RECORD: 68.0 seconds – Craig Boyce (03/08/04).
FIRST MEETING: 13 May 1996.
YEARS OF OPERATION: 1995 Demonstration; 1996 Conference League; 1997 Amateur League & Premier League; 1998-04 Premier League.

CLUB HONOURS

YOUNG SHIELD WINNERS: 1998, 2001.
PAIRS CHAMPIONS: 2002.
KNOCK-OUT CUP WINNERS: 2003.

RIDER ROSTER 2004

Craig BOYCE; Jason BUNYAN; Krister MARSH; Ray MORTON; Ulrich OSTERGAARD; Glen PHILLIPS; Sebastian TRESARRIEU.

OTHER APPEARANCES/GUESTS (official matches only):

Ben BARKER; James CLEMENT; Chris COURAGE; Jamie COURTNEY; Tony DART; Karlis EZERGAILIS; Chris JOHNSON; Mads KORNELIUSSEN; Kristian LUND; John MORRISON; Joel PARSONS; Shaun TACEY; Jamie WESTACOTT.

PREMIER LEAGUE

No	DATE	OPPONENTS	H/A	RESULT	BOYCE	BUNYAN	MARSH	TRESARRIEU	MORTON	PHILLIPS	JOHNSON	COURTNEY	OSTERGAARD	OTHERS
1	25/5	Newcastle	H	W53-38	12 (5)	R/R	4+1 (5)	13+1 (5)	5+1 (4)	17+1 (7)	2 (4)	–	–	–
2	1/6	Glasgow	H	W53-42	9 (5)	6+1 (4)	8+2 (4)	4 (2)	10+1 (5)	12+1 (6)	4+3 (4)	–	–	–
3	4/6	Edinburgh	A	L32-62	12 (5)	9 (6)	4+1 (5)	R/R	4+1 (6)	–	–	2 (5)	–	1 (3)
4	5/6	Berwick	A	L45-48	17 (5)	7+2 (5)	5+3 (4)	R/R	8+1 (6)	8+1 (6)	–	0 (4)	–	–
5	6/6	Glasgow	A	L34-58	12 (5)	10 (5)	4+2 (5)	R/R	6 (6)	2 (6)	–	0 (3)	–	–
6	15/6	Sheffield	H	W57-35	16 (6)	6+1 (4)	8+2 (5)	R/R	15+1 (6)	6+2 (4)	–	–	6+1 (5)	–
7	29/6	Hull	H	L44-49	16 (6)	8 (6)	4+2 (5)	R/R	0 (1)	11 (7)	–	–	5+2 (5)	–
8	2/7	Somerset	A	L44-49	16 (5)	3+2 (4)	7+2 (6)	–	R/R	2 (4)	–	–	13 (7)	3 (4)
9	3/7	Stoke	A	L38-56	10 (5)	5+1 (5)	13+1 (6)	–	R/R	2+1 (5)	–	–	3+2 (4)	5+1 (5)
10	13/7	Workington	H	D45-45	13 (5)	7+2 (5)	6+1 (5)	–	8 (4)	R/R	–	–	8+4 (6)	3+1 (5)
11	19/7	Exeter	A	L40-54	17 (5)	5+1 (4)	8+1 (6)	R/R	6 (4)	2 (4)	–	–	2+1 (6)	0 (1)
12	20/7	Berwick	H	W56-37*	14+1 (5)	8 (4)	8+3 (6)	R/R	10+1 (5)	7+2 (4)	–	–	9+1 (6)	–
13	24/7	Workington	A	L41-49	5+1 (4)	10 (5)	8+1 (6)	R/R	7+1 (5)	3+1 (4)	–	–	8+2 (6)	–
14	25/7	Newcastle	A	W49-46*	11 (5)	8+2 (4)	6+2 (5)	R/R	10+1 (5)	3+1 (4)	–	–	11+1 (7)	–
15	27/7	Stoke	H	W50-44	13 (5)	8+1 (4)	5 (6)	R/R	12+1 (6)	4+1 (4)	–	–	8+1 (5)	–

ISLE OF WIGHT: back row, left to right: Craig Boyce, Jed Stone (Team Manager), Sebastian Tresarrieu, Glen Phillips, Jason Bunyan, Krister Marsh, James Clement. Front, on bike: Ray Morton.

PREMIER LEAGUE continued

No	DATE	OPPONENTS	H/A	RESULT	BOYCE	BUNYAN	MARSH	TRESARRIEU	MORTON	PHILLIPS	JOHNSON	COURTNEY	OSTERGAARD	OTHERS
16	1/8	Newport	A	D45-45	11 (5)	14 (6)	8+2 (5)	R/R	1 (3)	4+1 (5)	–	–	7+2 (6)	–
17	3/8	Edinburgh	H	W65-31*	14+1 (5)	13 (5)	9+3 (5)	R/R	10+2 (5)	10+2 (5)	–	–	9+3 (5)	–
18	11/8	Hull	A	L46-48	10 (5)	7 (4)	2 (3)	16+1 (5)	1 (4)	2 (4)	–	–	8+1 (5)	–
19	19/8	Exeter	H	W63-31*	13+1 (5)	14+1 (5)	7+1 (4)	6+1 (4)	10+1 (4)	5+3 (4)	–	–	8+3 (4)	–
20	24/8	Somerset	H	W62-31*	12+1 (5)	11+1 (5)	8+3 (4)	8+2 (4)	9 (4)	5+3 (4)	–	–	9 (4)	–
21	26/8	Newport	H	W63-29*	10+1 (4)	12 (5)	9+3 (4)	3+1 (4)	8 (4)	9+2 (4)	–	–	12+2 (5)	–
22	31/8	King's Lynn	H	W66-29	10+4 (5)	14 (5)	7+2 (4)	8+3 (4)	8+2 (4)	10+1 (4)	–	–	9+2 (4)	–
23	7/9	Rye House	H	W63-32	14+1 (5)	15 (5)	4+2 (4)	10 (4)	4+1 (4)	8+2 (4)	–	–	8+2 (4)	–
24	10/9	King's Lynn	A	L39-57*	17 (5)	11 (5)	0 (3)	7+1 (5)	1+1 (4)	1 (4)	–	–	2 (4)	–
25	11/9	Rye House	A	L41-52*	15 (5)	6+2 (5)	3+2 (4)	6 (4)	7 (4)	2 (4)	–	–	2+1 (4)	–
26	13/9	Reading	A	L42-48	10+1 (5)	4+2 (4)	5+3 (4)	5 (4)	9 (5)	3+2 (4)	–	–	6+1 (4)	–
27	14/9	Reading	H	W55-40*	9+1 (5)	9+3 (6)	10+2 (4)	R/R	15+1 (6)	7+1 (4)	–	–	5+1 (5)	–
28	16/9	Sheffield	A	L39-55*	17 (6)	14+1 (6)	2+1 (5)	R/R	1 (5)	2 (4)	–	–	–	3 (4)

*Denotes bonus-point victory

DETAILS OF OTHER RIDERS:

Match No. 3: John Morrison 1 (3); Match No. 8: Mads Korneliussen 3 (4); Match No. 9: Mads Korneliussen 5+1 (5); Match No. 10: Shaun Tacey 3+1 (5); Match No. 11: Karlis Ezergailis 0 (1); Match No. 28: Joel Parsons 3 (4).

TACTICAL SUBSTITUTE AND TACTICAL RIDES, AS INCLUDED IN THE SCORES GRID:

Match No. 3: Bunyan 4 points (TR); Boyce 4 points (TR); Morton 0 points (TS); Match No. 4: Boyce 6 points (TR); Match No. 5: Boyce 4 points (TR); Morton 0 points (TR); Match No. 7: Boyce 6 points (TR); Match No. 8: Boyce 6 points (TR); Match No. 9: Boyce 4 points (TR); Marsh 4 points (TR); Match No. 11: Boyce 6 points (TR); Marsh 2 points (TR); Match No. 13: Marsh 0 points (TR); Match No. 18: Tresarrieu 6 points (TR); Ostergaard 2 points (TR); Match No. 24: Boyce 6 points (TR); Bunyan 4 points (TR); Tresarrieu 2 points (TS); Match No. 25: Boyce 4 points (TR); Tresarrieu 2 points (TR); Match No. 28: Boyce 4 points (TR); Bunyan 4 points (TR).

PREMIER LEAGUE AVERAGES

Rider	Mts	Rds	Pts	Bon	Tot	Avge	Max
Craig Boyce	28	141	330	13	343	9.73	3 paid
Sebastian Tresarrieu	11	45	81	10	91	8.09	–
Jason Bunyan	27	131	238	23	261	7.97	1 full; 1 paid
Ulrich Ostergaard	22	111	157	33	190	6.85	–
Ray Morton	26	119	185	17	202	6.79	–
Krister Marsh	28	132	169	48	217	6.58	2 paid
Glen Phillips	26	119	147	28	175	5.88	–
Chris Johnson	2	8	6	3	9	4.50	–
John Morrison	1	3	1	0	1	1.33	–
Jamie Courtney	3	12	2	0	2	0.67	–
Karlis Ezergailis	1	1	0	0	0	0.00	–
Guests	4	18	14	2	16	3.56	–

PREMIER TROPHY

No	DATE	OPPONENTS	H/A	RESULT	BOYCE	BUNYAN	TRESARRIEU	MARSH	MORTON	PHILLIPS	JOHNSON	OTHERS
1	2/4	Somerset	A	D45-45	14+1 (5)	7 (4)	8 (5)	1+1 (4)	7+1 (4)	7+1 (5)	1 (3)	–
2	5/4	Exeter	A	L33-59	10 (5)	7+1 (5)	2+1 (4)	4+1 (4)	4 (4)	5 (6)	1+1 (2)	–
3	11/4	Newport	A	L45-48	11+1 (5)	8+1 (5)	0 (3)	7+1 (4)	4 (3)	8+1 (5)	–	7+2 (5)
4	12/4	Reading†	A	L34-38	4+1 (3)	9+1 (4)	7 (4)	1 (2)	7 (3)	6+2 (5)	–	0 (3)
5	13/4	King's Lynn	H	W65-28	10+1 (4)	7+2 (4)	14+1 (5)	8+2 (4)	11+1 (5)	13+2 (5)	–	2+1 (3)
6	17/4	Rye House	A	L42-47	11+1 (5)	6 (4)	7+1 (5)	6 (4)	2+1 (4)	7+2 (5)	–	3+1 (3)
7	25/4	King's Lynn	A	L43-52*	16+1 (5)	11–2 (5)	8 (4)	0 (4)	3 (3)	4 (5)	–	1 (4)
8	18/5	Reading	H	D45-45	10 (5)	8 (6)	7+1 (4)	R/R	6+1 (4)	13+1 (7)	1 (4)	–
9	27/5	Exeter	H	W45-44	8+2 (5)	7 (4)	10 (5)	5+1 (4)	4+1 (4)	9 (5)	2+1 (3)	–
10	8/6	Rye House	H	W54-42*	14 (5)	7+4 (5)	R/R	11 (5)	14+2 (6)	5+3 (4)	3 (4)	–

*Denotes bonus-point victory

†Meeting abandoned after heat twelve, with the result permitted to stand.

NOTE: Two matches were not ridden: Isle of Wight *v.* Somerset; Isle of Wight *v.* Newport.

DETAILS OF OTHER RIDERS:

Match No. 3: Ben Barker 7+2 (5); Match No. 4: James Clement 0 (3); Match No. 5: Chris Courage 2+1 (3 ; Match No. 6: Jamie Westacott 3+1 (3); Match No. 7: Tony Dart 1 (4).

TACTICAL SUBSTITUTE AND TACTICAL RIDES, AS INCLUDED IN THE SCORES GRID:

Match No. 2: Bunyan 4 points (TS); Boyce 2 points (TR); Morton 0 points (TR); Match No. 7: Boyce 6 points (TR); Bunyan 4 points (TR).

PREMIER TROPHY AVERAGES

Rider	Mts	Rds	Pts	Bon	Tot	Avge	Max
Craig Boyce	10	47	104	8	112	9.53	1 paid
Jason Bunyan	10	46	73	11	84	7.30	–
Ben Barker	1	5	7	2	9	7.20	–
Ray Morton	10	40	62	7	69	6.90	–
Sebastian Tresarrieu	9	39	63	4	67	6.87	1 paid
Glen Phillips	10	52	77	12	89	6.85	1 paid
Krister Marsh	9	35	43	6	49	5.60	–
Jamie Westacott	1	3	3	1	4	5.33	–
Chris Courage	1	3	2	1	3	4.00	–
Chris Johnson	5	16	8	2	10	2.50	–
Tony Dart	1	4	1	0	1	1.00	–
James Clement	1	3	0	0	0	0.00	–

KNOCK-OUT CUP

No	DATE	OPPONENTS	H/A	RESULT	BOYCE	MARSH	BUNYAN	TRESARRIEU	MORTON	PHILLIPS	JOHNSON	COURTNEY	OSTERGAARD	OTHERS
1	11/5	King's Lynn	H	W63-29	10 (5)	9+1 (4)	7+2 (4)	13 (5)	7+2 (4)	13+1 (5)	4+1 (3)	–	–	–
2	12/5	King's Lynn	A	L39-56*	15 (5)	R/R	10+1 (6)	3 (5)	6 (5)	4+1 (4)	1 (4)	0 (1)	–	–
3	6/7	Rye House	H	W59-36	15 (5)	14+2 (6)	6 (4)	–	R/R	6+3 (5)	–	–	10+4 (6)	8 (4)
4	31/7	Rye House	A	L42-52*	11+1 (5)	9+1 (6)	6 (5)	R/R	4+1 (5)	3 (4)	–	–	9 (5)	–
5	2/9	Workington	H	W56-38	9+1 (4)	7+1 (4)	13+2 (5)	9 (5)	7 (4)	4+1 (4)	–	–	7+2 (4)	–
6	18/9	Workington	A	W46½-43½	7½(5)	6+1 (5)	10 (4)	9 (4)	5+1 (4)	4+3 (4)	–	–	5+2 (4)	–
7	20/10	Hull	A	L39-56	11+1 (5)	6+2 (5)	2 (4)	10+1 (5)	6 (4)	1+1 (3)	–	–	3 (4)	–
8	26/10	Hull	H	W52-43	9+1 (5)	9+1 (4)	12+1 (5)	7+1 (4)	6+2 (4)	4+2 (4)	–	–	5+1 (4)	–

*Denotes aggregate victory

DETAILS OF OTHER RIDERS:

Match No. 3: Kristian Lund 8 (4).

TACTICAL SUBSTITUTE AND TACTICAL RIDES, AS INCLUDED IN THE SCORES GRID:

Match No. 2: Boyce 6 points (TR); Morton 2 points (TR); Bunyan 2 points (TS); Match No. 4: Boyce 4 points (TR); Ostergaard 4 points (TR); Match No. 7: Boyce 6 points (TR); Tresarrieu 4 points (TR); Marsh 0 points (TS).

YOUNG SHIELD

No	DATE	OPPONENTS	H/A	RESULT	BOYCE	OSTERGAARD	MORTON	BUNYAN	TRESARRIEU	PHILLIPS	MARSH
1	25/9	Stoke	A	L40-52	3 (2)	4 (4)	4+1 (4)	10 (5)	9 (5)	6+2 (5)	4+3 (5)
2	28/9	Stoke	H	W59-32*	13 (5)	4 (4)	13+2 (5)	7+1 (4)	0 (0)	10+2 (6)	12+1 (6)
3	5/10	Reading	H	W53-45	12 (5)	6+2 (4)	8 (4)	6 (4)	10+3 (5)	6+1 (4)	5+2 (4)
4	10/10	Reading	A	L42-51	11 (5)	4+1 (4)	5+1 (4)	4+1 (4)	8 (5)	6 (4)	4+3 (4)

*Denotes aggregate victory

TACTICAL RIDE, AS INCLUDED IN THE SCORES GRID:

Match No. 1: Bunyan 4 points (TR).

OTHER MEETINGS

6 April: Inter-League Challenge

Isle of Wight 48 (Ray Morton 14; Craig Boyce 9+2; Jason Bunyan 8+1; Glen Phillips 7; Krister Marsh 5+1; Sebastian Tresarrieu 4; Steve Braidford 1) Swindon 42.

20 April: Premier Trophy

Isle of Wight 24 (Sebastian Tresarrieu 5; Craig Boyce 4; Jason Bunyan 4; Krister Marsh 3+2; Tony Dart 3+2; Glen Phillips 3; Ray Morton 2) Newport 15 – meeting abandoned after heat six.

12 August: Inter-League Challenge

Isle of Wight 42 (Craig Boyce 12+1; Jason Bunyan 11; Krister Marsh 8+2; Manuel Hauzinger 7+3; Glen Phillips 2+1; Sebastian Tresarrieu 2; Jamie Courtney 0; Ray Morton R/R) Poole 50.

17 August: Premier League

Isle of Wight 25 (Jason Bunyan 6; Krister Marsh 5+1; Craig Boyce 4; Sebastian Tresarrieu 3–1; Ray Morton 3; Glen Phillips 2+1; Ulrich Ostergaard 2+1) Newport 11 – meeting abandoned after heat six.

KING'S LYNN MONEY CENTRE STARS

NOTE: The information below relates only to the main King's Lynn team. For details of the second side, please refer to the Conference League section.

ADDRESS: Norfolk Arena, Saddlebow Road, King's Lynn, Norfolk, PE34 3AG.

PROMOTERS: Keith 'Buster' Chapman & Laurence Rogers, with the former assuming full control at the end of May 2004.

TRACK LENGTH: 342 metres.

TRACK RECORD: 57.6 seconds – Nicki Pedersen (11/09/02).

FIRST MEETING: 23 May 1965.

YEARS OF OPERATION: 1965 Open; 1966-67 British League; 1968-74 British League Division One; 1975-90 British League; 1991-94 British League Division One; 1995 Premier League; 1996 Training; 1997-02 Elite League; 2003-04 Premier League.

CLUB HONOURS

KNOCK-OUT CUP WINNERS: 1977, 2000.

INTER-LEAGUE KNOCK-OUT CUP WINNERS: 1978, 1980.

RIDER ROSTER 2004

Adam ALLOTT; James BRUNDLE; Kevin DOOLAN; Trevor HARDING; Paul LEE; Tom P. MADSEN; Darren MALLETT; Shaun TACEY; Tomas TOPINKA.

OTHER APPEARANCES/GUESTS (official matches only):

Tommy ALLEN; Craig BRANNEY; Chris NEATH; John OLIVER; Jamie ROBERTSON; Darren ROLPH; Mark THOMPSON.

PREMIER LEAGUE

No	DATE	OPPONENTS	H/A	RESULT	TOPINKA	TACEY	DOOLAN	ALLOTT	MADSEN	BRUNDLE	LEE	HARDING	OTHERS
1	2/6	Reading	H	W49-47	–	8+1 (4)	8+1 (5)	8 (4)	6+2 (4)	8+1 (5)	–	–	11+1 (8)
2	9/6	Somerset	H	W61-33	14+1 (5)	7+2 (4)	8+2 (5)	9 (4)	12 (4)	–	9+3 (4)	–	2 (4)
3	16/6	Stoke	H	W67-27	13+2 (5)	9+1 (4)	7+3 (4)	12 (4)	11+1 (5)	–	10+2 (4)	5+2 (4)	–
4	17/6	Glasgow	A	L38-56	11 (5)	2+2 (4)	9 (4)	3+2 (4)	4 (4)	–	8 (5)	1 (4)	–
5	18/6	Edinburgh	A	L38-55	0 (4)	8 (4)	13 (5)	1+1 (1)	3 (4)	–	9+2 (7)	4+1 (5)	–
6	4/7	Newport	A	L44-50	12 (5)	2+1 (4)	7+1 (4)	3 (4)	3 (4)	–	9+2 (4)	8–1 (5)	–
7	7/7	Glasgow†	H	W41-28*	8 (3)	1 (3)	6+1 (3)	5+2 (3)	6+1 (3)	–	5+1 (4)	10+1 (4)	–
8	14/7	Newcastle	H	W66-26	11 (4)	11+3 (5)	8+2 (4)	13 (5)	9+1 (4)	–	–	9–1 (4)	5+2 (4)
9	17/7	Stoke	A	L38-55*	9+1 (5)	11+2 (5)	7 (4)	2 (4)	4 (3)	–	–	3 (5)	2 (4)
10	21/7	Berwick	H	W61-35	13+2 (5)	13+2 (5)	8+2 (4)	10+1 (4)	9 (4)	–	–	4–1 (4)	4+1 (4)
11	31/7	Hull	A	L33-62	11+1 (5)	6+1 (4)	6 (4)	1 (4)	7 (6)	–	–	2 (4)	0 (3)
12	4/8	Edinburgh	H	W63-32*	9+2 (4)	10+2 (4)	11+1 (5)	11+1 (5)	9 (4)	–	11+5 (7)	2+1 (1)	–
13	9/8	Exeter	A	L38-55	3 (4)	18 (5)	9+3 (5)	2 (4)	4 (4)	–	2 (5)	0 (3)	–
14	11/8	Workington	H	W52-42	15 (5)	9+3 (5)	4 (3)	10 (4)	7 (4)	–	5+1 (6)	2 (3)	–

PREMIER LEAGUE continued

No	DATE	OPPONENTS	H/A	RESULT	TOPINKA	TACEY	DOOLAN	ALLOTT	MADSEN	BRUNDLE	LEE	HARDING	OTHERS
15	14/8	Workington	A	L36-54	11+1 (6)	11+1 (6)	R/R	6 (5)	3 (4)	–	3+1 (5)	2 (4)	–
16	20/8	Rye House	A	L35-58	12+1 (6)	12 (6)	R/R	0 (4)	–	1+1 (4)	7+2 (6)	3 (4)	–
17	28/8	Hull	H	W50-42	9+1 (5)	4+1 (5)	R/R	17 (6)	–	9+1 (6)	8+1 (5)	3+1 (3)	–
18	30/8	Reading	A	L39-56	11 (6)	6 (5)	R/R	9 (6)	–	1 (4)	7+3 (5)	5 (4)	–
19	31/8	Isle of Wight	A	L29-66	11 (6)	7 (6)	R/R	4 (5)	–	1 (4)	0 (3)	6 (6)	–
20	1/9	Rye House	H	W57-38	12 (6)	11+2 (5)	R/R	17+1 (6)	–	7+2 (5)	8+3 (5)	2 (3)	–
21	2/9	Sheffield	A	L38-56	11 (6)	10 (6)	R/R	6+3 (5)	–	0 (3)	10+1 (7)	1 (3)	–
22	4/9	Sheffield	H	W56-36*	17+1 (6)	10+2 (5)	R/R	17+1 (6)	–	1 (4)	6+1 (5)	5 (4)	–
23	8/9	Newport	H	W62-33*	14 (5)	12+1 (6)	R/R	16+1 (6)	–	7+1 (5)	8+2 (4)	5+1 (4)	–
24	10/9	Isle of Wight	H	W57-39	15+1 (6)	10+1 (5)	R/R	11 (5)	–	8+1 (4)	8+2 (5)	5+2 (5)	–
25	12/9	Newcastle	A	L39-57	17 (6)	1 (4)	R/R	16 (6)	–	1 (5)	4 (5)	0 (4)	–
26	15/9	Exeter	H	W64-29*	15 (5)	17+1 (6)	R/R	11+1 (5)	–	13+5 (6)	3 (4)	5 (4)	–
27	17/9	Somerset	A	L41-49*	15 (6)	9 (5)	R/R	4+1 (4)	–	2 (4)	9+3 (7)	2+2 (4)	–
28	18/9	Berwick	A	L29-65	10 (5)	10 (6)	R/R	0 (5)	–	0 (4)	8+1 (7)	1 (5)	–

*Denotes aggregate victory

†Meeting abandoned after heat twelve, with the result permitted to stand.

DETAILS OF OTHER RIDERS:

Match No. 1: Chris Neath 9 (5); Mark Thompson 2+1 (3); Match No. 2: John Oliver 2 (4); Match No. 8: Tommy Allen 5+2 (4); Match No. 9: Jamie Robertson 2 (4); Match No. 10: Darren Rolph 4+1 (4); Match No. 11: Craig Branney 0 (3).

TACTICAL SUBSTITUTE AND TACTICAL RIDES, AS INCLUDED IN THE SCORES GRID:

Match No. 4: Doolan 4 points (TR); Topinka 4 points (TR); Match No. 5: Doolan 4 points (TR); Lee 2 points (TR); Match No. 6: Lee 4 points (TR); Doolan 4 points (TR); Match No. 9: Doolan 4 points (TR); Topinka 2 points (TR); Match No. 11: Topinka 6 points (TR); Tacey 2 points (TR); Madsen 2 points (TS); Match No. 13: Tacey 6 points (TR); Doolan 2 points (TR); Match No. 15: Tacey 2 points (TR); Allott 0 points (TR); Match No. 16: Tacey 4 points (TR); Topinka 2 points (TR); Match No. 18: Allott 6 points (TR); Topinka 4 points (TR); Match No. 19: Topinka 6 points (TR); Tacey 4 points (TR); Match No. 21: Tacey 6 points (TR); Topinka 2 points (TR); Match No. 25: Topinka 6 points (TR); Allott 6 points (TR); Match No. 28: Topinka 4 points (TR); Tacey 4 points (TR).

PREMIER LEAGUE AVERAGES

Rider	Mts	Rds	Pts	Bon	Tot	Avge	Max
Tomas Topinka	27	139	291	14	305	8.78	2 full; 4 paid
Kevin Doolan	14	59	102	16	118	8.00	-
Shaun Tacey	28	136	231	29	260	7.65	1 full; 3 paid
Adam Allott	28	128	218	15	233	7.28	1 full; 2 paid
Tom P. Madsen	15	61	96	5	101	6.62	1 full
Paul Lee	23	119	154	36	190	6.39	2 paid
Darren Rolph	1	4	4	1	5	5.00	–
James Brundle	14	63	59	12	71	4.51	1 paid
Trevor Harding	26	103	95	14	109	4.23	–
Mark Thompson	1	3	2	1	3	4.00	–
John Oliver	1	4	2	0	2	2.00	–
Craig Branney	1	3	0	0	0	0.00	–
Guests	3	13	16	2	18	5.54	–

KING'S LYNN: back row, left to right: Tom P. Madsen, Shaun Tacey, Kevin Doolan, Paul Lee, Trevor Harding, Tommy Allen, Buster Chapman (Team Manager), Adam Allott. Front, on bike: Tomas Topinka.

PREMIER TROPHY

No	DATE	OPPONENTS	H/A	RESULT	MADSEN	ALLOTT	TACEY	HARDING	TOPINKA	BRUNDLE	MALLETT	OLIVER	ROLPH
1	24/3	Somerset	H	L43-49	7 (5)	10 (5)	7 (4)	0 (3)	7 (4)	8+1 (6)	4+2 (3)	–	–
2	26/3	Somerset	A	L34-60	–	10 (5)	4+1 (4)	2 (4)	11 (5)	4+1 (5)	1 (3)	2 (4)	–
3	28/3	Newport	A	L42-52	5 (4)	4+1 (4)	10 (6)	5+3 (4)	12 (5)	4+1 (4)	2+1 (3)	–	–
4	31/3	Reading	H	W49-45	4 (3)	8+2 (4)	8+2 (5)	2 (3)	10+1 (5)	14 (6)	3+1 (4)	–	–
5	12/4	Exeter	A	L29-65	1 (1)	3+1 (4)	9 (5)	0 (4)	11 (5)	5+1 (6)	0 (5)	–	–
6	13/4	Isle of Wight	A	L28-65	R/R	1+1 (5)	8 (6)	1 (4)	13 (6)	5 (5)	0 (4)	–	–
7	14/4	Exeter	H	W51-40	R/R	9+2 (5)	10+2 (6)	4+1 (4)	15 (6)	9 (5)	4+3 (4)	–	–
8	19/4	Reading	A	L38-58	R/R	6 (5)	2 (3)	9 (7)	17 (6)	1+1 (4)	3+1 (5)	–	–
9	24/4	Rye House	A	L37-58	5 (4)	3 (4)	8+1 (6)	0 (3)	15 (5)	6+1 (5)	0 (3)	–	–
10	25/4	Isle of Wight	H	W52-43	5+1 (3)	7+2 (5)	6+1 (4)	6+1 (4)	13 (5)	10 (4)	5+2 (5)	–	–
11	2/5	Rye House	H	D45-45	10 (4)	4+1 (4)	8 (5)	4+1 (4)	13+1 (5)	3 (4)	3 (4)	–	–
12	26/5	Newport	H	W50-45	12 (5)	9 (4)	6+1 (4)	6+1 (4)	9 (5)	6+2 (4)	–	–	2+1 (4)

TACTICAL SUBSTITUTE AND TACTICAL RIDES, AS INCLUDED IN THE SCORES GRID:

Match No. 2: Topinka 4 points (TR); Allott 4 points (TR); Match No. 3: Topinka 4 points (TR); Tacey 4 points (TS); Match No. 5: Topinka 4 points (TR); Tacey 4 points (TR); Match No. 6: Topinka 4 points (TR); Tacey 2 points (TR); Match No. 8: Topinka 6 points (TR); Harding 4 points (TS); Allott 2 points (TR); Match No. 9: Topinka 6 points (TR); Allott 2 points (TR); Tacey 2 points (TS).

PREMIER TROPHY AVERAGES

Rider	Mts	Rds	Pts	Bon	Tot	Avge	Max
Tomas Topinka	12	62	132	2	134	8.65	–
Tom P. Madsen	8	29	49	1	50	6.90	–
Shaun Tacey	12	58	80	8	88	6.07	–
Adam Allott	12	54	70	10	80	5.93	–
James Brundle	12	58	75	8	83	5.72	–
Trevor Harding	12	48	37	7	44	3.67	–
Darren Mallett	11	43	25	10	35	3.26	–
Darren Rolph	1	4	2	1	3	3.00	–
John Oliver	1	4	2	0	2	2.00	–

KNOCK-OUT CUP

No	DATE	OPPONENTS	H/A	RESULT	TOPINKA	HARDING	TACEY	ALLOTT	MADSEN	BRUNDLE	OLIVER	ROLPH
1	11/5	Isle of Wight	A	L29-63	9 (5)	2 (4)	2+1 (4)	6 (5)	5+1 (4)	5 (5)	0 (3)	–
2	12/5	Isle of Wight	H	W56-39	12 (5)	5+2 (4)	10+1 (5)	8+1 (4)	10+1 (4)	7+2 (4)	–	4+1 (4)

TACTICAL RIDES, AS INCLUDED IN THE SCORES GRID:

Match No. 1: Topinka 2 points (TR); Allott 2 points (TR).

YOUNG SHIELD

No	DATE	OPPONENTS	H/A	RESULT	TOPINKA	BRUNDLE	TACEY	ALLOTT	DOOLAN	HARDING	LEE
1	29/9	Workington	H	W52-41	15 (5)	0 (3)	9+1 (4)	4 (4)	7+1 (4)	3 (3)	14+2 (7)
2	9/10	Workington	A	L41-55	12 (5)	1 (3)	13 (5)	4+1 (4)	3 (4)	1 (4)	7+2 (5)

TACTICAL SUBSTITUTE AND TACTICAL RIDES, AS INCLUDED IN THE SCORES GRID:

Match No. 2: Topinka 6 points (TR); Tacey 4 points (TR); Lee 2 points (TS).

OTHER MEETINGS

13 March: A10 Trophy (first leg)

Rye House 55 King's Lynn 40 (Tom P. Madsen 12+1; Tomas Topinka 10; Shaun Tacey 8; Adam Allott 5+1; Darren Mallett 2; Trevor Harding 2; James Brundle 1+1).

17 March: A10 Trophy (second leg)

King's Lynn 42 (Adam Allott 13+2; Tomas Topinka 12; Tom P. Madsen 5+2 Shaun Tacey 5; James Brundle 4; Trevor Harding 2+1; Darren Mallett 1+1) Rye House 51 – Rye House won 106-82 on aggregate.

30 June: Premier League

King's Lynn 35 (Paul Lee 7+2; Shaun Tacey 6+2; Tom P. Madsen 6; Tomas Topinka 5; Trevor Harding 4+2; Kevin Doolan 4+1; Adam Allott 3) Exeter 22 – meeting abandoned after heat nine.

2 October: Young Shield quarter-final (second leg)

Workington 20 King's Lynn 10 (Kevin Doolan 4; Tomas Topinka 3; Paul Lee 1+1; Shaun Tacey 1; James Brundle 1; Adam Allott 0; Trevor Harding 0) – meeting abandoned after heat five.

INDIVIDUAL MEETINGS

21 March: Tomas Topinka Testimonial

QUALIFYING SCORES: Nicki Pedersen 11; Billy Janniro 9; Mark Loram 8; Hans N. Andersen 8; Adam Allott 7; Chris Louis 7; Travis McGowan 7; Tom P. Madsen 7; Stuart Robson 6; Trevor Harding 5; Chris Harris 5; Tomas Topinka 5; James Brundle 5; Bohumil Brhel 3; Jan Jaros 2; Toni Svab 1. FIRST SEMI-FINAL: 1st Loram; 2nd Pedersen; 3rd McGowan; 4th Allott. SECOND SEMI-FINAL: 1st Andersen; 2nd Louis; 3rd Janniro; 4th Madsen. CONSOLATION FINAL: 1st Janniro; 2nd McGowan; 3rd Allott; 4th Madsen. GRAND FINAL: 1st Loram; 2nd Pedersen; 3rd Andersen; 4th Louis.

19 May: Championship of Great Britain Semi-Final

1st Chris Neath (after run-off) 13; 2nd Andrew Moore 13; 3rd Andre Compton 12; Seemond Stephens 11; Glenn Cunningham 10; Michael Coles 9; Adam Allott 9; Danny Bird 8; Phil Morris 7; Shaun Tacey 7; Steve Masters 7; Ricky Ashworth 5; Ray Morton 3; James Brundle (Res) 3; David Meldrum 1; Kevin Little 1; Matt Read 0; Olly Allen 0.

28 July: Teng Tools Premier League Champions Chase

ELIMINATED IN ROUND ONE: Brent Werner; Cameron Woodward; Jan Staechmann; Ricky Ashworth; Claus Kristensen; Glenn Cunningham; Richard Hall; Pavel Ondrasik. ELIMINATED IN ROUND TWO: Josef Franc; Seemond Stephens; Adam Allott; Jason Bunyan; Simon Stead; Kevin Doolan; Garry Stead; Lubos Tomicek; Carl Stonehewer; Joel Parsons; Magnus Karlsson; Trent Leverington. ELIMINATED IN ROUND THREE: Chris Neath; Craig Boyce; Tom P. Madsen; Rory Schlein.

FIRST SEMI-FINAL: 1st Craig Watson; 2nd John Jorgensen; 3rd Andrew Moore; 4th Tomas Topinka.
SECOND SEMI-FINAL: 1st Matej Zagar; 2nd Jason Lyons; 3rd Shane Parker; 4th Andrew Appleton.
FINAL: 1st Watson; 2nd Jorgensen; 3rd Zagar; 4th Lyons.

21 October: Poultec Pride of the East

1st Davey Watt 14; 2nd Tomas Topinka (after run-off) 13; 3rd Craig Boyce 13; Adam Shields 10; Jason Lyons 10; Brent Werner 9; Shaun Tacey 9; Adam Allott 8; Craig Watson 8; Adam Skornicki 7; Kevin Doolan 5; Chris Neath 5; Paul Lee 4; James Brundle 2; Richard Hall 2; Ritchie Hawkins 1; Troy Batchelor (Res) 0.

NEWCASTLE TAP & SPILE NORTH SHIELDS DIAMONDS

NOTE: The information below relates only to the main Newcastle team. For details of the second side, please refer to the Conference League section.

ADDRESS: Brough Park Stadium, Fossway, Byker, Newcastle-upon-Tyne, Tyne and Wear, NE6 2XJ.
PROMOTERS: George English, Darryl Illingworth & Barry Wallace.
TRACK LENGTH: 300 metres.
TRACK RECORD: 62.1 seconds – Kenneth Bjerre (20/07/03).
FIRST MEETING: 17 May 1929.
YEARS OF OPERATION: 1929 English Dirt-track League; 1930 Open; 1938-39 National League Division Two; 1945 Open; 1946 Northern League; 1947-51 National League Division Two; 1961-64 Provincial League; 1965-67 British League; 1968-70 British League Division One; 1975-83 National League; 1984 British League; 1986-87 National League; 1989-90 National League; 1991-94 British League Division Two; 1997-04 Premier League.

NOTE: Although Newcastle have predominantly used 'Diamonds' as a nickname, there were three seasons when they ran with an alternative, namely 'Brough' in 1946, 'Magpies' in 1949, and 'Federation Specials' in 1986.

CLUB HONOURS

LEAGUE CHAMPIONS: 1964, 1976, 1982, 1983, 2001.
PAIRS CHAMPIONS: 1975.
FOUR-TEAM CHAMPIONS: 1976, 1982, 1983.
KNOCK-OUT CUP WINNERS: 1976, 1982.
SUPERNATIONAL WINNERS: 1982, 1983.
GOLD CUP WINNERS: 1991, 1992.

RIDER ROSTER 2004

Lee DICKEN; Richard JUUL; William LAWSON; Kevin LITTLE; Kristian LUND; Jason LYONS; Jamie ROBERTSON; Lee SMETHILLS; Scott SMITH; Lubos TOMICEK.

OTHER APPEARANCES/GUESTS (official matches only):

Jon ARMSTRONG; Carl DOWNS; Richard HALL; Danny HUGHES; Mario JIROUT; David MELDRUM; Jesper OLSEN; Michael PICKERING; George STANCL; Matthew WETHERS; Ben WILSON; Cameron WOODWARD.

PREMIER LEAGUE

No	DATE	OPPONENTS	H/A	RESULT	LITTLE	SMETHILLS	SMITH	JUUL	LUND	DICKEN	ROBERTSON	LAWSON	TOMICEK	LYONS	MELDRUM	OTHERS
1	24/5	Exeter	A	L32-64	1 (2)	11 (5)	2 (4)	3 (4)	3 (4)	9+1 (6)	3+1 (5)	–	–	–	–	–
2	25/5	Isle of Wight	A	L38-53	6 (4)	6+1 (5)	4 (4)	6+2 (4)	9 (5)	4+2 (4)	3 (4)	–	–	–	–	–
3	6/6	Reading	H	L47-48	15+1 (6)	–	6 (4)	11+1 (6)	R/R	4+1 (4)	6+2 (5)	5 (5)	–	–	–	–
4	11/6	Newport	A	L44-46	7 (5)	–	8+2 (5)	7+1 (4)	8 (5)	8+1 (4)	4+1 (4)	2 (3)	–	–	–	–
5	14/6	Newport†	H	W49-32*	9+1 (4)	–	4 (3)	8+1 (4)	9+1 (4)	–	7+2 (4)	7+1 (3)	5+2 (4)	–	–	–
6	17/6	Sheffield	A	L26-67	1 (4)	–	8 (7)	9+1 (6)	2+1 (4)	–	3 (5)	R/R	3 (4)	–	–	–
7	25/6	Edinburgh	A	L27-65	5 (5)	–	1 (4)	3 (4)	–	–	5+1 (4)	1 (4)	4 (4)	8 (5)	–	–
8	27/6	Edinburgh	H	W49-43	6+1 (5)	–	7+1 (4)	7 (4)	–	–	4+3 (4)	4+1 (4)	6+1 (4)	15 (5)	–	–
9	28/6	Reading	A	L38-57	9 (5)	–	3+1 (4)	6 (4)	–	–	2+2 (4)	4 (4)	2+2 (4)	12 (5)	–	–
10	5/7	Stoke	H	W50-43	9 (5)	–	4 (4)	10 (6)	–	–	4+2 (4)	5+2 (5)	R/R	18 (6)	–	–
11	11/7	Hull	H	L34-60	3 (4)	–	4+1 (5)	4+1 (4)	–	–	4 (4)	3 (4)	1 (4)	15 (5)	–	–
12	14/7	King's Lynn	A	L26-66	R/R	–	1 (4)	6 (5)	–	–	2 (5)	2+1 (5)	4 (6)	11 (5)	–	–
13	18/7	Somerset	H	W47-43	–	–	5+1 (5)	9+2 (6)	–	–	6+1 (5)	8+1 (5)	R/R	18 (6)	1 (3)	–
14	25/7	Isle of Wight	H	L46-49	–	–	4 (4)	9 (5)	–	–	3+1 (4)	6+1 (5)	5 (4)	18 (5)	1 (3)	–
15	31/7	Workington	A	L25-69	–	–	1 (5)	7 (5)	–	–	3 (4)	1 (3)	1 (4)	11 (5)	1 (4)	–
16	1/8	Berwick	H	L43-51	–	–	1 (3)	11 (5)	–	–	7+1 (4)	5+1 (6)	1 (3)	18 (6)	0 (3)	–
17	8/8	Rye House	H	L45-48	8 (4)	–	–	8+3 (5)	–	4+2 (4)	6+1 (4)	7 (5)	1 (3)	11 (5)	–	–
18	13/8	Somerset	A	L43-51	6 (4)	–	–	13+1 (5)	–	2 (4)	3+1 (6)	1+1 (3)	3 (3)	15 (5)	–	–
19	14/8	Rye House	A	L36-56	9 (5)	–	–	2 (4)	–	4+1 (4)	2+1 (4)	4 (4)	1+1 (4)	14 (5)	–	–
20	15/8	Sheffield	H	W52-44	3+1 (3)	–	–	9+1 (5)	–	5+2 (4)	7 (4)	6+2 (5)	7 (4)	15 (5)	–	–
21	22/8	Workington	H	L43-51	10+2 (5)	–	–	6+2 (4)	–	3+1 (4)	2+1 (5)	–	–	15 (5)	–	7 (7)
22	25/8	Hull	A	L31-60	3 (4)	–	–	2 (4)	–	5 (4)	1+1 (4)	3+1 (5)	–	16 (5)	–	1 (4)
23	29/8	Glasgow	A	L35-59	8 (5)	–	–	4+1 (4)	–	2+1 (4)	3+1 (4)	1+1 (4)	–	14 (5)	–	3 (4)
24	30/8	Glasgow	H	W49-47	10 (5)	–	–	5+2 (4)	–	5+2 (4)	9+4 (5)	4 (4)	–	10 (5)	–	6+1 (3)
25	5/9	Exeter	H	W49-45	8 (4)	–	–	9+3 (6)	–	4 (2)	7+2 (7)	7 (6)	–	14+1 (5)	–	R/R
26	12/9	King's Lynn	H	W57-39	–	–	–	10+3 (6)	–	–	11 (5)	4 (4)	–	18 (6)	–	14+4 (9)
27	15/9	Berwick	A	L35-59	–	–	–	7 (6)	–	–	4 (5)	0 (4)	–	–	–	24 (15)
28	18/9	Stoke	A	L37-58	–	–	–	10 (6)	–	–	2+1 (5)	2 (3)	–	17 (5)	–	6+2 (11)

*Denotes bonus-point victory

†Meeting abandoned after heat thirteen, with the result permitted to stand.

NEWCASTLE: back row, left to right: Jamie Robertson, Richard Juul, Lubos Tomicek. Front row: Scott Smith, Jason Lyons, William Lawson.

DETAILS OF OTHER RIDERS:

Match No. 21: Jesper Olsen 6 (4); Carl Downs 1 (3). Match No. 22: Jesper Olsen 1 (4); Match No. 23: Jesper Olsen 3 (4); Match No. 24: Jesper Olsen 6+1 (3); Match No. 25: Jesper Olsen R/R; Match No. 26: Matthew Wethers 9+1 (5); Cameron Woodward 5+3 (4); Jesper Olsen R/R; Match No. 27: George Stancl 18 (6); Richard Hall 3 (4); Ben Wilson 3 (5); Jesper Olsen R/R; Match No. 28: Cameron Woodward 5+1 (6); Jon Armstrong 1+1 (5); Jesper Olsen R/R.

TACTICAL SUBSTITUTE AND TACTICAL RIDES, AS INCLUDED IN THE SCORES GRID:

Match No. 1: Smethills 6 points (TR); Dicken 6 points (TR); Match No. 2: Juul 2 points (TR); Match No. 3: Little 6 points (TR); Juul 6 points (TR); Match No. 6: Juul 4 points (TR); Tomicek 2 points (TR); Match No. 7: Little 4 points (TR); Lyons 0 points (TR); Match No. 9: Lyons 6 points (TR); Little 4 points (TR); Match No. 11: Lyons 6 points (TR); Robertson 2 points (TR); Match No. 12: Lyons 2 points (TR); Juul 2 points (TR); Match No. 14: Lyons 6 points (TR); Juul 4 points (TR); Match No. 15: Lyons 6 points (TR); Juul 2 points (TR); Match No. 16: Lyons 4 points (TS); Juul 4 points (TR); Match No. 18: Juul 4 points (TR); Lyons 4 points (TR); Match No. 19: Little 4 points (TR); Lyons 2 points (TR); Match No. 21: Lyons 6 points (TR); Juul 2 points (TR); Match No. 22: Lyons 4 points (TR); Match No. 23: Lyons 4 points (TR); Little 4 points (TR); Match No. 27: Stancl 6 points (TR); Juul 2 points (TR); Match No. 28: Lyons 6 points (TR); Juul 4 points (TR).

PREMIER LEAGUE AVERAGES

Rider	Mts	Rds	Pts	Bon	Tot	Avge	Max
Jason Lyons	21	109	275	1	276	10.13	6 full; 1 paid
Richard Juul	28	135	183	25	208	6.16	–
Kristian Lund	5	22	31	2	33	6.00	–
Lee Smethills	2	10	14	1	15	6.00	–
Kevin Little	20	88	125	6	131	5.95	–
Lee Dicken	13	52	56	14	70	5.38	–
Jamie Robertson	28	127	122	30	152	4.79	–
Jesper Olsen	4	15	16	1	17	4.53	–
William Lawson	24	103	92	13	105	4.08	–
Scott Smith	16	69	63	6	69	4.00	–
Lubos Tomicek	14	55	43	6	49	3.56	–
Jon Armstrong	1	5	1	1	2	1.60	–
Carl Downs	1	3	1	0	1	1.33	–
David Meldrum	4	13	3	0	3	0.92	–
Guests	6	30	40	5	45	6.00	–

PREMIER TROPHY

No	DATE	OPPONENTS	H/A	RESULT	JIROUT	JUUL	HUGHES	SMETHILLS	LITTLE	LAWSON	ROBERTSON	SMITH	LUND	DICKEN	OTHERS
1	21/3	Berwick	H	L40-56	0 (4)	15 (6)	0 (3)	10 (4)	9+1 (5)	4+1 (4)	2+1 (4)	–	–	–	–
2	25/3	Sheffield	A	L30-65	2+2 (3)	7 (5)	1 (3)	12 (5)	2 (4)	3+1 (4)	3 (6)	–	–	–	–
3	31/3	Hull	A	L35-58	7 (4)	10 (5)	0 (3)	6 (4)	5+1 (5)	3+1 (4)	4+2 (5)	–	–	–	–
4	3/4	Berwick	A	L27-66	3 (3)	8+1 (5)	–	2 (4)	5 (4)	2 (4)	–	5 (5)	–	–	2+2 (5)
5	4/4	Sheffield	H	L42-51	3+3 (4)	10 (5)	–	12 (4)	7 (5)	4+2 (4)	5 (4)	1+1 (4)	–	–	–
6	11/4	Glasgow	A	L35-60	–	9 (6)	–	3+1 (5)	5 (5)	4 (5)	4+3 (5)	10 (6)	R/R	–	–
7	12/4	Glasgow	H	L38-56	–	10 (6)	–	4 (5)	14 (6)	2+1 (3)	6+2 (6)	2 (4)	R/R	–	–

PREMIER TROPHY continued

No	DATE	OPPONENTS	H/A	RESULT	JIROUT	JUUL	HUGHES	SMETHILLS	LITTLE	LAWSON	ROBERTSON	SMITH	LUND	DICKEN	OTHERS
8	25/4	Hull	H	L37-55	–	6 (5)	–	6+1 (4)	13 (5)	1+1 (4)	2 (3)	3 (4)	6 (5)	–	–
9	30/4	Edinburgh	A	L29-63	–	2 (4)	0 (3)	2 (4)	7+1 (5)	–	–	4 (4)	5 (5)	9+1 (5)	–
10	2/5	Workington	H	W49-47	–	6 (4)	–	6 (4)	9+1 (5)	–	5+2 (4)	4 (4)	11+1 (5)	8+1 (4)	–
11	9/5	Stoke	H	L40-51	–	8 (5)	–	3+2 (4)	10 (4)	–	1 (1)	1+1 (4)	10 (5)	7+1 (7)	–
12	21/5	Workington	A	L33-58	–	4+1 (4)	–	2+1 (4)	8 (5)	–	3 (4)	5 (4)	10 (5)	1+1 (4)	–
13	31/5	Edinburgh	H	L39-51	–	7+1 (5)	–	6 (4)	6+1 (5)	–	4+3 (4)	5+1 (4)	6+2 (4)	5+1 (4)	–
14	13/6	Stoke	A	L31-61	–	8 (5)	–	–	3 (4)	4+2 (4)	6+1 (5)	1+1 (4)	4 (4)	5 (4)	–

DETAILS OF OTHER RIDER:

Match No. 4: Michael Pickering 2+2 (5).

TACTICAL SUBSTITUTE AND TACTICAL RIDES, AS INCLUDED IN THE SCORES GRID:

Match No. 1: Little 4 points (TR); Smethills 4 points (TR); Juul 4 points (TS); Match No. 2: Smethills 6 points (TR); Juul 2 points (TR); Lawson 2 points (TS); Match No. 3: Juul 4 points (TR); Jirout 4 points (TR); Match No. 4: Juul 4 points (TR); Smith 2 points (TR); Match No. 5: Smethills 6 points (TR); Match No. 6: Smith 6 points (TR); Juul 4 points (TR); Match No. 7: Little 6 points (TR); Juul 2 points (TR); Match No. 8: Little 4 points (TR); Juul 0 points (TS); Lawson 0 points (TR); Match No. 9: Little 4 points (TR); Juul 0 points (TR); Match No. 11: Little 2 points (TR); Match No. 12: Lund 2 points (TR); Little 0 points (TR); Match No. 14: Juul 4 points (TR).

PREMIER TROPHY AVERAGES

Rider	Mts	Rds	Pts	Bon	Tot	Avge	Max
Kristian Lund	7	33	51	3	54	6.55	–
Kevin Little	14	67	93	5	98	5.85	–
Richard Juul	14	70	98	3	101	5.77	–
Lee Dicken	6	28	35	5	40	5.71	–
Lee Smethills	13	55	66	5	71	5.16	–
Jamie Robertson	12	51	45	14	59	4.63	–
Mario Jirout	5	18	13	5	18	4.00	–
William Lawson	9	36	26	9	35	3.89	–
Scott Smith	11	47	37	4	41	3.49	–
Michael Pickering	1	5	2	2	4	3.20	–
Danny Hughes	4	12	1	0	1	0.33	–

KNOCK-OUT CUP

No	DATE	OPPONENTS	H/A	RESULT	LITTLE	SMETHILLS	SMITH	JUUL	LUND	DICKEN	ROBERTSON
1	15/5	Rye House	A	L39-55	6 (4)	0 (3)	2 (4)	13+1 (5)	8 (5)	5+1 (5)	5 (4)
2	16/5	Rye House	H	L41-49	8+3 (5)	7+1 (4)	3+3 (4)	11 (5)	3 (4)	3+1 (4)	6 (4)

TACTICAL RIDES, AS INCLUDED IN THE SCORES GRID:

Match No. 1: Juul 6 points (TR); Lund 2 points (TR); Match No. 2: Little 2 points (TR).

OTHER MEETINGS

6 March: Carlos Villar Benefit

Edinburgh/Workington 32, Berwick 28, Glasgow 19, Newcastle 17 (Gary Havelock 5; Jamie Robertson 5; Josef Franc 3; Adrian Rymel 3; John Branney 1) – staged at Berwick.

14 March: Inter-League Challenge

Newcastle 41 (Jamie Robertson 10; Kevin Little 8+1; Lee Smethills 7+1; Richard Juul 6+2; Carl Stonehewer 6; William Lawson 4+2; Scott Smith R/R) Poole 49.

28 March: Richard Juul Testimonial

Newcastle Select 44 (Kenneth Bjerre 9; Bjarne Pedersen 9; Stuart Robson 8; Richard Juul 7; Rory Schlein 6+3; Kevin Little 3+1; Lee Smethills 2+1) Wolverhampton 45. Testimonial Trophy and Kenny Carter Remembrance Cup: FIRST SEMI-FINAL: 1st Bjarne Pedersen; 2nd Richard Juul; 3rd Kenneth Bjerre; 4th Stuart Robson. SECOND SEMI-FINAL: 1st Mikael Max; 2nd Sam Ermolenko; 3rd David Howe; 4th Adam Skornicki. FINAL: 1st Max; 2nd Pedersen; 3rd Juul; 4th Ermolenko.

INDIVIDUAL MEETING

26 September: George English Memorial Trophy

QUALIFYING SCORES: Jason Lyons 12; George Stancl 10; Jesper Olsen 8; Jamie Robertson 7; Richard Juul 5; Niklas Fridell 3; Josh Larsen 2; Andreas Lekander 1. FINAL: 1st Lyons; 2nd Stancl; 3rd Olsen; 4th Robertson.

NEWPORT WASPS

NOTE: The information below relates only to the main Newport team. For details of the second side, please refer to the Conference League section.

ADDRESS: Hayley Stadium, Plover Close, Longditch Road, Queensway Meadows, Newport, South Wales, NS19 4SU.

PROMOTER: Tim Stone.

TRACK LENGTH: 285 metres.

TRACK RECORD: 58.38 seconds – Craig Watson (03/08/03).

FIRST MEETING: 4 May 1997.

YEARS OF OPERATION: 1997-04 Premier League.

PREVIOUS VENUE: Somerton Park, Newport, South Wales.

YEARS OF OPERATION: 1964 Provincial League; 1965-67 British League; 1968-74 British League Division One; 1975-76 British League; 1977 National League.

NOTE: Newport did not use a nickname from 1973-76 inclusive, and in 1977, they were known as 'Dragons'.

CLUB HONOURS

PREMIER NATIONAL TROPHY WINNERS: 1999.

RIDER ROSTER 2004

Tony ATKIN; Barrie EVANS; Mads KORNELIUSSEN; Kristian LUND; Karl MASON; Pavel ONDRASIK; Craig WATSON; Carl WILKINSON.

OTHER APPEARANCES/GUESTS (official matches only):

Craig BRANNEY; Tom BROWN; Paul CLEWS; Neil COLLINS; Chris COURAGE; Karlis EZERGAILIS; Ritchie HAWKINS; Trent LEVERINGTON; Kauko NIEMINEN; John OLIVER; Jeremy PESTELL; Michael PICKERING; Luke PRIEST; Seemond STEPHENS.

PREMIER LEAGUE

No	DATE	OPPONENTS	H/A	RESULT	KORNELIUSSEN	WILKINSON	ONDRASIK	ATKIN	WATSON	PRIEST	MASON	EVANS	LUND	OTHERS
1	8/5	Workington	A	L28-65	11 (6)	4+1 (5)	R/R	6+1 (6)	6 (4)	1 (4)	0 (5)	–	–	–
2	9/5	Rye House	H	L42-47	9 (6)	8+1 (5)	R/R	0 (1)	15 (5)	5+2 (7)	5+1 (6)	–	–	–
3	30/5	Hull	H	L38-58	12+1 (5)	0 (5)	10 (5)	R/R	–	2+1 (6)	1 (4)	–	–	13 (5)
4	6/6	Stoke	H	L41-54	R/R	0 (2)	12 (6)	–	15+1 (5)	–	1 (4)	1 (6)	–	12+1 (5)
5	9/6	Hull	A	L35-61	10 (6)	–	–	R/R	16 (5)	–	2 (6)	1 (5)	–	6 (9)
6	11/6	Newcastle	H	W46-44	10 (5)	–	8+2 (5)	R/R	15 (5)	–	0 (4)	7+1 (6)	–	6 (5)
7	14/6	Newcastle†	A	L32-49	8+1 (4)	–	0 (4)	R/R	15 (4)	–	2 (4)	1 (5)	–	6 (5)
8	27/6	Exeter	H	W46-44	11 (5)	–	12+1 (5)	R/R	15 (5)	–	3+2 (5)	2 (5)	3 (5)	–
9	4/7	King's Lynn	H	W50-44	10 (5)	3 (5)	R/R	–	16 (6)	–	0 (3)	–	8+3 (5)	13+2 (6)
10	11/7	Workington	H	L44-46	6+1 (4)	7+1 (7)	5+2 (4)	R/R	13 (5)	–	–	3 (4)	10+2 (6)	–
11	15/7	Glasgow	A	L40-54	8 (5)	4+1 (6)	3+1 (4)	R/R	15 (5)	–	–	1+1 (4)	9+1 (6)	–
12	16/7	Edinburgh	A	L41-55	13 (5)	5+1 (5)	1 (3)	R/R	10 (5)	–	–	3+2 (6)	9+1 (6)	–
13	17/7	Berwick	A	L40-54	12 (6)	3+1 (5)	5+1 (4)	R/R	15 (5)	–	–	3 (5)	2+1 (5)	–
14	18/7	Edinburgh	H	W50-43	11+2 (6)	10+2 (6)	1 (3)	R/R	14 (5)	–	–	2+1 (5)	12+1 (5)	–
15	26/7	Reading	A	L42-48	10 (5)	6+1 (6)	6 (5)	R/R	10 (5)	–	–	3+2 (4)	7+2 (5)	–
16	1/8	Isle of Wight	H	D45-45	9+1 (5)	9+2 (7)	3+1 (4)	R/R	15 (5)	–	–	1 (4)	8 (5)	–
17	12/8	Sheffield	A	L26-65	9 (5)	4 (7)	4 (5)	R/R	–	–	–	0 (3)	5+1 (5)	4+1 (4)
18	16/8	Exeter	A	L27-65	12 (6)	2 (5)	6 (5)	–	R/R	–	3+1 (5)	–	2 (5)	2 (4)
19	22/8	Somerset	H	D45-45	11+1 (5)	5+1 (5)	2+2 (4)	5 (4)	10 (5)	–	4 (3)	–	8 (4)	–
20	26/8	Isle of Wight	A	L29-63	4 (4)	1+1 (4)	1 (4)	5 (4)	8 (5)	–	3+1 (4)	–	7 (5)	–
21	29/8	Sheffield	H	L43-46	7+1 (5)	4+2 (4)	4 (4)	4 (4)	12 (5)	–	3 (4)	–	9+1 (4)	–
22	5/9	Glasgow	H	W53-39	8+2 (5)	10+3 (5)	6 (4)	5+2 (4)	15 (5)	–	2+1 (3)	–	7+2 (4)	–
23	8/9	King's Lynn	A	L33-62	8 (5)	6 (5)	–	1 (4)	15 (5)	–	0 (4)	–	3 (4)	0 (3)
24	10/9	Somerset	A	L34-59	R/R	7+1 (6)	12+1 (5)	4 (6)	6 (5)	–	1 (4)	–	4+1 (5)	–
25	12/9	Reading	H	W50-43*	10+2 (5)	7+1 (4)	4 (4)	6+2 (4)	13 (5)	–	3+1 (4)	–	7 (4)	–
26	12/9	Berwick	H	W51-44	14+1 (6)	8+1 (4)	7 (5)	R/R	15 (5)	–	0 (5)	–	7+2 (5)	–
27	17/9	Stoke	A	L37-57	4 (4)	2+1 (5)	R/R	3+1 (4)	15 (5)	–	2 (5)	–	11 (6)	–
28	18/9	Rye House	A	L39-51	5 (4)	6+1 (7)	R/R	7+1 (4)	12 (5)	–	2+1 (4)	–	7+2 (6)	–

*Denotes bonus-point victory

†Meeting abandoned after heat thirteen, with the result permitted to stand.

NEWPORT: back row, left to right: Tony Atkin, Carl Wilkinson, Craig Watson, Pavel Ondrasik. Front row: Kristian Lund, Karl Mason, Mads Korneliussen.

DETAILS OF OTHER RIDERS:

Match No. 3: Seemond Stephens 13 (5); Match No. 4: Neil Collins 12+1 (5); Match No. 5: Paul Clews 6 (5); Michael Pickering 0 (4); Match No. 6: Ritchie Hawkins 6 (5); Match No. 7: Trent Leverington 6 (5); Match No. 9: Neil Collins 13+2 (6); Match No. 17: Neil Collins 4+1 (4); Match No. 18: Karlis Ezergailis 2 (4); Match No. 23: Jeremy Pestell 0 (3).

TACTICAL RIDES, AS INCLUDED IN THE SCORES GRID:

Match No. 1: Korneliussen 4 points (TR); Watson 2 points (TR); Match No. 3: Korneliussen 6 points (TR); Stephens 6 points (TR); Match No. 4: Watson 6 points (TR); Collins 4 points (TR): Match No. 5: Watson 6 points (TR); Korneliussen 6 points (TR); Match No. 7: Watson 6 points (TR); Match No. 11: Watson 6 points (TR); Korneliussen 2 points (TR); Match No. 12: Lund 6 points (TR); Korneliussen 6 points (TR); Match No. 13: Watson 6 points (TR); Korneliussen 4 points (TR); Match No. 17: Korneliussen 2 points (TR); Collins 0 points (TR); Match No. 18: Korneliussen 2 points (TR); Ondrasik 2 points (TR); Match No. 20: Atkin 2 points (TR); Korneliussen 2 points (TR); Match No. 23: Watson 6 points (TR); Korneliussen 4 points (TR); Match No. 24: Ondrasik 6 points (TR); Atkin 0 points (TR); Match No. 27: Lund 4 points (TR); Watson 4 points (TR); Match No. 28: Atkin 2 points (TR).

PREMIER LEAGUE AVERAGES

Rider	Mts	Rds	Pts	Bon	Tot	Avge	Max
Craig Watson	25	124	305	1	306	9.87	7 full
Mads Korneliussen	26	132	223	13	236	7.15	–
Kristian Lund	21	105	140	20	160	6.10	–
Pavel Ondrasik	21	92	108	11	119	5.17	–
Carl Wilkinson	24	125	121	23	144	4.61	–
Tony Atkin	11	45	44	7	51	4.53	–
Luke Priest	3	17	8	3	11	2.59	–
Barrie Evans	13	62	28	7	35	2.26	–
Karl Mason	20	86	37	8	45	2.09	–
Karlis Ezergailis	1	4	2	0	2	2.00	–
Jeremy Pestell	1	3	0	0	0	0.00	–
Michael Pickering	1	4	0	0	0	0.00	–
Guests	7	35	55	4	59	6.74	–

PREMIER TROPHY

No	DATE	OPPONENTS	H/A	RESULT	KORNELIUSSEN	WILKINSON	ATKIN	KUJAWA	WATSON	PRIEST	MASON	ONDRASIK	COURAGE	OTHERS
1	21/3	Exeter	H	L43-50	5+2 (5)	7 (5)	13 (7)	R/R	16 (5)	2 (4)	0 (4)	–	–	–
2	22/3	Exeter	A	L29-63	2 (6)	5 (5)	10 (5)	R/R	10 (5)	2+1 (6)	0 (3)	–	–	–
3	28/3	King's Lynn	H	W52-42	14+1 (5)	5+1 (4)	9 (4)	–	13+1 (5)	0 (4)	4+1 (4)	7 (4)	–	–
4	4/4	Reading	H	L38-58	11 (4)	–	5 (6)	–	14 (5)	0 (0)	1 (6)	4 (4)	–	3 (4)
5	10/4	Rye House	A	L27-66	6 (5)	3 (4)	2 (4)	–	6 (5)	–	2+1 (4)	4 (4)	4 (4)	–
6	11/4	Isle of Wight	H	W48-45	9+2 (5)	5+1 (4)	5+1 (4)	–	17 (5)	–	3 (4)	7+1 (4)	2 (4)	–
7	18/4	Rye House	H	L43-47	R/R	10 (6)	8+1 (5)	–	15 (6)	0 (3)	5 (5)	5+4 (5)	–	–
8	25/4	Somerset	H	L44-46	5 (5)	7 (4)	5+2 (4)	–	15 (5)	1+1 (3)	4+1 (5)	7 (4)	–	–
9	7/5	Somerset	A	L44-46	11+3 (5)	6+1 (4)	6+1 (4)	–	14 (5)	3+1 (5)	1 (5)	3+1 (2)	–	–
10	17/5	Reading	A	L41-54	9+1 (6)	4+2 (5)	–	–	6 (5)	4 (4)	5+3 (5)	R/R	–	13 (5)
11	26/5	King's Lynn	A	L45-50*	–	4 (5)	–	–	16 (5)	3+2 (6)	3+1 (3)	R/R	–	19+2 (11)

*Denotes bonus-point victory

NOTE: One match was not ridden: Isle of Wight *v.* Newport.

DETAILS OF OTHER RIDERS:

Match No. 4: Craig Branney 3 (4); Match No. 10: Kauko Nieminen 13 (5); Match No. 11: Kauko Nieminen 15 (6); John Oliver 4+2 (5).

TACTICAL SUBSTITUTE AND TACTICAL RIDES, AS INCLUDED IN THE SCORES GRID:

Match No. 1: Watson 6 points (TR); Korneliussen 0 points (TR); Atkin 0 points (TS); Match No. 2: Atkin 4 points (TR); Watson 0 points (TR); Match No. 4: Watson 6 points (TR); Korneliussen 6 points (TR); Atkin 0 points (TS); Match No. 5: Korneliussen 4 points (TR); Watson 2 points (TR); Match No. 6: Watson 6 points (TR); Match No. 10: Nieminen 6 points (TR); Korneliussen 4 points (TR); Match No. 11: Watson 6 points (TR); Nieminen 6 points (TR).

PREMIER TROPHY AVERAGES

Rider	Mts	Rds	Pts	Bon	Tot	Avge	Max
Craig Watson	11	56	129	1	130	9.29	1 full
Mads Korneliussen	9	46	65	9	74	6.43	1 paid
Pavel Ondrasik	7	27	37	6	43	6.37	–
Tony Atkin	9	43	61	5	66	6.14	–
Carl Wilkinson	10	46	56	5	61	5.30	–
John Oliver	1	5	4	2	6	4.80	–
Chris Courage	2	8	6	0	6	3.00	–
Craig Branney	1	4	3	0	3	3.00	–
Karl Mason	11	48	28	7	35	2.92	–
Luke Priest	9	35	15	5	20	2.29	–
Guests	2	11	22	0	22	8.00	–

KNOCK-OUT CUP

No	DATE	OPPONENTS	H/A	RESULT	KORNELIUSSEN	WILKINSON	ONDRASIK	ATKIN	WATSON	PRIEST	MASON	BROWN	OTHER
1	16/5	Exeter	H	L46-50	13+1 (6)	7+1 (5)	R/R	–	14 (5)	3 (4)	3+1 (5)	–	6 (5)
2	31/5	Exeter†	A	L19-53	4 (3)	4 (4)	6+1 (4)	R/R	–	2+1 (5)	0 (5)	3 (3)	–

†Meeting abandoned after heat twelve, with the result permitted to stand.

DETAILS OF OTHER RIDER:

Match No. 1: Paul Clews 6 (5).

TACTICAL RIDES, AS INCLUDED IN THE SCORES GRID:

Match No. 1: Korneliussen 6 points (TR); Watson 6 points (TR).

OTHER MEETINGS

14 March: Severn Bridge Trophy (first leg)

Newport 46 (Craig Watson 15; Tony Atkin 12; Mads Korneliussen 8+1; Karl Mason 6+1; Luke Priest 4+1; Carl Wilkinson 1; Dawid Kujawa 0) Somerset 44.

19 March: Severn Bridge Trophy (second leg)

Somerset 53 Newport 43 (Craig Watson 16+1; Tony Atkin 14; Mads Korneliussen 10+1; Karl Mason 2; Luke Priest 1; Barrie Evans 0; Dawid Kujawa R/R) – Somerset won 97-89 on aggregate.

20 April: Premier Trophy

Isle of Wight 24 Newport 15 (Mads Korneliussen 8; Craig Watson 5; Tony Atkin 1; Luke Priest 1; Carl Wilkinson 0; Pavel Ondrasik 0; Karl Mason 0) – meeting abandoned after heat six.

8 August: Premier League

Newport 17 (Kristian Lund 5; Craig Watson 3; Carl Wilkinson 3; Barrie Evans 3; Pavel Ondrasik 2+1; Mads Korneliussen 1+1; Tony Atkin R/R) Reading 13 – meeting abandoned after heat five.

17 August: Premier League

Isle of Wight 25 Newport 11 (Mads Korneliussen 3+1; Carl Wilkinson 3; Pavel Ondrasik 2; Roger Lobb 2; Karl Mason 1; Kristian Lund 0; Tony Atkin R/R) – meeting abandoned after heat six.

11 September: Premier League

Stoke 25 Newport 23 (Craig Watson 9; Kristian Lund 6+1; Tony Atkin 5; Carl Wilkinson 2; Pavel Ondrasik 1+1; Karl Mason 0; Mads Korneliussen R/R) – meeting abandoned after heat eight.

INDIVIDUAL MEETINGS

4 January: New Year Classic

QUALIFYING SCORES: David Howe 13; Chris Harris 12; Leigh Lanham 11; Brent Werner 11; Chris Neath 11; Adam Shields 8; Michael Coles 7; Tony Atkin 7; Carl Wilkinson 5; Andrew Appleton 4; Dawid Kujawa 1; Davey Watt 0; Karl Mason (Res) 0. FINAL: 1st Harris; 2nd Lanham; 3rd Werner; 4th Howe.

13 June: Welsh Open Championship

QUALIFYING SCORES: Craig Watson 13; Adam Shields 13; Chris Harris 11; Jesper B. Jensen 10; Danny Bird 10; Billy Hamill 9; Carl Stonehewer 9; David Howe 8; Niels-Kristian Iversen 8; Adam Skornicki 8; Andy Smith 7; Mads Korneliussen 4; Leigh Lanham 4; Phil Morris 4; Steve Johnston 2; Michael Coles 0. FINAL: 1st Watson; 2nd Harris; 3rd Shields; 4th Jensen. NOTE: Jensen qualified for the final after defeating Bird in a run-off.

READING EUPHONY RACERS

ADDRESS: Reading Stadium, Bennet Road, Smallmead, Reading, Berkshire, RG2 0JL.
PROMOTERS: Pat Bliss & Chris Shears.
TRACK LENGTH: 307 metres.
TRACK RECORD: 58.1 seconds – Per Jonsson (12/10/87).
FIRST MEETING: 28 April 1975.
YEARS OF OPERATION: 1975-90 British League; 1991-94 British League Division One; 1995-04 Premier League.

NOTE: Reading also ran a second team in the 1996 Conference League and the 1997 Amateur League. The 1996 side ran as 'Reading Ravens', whereas in 1997, the fixtures were shared with Swindon, under the banner of 'M4 Raven Sprockets'.

PREVIOUS VENUE: Reading Greyhound Stadium, Oxford Road, Tilehurst, Reading, Berkshire.
YEARS OF OPERATION: 1968-70 British League Division Two; 1971-73 British League Division One.

CLUB HONOURS

LEAGUE CHAMPIONS: 1980, 1990, 1992, 1997.
KNOCK-OUT CUP WINNERS: 1990, 1998.
PREMIERSHIP WINNERS: 1991, 1993.
BSPA CUP WINNERS: 1992.
FOUR-TEAM CHAMPIONS: 1993.
PAIRS CHAMPIONS: 2004.

RIDER ROSTER 2004

Andrew APPLETON; Danny BIRD; Steve BRAIDFORD; Chris MILLS; Phil MORRIS; Chris SCHRAMM; Jamie WESTACOTT; Matej ZAGAR.

OTHER APPEARANCES/GUESTS (official matches only):
Craig BOYCE; Eric CARRILLO; Simon CARTWRIGHT; Paul CLEWS; James COCKLE; Karlis EZERGAILIS; Trevor HARDING; Chris HARRIS; Malcolm HOLLOWAY; Chris JOHNSON; Leigh LANHAM; Mark LEMON; Danny NORTON; Shane PARKER; Joel PARSONS; Glen PHILLIPS; Frede SCHOTT; Garry STEAD; Cameron WOODWARD.

PREMIER LEAGUE

No	DATE	OPPONENTS	H/A	RESULT	BIRD	SCHRAMM	MORRIS	APPLETON	ZAGAR	BRAIDFORD	MILLS	WESTACOTT	OTHERS
1	14/4	Hull	A	L44-46	13 (5)	3 (4)	7+1 (4)	4 (4)	12 (5)	1 (3)	4+2 (5)	–	–
2	24/5	Hull	H	W51-39*	13+2 (5)	4 (4)	8 (4)	3 (4)	15 (5)	–	–	0 (3)	8+2 (5)
3	31/5	Glasgow	H	W53-44	11+1 (5)	6+1 (4)	10+1 (5)	10+1 (4)	–	–	6 (5)	1 (3)	9 (4)
4	2/6	King's Lynn	A	L47-49	16+1 (5)	1+1 (4)	7 (4)	7+1 (4)	–	–	2+1 (5)	–	14+1 (8)
5	5/6	Workington	A	L39-57	11 (5)	1+1 (4)	9 (5)	6 (4)	–	–	1 (4)	1 (4)	10+1 (5)

PREMIER LEAGUE continued

No	DATE	OPPONENTS	H/A	RESULT	BIRD	SCHRAMM	MORRIS	APPLETON	ZAGAR	BRAIDFORD	MILLS	WESTACOTT	OTHERS
6	6/6	Newcastle	A	W48-47	9+2 (5)	7+1 (4)	8 (4)	9+2 (4)	–	–	0 (4)	–	15 (9)
7	7/6	Rye House	H	W49-43	13 (5)	5+2 (4)	10+1 (5)	6+2 (4)	–	–	5+1 (5)	2+1 (3)	8+1 (4)
8	14/6	Sheffield	H	W50-45	13+1 (5)	6 (4)	13+1 (5)	7+2 (4)	–	–	2+1 (4)	2 (4)	7 (4)
9	28/6	Newcastle	H	W57-38*	14+1 (5)	5+2 (4)	10 (4)	12+3 (5)	7+1 (4)	2 (4)	7+1 (4)	–	–
10	10/7	Edinburgh	A	L42-47	12+1 (5)	2 (4)	7+1 (4)	4+1 (4)	–	–	6+1 (5)	–	11 (8)
11	19/7	Edinburgh	H	W55-39*	8+1 (4)	5+1 (4)	12+1 (5)	13+2 (5)	9 (4)	1 (4)	7+1 (4)	–	–
12	24/7	Berwick	A	L45-48	11+2 (5)	1+1 (2)	6 (4)	6 (4)	–	2+1 (4)	4+1 (6)	–	15+1 (5)
13	25/7	Glasgow	A	L45-51*	8 (4)	–	0 (1)	14+3 (7)	R/R	1+1 (6)	6 (7)	–	16 (5)
14	26/7	Newport	H	W48-42	R/R	–	–	16 (6)	13+3 (6)	2+1 (3)	6+1 (6)	–	11 (9)
15	29/7	Sheffield	A	L46-51*	R/R	–	–	12+2 (7)	14+1 (6)	0 (1)	3+1 (6)	–	17+1 (10)
16	6/8	Rye House	A	L44-49*	R/R	3+2 (5)	11+1 (5)	15 (6)	11+1 (6)	1 (3)	3 (5)	–	–
17	14/8	Stoke	A	W49-41	R/R	4+3 (5)	9 (5)	15+3 (6)	17 (6)	1+1 (3)	3 (5)	–	–
18	16/8	Berwick	H	W59-32*	R/R	10+3 (6)	15 (5)	11+1 (5)	17+1 (6)	2 (5)	4+1 (3)	–	–
19	20/8	Somerset	A	W52-42	R/R	4+1 (5)	8+1 (5)	16+1 (6)	15+1 (6)	1+1 (4)	–	–	8+2 (4)
20	26/8	Exeter	A	L47½-48½	R/R	3 (5)	8+1 (5)	15+2 (6)	19+1 (6)	–	–	–	2½ (8)
21	30/8	King's Lynn	H	W56-39*	14+1 (5)	6+1 (4)	12+1 (5)	8+2 (4)	11 (4)	–	–	–	5 (8)
22	1/9	Exeter	H	W58-36*	12 (4)	4 (4)	14+1 (5)	7+2 (4)	13 (5)	–	5+1 (4)	3+1 (4)	–
23	6/9	Somerset	H	W57-38*	11+1 (5)	9+1 (4)	6 (4)	12+3 (5)	12 (4)	–	5 (4)	2 (4)	–
24	12/9	Newport	A	L43-50	13 (5)	5 (4)	6 (4)	8+3 (5)	–	–	3+1 (4)	2 (4)	6 (4)
25	13/9	Isle of Wight	H	W48-42	14 (5)	1 (4)	10 (4)	7+1 (4)	12+2 (5)	–	3 (5)	1 (3)	–
26	14/9	Isle of Wight	A	L40-55	15+1 (5)	2+1 (4)	3 (4)	8+2 (5)	10 (5)	–	2 (4)	0 (3)	–
27	17/9	Workington	H	W56-37*	11+2 (5)	3 (4)	11 (4)	9 (4)	13+1 (5)	–	6+4 (5)	3 (3)	–
28	20/9	Stoke	H	W61-33*	12+2 (5)	8 (4)	13+1 (5)	7+1 (4)	10 (4)	–	8+1 (4)	3+1 (4)	–

*Denotes bonus-point victory

DETAILS OF OTHER RIDERS:

Match No. 2: Glen Phillips 8+2 (5); Match No. 3: Craig Boyce 9 (4); Match No. 4: Shane Parker 13+1 (5); James Cockle 1 (3); Match No. 5: Shane Parker 10+1 (5); Match No. 6: Leigh Lanham 14 (5); Danny Norton 1 (4); Match No. 7: Chris Harris 8+1 (4); Match No. 8: Leigh Lanham 7 (4); Match No. 10: Chris Harris 10 (5); Chris Johnson 1 (3); Match No. 12: Chris Harris 15+1 (5); Match No. 13: Chris Harris 16 (5); Match No. 14: Garry Stead 11 (5); Paul Clews 0 (4); Match No. 15: Garry Stead 13 (5); Simon Cartwright 4+1 (5); Match No. 19: Malcolm Holloway 8+2 (4); Match No. 20: Karlis Ezergailis 2½ (5); Malcolm Holloway 0 (3); Match No. 21: Cameron Woodward 4 (4); Chris Johnson 1 (4); Match No. 24: Mark Lemon 6 (4).

TACTICAL SUBSTITUTE AND TACTICAL RIDES, AS INCLUDED IN THE SCORES GRID:

Match No. 4: Parker 6 points (TR); Bird 6 points (TR); Match No. 5: Bird 6 points (TR); Parker 4 points (TS); Appleton 2 points (TR); Match No. 12: Harris 6 points (TR); Match No. 13: Harris 4 points (TR); Bird 4 points (TR); Appleton 4 points (TS); Match No. 15: Stead 6 points (TR); Zagar 4 points (TR); Appleton 4 points (TS); Match No. 16: Appleton 6 points (TR); Match No. 20: Appleton 6 points (TR); Zagar 6 points (TR); Match No. 24: Bird 4 points (TR); Lemon 2 points (TR); Match No. 26: Bird 6 points (TR); Appleton 2 points (TR); Zagar 2 points (TS).

READING: back row, left to right: Steve Braidford, Chris Mills, Jamie Westacott, Matej Zagar, Andrew Appleton, James Cockle. Front, kneeling: Danny Bird, Martin Davidson (Mascot), Chris Schramm. On bike: Phil Morris.

PREMIER LEAGUE AVERAGES

Rider	Mts	Rds	Pts	Bon	Tot	Avge	Max
Matej Zagar	18	92	224	12	236	10.26	2 full; 1 paid
Danny Bird	21	102	241	19	260	10.20	1 full; 3 paid
Andrew Appleton	28	134	255	40	295	8.81	4 paid
Phil Morris	26	114	233	12	245	8.60	1 full; 1 paid
Malcolm Holloway	2	7	8	2	10	5.71	–
Chris Schramm	25	104	108	22	130	5.00	–
Chris Mills	24	113	101	19	120	4.25	–
Jamie Westacott	12	42	20	3	23	2.19	–
Karlis Ezergailis	1	5	2½	0	2½	2.00	–
Steve Braidford	11	40	14	5	19	1.90	–
James Cockle	1	3	1	0	1	1.33	–
Chris Johnson	2	7	2	0	2	1.14	–
Danny Norton	1	4	1	0	1	1.00	–
Guests	16	74	134	7	141	7.62	–

PREMIER TROPHY

No	DATE	OPPONENTS	H/A	RESULT	BIRD	SCHRAMM	MORRIS	APPLETON	ZAGAR	BRAIDFORD	MILLS	COCKLE	WESTACOTT	OTHERS
1	20/3	Rye House	A	L37-56	9+1 (5)	3+1 (4)	4 (4)	5 (4)	12 (5)	1 (3)	3 (5)	–	–	–
2	22/3	Rye House	H	W48-45	18 (5)	5 (4)	4+2 (4)	5 (4)	10+1 (5)	0 (3)	6+2 (5)	–	–	–
3	31/3	King's Lynn	A	L45-49	13+1 (5)	2 (4)	3+1 (4)	6 (4)	17 (5)	–	4+1 (5)	0 (2)	–	–
4	4/4	Newport	A	W58-38	10 (4)	4+1 (4)	6+2 (4)	11 (5)	14 (5)	6+3 (4)	7 (4)	–	–	–
5	12/4	Isle of Wight†	H	W38-34	9 (3)	1+1 (4)	6+1 (3)	6+1 (4)	9 (3)	2+1 (3)	5 (4)	–	–	–
6	19/4	King's Lynn	H	W58-38*	11+1 (5)	6+3 (4)	9+3 (5)	9 (4)	11 (4)	6+1 (4)	6+2 (4)	–	–	–
7	23/4	Somerset	A	L41-48	10+1 (5)	5+1 (4)	6+1 (4)	3 (4)	11 (5)	2 (4)	4+3 (5)	–	–	–
8	26/4	Somerset	H	W52-38*	13+1 (5)	5 (4)	9 (4)	4+1 (4)	14+1 (5)	–	4+1 (5)	3 (3)	–	–
9	2/5	Exeter	H	W58-36	13+1 (5)	8+3 (4)	8+1 (4)	8 (4)	14+1 (5)	3 (4)	4+2 (4)	–	–	–
10	3/5	Exeter	A	L45-48*	9+1 (5)	3+1 (4)	4 (4)	6 (4)	18 (5)	0 (2)	5 (6)	–	–	–
11	17/5	Newport	H	W54-41*	14+1 (5)	7+1 (4)	9+1 (4)	9+2 (5)	12 (4)	–	0 (1)	–	3+1 (7)	–
12	18/5	Isle of Wight	A	D45-45*	10 (5)	4+2 (4)	9 (4)	6+1 (4)	11+2 (5)	4 (5)	–	–	1+1 (3)	–
13	11/7	Glasgow	A	L40-50	11 (5)	4+2 (4)	6+1 (4)	7+2 (4)	–	–	1 (4)	–	–	11+1 (9)
14	12/7	Glasgow	H	W57-36*	10+1 (5)	3+1 (4)	11 (4)	10+2 (4)	15 (5)	2 (3)	6+1 (5)	–	–	–
15	1/8	Exeter	H	W46-43	R/R	9+2 (5)	13+1 (6)	12+1 (6)	4 (3)	–	8+2 (7)	–	–	0 (3)
16	2/8	Exeter	A	L35-59	R/R	2 (5)	6+1 (5)	15 (6)	10 (6)	–	2 (5)	–	–	0 (3)

*Denotes bonus-point/aggregate victory

†Meeting abandoned after heat twelve, with the result permitted to stand.

DETAILS OF OTHER RIDERS:

Match No. 13: Frede Schott 7 (5); Chris Johnson 4+1 (4); Match No. 15: Danny Norton 0 (3); Match No. 16: Danny Norton 0 (3).

TACTICAL SUBSTITUTE AND TACTICAL RIDES, AS INCLUDED IN THE SCORES GRID:

Match No. 1: Zagar 6 points (TR); Bird 0 points (TR); Match No. 2: Bird 6 points (TR); Match No. 3: Zagar 6 points (TR); Bird 2 points (TR); Match No. 10: Zagar 6 points (TR); Match No. 16: Appleton 6 points (TR); Zagar 2 points (TR); Mills 0 points (TS).

PREMIER TROPHY AVERAGES

Rider	Mts	Rds	Pts	Bon	Tot	Avge	Max
Matej Zagar	15	70	172	5	177	10.11	3 full; 2 paid
Danny Bird	14	67	156	9	165	9.85	1 full; 1 paid
Phil Morris	16	67	113	15	128	7.64	–
Andrew Appleton	16	70	119	10	129	7.37	1 paid
Chris Schramm	16	66	71	19	90	5.45	–
Chris Johnson	1	4	4	1	5	5.00	–
Chris Mills	15	69	65	14	79	4.58	–
Steve Braidford	10	35	26	5	31	3.54	–
James Cockle	2	5	3	0	3	2.40	–
Jamie Westacott	2	10	4	2	6	2.40	–
Danny Norton	2	6	0	0	0	0.00	–
Guest	1	5	7	0	7	5.60	–

KNOCK-OUT CUP

No	DATE	OPPONENTS	H/A	RESULT	BIRD	SCHRAMM	MORRIS	APPLETON	ZAGAR	PARSONS	MILLS	BRAIDFORD	OTHERS
1	9/5	Glasgow	A	L43-47	8 (5)	5+2 (4)	8+1 (4)	4+1 (4)	9 (5)	5+2 (4)	4+2 (4)	–	–
2	10/5	Glasgow	H	W52-43*	11 (4)	4+1 (4)	10+1 (5)	6+1 (4)	12 (5)	5+2 (4)	4+1 (4)	–	–
3	18/8	Hull	A	L39-53	R/R	5+1 (5)	11 (6)	5 (5)	17+1 (7)	–	1 (3)	0 ([illegible])	–
4	23/8	Hull	H	W51-42	R/R	4+1 (5)	21 (6)	9+1 (5)	15+1 (6)	–	–	1 ([illegible])	1 (4)

*Denotes aggregate victory

DETAILS OF OTHER RIDER:

Match No. 4: Eric Carrillo 1 (4).

TACTICAL SUBSTITUTE AND TACTICAL RIDES, AS INCLUDED IN THE SCORES GRID:

Match No. 3: Zagar 2 points (TS); Morris 2 points (TR); Appleton 0 points (TR); Match No. 4: Morris 6 points (TR).

YOUNG SHIELD

No	DATE	OPPONENTS	H/A	RESULT	BIRD	APPLETON	SCHRAMM	MORRIS	ZAGAR	WESTACOTT	MILLS	OTHERS
1	27/9	Sheffield	H	W58-34	10+2 (5)	8+2 (4)	9+1 (4)	8+1 (4)	15 (5)	1 (3)	–	7+4 (5)
2	30/9	Sheffield	A	L41-56*	15 (5)	2+1 (4)	0 (3)	8 (5)	13+1 (5)	–	–	3 (3)
3	5/10	Isle of Wight	A	L45-53	9+2 (4)	12+1 (5)	2 (4)	5 (4)	16 (6)	0 (3)	–	1 (4)
4	10/10	Isle of Wight	H	W51-42*	15 (5)	7+2 (4)	1+1 (4)	10 (4)	14+1 (5)	0 (3)	–	4 (5)
5	25/10	Hull	H	L41-52	4+1 (5)	6 (3)	1 (3)	4 (4)	13 (5)	1 (3)	12+4 (7)	–
6	27/10	Hull	A	L44-52	13 (6)	R/R	4+1 (4)	10 (5)	13 (5)	1 (6)	3 (4)	–

*Denotes aggregate victory

DETAILS OF OTHER RIDERS:

Match No. 1: Cameron Woodward 7+4 (5); Match No. 2: Cameron Woodward 3 (5); Danny Norton 0 (3); Match No. 3: Trevor Harding 1 (4); Match No. 4: Trevor Harding 4 (5).

TACTICAL SUBSTITUTE AND TACTICAL RIDES, AS INCLUDED IN THE SCORES GRID:

Match No. 2: Bird 6 points (TR); Zagar 6 points (TR); Morris 2 points (TS); Match No. 3: Bird 6 points (TR); Zagar 6 points (TS); Appleton 4 points (TR); Match No. 4: Bird 6 points (TR); Match No. 5: Zagar 6 points (TR); Bird 0 points (TR); Match No. 6: Bird 6 points (TR); Zagar 6 points (TR).

OTHER MEETINGS

15 March: Challenge

Reading 56 (Danny Bird 13+2; Matej Zagar 12; Phil Morris 11+1; Andrew Appleton 8+1; Chris Schramm 5+1; Chris Mills 5+1; Steve Braidford 2+1) King's Lynn 38.

8 August: Premier League

Newport 17 Reading 13 (Andrew Appleton 6; Chris Schramm 2; Matej Zagar 2; Steve Braidford 2; Chris Mills 1+1; Phil Morris 0; Danny Bird R/R) – meeting abandoned after heat five.

INDIVIDUAL MEETING

31 October: Euphony Classic

1st Adam Shields (after run-off) 14; 2nd Danny Bird 14; 3rd Davey Watt (after run-off) 11; Matej Zagar 11; Phil Morris 9; Chris Harris 9; Brent Werner 9; Craig Boyce 8; Leigh Lanham 8; Chris Neath 7; Mark Lemon 6; Chris Mills 5; Adam Allott 3; Chris Schramm 3; Jamie Smith 3; Shane Colvin 0.

RYE HOUSE SILVER SKI ROCKETS

NOTE: The information below relates only to the main Rye House team. For details of the second side, please refer to the Conference League section.

ADDRESS: Rye House Stadium, Rye Road, Hoddesdon, Hertfordshire, EN11 0EH.
PROMOTER: Len Silver.
TRACK LENGTH: 271 metres.
TRACK RECORD: 55.8 seconds – Chris Harris (19/06/04).
FIRST MEETING: 3 August 1958.
YEARS OF OPERATION: 1958 Open; 1959 Southern Area League; 1960-66 Open & Training; 1967 Training; 1969-73 Open & Training; 1974 British League Division Two; 1975-90 National League; 1991-93 British League Division Two; 1999-01; Conference League; 2002-04 Premier League.

NOTE: In 1999, Rye House staged their home matches at Eastbourne, King's Lynn and Mildenhall.

PREVIOUS VENUE: Hoddesdon Stadium, Rye Road, Hoddesdon, Hertfordshire
YEARS OF OPERATION: 1935 Open & Training; 1936-37 Open; 1938 Sunday Dirt-track League; 1939-43 Open; 1945-53 Open; 1954-57 Southern Area League.

NOTE: Rye House first acquired the 'Rockets' moniker in 1974, having previously been known as 'Roosters' in 1955 and 'Red Devils' from 1960-73.

CLUB HONOURS

KNOCK-OUT CUP WINNERS: 1979.
LEAGUE CHAMPIONS: 1980.

RIDER ROSTER 2004

Tommy ALLEN; Luke BOWEN; Steve BOXALL; Jason KING; Steve MASTERS; Chris NEATH; Scott ROBSON; Davey WATT; Brent WERNER.

OTHER APPEARANCES/GUESTS (official matches only):

Karlis EZERGAILIS; Mads KORNELIUSSEN; Kevin LITTLE; Joel PARSONS; Matt READ; Jamie SMITH; Cameron WOODWARD.

PREMIER LEAGUE

No	DATE	OPPONENTS	H/A	RESULT	NEATH	MASTERS	ROBSON	WERNER	WATT	ALLEN	BOXALL	KING	BOWEN	OTHERS
1	12/4	Sheffield	H	W52-42	13+1 (5)	6+1 (4)	11 (5)	2+1 (4)	9 (4)	3 (4)	8+1 (4)	–	–	–
2	9/5	Newport	A	W47-42	6+1 (4)	4+1 (4)	6+3 (4)	11 (5)	10 (5)	10+3 (5)	0 (3)	–	–	–
3	22/5	Workington	H	W56-39	7 (4)	<u>9+3 (4)</u>	8+1 (4)	10+1 (5)	12+1 (5)	8+1 (4)	2+1 (4)	–	–	–
4	28/5	Edinburgh	A	W46-44	8 (5)	4+1 (4)	7+1 (4)	8+1 (4)	10 (4)	4+1 (4)	5+4 (5)	–	–	–
5	29/5	Berwick	A	L42-53	4+1 (5)	3 (5)	11 (6)	16 (6)	R/R	1 (3)	2+1 (5)	–	–	–
6	5/6	Hull	H	L44-51	R/R	–	8+3 (5)	18 (6)	9 (5)	4 (5)	1+1 (4)	–	–	4 (5)

PREMIER LEAGUE continued

No	DATE	OPPONENTS	H/A	RESULT	NEATH	MASTERS	ROBSON	WERNER	WATT	ALLEN	BOXALL	KING	BOWEN	OTHERS
7	7/6	Reading	A	L43-49	13 (5)	R/R	3+1 (4)	18 (6)	6 (4)	3 (7)	0 (4)	–	–	–
8	13/6	Berwick	H	W48-42	14+3 (6)	–	9 (5)	14 (6)	R/R	2+1 (4)	3+1 (5)	–	–	6+2 (5)
9	19/6	Exeter	H	W45-44	6+1 (5)	–	16 (6)	12 (6)	R/R	4+1 (4)	3+1 (4)	–	–	4+1 (5)
10	2/7	Workington	A	L34-58	3+1 (5)	–	16 (6)	6 (5)	R/R	1 (4)	2+1 (5)	–	–	6 (5)
11	3/7	Somerset	H	W49-41	14 (6)	–	6+1 (5)	13+2 (5)	R/R	1 (3)	8 (6)	–	–	7+1 (5)
12	16/7	Somerset	A	L40-52	7+1 (4)	–	11 (5)	9 (5)	5 (4)	1 (4)	2+1 (4)	5+1 (4)	–	–
13	17/7	Edinburgh	H	W50-40*	10 (4)	–	5+2 (4)	8+1 (5)	14 (5)	8 (5)	4+1 (4)	1+1 (3)	–	–
14	4/8	Hull	A	L32-62	10 (5)	–	3+1 (4)	2 (5)	13 (5)	1 (4)	2 (4)	1+1 (3)	–	–
15	6/8	Reading	H	W49-44	7+1 (4)	–	9+2 (5)	6 (4)	14+1 (5)	5+2 (4)	6+1 (5)	2+2 (3)	–	–
16	8/8	Newcastle	A	W48-45	9+2 (5)	–	16+1 (5)	7 (4)	6+2 (4)	3 (4)	6+1 (5)	1+1 (3)	–	–
17	14/8	Newcastle	H	W56-36*	10+2 (5)	8+2 (4)	R/R	11+2 (5)	10+2 (5)	9+1 (6)	8 (5)	–	–	–
18	19/8	Sheffield	A	L25-69	3 (4)	0 (3)	R/R	9 (5)	11 (6)	2 (6)	0 (6)	–	–	–
19	20/8	King's Lynn	H	W58-35	5+1 (4)	10+1 (5)	11 (4)	13+1 (5)	8+3 (4)	6+1 (4)	5+1 (4)	–	–	–
20	22/8	Glasgow	A	L47-48	5+1 (4)	12 (4)	8+1 (5)	5+1 (4)	10+1 (5)	3 (3)	4+1 (5)	–	–	–
21	28/8	Stoke	A	L40-56	6 (5)	1+1 (4)	1 (3)	5 (4)	12 (5)	–	–	–	1 (3)	14+2 (6)
22	30/8	Stoke	H	W50-45	2 (4)	11+1 (5)	5+2 (4)	9 (4)	11+1 (5)	–	9 (4)	–	3+2 (4)	–
23	1/9	King's Lynn	A	L38-57*	8 (5)	0 (3)	3 (4)	7 (5)	13+1 (5)	7+2 (5)	–	–	0 (3)	–
24	4/9	Glasgow	H	W51-41*	5+1 (4)	9 (4)	10+1 (5)	7+1 (4)	11+1 (5)	4 (4)	5 (4)	–	–	–
25	7/9	Isle of Wight	A	L32-63	2+1 (4)	6 (4)	1 (4)	6 (5)	12 (5)	0 (3)	5+2 (5)	–	–	–
26	11/9	Isle of Wight	H	W52-41	R/R	7+3 (5)	5+1 (5)	12+1 (6)	17 (6)	10+2 (4)	–	–	1 (4)	–
27	13/9	Exeter	A	L18-75	R/R	1 (3)	1 (3)	5 (5)	2 (4)	5 (5)	–	–	0 (5)	4 (5)
28	18/9	Newport	H	W51-39*	7+1 (4)	9+2 (5)	8 (4)	10+1 (5)	6 (4)	10+1 (5)	–	–	1 (3)	–

*Denotes bonus-point victory

DETAILS OF OTHER RIDERS:

Match No. 6: Matt Read 4 (5); Match No. 8: Joel Parsons 6+2 (5); Match No. 9: Jamie Smith 4+1 (5); Match No. 10: Kevin Little 6 (5); Match No. 11: Kevin Little 7+1 (5); Match No. 21: Cameron Woodward 14+2 (6); Match No. 27: Karlis Ezergailis 4 (5).

TACTICAL SUBSTITUTE AND TACTICAL RIDES, AS INCLUDED IN THE SCORES GRID:

Match No. 5: Werner 6 points (TR); Robson 4 points (TR); Match No. 6: Werner 6 points (TR); Robson 4 points (TR); Match No. 7: Werner 6 points (TR); Match No. 10: Robson 4 points (TR); Werner 0 points (TR); Match No. 12: Robson 4 points (TR); Match No. 14: Neath 4 points (TR); Watt 4 points (TR); Werner 0 points (TS); Match No. 16: Robson 6 points (TR); Match No. 18: Werner 6 points (TR); Watt 2 points (TR); Match No. 20: Masters 6 points (TR); Watt 4 points (TR); Match No. 21: Woodward 6 points (TR); Watt 6 points (TR); Match No. 23: Watt 6 points (TR); Werner 2 points (TR); Neath 2 points (TS); Match No. 25: Watt 6 points (TR); Masters 4 points (TR); Match No. 27: Allen 2 points (TR); Ezergailis 2 points (TS); Werner 2 points (TR).

PREMIER LEAGUE AVERAGES

Rider	Mts	Rds	Pts	Bon	Tot	Avge	Max
Davey Watt	23	109	217	13	230	8.44	1 paid
Brent Werner	28	138	245	13	258	7.48	1 paid
Scott Robson	26	118	187	21	208	7.05	–
Chris Neath	25	115	181	19	200	6.96	–
Steve Masters	17	70	100	16	116	6.63	1 paid

Rider	Mts	Rds	Pts	Bon	Tot	Avge	Max
Tommy Allen	26	113	114	16	130	4.60	1 paid
Steve Boxall	23	104	90	19	109	4.19	–
Jason King	5	16	10	6	16	4.00	–
Karlis Ezergailis	1	5	3	0	3	2.40	–
Luke Bowen	6	22	6	2	8	1.45	–
Guests	6	31	38	6	44	5.68	–

PREMIER TROPHY

No	DATE	OPPONENTS	H/A	RESULT	NEATH	MASTERS	ROBSON	WERNER	WATT	ALLEN	BOXALL	BOWEN	OTHERS
1	20/3	Reading	H	W56-37	9+2 (5)	10 (4)	7+3 (4)	13 (5)	7+2 (4)	7+1 (4)	3+2 (4)	–	–
2	22/3	Reading	A	L45-48*	8 (5)	2+1 (4)	6+1 (4)	13 (5)	8 (4)	5+1 (6)	3+1 (2)	–	–
3	27/3	Exeter	H	W51-42	9+1 (4)	7+3 (5)	12+1 (5)	8+1 (4)	9 (4)	1+1 (4)	5 (4)	–	–
4	10/4	Newport	H	W66-27	13+2 (5)	7+2 (3)	9+3 (4)	8+1 (3)	15 (5)	5 (4)	9+1 (6)	–	–
5	17/4	Isle of Wight	H	W47-42	11+2 (5)	7 (4)	12+1 (5)	7+2 (4)	7 (4)	1 (4)	2+1 (4)	–	–
6	18/4	Newport	A	W47-43*	12 (5)	4+1 (3)	1+1 (3)	12+1 (5)	3 (4)	12+1 (6)	3+2 (4)	–	–
7	24/4	King's Lynn	H	W58-37	13+1 (5)	6+1 (4)	8 (4)	7+2 (4)	11+2 (5)	5+1 (4)	8+1 (4)	–	–
8	26/4	Exeter	A	L26-67	12 (5)	0 (3)	6 (4)	R/R	3 (5)	2 (6)	2+1 (5)	–	1 (3)
9	2/5	King's Lynn	A	D45-45*	13 (5)	5 (4)	2 (3)	4+2 (4)	7 (4)	6+1 (4)	8+1 (6)	–	–
10	8/5	Somerset	H	W49-44	R/R	6+2 (5)	8+1 (5)	16+1 (6)	14+1 (6)	3 (4)	2 (4)	–	–
11	4/6	Somerset	A	L37-56	R/R	2 (1)	7+1 (6)	8+1 (6)	10+1 (5)	10+2 (6)	0 (6)	–	–
12	8/6	Isle of Wight	A	L42-54	11+1 (5)	R/R	0 (4)	15 (6)	3 (3)	7 (5)	2 (4)	4 ([illegible])	–

*Denotes bonus-point victory

DETAILS OF OTHER RIDER:

Match No. 8: Joel Parsons 1 (3).

TACTICAL SUBSTITUTE AND TACTICAL RIDES, AS INCLUDED IN THE SCORES GRID:

Match No. 8: Neath 4 points (TR); Robson 2 points (TR); Match No. 11: Robson 2 points (TS); Watt 2 points (TR); Allen 2 points (TR); Match No. 12: Neath 6 points (TR); Bowen 4 points (TS); Werner 2 points (TR).

PREMIER TROPHY AVERAGES

Rider	Mts	Rds	Pts	Bon	Tot	Avge	Max
Chris Neath	10	49	106	9	115	9.39	1 paid
Brent Werner	11	52	110	11	121	9.31	–
Davey Watt	12	53	96	6	102	7.70	1 full
Scott Robson	12	51	76	12	88	6.90	1 paid
Steve Masters	11	40	56	10	66	6.60	–
Tommy Allen	12	57	63	8	71	4.98	–
Steve Boxall	12	53	47	10	57	4.30	–
Luke Bowen	1	3	2	0	2	2.67	–
Joel Parsons	1	3	1	0	1	1.33	–

KNOCK-OUT CUP

No	DATE	OPPONENTS	H/A	RESULT	NEATH	MASTERS	ROBSON	WERNER	WATT	ALLEN	BOXALL	PARSONS	KING	OTHERS
1	15/5	Newcastle	H	W55-39	10 (4)	7+3 (4)	7+2 (4)	13 (5)	11+2 (5)	4+1 (4)	3+1 (4)	–	–	–
2	16/5	Newcastle	A	W49-41*	12 (4)	4+1 (4)	5+1 (4)	7+2 (5)	15 (5)	2 (4)	–	4+2 (4)	–	–
3	6/7	Isle of Wight	A	L36-59	3 (5)	–	8+2 (5)	12 (5)	R/R	1 (4)	0 (5)	–	–	12 (6)
4	31/7	Isle of Wight	H	W52-42	10 (4)	–	8+3 (4)	13 (5)	12+1 (5)	3+1 (4)	6 (5)	–	0 (3)	–

*Denotes aggregate victory

DETAILS OF OTHER RIDER:

Match No. 3: Mads Korneliussen 12 (6).

TACTICAL RIDES, AS INCLUDED IN THE SCORES GRID:

Match No. 3: Werner 6 points (TR); Korneliussen 4 points (TR).

YOUNG SHIELD

No	DATE	OPPONENTS	H/A	RESULT	NEATH	MASTERS	WATT	ROBSON	WERNER	BOXALL	ALLEN	BOWEN
1	25/9	Hull	H	W47-44	11+1 (5)	4 (4)	9 (4)	3+1 (4)	12+2 (5)	0 (2)	8+1 (6)	–
2	29/9	Hull	A	L42-52	3+1 (4)	1 (3)	13 (5)	5+1 (5)	14 (5)	–	5 (5)	1 (3)

TACTICAL SUBSTITUTE AND TACTICAL RIDES, AS INCLUDED IN THE SCORES GRID:

Match No. 2: Watt 6 points (TR); Werner 2 points (TR); Robson 0 points (TS).

OTHER MEETINGS

13 March: A10 Trophy (first leg)

Rye House 55 (Chris Neath 13+1; Steve Masters 10+2; Steve Boxall 7+2; Scott Robson 7+1; Tommy Allen 7+1; Brent Werner 6+2; Davey Watt 5) King's Lynn 40.

17 March: A10 Trophy (second leg)

King's Lynn 42 Rye House 51 (Davey Watt 14; Chris Neath 10+1; Brent Werner 8+1; Scott Robson 6+2; Steve Boxall 6+1; Tommy Allen 5+1; Steve Masters 2+1) – Rye House won 106-82 on aggregate.

31 May: Inter-League Challenge

Rye House 46 (Brent Werner 17; Chris Neath 14+2; Joel Parsons 7; Tommy Allen 3+1; Steve Masters 2+1; Scott Robson 2; Luke Bowen 1+1; Davey Watt R/R) Eastbourne 45.

2 September: Challenge

Ipswich 60 Rye House 33 (Steve Masters 10+1; Chris Neath 7+2; Davey Watt 4; Brent Werner 4; Tommy Allen 4; Scott Robson 3; Luke Bowen 1+1).

9 October: Scott Robson Testimonial

Scott's Red Devils 53 (Billy Hamill 11+1; Brent Werner 10; Davey Watt 9+1; Chris Neath 8+2; Steve Masters 7+1; Scott Robson 5+2; Tommy Allen 3) Stuart's Blue Angels 33 (Leigh Lanham 9+1; Craig Boyce 6+1; Stuart Robson 4+1; Joe Screen 4; Jason Bunyan 4; Kevin Little 3+1; Edward Kennett 3).

RYE HOUSE: back row, left to right: Steve Masters, Davey Watt, Steve Boxall, Tommy Allen. Front row: Chris Neath, Scott Robson, Brent Werner.

INDIVIDUAL MEETING

30 October: Sainsbury's Ace of Herts Championship

1st Stuart Robson 14; 2nd Edward Kennett (after run-off) 12; 3rd Adam Shields 12; Davey Watt 11; Craig Boyce 9; Chris Neath 9; Leigh Lanham 9; Mark Lemon 9; Brent Werner 8; Scott Robson 7; Daniel King 5; Steve Masters 4; Jason King 4; Jamie Smith 3; Tommy Allen 3; Harland Cook 1; Barry Burchatt 0.

SHEFFIELD PIRTEK TIGERS

NOTE: The information below relates only to the main Sheffield team. For details of the second side, please refer to the Conference League section.

ADDRESS: Owlerton Sports Stadium, Penistone Road, Owlerton, Sheffield, South Yorkshire, S6 2DE.
PROMOTERS: Neil Machin & Malcolm Wright.
TRACK LENGTH: 361 metres.
TRACK RECORD: 59.5 seconds – Simon Stead (08/08/04).
FIRST MEETING: 30 March 1929.
YEARS OF OPERATION: 1929 English Dirt-track League; 1930-31 Northern League; 1932 Speedway National Association Trophy; 1933 National League; 1938-39 National League Division Two; 1945 Open; 1946 Northern League; 1947-50 National League Division Two; 1951-52 Open; 1960-64 Provincial League; 1965-67 British League; 1968-74 British League Division One; 1975-88 British League; 1991-94 British League Division Two; 1995-04 Premier League.

CLUB HONOURS

BRITISH SPEEDWAY CUP (DIVISION TWO) WINNERS: 1947.
KNOCK-OUT CUP WINNERS: 1974, 2002.
FOUR-TEAM CHAMPIONS: 1999, 2000.
LEAGUE CHAMPIONS: 1999, 2002.
YOUNG SHIELD WINNERS: 1999, 2002.
PREMIERSHIP WINNERS: 2000.

RIDER ROSTER 2004

Ricky ASHWORTH; James BIRKINSHAW; Andre COMPTON; Richard HALL; Andrew MOORE; Ben WILSON; Sean WILSON.

OTHER APPEARANCES/GUESTS (official matches only):

Ross BRADY; Jason BUNYAN; James COCKLE; Shane COLVIN; Benji COMPTON; John JORGENSEN; Magnus KARLSSON; Shane PARKER; Paul PICKERING; Emiliano SANCHEZ; Rory SCHLEIN; Jan STAECHMANN; George STANCL; Simon STEAD; Mark THOMPSON; Paul THORP; Craig WATSON.

PREMIER LEAGUE

No	DATE	OPPONENTS	H/A	RESULT	S. WILSON	BIRKINSHAW	ASHWORTH	MOORE	A. COMPTON	B. WILSON	HALL	COLVIN	OTHERS
1	12/4	Rye House	A	L42-52	13 (5)	0 (4)	3+3 (4)	13+1 (5)	4+1 (4)	–	3+1 (4)	–	6 (4)
2	13/5	Exeter	H	W57-38	R/R	5+2 (4)	12+1 (5)	13+2 (6)	18 (6)	4 (4)	5+2 (5)	–	–
3	20/5	Somerset	H	W54-42	R/R	7+1 (4)	17+1 (6)	6+1 (4)	13 (6)	6 (5)	5+4 (5)	–	–
4	10/6	Glasgow	H	W55-41	–	2+1 (4)	11+1 (5)	11+1 (5)	9+1 (4)	5+2 (4)	7+1 (4)	–	10 (4)
5	14/6	Reading	A	L45-50	–	3 (4)	8+2 (4)	6 (4)	7+1 (5)	3+1 (4)	5+1 (4)	–	13 (5)
6	15/6	Isle of Wight	A	L35-57	–	0 (3)	6 (4)	1+1 (4)	8 (5)	2 (3)	6+1 (6)	–	12 (5)
7	17/6	Newcastle	H	W67-26	R/R	12+3 (5)	11+1 (5)	12+3 (5)	11+1 (5)	8+1 (5)	13+2 (5)	–	–
8	19/6	Workington	A	L44-51	–	3 (4)	11 (5)	4+1 (4)	11 (5)	3+1 (3)	6+1 (5)	–	6 (4)
9	1/7	Berwick	H	W55-38	–	–	7+1 (4)	9+1 (4)	14+1 (5)	5 (4)	5+1 (4)	1 (4)	14+1 (5)
10	10/7	Berwick	A	L37-57	–	–	12 (5)	6+3 (4)	5+1 (4)	2 (4)	3+1 (4)	–	9 (9)
11	14/7	Hull	A	L40-54	–	–	16 (5)	3 (4)	6 (4)	4 (4)	3+3 (4)	2 (4)	6+1 (5)
12	18/7	Glasgow	A	L42-51*	–	1+1 (4)	8+1 (5)	4+1 (4)	11+1 (5)	2 (4)	3+1 (4)	–	13 (4)
13	23/7	Somerset	A	L39-51*	–	1 (4)	7+1 (5)	5+2 (4)	5 (4)	8+1 (5)	0 (3)	–	13 (5)
14	29/7	Reading	H	W51-46	–	6 (4)	17 (6)	5+2 (5)	R/R	3 (4)	4+1 (5)	–	16+1 (6)
15	7/8	Stoke	A	L30-62	–	5+1 (5)	5 (4)	2 (4)	6 (5)	0 (3)	4+1 (4)	–	8 (5)
16	8/8	Hull	H	W52-38	–	2 (4)	8 (4)	5+1 (4)	12+1 (5)	6+2 (4)	4+1 (4)	–	15 (5)
17	12/8	Newport	H	W65-26	R/R	10+4 (5)	15 (5)	8+3 (5)	17 (6)	6+3 (4)	9+1 (5)	–	–
18	15/8	Newcastle	A	L44-52*	–	1 (4)	15 (6)	R/R	9 (4)	4 (7)	5 (5)	–	10 (4)
19	19/8	Rye House	H	W69-25*	–	9+2 (5)	12 (4)	R/R	14+1 (5)	13+2 (6)	11+5 (6)	–	10+1 (4)
20	26/8	Edinburgh	H	W65-27	–	6+3 (5)	16+1 (6)	R/R	14+1 (5)	10+1 (5)	8+4 (5)	–	11+1 (4)
21	29/8	Newport	A	W46-43*	–	0 (3)	13+1 (6)	R/R	11 (5)	8+1 (7)	7+2 (5)	–	7+1 (4)
22	30/8	Exeter	A	L36-59	–	8+2 (6)	2+1 (5)	R/R	10 (5)	2+2 (4)	5+1 (5)	–	9+1 (5)
23	2/9	King's Lynn	H	W56-38	–	8+2 (5)	16+1 (6)	R/R	14+1 (5)	3+1 (5)	4+1 (5)	–	11+1 (4)
24	3/9	Edinburgh	A	L39-54*	–	3 (4)	12 (5)	R/R	10 (5)	4+3 (6)	0 (5)	–	10 (5)
25	4/9	King's Lynn	A	L36-56	–	1+1 (4)	9+1 (5)	R/R	8 (5)	9+1 (7)	4+1 (5)	–	5+1 (4)
26	9/9	Workington	H	L44-46	–	12+3 (7)	14 (6)	R/R	7 (5)	4+2 (4)	3 (5)	–	4 (4)
27	12/9	Stoke†	H	W44-33	–	10+1 (5)	11 (4)	R/R	9 (3)	8+4 (6)	–	–	6+1 (6)
28	16/9	Isle of Wight	H	W55-39	–	5+1 (4)	13 (6)	R/R	14 (5)	11+1 (5)	5+3 (5)	–	7 (4)

*Denotes bonus-point victory

†Meeting abandoned after heat twelve, with the result permitted to stand.

DETAILS OF OTHER RIDERS:

Match No. 1: James Cockle 6 (4); Match No. 4: Simon Stead 10 (4); Match No. 5: Simon Stead 13 (5); Match No. 6: Craig Watson 12 (5); Match No. 8: Simon Stead 14+1 (5); Rory Schlein 6 (4); Match No. 10: Paul Pickering 8 (5); Mark Thompson 1 (4); Match No. 11: Jan Staechmann 6+1 (5); Match No. 12: Simon Stead 13 (4); Match No. 13: Craig Watson 13 (5); Match No. 14: Simon Stead 16+1 (6); Match No. 15: George Stancl 8 (5); Match No. 16: Simon Stead 15 (5); Match No. 18: Ross Brady 10 (4); Match No. 19: Magnus Karlsson 10+1 (4); Match No. 20: Simon Stead 11+1 (4); Match No. 21: Jason Bunyan 7+1 (4); Match No. 22: Jason Bunyan 9+1 (5); Match No. 23: Paul Thorp 11+1 (4); Match No. 24: Shane Parker 10 (5); Match No. 25: John Jorgensen 5+1 (4); Match No. 26: Shane Parker 4 (4); Match No. 27: Paul Thorp 4 (3); Benji Compton 2+1 (3); Match No. 28: George Stancl 7 (4).

TACTICAL SUBSTITUTE AND TACTICAL RIDES, AS INCLUDED IN THE SCORES GRID:

Match No. 1: Moore 4 points (TR); S. Wilson 4 points (TR); Match No. 5: Ashworth 6 points (TR); Stead 4 points (TR); Match No. 6: Watson 2 points (TR); Ashworth 2 points (TR); Match No. 8: Ashworth 6 points (TR); Compton 4 points (TR); Match No. 10: Ashworth 6 points (TR); Pickering 2 points (TR); Match No. 11: Ashworth 6 points (TR); Moore 2 points (TR); Match No. 12: Stead 6 points (TR); Match No. 15: Moore 2 points (TR); Ashworth 2 points (TR); Match No. 18: A. Compton 6 points (TR); Ashworth 6 points (TR); Match No. 22: A. Compton 4 points (TR); Bunyan 4 points (TR); Birkinshaw 2 points (TS); Match No. 24: Ashworth 6 points (TR); A. Compton 0 points (TR); Match No. 25: Jorgensen 2 points (TR); Ashworth 2 points (TR).

PREMIER LEAGUE AVERAGES

Rider	Mts	Rds	Pts	Bon	Tot	Avge	Max
Sean Wilson	1	5	11	0	11	8.80	–
Ricky Ashworth	28	140	286	17	303	8.66	2 full; 1 paid
Andre Compton	27	130	270	11	281	8.65	1 full; 4 paid
Andrew Moore	17	75	109	23	132	7.04	1 paid
James Cockle	1	4	6	0	6	6.00	–
Richard Hall	27	126	137	40	177	5.62	1 paid
Ben Wilson	27	126	143	29	172	5.46	–
James Birkinshaw	25	110	119	28	147	5.35	1 paid
Benji Compton	1	3	2	1	3	4.00	–
Shane Colvin	2	8	3	0	3	1.50	–
Mark Thompson	1	4	1	0	1	1.00	–
Guests	23	103	212	9	221	8.58	1 full; 3 paid

PREMIER TROPHY

No	DATE	OPPONENTS	H/A	RESULT	S. WILSON	BIRKINSHAW	ASHWORTH	MOORE	A. COMPTON	B. WILSON	HALL	COLVIN	OTHERS
1	18/3	Workington	H	W52-42	12+1 (5)	6+2 (4)	11 (5)	7+2 (4)	9 (4)	4 (4)	3 (4)	–	–
2	25/3	Newcastle	H	W65-30	12 (4)	7+2 (4)	14+1 (5)	9+2 (4)	11+1 (4)	2+1 (4)	10+3 (5)	–	–
3	27/3	Stoke	A	L38-54	8 (5)	3 (4)	8 (4)	1 (4)	10+1 (5)	1+1 (3)	7+1 (5)	–	–
4	1/4	Stoke	H	W59-35*	13+1 (5)	6+1 (4)	10+1 (4)	9+2 (4)	10+1 (5)	5 (4)	6+3 (4)	–	–
5	4/4	Newcastle	A	W51-42*	14+1 (5)	2+1 (4)	9 (4)	5+1 (3)	12+2 (5)	6 (5)	3 (4)	–	–
6	15/4	Edinburgh	H	W63-32	14+1 (5)	8+2 (4)	7+1 (4)	9+1 (4)	14+1 (5)	6 (4)	5+1 (4)	–	–
7	16/4	Edinburgh	A	L42-47*	10 (5)	1+1 (3)	4 (4)	9+1 (4)	11 (5)	2+2 (4)	5 (5)	–	–
8	22/4	Glasgow	H	W53-40	14+1 (5)	6+1 (4)	7+1 (4)	7 (4)	13+1 (5)	3 (3)	3+1 (5)	–	–
9	24/4	Workington	A	L40-55	13 (5)	3 (4)	4+1 (4)	12+1 (5)	4+2 (4)	2 (4)	2 (4)	–	–

No	DATE	OPPONENTS	H/A	RESULT	S. WILSON	BIRKINSHAW	ASHWORTH	MOORE	A. COMPTON	B. WILSON	HALL	COLVIN	OTHERS
10	25/4	Glasgow	A	L41-49*	11 (5)	2+2 (4)	6+1 (5)	5+2 (4)	6 (4)	6 (4)	5+1 (4)	–	–
11	28/4	Hull	A	L37-57	10 (5)	0 (1)	5 (4)	4 (4)	6 (5)	1 (4)	11 (7)	–	–
12	6/5	Berwick	H	W67-25	–	9+3 (4)	13+2 (5)	8+1 (4)	15 (5)	6+1 (4)	6+1 (4)	–	10+2 (4)
13	15/5	Berwick	A	L43-47*	–	2 (5)	9 (5)	4 (4)	10 (4)	4+1 (4)	2 (4)	–	12+2 (5)
14	3/6	Hull	H	W55-40	–	4+1 (4)	10 (4)	9+1 (5)	13+1 (5)	3+2 (4)	5+2 (4)	–	11 (4)
15	21/6	Exeter	A	L30-64	–	–	1 (3)	3 (4)	6 (5)	3+1 (5)	2 (4)	3 (4)	12 (5)
16	24/6	Exeter	H	W56-38	–	–	R/R	13+1 (5)	16+2 (6)	9 (5)	6+3 (6)	2+1 (4)	10+1 (4)

*Denotes bonus-point victory

DETAILS OF OTHER RIDERS:

Match No. 12: Shane Parker 10+2 (4); Match No. 13: George Stancl 12+2 (5); Match No. 14: Craig Watson 11 (4); Match No. 15: Craig Watson 12 (5); Match No. 16: Craig Watson 10+1 (4).

TACTICAL RIDES, AS INCLUDED IN THE SCORES GRID:

Match No. 3: Ashworth 2 points (TR); Hall 2 points (TR); Match No. 9: Moore 6 points (TR); S. Wilson 4 points (TR); Match No. 11: Hall 4 points (TR); S. Wilson 4 points (TR); Match No. 15: Watson 6 points (TR); A. Compton 2 points (TR)

PREMIER TROPHY AVERAGES

Rider	Mts	Rds	Pts	Bon	Tot	Avge	Max
Sean Wilson	11	54	127	5	132	9.78	1 full; 3 paid
Andre Compton	16	76	165	12	177	9.32	1 full; 3 paid
Ricky Ashworth	15	64	117	8	125	7.81	2 paid
Andrew Moore	16	66	111	15	126	7.64	–
James Birkinshaw	14	53	59	16	75	5.66	1 paid
Richard Hall	16	73	78	16	94	5.15	–
Ben Wilson	16	65	63	9	72	4.43	–
Shane Colvin	2	8	5	1	6	3.00	–
Guests	5	22	52	5	57	10.36	1 paid

KNOCK-OUT CUP

No	DATE	OPPONENTS	H/A	RESULT	MOORE	HALL	ASHWORTH	A. COMPTON	BIRKINSHAW	B. WILSON	OTHERS
1	22/7	Exeter	H	W57-37	14+1 (5)	5+2 (4)	11 (4)	14+1 (5)	2+1 (5)	7 (4)	4 (4)
2	26/7	Exeter	A	L29-62	6 (5)	7 (5)	5 (4)	5 (3)	5+1 (6)	0 (4)	1 (3)

DETAILS OF OTHER RIDERS:

Match No. 1: Craig Watson 4 (4); Match No. 2: Paul Pickering 1 (3).

TACTICAL RIDES, AS INCLUDED IN THE SCORES GRID:

Match No. 2: A. Compton 2 points (TR); Pickering 0 points (TR).

SHEFFIELD: back row, left to right: James Birkinshaw, Andre Compton, Ricky Ashworth, Ben Wilson, Richard Hall, Andrew Moore. Front, on bike: Sean Wilson.

YOUNG SHIELD

No	DATE	OPPONENTS	H/A	RESULT	S. WILSON	MOORE	HALL	ASHWORTH	A. COMPTON	BIRKINSHAW	B. WILSON	OTHERS
1	27/9	Reading	A	L34-58	–	–	6 (6)	2+1 (4)	R/R	3 (5)	6+2 (5)	17+1 (10)
2	30/9	Reading	H	W56-41	–	–	8+1 (5)	11 (5)	R/R	7+2 (5)	7+2 (4)	23+1 (11)

DETAILS OF OTHER RIDERS:

Match No. 1: George Stancl 13 (6); Emiliano Sanchez 4+1 (4); Match No. 2: Jason Bunyan 15 (6); Rory Schlein 8+1 (5).

TACTICAL RIDES, AS INCLUDED IN THE SCORES GRID:

Match No. 1: Stancl 4 points (TR); Ashworth 0 points (TR).

OTHER MEETINGS

10 March: Challenge (first leg)

Hull 46 Sheffield 44 (Sean Wilson 14; Ricky Ashworth 7; Richard Hall 6+1; Andrew Moore 5+2; Andre Compton 5+1; James Birkinshaw 5; Ben Wilson 2).

11 March: Challenge (second leg)

Sheffield 52 (Sean Wilson 14; Andrew Moore 9+2; Andre Compton 9; Ricky Ashworth 7+1; James Birkinshaw 6+3; Richard Hall 5; Ben Wilson 2+1) Hull 43 – Sheffield won 96-89 on aggregate.

9 April: Seventy-Five-Year Celebration

Sheffield 57 (Andre Compton 13+2; Sean Wilson 13+1; Ricky Ashworth 10+1; Andrew Moore 8+1; James Birkinshaw 7+1; Richard Hall 3+1; Ben Wilson 3) The Stars 35 (Billy Hamill 10; Robbie Kessler 6+1; George Stancl 6; Paul Lee 6; Adam Allott 4+1; Simon Cartwright 2+1; Mirko Wolter 1+1).

INDIVIDUAL MEETING

17 October: Teng Tools Northern Classic

QUALIFYING SCORES: Simon Stead 15; Magnus Karlsson 13; Ricky Ashworth 12; Sam Ermolenko 10; Adam Allott 10; Craig Boyce 10; Mark Lemon 7; Brent Werner 7; Richard Hall 7; Robbie Kessler 6; Jason Bunyan 5; Ben Wilson 5; Jason Lyons 5; Adam Skornicki 5; James Birkinshaw 2; Ritchie Hawkins 1. SEMI-FINAL: 1st Ermolenko; 2nd Boyce; 3rd Ashworth; 4th Allott. FINAL: 1st Stead; 2nd Karlsson; 3rd Ermolenko; 4th Boyce.

SOMERSET ORCHARD FM REBELS

ADDRESS: Oak Tree Arena, Edithmead, nr. Highbridge, Somerset.
PROMOTERS: Peter Toogood & Andy Hewlett.
TRACK LENGTH: 300 metres.
TRACK RECORD: 56.40 seconds – Kenneth Bjerre (20/05/03).
FIRST MEETING: 2 June 2000.
YEARS OF OPERATION: 2000-01 Conference League; 2002-04 Premier League.

CLUB HONOURS

CONFERENCE TROPHY WINNERS: 2001.
KNOCK-OUT CUP WINNERS: 2001.

RIDER ROSTER 2004

Steve BISHOP; Neil COLLINS; Glenn CUNNINGHAM; Paul FRY; John JORGENSEN; Matt READ; Lee SMART; Jamie SMITH; Simon WALKER.

OTHER APPEARANCES/GUESTS (official matches only):

Olly ALLEN; Adam ALLOTT; Simon CARTWRIGHT; Ritchie HAWKINS; Malcolm HOLLOWAY; Danny HUGHES; Chris JOHNSON; John OLIVER; Scott SMITH; Carl WILKINSON.

PREMIER LEAGUE

No	DATE	OPPONENTS	H/A	RESULT	JORGENSEN	READ	COLLINS	CUNNINGHAM	FRY	SMART	SMITH	WALKER	BISHOP	OTHERS
1	17/5	Exeter	A	L31-62	3 (4)	R/R	1 (5)	10 (6)	9 (5)	1+1 (4)	–	–	–	7+1 (6)
2	20/5	Sheffield	A	L42-54	13 (5)	R/R	11 (6)	4+1 (5)	8+1 (5)	–	3+1 (5)	–	–	3+1 (5)
3	21/5	Berwick	H	W51-41	<u>15 (5)</u>	R/R	9+2 (5)	11 (5)	12+1 (5)	3 (4)	–	–	–	1 (6)
4	26/5	Hull	A	L38-55	5 (5)	0 (4)	5+3 (4)	12 (5)	7 (4)	–	8+1 (5)	1 (3)	–	–
5	28/5	Workington	H	W54-41	10 (4)	6+1 (4)	7 (4)	13+1 (5)	11+1 (5)	–	5+1 (4)	2+1 (4)	–	–
6	9/6	King's Lynn	A	L33-61	13 (5)	1+1 (4)	5+1 (4)	6 (4)	4+1 (5)	–	3+2 (4)	1 (4)	–	–
7	11/6	Glasgow	H	W46-44	<u>15 (5)</u>	2+1 (4)	5+1 (4)	11 (5)	9+1 (4)	–	4 (4)	0 (4)	–	–
8	18/6	Hull	H	L44-53	10 (5)	2 (4)	9+2 (5)	14 (5)	4 (4)	–	3 (4)	2 (3)	–	–
9	2/7	Isle of Wight	H	W49-44	12 (5)	6+1 (5)	5+2 (4)	–	10 (4)	–	5+3 (4)	1+1 (3)	–	10 (5)
10	3/7	Rye House	A	L41-49	1 (4)	12+3 (7)	12+1 (6)	–	10 (6)	–	R/R	–	–	6+1 (7)
11	16/7	Rye House	H	W52-40*	9+2 (5)	–	6 (4)	13 (5)	9+1 (4)	–	4+1 (4)	9+2 (5)	–	2+1 (3)
12	17/7	Workington	A	L35-58	6 (5)	–	10+2 (5)	4+1 (4)	4 (4)	–	5 (4)	0 (3)	–	6+1 (5)
13	18/7	Newcastle	A	L43-47	8 (5)	–	8+2 (5)	7+1 (4)	0 (1)	–	7 (4)	2+1 (4)	–	11+2 (7)
14	23/7	Sheffield	H	W51-39	17 (6)	–	6+2 (5)	10 (5)	R/R	–	10+1 (5)	1+1 (3)	–	7+1 (6)
15	30/7	Exeter	H	W55-39	14 (5)	–	5+2 (4)	10+1 (4)	8 (4)	–	8+1 (4)	5+1 (4)	5+2 (5)	–
16	31/7	Stoke	A	L32-62	8 (5)	–	5+1 (5)	9+1 (5)	6 (5)	0 (1)	R/R	0 (3)	4+2 (7)	–
17	6/8	Edinburgh	A	L39-55	10+2 (5)	–	5+1 (4)	5 (4)	9 (5)	–	3+1 (4)	1 (3)	6+2 (5)	–
18	7/8	Berwick	A	L42-53	7+1 (4)	–	4+1 (4)	14+1 (5)	14 (5)	–	2 (4)	0 (3)	1 (5)	–

No	DATE	OPPONENTS	H/A	RESULT	JORGENSEN	READ	COLLINS	CUNNINGHAM	FRY	SMART	SMITH	WALKER	BISHOP	OTHERS
19	8/8	Glasgow	A	L42-54	9 (5)	–	8+4 (5)	5 (4)	1 (2)	–	11 (5)	4 (4)	4+1 (5)	–
20	13/8	Newcastle	H	W51-43*	11+1 (5)	–	6+2 (4)	7+1 (5)	10 (4)	–	6+2 (4)	4 (4)	7 (4)	–
21	20/8	Reading	H	L42-52	14 (5)	–	6+2 (5)	0 (4)	9+1 (5)	–	R/R	2 (4)	11+2 (7)	–
22	22/8	Newport	A	D45-45	10 (4)	–	8+3 (5)	11 (5)	10 (5)	–	R/R	–	3+2 (6)	3 (5)
23	24/8	Isle of Wight	A	L31-62	9 (5)	–	9+1 (5)	6 (4)	2+1 (4)	0 (4)	4 (4)	–	1 (4)	–
24	25/8	Edinburgh	H	W61-33*	15 (5)	–	6+3 (4)	11+1 (5)	9+1 (4)	–	5+1 (4)	7 (4)	8+1 (4)	–
25	3/9	Stoke	H	W50-43	11+2 (5)	6+2 (5)	5+1 (4)	14+1 (5)	6+2 (4)	–	6 (4)	2+1 (3)	–	–
26	6/9	Reading	A	L38-57	8+1 (5)	–	6 (4)	7 (4)	11+2 (5)	–	2 (4)	0 (3)	4+1 (5)	–
27	10/9	Newport	H	W59-34*	6 (4)	–	10+1 (4)	12+2 (5)	13+2 (5)	–	7 (4)	5+3 (4)	6+2 (4)	–
28	17/9	King's Lynn	H	W49-41	14 (5)	–	6+2 (4)	4+1 (4)	12 (5)	–	6+1 (4)	4 (4)	–	3+1 (4)

*Denotes bonus-point victory

DETAILS OF OTHER RIDERS:

Match No. 1: Adam Allott 7+1 (6); Match No. 2: Danny Hughes 3+1 (5); Match No. 3: Adam Allott 1 (6); Match No. 9: Olly Allen 10 (5); Match No. 10: Olly Allen 5+1 (4); Chris Johnson 1 (3); Match No. 11: Ritchie Hawkins 2+1 (3); Match No. 12: Scott Smith 6+1 (5); Match No. 13: Simon Cartwright 11+2 (7); Match No. 14: Carl Wilkinson 7+1 (6); Match No. 22: Chris Johnson 3 (5); Match No. 28: Malcolm Holloway 3+1 (4).

TACTICAL SUBSTITUTE AND TACTICAL RIDES, AS INCLUDED IN THE SCORES GRID:

Match No. 1: Fry 4 points (TR); Cunningham 2 points (TR); Match No. 2: Collins 6 points (TR); Jorgensen 6 points (TR); Fry 2 points (TS); Match No. 4: Fry 4 points (TR); Cunningham 2 points (TR); Match No. 6: Jorgensen 4 points (TR); Cunningham 4 points (TR); Match No. 8: Cunningham 6 points (TR); Jorgensen 6 points (TR); Collins 2 points (TS); Match No. 12: Collins 6 points (TR); Fry 0 points (TR); Match No. 16: Collins 4 points (TR); Jorgensen 4 points (TR); Match No. 17: Jorgensen 4 points (TR); Fry 4 points (TR); Match No. 18: Fry 6 points (TR); Cunningham 4 points (TR); Match No. 19: Smith 6 points (TR); Jorgensen 4 points (TR); Collins 2 points (TS); Match No. 21: Jorgensen 6 points (TR); Bishop 4 points (TR); Match No. 23: Cunningham 4 points (TR); Jorgensen 2 points (TR); Match No. 26: Fry 6 points (TR); Cunningham 4 points (TR).

PREMIER LEAGUE AVERAGES

Rider	Mts	Rds	Pts	Bon	Tot	Avge	Max
John Jorgensen	28	135	265	9	274	8.12	3 full
Glenn Cunningham	26	121	217	13	230	7.60	1 paid
Paul Fry	27	118	204	15	219	7.42	1 paid
Neil Collins	28	127	178	42	220	6.93	–
Jamie Smith	22	92	114	16	130	5.65	–
Steve Bishop	12	61	58	15	73	4.79	–
Matt Read	8	37	35	9	44	4.76	–
Malcolm Holloway	1	4	3	1	4	4.00	–
Simon Walker	22	79	53	11	64	3.24	–
Danny Hughes	1	5	3	1	4	3.20	–
Chris Johnson	2	8	4	0	4	2.00	–
Lee Smart	4	13	4	1	5	1.54	–
Guests	8	42	49	7	56	5.33	–

PREMIER TROPHY

No	DATE	OPPONENTS	H/A	RESULT	JORGENSEN	READ	COLLINS	CUNNINGHAM	FRY	SMITH	WALKER	SMART
1	24/3	King's Lynn	A	W49-43	15 (5)	4 (4)	8 (4)	7+1 (4)	12+1 (5)	2 (5)	1 (3)	–
2	26/3	Kings Lynn	H	W60-34*	13+1 (5)	5+1 (4)	11+2 (5)	11+1 (4)	8+2 (4)	9 (4)	3+1 (4)	–
3	29/3	Exeter	A	L35-60	10 (4)	0 (4)	3 (4)	3 (4)	15 (5)	1+1 (5)	3 (5)	–
4	2/4	Isle of Wight	H	D45-45	9 (5)	5+1 (4)	1 (4)	13 (5)	6+1 (4)	9+1 (5)	2 (3)	–
5	9/4	Exeter	H	L44-45	5+2 (4)	9 (5)	5 (4)	12 (5)	8+1 (4)	0 (1)	5 (6)	–
6	23/4	Reading	H	W48-41	9 (5)	5+1 (4)	6+2 (4)	10 (5)	7 (4)	11+1 (5)	0 (3)	–
7	25/4	Newport	A	W46-44	4+1 (4)	3+1 (4)	10+3 (5)	12+1 (5)	9 (4)	6+1 (5)	2+1 (3)	–
8	26/4	Reading	A	L38-52	11 (5)	3+1 (4)	1+1 (4)	11 (5)	7 (4)	3 (5)	2 (3)	–
9	7/5	Newport	H	W46-44*	5 (5)	5+1 (4)	4 (4)	12 (4)	7 (5)	11+3 (5)	–	2+1 (3)
10	8/5	Rye House	A	L44-49	6 (4)	R/R	10 (6)	9+2 (6)	4 (4)	14+2 (7)	–	1 (3)
11	4/6	Rye House	H	W56-37*	12 (5)	9+2 (4)	5+2 (5)	10+1 (4)	9+1 (5)	6+1 (4)	5 (3)	–

*Denotes bonus-point victory

NOTE: One match was not ridden: Isle of Wight *v.* Somerset.

TACTICAL RIDES, AS INCLUDED IN THE SCORES GRID:

Match No. 1: Jorgensen 6 points (TR); Match No. 3: Jorgensen 6 points (TR); Fry 4 points (TR); Match No. 8: Cunningham 4 points (TR); Jorgensen 2 points (TR); Match No. 10: Collins 6 points (TR).

PREMIER TROPHY AVERAGES

Rider	Mts	Rds	Pts	Bon	Tot	Avge	Max
Glenn Cunningham	11	51	108	6	114	8.94	1 full; 1 paid
Paul Fry	11	48	90	6	96	8.00	–
John Jorgensen	11	51	92	4	96	7.53	–
Jamie Smith	11	51	72	10	82	6.43	–
Neil Collins	11	49	61	10	71	5.80	–
Matt Read	10	41	48	8	56	5.46	–
Simon Walker	9	33	23	2	25	3.03	–
Lee Smart	2	6	3	1	4	2.67	–

KNOCK-OUT CUP

No	DATE	OPPONENTS	H/A	RESULT	JORGENSEN	READ	COLLINS	CUNNINGHAM	FRY	SMITH	OLIVER	WALKER
1	14/5	Stoke	H	W48-42	9+2 (5)	R/R	5+2 (5)	15 (6)	8+1 (4)	11+3 (7)	0 (3)	–
2	15/5	Stoke	A	W46-44*	6 (4)	R/R	8+2 (5)	12+1 (6)	5 (5)	13+4 (7)	2+1 (3)	–
3	25/6	Workington	H	W48-44	13 (5)	5+1 (4)	9+2 (5)	8 (4)	9 (5)	3+1 (4)	–	1+1 (3)
4	26/6	Workington	A	L40-54	7+1 (4)	7+2 (6)	13+1 (6)	5 (4)	6 (4)	0 (3)	–	2 (3)

*Denotes aggregate victory

TACTICAL SUBSTITUTE AND TACTICAL RIDES, AS INCLUDED IN THE SCORES GRID:

Match No. 4: Jorgensen 4 points (TR); Collins 4 points (TR); Read 0 points (TS).

SOMERSET: back row, left to right: Glenn Cunningham, Matt Read, Mick Bell (Team Manager), Neil Collins, John Jorgensen. Front, kneeling: Jamie Smith, Simon Walker. On bike: Paul Fry.

OTHER MEETINGS

14 March: Severn Bridge Trophy (first leg)

Newport 46 Somerset 44 (Glenn Cunningham 11; Jamie Smith 8+1; John Jorgensen 7+1; Matt Read 7+1; Paul Fry 6; Neil Collins 4+2; Simon Walker 1).

19 March: Severn Bridge Trophy (second leg)

Somerset 53 (Glenn Cunningham 12; Jamie Smith 9+1; John Jorgensen 9; Matt Read 7+2; Paul Fry 6; Simon Walker 5+3; Neil Collins 5+1) Newport 43 – Somerset won 97-89 on aggregate.

INDIVIDUAL MEETING

24 September: Glenn Cunningham Testimonial

QUALIFYING SCORES: Jason Crump 14; Magnus Zetterstrom 13; Craig Boyce 12; Paul Fry 12; Mark Lemon 10; David Ruud 9; John Jorgensen 8; Brent Werner 8; Stephan Katt 7; Leigh Lanham 7; Chris Neath 6; Steve Bishop 6; Phil Morris 3; Shane Parker 3; Neil Collins 1; Steve Masters 1; Simon Walker (Res) 1. FINAL: 1st Crump; 2nd Zetterstrom; 3rd Boyce; 4th Fry.

STOKE EASY-RIDER POTTERS

NOTE: The information below relates only to the main Stoke team. For details of the second side, please refer to the Conference League section.

ADDRESS: Chesterton Stadium, Loomer Road, Chesterton, Newcastle-under-Lyme, Staffordshire, ST5 7LB.

PROMOTER: Dave Tattum.

TRACK LENGTH: 312 metres.

TRACK RECORD: 61.0 seconds – Billy Hamill (11/09/96).

FIRST MEETING: 12 April 1973.

YEARS OF OPERATION: 1972 Training; 1973-74 British League Division Two; 1975-90 National League; 1991-92 British League Division Two; 1994 British League Division Three; 1995 Academy League; 1996-04 Premier League.

NOTES: (1) The team rode under the name of 'Chesterton' in 1973; (2) The team rode under the name of 'Cradley Heath & Stoke' in 1996.

PREVIOUS VENUE: Hanley Stadium, Sun Street, Hanley, Staffordshire.

YEARS OF OPERATION: 1929 English Dirt-track League & Open; 1939 National League Division Two; 1947-49 National League Division Three; 1950-53 National League Division Two; 1960-63 Provincial League.

CLUB HONOURS

LEAGUE CHAMPIONS: 1949.
PAIRS CHAMPIONS: 1984, 1988, 1989.
FOUR-TEAM CHAMPIONS: 1990.

RIDER ROSTER 2004

Paul CLEWS; Daniel GIFFARD; Rob GRANT jr; Robbie KESSLER; Trent LEVERINGTON; Alan MOGRIDGE; Paul PICKERING; Jan STAECHMANN.

OTHER APPEARANCES/GUESTS (official matches only):
Tom BROWN; Justin ELKINS; Paul FRY; Jack HARGREAVES; Chris MILLS; Luke PRIEST.

PREMIER LEAGUE

No	DATE	OPPONENTS	H/A	RESULT	KESSLER	CLEWS	PICKERING	MOGRIDGE	STAECHMANN	GRANT Jr	LEVERINGTON	OTHERS
1	22/5	Berwick	H	W55-39	R/R	5+1 (5)	16+1 (6)	9+2 (5)	18 (6)	2+1 (4)	5 (4)	–
2	29/5	Workington	H	W56-37	R/R	8+1 (5)	16 (6)	7 (5)	13+2 (5)	7+4 (5)	5 (4)	–
3	31/5	Workington	A	L42-52*	R/R	0 (5)	16 (6)	13 (6)	7+2 (5)	3+1 (4)	3 (4)	–
4	5/6	Exeter	H	W57-36	9+1 (4)	7+2 (4)	8+1 (4)	13+1 (5)	10+1 (5)	6+2 (4)	4+1 (4)	–
5	6/6	Newport	A	W54-41	7+1 (4)	6+1 (4)	12 (5)	11+1 (5)	6 (3)	–	7+2 (5)	5+3 (4)
6	7/6	Exeter	A	W50-43*	0 (3)	3+1 (4)	12 (5)	14 (5)	–	–	12+2 (6)	9+1 (7)
7	16/6	King's Lynn	A	L27-67	7+1 (6)	1 (4)	R/R	7 (6)	9 (5)	–	3+1 (5)	0 (4)
8	19/6	Glasgow	H	W52-40	8 (4)	4 (4)	9 (4)	11+2 (5)	13+1 (5)	–	6 (5)	1 (3)
9	27/6	Glasgow	A	L39-54	7 (5)	2+1 (4)	8+1 (4)	8+1 (5)	9 (5)	–	1+1 (2)	4+[illegible] (5)
10	30/6	Hull	A	L46-50	5 (4)	3 (4)	9 (4)	13+1 (5)	11 (5)	2+2 (4)	3 (4)	–
11	3/7	Isle of Wight	H	W56-38	10+1 (4)	6+1 (4)	15 (5)	9+2 (4)	11+2 (5)	5 (5)	0 (3)	–
12	5/7	Newcastle	A	L43-50	1+1 (4)	3+2 (4)	7 (4)	14+1 (5)	12 (5)	1 (3)	5 (5)	–
13	17/7	King's Lynn	H	W55-38	10+1 (5)	5 (4)	8+1 (4)	7+2 (4)	15 (5)	3+1 (4)	7+1 (4)	–
14	24/7	Edinburgh	H	W51-39	8+1 (4)	1 (3)	13 (5)	8+2 (4)	8+1 (5)	5 (4)	8 (5)	–
15	27/7	Isle of Wight	A	L44-50*	4+2 (4)	3 (4)	3 (4)	13+1 (5)	10+1 (5)	1+1 (3)	10+1 (5)	–
16	31/7	Somerset	H	W62-32	10+2 (5)	8+2 (4)	10+1 (4)	14+1 (5)	11 (4)	2+1 (4)	7+1 (4)	–
17	7/8	Sheffield	H	W62-30	11+1 (4)	9+1 (4)	12 (5)	8+2 (4)	13+1 (5)	4+1 (4)	5 (4)	–
18	14/8	Reading	H	L41-49	4+3 (4)	4 (3)	7 (4)	10 (5)	8 (5)	1+1 (3)	7 (6)	–
19	22/8	Hull	H	L42-52	3+1 (4)	10+1 (5)	1 (4)	9 (5)	17 (5)	1 (3)	1+1 (4)	–
20	28/8	Rye House	H	W56-40	5 (4)	8+1 (5)	15 (5)	13+2 (5)	9+1 (4)	2+1 (3)	4 (4)	–
21	30/8	Rye House	A	L45-50*	1+1 (3)	7+2 (5)	9+1 (5)	13+1 (5)	10+1 (5)	2 (4)	3 (3)	–
22	3/9	Somerset	A	L43-50*	11+1 (5)	8+1 (6)	2 (4)	10+1 (5)	7 (4)	0 (3)	5+2 (4)	–
23	4/9	Berwick	A	W49-48*	10+1 (4)	6+3 (5)	9+1 (4)	8+1 (5)	11 (5)	1 (3)	4+2 (4)	–
24	10/9	Edinburgh†	A	L20-64	6 (4)	3 (4)	2 (4)	0 (3)	4 (3)	2+1 (6)	3 (4)	–
25	12/9	Sheffield#	A	L33-44*	12 (5)	5+1 (4)	R/R	6+1 (4)	9 (4)	0 (3)	1 (4)	–
26	17/9	Newport	H	W57-37*	10+1 (5)	10+1 (4)	10 (4)	6+1 (4)	13 (5)	3+1 (4)	5+1 (4)	–
27	18/9	Newcastle	H	W58-37*	6+2 (4)	12+2 (5)	8 (4)	12+2 (5)	11+1 (5)	2 (3)	7+2 (4)	–
28	20/9	Reading	A	L33-61	3 (4)	3 (4)	11 (5)	9+1 (5)	5 (4)	0 (4)	2+2 (4)	–

*Denotes bonus-point victory †Meeting abandoned after heat fourteen, with the result permitted to stand.

#Meeting abandoned after heat twelve, with the result permitted to stand.

STOKE: back row, left to right: Paul Clews, Jan Staechmann, Alan Mogridge. Front, kneeling: Daniel Giffard, Rob Grant jr. On bike: Paul Pickering.

DETAILS OF OTHER RIDERS:

Match No. 5: Tom Brown 5+3 (4); Match No. 6: Paul Fry 8+1 (4); Justin Elkins 1 (3); Match No. 7: Justin Elkins 0 (4); Match No. 8: Luke Priest 1 (3); Match No. 9: Tom Brown 4+1 (5).

TACTICAL SUBSTITUTE AND TACTICAL RIDES, AS INCLUDED IN THE SCORES GRID:

Match No. 3: Pickering 4 points (TR); Mogridge 4 points (TR); Staechmann 2 points (TS); Match No. 7: Staechmann 4 points (TR); Mogridge 4 points (TR); Match No. 9: Pickering 4 points (TR); Staechmann 2 points (TS); Match No. 10: Pickering 6 points (TR); Mogridge 6 points (TR); Match No. 12: Mogridge 6 points (TR); Pickering 0 points (TR); Match No. 15: Mogridge 4 points (TR); Leverington 4 points (TR); Match No. 19: Staechmann 6 points (TR); Mogridge 4 points (TR); Match No. 21: Mogridge 6 points (TR); Pickering 2 points (TR); Staechmann 2 points (TS); Match No. 22: Mogridge 6 points (TR); Match No. 25: Kessler 6 points (TR); Staechmann 4 points (TR); Match No. 28: Pickering 4 points (TR); Mogridge 4 points (TR).

PREMIER LEAGUE AVERAGES

Rider	Mts	Rds	Pts	Bon	Tot	Avge	Max
Jan Staechmann	27	127	270	14	284	8.94	2 full; 1 paid
Alan Mogridge	28	134	253	29	282	8.42	2 paid
Paul Pickering	26	118	238	7	245	8.31	2 full
Robbie Kessler	25	106	165	22	187	7.06	1 paid
Paul Clews	28	120	150	25	175	5.83	–
Tom Brown	2	9	9	4	13	5.78	–
Trent Leverington	28	118	131	20	151	5.12	–
Rob Grant jr	23	87	55	18	73	3.36	–
Luke Priest	1	3	1	0	1	1.33	–
Justin Elkins	2	7	1	0	1	0.57	–
Guest	1	4	8	1	9	9.00	–

PREMIER TROPHY

No	DATE	OPPONENTS	H/A	RESULT	KESSLER	CLEWS	PICKERING	MOGRIDGE	STAECHMANN	GRANT Jr	GIFFARD	LEVERINGTON	OTHERS
1	27/3	Sheffield	H	W54-38	8 (4)	5+1 (4)	13 (5)	5+2 (4)	12+1 (5)	11+1 (5)	0 (3)	–	–
2	1/4	Sheffield	A	L35-59	4+1 (4)	5 (4)	14 (5)	4+1 (4)	7 (5)	1 (4)	0 (4)	–	–
3	10/4	Hull	H	W50-45	4+1 (4)	8 (4)	11+1 (5)	5 (4)	11+1 (5)	6+1 (4)	5 (4)	–	–
4	14/4	Berwick	A	L44-49	7 (4)	1+1 (4)	14 (5)	7+1 (4)	9+1 (5)	5 (5)	1 (3)	–	–
5	17/4	Berwick	H	W54-36*	4 (4)	8 (4)	9 (4)	11+3 (5)	14 (5)	5+2 (4)	3 (4)	–	–
6	23/4	Edinburgh	A	L34-59	3 (4)	4+1 (4)	10+1 (5)	3+1 (4)	7 (4)	6+2 (6)	1+1 (3)	–	–
7	24/4	Glasgow	H	D45-45	5+1 (4)	3+1 (4)	10 (5)	4+2 (4)	13 (5)	6 (4)	4+3 (4)	–	–
8	1/5	Workington	H	W48-44	4+1 (4)	3+1 (3)	14 (5)	8+2 (4)	11+1 (5)	–	6 (6)	–	2 (3)
9	3/5	Workington	A	L41-54	7 (4)	3+1 (5)	15 (5)	R/R	14+1 (5)	1 (7)	1+1 (4)	–	–
10	5/5	Hull	A	L44-50	1 (1)	2 (4)	11 (5)	7+2 (4)	14 (5)	9+1 (7)	0 (4)	–	–
11	9/5	Newcastle	A	W51-40	R/R	5+1 (5)	11 (5)	15+1 (6)	14+1 (6)	3+1 (2)	3+1 (6)	–	–
12	23/5	Glasgow	A	L43-50	R/R	6+1 (6)	17 (6)	5+1 (5)	6 (5)	3+2 (4)	–	6–1 (4)	–
13	30/5	Edinburgh	H	L47-48	R/R	6+2 (5)	12 (6)	11+1 (5)	11 (5)	2 (3)	–	5–1 (6)	–
14	13/6	Newcastle	H	W61-31*	15+2 (6)	9+2 (5)	R/R	13+2 (5)	18 (6)	–	–	5–1 (4)	1 (4)

*Denotes bonus-point victory

DETAILS OF OTHER RIDERS:

Match No. 8: Chris Mills 2 (3); Match No. 14: Jack Hargreaves 1 (4).

TACTICAL RIDES, AS INCLUDED IN THE SCORES GRID:

Match No. 2: Pickering 6 points (TR); Staechmann 2 points (TR); Match No. 4: Pickering 6 points (TR); Match No. 6: Pickering 4 points (TR); Staechmann 2 points (TR); Match No. 9: Staechmann 6 points (TR); Pickering 4 points (TR); Match No. 10: Pickering 4 points (TR); Staechmann 4 points (TR); Match No. 12: Pickering 6 points (TR).

PREMIER TROPHY AVERAGES

Rider	Mts	Rds	Pts	Bon	Tot	Avge	Max
Jan Staechmann	14	71	154	6	160	9.01	1 full
Paul Pickering	13	66	146	2	148	8.97	–
Alan Mogridge	13	58	98	19	117	8.07	1 paid
Robbie Kessler	11	43	62	6	68	6.33	–
Trent Leverington	3	14	16	3	19	5.43	–
Paul Clews	14	61	68	12	80	5.25	–
Rob Grant jr	12	55	58	10	68	4.95	–
Daniel Giffard	11	45	24	6	30	2.67	–
Jack Hargreaves	1	4	1	0	1	1.00	–
Guest	1	3	2	0	2	2.67	–

KNOCK-OUT CUP

No	DATE	OPPONENTS	H/A	RESULT	KESSLER	CLEWS	PICKERING	MOGRIDGE	STAECHMANN	LEVERINGTON	GIFFARD
1	14/5	Somerset	A	L42-48	R/R	0 (4)	7 (5)	11+1 (6)	15 (6)	7+3 (6)	2 (3)
2	15/5	Somerset	H	L44-46	R/R	6+1 (5)	15 (6)	5+1 (5)	16 (6)	2 (5)	0 (3)

YOUNG SHIELD

No	DATE	OPPONENTS	H/A	RESULT	PICKERING	LEVERINGTON	KESSLER	MOGRIDGE	STAECHMANN	GRANT Jr	CLEWS	ELKINS
1	25/9	Isle of Wight	H	W52-40	7 (4)	5 (4)	5+2 (4)	15 (5)	11+2 (5)	0 (3)	9 (5)	–
2	28/9	Isle of Wight	A	L32-59	2 (1)	4 (4)	3+1 (4)	7 (4)	11 (5)	–	3+1 (6)	2 (6)

TACTICAL RIDES, AS INCLUDED IN THE SCORES GRID:

Match No. 2: Staechmann 4 points (TR); Mogridge 0 points (TR).

OTHER MEETINGS

13 March: Challenge

Stoke 53 (Jan Staechmann 14+1; Paul Pickering 11; Rob Grant jr 9; Paul Clews 7+1; Robbie Kessler 6; Alan Mogridge 4+1; Daniel Giffard 2) Stoke Guests 44 (Andy Smith 15; Neil Collins 10+2; Phil Morris 7; Lee Dicken 5+2; Tony Atkin 4+1; Shane Colvin 3+1; Luke Priest 0).

21 March: Staechmann Slideshow (Jan Staechmann Testimonial)

Stoke Select 22 (Joe Screen 6; Leigh Adams 5; Paul Pickering 5; Jan Staechmann 5; Jonathon Bethell 1), Long Eaton Select 14 (Carl Stonehewer 5; Steve Johnston 4; Peter Karlsson 3; James Wright 2; Jason Bunyan 0), Oxford Select 10, Wolverhampton Select 8 – meeting abandoned after heat nine.

4 April: Premier Trophy

Glasgow 16 Stoke 8 (Rob Grant jr 3+1; Paul Pickering 3; Jan Staechmann 2; Paul Clews 0; Alan Mogridge 0; Benji Compton 0; Robbie Kessler R/R) – meeting abandoned after heat four.

11 September: Premier League

Stoke 25 (Paul Clews 8; Jan Staechmann 4+1; Paul Pickering 4; Trent Leverington 3+2; Alan Mogridge 3; Robbie Kessler 2; Rob Grant jr 1) Newport 23 – meeting abandoned after heat eight.

INDIVIDUAL MEETING

24 October: Wedgwood Pride Of The Potteries

QUALIFYING SCORES: Paul Pickering 11; Jan Staechmann 11; Mark Lemon 9; Alan Mogridge 8; Adam Skornicki 8; Rob Grant jr 7; Adam Allott 6; Paul Clews 5; Ricky Ashworth 5; Tony Atkin 1; Jack Hargreaves 0. FIRST SEMI-FINAL: 1st Allott; 2nd Lemon; 3rd Mogridge; 4th Staechmann. SECOND SEMI-FINAL: 1st Skornicki; 2nd Pickering; 3rd Clews; 4th Grant jr. FINAL: 1st Lemon; 2nd Allott; 3rd Skornicki; 4th Pickering

WORKINGTON THOMAS ARMSTRONG COMETS

ADDRESS: Derwent Park Stadium, Workington, Cumbria, CA14 2HG.
PROMOTERS: Tony Mole, Ian Thomas & Redvers Mole.
TRACK LENGTH: 364 metres.
TRACK RECORD: 64.1 seconds – Simon Stead (17/07/04).
FIRST MEETING: 3 April 1970.
YEARS OF OPERATION: 1970-74 British League Division Two; 1975-81 National League; 1985 Open; 1987 National League; 1994 Demonstration; 1999-04 Premier League.
NOTE: In 1987, the track was occupied by 'Glasgow Tigers', who later that year became known as 'Workington Tigers'.

CLUB HONOURS

PAIRS CHAMPIONS: 1999, 2000, 2001, 2003.
FOUR-TEAM CHAMPIONS: 2001, 2004.

RIDER ROSTER 2004

Aidan COLLINS; Rusty HARRISON; Kauko NIEMINEN; Simon STEAD; Carl STONEHEWER; Brett WOODIFIELD; James WRIGHT.

OTHER APPEARANCES/GUESTS (official matches only):
Paul COOPER, Jason LYONS; Glen PHILLIPS; Chris SCHRAMM; Blair SCOTT.

PREMIER LEAGUE

No	DATE	OPPONENTS	H/A	RESULT	STONEHEWER	WOODIFIELD	HARRISON	NIEMINEN	STEAD	WRIGHT	COLLINS	OTHERS
1	8/5	Newport	H	W65-28	16+1 (6)	5+2 (4)	12+3 (6)	13+1 (5)	R/R	10+2 (5)	9+2 (4)	–
2	22/5	Rye House	A	L39-56	16 (6)	–	10+1 (6)	4 (5)	R/R	4 (5)	4 (4)	1+1 (4)
3	28/5	Somerset	A	L41-54	16 (6)	3 (5)	1 (3)	12 (6)	R/R	2 (4)	7+1 (6)	–
4	29/5	Stoke	A	L37-56	13+1 (6)	11 (7)	6+1 (6)	5+2 (5)	R/R	2+1 (3)	0 (3)	–
5	31/5	Stoke	H	W52-42	11 (5)	4 (4)	9 (5)	7+1 (4)	9 (4)	5 (4)	7+2 (4)	–
6	5/6	Reading	H	W57-39	13+2 (5)	7 (4)	8+1 (4)	6 (4)	13+1 (5)	6+2 (4)	4+1 (4)	–
7	19/6	Sheffield	H	W51-44	12+2 (5)	4 (4)	6+1 (4)	9+1 (4)	15 (5)	1 (4)	4+2 (4)	–
8	2/7	Rye House	H	W58-34*	12+1 (5)	4+1 (3)	3+1 (4)	10 (4)	13+2 (5)	10+2 (5)	6+3 (4)	–
9	7/7	Hull	A	L44-46	14 (5)	6+1 (5)	3+1 (4)	7 (4)	9 (5)	2 (4)	3+1 (3)	–
10	10/7	Glasgow	H	W68-25	13+2 (5)	9+1 (4)	12+3 (5)	10 (4)	12 (4)	7+3 (4)	5 (4)	–
11	11/7	Newport	A	W46-44*	5+2 (4)	19+1 (7)	0 (3)	8+1 (5)	9+1 (5)	3+1 (3)	2 (3)	–
12	12/7	Exeter	A	L39-56	3 (5)	12 (5)	5 (5)	1 (3)	14+2 (5)	1+1 (3)	3+1 (4)	–
13	13/7	Isle of Wight	A	D45-45	11+2 (5)	6+1 (4)	6 (4)	7+1 (4)	12 (5)	0 (4)	3 (4)	–
14	17/7	Somerset	H	W58-35*	14+1 (5)	3+2 (4)	6+1 (4)	11+1 (4)	14+1 (5)	8 (5)	2 (3)	–
15	24/7	Isle of Wight	H	W49-41*	14+1 (5)	3 (5)	9+2 (5)	R/R	12 (4)	9+1 (7)	2+1 (4)	–
16	31/7	Newcastle	H	W69-25	12+1 (5)	10+2 (4)	7+4 (4)	10+1 (4)	15 (5)	8+2 (4)	7+1 (4)	–

WORKINGTON: back row, left to right: Rusty Harrison, Aidan Collins, Brett Woodifield, Simon Stead. Front, kneeling: James Wright, Kauko Nieminen. On bike: Carl Stonehewer.

PREMIER LEAGUE continued

No	DATE	OPPONENTS	H/A	RESULT	STONEHEWER	WOODIFIELD	HARRISON	NIEMINEN	STEAD	WRIGHT	COLLINS	OTHERS
17	7/8	Edinburgh	H	W65-30	12+2 (5)	10+1 (4)	7+2 (4)	10 (4)	14+1 (5)	6+2 (4)	6+1 (4)	–
18	11/8	King's Lynn	A	L42-52	11+1 (5)	11+3 (6)	2+1 (4)	6 (4)	10 (5)	1 (3)	1 (3)	–
19	14/8	King's Lynn	H	W54-36*	9+1 (5)	7 (4)	4+1 (4)	6+2 (4)	15 (5)	7+2 (4)	6 (4)	–
20	22/8	Newcastle	A	W51-43*	10+1 (5)	11+2 (5)	10+1 (5)	5 (4)	10+1 (4)	5+2 (4)	0 (3)	–
21	27/8	Edinburgh	A	L43-53*	12+1 (5)	8+1 (5)	5 (4)	2 (4)	13 (5)	3 (4)	0 (3)	–
22	28/8	Berwick	A	L44-49	8+1 (5)	8+1 (5)	5+1 (4)	3 (4)	17 (5)	–	1 (3)	2+1 (4)
23	30/8	Berwick	H	W60-33*	13+2 (5)	5+2 (4)	7+1 (4)	6 (4)	12 (4)	7+1 (4)	10+1 (5)	–
24	4/9	Exeter	H	W66-26*	14+1 (5)	6+1 (4)	10+2 (4)	10 (4)	11+1 (5)	8+3 (4)	7+2 (4)	–
25	9/9	Sheffield	A	W46-44*	10+1 (5)	5+3 (4)	9 (4)	0 (3)	15 (5)	6+1 (6)	1 (3)	–
26	11/9	Hull	H	W53-43*	12+3 (5)	1 (3)	8+1 (4)	5+1 (4)	15 (5)	9+1 (5)	3+1 (4)	–
27	12/9	Glasgow	A	W46-44*	7 (5)	6 (4)	7 (4)	2 (3)	13 (5)	4+2 (4)	7+3 (5)	–
28	17/9	Reading	A	L37-56	10 (5)	2+1 (3)	2+2 (4)	9 (5)	8 (4)	5+2 (6)	1 (3)	–

*Denotes bonus-point victory

DETAILS OF OTHER RIDERS:

Match No. 2: Chris Schramm 1+1 (4); Match No. 22: Blair Scott 2+1 (4).

TACTICAL RIDES, AS INCLUDED IN THE SCORES GRID:

Match No. 2: Harrison 6 points (TR); Stonehewer 4 points (TR); Match No. 3: Stonehewer 6 points (TR); Nieminen 4 points (TR); Match No. 4: Stonehewer 6 points (TR); Woodifield 0 points (TR); Match No. 12: Stead 6 points (TR); Woodifield 4 points (TR); Match No. 13: Nieminen 2 points (TR); Match No. 18: Stonehewer 6 points (TR); Stead 4 points (TR); Match No. 21: Stead 6 points (TR); Stonehewer 6 points (TR); Match No. 22: Stead 6 points (TR); Match No. 28: Stead 4 points (TR); Stonehewer 4 points (TR).

PREMIER LEAGUE AVERAGES

Rider	Mts	Rds	Pts	Bon	Tot	Avge	Max
Simon Stead	24	114	287	10	297	10.42	8 full; 3 paid
Carl Stonehewer	28	143	307	30	337	9.43	7 paid
Brett Woodifield	27	120	184	26	210	7.00	1 paid
Kauko Nieminen	27	112	181	12	193	6.89	1 paid
Rusty Harrison	28	121	176	31	207	6.84	2 paid
James Wright	27	116	139	31	170	5.86	–
Aidan Collins	28	106	111	23	134	5.06	–
Blair Scott	1	4	2	1	3	3.00	–
Guest	1	4	1	1	2	2.00	–

PREMIER TROPHY

No	DATE	OPPONENTS	H/A	RESULT	STONEHEWER	WOODIFIELD	HARRISON	NIEMINEN	STEAD	COLLINS	WRIGHT	COOPER	OTHERS
1	17/3	Hull	A	L44-49	21 (6)	7+1 (5)	1 (4)	8 (6)	R/R	5 (5)	2+1 (4)	–	–
2	18/3	Sheffield	A	L42-52	16 (6)	8+1 (6)	7+1 (5)	6 (5)	R/R	5+1 (5)	0 (3)	–	–
3	20/3	Edinburgh	H	W50-46	17 (6)	7+2 (5)	8+2 (6)	9+2 (5)	R/R	8+1 (5)	1+1 (3)	–	–
4	27/3	Glasgow	H	W59-35	17+1 (6)	7+1 (5)	5+1 (4)	14 (6)	R/R	11+1 (5)	5+2 (4)	–	–

No	DATE	OPPONENTS	H/A	RESULT	STONEHEWER	WOODIFIELD	HARRISON	NIEMINEN	STEAD	COLLINS	WRIGHT	COOPER	OTHERS
5	3/4	Hull	H	W58-35*	15 (5)	5+2 (5)	15 (6)	7+1 (5)	R/R	11+2 (5)	–	5+2 (4)	–
6	9/4	Edinburgh	A	L40-54	13 (6)	2+2 (4)	6 (5)	4+3 (5)	R/R	14+2 (7)	1 (3)	–	–
7	10/4	Berwick	A	L36-58	18 (6)	2+1 (5)	4 (6)	1 (4)	R/R	11+1 (6)	0 (3)	–	–
8	12/4	Berwick	H	W60-32*	15 (6)	9+3 (5)	8+2 (5)	13+2 (6)	R/R	11+2 (5)	4+2 (3)	–	–
9	24/4	Sheffield	H	W55-40*	15 (6)	7+3 (5)	14+1 (6)	6+1 (5)	R/R	–	6+1 (4)	–	7+1 (4)
10	1/5	Stoke	A	L44-48	18 (6)	4+1 (5)	4+1 (6)	10 (5)	R/R	7+3 (5)	–	1 (3)	–
11	2/5	Newcastle	A	L47-49	21 (6)	3 (5)	13+1 (6)	2 (5)	R/R	0 (3)	8+1 (5)	–	–
12	3/5	Stoke	H	W54-41*	18 (6)	3 (4)	9+1 (6)	6+3 (5)	R/R	9+1 (4)	9+2 (5)	–	–
13	16/5	Glasgow	A	L46-47*	13 (6)	4+1 (5)	9+1 (6)	9 (5)	R/R	6+3 (4)	5+2 (4)	–	–
14	21/5	Newcastle	H	W58-33*	15+1 (6)	5+1 (4)	14+2 (6)	11+3 (5)	R/R	5+2 (4)	8+2 (5)	–	–

*Denotes bonus-point victory

DETAILS OF OTHER RIDER:

Match No. 9: Glen Phillips 7+1 (4).

TACTICAL RIDES, AS INCLUDED IN THE SCORES GRID:

Match No. 1: Stonehewer 6 points (TR); Match No. 2: Stonehewer 4 points (TR); Harrison 4 points (TR); Match No. 6: Collins 4 points (TR); Stonehewer 4 points (TR); Match No. 7: Stonehewer 4 points (TR); Collins 4 points (TR); Match No. 10: Stonehewer 4 points (TR); Match No. 11: Stonehewer 6 points (TR); Harrison 6 points (TR); Match No. 13: Stonehewer 6 points (TR).

PREMIER TROPHY AVERAGES

Rider	Mts	Rds	Pts	Bon	Tot	Avge	Max
Carl Stonehewer	14	83	215	2	217	10.46	4 full; 1 paid
Aidan Collins	13	63	99	19	118	7.49	–
Kauko Nieminen	14	72	106	15	121	6.72	–
Rusty Harrison	14	77	112	13	125	6.49	–
James Wright	12	46	49	14	63	5.48	–
Brett Woodifield	14	68	73	19	92	5.41	–
Paul Cooper	2	7	6	2	8	4.57	–
Guest	1	4	7	1	8	8.00	–

KNOCK-OUT CUP

No	DATE	OPPONENTS	H/A	RESULT	STONEHEWER	WOODIFIELD	HARRISON	NIEMINEN	STEAD	WRIGHT	COLLINS
1	14/5	Edinburgh	A	L43-50	18 (6)	5+1 (5)	5+1 (6)	7 (5)	R/R	7+1 (5)	1+1 (3)
2	15/5	Edinburgh	H	W57-35*	14+1 (6)	11+1 (5)	7+1 (5)	11+1 (6)	R/R	6+2 (4)	8+1 (4)
3	25/6	Somerset	A	L44-48	15+1 (5)	3 (5)	5+3 (4)	7 (4)	9+1 (5)	3 (4)	2 (3)
4	26/6	Somerset	H	W54-40*	17+1 (6)	5 (5)	13+2 (6)	11+2 (5)	R/R	3 (4)	5+1 (4)
5	2/9	Isle of Wight	A	L38-56	15 (5)	0 (3)	5 (4)	5+1 (4)	5 (5)	2 (4)	6 (5)
6	18/9	Isle of Wight	H	L43½-46½	12 (5)	1 (4)	4+2 (4)	9 (4)	13 (5)	4½+1 (5)	0 (3)

*Denotes aggregate victory

TACTICAL RIDES, AS INCLUDED IN THE SCORES GRID:

Match No. 1: Stonehewer 4 points (TR); Nieminen 2 points (TR); Match No. 3: Stonehewer 4 points (TR); Match No. 5: Stonehewer 6 points (TR); Stead 2 points (TR).

YOUNG SHIELD

No	DATE	OPPONENTS	H/A	RESULT	STONEHEWER	WOODIFIELD	HARRISON	NIEMINEN	STEAD	WRIGHT	COLLINS	OTHERS
1	29/9	King's Lynn	A	L41-52	4+4 (5)	8 (4)	7 (4)	0 (0)	–	9+3 (7)	1+1 (5)	12 (5)
2	9/10	King's Lynn	H	W55-41*	13+1 (6)	7+1 (5)	11+1 (5)	R/R	–	3 (2)	9+2 (7)	12+1 (5)
3	16/10	Hull	H	W52-44	13+2 (6)	6+1 (4)	6 (5)	R/R	15 (5)	6+1 (6)	6+3 (4)	–
4	20/10	Hull	A	L42-52	18+1 (6)	6 (5)	3 (4)	R/R	10 (5)	0 (4)	5+1 (6)	–

*Denotes aggregate victory

DETAILS OF OTHER RIDERS:

Match No. 1: Jason Lyons 12 (5); Match No. 2: Jason Lyons 12+1 (5).

TACTICAL RIDES, AS INCLUDED IN THE SCORES GRID:

Match No. 1: Lyons 4 points (TR); Wright 2 points (TR); Match No. 4: Stonehewer 6 points (TR); Stead 2 points (TR).

OTHER MEETINGS

6 March: Carlos Villar Benefit

Edinburgh/Workington 32 (Simon Stead 12; Carl Stonehewer 9; Paul Cooper 7; Simon Cartwright 4; Steven McAllister DNR), Berwick 28, Glasgow 19, Newcastle 17 – staged at Berwick.

13 March: Challenge

Workington 66 (Aidan Collins 14+2; Brett Woodifield 14+1; Rusty Harrison 13+2; James Wright 9+5; Carl Stonehewer 8+1; Kauko Nieminen 8; Simon Stead 0) Valsarna 27 (Stefan Danno 15; Johan Engman 7; Niklas Fridell 2+1; Rene Lethinen 2; Anders Agmell 1; Peter I. Karlsson 0; Adam Skornicki R/R).

2 October: Young Shield quarter-final (second leg)

Workington 20 (Carl Stonehewer 6; Rusty Harrison 5+1; Aidan Collins 3+2; James Wright 3; Jason Lyons 2; Brett Woodifield 1; Kauko Nieminen R/R) King's Lynn 10 – meeting abandoned after heat five.

13 October: Young Shield semi-final (first leg)

Hull 33 Workington 15 (Carl Stonehewer 7; Simon Stead 4; Aidan Collins 4; Brett Woodifield 0; Rusty Harrison 0; James Wright 0; Kauko Nieminen R/R) – meeting abandoned after heat eight.

INDIVIDUAL MEETING

25 September: Cumberland Classic

1st Jason Lyons 13; 2nd Rory Schlein 12; 3rd James Wright 11; Stuart Robson 11; Kauko Nieminen 10; Carl Stonehewer 10; Fredrik Lindgren 9; Aidan Collins 8; Rusty Harrison 7; Brett Woodifield 7; Shane Parker 6; Richard Juul 5; David Howe 4; Phil Morris 4; John Branney (Res) 3; Ford Keane 0; Henning Loof 0; Kriss Irving (Res) 0.

CONFERENCE LEAGUE
2004

RACING DIARY OF THE SEASON

MARCH

13 Torrents of the wet stuff wash out Boston's much-anticipated challenge match versus Mildenhall.

14 Three-Team Tournament fare sees Rye House dominate proceedings to register 45 points and take victory over King's Lynn (32) and Peterborough (30) at the East of England Showground, with Steve Boxall carding maximum points (12) for the Raiders.

16 With the Saddlebow Road circuit in a waterlogged state, Boston's intriguing challenge match against Mildenhall is again regrettably called off. Weymouth kick-off with a narrow 47-46 challenge-match success over a dogged Swindon outfit.

20 Mildenhall's opening challenge fixture versus Boston lasts just one heat before heavy rain causes an early curtailment, with the visitors leading 5-1.

21 The Queensway Meadows raceway serves up an entertaining encounter, with Newport and Weymouth finally ending all-square at 45-45 in the season's first league meeting. Scott Pegler is in top form for the Mavericks, romping to an unbeaten six-ride full house (18).

24 The Tommy Jansson Memorial Shield is postponed at lunchtime, due to a waterlogged Wimbledon circuit.

26 Chris Courage nets 14 points to win the Wessex Rosebowl at Weymouth, with Jason Prynne finishing as runner-up a single point behind.

28 Carmarthen begin their third season of racing, but suffer a hefty 57-36 Conference League loss at the hands of a solid-looking Boston septet. Mildenhall overcome an early deficit to defeat Newcastle 54-38 in the league at West Row.

31 Wimbledon suffer a 48-45 league reverse at the hands of reigning Champions Mildenhall.

APRIL

2 Weymouth are beaten 48-42 by visiting Carmarthen in exciting league fare at the Wessex Stadium.

3 Richard Hall comes out on top in the British Under-21 Championship qualifier at Buxton, with Ben Wilson and Jamie Robertson filling the other podium positions.

4 Newport's league clash against Oxford lasts just three heats, before the rain intervenes with the visitors holding an 11-7 advantage. The second qualifier for the British Under-21 Championship is curtailed by rain at Mildenhall after sixteen heats. At the time, Daniel King is holding sway from Steve Boxall and Lee Smart.

7 Understrength Stoke suffer a 51-41 league reverse at the hands of visiting Newcastle. At Plough Lane, Wimbledon post a conclusive 57-38 Conference Trophy victory over Buxton.

9 League activity sees Carmarthen defeat Newport 57-37 in a one-sided Welsh derby at the United Counties Showground. Weymouth win 53-41 against Stoke in the first leg of their Knock-Out Cup tie. Led by a full 15-pointer from Daniel King, Mildenhall claim a 53-42 victory at Boston in an action-packed challenge match.

10 Armadale race their first-ever Conference League fixture and just shade a 49-44 success against Buxton.

11 Buxton quickly gain revenge over Armadale, winning the return league match 47-45, with Trent Leverington scoring the lot (15). The league action continues at West Row, where Mildenhall get the better of a full-blooded encounter to defeat Rye House 53-40. There's more thrilling speedway at Saddlebow Road, as Boston beat Wimbledon 52-43 in the day's third league match.

12 Tommy Allen bags a 15-point maximum, as Rye House ease to a 55-38 win over Boston in the Conference League.

14 Wimbledon win 54-40 against Carmarthen in a fully committed league clash at Plough Lane.

16 Peterborough announce their immediate withdrawal from the Conference Trophy, due to the problems in securing the necessary support services for Sunday meetings. Thanks to steady rain, Weymouth's league encounter with Boston is curtailed after nine heats, with the Barracuda-Braves holding a 30-24 advantage.

17 Rain halts Armadale's league match against Weymouth, but with twelve heats completed the result stands as a 53-21 success for the Devils.

18 Despite a mid-match fightback, Newport still go down to a 52-41 league defeat at the hands of Rye House. Mildenhall's Knock-Out Cup tie versus Carmarthen sees thirteen heats completed, before rains cuts the contest short. The result stands as a 52-31 victory for the Fen Tigers, with Daniel King unbeaten on a tally of 11+1 points. Three scheduled league fixtures are postponed due to the effects of rain: Buxton *v.* Stoke, Boston *v.* Oxford and Newcastle *v.* Weymouth.

19 Coventry stage their first-ever Conference Trophy meeting, but suffer a 51-40 loss to visiting Wimbledon, for whom both Wayne Broadhurst (15) and Barrie Evans (12+3) ride unbeaten.

21 Wimbledon's Conference Trophy match against Coventry is postponed due to a waterlogged Plough Lane raceway.

25 Buxton defeat a battling Coventry outfit 53-44 in the Conference Trophy. Undefeated totals from Daniel King (15) and Paul Lee (12+3) help Mildenhall to a 59-36 victory against Wimbledon in the league.

28 Stoke's Conference League match against Swindon is called off due to heavy rain. Wimbledon's league match versus Armadale is also a victim of wet weather.

30 The rain continues to wreak havoc, with the day's two scheduled league meetings called off: Oxford *v.* Armadale and Weymouth *v.* Buxton.

MAY

1 Armadale crush Newport 62-31 in the league, with Derek Sneddon (14+1) and Matthew Wethers (12) remaining unbeaten by an opponent.

2 Mildenhall race to a comfortable 60-32 league success over Weymouth. At Saddlebow Road, Darren Rolph bags a paid maximum (14+1) as Boston defeat Rye House 57-36 in the league. William Lawson cleans up (15), as Newcastle register a 58-38 league win over Newport.

3 Weymouth trail for much of the meeting, before going down 47-45 to visiting Wimbledon in an eventful league encounter. Following the match, thirteen-year-old Joshua Auty races to victory from Shane Waldron in the first round of the new British Under-15 Championship. Carmarthen suffer a 53-42 reverse to Mildenhall, as the Fen Tigers claim an aggregate Knock-Out Cup triumph.

5 Mark Burrows' Testimonial is unfortunately postponed, due to a waterlogged Wimbledon circuit.

7 Weymouth narrowly defeat Buxton 47-42 in an exciting league encounter at the Wessex Stadium, with visiting rider James Wright establishing a new track record of 54.7 seconds for the 223-metre circuit.

8 Armadale plays host to the second round of the British Under-15 Championship and it's Shane Waldron who takes victory ahead of Simon Lambert and Kyle Hughes.

9 Led by unbeaten tallies from James Wright (15) and Trent Leverington (13+2), Buxton claim a 52-39 league win over Boston. The match is marred by a sickening third-heat crash involving Benji Compton and Darren Mallett, which results in the latter being airlifted to hospital after breaking both a wrist and an ankle. Mildenhall race to a 56-39 success against Sheffield in the Conference Trophy, with Paul Lee netting a full points quota (15).

10 Despite sunny skies above the Abbey Stadium, Swindon's opening league fixture against Carmarthen is called off at 2.30 p.m., due to the effects of heavy weekend rainfall.

12 Stoke suffer a 47-42 reverse to visiting Weymouth, as the Wildcats progress to the next round in the Knock-Out Cup. Great Britain's Under-21 side shows no mercy as they steam to a 61-33 victory in a challenge match against Wimbledon at Plough Lane.

14 Chris Schramm's 15-point maximum helps Oxford to a comfortable 57-34 league success over local rivals Swindon. Over in West Wales, Carmarthen's first-ever Friday night meeting results in a 63-27 league success over Newcastle, with both Steve Bishop (18) and Dean Felton (13+2) remaining unbeaten. Weymouth lose 52-43 to Mildenhall in the Conference Trophy, with visiting number one Paul Lee setting a new best time for the circuit of 53.5 seconds in heat five. This comes after home man David Mason had beaten the previous best time when clocking 54.3 seconds in the opening race.

16 Non-league Sittingbourne put up a valiant effort before going down 53-40 to Wimbledon in the first leg of their Knock-Out Cup tie. Paul Lee establishes his second track record in three days when timed at 50.25 seconds in the opening heat of Mildenhall's comfortable 59-36 league win against Swindon at West Row. Meanwhile, ex-Swindon man and recently crowned British Under-21 Champion Ritchie Hawkins bags a paid maximum (11+1) for the victorious Fen men. William Lawson thunders to maximum points (21) and sets a new Conference League track record of 64.6 seconds for the Brough Park raceway, but his efforts can't prevent Newcastle from slipping to a 53-42 defeat at the hands of Rye House. At the Norfolk Arena, Richie Dennis' paid maximum (14+1) helps Boston ease to a 57-36 league win against Stoke.

17 Double-header Conference Trophy fare at Owlerton sees Sheffield register a brace of wins, 58-36 against Wimbledon and 60-34 versus Weymouth. Richard Hall posts 15 and 12-point maximums respectively, while Ben Wilson nets identical unbeaten tallies of 13+2 points in both matches. Also weighing in with a paid full house is Paul Cooper (13+2) in the first match. Swindon make a losing start to their home league programme, going down 47-42 to Carmarthen in a thrilling tussle.

19 Wimbledon defeat Sittingbourne 55-38 for a comfortable passage through to the next round of the Knock-Out Cup.

21 David Mason nets an unbeaten 14+1 points as Weymouth record a 55-37 league victory over Newport.

22 Matthew Wethers sets a new Conference League track record of 57.84 seconds, but Armadale can't prevent visiting Mildenhall from winning 49-45.

23 Terrific Sunday afternoon league fare at Buxton results in a hard-fought 51-45 success for the homesters versus the Oxford Academy. In a double dose of league activity at Brough Park, Newcastle are soundly beaten 55-40 in the first match, as Mildenhall make it eight wins out of eight. The second meeting sees the Gems win 45-44 in a thriller against Weymouth. At Saddlebow Road, Boston retain second spot in the league standings courtesy of a 55-40 success against Armadale.

24 Karl Mason scores maximum points (15) and establishes a new Conference-level track record at Brandon as Coventry register a 61-35 challenge-match success over Belle Vue Colts. Swindon battle valiantly before suffering a 50-44 league loss to visiting Armadale, with both Matthew Wethers (17+1) and Gary Phelps (15) remaining unbeaten for the victorious Devils.

25 After coming from behind on three occasions, Stoke narrowly defeat Armadale 46-44. For the Devils, Matthew Wethers at least has the satisfaction of establishing a new Conference League track record of 64.4 seconds.

26 'Buzz' Burrows romps to maximum points (18), as Wimbledon claim a 55-43 league success over Newcastle.

27 The prestigious Top Gun Championship at Sheffield results in victory for Ben Wilson from Richard Hall, Paul Cooper and Mark Thompson.

28 A last-heat 4-2 gives Stoke a 48-46 win at Oxford in a pulsating league encounter. Further domestic activity at the Wessex Stadium sees Weymouth triumph 51-44 versus Newcastle.

29 Armadale overcome dogged resistance to beat Boston 48-42, with Matthew Wethers bagging another league maximum (15). Rye House race to a 50-42 league victory against Carmarthen.

30 Buxton have no answers as visiting Mildenhall sweep to a 56-38 league victory, with Ritchie Hawkins remaining unbeaten (13+2). Meanwhile, at the United Counties Showground, Carmarthen are swamped 62-29 by Oxford in a one-sided league match. The victorious Silver Machine Academy are headed by paid maximums from Danny Norton (16+2) and Chris Schramm (14+1).

31 Mildenhall make it ten league wins out of ten as they convincingly defeat Buxton 57-35, aided by undefeated tallies from Lee Smart (16+2), Jon Armstrong (11+1) and Paul Lee (10+2). The victory is marred, however, by a frightening eleventh-heat crash, which leaves young Adam Roynon nursing two broken wrists. Depleted Rye House reveal great character in registering a 52-41 Bank Holiday league win against Wimbledon.

JUNE

2 Wimbledon not only host, but also win the inaugural Conference League Pairs Championship ahead of Mildenhall, thanks to the last-heat heroics of Mark Burrows and Barrie Evans in gaining maximum points over Ritchie Hawkins and Jon Armstrong.

4 A topsy-turvy league match finally results in victory for Weymouth against Swindon by a 48-47 scoreline.

5 Matthew Wethers' 18-point full house helps Armadale to a 58-37 league victory versus Wimbledon.

6 Newport claim their first league win of the season, narrowly beating Stoke 47-46 in a thriller at Queensway Meadows. It's tight league fare at Hi-Edge too, with Buxton finally defeating Carmarthen 46-44. The talented James Wright leaves his mark on the match,

firstly equalling the track record in heat one (54.0 seconds), prior to rocketing around the 240-metre circuit in heat six and clocking a new best time of 53.5 seconds. After ten straight wins in the league, Mildenhall surprisingly lose 47-45 at home to a determined Boston outfit. A twelfth-heat crash forces the abandonment of Newcastle's league match against Wimbledon, but the result stands as a 41-31 success for the Dons.

7 Swindon look like further denting Mildenhall's impressive record until a last-heat 5-1 turns the league match in the Fen Tigers' favour, giving a final result of 47-46. Former Swindon rider Ritchie Hawkins lowers his own Conference League track record to 68.02 seconds on his way to a marvellous 21-point maximum for the Suffolk side. Paul Cooper plunders a paid maximum (13+2) as Sheffield race to a 57-37 Conference Trophy success over King's Lynn in the first part of a double-header. The second match, against Coventry, is halted on the opening lap of heat twelve when a dreadful crash leaves Michael Mitchell and Steve Clarke with serious injuries. Despite Sheffield holding an unassailable 44-22 advantage, the result is not allowed to stand.

9 Stoke comfortably beat Carmarthen 58-36 in the league at Loomer Road. There's further league action at Wimbledon, with visiting Oxford coming from behind to edge a 48-47 victory in a thrilling encounter.

11 The Wessex Stadium hosts the Vic Harding Memorial meeting, with Hackney and Sunderland finishing all-square on 25 points apiece ahead of host side Weymouth (20). The second-half event sees Jack Gledhill take victory from Lee Smart, Chris Ferguson and Ben Powell in the final of the Memorial Trophy, held in memory of the rider who tragically died the day after crashing at Hackney on 8 June 1979.

13 Led by James Wright's second league maximum (15), Buxton ease to a 55-40 victory over Newport. At the United Counties Showground, Carmarthen lose 45-42 as Mildenhall collect their twelfth league success in thirteen matches. Joel Parsons nets an untroubled maximum (12), as Rye House romp to a 61-30 victory over Weymouth in the league. Individual fare at King's Lynn sees Richard Hall tally 14 points to take the Lincolnshire Trophy ahead of Peter Boast (13) and Mark Thompson (13).

14 Coventry are unable to prevent King's Lynn from sprinting to a 53-39 success in the Conference Trophy at Brandon.

16 League fare sees Weymouth win 47-43 at Wimbledon, with former Don Daniel Giffard plundering maximum points (15) for the victorious Wildcats.

18 Richard Hall cards a six-ride full house (18) as Boston dismiss Newport 67-24 in the Conference League. The day's other league match results in a 59-34 success for Weymouth over Rye House.

19 Armadale's league fixture against Swindon is called off after heavy overnight rain.

20 At Sittingbourne, the Nathan Gaymer Memorial Trophy is won in fine style by maximum man Chris Ferguson (15), with Matthew Wright (14) and James Theobald (13) filling the other podium positions. Buxton's league match against Wimbledon falls victim to a waterlogged track. A double dose of league activity at Brough Park firstly sees Newcastle defeat Swindon 53-39, with Jamie Robertson remaining unbeaten (14+1). In the second match, visiting Boston are never headed as they claim a 49-47 success. Led by unbeaten scores from Jason King (12), Jon Armstrong (11+1) and Lee Smart (9+3), mighty Mildenhall cruise to a 66-26 victory against Newport, thereby remaining head and shoulders above the rest in the league standings.

23 Stoke's league match versus Newport is postponed due to a waterlogged Loomer Road

circuit. For a second time, Buzz Burrows' much-anticipated Testimonial is unfortunately washed out at Wimbledon.

25 Boston defeat Rye House in the first leg of their Knock-Out Cup tie. Further KOC action sees Oxford swamp Buxton 61-31, with Chris Schramm (18), Craig Branney (15) and Danny Norton (12+3) remaining unbeaten. Also in the Knock-Out Cup, a cracker at the Wessex Stadium sees visiting Wimbledon triumph 48-47 against Weymouth.

26 The Knock-Out Cup match between Rye House and Boston is a casualty of rain at Hoddesdon. Stoke race to a 57-36 victory over Swindon in the league at Loomer Road, with veteran visiting skipper Malcolm Holloway clocking a new CL track record of 63.8 seconds in the opening heat.

27 Aided by unbeaten tallies from Karl Mason (15) and Scott Pegler (11+1), Newport win 46-44 against Welsh rivals Carmarthen in a thrilling league contest at Queensway Meadows. James Wright lowers the Buxton track record to 52.9 seconds and goes on to net maximum points (15) in an enthralling Knock-Out Cup fixture versus Oxford. The youngster's efforts help the Hitmen to a 50-44 success, but it's the visitors who go through on aggregate. With Mildenhall leading 43-17 after ten heats, their KOC clash against King's Lynn is abandoned due to rain. Newcastle put up a brave fight before going down to a 48-41 defeat at the hands of visiting Armadale in exciting league fare at Brough Park.

28 Mildenhall's strong opening pairing of Ritchie Hawkins (15) and Jon Armstrong (11+4) plunder maximums as the Fen Tigers win 54-39 in the Conference Trophy at Coventry. In a blistering performance, Hawkins also lowers Brandon's CL track record to 61.4 seconds, amazingly shaving 1.3 seconds off the previous best time!

30 Led by a paid maximum from Mark Burrows (13+2), Wimbledon beat Coventry 55-39 in the Conference Trophy.

JULY

2 Run amid driving rain, Conference League activity sees Weymouth chalk up a 57-36 victory against Stoke.

4 It's wholly entertaining at Sittingbourne as Edward Kennett clocks a new track record of 58.4 seconds during the aptly-titled Festival of Speed team event. Wimbledon and Swindon win their respective groups, with Weymouth joining them in the final as the best runners-up. Victory in the final subsequently goes the way of Wimbledon (21) from Weymouth (20) and Swindon (13). Second-in-the-table Boston run riot at Queensway Meadows, thrashing Newport 66-26, with unbeaten totals from Richard Hall (15), James Cockle (14+1) and Darren Rolph (11+1). A double dose of action at Buxton firstly results in a 50-45 success for the homesters versus Newcastle, as James Wright nets his second successive league maximum (15). The picturesque venue then plays host to the fourth round of the British Under-15 Championship, with a 15-point maximum giving victory to Josh Auty from joint runners-up Simon Lambert and Shane Waldron (13). Reigning Conference League Champions Mildenhall continue their march towards another title, easily dispatching Stoke 59-36. The victorious Fen Tigers boast three men with unbeaten tallies in Jason King (14+1), Jon Armstrong (12) and Ritchie Hawkins (11+4).

7 Wimbledon's Conference Trophy clash with Sheffield is postponed due to a waterlogged Plough Lane circuit.

9 The league match between Weymouth and Boston is an unfortunate casualty of heavy

rainfall. Led by a maximum from Blair Scott (15), Armadale comfortably collect the league points against Rye House, winning 59-31.

11 Mildenhall claim a 52-43 success against Wimbledon in the Conference Trophy at West Row. Despite brave resistance, Newport can't prevent visiting Buxton from winning 48-42 in pulsating league fare. In a Saddlebow Road thriller, second-in-the-table Boston are shocked as basement-club Swindon steal away with a 47-43 victory.

12 Having collected their first league success of the campaign the previous evening, Swindon make it two on the trot, romping to a 65-27 victory against a youthful Newport septet. Remarkably, the Sprockets' entire top five all go through the card unbeaten: Mark Thompson (12), Malcolm Holloway (11+1), Simon Walker (11+1), Danny Warwick (10+2) and Chris Johnson (9+3).

14 Stoke and Boston battle to a 45-45 draw in thrilling league contest at Loomer Road. Wimbledon post a huge 65-25 league victory over Newport, aided by paid maximum returns from Barrie Evans (14+1), Mark Burrows (11+1) and Matthew Wright (9+3).

16 With rain forecast, Carmarthen make an early decision to postpone their league clash with Buxton.

17 Rye House have little difficulty in collecting a 54-39 success over Armadale in the league at Hoddesdon.

18 Mildenhall's league match versus Oxford is called off at 1 p.m., due to a waterlogged circuit. Buxton have no answers as visiting Rye House run riot to win their league encounter 54-36, with both Tommy Allen (12) and Steve Boxall (11+1) remaining unbeaten for the Raiders. Newport suffer their fifth loss in a row as Armadale triumph 53-39 at Queensway Meadows. The Scottish side consolidate third spot in the league standings as a result, their win including unbeaten totals from Derek Sneddon (12), Blair Scott (12) and Matthew Wethers (11+1). A third straight win takes Swindon off the foot of the Conference League table, their 53-41 success over Wimbledon featuring maximums from Mark Thompson (15) and Trevor Harding (12).

20 Weymouth make it four league wins on the trot, but they're made to fight for it before finally beating Armadale 46-45.

21 Mark Burrows cards another paid maximum (14+1), as Wimbledon defeat Weymouth 56-38 and ease through to the next stage of the Knock-Out Cup.

23 Riding their second home match in four days, Weymouth narrowly beat Wimbledon 48-45 in the Conference Trophy.

24 Knock-Out Cup fare at Hoddesdon results in a 51-44 win for visiting Boston over Rye House and a place in the next round for the Barracuda-Braves.

25 Morning rain unfortunately leads to the postponement of the Conference Trophy match between Buxton and Mildenhall. At the United Counties Showground, Carmarthen determinedly overturn a ten-point deficit to defeat Stoke 50-42 in a pulsating league encounter. Newport remain in the cellar position as visiting Oxford win 52-41, with Craig Branney recording a brilliant six-ride maximum (18).

28 Stoke lose 48-42 at the hands of Buxton in a thrilling league tussle. Wimbledon go top of the Conference Trophy standings with a 53-41 success over King's Lynn.

30 Conference Trophy action at the Wessex Stadium results in a 64-29 success for Weymouth against Coventry, with David Mason (10+2) paid for a maximum.

31 A Scottish Junior Cup encounter brings the month to a close at Armadale, with Ashfield holding the homesters to a 48-48 draw.

AUGUST

1 James Wright storms through the card (18), as Buxton complete a quick-fire league double over near-neighbours Stoke, winning 47-42. Despite the absence of several riders, Swindon claim a hard-earned 46-43 success at Carmarthen in an exciting league clash. Top-of-the-table Mildenhall are pushed all the way before defeating third-placed Armadale 47-46.

2 Coventry suffer their seventh Conference Trophy loss in seven attempts, as visiting Buxton steal away with a 48-45 victory under their belts. James Wright hits a fabulous 21-point maximum for the Hitmen and twice clocks a new CL track record of 61.3 seconds for the Brandon circuit. Staying with the Conference Trophy, Sheffield narrowly defeat Mildenhall 47-46. Despite losing, the Fen Tigers collect the aggregate bonus point and jump to the head of the table. The match also sees home man Richard Hall lower Owlerton's CL track record to 62.0 seconds in heat six.

4 Stoke's league encounter with Weymouth is a casualty of prolonged rainfall. Pulsating league fare at Plough Lane finally results in a narrow 47-46 win for Wimbledon versus Boston. Unpleasant scenes regarding the events of heat fourteen see riders, fans and mechanics involved in a melee, which subsequently result in SCB bans, suspended for fifteen months, being handed out to the home duo of Marc Norris and James Clement, plus the visiting pair of James Cockle and Richie Dennis.

6 David Mason races to a classy maximum (15) to win the Weymouth Open Championship ahead of Justin Elkins (14) and Lee Smart (13).

7 Mildenhall lose only for the second time in seventeen league matches, as Rye House romp to a 56-36 success at Hoddesdon.

8 James Wright bags an immaculate 18-point maximum as Buxton defeat Swindon 56-38 in CL action. A torrential downpour forces the abandonment of Carmarthen's league fixture against Armadale after six heats, with the visitors holding a 22-13 advantage. Unfortunately, it also washes out the British Under-15 Championship round which was scheduled to follow. In the Knock-Out Cup, Mildenhall cruise to a 63-27 success over King's Lynn, helped on their way by maximums from James Brundle (12) and Ritchie Hawkins (11+1).

9 Mark Burrows thunders to maximum points (15), as Wimbledon beat Armadale 59-37 on league business at their plush Plough Lane home.

11 Stoke's Conference League match versus Newport is postponed, with the circuit under water following heavy rainfall. Reserve Andre Cross lands a maximum as Wimbledon return to the head of the Conference Trophy standings with a narrow 51-45 victory over Sheffield.

13 After losing only their second league match of the campaign at Rye House six days previously, Mildenhall return to winning ways at Weymouth, scorching to a 58-35 success.

14 Armadale cruise to a comfortable 67-27 win against Carmarthen in the league, with Blair Scott (15), Barry Campbell (12) and Derek Sneddon (11+1) all notching unbeaten tallies. Rye House also post a big league win, with Tommy Allen (12) and Barry Burchatt (11+4) bagging maximums as they defeat Newcastle 62-33.

15 Newport's league encounter with Swindon is washed away by heavy storms. James Wright nets his third maximum (18) on the bounce, as Buxton collect a 59-33 victory over Weymouth and jump to second place in the table. Mildenhall lose 49-43 to Great Britain Under-21s in an entertaining challenge at West Row. Newcastle plunder the league points, courtesy of a 52-43 success against Carmarthen at Brough Park.

17 Weymouth's league match against Oxford is called off due to a waterlogged circuit.

18 Rain is the only winner as both the day's scheduled matches are washed out: Stoke *v.* Newport (CL) and Wimbledon *v.* Mildenhall (CT).

19 Boston's league match against Buxton is yet another victim of the summer rain. Meanwhile, at Oxford, a planned double-header sees just one match completed, as the Silver Machine Academy defeat Weymouth 54-39, aided no end by Craig Branney's six-ride paid maximum (17+1). The second meeting versus Newport is unfortunately postponed following a downpour.

21 A terrific Conference Trophy match finally results in a hard-fought 48-45 victory for Buxton against Mildenhall, with James Wright netting yet another 18-point maximum. A powerful Rye House septet romp to a 65-26 success over Swindon in the league, with Steve Boxall (12), Tommy Allen (12) and Joel Parsons (10+2) steaming to maximums.

22 Barrie Evans scores a full house (12), as Wimbledon run riot to win their league match at Carmarthen 55-38. Led by maximums from James Brundle (12) and Jon Armstrong (10+2), Mildenhall jump back to the top of the Conference Trophy standings courtesy of a 53-42 victory against Weymouth. At Brough Park, high-flying Buxton triumph for the fifth league match in a row, winning narrowly 46-44, with James Wright going through the card once more (18).

24 Oxford come from behind to win a terrific league clash 48-45 at Weymouth.

25 Mildenhall are handed a walkover through to the semi-final of the Knock-Out Cup after King's Lynn are unable to find a date to stage their leg of the second-round tie. Due to the time curfew, Wimbledon's Conference Trophy match versus Weymouth is abandoned after fourteen heats, with the 42-42 scoreline standing. Dons' number one Barrie Evans is credited with a paid maximum (11+1), as his side again return to the head of the standings.

27 Weymouth's scheduled 50th Anniversary meeting is unfortunately washed out at lunchtime.

28 Buxton's James Wright rides brilliantly to win the Conference League Riders' Championship at Rye House. He tallies 14 points to finish ahead of Mark Burrows and Richard Hall; the Wimbledon racer claiming second spot after a run-off.

29 Conference Trophy action sees Buxton defeat Wimbledon 55-39, with CLRC Champion James Wright hitting another maximum (18). Due to a lack of medical cover, Newport's league encounter with Mildenhall is curtailed after fourteen heats. The result stands as a 55-29 victory to the Fen Tigers, with Jon Armstrong sat on maximum points (12). Solid scoring paves the way as Swindon beat a depleted Boston outfit 55-40 in an entertaining league clash.

30 Bank Holiday league fare sees David Mason (14+1) and Wayne Barrett (13+2) net unbeaten tallies, as Weymouth comfortably defeat Boston 55-40. Rye House collect their sixth league victory on the bounce, winning 51-38 against Stoke, with Steve Boxall hitting a five-ride full house (15). Tony Dart's 12-point maximum greatly assists runaway league leaders Mildenhall to a 55-38 success over Carmarthen.

SEPTEMBER

1 Jon Armstrong wins the Yorkshire Junior Open Championship, beating Joel Parsons in a title run-off, after finishing level on 14 points. In a thriller at Loomer Road, Stoke come from behind to collect the league points, winning 48-45 against Oxford. Meanwhile, in the Knock-Out Cup, Boston run riot to win 56-38 at Wimbledon in the first leg of the semi-final.

2 The first part of a league double-header at Blunsdon sees Swindon defeat Newcastle 58-37, with both Chris Johnson (14+1) and Nathan Irwin (9+3) paid for maximums. Johnson is again unbeaten in the second match (15), with Simon Walker joining him on an unbeaten tally (11+1), as the Sprockets beat Buxton 59-36.

3 A double dose of league activity at Cowley results firstly in a 58-35 success for Oxford versus Boston, with Chris Schramm scoring the lot (15). Schramm again hits a five-ride full house (15) in the second fixture, with Craig Branney also unbeaten (14+1), as Oxford wallop Newcastle 61-29.

4 Armadale overpower a weakened Swindon side to win their league encounter 59-33, with Matthew Wethers (12), Derek Sneddon (12), Andrew Tully (11+4) and Sean Stoddart (10+2) all scoring maximums. In the Conference Trophy, Sheffield win 47-43 at King's Lynn, with Richard Hall romping to a full 18-point tally. Justin Elkins sets a new CL track record at Loomer Road on his way to maximum points (15), as Stoke defeat Wimbledon 51-42.

5 Buxton post their fifth successive Conference Trophy victory, beating Sheffield 52-44. Rye House jump to second place in the league standings, courtesy of a 54-40 victory at Carmarthen. It's double the fun at West Row, where Mildenhall initially beat Oxford 51-43 in the first leg of the Knock-Out Cup final. The second match sees the Fen Tigers maintain top spot in the Conference Trophy, beating King's Lynn 56-38, with Jon Armstrong (11+1) plundering a paid maximum. After seven straight league defeats, Newport come good to win 47-43 against Wimbledon. Boston's league match with Oxford is abandoned following a last-race crash, with the result standing after heat fourteen as a 52-33 success for the visitors. Completing a busy day, Newcastle claim a 50-43 win versus Stoke in an exciting league affair, with David Meldrum and Jamie Robertson scoring identical paid maximums (11+1).

6 Part one of a double-header at Sheffield sees the homesters win 49-40 against Coventry in the Conference Trophy, with Paul Cooper paid for maximum points (13+2). The second portion of the double bill sees Josh Auty race to a full maximum (15) to win the fifth round of the British Under-15 Championship, with Gary Cottham claiming second place after defeating Matt Bates in a run-off, both lads having tallied 12 points.

8 League activity at Stoke sees Jon Armstrong pocket a paid maximum (14+1), as Mildenhall secure a thrilling 50-45 victory. Due to an horrific crash involving visiting rider Barry Burchatt and the subsequent lack of paramedic cover, Wimbledon's league encounter against Rye House is abandoned inconclusively after eleven heats, with the visitors holding a 35-31 advantage.

10 Heavy rain curtails Weymouth's Conference Trophy fixture versus Sheffield after just one heat, with the homesters leading 5-1.

12 Buxton edge to a 49-47 success over a determined King's Lynn side in rip-roaring Conference Trophy action. The first part of a scheduled league double-header sees Swindon lose 47-43 to Stoke, as Justin Elkins zips to a full 18-pointer for the triumphant visitors in a rain-affected meeting. With track conditions deteriorating, the second match against Oxford is postponed following a lengthy consultation among the riders.

15 Buxton's James Wright blazes a trail to his eighth league maximum of the season (21), but his efforts can't prevent home boys Wimbledon from winning an entertaining encounter 51-44.

17 Oxford's scheduled league double-header versus Mildenhall and Carmarthen unfortunately

falls foul to inclement weather. Similarly, Weymouth's Conference Trophy match against King's Lynn becomes another statistic of a rain-ravaged season.

18 Armadale are in cruise control as they hammer Newcastle 65-25 in a one-sided league fixture, their scoring headed by maximums from Matthew Wethers (12), Blair Scott (11+1), Derek Sneddon (11+1) and Gary Beaton (9+3). The Norfolk Arena plays host to a double dose of Conference Trophy activity, with King's Lynn going down to a 47-43 loss at the hands of Weymouth in the first match, despite Craig Branney's wonderful six-ride full house (18). Match number two sees the Starlets suffer their sixth successive defeat, as Wimbledon come out on top by a 55-41 scoreline. The win takes the Londoners to top spot in the Trophy standings, above Mildenhall. Returning to league action, the day's other match results in a thumping 64-31 success for Rye House against Newport, with Joel Parsons (17+1) and Tommy Allen (12) carding maximums.

19 Double-headers are the order of the day, with Carmarthen firstly losing 48-42 to visiting Weymouth in the league. The super Welsh venue then plays host to round six of the British Under-15 Championship, with a maximum (15) giving Shane Waldron victory from Josh Auty (13) and Simon Lambert (12). At Mildenhall, a brace of Conference Trophy wins sees the Fen Tigers return to top spot in the table. Jon Armstrong hits an unbeaten tally (11+1), as they defeat Buxton 52-40 in the first match and he follows it up with a replica performance in a 54-41 success over Coventry. Meanwhile, joining Armstrong on maximum points in the second match is flying reserve Lee Smart (12).

22 A saturated track forces Stoke to postpone their league match against Rye House in mid-morning. The weather is better in the capital, however, and a last-heat 5-1 gives Wimbledon a 48-45 victory over Mildenhall in the Conference Trophy. In winning heat fifteen, Mark Burrows completes an excellent maximum (15) for the victorious Dons.

23 In the Conference Trophy, Sheffield overcome dogged resistance to defeat Buxton 50-43. League action at Blunsdon results in a well-earned 55-39 victory for Swindon against Weymouth, with Trevor Harding netting a scintillating paid maximum (14+1).

24 Richard Hall races to an unbeaten tally (18), as Boston beat Wimbledon 54-43 to claim their place in the Knock-Out Cup final. Craig Branney bags a maximum (15), as Oxford come from behind to win 48-42 against a determined Rye House in thrilling league fare. Before an appreciative audience, Weymouth ease to a 52-43 victory against Buxton in the Conference Trophy.

25 Armadale get the better of a last-heat decider to defeat Oxford 44-43 in a rip-roaring league tussle.

26 Newport collect only their fourth league victory of the season beating injury-hit Swindon 49-43 at Queensway Meadows. James Wright registers yet another maximum (15) and helps Buxton to a convincing 53-39 Conference Trophy success over Weymouth. At Ashfield, pre-meeting favourite Sean Stoddart drops just one point (14) to win the Heathersfield Golden Helmet, with Gary Flint (13) and Gary Beaton (12) completing the top three. Craig Branney returns to his old Newcastle stamping-ground to score maximum points (18) for Oxford, as the Silver Machine Academy win the league fixture 53-39. Concluding a busy day, Boston storm to a 65-28 victory over Carmarthen in the league, with Richard Hall (15), James Cockle (13+2) and Darren Rolph (11+1) coasting to unbeaten returns.

27 A double dose of Conference Trophy action at Brandon results in two more defeats for Coventry, the Cougars taking their unenviable record to eleven losses out of eleven. They

go down narrowly, 47-46, to Weymouth in the first, with Sheffield subsequently winning the second fixture 47-43.

29 King's Lynn notch only their second Conference Trophy win of the season, beating Buxton 48-42. Both Barrie Evans (12) and Mark Burrows (11+1) remain unbeaten as Wimbledon romp to a 62-32 success over Stoke in the league.

OCTOBER

1 Rain washes out Weymouth's Conference Trophy encounter with Sheffield. The first part of a double-header sees Oxford narrowly win 45-43 in a rain-affected league match against Wimbledon. Unfortunately, with a curfew to adhere to, there simply isn't sufficient time to stage the scheduled second league fixture versus Buxton. Armadale comfortably beat Stoke 46-27 in a league match curtailed after twelve heats, due to rain. Boston's league fixture is also abandoned, the Barracuda-Braves claiming a 48-31 victory against Newcastle after thirteen heats, with Richard Hall recording maximum points (12).

2 Rye House just shade a rip-roaring Conference League match 47-46 against Oxford. Still in the league, it's not so tight at Loomer Road, as Stoke ease to a 57-38 success over Newport.

3 Three of the day's scheduled league meetings are rained off, namely Newport *v.* Newcastle, Buxton *v.* Wimbledon and Swindon *v.* Rye House. The 'Men in Black' vintage meeting also falls victim to poor weather at Carmarthen. Just one track sees any action and it's jubilation time at Mildenhall as the Fen Tigers beat Oxford 55-37 to clinch back-to-back Conference League titles.

6 The rains curtail Wimbledon's league match against Rye House after just two heats, with the Dons holding an 8-3 advantage at the time. The first part of a Conference Trophy double bill at King's Lynn results in a 48-44 victory for Mildenhall, as the Fen Tigers clinch top spot and add another piece of silverware to their display cabinet. The Starlets gain a 50-45 win over Coventry in the second match, giving the Cougars the unenviable record of having lost all twelve of their matches.

7 Conference League Riders' Champion James Wright wins the Steel City Championship at Sheffield, beating Ben Wilson, David Meldrum and Richard Hall in the final.

8 Oxford record a brace of league victories at Cowley, firstly dispatching bottom-of-the-table Newport 62-34 and then defeating high-flying Armadale 58-37. No fewer than four homesters register maximums against the Mavericks, namely: Chris Schramm (15), Danny Norton (12+3), Craig Branney (12) and Jamie Courtney (10+2), with only Branney keeping his unbeaten run going in the second match (14+1). Boston complete a wonderful league double over Champions Mildenhall, winning 52-42 at the Norfolk Arena. Stoke fail to contain Rye House, as the visitors complete a smash-and-grab raid to win the league encounter 49-41.

9 In an effort to avoid forecasted rainfall, promoter Brian White's decision to bring the start time of Weymouth's prestigious 50th Anniversary meeting forward proves spot on. Starting six hours earlier than scheduled at 12 p.m., Great Britain Under-21s race to a 54-39 victory over the Rest of the World. Carmarthen suffer their ninth successive league loss, going down 46-44 to visiting Armadale.

10 At Mildenhall, the first part of an individual double-header sees fourteen-year-old wonder boy Josh Auty clean-up with maximum points (15) to take victory in the final of the inaugural British Under-15 Championship. Second place overall goes to Shane Waldron,

with Simon Lambert finishing third. The day's other showpiece event, the Bert Harkins'-sponsored Bronze Helmet, boils down to a head-to-head final involving Wimbledon's Mark Burrows and Mildenhall's Jon Armstrong, with the home representative brilliantly coming from behind in mid-race to triumph.

11 Boston's penultimate league match eventually ends in a 50-44 victory against a depleted, but nonetheless determined, Weymouth outfit.

13 Rain is the only victor, as Oxford's scheduled CL and KOC double-header against Mildenhall gets washed away. The prestigious Laurels meeting at Wimbledon is also postponed after lunchtime rainfall.

14 Following heavy overnight rain, Swindon's Conference League double bill versus Rye House and Oxford is called off shortly after 10 a.m.

15 Two matches are lost to the weather: Boston *v.* Buxton (CL) and Weymouth *v.* King's Lynn (CT). The combination of a lighting failure and rain causes the abandonment of Scotland's international versus Great Britain Under-21s at Armadale after just two heats, with the Brits holding a 7-5 advantage.

16 At Carmarthen, the Inter-Nations Fours are won by England (38), ahead of Scotland (33), World Select (32) and Wales (25). Scotland's Blair Scott is the meeting's star man with a 12-point full house. Twelve heats are completed at Rye House before the league match versus Buxton is abandoned after injuries to Lee Derbyshire and Barry Burchatt leave insufficient medical cover. The result stands as a 42-33 victory to the homesters, with both Harland Cook (16+2) and Tommy Allen (12) unbeaten. Stoke pull clear in the latter stages to beat Weymouth 50-40 in an ultra-competitive league fixture at Loomer Road.

17 Great Britain Under-21s wallop the Rest of the World 64-30 at Newport, with Chris Schramm (14+1), Karl Mason (12+3) and Tommy Allen (12) hitting maximums. The second part of an entertaining double dose of racing sees Newport Under-15s draw 36-36 with Cardiff Under-15s. The day's other fixture is another victim of adverse weather: Buxton *v.* Wimbledon (CL).

18 At Wolverhampton, Daniel King nets a superb maximum (15) to land the British Under-18 Championship ahead of James Wright (14) and Edward Kennett (12).

20 Mark Burrows' Testimonial is unluckily washed out for a third time at Wimbledon and it is subsequently decided to stage the event in 2005. Oxford's scheduled CL double-header versus Carmarthen and Buxton is another victim of dreadful weather.

21 A broken knee sustained by Rye House's Luke Bowen in the third heat causes a long delay at Swindon, with the depleted Sprockets eventually conceding defeat in the league match at 49-39 in arrears, with a race to spare. The second part of another Blunsdon double-header sees Oxford claim the league points courtesy of a 52-41 success. Both victorious visitors boast maximum men on the night: Tommy Allen (15) in the first match and Chris Schramm (also 15) in the second.

22 An exciting double meeting at Oxford twice pitches the Silver Machine Academy against mighty Mildenhall, firstly in the Knock-Out Cup semi-final and then in the league. The initial match features a terrific comeback from the visitors and, although the Fen Tigers go down 48-45, it is they who reach the Knock-Out Cup final on aggregate. The second match sees Mildenhall take control and when home man Danny Norton badly damages the air safety barrier in heat twelve, the meeting is abandoned with the visitors holding a decisive 43-32 advantage. Meanwhile, Boston survive a stern test to beat Buxton 48-42 in a full-blooded league encounter at Saddlebow Road.

23 Amid wet conditions, Buxton post a 48-41 success over Wimbledon, with James Wright subsequently defeating Mark Burrows to also scoop the league bonus point for the Hitmen.

24 Due to a waterlogged circuit, Carmarthen's league match versus Buxton is called off twenty-four hours in advance. Having run out of dates because of all the wet weather, Wimbledon switch their 'home' match against Rye House to Hoddesdon. The Raiders take advantage to win 53-43, with Tommy Allen cantering to a fabulous full 18-pointer, as his side guarantee themselves the runners-up spot in the league. David Mason scores a paid maximum (14+1), as Weymouth complete their Conference Trophy fixtures by defeating Sheffield 56-39.

27 Wimbledon's season ends in a damp squib, with the Laurels again being postponed due to wet conditions in SW17. It's much better at King's Lynn, however, as Richard Hall races to an impressive five-ride maximum to take victory ahead of James Brundle (14) and Craig Branney (12) in the David Nix Memorial.

29 Weymouth's final Conference Trophy fixture of the season, against King's Lynn, is unfortunately called off due to a floodlight failure. Amid threatening skies and with Oxford holding an unassailable lead, their league encounter against Carmarthen is declared a 44-31 result after twelve heats in order to allow the second part of a double-header to go ahead. Buxton provide the opposition for the other league match, but it's third-in-the-table Oxford who come out on top by 51 points to 44. There are two maximum men on the night: Ricky Scarboro (9+3) for the Silver Machine Academy in the first match and Buxton's brilliant Conference League Riders' Champion James Wright (21) in the second. At Armadale, the second attempt to stage the international between Scotland and Great Britain Under-21s only lasts four heats, before rain calls a halt with the Brits leading 14-8. It's first blood to Mildenhall in the Knock-Out Cup final, as they win a fully committed encounter 47-46 at Boston.

30 At Stoke, the remarkable James Wright adds the Pride of the Conference League to his growing list of titles, winning the final ahead of Tom Brown, Rob Grant jr and Benji Compton.

31 Although Sittingbourne defeat a league Select 42-35 in an entertaining challenge match at their Old Gun Site venue, they are unable to stop Matthew Wright from notching maximum points (18) for the opposition. Carmarthen and Buxton fight out a 46-46 draw in a hugely entertaining final league fixture of the season at the United Counties Showground. Newcastle end their season in style, easing to a 53-43 win at Newport. Ugly crowd scenes mar the second leg of the Knock-Out Cup final at Mildenhall, as Boston walk out after six heats in protest over track conditions, leaving the Fen Tigers to collect nine successive 5-0s on their way to a mammoth 69-12 victory. Adam Roynon (15), Jon Armstrong (12), Tony Dart (11+4) and James Brundle (11+1) all remain unbeaten, as Mildenhall add the Knock-Out Cup to their earlier triumphs of the League Championship, Conference Trophy and Four-Team Championship. Boston team manager Malcolm Vasey, together with riders James Cockle, Robert Hollingworth, Simon Lambert, Darren Mallett and Darren Rolph all receive £250 fines from referee Mick Bates, with both Richard Hall and Ben Powell exonerated by the meeting official. The hastily rearranged Conference Trophy match sees Weymouth overpower King's Lynn 62-31, with Daniel Giffard (12), Chris Courage (12) and David Mason (11+1) all remaining undefeated.

CONFERENCE LEAGUE TABLE

	Mts	Won	Drn	Lst	For	Agn	Pts	Bon	Tot
Mildenhall	24	21	0	3	1254	952	42	10	52
Rye House	24	19	0	5	1206	991	38	9	47
Oxford	24	17	0	7	1199	979	34	10	44
Armadale	24	15	0	9	1185	990	30	8	38
Boston	24	14	1	9	1171	1034	29	8	37
Buxton	24	13	1	10	1093	1100	27	7	34
Wimbledon	24	11	0	13	1138	1080	22	6	28
Weymouth	24	10	1	13	1047	1143	21	5	26
Stoke	24	9	1	14	1054	1139	19	4	23
Swindon	24	8	0	16	1063	1158	16	5	21
Newcastle	24	7	0	17	998	1203	14	2	16
Carmarthen	24	5	1	18	998	1187	11	4	15
Newport	24	4	1	19	883	1333	9	0	9

CONFERENCE TROPHY TABLE

	Mts	Won	Drn	Lst	For	Agn	Pts	Bon	Tot
Mildenhall	12	9	0	3	613	512	18	6	24
Sheffield	12	8	0	4	582	537	16	4	20
Weymouth	12	7	1	4	576	536	15	3	18
Wimbledon	12	7	1	4	575	544	15	3	18
Buxton	12	7	0	5	564	562	14	3	17
King's Lynn	12	3	0	9	516	600	6	2	8
Coventry	12	0	0	12	490	625	0	0	0

KNOCK-OUT CUP

ROUND ONE

Sittingbourne	40	Wimbledon	53	
Wimbledon	55	Sittingbourne	38	(Wimbledon won 108-78 on aggregate)
Weymouth	53	Stoke	41	
Stoke	42	Weymouth	47	(Weymouth won 100-83 on aggregate)
Mildenhall	52	Carmarthen	31	
Carmarthen	42	Mildenhall	53	(Mildenhall won 105-73 on aggregate)

ROUND TWO

Boston	48	Rye House	42	
Rye House	44	Boston	51	(Boston won 99-86 on aggregate)
Oxford	61	Buxton	31	
Buxton	50	Oxford	44	(Oxford won 105-81 on aggregate)
Weymouth	47	Wimbledon	48	
Wimbledon	56	Weymouth	38	(Wimbledon won 104-85 on aggregate)
Mildenhall	63	King's Lynn	27	
King's Lynn	–	Mildenhall	–	(Mildenhall given walkover through after King's Lynn conceded the tie)

SEMI-FINAL

Wimbledon	38	Boston	56	
Boston	54	Wimbledon	43	(Boston won 110-81 on aggregate)
Mildenhall	51	Oxford	43	
Oxford	48	Mildenhall	45	(Mildenhall won 96-91 on aggregate)

FINAL

Boston	46	Mildenhall	47	
Mildenhall	69	Boston	12	(Mildenhall won 116-58 on aggregate)

ARMADALE AWG DALE DEVILS

NOTE: The information below relates only to the second Edinburgh team. For details of the main side, please refer to the Premier League section.

ADDRESS: Armadale Stadium, 2 Bathgate Road, Armadale, West Lothian, EH48 2PD.
CLUB CHAIRMEN: John Campbell & Graham Maben.
TRACK LENGTH: 260 metres.
CL TRACK RECORD: 57.7 seconds – Matthew Wethers (25/09/04).
FIRST MEETING: 31 May 2003.
YEARS OF OPERATION: 2003 Conference Trophy; 2004 Conference League.

CLUB HONOURS

None.

RIDER ROSTER 2004

Gary BEATON; Barry CAMPBELL; Adam McKINNA; Blair SCOTT; Carl SHIELD; Derek SNEDDON; Sean STODDART; Andrew TULLY; Matthew WETHERS.

OTHER APPEARANCES/GUESTS (official matches only):

John MacPHAIL; Steven McALLISTER; James McBAIN; Keith MABEN; Gary PHELPS.

CONFERENCE LEAGUE

No	DATE	OPPONENTS	H/A	RESULT	WETHERS	BEATON	SHIELD	SNEDDON	TULLY	STODDART	MABEN	SCOTT	CAMPBELL	PHELPS	McKINNA	OTHERS
1	10/4	Buxton	H	W49-44	R/R	10 (4)	12 (5)	12+1 (5)	5+2 (6)	8+1 (4)	1+1 (3)	–	–	–	–	1 (3)
2	11/4	Buxton	A	L45-47*	R/R	6+3 (5)	11 (6)	7+1 (6)	6+1 (5)	13+3 (6)	–	–	–	–	–	2 (2)
3	17/4	Weymouth†	H	W53-21	R/R	9+1 (4)	6+3 (3)	11 (4)	4+2 (4)	8+2 (4)	–	15 (5)	–	–	–	–
4	1/5	Newport	H	W62-31	12 (4)	6+2 (4)	8+3 (4)	14+1 (5)	1+1 (4)	8+2 (4)	–	13 (5)	–	–	–	–
5	22/5	Mildenhall	H	L45-49	15 (5)	8+1 (5)	3+2 (4)	10 (5)	1 (3)	2+1 (4)	–	–	6 (4)	–	–	–
6	23/5	Boston	A	L40-55	18 (6)	6+1 (6)	2 (4)	12 (6)	0 (1)	2+1 (6)	0 (1)	–	R/R	–	–	–
7	24/5	Swindon	A	W50-44	17+1 (6)	3 (4)	4 (4)	11+1 (5)	0 (1)	0 (5)	–	–	R/R	15 (5)	–	–
8	25/5	Stoke	A	L44-46	17 (6)	5 (6)	3+1 (4)	8+2 (5)	0 (1)	0 (2)	–	–	R/R	11+1 (6)	–	–
9	29/5	Boston	H	W48-42	15 (5)	2+1 (4)	6+1 (4)	12+1 (5)	1 (3)	5 (5)	–	–	–	7 (4)	–	–
10	5/6	Wimbledon	H	W58-37	18 (6)	4+1 (3)	–	R/R	6+3 (5)	15 (7)	1 (3)	–	14+2 (6)	–	–	–
11	27/6	Newcastle	A	W48-41	5 (4)	4 (4)	–	12+1 (5)	5+2 (5)	–	–	14 (5)	6+[illegible] (4)	–	–	2 (3)
12	9/7	Rye House	H	W59-31	13+1 (5)	4+2 (4)	–	9 (4)	9+2 (4)	4+1 (4)	–	15 (5)	5+1 (4)	–	–	–
13	17/7	Rye House	A	L39-54*	R/R	4 (4)	–	8 (6)	2+2 (6)	5 (5)	–	19 (6)	–	–	1 (3)	–
14	18/7	Newport	A	W53-39*	11+1 (4)	1 (4)	–	12 (4)	4+2 (5)	10+1 (5)	–	12 (4)	–	–	3+1 (4)	–
15	20/7	Weymouth	A	L45-46*	13 (5)	5+1 (4)	–	5 (4)	3+1 (4)	2 (5)	–	15 (5)	–	–	2 (3)	–
16	1/8	Mildenhall	A	L46-47	2 (2)	2+1 (3)	–	9+1 (5)	3 (5)	14+4 (7)	–	10 (5)	6 (4)	–	–	–
17	9/8	Wimbledon	A	L37-59	R/R	0 (3)	–	13 (6)	0 (4)	8+1 (7)	–	15 (6)	–	–	1 (4)	–
18	14/8	Carmarthen	H	W67-27	–	6+3 (4)	–	11+1 (4)	7+2 (4)	11+2 (5)	–	15 (5)	12 (4)	–	5+2 (4)	–

CONFERENCE LEAGUE continued

No	DATE	OPPONENTS	H/A	RESULT	WETHERS	BEATON	SHIELD	SNEDDON	TULLY	STODDART	MABEN	SCOTT	CAMPBELL	PHELPS	McKINNA	OTHERS
19	4/9	Swindon	H	W59-33*	12 (4)	1 (4)	–	12 (4)	11+4 (5)	10+2 (4)	–	11+1 (5)	–	–	–	2 (4)
20	18/9	Newcastle	H	W65-25*	12 (4)	9+3 (4)	–	11+1 (4)	5+1 (5)	11+2 (5)	–	11+1 (4)	–	–	6+1 (4)	–
21	25/9	Oxford	H	W44-43	14 (5)	5+2 (4)	–	6+1 (4)	4+2 (5)	7 (6)	–	8 (5)	0 (1)	–	–	–
22	1/10	Stoke†	H	W46-27*	8 (3)	2+1 (3)	–	2 (3)	8+1 (4)	9+1 (4)	–	8+1 (3)	–	–	9+2 (4)	–
23	8/10	Oxford	A	L37-58	10+1 (5)	2+1 (4)	–	13+1 (5)	1+1 (4)	2 (4)	–	8 (4)	–	–	1 (4)	–
24	9/10	Carmarthen	A	W46-44*	11 (4)	1 (4)	–	7+1 (4)	4+1 (5)	8 (5)	–	11 (4)	–	–	4 (4)	–

*Denotes bonus-point victory

†Meeting abandoned after heat twelve, with the result permitted to stand.

DETAILS OF OTHER RIDERS:

Match No. 1: Steven McAllister 1 (3); Match No. 2: Steven McAllister 2 (2); Match No. 11: John MacPhail 2 (3); Match No. 19: James McBain 2 (4).

TACTICAL RIDES, AS INCLUDED IN THE SCORES GRID:

Match No. 2: Stoddart 6 points (TR); Match No. 5: Sneddon 4 points (TR); Wethers 4 points (TR); Match No. 6: Wethers 6 points (TR); Sneddon 4 points (TR); Match No. 13: Scott 6 points (TR); Sneddon 4 points (TR); Match No. 15: Wethers 6 points (TR); Match No. 16: Stoddart 6 points (TR); Match No. 17: Scott 6 points (TR); Sneddon 6 points (TR); Match No. 23: Sneddon 6 points (TR); Scott 4 points (TR).

CONFERENCE LEAGUE AVERAGES

Rider	Mts	Rds	Pts	Bon	Tot	Avge	Max
Matthew Wethers	18	83	215	4	219	10.55	5 full; 2 paid
Blair Scott	16	76	192	3	195	10.26	5 full; 1 paid
Gary Phelps	3	15	33	1	34	9.07	1 full
Derek Sneddon	23	108	215	14	229	8.48	2 full; 3 paid
Barry Campbell	7	27	49	4	53	7.85	1 full
Carl Shield	9	38	55	10	65	6.84	–
Sean Stoddart	23	113	156	24	180	6.37	1 paid
Gary Beaton	24	98	105	24	129	5.27	1 paid
Andrew Tully	24	98	90	30	120	4.90	1 paid
Adam McKinna	9	34	32	6	38	4.47	–
John MacPhail	1	3	2	0	2	2.67	–
Steven McAllister	2	5	3	0	3	2.40	–
James McBain	1	4	2	0	2	2.00	–
Keith Maben	3	7	2	1	3	1.71	–

OTHER MEETINGS

4 July: Festival of Speed (staged at Sittingbourne)

FIRST SEMI-FINAL: Wimbledon 24, Weymouth 19, Coventry 11. SECOND SEMI-FINAL: Swindon 24, Armadale 16 (Blair Scott 8; Gary Beaton 6; Andrew Tully 1+1; Keith Maben 1), Sittingbourne 14. FINAL: Wimbledon 21, Weymouth 20, Swindon 13.

ARMADALE: back row, left to right: Gary Beaton, Derek Sneddon, Alan Robertson (Team Manager), Blair Scott, Sean Stoddart. Front row: Andrew Tully, Matthew Wethers, Adam McKinna.

31 July: Scottish Junior Cup

Armadale 48 (Blair Scott 15; Derek Sneddon 14+1; Sean Stoddart 10; Andrew Tully 5+1; Keith Maben 4; Colin McDonald 0; Cal McDade 0) Ashfield 48 (Barry Campbell 11; David McAllan 11; Gary Beaton 10+1; Adam McKinna 7+2; Kriss Irving 5+2; James McBain 3+1; Kieran Morris 1).

8 August: Conference League

Carmarthen 13 Armadale 22 (Blair Scott 6; Derek Sneddon 6; Gary Beaton 3; Andrew Tully 3; Sean Stoddart 3; Adam McKinna 1; Barry Campbell R/R) – meeting abandoned after heat six.

15 October: Conference League International

Scotland 5 (William Lawson 3; Gary Beaton 1; Sean Stoddart 1; Andrew Tully 0; Derek Sneddon DNR; Blair Scott DNR; David McAllan DNR) Great Britain Under-21 7 (Jamie Westacott 3; Jamie Courtney 2+1; Ritchie Hawkins 2; John Branney 0; Jamie Robertson DNR; Lee Smart DNR; Ben Wilson DNR) – meeting abandoned after heat two.

29 October: Conference League International

Scotland 8 (Blair Scott 3; Gary Beaton 2; Sean Stoddart 2; Andrew Tully 1+1; William Lawson 0; Derek Sneddon 0; David McAllan 0) Great Britain Under-21 14 (Shane Waldron 6; Rob Grant jr 3; Ben Wilson 2+1; John Branney 2; Karl Mason 1; Jamie Robertson 0; Benji Compton 0) – meeting abandoned after heat four.

INDIVIDUAL MEETING

8 May: British Under-15 Championship (Second Round)

1st Shane Waldron 14; 2nd Simon Lambert 14; 3rd Kyle Hughes 12; Josh Auty 11; Gary Cottham 10; Matthew Bates 10; Scott Campos 8; James Humby 6; Grant Hayes 5; George Piper 5; Sam Hurst 5; Ben Thompson 5; Ben Hopwood 4; Chris Widman 2; Connor Scott 1; Peter Gemmill DNR. A run-off for first place wasn't staged as Lambert had suffered an injury, so Waldron was awarded top spot. Series points: 1st Waldron 32; 2nd Auty 30; 3rd Lambert 28; Campos 24; Cottham 23; Hughes 23; Bates 23; Humby 21; Piper 16; Hurst 16; Hopwood 10; Hayes 8; Thompson 8; Aaron Baseby 6; Joe Reynolds 4; Lewis Bridger 3; Widman 3; Trevor Heath 2; Scott 2; Tim Webster 1; Ben Hannon 1; Andy Braithwaite 1.

BOSTON N.C. WILLIAMS & SON INSURANCE BARRACUDA-BRAVES

ADDRESS: Norfolk Arena, Saddlebow Road, King's Lynn, Norfolk, PE34 3AG.
CLUB CHAIRMEN: Stephen Lambert, Malcolm Vasey & Mick Smith.
TRACK LENGTH: 342 metres.
CL TRACK RECORD: 60.0 seconds – Trevor Harding (15/06/03).
FIRST MEETING: 1 April 2000.
YEARS OF OPERATION: 2000-04 Conference League.

PREVIOUS VENUE: Boston Sports Stadium, New Hammond Beck Road, Boston, Lincolnshire.
YEARS OF OPERATION: 1970-74 British League Division Two; 1975-84 National League; 1986-87 National League.

CLUB HONOURS

LEAGUE CHAMPIONS: 1973.
KNOCK-OUT CUP WINNERS: 1973, 2000.
PAIRS CHAMPIONS: 1977.
CONFERENCE TROPHY WINNERS: 2003.

RIDER ROSTER 2004

James COCKLE; Richie DENNIS; Wayne DUNWORTH; Richard HALL; Robert HOLLINGWORTH; Simon LAMBERT; David McALLAN; Darren MALLETT; John OLIVER; Darren ROLPH.

OTHER APPEARANCES/GUESTS (official matches only):
Shane COLVIN; Dean GARROD; Ben POWELL; Mark RICHARDSON.

CONFERENCE LEAGUE

No	DATE	OPPONENTS	H/A	RESULT	HALL	COCKLE	HOLLINGWORTH	DENNIS	McALLAN	ROLPH	OLIVER	MALLETT	LAMBERT	DUNWORTH	POWELL	OTHERS
1	28/3	Carmarthen	A	W57-36	12 (5)	9+3 (5)	3 (3)	5+2 (4)	7+2 (4)	13+1 (5)	8+1 (4)	–	–	–	–	–
2	11/4	Wimbledon	H	W52-43	13 (5)	3 (4)	–	4+2 (4)	8 (4)	9+2 (4)	4+1 (4)	11 (5)	–	–	–	–
3	12/4	Rye House	A	L38-55	11 (5)	1+1 (4)	2+1 (4)	4 (4)	9 (5)	9+1 (5)	2+2 (3)	–	–	–	–	–
4	2/5	Rye House	H	W57-36*	11 (5)	4+2 (4)	–	5+1 (4)	5+2 (4)	14+1 (5)	10+1 (4)	8+1 (4)	–	–	–	–
5	9/5	Buxton	A	L39-52	–	2 (3)	4+1 (3)	7+1 (5)	8+1 (5)	11+3 (7)	7 (7)	0 (0)	–	–	–	–
6	16/5	Stoke	H	W57-36	–	5+2 (3)	8+1 (4)	14+1 (5)	6+3 (4)	15+1 (6)	7+1 (5)	R/R	2–1 (3)	–	–	–
7	23/5	Armadale	H	W55-40	11 (5)	9+1 (4)	4+1 (3)	7+2 (4)	12+1 (5)	10+2 (5)	2 (4)	–	–	–	–	–
8	29/5	Armadale	A	L42-48*	R/R	10 (6)	0 (4)	0 (2)	12 (6)	16+2 (7)	4+3 (5)	–	–	–	–	–
9	6/6	Mildenhall	A	W47-45	12 (6)	5+2 (4)	7+1 (4)	–	10+1 (6)	1 (3)	12+2 (7)	R/R	–	–	–	–
10	18/6	Newport	H	W67-24	18 (6)	11+3 (5)	9 (4)	–	8+2 (4)	10+2 (5)	–	R/R	8–3 (4)	3+1 (2)	–	–
11	20/6	Newcastle	A	W49-47	13 (6)	9+1 (5)	3+2 (4)	–	11 (6)	11+2 (6)	–	R/R	2 (3)	–	–	–

BOSTON: back row, left to right: Darren Mallett, Darren Rolph, Malcolm Vasey (Team Manager), Simon Lambert, Stephen Lambert (Chairman), James Cockle. Front, kneeling: Robert Hollingworth, Ben Wilson. On bike: Richard Hall.

CONFERENCE LEAGUE continued

No	DATE	OPPONENTS	H/A	RESULT	HALL	COCKLE	HOLLINGWORTH	DENNIS	McALLAN	ROLPH	OLIVER	MALLETT	LAMBERT	DUNWORTH	POWELL	OTHERS
12	4/7	Newport	A	W66-26*	15 (5)	14+1 (5)	8+2 (4)	4+1 (4)	8+3 (4)	11+1 (4)	–	–	–	6+2 (4)	–	–
13	11/7	Swindon	H	L43-47	12+1 (5)	8+1 (5)	2+1 (4)	6 (4)	4+1 (4)	9 (5)	–	–	2+1 (3)	–	–	–
14	14/7	Stoke	A	D45-45*	R/R	15+2 (7)	7+1 (5)	4 (4)	8+1 (5)	10+1 (6)	–	–	1+1 (3)	–	–	–
15	4/8	Wimbledon	A	L46-47*	6 (3)	5+1 (5)	7 (4)	5+1 (3)	11 (5)	8+2 (5)	–	–	4 (5)	–	–	–
16	29/8	Swindon	A	L40-55	–	–	8+1 (6)	16 (7)	–	12+1 (5)	–	R/R	3 (5)	1+1 (4)	–	–
17	30/8	Weymouth	A	L40-55	13 (6)	–	6 (5)	12+3 (6)	–	R/R	–	–	6+1 (6)	3 (4)	–	0 (3)
18	3/9	Oxford	A	L35-58	R/R	13+2 (6)	2+1 (4)	4 (5)	–	12 (6)	–	–	3+1 (5)	1 (4)	–	–
19	5/9	Oxford †	H	L33-52	12 (5)	–	4 (4)	7 (5)	–	5+1 (5)	–	R/R	3 (6)	1 (3)	–	1 (1)
20	26/9	Carmarthen	H	W65-28*	15 (5)	13+2 (5)	9+1 (4)	–	–	11+1 (4)	–	8+2 (4)	9+3 (5)	0 (3)	–	–
21	1/10	Newcastle +	H	W48-31*	12 (4)	7 (3)	8+1 (4)	–	–	6+1 (4)	–	7+1 (3)	4+1 (4)	–	4 (4)	–
22	8/10	Mildenhall	H	W52-42*	16 (6)	8+1 (7)	7+2 (4)	–	–	R/R	–	10 (5)	10+2 (5)	–	–	1 (3)
23	11/10	Weymouth	H	W50-44	13+1 (5)	11+1 (6)	7+2 (4)	–	–	6 (4)	–	6+1 (4)	5 (4)	–	–	2+1 (3)
24	22/10	Buxton	H	W48-42	16 (6)	11+1 (5)	8+2 (5)	–	–	4+1 (4)	–	R/R	0 (5)	–	9 (5)	–

*Denotes bonus-point victory

†Meeting abandoned after heat fourteen, with the result permitted to stand.

+Meeting abandoned after heat thirteen, with the result permitted to stand.

DETAILS OF OTHER RIDERS:

Match No. 17: Mark Richardson 0 (3); Match No. 19: Mark Richardson 1 (1); Match No. 22: Dean Garrod ~ (3); Match No. 23: Dean Garrod 2+1 (3).

TACTICAL SUBSTITUTE AND TACTICAL RIDES, AS INCLUDED IN THE SCORES GRID:

Match No. 3: Rolph 4 points (TR); Hall 4 points (TR); Match No. 5: McAllan 4 points (TR); Rolph 0 points (TS); Match No. 16: Rolph 6 points (TR); Dennis 4 points (TS); Match No. 17: Hall 6 points (TR); Dennis 6 points (TR); Match No. 18: Rolph 4 points (TR); Cockle 2 points (TR); Match No. 19: Rolph 2 points (TR); Hall 0 points (TR).

CONFERENCE LEAGUE AVERAGES

Rider	Mts	Rds	Pts	Bon	Tot	Avge	Max
Richard Hall	18	93	226	2	228	9.81	4 full
Darren Mallett	7	25	50	5	55	8.80	–
Darren Rolph	22	110	205	26	231	8.40	3 paid
David McAllan	15	71	125	17	142	8.00	–
James Cockle	21	101	172	27	199	7.88	2 paid
Richie Dennis	16	70	99	14	113	6.46	1 paid
Robert Hollingworth	22	90	123	21	144	6.40	–
John Oliver	9	43	56	11	67	6.23	–
Ben Powell	2	9	13	0	13	5.78	–
Simon Lambert	15	66	62	14	76	4.61	–
Wayne Dunworth	7	24	15	4	19	3.17	–
Dean Garrod	2	6	3	1	4	2.67	–
Mark Richardson	2	4	1	0	1	1.00	–

KNOCK-OUT CUP

No	DATE	OPPONENTS	H/A	RESULT	HALL	MALLETT	HOLLINGWORTH	COCKLE	McALLAN	ROLPH	LAMBERT	DENNIS	DUNWORTH	COLVIN	POWELL
1	25/6	Rye House	H	W48-42	15 (6)	R/R	5+2 (4)	5 (4)	8+2 (6)	13+3 (7)	2+2 (3)	–	–	–	–
2	24/7	Rye House	A	W51-44*	R/R	–	7+1 (5)	13+2 (6)	13+2 (6)	14 (6)	–	3 (4)	1 (3)	–	–
3	1/9	Wimbledon	A	W56-38	15 (6)	–	8+2 (5)	16+1 (6)	–	11+2 (5)	2 (3)	4 (4)	–	R/R	–
4	24/9	Wimbledon	H	W54-43*	18 (6)	R/R	6+1 (4)	9 (6)	–	6 (5)	5+3 (4)	–	–	–	10+1 (5)
5	29/10	Mildenhall	H	L46-47	17+1 (6)	8 (4)	1 (3)	15+2 (7)	–	2 (4)	1 (3)	–	–	–	2 (3)
6	31/10	Mildenhall	A	L12-69	2 (2)	0 (1)	1 (1)	0 (2)	–	2+1 (2)	3+1 (2)	–	–	–	4 (2)

*Denotes aggregate victory

OTHER MEETINGS

20 March: Conference Challenge

Mildenhall 1 Boston 5 (James Cockle 3; Darren Mallett 2; Luke Clifton DNR; Richie Dennis DNR; David McAllan DNR; Darren Rolph DNR; John Oliver DNR) – meeting abandoned after heat one.

9 April: Conference Challenge

Boston 42 (Darren Rolph 12; Darren Mallett 9; Robert Hollingworth 7+2; Richie Dennis 5; Luke Clifton 4; James Cockle 3+1; John Oliver 2+1) Mildenhall 53.

16 April: Conference League

Weymouth 24 Boston 30 (David McAllan 8+1; Darren Rolph 6+1; James Cockle 5; Robert Hollingworth 5; Darren Mallett 3+2; John Oliver 3; Richard Hall R/R) – meeting abandoned after heat nine.

INDIVIDUAL MEETING

13 June: Lincolnshire Trophy

1st Richard Hall 14; 2nd Peter Boast (on countback) 13; 3rd Mark Thompson 13; David McAllan 11; James Cockle 9; Simon Lambert 9; Ricky Scarboro 9; Darren Rolph 8; Dean Garrod 7; John Oliver 7; Robert Hollingworth 6; Wayne Dunworth 5; Roger Dickerson 3; Paul Knott 3; Scott Campos 2; Keith Maben 0.

BUXTON HITMEN

ADDRESS: Buxton Raceway, Dale Head Lane, Axe Edge, nr. Buxton, Derbyshire.
CLUB CHAIRMEN: Richard Moss & Jayne Moss.
TRACK LENGTH: 240 metres.
TRACK RECORD: 52.9 seconds – James Wright (27/06/04).
FIRST MEETING: 19 May 1996.
YEARS OF OPERATION: 1996 Conference League; 1997 Amateur League; 1998-04 Conference League.

PREVIOUS VENUE: Buxton Stadium, off A53 Leek-to-Buxton Road, Buxton, Derbyshire.
YEARS OF OPERATION: 1994 British League Division Three; 1995 Academy League.

CLUB HONOURS

KNOCK-OUT CUP WINNERS: 2002.

RIDER ROSTER 2004

Carl BELFIELD; Jonathon BETHELL; Alan BROWN; Paul BURNETT; Benji COMFTON; Lee DERBYSHIRE; Ross PARKER; Paul SHARPLES; Charles WRIGHT; James WRIGHT.

OTHER APPEARANCES/GUESTS (official matches only):
James BIRKINSHAW; Scott CHESTER; Thomas HILL; Trent LEVERINGTON; Joe REYNOLDS.

CONFERENCE LEAGUE

No	DATE	OPPONENTS	H/A	RESULT	J. WRIGHT	BURNETT	BETHELL	COMPTON	LEVERINGTON	BROWN	SHARPLES	C. WRIGHT	BELFIELD	HILL	DERBYSHIRE	OTHERS
1	10/4	Armadale	A	L44-49	R/R	6+1 (4)	9+1 (5)	5 (5)	19 (6)	3 (4)	1+1 (4)	1+1 (2)	–	–	–	–
2	11/4	Armadale	H	W47-45	11+1 (5)	2 (3)	10+1 (4)	4 (4)	15 (5)	2 (4)	3+1 (5)	–	–	–	–	–
3	7/5	Weymouth	A	L42-47	11 (5)	4+1 (4)	8 (4)	3+1 (4)	12 (5)	0 (4)	4+2 (5)	–	–	–	–	–
4	9/5	Boston	H	W52-39	15 (5)	4+2 (4)	11 (4)	0 (4)	13+2 (5)	2 (3)	7+2 (5)	–	–	–	–	–
5	23/5	Oxford	H	W51-45	13 (5)	8+2 (4)	10+1 (5)	6+1 (4)	–	2+1 (4)	7 (4)	5+3 (4)	–	–	–	–
6	30/5	Mildenhall	H	L38-56	10 (6)	6+1 (4)	9 (4)	4 (4)	–	2+1 (3)	–	5 (5)	2+1 (4)	–	–	–
7	31/5	Mildenhall	A	L35-57	–	9+2 (6)	7+1 (5)	13 (6)	–	R/R	–	3+1 (5)	1+1 (4)	2+1 (4)	–	–
8	6/6	Carmarthen	H	W46-44	13 (5)	8+1 (4)	7 (5)	6+1 (4)	–	–	–	8+2 (5)	4+3 (4)	0 (3)	–	–
9	13/6	Newport	H	W55-40	15 (5)	8+3 (4)	5+1 (4)	10+1 (5)	–	–	3+1 (4)	6+1 (4)	8+1 (4)	–	–	–
10	4/7	Newcastle	H	W50-45	15 (5)	3+1 (3)	6 (4)	7+1 (4)	–	2+1 (3)	–	6+2 (5)	11–1 (6)	–	–	–
11	11/7	Newport	A	W48-42*	14 (5)	5 (4)	4 (4)	2 (3)	–	–	–	4+1 (4)	8+2 (5)	–	–	11+1 (5)
12	18/7	Rye House	H	L36-54	12 (5)	4 (4)	5 (4)	8 (5)	–	1+1 (3)	–	0 (3)	6–2 (6)	–	–	–
13	28/7	Stoke	A	W48-42	15 (6)	8 (5)	5+1 (5)	7+1 (4)	–	0 (2)	–	5+2 (4)	8–1 (4)	–	R/R	–
14	1/8	Stoke	H	W47-42*	18 (6)	8 (5)	11+1 (6)	3+1 (5)	–	–	–	3 (4)	4–1 (4)	–	R/R	–
15	8/8	Swindon	H	W56-38	18 (6)	8+2 (5)	4 (4)	9+3 (5)	–	–	–	9+2 (5)	8 (5)	–	R/R	–
16	15/8	Weymouth	H	W59-33*	18 (6)	8+1 (4)	9+2 (5)	12+2 (5)	–	–	–	5+3 (4)	7 (5)	0 (1)	R/R	–

CONFERENCE LEAGUE continued

No	DATE	OPPONENTS	H/A	RESULT	J. WRIGHT	BURNETT	BETHELL	COMPTON	LEVERINGTON	BROWN	SHARPLES	C. WRIGHT	BELFIELD	HILL	DERBYSHIRE	OTHERS
17	22/8	Newcastle	A	W46-44*	18 (6)	8 (6)	0 (1)	5+3 (5)	–	–	–	2 (5)	13 (7)	–	R/R	–
18	2/9	Swindon	A	L36-59	–	12+1 (6)	–	7 (6)	–	–	–	3+2 (5)	13 (7)	0 (3)	R/R	1+1 (3)
19	15/9	Wimbledon	A	L44-51	21 (6)	1 (3)	4+1 (4)	7 (4)	–	–	–	2 (4)	8 (5)	–	1 (4)	–
20	16/10	Rye House†	A	L33-42	R/R	0 (3)	8 (4)	9+2 (5)	–	–	–	–	7+1 (5)	–	5 (4)	4+2 (3)
21	22/10	Boston	A	L42-48*	17 (6)	5 (5)	6+2 (5)	6 (4)	–	–	–	–	6+1 (6)	–	R/R	2+1 (4)
22	23/10	Wimbledon	H	W48-41*	17 (6)	3 (3)	10+1 (5)	5+1 (5)	–	–	–	–	7 (7)	–	R/R	6+3 (4)
23	29/10	Oxford	A	L44-51	21 (6)	–	2 (2)	–	–	–	–	–	10+1 (7)	1+1 (4)	R/R	10+2 (11)
24	31/10	Carmarthen	A	D46-46*	19 (6)	–	10+1 (5)	11 (6)	–	–	–	–	6+1 (6)	–	R/R	0 (7)

*Denotes bonus-point victory

†Meeting abandoned after heat twelve, with the result permitted to stand.

DETAILS OF OTHER RIDERS:

Match No. 11: James Birkinshaw 11+1 (5); Match No. 18: Scott Chester 1+1 (3); Match No. 20: Ross Parker 4+2 (3); Match No. 21: Ross Parker 2+1 (4); Match No. 22: Ross Parker 6+3 (4); Match No. 23: Ross Parker 8+1 (7); Joe Reynolds 2+1 (4); Match No. 24: Joe Reynolds 0 (3); Ross Parker 0 (4).

TACTICAL SUBSTITUTE AND TACTICAL RIDES, AS INCLUDED IN THE SCORES GRID:

Match No. 1: Leverington 6 points (TR); Match No. 6: Bethell 6 points (TR); Burnett 4 points (TR); J. Wright 0 points (TS); Match No. 7: Compton 4 points (TR); Bethell 4 points (TR); Match No. 12: Compton 4 points (TR); J. Wright 2 points (TR); Match No. 13: Burnett 6 points (TR); Belfield 4 points (TR); Match No. 19: J. Wright 6 points (TR); Compton 4 points (TR); Match No. 20: Compton 4 points (TR); Bethell 4 points (TR); Match No. 23: J. Wright 6 points (TR); Belfield 4 points (TR); Match No. 24: J. Wright 6 points (TR).

CONFERENCE LEAGUE AVERAGES

Rider	Mts	Rds	Pts	Bon	Tot	Avge	Max
Trent Leverington	4	21	56	2	58	11.05	1 full; 1 paid
James Wright	20	111	301	1	302	10.88	9 full
James Birkinshaw	1	5	11	1	12	9.60	–
Jonathon Bethell	23	98	153	14	167	6.82	–
Paul Burnett	22	93	123	18	141	6.06	–
Benji Compton	23	106	141	18	159	6.00	–
Carl Belfield	19	101	133	17	150	5.94	–
Charles Wright	16	68	67	20	87	5.12	–
Ross Parker	5	22	20	7	27	4.91	–
Paul Sharples	6	27	25	7	32	4.74	–
Lee Derbyshire	2	8	6	0	6	3.00	–
Scott Chester	1	3	1	1	2	2.67	–
Alan Brown	9	30	14	4	18	2.40	–
Joe Reynolds	2	7	2	1	3	1.71	–
Thomas Hill	5	15	3	2	5	1.33	–

BUXTON: back row, left to right: Jack Lee (Team Manager), James Wright, Lee Derbyshire, Charles Wright, Jonathon Bethell, Joe Reynolds, Paul Burnett. Front row: Benji Compton, Carl Belfield, Alan Brown.

CONFERENCE TROPHY

No	DATE	OPPONENTS	H/A	RESULT	J. WRIGHT	C. WRIGHT	DERBYSHIRE	COMPTON	BURNETT	BROWN	SHARPLES	BETHELL	BELFIELD	HILL	REYNOLDS	OTHERS
1	7/4	Wimbledon	A	L38-57	19 (6)	2 (5)	R/R	12+1 (6)	1 (4)	3 (5)	1 (4)	–	–	–	–	–
2	25/4	Coventry	H	W53-44	12 (5)	–	–	3+2 (4)	7+3 (4)	4+1 (4)	6+1 (4)	9 (4)	–	–	–	12 (5)
3	2/8	Coventry	A	W48-45*	21 (6)	2 (3)	R/R	9+1 (6)	4+2 (4)	–	–	6 (5)	6+1 (6)	–	–	–
4	21/8	Mildenhall	H	W48-45	18 (6)	3 (3)	R/R	10+1 (6)	2+1 (4)	–	–	2+1 (4)	13 (7)	–	–	–
5	29/8	Wimbledon	H	W55-39	18 (6)	8+2 (4)	R/R	10+1 (5)	8+1 (5)	–	–	–	11+3 (7)	0 (3)	–	–
6	5/9	Sheffield	H	W52-44	14 (6)	6+1 (5)	R/R	5+4 (6)	9 (4)	–	–	11 (5)	7+2 (4)	–	–	–
7	12/9	King's Lynn	H	W49-47	R/R	9+3 (5)	5+2 (4)	10 (6)	9+2 (4)	–	–	6+1 (5)	10+1 (6)	–	–	–
8	19/9	Mildenhall	A	L40-52	15 (5)	4 (5)	7+2 (5)	3 (4)	–	–	–	4 (4)	7+1 (4)	0 (3)	–	–
9	23/9	Sheffield	A	L43-50*	16 (5)	3+1 (4)	5+1 (4)	7 (5)	3 (4)	–	–	0 (3)	9+2 (5)	–	–	–
10	24/9	Weymouth	A	L43-52	17 (5)	0 (1)	1 (4)	3+1 (4)	2 (4)	–	–	7+2 (5)	13+1 (7)	–	–	–
11	26/9	Weymouth	H	W53-39*	15 (5)	–	8 (4)	5+1 (4)	0 (0)	–	–	7+2 (5)	15+3 (7)	–	3+1 (5)	–
12	29/9	King's Lynn	A	L42-48	12 (4)	–	6 (4)	5+1 (4)	–	–	–	9+1 (4)	10 (7)	–	0 (3)	0 (4)

*Denotes bonus-point victory

NOTE: James Wright is not credited with a maximum in the away match at King's Lynn, as he suffered a fall in the original running of heat fifteen and was unable to take part in the rerun.

DETAILS OF OTHER RIDERS:

Match No. 2: Trent Leverington 12 (5); Match No. 12: Ross Parker 0 (4).

TACTICAL RIDES, AS INCLUDED IN THE SCORES GRID:

Match No. 1: J. Wright 6 points (TR); Compton 4 points (TR); Match No. 3: J. Wright 6 points (TR); Match No. 8: J. Wright 6 points (TR); Belfield 0 points (TR); Match No. 9: J. Wright 6 points (TR); Match No. 10: J. Wright 6 points (TR); Belfield 4 points (TR).

CONFERENCE TROPHY AVERAGES

Rider	Mts	Rds	Pts	Bon	Tot	Avge	Max
James Wright	11	59	162	0	162	10.98	4 full
Trent Leverington	1	5	12	0	12	9.60	–
Carl Belfield	10	60	99	14	113	7.53	–
Benji Compton	12	60	80	13	93	6.20	–
Jonathon Bethell	10	44	61	7	68	6.18	–
Lee Derbyshire	6	25	32	5	37	5.92	–
Paul Burnett	10	37	45	9	54	5.84	–
Charles Wright	9	35	37	7	44	5.03	–
Paul Sharples	2	8	7	1	8	4.00	–
Alan Brown	2	9	7	1	8	3.56	–
Joe Reynolds	2	8	3	1	4	2.00	–
Thomas Hill	2	6	0	0	0	0.00	–
Ross Parker	1	4	0	0	0	0.00	–

KNOCK-OUT CUP

No	DATE	OPPONENTS	H/A	RESULT	BURNETT	J. WRIGHT	COMPTON	BROWN	BETHELL	BELFIELD	C. WRIGHT
1	25/6	Oxford	A	L31-61	9 (5)	R/R	6+1 (6)	3 (4)	9+2 (7)	4 (6)	0 (1)
2	27/6	Oxford	H	W50-44	2+1 (3)	15 (5)	8+1 (4)	3+1 (3)	8 (5)	5+2 (4)	9+2 (6)

TACTICAL SUBSTITUTE AND TACTICAL RIDES, AS INCLUDED IN THE SCORES GRID:

Match No. 1: Burnett 4 points (TR); Compton 4 points (TR); Bethell 2 points (TS).

INDIVIDUAL MEETINGS

3 April: British Under-21 Championship Qualifying Round

1st Richard Hall 13 (on countback); 2nd Ben Wilson 13; 3rd Jamie Robertson 12 (on countback); James Wright 12; Rob Grant jr 12; Chris Schramm 10; Adam Roynon 7; Danny Hughes 7; Tom Brown 6; Chris Mills 5; Steve Braidford 5; Daniel Giffard 5; Jamie Courtney 4; Luke Priest 3; Benji Compton 2; John Branney 2; Charles Wright (Res) 1.

4 July: British Under-15 Championship (Fourth Round)

1st Josh Auty 15; =2nd Simon Lambert; Shane Waldron 13; Matthew Bates 11; Gary Cottham 10; Scott Campos 10; Kyle Hughes 10; Lewis Bridger 9; Sam Hurst 8; George Piper 6; James Humby 4; Connor Scott 3; Ben Hopwood 3; Joe Reynolds 2; Aaron Baseby 2; Ben Thompson 1. SERIES POINTS (best three rounds count): 1st Auty 49; =2nd Lambert, Waldron 47; Bates 39; Cottham 39; Hughes 38; Campos 37; Humby 27; Piper 25; Hurst 24; Bridger 21; Hopwood 15; Grant Hayes 13; Baseby 10; Trevor Heath 9; Thompson 9; Reynolds 7; Scott 7; Dean Hargrave 4; Ben Hannon 4; Tim Webster 4; Chris Widman 3; Andy Braithwaite 1; Shawn Taylor 1.

CARMARTHEN DRAGONS

ADDRESS: United Counties Showground, Nantyci, Carmarthen, West Wales, SA33 5DR.
CLUB CHAIRMAN: Nigel Meakins.
TRACK LENGTH: 242 metres.
TRACK RECORD: 56.83 seconds – Ritchie Hawkins (06/04/03).
FIRST MEETING: 21 April 2002.
YEARS OF OPERATION: 2002-04 Conference League.

CLUB HONOURS

None.

RIDER ROSTER 2004

Steve BISHOP; Dean FELTON; Darren HATTON; Chris HUNT; Steven JONES; Gordon MEAKINS; Ben POWELL; Darren PUGH.

OTHER APPEARANCES/GUESTS (official matches only):

Shane COLVIN; Andrew JACKSON; Ben WILSON.

CONFERENCE LEAGUE

No	DATE	OPPONENTS	H/A	RESULT	POWELL	MEAKINS	COLVIN	FELTON	HUNT	HATTON	PUGH	BISHOP	WILSON	JACKSON	JONES
1	28/3	Boston	H	L36-57	2 (3)	3 (4)	13 (5)	7+1 (6)	5+1 (4)	3 (4)	3 (4)	–	–	–	–
2	2/4	Weymouth	A	W48-42	11+1 (5)	1 (4)	–	5+4 (4)	1+1 (2)	4+1 (4)	13 (6)	13 (5)	–	–	–
3	9/4	Newport	H	W57-37	5+1 (4)	–	10+2 (5)	10 (4)	5+3 (4)	7+1 (4)	6+2 (4)	14 (5)	–	–	–
4	14/4	Wimbledon	A	L40-54	9+1 (6)	4+2 (5)	8 (6)	9 (4)	7+1 (5)	3+1 (4)	–	R/R	–	–	–
5	14/5	Newcastle	H	W63-27	9+1 (5)	5 (4)	R/R	13+2 (5)	9+2 (4)	2 (2)	7+2 (4)	18 (6)	–	–	–
6	17/5	Swindon	A	W47-42	8 (5)	2+1 (3)	2+2 (4)	7 (4)	1 (3)	–	13+1 (6)	14 (5)	–	–	–
7	29/5	Rye House	A	L42-50	3+1 (4)	4 (5)	–	7+3 (4)	5+1 (4)	–	0 (3)	7 (5)	16 (5)	–	–
8	30/5	Oxford	H	L29-62	5 (4)	1 (3)	–	4 (6)	5+1 (5)	–	6+1 (5)	8 (6)	R/R	–	–
9	6/6	Buxton	A	L44-46	2+1 (4)	2+1 (4)	–	4 (4)	9 (4)	–	–	13 (5)	13+1 (5)	1 (4)	–
10	9/6	Stoke	A	L36-58	13 (5)	2+1 (3)	–	9+1 (5)	1 (4)	3 (4)	7 (5)	–	–	1 (4)	–
11	13/6	Mildenhall	H	L42-46	7+1 (6)	–	–	7+1 (5)	6+2 (5)	1+1 (3)	7+1 (5)	14 (6)	R/R	–	–
12	27/6	Newport	A	L44-46*	6+1 (6)	4+3 (3)	–	9+2 (5)	5+1 (4)	1+1 (1)	7 (5)	12 (6)	R/R	–	–
13	25/7	Stoke	H	W50-42	R/R	–	–	11+1 (6)	2 (4)	2+1 (3)	10+2 (6)	19 (6)	–	–	6+2 (5)
14	1/8	Swindon	H	L43-46*	12 (6)	5+1 (6)	–	14+1 (6)	1 (1)	5+1 (6)	–	R/R	–	–	6 (5)
15	14/8	Armadale	A	L27-67	4 (4)	1 (4)	–	7+2 (4)	–	2 (5)	1 (3)	–	9+1 (5)	–	3 (5)
16	15/8	Newcastle	A	L43-52*	11+1 (5)	1 (4)	–	10 (4)	–	1+1 (4)	4 (4)	–	11+1 (5)	–	5+1 (4)
17	22/8	Wimbledon	H	L38-55	7 (6)	2+1 (3)	–	15+1 (6)	3+2 (5)	4 (4)	–	–	R/R	–	7 (6)
18	30/8	Mildenhall	A	L38-55	–	2+1 (4)	–	7 (4)	3 (4)	2+1 (3)	9 (6)	12+1 (5)	–	–	3+1 (4)
19	5/9	Rye House	H	L40-54	–	2+1 (3)	–	9 (5)	2+1 (4)	8+2 (7)	0 (1)	12 (5)	–	–	7 (5)

CARMARTHEN: back row, left to right: Nigel Meakins (Team Manager), Ben Wilson, Dean Felton, Darren Pugh, Gordon Meakins. Front, kneeling: Shane Colvin, Steve Bishop. On bike: Chris Hunt.

CONFERENCE LEAGUE continued

No	DATE	OPPONENTS	H/A	RESULT	POWELL	MEAKINS	COLVIN	FELTON	HUNT	HATTON	PUGH	BISHOP	WILSON	JACKSON	JONES
20	19/9	Weymouth	H	L42-48*	–	0 (4)	–	12 (6)	6 (5)	3+1 (5)	–	15 (6)	R/R	–	6+1 (5)
21	26/9	Boston	A	L28-65	–	2 (4)	–	6+1 (5)	2+1 (5)	3 (5)	–	6 (5)	R/R	–	9 (6)
22	9/10	Armadale	H	L44-46	–	0 (3)	–	13+1 (6)	5+1 (5)	5+1 (5)	–	15 (6)	R/R	–	6+1 (5)
23	29/10	Oxford†	A	L31-44	–	2+1 (3)	–	4+1 (4)	3+1 (4)	5+1 (5)	–	11 (4)	R/R	–	6 (4)
24	31/10	Buxton	H	D46-46	–	5+1 (4)	–	11+1 (6)	4 (4)	7 (6)	–	17 (6)	R/R	–	2+2 (4)

*Denotes bonus-point victory

†Meeting abandoned after heat twelve, with the result permitted to stand.

TACTICAL SUBSTITUTE AND TACTICAL RIDES, AS INCLUDED IN THE SCORES GRID:

Match No. 1: Colvin 6 points (TR); Powell 0 points (TR); Felton 0 points (TS); Match No. 4: Colvin 4 points (TR); Felton 4 points (TR); Match No. 7: Wilson 6 points (TR); Match No. 8: Bishop 2 points (TR); Powell 0 points (TR); Match No. 10: Powell 6 points (TR); Felton 2 points (TR); Match No. 13: Bishop 6 points (TR); Match No. 15: Wilson 4 points (TR); Felton 4 points (TR); Match No. 16: Wilson 6 points (TR); Powell 4 points (TR); Match No. 17: Felton 6 points (TR); Jones 2 points (TR); Powell 0 points (TS); Match No. 18: Felton 4 points (TR); Bishop 2 points (TR); Match No. 19: Bishop 4 points (TR); Jones 2 points (TR); Felton 2 points (TS); Match No. 21: Jones 4 points (TR); Bishop 2 points (TR); Match No. 23: Bishop 4 points (TR); Jones 2 points (TR).

CONFERENCE LEAGUE AVERAGES

Rider	Mts	Rds	Pts	Bon	Tot	Avge	Max
Steve Bishop	17	92	210	1	211	9.17	1 full
Ben Wilson	4	20	41	3	44	8.80	–
Dean Felton	24	118	199	23	222	7.53	1 paid
Shane Colvin	4	20	28	4	32	6.40	–
Darren Pugh	15	67	93	9	102	6.09	–
Ben Powell	16	78	109	9	118	6.05	–
Chris Hunt	22	89	90	19	109	4.90	–
Steven Jones	12	58	61	8	69	4.76	–
Darren Hatton	20	84	71	14	85	4.05	–
Gordon Meakins	21	80	50	14	64	3.20	–
Andrew Jackson	2	8	2	0	2	1.00	–

KNOCK-OUT CUP

No	DATE	OPPONENTS	H/A	RESULT	POWELL	HUNT	MEAKINS	FELTON	BISHOP	PUGH	HATTON	JACKSON
1	18/4	Mildenhall†	A	L31-52	10 (4)	2 (4)	2 (4)	3 (3)	11 (4)	2 (4)	1 (3)	–
2	3/5	Mildenhall	H	L42-53	11+1 (5)	3+1 (4)	–	6 (5)	15 (5)	4 (3)	2+1 (4)	1+1 (4)

†Meeting abandoned after heat thirteen, with the result permitted to stand.

TACTICAL SUBSTITUTE AND TACTICAL RIDES, AS INCLUDED IN THE SCORES GRID:

Match No. 1: Powell 6 points (TR); Bishop 4 points (TR); Match No. 2: Powell 6 points (TR); Bishop 4 points (TR); Felton 0 points (TS).

OTHER MEETINGS

8 August: Conference League

Carmarthen 13 (Darren Pugh 6; Gordon Meakins 4; Dean Felton 3+1; Ben Powell 0; Steven Jones 0; Darren Hatton 0; Chris Hunt R/R) Armadale 22 – meeting abandoned after heat six.

16 October: Inter-Nations Fours

England 38 (Jamie Robertson 9; Chris Schramm 8; Dean Felton 7; Craig Branney 7; Chris Hunt 7), Scotland 33 (Blair Scott 12; Adam McKinna 11; William Lawson 8; Andrew Tully 2), World Select 32 (Lee Smart 9; James Theobald 7; Karol Malecha 6; Karlis Ezergailis 6; Steven Jones 4), Wales 25 (Jamie Westacott 11; Mark Burrows 7; Gordon Meakins 3; Matthew Wright 2; Darren Hatton 2).

INDIVIDUAL MEETING

19 September: British Under-15 Championship (Sixth Round)

1st Shane Waldron 15; 2nd Josh Auty 13; =3rd Simon Lambert, Gary Cottham 12; Lewis Bridger 10; Matt Bates 10; George Piper 7; Chris Widman 7; Grant Hayes 6; James Humby 5; Gavin Wrigley 5; Joe Reynolds 5; Sam Hurst 5; Tim Webster 4; Andy Braithwaite 1; Connor Scott (Res) 1; Scott Meakins (Res) 1; Dan Kirkman 0. SERIES POINTS (best three rounds count): 1st Auty 51; 2nd Waldron 49; 3rd Lambert 47; Cottham 43; Bates 42; Hughes 38; Campos 37; Bridger 30; Hurst 29; Humby 28; Piper 27; Hayes 25; Reynolds 18; Ben Hopwood 15; Widman 13; Ben Thompson 12; Aaron Baseby 10; Scott 10; Trevor Heath 9; Webster 7; Wrigley 7; Braithwaite 6; Dean Hargrave 4; Ben Hannon 4; Meakins 2; Shawn Taylor 1; Kirkman 1.

COVENTRY DLG COUGARS

NOTE: The information below relates only to the second Coventry team. For details of the main side, please refer to the Elite League section.

ADDRESS: Coventry International Motor Speedway, Rugby Road, Brandon, nr. Coventry, Warwickshire, CV8 3GJ.
CLUB CHAIRMAN: Des Quinney.
TRACK LENGTH: 303 metres.
CL TRACK RECORD: 61.3 seconds – James Wright (2/08/04).
FIRST MEETING: 19 April 2004.
YEARS OF OPERATION: 2004 Conference Trophy.

CLUB HONOURS

None.

RIDER ROSTER 2004

Darren ANDREWS; Ben BARKER; Tom BROWN; Harland COOK; Karl MASON; Jeremy PESTELL.

OTHER APPEARANCES/GUESTS (official matches only):

Matt BATES; Carl DOWNS; Karlis EZERGAILIS; Danny HUGHES; Lawrence NEEDS; Ben POWELL; Ricky SCARBORO.

CONFERENCE TROPHY

No	DATE	OPPONENTS	H/A	RESULT	BROWN	DOWNS	BARKER	ANDREWS	MASON	NEEDS	PESTELL	HUGHES	POWELL	COOK	EZERGAILIS	OTHERS
1	19/4	Wimbledon	H	L40-51	6 (5)	2+2 (4)	7+2 (5)	9+1 (4)	6 (4)	2+1 (3)	8+3 (5)	–	–	–	–	–
2	25/4	Buxton	A	L44-53	12 (6)	2+2 (3)	3 (3)	13 (4)	–	2+1 (5)	0 (4)	12+3 (5)	–	–	–	–
3	14/6	King's Lynn	H	L39-53	15 (6)	–	R/R	9+2 (6)	–	–	1+1 (5)	1 (3)	3 (2)	10+1 (7)	–	–
4	28/6	Mildenhall	H	L39-54	8+1 (7)	–	3 (5)	10+1 (5)	11 (6)	–	1 (3)	–	R/R	6 (4)	–	–
5	30/6	Wimbledon	A	L39-55	9 (6)	–	4+3 (5)	5 (5)	13 (6)	–	0 (1)	–	–	8+1 (5)	–	R/R
6	30/7	Weymouth	A	L29-64	12 (6)	–	R/R	–	2 (4)	–	1 (4)	–	–	3 (6)	10+1 (6)	1 (4)
7	2/8	Buxton	H	L45-48	10 (5)	–	5+1 (4)	8+2 (4)	5 (3)	–	5+2 (5)	–	–	6 (4)	6 (5)	–
8	6/9	Sheffield	A	L40-49	9+1 (6)	–	R/R	2 (3)	6+2 (5)	–	1 (3)	–	7 (6)	–	15+2 (7)	–
9	19/9	Mildenhall	A	L41-54	15+1 (6)	–	10 (6)	0 (3)	1+1 (4)	–	–	–	R/R	10 (6)	5+3 (5)	–
10	27/9	Weymouth	H	L46-47	19 (6)	–	R/R	2+1 (4)	12+2 (6)	–	1 (4)	–	6 (5)	6+1 (5)	–	–
11	27/9	Sheffield	H	L43-47	11 (6)	–	R/R	3+1 (4)	6+1 (6)	–	5+3 (4)	–	6 (4)	12+1 (6)	–	–
12	6/10	King's Lynn	A	L45-50	–	–	4+1 (5)	4+1 (4)	11 (5)	–	5+1 (5)	–	R/R	–	18+1 (7)	3 (4)

*Denotes bonus-point victory

DETAILS OF OTHER RIDERS:

Match No. 5: Nick Simmons R/R; Match No. 6: Matt Bates 1 (4); Match No. 12: Ricky Scarboro 3 (4).

COVENTRY: back row, left to right: Jeremy Pestell, Darren Andrews, Danny Hughes, Tom Brown. Front row: Carl Downs, Ben Barker, Lawrence Needs.

TACTICAL SUBSTITUTE AND TACTICAL RIDES, AS INCLUDED IN THE SCORES GRID:

Match No. 1: Andrews 4 points (TR); Match No. 2: Hughes 6 points (TR); Andrews 6 points (TR); Brown 4 points (TS); Match No. 3: Brown 6 points (TR); Powell 0 points (TR); Match No. 4: Mason 2 points (TR); Andrews 2 points (TR); Brown 2 points (TS); Match No. 5: Mason 6 points (TR); Andrews 2 points (TR); Match No. 6: Brown 6 points (TR); Mason 0 points (TR); Match No. 9: Brown 6 points (TR); Barker 4 points (TR); Match No. 10: Brown 6 points (TR); Match No. 12: Ezergailis 6 points (TR); Mason 4 points (TR).

CONFERENCE TROPHY AVERAGES

Rider	Mts	Rds	Pts	Bon	Tot	Avge	Max
Karlis Ezergailis	5	30	51	7	58	7.73	–
Tom Brown	11	65	111	3	114	7.02	–
Danny Hughes	2	8	10	3	13	6.50	–
Harland Cook	8	43	61	4	65	6.05	–
Karl Mason	10	49	67	6	73	5.96	–
Darren Andrews	11	46	58	9	67	5.83	–
Ben Powell	4	17	22	0	22	5.18	–
Ben Barker	7	33	34	7	41	4.97	–
Carl Downs	2	7	4	4	8	4.57	–
Jeremy Pestell	11	43	28	10	38	3.53	–
Lawrence Needs	2	8	4	2	6	3.00	–
Ricky Scarboro	1	4	3	0	3	3.00	–
Matt Bates	1	4	1	0	1	1.00	–

OTHER MEETINGS

24 May: Conference Challenge

Coventry 61 (Karl Mason 15; Tom Brown 11+2; Harland Cook 9+1; Darren Andrews 8+2; Ben Barker 8+1; Danny Hughes 6+2; Steve Clarke 4) Belle Vue Colts 35 (Adam Roynon 14; John Oliver 10; Lee Smart 4+1; Jonathon Bethell 3; Paul Burnett 2+1; Paul Sharples 2+1; Charlie Wright 0).

7 June: Conference Trophy

Sheffield 44 Coventry 22 (Tom Brown 6; Ben Powell 5; Karl Mason 5; Danny Hughes 2; Jeremy Pestell 2; Darren Andrews 1+1; Steve Clarke 1) – meeting abandoned after heat eleven.

4 July: Festival of Speed (staged at Sittingbourne)

FIRST SEMI-FINAL: Wimbledon 24, Weymouth 19, Coventry 11 (Harland Cook 5; Ricky Scarboro 3+1; Karlis Ezergailis 2; Lewis Dallaway (Res) 1; Sam Martin 0). SECOND SEMI-FINAL: Swindon 24, Armadale 16, Sittingbourne 14. FINAL: Wimbledon 21, Weymouth 20, Swindon 13.

KING'S LYNN STARLETS

NOTE: The information below relates only to the second King's Lynn team. For details of the main side, please refer to the Premier League section.

ADDRESS: Norfolk Arena, Saddlebow Road, King's Lynn, Norfolk, PE34 3AG.
CLUB CHAIRMEN: Keith 'Buster' Chapman & Laurence Rogers.
TRACK LENGTH: 342 metres.
CL TRACK RECORD: 60.0 seconds – Trevor Harding (15/06/03).
FIRST MEETING: 11 May 1969.
YEARS OF OPERATION: 1969-70 British League Division Two; 1997 Amateur League; 1998-99 Conference League; 2004 Conference Trophy.

NOTE: The Amateur League team of 1997 shared their fixtures with Ipswich and rode under the name of 'Anglian Angels'. The Conference League side of 1998 was known as 'Norfolk Braves', whereas in 1999, they rode as 'King's Lynn Braves'.

CLUB HONOURS

None.

RIDER ROSTER 2004

Craig BRANNEY; John BRANNEY; Daniel HARDING; Daniel HODGSON.

OTHER APPEARANCES/GUESTS (official matches only):

Marc ANDREWS; Luke BOWEN; Scott CHESTER; Lewis DALLAWAY; Richie DENNIS; Wayne DUNWORTH; Dean FELTON; Jordan FRAMPTON; Dean GARROD; Trevor HARDING; Sam HURST; Chris JOHNSON; Paul KNOTT; Simon LAMBERT; Darren MALLETT; John OLIVER; Joel PARSONS; Michael PICKERING; James PURCHASE; Darren ROLPH; James THEOBALD; Mark THOMPSON; Simon WALKER; Danny WARWICK; Tim WEBSTER; Dean WILSON.

CONFERENCE TROPHY

No	DATE	OPPONENTS	H/A	RESULT	C. BRANNEY	HODGSON	J. BRANNEY	MALLETT	T. HARDING	D. HARDING	KNOTT	ROLPH	THOMPSON	DENNIS	GARROD	OTHERS
1	7/6	Sheffield	A	L37-57	12 (6)	2 (4)	6 (5)	R/R	14 (5)	1+1 (5)	2 (5)	–	–	–	–	–
2	14/6	Coventry	A	W53-39	10 (5)	8+1 (5)	–	R/R	–	1 (2)	5+2 (5)	10 (5)	14 (5)	–	–	5+1 (3)
3	28/7	Wimbledon	A	L41-53	11 (6)	1+1 (4)	5+2 (5)	–	–	2 (4)	–	–	R/F	14 (6)	–	8+1 (5)
4	4/9	Sheffield	H	L43-47	8 (4)	1+1 (4)	4 (4)	–	7 (5)	6+2 (4)	–	–	–	12 (5)	5+2 (4)	–
5	5/9	Mildenhall	A	L38-56	R/R	1 (4)	–	–	11 (5)	7+2 (6)	–	–	–	–	3+1 (6)	16 (8)
6	12/9	Buxton	A	L47-49	R/R	–	6+1 (5)	–	–	–	–	–	–	–	–	41+3 (22)
7	18/9	Weymouth	H	L43-47	18 (6)	–	–	–	–	3 (6)	–	11 (6)	3 (3)	–	4 (5)	4 (4)
8	18/9	Wimbledon	H	L41-55	14 (5)	–	–	–	–	7+1 (6)	–	11 (5)	5 (3)	–	3+1 (5)	1 (6)
9	29/9	Buxton	H	W48-42*	15 (6)	2 (4)	10 (5)	9+2 (6)	–	–	–	7+2 (5)	–	–	–	5+2 (4)
10	6/10	Mildenhall	H	L44-48	14 (6)	0 (3)	–	2 (4)	–	–	–	–	–	–	–	28+3 (17)
11	6/10	Coventry	H	W50-45*	13+2 (6)	1 (3)	–	11+2 (5)	–	–	–	–	–	–	–	25+2 (16)
12	31/10	Weymouth	A	L31-62	–	–	–	–	–	–	–	–	–	–	–	31+3 (30)

*Denotes bonus-point victory

DETAILS OF OTHER RIDERS:

Match No. 2: John Oliver 5+1 (3); Match No. 3: Dean Felton 8+1 (5); Match No. 5: Chris Johnson 16 (6); Lewis Dallaway 0 (2); Match No. 6: Joel Parsons 19+1 (6); Dean Felton 18+1 (6); Simon Lambert 4+1 (6); Scott Chester 0 (4), Lewis Dallaway 0 (0); Match No. 7: Wayne Dunworth 4 (4); Joel Parsons R/R; Match No. 8: Wayne Dunworth 1 (4); Dean Wilson 0 (2); Joel Parsons R/R; Match No. 9: Simon Lambert 5+2 (4); Joel Parsons R/R; Match No. 10: Simon Walker 15 (6); Simon Lambert 9+2 (6); Dean Felton 4+1 (5); Joel Parsons R/R; Match No. 11: Simon Walker 9+1 (4); Dean Felton 7+1 (4); Simon Lambert 7 (6); Wayne Dunworth 2 (2); Joel Parsons R/R; Match No. 12: Danny Warwick 11+1 (6); Sam Hurst 11 (6); Jordan Frampton 5+1 (5); James Purchase 3+1 (5); Marc Andrews 1 (4); Tim Webster 0 (4); Dean Felton R/R.

TACTICAL RIDES, AS INCLUDED IN THE SCORES GRID:

Match No. 1: T. Harding 6 points (TR); J. Branney 2 points (TR); Match No. 3: Dennis 6 points (TR); Felton 4 points (TR); Match No. 5: Johnson 6 points (TR); T. Harding 2 points (TR); Match No. 6: Parsons 6 points (TR); Felton 6 points (TR); Match No. 8: Rolph 6 points (TR); C. Branney 6 points (TR); Match No. 12: Hurst 4 points (TR); Warwick 2 points (TR).

CONFERENCE TROPHY AVERAGES

Rider	Mts	Rds	Pts	Bon	Tot	Avge	Max
Joel Parsons	1	6	16	1	17	11.33	–
Simon Walker	2	10	24	1	25	10.00	–
Craig Branney	9	50	112	2	114	9.12	1 full
Chris Johnson	1	6	13	0	13	8.67	–
Richie Dennis	2	11	23	0	23	8.36	–
John Oliver	1	3	5	1	6	8.00	–
Mark Thompson	3	11	22	0	22	8.00	–
Trevor Harding	3	15	28	0	28	7.47	–
Danny Warwick	1	6	10	1	11	7.33	–
Darren Rolph	4	21	36	2	38	7.24	–
Dean Felton	4	20	32	4	36	7.20	–
Darren Mallett	3	15	22	4	26	6.93	–
Sam Hurst	1	6	9	0	9	6.00	–
John Branney	5	24	30	3	33	5.50	–
Simon Lambert	4	22	25	5	30	5.45	–
Jordan Frampton	1	5	5	1	6	4.80	–
Daniel Harding	7	33	27	6	33	4.00	–
Dean Garrod	4	20	15	4	19	3.80	–
Paul Knott	2	10	7	2	9	3.60	–
James Purchase	1	5	3	1	4	3.20	–
Wayne Dunworth	3	10	7	0	7	2.80	–
Daniel Hodgson	8	31	16	3	19	2.45	–
Marc Andrews	1	4	1	0	1	1.00	–
Scott Chester	1	4	0	0	0	0.00	–
Lewis Dallaway	2	2	0	0	0	0.00	–
Tim Webster	1	4	0	0	0	0.00	–
Dean Wilson	1	2	0	0	0	0.00	–

KING'S LYNN: back row, left to right: Laurence Rogers (Team Manager), Wayne Davies, Joel Parsons, Scott Chester, John Branney. Front row: Lewis Dallaway, Dean Felton, Simon Lambert.

KNOCK-OUT CUP

No	DATE	OPPONENTS	H/A	RESULT	THEOBALD	GARROD	J. BRANNEY	THOMPSON	BOWEN	HODGSON	PICKERING
1	8/8	Mildenhall	A	L27-63	3 (5)	7 (5)	5 (5)	R/R	9 (6)	0 (3)	3+2 (6)

NOTE: Mildenhall were given a walkover through to the semi-final of the Knock-Out Cup after King's Lynn were unable to find a date for their home leg of the second round tie.

TACTICAL RIDE, AS INCLUDED IN THE SCORES GRID:

Match No. 1: J. Branney 2 points (TR).

OTHER MEETINGS

14 March: Three-Team Tournament

Peterborough 30 (Richie Dennis 10; Danny Norton 9; Adam Pryer 6; Steve Clarke 2+1; Adam Roynon 2; James Purchase 1+1), Rye House 45, King's Lynn 32 (Chris Mills 9; Darren Mallett 8; Darren Rolph 5+1; John Oliver 4+3; Paul Knott 4; Daniel Hodgson 2) – staged at Peterborough.

27 June: Knock-Out Cup second round (first leg)

Mildenhall 43 King's Lynn 17 (Trevor Harding 6; Chris Johnson 4; Dean Garrod 2; Mark Thompson 2; Daniel Hodgson 2; Daniel Harding 1; Lewis Dallaway 0; Luke Clifton R/R) – meeting abandoned after heat ten.

INDIVIDUAL MEETING

27 October: David Nix Memorial

1st Richard Hall 15; 2nd James Brundle 14; 3rd Craig Branney 12; Darren Rolph 10; Jamie Robertson 9; Karl Mason 9; Darren Mallett 8; Ben Barker 7; Tom Brown 7; Benji Compton 6; Simon Walker 5; John Branney 5; Ritchie Hawkins 4; Jonathon Bethell 4; Simon Lambert 3; Mark Richardson 2.

MILDENHALL SUPERIOR EXTERIORS FEN TIGERS

ADDRESS: Mildenhall Stadium, Hayland Drove, West Row Fen, Mildenhall, Suffolk, IP28 8QU.

CLUB CHAIRMEN: Graham Drury & Denise Drury.

TRACK LENGTH: 260 metres.

TRACK RECORD: 50.25 seconds – Paul Lee (16/05/04).

FIRST MEETING: 18 May 1975.

YEARS OF OPERATION: 1973 Training; 1974 Open & Training; 1975-89 National League; 1990-91 Training; 1992 British League Division Two; 1994 British League Division Three; 1995 Academy League; 1996 Conference League; 1997 Amateur League; 1998-04 Conference League.

CLUB HONOURS

LEAGUE CHAMPIONS: 1979, 2003, 2004.

FOUR-TEAM CHAMPIONS: 1984, 1987, 2004.

PAIRS CHAMPIONS: 1987.

LEAGUE CUP WINNERS: 2000.

CONFERENCE TROPHY WINNERS: 2002, 2004.

KNOCK-OUT CUP WINNERS: 2003, 2004.

RIDER ROSTER 2004

Jon ARMSTRONG; James BRUNDLE; Tony DART; Ritchie HAWKINS; Kyle HUGHES; Jason KING; Paul LEE; James MANN; Gary PHELPS; Adam ROYNON; Lee SMART; Darren SMITH.

OTHER APPEARANCES/GUESTS (official matches only):

Carl BALDWIN; Danny BETSON; Daniel BLAKE; Scott CAMPOS; Chris COLLINS; John DOHERTY; Daniel KING; Billy LEGG; Keith MABEN; Rob SMITH; James THEOBALD.

CONFERENCE LEAGUE

No	DATE	OPPONENTS	H/A	RESULT	HAWKINS	J. KING	LEE	SMITH	SMART	BRUNDLE	DART	ROYNON	ARMSTRONG	PHELPS	HUGHES	OTHERS
1	28/3	Newcastle	H	W54-38	10+1 (5)	8+1 (4)	8+1 (4)	4+1 (4)	12+1 (5)	–	–	–	–	–	–	12+2 (8)
2	31/3	Wimbledon	A	W48-45	8+3 (5)	12+1 (5)	13 (6)	1 (3)	2+2 (5)	R/R	–	–	–	–	–	12 (6)
3	11/4	Rye House	H	W53-40	6+2 (4)	8 (4)	11+1 (5)	9+2 (5)	11+3 (5)	2+1 (4)	–	–	–	–	–	6 (3)
4	25/4	Wimbledon	H	W59-36*	9+2 (5)	8+1 (4)	12+3 (5)	7+1 (6)	8+2 (5)	R/R	–	–	–	–	–	15 (5)
5	2/5	Weymouth	H	W60-32	9+1 (4)	13 (5)	8+1 (4)	–	11+1 (6)	R/R	10+3 (5)	9+4 (6)	–	–	–	–
6	16/5	Swindon	H	W59-36	11+1 (4)	–	10+1 (4)	7 (5)	7+4 (4)	–	9 (5)	9+2 (4)	6+[illegible] (4)	–	–	–
7	22/5	Armadale	A	W49-45	–	R/R	15+1 (6)	–	2 (4)	15+1 (6)	–	9+3 (6)	8 (5)	–	–	0 (3)
8	23/5	Newcastle	A	W55-40*	9+3 (5)	R/R	10 (4)	–	10 (6)	10+1 (4)	–	7+3 (6)	9+[illegible] (5)	–	–	–
9	30/5	Buxton	A	W56-38	13+2 (5)	–	5 (3)	0 (3)	11 (6)	9 (4)	–	7+3 (5)	11+1 (4)	–	–	–
10	31/5	Buxton	H	W57-35*	–	R/R	10+2 (4)	5+1 (4)	16+2 (6)	–	9 (5)	4 (3)	11+1 (4)	–	–	2 (4)

CONFERENCE LEAGUE continued

No	DATE	OPPONENTS	H/A	RESULT	HAWKINS	J. KING	LEE	SMITH	SMART	BRUNDLE	DART	ROYNON	ARMSTRONG	PHELPS	HUGHES	OTHERS
11	6/6	Boston	H	L45-47	7 (5)	R/R	18 (6)	2 (3)	3 (5)	–	3 (5)	–	12+2 (6)	–	–	–
12	7/6	Swindon	A	W47-46*	21 (6)	R/R	–	0 (3)	9+1 (7)	–	6+1 (5)	–	11+2 (6)	–	–	0 (3)
13	13/6	Carmarthen	A	W46-42	–	R/R	–	0 (3)	12 (7)	–	10 (5)	–	17 (6)	7+3 (5)	–	0 (4)
14	20/6	Newport	H	W66-26	–	12 (4)	–	6+1 (5)	9+3 (4)	–	14 (5)	–	11+1 (4)	7+3 (4)	7+1 (4)	7+1 (4)
15	4/7	Stoke	H	W59-36	11+4 (5)	14+1 (5)	–	5+1 (4)	–	–	9+1 (4)	–	12 (4)	7+1 (4)	–	1 (4)
16	1/8	Armadale	H	W47-46*	R/R	–	–	–	8+2 (7)	–	5+1 (5)	–	17 (6)	9+1 (6)	0 (1)	8+3 (5)
17	7/8	Rye House	A	L36-56	R/R	–	–	–	4+1 (7)	9 (6)	15 (6)	–	6 (4)	–	0 (4)	2+1 (3)
18	13/8	Weymouth	A	W58-35*	10+1 (4)	–	–	–	11+1 (5)	11 (4)	11+3 (5)	–	8+1 (4)	–	2 (3)	5+2 (5)
19	29/8	Newport†	A	W55-29*	10+1 (4)	–	–	–	7+2 (4)	–	8 (4)	–	12 (4)	7+1 (4)	6+3 (4)	5 (4)
20	30/8	Carmarthen	H	W55-38*	–	–	–	–	11+2 (5)	R/R	12 (4)	–	14 (5)	–	8+3 (5)	10+3 (11)
21	8/9	Stoke	A	W50-45*	R/R	–	–	–	18 (7)	–	6+1 (5)	–	14+1 (5)	–	2 (4)	10+1 (9)
22	3/10	Oxford	H	W55-37	14 (5)	10 (4)	–	–	8+2 (6)	2+1 (3)	10+2 (5)	–	9+2 (4)	–	2 (3)	–
23	8/10	Boston	A	L42-52	13 (6)	3 (4)	–	–	4 (4)	–	2+1 (4)	–	14 (5)	–	–	6+2 (7)
24	22/10	Oxford$^{\Delta}$	A	W43-32*	8+1 (4)	R/R	–	–	10+1 (4)	14 (5)	–	–	4+2 (3)	–	2+1 (4)	5+2 (4)

*Denotes bonus-point victory

†Meeting abandoned after heat fourteen, with the result permitted to stand.

$^{\Delta}$Meeting abandoned after heat twelve, with the result permitted to stand.

DETAILS OF OTHER RIDERS:

Match No. 1: Chris Collins 10+1 (5); Carl Baldwin 2+1 (3); Match No. 2: Chris Collins 12 (6); Match No. 3: Chris Collins 6 (3); Match No. 4: Daniel King 15 (5); Match No. 7: Keith Maben 0 (3); Match No. 10: Scott Campos 2 (4); Match No. 12: Billy Legg 0 (3); Match No. 13: John Doherty 0 (4); Match No. 15: Danny Betson 1 (4); Match No. 16: James Mann 8+3 (5); Match No. 17: James Theobald 2+1 (3); Match No. 18: James Mann 5+2 (5); Match No. 19: James Mann 5 (4); Match No. 20: James Mann 8+3 (4); Rob Smith 2 (5); Daniel Blake 0 (2); Match No. 21: James Mann 9+1 (5); Danny Betson 1 (4); Match No. 23: James Mann 4+1 (4); Rob Smith 2+1 (3); Match No. 24: James Mann 5+2 (4).

TACTICAL SUBSTITUTE AND TACTICAL RIDES, AS INCLUDED IN THE SCORES GRID:

Match No. 11: Lee 6 points (TR); Match No. 12: Hawkins 6 points (TR); Match No. 17: Dart 6 points (TR); Armstrong 0 points (TR); Match No. 23: Armstrong 6 points (TR); Hawkins 2 points (TS); J. King 0 points (TR).

CONFERENCE LEAGUE AVERAGES

Rider	Mts	Rds	Pts	Bon	Tot	Avge	Max
Daniel King	1	5	15	0	15	12.00	1 full
Paul Lee	11	51	117	10	127	9.96	2 paid
Jon Armstrong	19	88	203	15	218	9.91	2 full; 4 paid
Ritchie Hawkins	16	76	165	22	187	9.84	1 full; 3 paid
Jason King	9	39	88	4	92	9.44	1 full; 1 paid
James Brundle	8	36	72	4	76	8.44	–
Chris Collins	3	14	28	1	29	8.29	–
Gary Phelps	5	23	37	9	46	8.00	–
Adam Roynon	6	30	45	15	60	8.00	–
Tony Dart	16	77	136	13	149	7.74	1 full
Lee Smart	23	124	204	30	234	7.55	2 paid

Rider	Mts	Rds	Pts	Bon	Tot	Avge	Max
James Mann	7	31	44	12	56	7.23	–
Kyle Hughes	9	32	29	8	37	4.63	–
Darren Smith	12	48	46	7	53	4.42	–
Carl Baldwin	1	3	2	1	3	4.00	–
James Theobald	1	3	2	1	3	4.00	–
Rob Smith	2	8	4	1	5	2.50	–
Scott Campos	1	4	2	0	2	2.00	–
Danny Betson	2	8	2	0	2	1.00	–
Daniel Blake	1	2	0	0	0	0.00	–
John Doherty	1	4	0	0	0	0.00	–
Billy Legg	1	3	0	0	0	0.00	–
Keith Maben	1	3	0	0	0	0.00	–

CONFERENCE TROPHY

No	DATE	OPPONENTS	H/A	RESULT	LEE	SMITH	HAWKINS	DART	J. KING	ROYNON	SMART	ARMSTRONG	HUGHES	PHELPS	MANN	OTHERS
1	9/5	Sheffield	H	W56-39	15 (5)	3 (4)	9+1 (5)	10 (4)	9 (4)	6+1 (4)	4+2 (4)	–	–	–	–	–
2	14/5	Weymouth	A	W52-43	8+1 (5)	–	16 (6)	3+1 (4)	R/R	8+1 (5)	5+2 (5)	12 (5)	–	–	–	–
3	28/6	Coventry	A	W54-39	–	5+1 (4)	15 (5)	7 (4)	10+1 (4)	–	4 (4)	11+4 (5)	2 (4)	–	–	–
4	11/7	Wimbledon	H	W52-43	–	2 (4)	10+4 (5)	10 (4)	8 (3)	–	–	14 (5)	3+2 (5)	5+1 (4)	–	–
5	2/8	Sheffield	A	L46-47	–	–	1[illegible] (5)	8 (4)	–	–	11+1 (5)	6+1 (5)	1 (3)	3+3 (4)	6+3 (4)	–
6	21/8	Buxton	A	L45-48	–	–	9+4 (6)	–	R/R	–	11+2 (6)	16 (6)	0 (3)	7 (5)	2+1 (4)	–
7	22/8	Weymouth	H	W53-42*	–	–	–	8 (4)	–	–	9+2 (5)	10+2 (4)	2 (4)	7+2 (4)	5+2 (5)	12 (4)
8	5/9	King's Lynn	H	W56-38	–	–	–	4 (3)	8 (4)	–	10+1 (4)	11+1 (4)	5+3 (5)	–	9+1 (5)	9+3 (5)
9	19/9	Buxton	H	W52-40*	–	–	10+1 (4)	–	10 (4)	4+2 (5)	8+1 (4)	11+1 (4)	3+1 (5)	–	6 (4)	–
10	19/9	Coventry	H	W54-41*	–	–	–	–	8 (4)	3 (4)	12 (4)	11+1 (4)	–	–	8+2 (5)	12+2 (9)
11	22/9	Wimbledon	A	L45-48*	–	–	R/R	6 (5)	7+2 (5)	0 (2)	16+1 (7)	13 (6)	–	–	3+2 (4)	–
12	6/10	King's Lynn	A	W48-44*	–	–	17 (5)	6+1 (4)	–	–	7+1 (5)	4 (4)	0 (3)	–	10+1 (5)	4+1 (4)

*Denotes bonus-point victory

DETAILS OF OTHER RIDERS:

Match No. 7: James Brundle 12 (4); Match No. 8: Danny Betson 9+3 (5); Match No. 10: James Brundle 11+1 (5); Danny Betson 1+1 (4); Match No. 12: James Brundle 4+1 (4).

TACTICAL RIDES, AS INCLUDED IN THE SCORES GRID:

Match No. 6: Armstrong 6 points (TR); Match No. 11: Armstrong 6 points (TR); Match No. 12: Hawkins 6 points (TR).

CONFERENCE TROPHY AVERAGES

Rider	Mts	Rds	Pts	Bon	Tot	Avge	Max
Ritchie Hawkins	8	41	94	10	104	10.15	1 full
Paul Lee	2	10	23	1	24	9.60	1 full
Jon Armstrong	11	52	113	10	123	9.46	5 paid
Jason King	7	28	60	3	63	9.00	–

MILDENHALL: back row, left to right: Jason King, James Mann, Graham Drury (Team Manager), Lee Smart, Kyle Hughes. Front, kneeling: James Brundle, Jon Armstrong. On bike: Ritchie Hawkins.

Rider	Mts	Rds	Pts	Bon	Tot	Avge	Max
James Brundle	3	13	27	2	29	8.92	1 full
Lee Smart	11	53	97	13	110	8.30	1 full
Tony Dart	9	36	62	2	64	7.11	–
James Mann	8	36	49	12	61	6.78	–
Gary Phelps	4	17	22	6	28	6.59	–
Danny Betson	2	9	10	4	14	6.22	–
Adam Roynon	5	20	21	4	25	5.00	–
Darren Smith	3	12	10	1	11	3.67	–
Kyle Hughes	8	32	16	6	22	2.75	–

KNOCK-OUT CUP

No	DATE	OPPONENTS	H/A	RESULT	LEE	D. KING	HAWKINS	COLLINS	J. KING	SMART	BRUNDLE	DART	ROYNON	MANN	ARMSTRONG	OTHERS
1	18/4	Carmarthen†	H	W52-31	7+1 (4)	11+1 (4)	7+2 (4)	6+1 (3)	5 (3)	13+1 (5)	–	–	–	–	–	3+1 (3)
2	3/5	Carmarthen	A	W53-42*	8+1 (4)	–	14 (5)	–	8 (4)	4 (4)	9+2 (4)	3+1 (4)	7+3 (5)	–	–	–
3	8/8	King's Lynn	H	W63-27+	–	–	11+1 (4)	–	–	8+1 (5)	12 (4)	8+1 (4)	–	7+4 (4)	9+2 (4)	8+2 (5)
4	5/9	Oxford	H	W51-43	–	–	12+2 (5)	–	8+1 (4)	4+1 (5)	9 (4)	8 (4)	–	–	10+2 (5)	0 (3)
5	22/10	Oxford	A	L45-48*	–	–	15+2 (5)	–	5 (4)	7 (5)	8 (5)	–	–	4 (4)	5+2 (4)	1+1 (3)
6	29/10	Boston	A	W47-46	–	–	10+2 (5)	–	9 (4)	4 (4)	10 (5)	1+1 (4)	4+2 (4)	–	9+1 (4)	–
7	31/10	Boston	H	W69-12*	–	–	5+2 (4)	–	6+3 (4)	9+1 (4)	11+1 (4)	11+4 (5)	15 (5)	–	12 (4)	–

*Denotes aggregate victory

†Meeting abandoned after heat thirteen, with the result permitted to stand.

+Mildenhall were given a walkover through to the semi-final of the Knock-Out Cup after King's Lynn conceded their leg of the second-round tie, having been unable to find a suitable staging date.

DETAILS OF OTHER RIDERS:

Match No. 1: Darren Smith 3+1 (3); Match No. 3: Danny Betson 8+2 (5); Match No. 4: Kyle Hughes 0 (3); Match No. 5: Kyle Hughes 1+1 (3).

TACTICAL RIDE, AS INCLUDED IN THE SCORES GRID:

Match No. 5: Hawkins 6 points (TR).

OTHER MEETINGS

20 March: Conference Challenge

Mildenhall 1 (Ritchie Hawkins 1; James Brundle 0; Jason King DNR; Chris Collins DNR; Paul Lee DNR; Darren Smith DNR; Lee Smart DNR) Boston 5 – meeting abandoned after heat one.

9 April: Conference Challenge

Boston 42 Mildenhall 53 (Daniel King 15; Jason King 12+2; Ritchie Hawkins 8; James Brundle 7+2; Chris Collins 5; Lee Smart 4; Darren Smith 2+1).

27 June: Knock-Out Cup second round (first leg)

Mildenhall 43 (Gary Phelps 10+2; Jon Armstrong 8+1; Tony Dart 6+1; Jason King 6; Lee Smart 5+1; Kyle Hughes 4+2; Ritchie Hawkins 4+1) King's Lynn 17 – meeting abandoned after heat ten.

15 August: Challenge

Mildenhall 43 (Ritchie Hawkins 11+1; Jon Armstrong 10; Jason King 7+1; Gary Phelps 7; James Mann 4; Danny Betson 3; Kyle Hughes 1) Great Britain Under-21 49 (James Brundle 12+1; Steve Boxall 11+1; Lee Smart 8+1; Chris Schramm 6; Tommy Allen 5+1; Jack Hargreaves 4+1; Tom Brown 3).

INDIVIDUAL MEETINGS

4 April: British Under-21 Championship Qualifying Round

1st Daniel King 12; 2nd Steve Boxall 10; 3rd Lee Smart 9; James Brundle 9; Darren Mallett 6; Ben Barker 6; Barrie Evans 6; James Cockle 5; Luke Bowen 5; Tommy Allen 5; Richie Dennis 5; Adam Pryer 5; Chris Johnson 4; Danny Warwick 4; Carl Downs 3; Matthew Wright 0 – meeting abandoned after heat sixteen. A run-off to determine the last qualifying place for the final was subsequently staged at Peterborough on 9 April and resulted in a victory for Mallett, with Barker in second place and Evans third.

10 October: British Under-15 Championship Final

1st Josh Auty 15; 2nd Simon Lambert 13; =3rd Shane Waldron, Kyle Hughes 12; Lewis Bridger 11; Gary Cottham 10; Matt Bates 8; George Piper 7; Sam Hurst 6; James Humby 6; Scott Campos 5; Joe Reynolds 5; Grant Hayes 5; Ben Thompson 3; Chris Widman 2; Ben Hopwood 0; Connor Scott (Res) 0; Aaron Baseby (Res) 0. OVERALL SERIES POINTS: 1st Auty 68; 2nd Waldron 63; 3rd Lambert 62; Cottham 54; Hughes 52; Bates 52; Campos 43; Bridger 42; Hurst 37; Humby 36; Piper 36; Hayes 31; Reynolds 24; Hopwood 16; Widman 15; Thompson 15; Baseby 11; Scott 11; Trevor Heath 9; Tim Webster 7; Gavin Wrigley 7; Andy Braithwaite 6; Dean Hargrave 4; Ben Hannon 4; Scott Meakins 2; Shawn Taylor 1; Dan Kirkman 1.

10 October: Bert Harkins' Bronze Helmet

QUALIFYING SCORES: Jon Armstrong 12; James Brundle 12; Tommy Allen 11; Richard Hall 11; Blair Scott 11: David Mason 11; Mark Burrows 8; Benji Compton 7; Darren Rolph 7; Barry Burchatt 7; Danny Warwick 5; Matthew Wright 5; Dean Felton 5; Karlis Ezergailis 4; Craig Branney 2; Michael Pickering 1. FIRST SEMI-FINAL: 1st Armstrong; 2nd Mason; 3rd Compton; 4th Brundle. SECOND SEMI-FINAL: 1st Burrows; 2nd Scott; 3rd Hall; 4th Allen. FINAL: 1st Armstrong; 2nd Burrows.

NEWCASTLE ULTRAFAST GEMS

NOTE: The information below relates only to the second Newcastle team. For details of the main side, please refer to the Premier League section.

ADDRESS: Brough Park Stadium, Fossway, Byker, Newcastle-upon-Tyne, Tyne and Wear, NE6 2XJ.
CLUB CHAIRMAN: Kenny Smith.
TRACK LENGTH: 300 metres.
CL TRACK RECORD: 64.6 seconds – William Lawson (16/05/04).
FIRST MEETING: 7 April 2002.
YEARS OF OPERATION: 2002-04 Conference League.

CLUB HONOURS

None.

RIDER ROSTER 2004

Byron BEKKER; John BRANNEY; Lee DICKEN; Carl DOWNS; Danny HUGHES; Kriss IRVING; Karl LANGLEY; David MELDRUM; Michael PICKERING; Jamie ROBERTSON; Paul SHARPLES.

OTHER APPEARANCES/GUESTS (official matches only):

Corey BLACKMAN; David HAIGH; Ashley JOHNSON; William LAWSON; John MacPHAIL; John MORRISON; Scott NETTLESHIP; Phil PICKERING; Adam ROYNON; David SPEIGHT.

CONFERENCE LEAGUE

No	DATE	OPPONENTS	H/A	RESULT	DICKEN	BRANNEY	HUGHES	ROBERTSON	M. PICKERING	LANGLEY	LAWSON	JOHNSON	HAIGH	IRVING	BLACKMAN	OTHERS
1	28/3	Mildenhall	A	L38-54	14+1 (5)	1 (4)	5 (4)	11 (5)	1 (3)	–	–	–	–	–	–	6 (9)
2	7/4	Stoke	A	W51-41	12+1 (5)	10+1 (5)	7 (4)	8 (4)	4+1 (4)	4+1 (4)	–	–	–	–	–	6+1 (4)
3	2/5	Newport	H	W58-38	–	10 (5)	9+2 (4)	10+1 (4)	5+1 (4)	5+1 (4)	<u>15 (5)</u>	4+3 (4)	–	–	–	–
4	14/5	Carmarthen	A	L27-63	–	4 (5)	–	7 (5)	10 (7)	0 (3)	R/R	4+1 (5)	2+1 (5)	–	–	–
5	16/5	Rye House	H	L42-53	–	11+1 (7)	6+1 (5)	R/R	1 (4)	–	<u>21 (6)</u>	1 (4)	–	2 (4)	–	–
6	23/5	Mildenhall	H	L40-55	–	6 (4)	2 (4)	12+2 (5)	–	1+1 (4)	15 (5)	3 (5)	–	1 (3)	–	–
7	23/5	Weymouth	H	W45-44	–	8 (4)	5+2 (4)	11+1 (5)	–	4+1 (5)	12 (5)	5 (6)	–	0 (1)	–	–
8	26/5	Wimbledon	A	L43-55	–	9 (4)	7+1 (4)	9 (5)	–	1 (4)	–	0 (3)	–	2+1 (4)	15+1 (6)	–
9	28/5	Weymouth	A	L44-51	–	3+1 (4)	10 (4)	14+1 (5)	–	0 (3)	–	0 (3)	–	5 (5)	12 (6)	–
10	6/6	Wimbledon†	H	L31-41	–	9 (4)	–	9 (4)	8+1 (5)	–	–	4 (5)	0 (3)	1 (3)	R/R	–
11	20/6	Swindon	H	W53-39	13 (5)	5 (4)	–	<u>14+1 (5)</u>	7 (4)	0 (4)	–	–	3+ (4)	–	11 (4)	–
12	20/6	Boston	H	L47-49	13+2 (5)	4 (4)	–	10 (5)	4+1 (4)	1+1 (4)	–	–	–	2 (4)	13 (4)	–
13	27/6	Armadale	H	L41-48	9 (6)	7 (5)	–	13+1 (6)	9+1 (5)	–	–	–	1 (3)	–	R/R	2 (5)
14	4/7	Buxton	A	L45-50	15 (5)	8 (4)	1 (3)	8+2 (5)	5 (4)	–	–	–	–	–	–	8+2 (9)
15	14/8	Rye House	A	L33-62	–	10 (6)	–	R/R	0 (3)	–	–	–	–	–	–	23+3 (21)
16	15/8	Carmarthen	H	W52-43	–	7+1 (5)	–	11 (4)	–	–	–	–	–	–	–	34+5 (21)

NEWCASTLE: back row, left to right: Byron Bekker, Paul Sharples, Kenny Smith (Team Manager), John Branney, Jamie Robertson, Carl Downs. Front row: Michael Pickering, David Meldrum.

CONFERENCE LEAGUE continued

No	DATE	OPPONENTS	H/A	RESULT	DICKEN	BRANNEY	HUGHES	ROBERTSON	M. PICKERING	LANGLEY	LAWSON	JOHNSON	HAIGH	IRVING	BLACKMAN	OTHERS
17	22/8	Buxton	H	L44-46	–	13+3 (6)	–	R/R	–	–	–	–	–	–	–	31+2 (24)
18	2/9	Swindon	A	L37-58	–	6 (4)	–	6 (5)	0 (3)	–	–	–	–	–	–	25+3 (18)
19	3/9	Oxford	A	L29-61	–	4+1 (4)	–	4 (4)	0 (3)	–	–	–	–	–	–	21+1 (19)
20	5/9	Stoke	H	W50-43*	–	14 (5)	–	11+1 (4)	1 (4)	–	–	–	–	–	–	24+4 (17)
21	18/9	Armadale	A	L25-65	–	12 (6)	–	R/R	–	–	–	–	1 (4)	–	–	12+1 (20)
22	26/9	Oxford	H	L39-53	–	10 (4)	–	7 (4)	5 (6)	–	–	–	–	–	–	17+5 (16)
23	1/10	Boston+	A	L31-48	–	7 (4)	–	7 (4)	6+2 (4)	–	–	–	–	–	–	11+1 (13)
24	31/10	Newport	A	W53-43*	–	11+1 (6)	–	16 (6)	5 (4)	–	–	–	–	–	–	21+9 (14)

*Denotes bonus-point victory

†Meeting abandoned after heat twelve, with the result permitted to stand.

+Meeting abandoned after heat thirteen, with the result permitted to stand.

DETAILS OF OTHER RIDERS:

Match No. 1: Adam Roynon 6 (5); David Speight 0 (4); Match No. 2: Adam Roynon 6+1 (4); Match No. 13: John Morrison 2 (5); Match No. 14: Paul Sharples 6+1 (5); John Morrison 2+1 (4); Match No. 15: Carl Downs 13 (6); Byron Bekker 5+1 (6); Paul Sharples 3+2 (4); John Morrison 2 (5); Match No. 16: David Meldrum 13+1 (5); Carl Downs 7+1 (4); Paul Sharples 7+1 (7); Byron Bekker 6+1 (3); John Morrison 1+1 (2); Match No. 17: David Meldrum 13+1 (6); Byron Bekker 12+1 (6); Carl Downs 6 (5); Scott Nettleship 0 (3); Paul Sharples 0 (4); Match No. 18: David Meldrum 15 (5); Paul Sharples 5+1 (5); Byron Bekker 3 (4); Carl Downs 2+2 (4); Match No. 19: David Meldrum 10 (5); Byron Bekker 5+1 (5); Paul Sharples 4 (5); Carl Downs 2 (4); Match No. 20: David Meldrum 11+1 (4); Paul Sharples 6+2 (6); Carl Downs 4+1 (4); Byron Bekker 3 (3); Match No. 21: Byron Bekker 5 (7); David Meldrum 4 (5); Carl Downs 2+1 (5); John MacPhail 1 (3); Match No. 22: Paul Sharples 7 (5); David Meldrum 5+1 (3); Carl Downs 4+3 (5); Scott Nettleship 1+1 (3); Match No. 23: David Meldrum 8+1 (4); Phil Pickering 2 (4); Paul Sharples 1 (2); Carl Downs 0 (3); Match No. 24: Paul Sharples 10+2 (6); Carl Downs 7+4 (5); Phil Pickering 4+3 (3); David Meldrum R/R.

TACTICAL SUBSTITUTE AND TACTICAL RIDES, AS INCLUDED IN THE SCORES GRID:

Match No. 1: Dicken 4 points (TR); Robertson 0 points (TR); Match No. 4: Branney 2 points (TR); Robertson 0 points (TR); Match No. 5: Lawson 6 points (TR); Hughes 2 points (TR); Branney 2 points (TS); Match No. 6: Lawson 6 points (TR); Robertson 4 points (TR); Match No. 8: Blackman 6 points (TS); Hughes 6 points (TR); Branney 4 points (TR); Match No. 9: Robertson 6 points (TR); Blackman 4 points (TS); Match No. 12: Dicken 6 points (TR); Blackman 6 points (TR); Match No. 14: Robertson 6 points (TR); Dicken 6 points (TR); Match No. 15: Downs 6 points (TR); Branney 4 points (TR); Match No. 18: Meldrum 6 points (TR); Robertson 4 points (TR); Match No. 19: Meldrum 2 points (TR); Robertson 0 points (TR); Match No. 21: Branney 2 points (TR); Meldrum 0 points (TR); Match No. 22: Branney 4 points (TR); Robertson 0 points (TR); Match No. 23: Meldrum 4 points (TR).

CONFERENCE LEAGUE AVERAGES

Rider	Mts	Rds	Pts	Bon	Tot	Avge	Max
William Lawson	4	21	57	0	57	10.86	2 full
Lee Dicken	6	31	68	4	72	9.29	–
Corey Blackman	4	20	43	1	44	8.80	–
David Meldrum	8	37	73	5	78	8.43	1 paid
Jamie Robertson	20	94	188	10	198	8.43	2 paid
John Branney	24	113	180	9	189	6.69	–
Danny Hughes	9	36	48	6	54	6.00	–
Adam Roynon	2	9	12	1	13	5.78	–

Rider	Mts	Rds	Pts	Bon	Tot	Avge	Max
Phil Pickering	2	7	6	3	9	5.14	–
Byron Bekker	7	34	39	4	43	5.06	–
Carl Downs	10	45	44	12	56	4.98	–
Paul Sharples	10	49	49	9	58	4.73	–
Michael Pickering	17	71	71	7	78	4.39	–
Ashley Johnson	8	35	21	4	25	2.86	–
Karl Langley	9	35	16	5	21	2.40	–
Kriss Irving	7	24	13	1	14	2.33	–
John Morrison	4	16	7	2	9	2.25	–
David Haigh	5	19	7	2	9	1.89	–
John MacPhail	1	3	1	0	1	1.33	–
Scott Nettleship	2	6	1	1	2	1.33	–
David Speight	1	4	0	0	0	0.00	–

NEWPORT GMB MAVERICKS

NOTE: The information below relates only to the second Newport team. For details of the main side, please refer to the Premier League section.

ADDRESS: Hayley Stadium, Plover Close, Longditch Road, Queensway Meadows, Newport, South Wales, NS19 4SU.
CLUB CHAIRMAN: Tim Stone.
TRACK LENGTH: 285 metres.
CL TRACK RECORD: 60.27 Scott Pegler (09/09/00).
FIRST MEETING: 30 May 1997.
YEARS OF OPERATION: 1997 Amateur League; 1998–04 Conference League.

CLUB HONOURS

LEAGUE CHAMPIONS: 1999.

RIDER ROSTER 2004

Russell BARNETT; Paul CANDY; Karlis EZERGAILIS; Sam HURST; Billy LEGG; Nick MALLETT; Karl MASON; Scott PEGLER; Matt TUTTON; Jamie WESTACOTT.

OTHER APPEARANCES/GUESTS (official matches only):
Thomas HILL; David MINALL.

CONFERENCE LEAGUE

No	DATE	OPPONENTS	H/A	RESULT	PEGLER	LEGG	MALLETT	BARNETT	MASON	WESTACOTT	MINALL	CANDY	TILTON	HURST	EZERGAILIS	OTHERS
1	21/3	Weymouth	H	D45-45	18 (6)	2 (5)	4+2 (5)	3+1 (5)	R/R	14 (6)	4 (4)	–	–	–	–	–
2	9/4	Carmarthen	A	L37-57	13 (5)	–	0 (3)	0 (4)	3 (4)	17+1 (7)	–	4+1 (4)	–	–	–	–
3	18/4	Rye House	H	L41-52	14 (5)	–	1 (5)	1 (3)	4+1 (3)	16 (6)	–	2+1 (4)	3 (4)	–	–	–
4	1/5	Armadale	A	L31-62	R/R	–	3+1 (5)	0 (4)	12 (6)	12+1 (6)	–	4 (5)	–	0 (4)	–	–
5	2/5	Newcastle	A	L38-58	R/R	–	2 (5)	0 (4)	13+1 (6)	20+1 (7)	–	3 (4)	–	0 (4)	–	–
6	21/5	Weymouth	A	L37-55	10 (5)	–	–	1 (4)	4+1 (4)	12 (6)	–	8+1 (4)	1 (3)	1+1 (4)	–	–
7	6/6	Stoke	H	W47-46	7+1 (4)	–	2 (3)	–	12+1 (5)	16+3 (7)	–	4 (4)	0 (3)	–	6+1 (4)	–
8	13/6	Buxton	A	L40-55	R/R	–	0 (6)	–	17+1 (6)	14+3 (6)	–	–	2 (4)	4 (4)	–	3+1 (4)
9	18/6	Boston	A	L24-67	R/R	0 (4)	2 (5)	–	12 (6)	–	–	5 (5)	1 (4)	4 (6)	–	–
10	20/6	Mildenhall	A	L26-66	8 (5)	0 (4)	3 (4)	1+1 (4)	8 (5)	–	–	6 (4)	–	0 (4)	–	–
11	27/6	Carmarthen	H	W46-44	11+1 (4)	2 (4)	3 (4)	–	15 (5)	13+1 (6)	–	1 (4)	–	1 (3)	–	–
12	4/7	Boston	H	L26-66	R/R	2 (6)	–	0 (4)	0 (1)	10 (6)	–	10 (6)	4 (7)	–	–	–
13	11/7	Buxton	H	L42-48	R/R	2 (4)	–	–	12+1 (6)	9 (4)	–	6+1 (5)	–	1 (4)	12+2 (7)	–
14	12/7	Swindon	A	L27-65	–	1 (4)	–	–	6 (5)	4 (4)	–	2+1 (4)	3 (4)	0 (3)	11+1 (7)	–
15	14/7	Wimbledon	A	L25-65	–	3 (4)	–	–	0 (0)	8 (5)	–	2 (4)	3+1 (4)	2 (6)	7 (7)	–
16	18/7	Armadale	H	L39-53	R/R	2 (4)	–	–	15+1 (6)	6+2 (5)	–	–	5+1 (4)	2+1 (4)	9+2 (7)	–
17	25/7	Oxford	H	L41-52	R/R	0 (4)	–	–	16+1 (6)	8+1 (4)	–	4 (4)	–	2 (5)	11+3 (7)	–
18	29/8	Mildenhall†	H	L29-55	5+1 (4)	–	1 (2)	–	8 (4)	4 (4)	–	2 (4)	–	0 (4)	9 (5)	–
19	5/9	Wimbledon	H	W47-43	14 (5)	1 (4)	–	0 (4)	8 (3)	13+1 (5)	–	–	–	3 (4)	8+1 (5)	–
20	18/9	Rye House	A	L31-64	R/R	1 (4)	–	–	11 (5)	1 (4)	–	2 (5)	–	3 (5)	13+1 (7)	–
21	26/9	Swindon	H	W49-43	10 (4)	1+1 (4)	–	–	9+2 (5)	8 (4)	–	–	3+1 (3)	1+1 (4)	17 (6)	–
22	2/10	Stoke	A	L38-57	7+1 (4)	1 (4)	–	–	10+1 (6)	10 (5)	–	–	3 (3)	1 (4)	6+2 (4)	–
23	8/10	Oxford	A	L34-62	11 (5)	0 (4)	–	1 (4)	10+2 (6)	1 (3)	–	–	–	3+1 (4)	8 (4)	–
24	31/10	Newcastle	H	L43-53	12+1 (5)	2 (4)	–	1 (4)	10 (4)	17 (5)	–	–	1 (5)	0 (3)	–	–

†Meeting abandoned after heat fourteen, with the result permitted to stand.

DETAILS OF OTHER RIDER:

Match No. 8: Thomas Hill 3+1 (4).

TACTICAL SUBSTITUTE AND TACTICAL RIDES, AS INCLUDED IN THE SCORES GRID:

Match No. 2: Westacott 6 points (TR); Pegler 4 points (TR); Match No. 3: Pegler 6 points (TR); Match No. 4: Mason 6 points (TR); Westacott 6 points (TR); Match No. 5: Mason 6 points (TR); Westacott 6 points (TR); Match No. 6: Candy 2 points (TR); Pegler 2 points (TR); Match No. 7: Pegler 6 points (TR); Match No. 8: Mason 6 points (TR); Westacott 4 points (TR); Match No. 9: Mason 6 points (TR); Match No. 10: Pegler 2 points (TR); Mason 2 points (TR); Match No. 12: Westacott 2 points (TR); Candy 2 points (TR); Match No. 14: Ezergailis 4 points (TR); Mason 0 points (TR); Match No. 15: Westacott 2 points (TR); Ezergailis 0 points (TR); Match No. 16: Mason 6 points (TR); Match No. 17: Mason 6 points (TR); Match No. 18: Mason 2 points (TR); Pegler 0 points (TR); Match No. 20: Mason 6 points (TR); Ezergailis 6 points (TR); Match No. 22: Pegler 4 points (TR); Mason 4 points (TS); Ezergailis 2 points (TR); Match No. 23: Ezergailis 4 points (TR); Mason 4 points (TS); Pegler 4 points (TR); Match No. 24: Pegler 6 points (TR); Westacott 6 points (TR).

NEWPORT: back row, left to right: Billy Legg, Sam Hurst, Karlis Ezergailis, Jamie Westacott, Karl Mason, Russell Barnett. Front, on bike: Scott Pegler.

CONFERENCE LEAGUE AVERAGES

Rider	Mts	Rds	Pts	Bon	Tot	Avge	Max
Scott Pegler	13	61	123	5	128	8.39	1 full 1 paid
Jamie Westacott	22	115	217	14	231	8.03	–
Karl Mason	23	107	188	13	201	7.51	1 full
Karlis Ezergailis	12	70	109	13	122	6.97	–
Thomas Hill	1	4	3	1	4	4.00	–
David Minall	1	4	4	0	4	4.00	–
Paul Candy	16	70	63	5	68	3.89	–
Matt Tutton	12	48	29	3	32	2.67	–
Nick Mallett	11	47	21	3	24	2.04	–
Sam Hurst	19	79	28	4	32	1.62	–
Billy Legg	16	67	20	1	21	1.25	–
Russell Barnett	11	44	8	2	10	0.91	–

OTHER MEETINGS

4 April: Conference League

Newport 7 (Scott Pegler 3; Nick Mallett 2; Matt Tutton 1+1; David Gough 1; Russell Barnett 0; Billy Legg 0; Karl Mason DNR) Oxford 11 – meeting abandoned after heat three.

17 October: Conference League International

Great Britain Under-21 64 (Chris Schramm 14+1; Karl Mason 12+3; Tommy Allen 12; Ben Barker 12; Jamie Westacott 10+3; Barry Burchatt 4+1; Daniel Giffard 0) Rest of the World 30 (Tom Brown 8+1; Karlis Ezergailis 8; Troy Batchelor 7; Danny Warwick 3; Chris Ferguson 2+1; Luke Priest 2; Trevor Harding R/R).

17 October: Under-15 Challenge

Newport 36 (Kyle Hughes 11; Sam Hurst 10; Grant Hayes 8+3; Daniel Greenwood 4+1; Ben Hopwood 3+2; Josh Auty R/R) Cardiff 36 (Lewis Bridger 14; Matt Bates 12; James Humby 5; Ben Thompson 4+1; George Piper 1+1; Connor Scott R/R).

OXFORD SILVER MACHINE ACADEMY

NOTE: The information below relates only to the second Oxford team. For details of the main side, please refer to the Elite League section.

ADDRESS: Oxford Stadium, Sandy Lane, Cowley, Oxford, OX4 6LJ.
CLUB CHAIRMAN: Nigel Wagstaff.
TRACK LENGTH: 297 metres.
CL TRACK RECORD: 60.89 seconds – Andy Smith (06/06/03).
FIRST MEETING: 25 May 1997.
YEARS OF OPERATION: 1997 Amateur League; 2003-04 Conference League.

CLUB HONOURS

None.

RIDER ROSTER 2004

Ben BARKER; Craig BRANNEY; Jamie COURTNEY; Sam MARTIN; Chris MILLS; Jason NEWITT; Danny NORTON; Chris SCHRAMM.

OTHER APPEARANCES/GUESTS (official matches only):

Paul COOPER; Carl DOWNS; Gary FLINT; James HUMBY; Ricky SCARBORO; Mark WOODS.

CONFERENCE LEAGUE

No	DATE	OPPONENTS	H/A	RESULT	MILLS	BARKER	NORTON	BRANNEY	SCHRAMM	MARTIN	WOODS	DOWNS	NEWITT	COURTNEY	SCARBORO	OTHERS
1	14/5	Swindon	H	W57-34	10+1 (4)	4+1 (4)	8+3 (4)	12+1 (5)	15 (5)	5+2 (5)	3+1 (3)	–	–	–	–	–
2	23/5	Buxton	A	L45-51	–	9 (4)	7+1 (4)	8+1 (5)	15 (5)	4+1 (7)	1 (3)	1 (2)	–	–	–	–
3	28/5	Stoke	H	L46-48	11 (4)	–	5+2 (4)	9 (5)	16+1 (5)	4 (5)	0 (3)	1 (4)	–	–	–	–
4	30/5	Carmarthen	A	W62-29	13+1 (5)	R/R	16+2 (6)	13+4 (6)	14+1 (5)	5 (4)	–	–	1 (4)	–	–	–
5	9/6	Wimbledon	A	W48-47	11+4 (6)	R/R	5+1 (5)	15 (6)	12 (5)	4+1 (5)	1 (3)	–	–	–	–	–
6	25/7	Newport	A	W52-41	R/R	5+1 (5)	14 (6)	18 (6)	–	5+4 (5)	–	–	2 (3)	8+2 (5)	–	–
7	20/8	Weymouth	H	W54-39	R/R	6+1 (5)	14 (6)	17+1 (6)	–	2 (4)	–	–	–	13+1 (5)	2 (4)	–
8	24/8	Weymouth	A	W48-45*	R/R	7+3 (5)	2 (5)	14 (6)	13 (6)	2 (3)	–	–	–	10 (6)	–	–
9	1/9	Stoke	A	L45-48	R/R	9+1 (5)	13 (6)	12 (6)	–	2 (4)	–	–	–	7+2 (5)	2 (4)	–
10	3/9	Boston	H	W58-35	11+1 (5)	5+2 (4)	11 (4)	7+2 (4)	15 (5)	2+1 (4)	–	–	–	7+2 (4)	–	–
11	3/9	Newcastle	H	W61-29	5+1 (4)	9+1 (4)	8+3 (4)	14+1 (5)	15 (5)	1 (3)	–	–	–	9+3 (5)	–	–
12	5/9	Boston†	A	W52-33*	10+1 (4)	4 (4)	8+3 (4)	11 (4)	10 (4)	1+1 (3)	–	–	–	8+4 (5)	–	–
13	24/9	Rye House	H	W48-42	0 (0)	7+2 (4)	2+1 (4)	15 (5)	7+1 (5)	2 (5)	–	–	–	15+1 (7)	–	–
14	25/9	Armadale	A	L43-44	R/R	–	6+2 (5)	13 (6)	9+1 (6)	3 (4)	–	–	1 (3)	11 (6)	–	–
15	26/9	Newcastle	A	W53-39*	R/R	4 (3)	5 (5)	18 (6)	16+1 (6)	4 (5)	–	–	–	6+1 (5)	–	–
16	1/10	Wimbledon	H	W45-43*	R/R	6+1 (5)	0 (3)	16 (6)	13+1 (6)	3+2 (4)	–	–	–	7+1 (6)	–	–
17	2/10	Rye House	A	L46-47*	R/R	5+3 (5)	4+1 (5)	14 (6)	15+2 (6)	3 (3)	–	–	–	5 (5)	–	–

OXFORD: back row, left to right: Jamie Courtney, Jason Newitt, Chris Mills, Danny Norton, Craig Branney. Front row: Ben Barker, Chris Schramm, Sam Martin.

CONFERENCE LEAGUE continued

No	DATE	OPPONENTS	H/A	RESULT	MILLS	BARKER	NORTON	BRANNEY	SCHRAMM	MARTIN	WOODS	DOWNS	NEWITT	COURTNEY	SCARBORO	OTHERS
18	3/10	Mildenhall	A	L37-55	R/R	4+1 (5)	3 (4)	8+1 (5)	14+1 (6)	1+1 (3)	–	–	–	7 (7)	–	–
19	8/10	Newport	H	W62-34*	R/R	7 (5)	12+3 (5)	12 (4)	15 (5)	6+2 (4)	–	–	0 (3)	10+2 (4)	–	–
20	8/10	Armadale	H	W58-37*	R/R	5+1 (6)	8+2 (5)	14+1 (5)	13+2 (6)	0 (1)	–	–	–	18+2 (7)	–	–
21	21/10	Swindon	A	W52-41*	8 (4)	5+3 (4)	9+1 (5)	–	15 (5)	–	–	–	1 (3)	7+1 (5)	7+3 (4)	–
22	22/10	Mildenhall$^{\Delta}$	H	L32-43	8 (4)	1+1 (4)	5 (4)	4+1 (3)	9 (3)	–	–	–	0 (3)	5 (3)	–	–
23	29/10	Carmarthen$^{\Delta}$	H	W44-31*	–	9+2 (4)	9 (3)	7+1 (3)	–	–	–	–	–	–	9+3 (4)	10 (10)
24	29/10	Buxton	H	W51-44*	–	6+2 (4)	11+1 (5)	12 (5)	–	–	–	–	–	–	7+3 (4)	15+3 (12)

*Denotes bonus-point victory

†Meeting abandoned after heat fourteen, with the result permitted to stand.

$^{\Delta}$Meeting abandoned after heat twelve, with the result permitted to stand.

DETAILS OF OTHER RIDERS:

Match No. 23: Paul Cooper 6 (3); Gary Flint 4 (4); James Humby 0 (3); Match No. 24: Paul Cooper 8+2 (4); Gary Flint 4 (4); James Humby 3+1 (4).

TACTICAL RIDES, AS INCLUDED IN THE SCORES GRID:

Match No. 2: Schramm 6 points (TR); Barker 6 points (TR); Match No. 3: Schramm 6 points (TR); Mills 4 points (TR); Match No. 5: Schramm 6 points (TR); Branney 6 points (TR); Match No. 8: Schramm 6 points (TR); Match No. 17: Schramm 6 points (TR); Match No. 18: Schramm 4 points (TR); Branney 0 points (TR); Match No. 22: Schramm 6 points (TR); Mills 2 points (TR).

CONFERENCE LEAGUE AVERAGES

Rider	Mts	Rds	Pts	Bon	Tot	Avge	Max
Craig Branney	23	118	280	14	294	9.97	4 full; 3 paid
Chris Schramm	19	99	231	11	242	9.78	5 full; 1 paid
Chris Mills	10	40	84	9	93	9.30	–
Paul Cooper	2	7	14	2	16	9.14	–
Jamie Courtney	17	90	153	22	175	7.78	1 paid
Danny Norton	24	111	185	26	211	7.60	2 paid
Ricky Scarboro	5	20	27	9	36	7.20	1 paid
Ben Barker	20	89	114	26	140	6.29	–
Gary Flint	2	8	8	0	8	4.00	–
Sam Martin	20	81	59	15	74	3.65	–
James Humby	2	7	3	1	4	2.29	–
Mark Woods	4	12	5	1	6	2.00	–
Carl Downs	2	6	2	0	2	1.33	–
Jason Newitt	6	19	5	0	5	1.05	–

KNOCK-OUT CUP

No	DATE	OPPONENTS	H/A	RESULT	MILLS	BARKER	NORTON	BRANNEY	SCHRAMM	MARTIN	WOODS	NEWITT	COURTNEY
1	25/6	Buxton	H	W61-31	8+4 (5)	R/R	12+3 (5)	15 (5)	18 (6)	5+1 (5)	3 (4)	–	–
2	27/6	Buxton	A	L44-50*	11 (5)	5+1 (4)	3+1 (4)	13+1 (5)	4 (4)	6 (3)	–	2 (5)	–
3	5/9	Mildenhall	A	L43-51	7 (3)	3 (4)	3 (4)	11 (5)	11 (5)	2+1 (4)	–	–	6 (5)
4	22/10	Mildenhall	H	W48-45	9+2 (5)	6+2 (4)	10 (4)	6 (4)	9 (5)	–	–	0 (3)	8+1 (5)

*Denotes aggregate victory

TACTICAL RIDES, AS INCLUDED IN THE SCORES GRID:

Match No. 2: Mills 6 points (TR); Branney 6 points (TR); Match No. 3: Branney 6 points (TR); Mills 2 points (TR).

OTHER MEETING

4 April: Conference League

Newport 7 Oxford 11 (Chris Mills 3; Mark Woods 3; Wayne Barrett 2+1; Chris Schramm 2; Craig Branney 1+1; John Markham 0; Ben Barker R/R) – meeting abandoned after heat three.

RYE HOUSE ELMSIDE RAIDERS

NOTE: The information below relates only to the second Rye House team. For details of the main side, please refer to the Premier League section.

ADDRESS: Rye House Stadium, Rye Road, Hoddesdon, Hertfordshire, EN11 0EH.

CLUB CHAIRMEN: Len Silver & Hazal Naylor.

TRACK LENGTH: 271 metres.

FIRST MEETING: 1 April 2002.

CL TRACK RECORD: 57.0 seconds – Edward Kennett (21/04/03).

YEARS OF OPERATION: 2002-04 Conference League.

CLUB HONOURS

FOUR-TEAM CHAMPIONS: 2003.

RIDER ROSTER 2004

Tommy ALLEN; Mark BASEBY; Luke BOWEN; Steve BOXALL; Barry BURCHATT; Harland COOK; Gary COTTHAM; Joel PARSONS.

OTHER APPEARANCES/GUESTS (official matches only):

Scott CAMPOS; Luke CLIFTON; Alan FERROW; Robert MEAR; Karl WHITE.

CONFERENCE LEAGUE

No	DATE	OPPONENTS	H/A	RESULT	ALLEN	WHITE	BOXALL	BOWEN	PARSONS	COOK	BURCHATT	MEAR	BASEBY	CLIFTON	COTTHAM	OTHERS
1	11/4	Mildenhall	A	L40-53	12 (6)	0 (0)	10+2 (5)	4 (4)	9+1 (4)	3+1 (5)	2 (6)	–	–	–	–	–
2	12/4	Boston	H	W55-38	15 (5)	–	11 (4)	2+1 (3)	12+1 (5)	7 (4)	7 (6)	1 (3)	–	–	–	–
3	18/4	Newport	A	W52-41	9 (4)	–	6 (3)	–	13+1 (5)	5+4 (4)	11 (6)	2 (4)	6+1 (4)	–	–	–
4	2/5	Boston	A	L36-57	15 (5)	–	7 (4)	4+1 (4)	7+2 (5)	1 (4)	2 (4)	–	0 (4)	–	–	–
5	16/5	Newcastle	A	W53-42	12+1 (5)	–	R/R	10+1 (5)	12 (5)	3+2 (4)	11+3 (6)	–	–	5+2 (5)	–	–
6	29/5	Carmarthen	H	W50-42	–	–	R/R	13+1 (6)	15+1 (6)	6 (5)	10+1 (7)	–	0 (3)	6+1 (3)	–	–
7	31/5	Wimbledon	H	W52-41	–	–	R/R	11+1 (6)	13+1 (6)	16+3 (7)	11+2 (7)	–	1 (3)	–	–	–
8	13/6	Weymouth	H	W61-30	0 (0)	–	14 (5)	9+3 (5)	12 (4)	8+1 (5)	15+3 (7)	–	3+1 (4)	–	–	–
9	18/6	Weymouth	A	L34-59*	–	–	21 (6)	1 (3)	R/R	4 (6)	6 (7)	–	0 (5)	–	–	2+1 (4)
10	9/7	Armadale	A	L31-59	4 (4)	–	8 (5)	5+3 (5)	5 (3)	1 (4)	7+1 (6)	–	–	–	–	1 (3)
11	17/7	Armadale	H	W54-39	8 (4)	1+1 (3)	14 (5)	4 (4)	9+1 (4)	8+1 (5)	10+2 (5)	–	–	–	–	–
12	18/7	Buxton	A	W54-36	12 (4)	–	11+1 (4)	4 (4)	9 (4)	7+2 (5)	10+2 (5)	–	1+1 (4)	–	–	–
13	7/8	Mildenhall	H	W56-36*	13+1 (5)	–	8 (4)	6 (4)	12+2 (5)	6 (4)	10+4 (5)	–	1+1 (3)	–	–	–
14	14/8	Newcastle	H	W62-33*	12 (4)	–	9 (4)	13+2 (6)	R/R	10+1 (5)	11+4 (5)	–	0 (2)	7+2 (4)	–	–
15	21/8	Swindon	H	W65-26	12 (4)	–	12 (4)	10+4 (5)	10+2 (4)	11+1 (5)	8+2 (5)	–	–	2+1 (3)	–	–
16	30/8	Stoke	H	W51-38	–	–	15 (5)	10+3 (6)	R/R	6 (5)	16+1 (7)	1 (3)	3+2 (4)	–	–	–
17	5/9	Carmarthen	A	W54-40*	10+1 (4)	–	9 (4)	6 (4)	11 (4)	14+3 (6)	3 (4)	–	1 (4)	–	–	–
18	18/9	Newport	H	W64-31*	12 (4)	–	R/R	7+2 (4)	17+1 (6)	10+3 (5)	6+3 (4)	–	5+2 (3)	–	7+1 (4)	–
19	24/9	Oxford	A	L42-48	16 (6)	–	R/R	4+2 (5)	9 (6)	10+2 (7)	2+1 (3)	–	–	–	1 (3)	–
20	2/10	Oxford	H	W47-46	15 (6)	–	R/R	5+1 (5)	9 (5)	8+1 (6)	9+1 (5)	–	–	–	1 (3)	–
21	8/10	Stoke	A	W49-41*	12 (6)	–	R/R	11+2 (6)	7+2 (5)	3+1 (3)	16+1 (7)	–	–	–	0 (3)	–
22	16/10	Buxton†	H	W42-33*	12 (4)	–	R/R	9 (5)	–	16+2 (6)	4 (5)	–	0 (2)	–	1 (2)	–
23	21/10	Swindon$^{\Delta}$	A	W49-39*	15 (5)	–	R/R	3 (2)	13 (5)	7+1 (6)	7+2 (6)	–	–	–	4 (4)	–
24	24/10	Wimbledon	A®	W53-43*	18 (6)	–	R/R	–	13 (5)	12+1 (7)	8+2 (6)	–	0 (3)	–	2+1 (3)	–

*Denotes bonus-point victory

†Meeting abandoned after heat twelve, with the result permitted to stand.

$^{\Delta}$Meeting abandoned after heat fourteen, with the result permitted to stand.

®Match raced at Rye House.

DETAILS OF OTHER RIDERS:

Match No. 9: Scott Campos 2+1 (4); Match No. 10: Alan Ferrow 1 (3).

TACTICAL SUBSTITUTE AND TACTICAL RIDES, AS INCLUDED IN THE SCORES GRID:

Match No. 1: Parsons 6 points (TR); Allen 2 points (TS); Boxall 0 points (TR); Match No. 4: Allen 6 points (TR); Boxall 0 points (TR); Match No. 9: Boxall 6 points (TR); Bowen 0 points (TR); Match No. 10: Boxall 0 points (TR); Parsons 0 points (TR).

RYE HOUSE: back row, left to right: Gary Cottham, John Sampford (Team Manager), Joel Parsons, Tommy Allen. Front row: Barry Burchatt, Luke Bowen, Harland Cook.

CONFERENCE LEAGUE AVERAGES

Rider	Mts	Rds	Pts	Bon	Tot	Avge	Max
Tommy Allen	20	91	230	3	233	10.24	8 full
Steve Boxall	14	62	152	3	155	10.00	3 full; 1 paid
Joel Parsons	20	96	214	15	229	9.54	1 full; 2 paid
Barry Burchatt	24	134	202	35	237	7.07	1 paid
Luke Bowen	22	101	151	27	178	7.05	–
Luke Clifton	4	15	20	6	26	6.93	–
Harland Cook	24	123	182	30	212	6.89	1 paid
Gary Cottham	7	22	16	2	18	3.27	–
Scott Campos	1	4	2	1	3	3.00	–
Karl White	2	3	1	1	2	2.67	–
Mark Baseby	14	48	21	8	29	2.42	–
Robert Mear	3	10	4	0	4	1.60	–
Alan Ferrow	1	3	1	0	1	1.33	–

KNOCK-OUT CUP

No	DATE	OPPONENTS	H/A	RESULT	PARSONS	BOXALL	BASEBY	ALLEN	COOK	BURCHATT	BOWEN	CLIFTON	OTHERS
1	25/6	Boston	A	L42-48	10 (4)	11 (5)	1+1 (3)	11 (4)	3 (4)	6+2 (7)	–	–	0 (3)
2	24/7	Boston	H	L44-51	R/R	–	2 (3)	12+1 (6)	1+1 (3)	12+2 (7)	14 (6)	3 (5)	–

DETAILS OF OTHER RIDER:

Match No. 1: Scott Campos 0 (3).

TACTICAL RIDES, AS INCLUDED IN THE SCORES GRID:

Match No. 2: Bowen 6 points (TR); Allen 4 points (TR).

OTHER MEETINGS

14 March: Three-Team Tournament

Peterborough 30 (Richie Dennis 10; Danny Norton 9; Adam Pryer 6; Steve Clarke 2+1; Adam Roynon 2; James Purchase 1+1), Rye House 45 (Steve Boxall 12; Luke Bowen 11; Tommy Allen 9; Joel Parsons 8+3; Barry Burchatt 3+1; Harland Cook 2), King's Lynn 32 – staged at Peterborough.

8 September: Conference League

Wimbledon 31 Rye House 35 (Tommy Allen 11; Harland Cook 10+1; Luke Bowen 8; Steve Boxall 3; Barry Burchatt 2+1; Mark Baseby 1; Joel Parsons R/R) – meeting abandoned after heat eleven.

6 October: Conference League

Wimbledon 8 Rye House 3 (Tommy Allen 3; Gary Cottham 0; Harland Cook 0; Barry Burchatt 0; Luke Bowen DNR; Karl White DNR; Steve Boxall R/R) – meeting abandoned after heat two.

SHEFFIELD PIRTEK PROWLERS

NOTE: The information below relates only to the second Sheffield team. For details of the main side, please refer to the Premier League section.

ADDRESS: Owlerton Sports Stadium, Penistone Road, Owlerton, Sheffield, South Yorkshire, S6 2DE.

CLUB CHAIRMEN: Neil Machin & Malcolm Wright.

TRACK LENGTH: 361 metres.

CL TRACK RECORD: 62.0 seconds – Richard Hall (02/08/04).

FIRST MEETING: 25 April 1996.

YEARS OF OPERATION: 1996 Conference League; 2000-03 Conference League; 2004 Conference Trophy.

CLUB HONOURS

LEAGUE CHAMPIONS: 2000, 2001.

RIDER ROSTER 2004

Paul COOPER; Richard HALL; Karl LANGLEY; Michael MITCHELL; Luke PRIEST; David SPEIGHT; Ben WILSON.

OTHER APPEARANCES/GUESTS (official matches only):

Wayne CARTER; James COCKLE; Gary FLINT; Jordan FRAMPTON; Grant HAYES; Trevor HEATH; Mark RICHARDSON; Carl SHIELD.

CONFERENCE TROPHY

No	DATE	OPPONENTS	H/A	RESULT	HALL	SHIELD	WILSON	SPEIGHT	COOPER	MITCHELL	COCKLE	PRIEST	LANGLEY	FLINT	CARTER	OTHERS
1	9/5	Mildenhall	A	L39-56	16 (7)	1+1 (4)	6+2 (6)	0 (3)	15+1 (7)	1 (3)	–	–	–	–	–	R/R
2	17/5	Wimbledon	H	W58-36	15 (5)	6+2 (4)	13+2 (5)	5 (4)	13+2 (5)	2 (3)	4+1 (4)	–	–	–	–	–
3	17/5	Weymouth	H	W60-34	12 (4)	5 (4)	13+2 (5)	5+1 (3)	11+1 (5)	6+2 (4)	8+1 (5)	–	–	–	–	–
4	7/6	King's Lynn	H	W57-37	14 (5)	–	8+1 (4)	8+1 (4)	13+2 (5)	6+1 (4)	4+4 (4)	4+1 (4)	–	–	–	–
5	2/8	Mildenhall	H	W47-46	16+1 (5)	–	13 (5)	2 (4)	9 (4)	–	–	5+1 (4)	2 (5)	0 (3)	–	–
6	11/8	Wimbledon	A	L45-51*	14 (6)	–	17+2 (6)	3+1 (5)	R/R	–	–	8+1 (5)	1 (4)	–	–	2 (4)
7	4/9	King's Lynn	A	W47-43*	18 (6)	–	13+1 (6)	7 (5)	R/R	–	–	–	4+2 (6)	2 (4)	–	3+1 (4)
8	5/9	Buxton	A	L44-52	R/R	–	15+2 (6)	2 (4)	–	–	–	9+1 (5)	1 (6)	0 (3)	17 (6)	–
9	6/9	Coventry	H	W49-40	12 (5)	–	8+1 (4)	2 (4)	13+2 (5)	2+1 (4)	–	7 (4)	5 (4)	–	–	–
10	23/9	Buxton	H	W50-43	14 (5)	–	6 (5)	5+1 (4)	11 (4)	0 (3)	–	7+2 (4)	7+1 (5)	–	–	–
11	27/9	Coventry	A	W47-43*	R/R	–	–	6 (5)	13+1 (6)	4+3 (7)	–	7+1 (5)	–	–	17 (6)	0 (1)
12	24/10	Weymouth	A	L39-56*	R/R	–	14 (6)	–	–	8+1 (6)	–	13+1 (6)	–	–	–	4+2 (9)

*Denotes bonus-point victory

DETAILS OF OTHER RIDERS:

Match No. 1: Corey Blackman R/R; Match No. 6: Trevor Heath 2 (4); Match No. 7: Mark Richardson 3+1 (4); Match No. 11: Mark Richardson 0 (1); Match No. 12: Jordan Frampton 3+2 (5); Grant Hayes 1 (4).

TACTICAL SUBSTITUTE AND TACTICAL RIDES, AS INCLUDED IN THE SCORES GRID:

Match No. 1: Cooper 6 points (TR); Hall 4 points (TR); Match No. 5: Hall 6 points (TR); Match No. 6: Wilson 6 points (TR); Hall 6 points (TR); Match No. 8: Priest 6 points (TR); Carter 4 points (TR); Wilson 4 points (TS); Match No. 12: Wilson 6 points (TR); Priest 4 points (TR).

CONFERENCE TROPHY AVERAGES

Rider	Mts	Rds	Pts	Bon	Tot	Avge	Max
Wayne Carter	2	12	32	0	32	10.67	–
Richard Hall	9	48	123	1	124	10.33	3 full
Paul Cooper	8	41	95	9	104	10.15	3 paid
Ben Wilson	11	58	118	13	131	9.03	2 paid
Luke Priest	8	37	55	8	63	6.81	–
James Cockle	3	13	16	6	22	6.77	–
Carl Shield	3	12	12	3	15	5.00	–
David Speight	11	45	45	4	49	4.36	–
Michael Mitchell	8	34	29	8	37	4.35	–
Jordan Frampton	1	5	3	2	5	4.00	–
Mark Richardson	2	5	3	1	4	3.20	–
Karl Langley	6	30	20	3	23	3.07	–
Trevor Heath	1	4	2	0	2	2.00	–
Grant Hayes	1	4	1	0	1	1.00	–
Gary Flint	3	10	2	0	2	0.80	–

OTHER MEETINGS

7 June: Conference Trophy

Sheffield 44 (Richard Hall 9; Ben Wilson 8+1; Luke Priest 7+1; David Speight 7+1; Paul Cooper 5+1; Michael Mitchell 5+1; James Cockle 3) Coventry 22 – meeting abandoned after heat eleven.

10 September: Conference Trophy

Weymouth 5 Sheffield 1 (David Speight 1; Richard Hall 0; Luke Priest DNR; Ben Wilson DNR; Michael Mitchell DNR; Matt Bates DNR; Paul Cooper R/R) – meeting abandoned after heat one.

INDIVIDUAL MEETINGS

27 May: Jeff Hall Suzuki Top Gun Championship

QUALIFYING SCORES: Ben Wilson 14; Richard Hall 14; Paul Cooper 13; Mark Thompson 11; James Cockle 10; Ritchie Hawkins 10; Barrie Evans 8; Rob Grant jr 8; David Speight 6; Richie Dennis 6; Michael Mitchell 5; Benji Compton 5; John Oliver 4; Luke Priest 2; Corey Blackman 2; Ben Powell 0. SEMI-FINAL: 1st Thompson; 2nd Hawkins; 3rd Cockle; 4th Cooper. FINAL: 1st Wilson; 2nd Hall; 3rd Hawkins; 4th Thompson.

SHEFFIELD: back row, left to right: Michael Mitchell, James Cockle, Richard Hall, Paul Cooper, Carl Shield, David Speight. On bike: Ben Wilson.

6 September: British Under-15 Championship (Fifth Round)

1st Josh Auty 15; 2nd Gary Cottham (after run-off) 12; 3rd Matt Bates 12; Shane Waldron 11; Sam Hurst 11; Kyle Hughes 10; Simon Lambert 9; Grant Hayes 7; Lewis Bridger 6; Scott Campos 5; Joe Reynolds 5; James Humby 5; Ben Hopwood 3; George Piper 2; Connor Scott 2; Ben Thompson 2; Andrew Braithwaite (Res) 2. SERIES POINTS (best three rounds count): 1st Auty 51; =2nd Lambert, Waldron 47; Bates 42; Cottham 42; Hughes 38; Campos 37; Hurst 29; Humby 28; Bridger 26; Piper 25; Hayes 22; Hopwood 15; Reynolds 14; Thompson 12; Aaron Baseby 10; Scott 10; Trevor Heath 9; Dean Hargrave 4; Ben Hannon 4; Tim Webster 4; Braithwaite 4; Chris Widman 3; Shawn Taylor 1.

7 October: Steel City Championship

QUALIFYING SCORES: Ben Wilson 15; Danny Norton 13; Richard Hall 13; James Wright 12; David Meldrum 9; Luke Priest 9; Benji Compton 8; David Speight 7; Lee Smart 6; Paul Cooper 6; Chris Ferguson 5; Lee Derbyshire 4; Carl Belfield 4; Gary Flint 4; Kyle Hughes 2; Darren Rolph 1; Mark Richardson (Res) 1; Grant Hayes (Res) 1. SEMI-FINAL: 1st Wright; 2nd Meldrum; 3rd Priest; 4th Norton. FINAL: 1st Wright; 2nd Wilson; 3rd Meldrum; 4th Hall.

SITTINGBOURNE SET LIGHTING CRUSADERS

ADDRESS: The Old Gun Site, Old Ferry Road, Iwade, Sittingbourne, Kent, ME9 8SP.
CLUB CHAIRMAN: Graham Arnold.
TRACK LENGTH: 251 metres.
TRACK RECORD: 58.4 seconds – Edward Kennett (04/07/04).
FIRST MEETING: 5 November 1972.
YEARS OF OPERATION: 1971 Training; 1972-93 Open & Training; 1994 British League Division Three; 1995 Academy League; 1996 Conference League; 1997-03 Open & Training; 2004 Conference League Knock-Out Cup, Open & Training.

CLUB HONOURS

None.

RIDER ROSTER 2004

Mark BASEBY; Peter BOAST; Shane COLVIN; Carl DOWNS; Dean GARROD; Chris GEER; Malcolm HOLLOWAY; James THEOBALD.

The programme from Sittingbourne's only official home fixture in 2004.

KNOCK-OUT CUP

No	DATE	OPPONENTS	H/A	RESULT	COLVIN	DOWNS	BRAIDFORD	GARROD	BOAST	THEOBALD	BASEBY	GEER	HOLLOWAY
1	16/5	Wimbledon	H	L40-53	15 (6)	1 (3)	R/R	7+2 (4)	7 (6)	6 (5)	0 (4)	4 (2)	–
2	19/5	Wimbledon	A	L38-55	8+1 (6)	2 (4)	R/R	3 (4)	–	1 (4)	–	6+1 (6)	18 (6)

TACTICAL RIDES, AS INCLUDED IN THE SCORES GRID:

Match No. 1: Geer 4 points (TR); Colvin 4 points (TR); Match No. 2: Holloway 6 points (TR); Colvin 0 points (TR).

OTHER MEETINGS

4 July: Festival of Speed

FIRST SEMI-FINAL: Wimbledon 24, Weymouth 19, Coventry 11. SECOND SEMI-FINAL: Swindon 24, Armadale 16, Sittingbourne 14 (Edward Kennett 9; Dean Garrod 3; Chris Geer 1; James Theobald 1). FINAL: Wimbledon 21, Weymouth 20, Swindon 13.

31 October: Challenge

Sittingbourne 42 (James Theobald 10+1; Mark Baseby 8+2; Harland Cook 8+1; Lance Stott 7+3; Martyn Sturgeon 6+2; Keith Yorke 3+2; R/R at number three) League Select 35 (Matthew Wright 18; Barry Burchatt 11; Gary Cottham 5; Karl Rushen 1+1; Martin Elliott 0; Danny Betson 0; Lee Lingham 0; R/R at number one).

INDIVIDUAL MEETINGS

6 June: British Under-15 Championship (Third Round)

1st Simon Lambert (after run-off) 14; 2nd Josh Auty 14; 3rd Gary Cottham 12; Matt Bates 11; Shane Waldron 11; Kyle Hughes 10; Scott Campos 9; Lewis Bridger 7; George Piper 7; Sam Hurst 5; Trevor Heath 5; Grant Hayes 4; Dean Hargrave (Res) 3; Ben Hannon 2; Tim Webster 2; Aaron Baseby 1; Shawn Taylor (Res) 1; James Humby 0. SERIES POINTS (best three rounds count): =1st Auty, Waldron, Lambert 45; Cottham 37; Bates 36; Campos 34; Hughes 34; Piper 25; Hurst 23; Humby 22; Hayes 13; Bridger 12; Ben Hopwood 10; Heath 9; Ben Thompson 8; Baseby 8; Webster 4; Hannon 4; Joe Reynolds 4; Hargrave 4; Chris Widman 3; Connor Scott 2; Andy Braithwaite 1; Taylor 1.

20 June: Nathan Gaymer Memorial Trophy

1st Chris Ferguson 15; 2nd Matthew Wright 14; 3rd James Theobald 13; Sam Martin 12; James Purchase 11; Jon Stevens 10; Keith Yorke 9; Lee Strudwick 5; Martin Elliott 5; Daniel Blake 5; Robert Smith (Res) 5; Jordan Frampton 4; Lee Lingham 3; Alan Fenn-Smith 3; Jason Taylor 1; Adam Filmer 1; Daniel Hunt (Res) 1; John Markham 0.

13 November: SCB Referees' Track Day

D-FINAL: 1st Mick Posselwhite; 2nd Tony Steele; 3rd Phil Griffin. C-FINAL: 1st Dale Entwistle; 2nd Chris Durno; 3rd Jim McGregor. B-FINAL: 1st Richard Williams; 2nd Jim Lawrence; 3rd David Peet; 4th Paul Carrington. A-FINAL: 1st Rod Smith; 2nd Jim Lawrence; =3rd Chris Gay, Richard Williams (dead-heat).

STOKE EASY-RIDER SPITFIRES

NOTE: The information below relates only to the second Stoke team. For details of the main side, please refer to the Premier League section.

ADDRESS: Chesterton Stadium, Loomer Road, Chesterton, Newcastle-under-Lyme, Staffordshire, ST5 7LB.
CLUB CHAIRMAN: Dave Tattum.
TRACK LENGTH: 312 metres.
CL TRACK RECORD: 63.6 seconds – Justin Elkins (04/09/04).
FIRST MEETING: 13 April 2003.
YEARS OF OPERATION: 2003 Conference Trophy; 2004 Conference League.

CLUB HONOURS

None.

RIDER ROSTER 2004

Darren ANDREWS; Tom BROWN; Justin ELKINS; Rob GRANT jr; Jack HARGREAVES; Michael MITCHELL; Luke PRIEST.

OTHER APPEARANCES/GUESTS (official matches only):

Marc ANDREWS; Andrew BLACKBURN; Clayton CHUBB; Gary FLINT; Daniel GIFFARD; Rob GRANT sr; David HAIGH; Lee HODGSON; James HUMBY; Kriss IRVING; Andrew JACKSON; John MacPHAIL; Jamie NICOL; David SPEIGHT.

CONFERENCE LEAGUE

No	DATE	OPPONENTS	H/A	RESULT	BLACKBURN	ANDREWS	BROWN	GRANT jr	GIFFARD	MITCHELL	HARGREAVES	ELKINS	PRIEST	HODGSON	OTHERS
1	7/4	Newcastle	H	L41-51	1+1 (3)	3 (5)	9+1 (6)	R/R	15+1 (6)	2+1 (5)	11 (5)	–	–	–	–
2	16/5	Boston	A	L36-57	–	3 (4)	6 (6)	R/R	3 (4)	1 (3)	3+1 (7)	20 (6)	–	–	–
3	25/5	Armadale	H	W46-44	–	5+1 (4)	8 (5)	8+2 (5)	–	2 (3)	8+2 (5)	7+1 (4)	8 ([illegible])	–	–
4	28/5	Oxford	A	W48-46	–	7+2 (5)	10+1 (6)	–	R/R	2+1 (3)	10+1 (5)	12 (6)	7+3 (5)	–	–
5	6/6	Newport	A	L46-47	–	5 (4)	11+1 (6)	R/R	–	6+2 (4)	4+1 (5)	14 (6)	6+2 (5)	–	–
6	9/6	Carmarthen	H	W58-36	0 (3)	12+1 (5)	12+1 (6)	R/R	–	–	11+2 (6)	14+1 (5)	9+3 (5)	–	–
7	26/6	Swindon	H	W57-36	–	8+4 (5)	8 (5)	R/R	–	–	11+3 (5)	16+1 (6)	13+1 (6)	–	1 (2)
8	2/7	Weymouth	A	L36-57	–	0 (4)	–	R/R	–	–	9+1 (6)	16 (6)	10 (7)	–	1 (4)
9	4/7	Mildenhall	A	L36-59	1+1 (4)	2+2 (4)	5 (6)	R/R	–	–	7+1 (5)	8 (5)	13+1 (6)	–	–
10	14/7	Boston	H	D45-45	0 (3)	1+1 (4)	11 (6)	R/R	–	–	10+2 (6)	14 (6)	9 (5)	–	–
11	25/7	Carmarthen	A	L42-50*	–	1 (4)	11 (6)	R/R	–	–	9+1 (5)	9 (5)	11 (5)	–	1 (4)
12	28/7	Buxton	H	L42-48	–	1+1 (2)	11+1 (6)	R/R	–	–	6+1 (6)	17 (6)	4 (5)	–	3 (4)
13	1/8	Buxton	A	L42-47	0 (2)	2 (4)	8+2 (6)	R/R	–	–	15+1 (7)	11 (5)	6 (5)	–	–
14	30/8	Rye House	A	L38-51	–	–	9+1 (5)	8 (4)	–	4+3 (5)	11+1 (6)	0 (3)	4 (4)	2+1 (4)	2+1 (4)
15	1/9	Oxford	H	W48-45*	–	1+1 (3)	8 (4)	–	–	0 (3)	12 (7)	16 (5)	6+1 (4)	5+2 (4)	–

CONFERENCE LEAGUE continued

No	DATE	OPPONENTS	H/A	RESULT	BLACKBURN	ANDREWS	BROWN	GRANT jr	GIFFARD	MITCHELL	HARGREAVES	ELKINS	PRIEST	HODGSON	OTHERS
16	4/9	Wimbledon	H	W51-42	–	1 (3)	9+2 (5)	–	–	3+2 (3)	13 (6)	<u>15 (5)</u>	7+1 (4)	3+3 (4)	–
17	5/9	Newcastle	A	L43-50	–	5+2 (4)	7 (5)	5+3 (4)	–	3+1 (4)	16+1 (6)	7 (4)	–	–	–
18	8/9	Mildenhall	H	L45-50	–	2 (3)	4 (4)	–	–	0 (3)	17+2 (7)	14 (5)	6+1 (4)	2 (4)	–
19	12/9	Swindon	A	W47-43*	–	0 (4)	6+1 (5)	R/R	–	1 (3)	15+1 (7)	<u>18 (6)</u>	7+1 (5)	–	–
20	29/9	Wimbledon	A	L32-62	–	3 (4)	6+1 (6)	–	–	1 (4)	9 (7)	6 (3)	7 (6)	R/R	–
21	1/10	Armadale†	A	L27-46	–	–	–	7 (3)	–	0 (4)	–	9 (3)	–	–	11 (14)
22	2/10	Newport	H	W57-38*	–	2 (4)	13+1 (5)	–	–	3+1 (4)	15 (5)	11+1 (5)	9+2 (4)	4 (3)	–
23	8/10	Rye House	H	L41-49	–	–	8 (4)	11 (5)	–	–	–	10 (5)	5+1 (4)	–	7+2 (12)
24	16/10	Weymouth	H	W50-40	–	–	7 (4)	12+1 (5)	–	4+3 (4)	–	14 (5)	5+2 (4)	–	8+4 (8)

*Denotes bonus-point victory

†Meeting abandoned after heat twelve, with the result permitted to stand.

NOTES: (1) Justin Elkins is not credited with a paid maximum in the home match versus Carmarthen as he missed a programmed ride (heat ten) through a two-minute exclusion; (2) Jack Hargreaves is not credited with a full maximum in the home fixture against Newport due to a two-minute exclusion in his second programmed ride (heat four).

DETAILS OF OTHER RIDERS:

Match No. 7: Jamie Nicol 1 (2); Match No. 8: Marc Andrews 1 (4); James Humby 0 (0); Match No. 11: Andrew Jackson 1 (4); Match No. 12: Andrew Jackson 3 (4); Match No. 21: David Haigh 4 (4); Kriss Irving 4 (4); Rob Grant sr 2 (3); John MacPhail 1 (3); Match No. 23: David Speight 4+2 (4); Gary Flint 2 (4); Kriss Irving 1 (4); Match No. 24: Kriss Irving 5+2 (4); David Speight 3+2 (4).

TACTICAL SUBSTITUTE AND TACTICAL RIDES, AS INCLUDED IN THE SCORES GRID:

Match No. 1: Giffard 4 points (TR); Brown 0 points (TR); Match No. 2: Elkins 6 points (TR); Hargreaves 0 points (TR); Match No. 8: Elkins 4 points (TR); Priest 2 points (TS); Hargreaves 0 points (TR); Match No. 9: Priest 6 points (TR); Elkins 4 points (TR); Match No. 15: Elkins 6 points (TR); Match No. 17: Hargreaves 6 points (TR); Match No. 18: Elkins 6 points (TR); Hargreaves 4 points (TR); Match No. 20: Elkins 6 points (TR); Brown 2 points (TR); Match No. 21: Elkins 6 points (TR).

CONFERENCE LEAGUE AVERAGES

Rider	Mts	Rds	Pts	Bon	Tot	Avge	Max
Justin Elkins	23	115	259	4	263	9.15	2 Full
Rob Grant jr	6	26	51	6	57	8.77	–
Jack Hargreaves	21	124	217	22	239	7.71	–
Luke Priest	20	97	148	19	167	6.89	–
Tom Brown	22	117	186	13	199	6.80	–
Daniel Giffard	2	10	16	1	17	6.80	–
David Speight	2	8	7	4	11	5.50	–
Lee Hodgson	5	19	16	6	22	4.63	–
Darren Andrews	20	79	64	15	79	4.00	–
David Haigh	1	4	4	0	4	4.00	–
Kriss Irving	3	12	10	2	12	4.00	–
Michael Mitchell	15	55	32	14	46	3.35	–
Rob Grant sr	1	3	2	0	2	2.67	–
Gary Flint	1	4	2	0	2	2.00	–
Andrew Jackson	2	8	4	0	4	2.00	–

STOKE: back row, left to right: Michael Mitchell, Jack Hargreaves, Clayton Chubb, Justin Elkins. Front row: Daniel Giffard, Darren Andrews.

Rider	Mts	Rds	Pts	Bon	Tot	Avge	Max
Jamie Nicol	1	2	1	0	1	2.00	–
John MacPhail	1	3	1	0	1	1.33	–
Andrew Blackburn	5	15	2	2	4	1.07	–
Marc Andrews	1	4	1	0	1	1.00	–
James Humby	1	0	0	0	0	0.00	–

KNOCK-OUT CUP

No	DATE	OPPONENTS	H/A	RESULT	ELKINS	ANDREWS	BROWN	CHUBB	GIFFARD	MITCHELL	HARGREAVES	PRIEST
1	9/4	Weymouth	A	L41-53	16 (6)	0 (2)	R/R	1 (4)	10 (6)	4+1 (6)	10 (7)	–
2	12/5	Weymouth	H	L42-47	5+1 (4)	3+1 (3)	9+1 (5)	–	5 (4)	2+2 (3)	10+1 (6)	8+2 (5)

TACTICAL RIDES, AS INCLUDED IN THE SCORES GRID:

Match No. 1: Elkins 4 points (TR); Hargreaves 4 points (TR).

INDIVIDUAL MEETING

30 October: Pride Of The Conference League

QUALIFYING SCORES: Justin Elkins 12; James Wright 11; Tom Brown 8; Daniel Giffard 8; Rob Grant jr 7; Robert Hollingworth 7; Benji Compton 5; Luke Priest 4; Rob Grant sr 4; Jack Hargreaves 3; Jonathon Bethell 3; Michael Mitchell 3; Andrew Blackburn (Res) 0; David Speight (Res) 0. FIRST SEMI-FINAL: 1st Grant jr; 2nd Compton; 3rd Giffard; 4th Elkins. SECOND SEMI-FINAL: 1st Wright; 2nd Brown; 3rd Priest; 4th Hollingworth. FINAL: 1st Wright; 2nd Brown; 3rd Grant jr; 4th Compton.

1 Hans N. Andersen adjusts his helmet prior to the practice for the Danish Grand Prix at Parken, Copenhagen.

tservice.no
king Ship Hamar
WWW.SPEEDWAYWORLD.TV
ULLEVI TICNET.SE
VEIDEC
www.wroclaw.pl
SELEK

BN PRODUCTS.DK
RÅD & DÅD BYGGECENTER
i4
21

This page

4 The Hull pairing of Ross Brady (yellow/black), Emil Kramer (green) lead the charge to the first turn from Reading representatives Andrew Appleton (red) and Glen Phillips (blue) during the Premier League clash at Smallmead.

5 Wolverhampton's David Howe takes the inside line against Antonio Lindback of Poole during the Elite League Play-Off final at Wimborne Road.

Opposite page

2 Tony Rickardsson (blue) dices with Bjarne Pedersen (white) during the European Grand Prix at Wroclaw, Poland.

3 Jesper B. Jensen makes adjustments to his steed during the practice session for the British Grand Prix.

6 Action from the Championship of Great Britain at Oxford, as Joe Screen (red) leads the charge from Andre Compton (blue) and Dean Barker (yellow/black), with Michael Coles (green) at the rear.

7 Poland's Grzegorz Walasek caught in flight during the dramatic Speedway World Cup Race-Off at Poole.

8 Ricky Ashworth burns up the track on Peterborough's Press and Practice Day.

9 From left to right, Magnus Zetterstrom, Jesper B. Jensen, Matej Ferjan and Kim Jansson wait for the tapes to rise during the Knock-Out Cup final at Ipswich.

This page

10 A smiling Dean Barker, pictured at the Arena-Essex Press and Practice Day.

11 Jason Crump leads fellow Aussie Leigh Adams in atrocious conditions during the Czech Republic Grand Prix at Prague.

Opposite page

12 An airborne Antonio Lindback (yellow/black) of Poole leaves the gate alongside Ipswich's Daniel King (blue) during the first leg of the Knock-Out Cup final at Foxhall Heath.

13 Multi-World Champion Tony Rickardsson (yellow/black) takes the impact as Nicki Pedersen (red) and Scott Nicholls (white) clash in the British Grand Prix at the magical Millennium Stadium, Cardiff.

POOLE
ARROW
SCOTT
MARTIN & ELAINE COOMBS
MYRA & HARRY DIXON
ADVANCE EUROPA
SKY

8.COM
888.C
commercial vehicles
VEIDEC
PEUGEOT SKANDERBORG

14 Workington's Simon Stead putting on the style during the Champions Chase at King's Lynn.

15 Always exciting Pole Tomasz Gollob (red) heads Bohumil Brhel (yellow/black) and Jesper B. Jensen (blue) at the Scandinavian Grand Prix in Gothenburg.

16 Craig Boyce races inside Tomas Topinka during the Champions Chase at King's Lynn.

17 Five times World Champion Tony Rickardsson holds a team talk with his pit crew.

18 Sam Ermolenko of Wolverhampton heads Matej Ferjan and Magnus Karlsson during the Elite League Play-Off final at Poole.

19 Andreas Jonsson stylishly leads from Kaj Laukkanen and Scott Nicholls at the European Grand Prix in Poland.

20 Poole's Bjarne Pedersen crashes alarmingly at Oxford.

21 Up, up and away with Danny Bird at Reading's Press and Practice Day.

22 Hans N. Andersen (17) leads from Lukas Dryml (13) during the European Grand Prix at Wroclaw, Poland.

23 Super Swede Andreas Jonsson holds aloft the chequered flag following a race victory at the Norwegian Grand Prix.

24 Peterborough's Lukas Dryml holds the advantage over the Ipswich duo of Jesper B. Jensen (green) and Chris Louis (yellow/black) during the Air-Tek Challenge at the East of England Showground.

25 Brilliant action from the final of the Danish Grand Prix in Copenhagen, as Jason Crump (white) leads the way from Andreas Jonsson (red) and Greg Hancock (yellow/black).

26 Local derby action from Cowley, as Swindon's Charlie Gjedde (green) and Olly Allen (yellow/black) leave the gate with the Oxford duo of Travis McGowan (blue) and Niels-Kristian Iversen (red).

27 Leigh Adams of Swindon – the Elite League's top man in 2004.

28 Oxford's influential captain Greg Hancock shows his style at Cowley.

TEAM ARTDEANS SWINDON SPROCKETS

NOTE: The information below relates only to the second Swindon team. For details of the main side, please refer to the Elite League section.

ADDRESS: Swindon Stadium, Blunsdon, nr. Swindon, Wiltshire, SN25 4DN.
CLUB CHAIRMAN: Martin Satchell.
TRACK LENGTH: 361.2 metres.
CL TRACK RECORD: 68.02 seconds – Ritchie Hawkins (07/06/04).
FIRST MEETING: 12 May 1996.
YEARS OF OPERATION: 1996 Conference League; 1997 Amateur League (fixtures shared with Reading, under the banner of 'M4 Raven Sprockets'); 2002 Conference Trophy; 2003-04 Conference League.

CLUB HONOURS

None.

RIDER ROSTER 2004

Jordan FRAMPTON; Daniel HARDING; Malcolm HOLLOWAY; Nathan IRWIN; Chris JOHNSON; James PURCHASE; Mark THOMPSON; Simon WALKER; Danny WARWICK.

OTHER APPEARANCES/GUESTS (official matches only):

Marc ANDREWS; Danny BETSON; Steve BRAIDFORD; Wayne CARTER; Jamie COURTNEY; Martin ELLIOTT; Trevor HARDING; Cal McDADE; John MORRISON; Jason PRYNNE.

CONFERENCE LEAGUE

No	DATE	OPPONENTS	H/A	RESULT	HOLLOWAY	WARWICK	BRAIDFORD	COURTNEY	JOHNSON	PURCHASE	FRAMPTON	D. HARDING	IRWIN	WALKER	THOMPSON	OTHERS
1	14/5	Oxford	A	L34-57	6 (4)	3 (4)	R/R	7 (5)	6 (5)	6+1 (4)	2 (4)	4+3 (4)	–	–	–	2 (4)
2	16/5	Mildenhall	A	L36-59	16 (5)	3+1 (4)	R/R	7 (6)	8 (5)	1 (4)	1+1 (2)	0 (4)	–	–	–	1+1 (2)
3	17/5	Carmarthen	H	L42-47	13 (6)	6+1 (4)	R/R	9+1 (6)	8 (5)	4+1 (5)	–	1 (3)	1+1 (1)	–	–	–
4	24/5	Armadale	H	L44-50	16 (7)	7+1 (5)	R/R	–	9+2 (6)	1 (3)	–	–	6+3 (5)	5 (4)	–	–
5	4/6	Weymouth	A	L47-48	13 (5)	9+1 (4)	–	–	9 (4)	2+1 (4)	1 (4)	–	6+ (5)	–	7 (5)	1 (4)
6	7/6	Mildenhall	H	L46-47	12+2 (6)	6+3 (5)	R/R	7 (4)	–	–	–	–	3+1 (4)	10+1 (5)	8+1 (6)	–
7	20/6	Newcastle	A	L39-53	11 (4)	8+1 (5)	6 (4)	–	5+1 (5)	–	–	–	3+3 (5)	–	3 (4)	3 (3)
8	26/6	Stoke	A	L36-57	10 (5)	2+1 (4)	5 (4)	–	4+1 (4)	–	–	1+1 (4)	3 (4)	–	11+1 (5)	–
9	11/7	Boston	A	W47-43	11+1 (5)	5+2 (4)	–	–	–	–	–	0 (3)	3 (5)	9+1 (4)	8+1 (4)	–
10	12/7	Newport	H	W65-27	11+1 (4)	10+2 (4)	–	–	9+3 (4)	–	–	4+1 (5)	8+1 (5)	11+1 (4)	12 (4)	–
11	18/7	Wimbledon	H	W53-41	9+1 (5)	7+2 (4)	–	–	0 (1)	–	–	1 (5)	9+1 (6)	–	15 (5)	–
12	26/7	Wimbledon	A	L38-57	20 (6)	11 (6)	R/R	–	–	–	4 (6)	2 (5)	1 (4)	–	–	4 (9)
13	1/8	Carmarthen	A	W46-43	7 (6)	8 (5)	–	–	14+3 (6)	–	2+2 (4)	4+2 (4)	11–1 (5)	–	R/R	–
14	8/8	Buxton	A	L38-56	13 (5)	7 (4)	–	–	8 (5)	4+1 (4)	1 (4)	3 (5)	2 (4)	–	–	–
15	21/8	Rye House	A	L26-65	6 (5)	1 (4)	0 (1)	–	9+2 (5)	–	–	0 (5)	7+1 (7)	3 (3)	–	–

CONFERENCE LEAGUE continued

No	DATE	OPPONENTS	H/A	RESULT	HOLLOWAY	WARWICK	BRAIDFORD	COURTNEY	JOHNSON	PURCHASE	FRAMPTON	D. HARDING	IRWIN	WALKER	THOMPSON	OTHERS
16	29/8	Boston	H	W55-40*	6 (2)	6+1 (4)	–	–	11+3 (5)	–	–	5+2 (5)	9+1 (5)	11 (5)	–	7+1 (4)
17	2/9	Newcastle	H	W58-37*	10 (4)	9+2 (6)	R/R	–	14+1 (5)	4+1 (3)	1 (4)	–	9+3 (4)	11 (4)	–	–
18	2/9	Buxton	H	W59-36*	11+1 (5)	8+2 (4)	–	–	15 (5)	2 (4)	2 (3)	–	10+1 (5)	11+1 (4)	–	–
19	4/9	Armadale	A	L33-59	R/R	10+2 (6)	–	–	13 (6)	5 (4)	0 (4)	–	4+2 (6)	–	–	1+1 (4)
20	12/9	Stoke	H	L43-47	13+2 (6)	3+2 (5)	R/R	–	5+1 (3)	–	1 (3)	0 (1)	11+1 (7)	10 (5)	–	–
21	23/9	Weymouth	H	W55-39*	11 (4)	5 (4)	–	–	–	–	–	2+1 (4)	8+2 (5)	9+1 (4)	6 (4)	14+1 (5)
22	26/9	Newport	A	L43-49*	6 (3)	6 (5)	–	–	–	–	1+1 (4)	–	5+3 (7)	7 (4)	0 (1)	18 (6)
23	21/10	Rye House†	H	L39-49	–	11+1 (5)	R/R	–	–	3 (4)	2+1 (4)	–	2 (4)	12 (4)	–	9+1 (7)
24	21/10	Oxford	H	L41-52	–	15 (5)	R/R	–	–	2+1 (4)	1 (5)	–	8 (6)	9+1 (4)	–	6 (6)

*Denotes bonus-point victory

†Meeting abandoned after heat fourteen, with the result permitted to stand.

DETAILS OF OTHER RIDERS:

Match No. 7: John Morrison 3 (3); Match No. 9: Trevor Harding 11+1 (5); Match No. 11: Trevor Harding 12 (4); Match No. 12: Martin Elliott 0 (3); Match No. 13: Marc Andrews 0 (1); Match No. 16: Jason Prynne 7+1 (4); Match No. 19: Marc Andrews 1+1 (3); Cal McDade 0 (1); Match No. 21: Trevor Harding 14+1 (5); Match No. 22: Trevor Harding 18 (6); Match No. 23: Wayne Carter 9+1 (5); Danny Betson 0 (2); Match No. 24: Wayne Carter 5 (4); Marc Andrews 1 (2).

TACTICAL SUBSTITUTE AND TACTICAL RIDES, AS INCLUDED IN THE SCORES GRID:

Match No. 1: Johnson 2 points (TR); Holloway 0 points (TR); Match No. 2: Holloway 6 points (TR); Johnson 2 points (TR); Courtney 2 points (TS); Match No. 4: Holloway 6 points (TS); Johnson 4 points (TR); Walker 0 points (TR); Match No. 5: Warwick 6 points (TR); Thompson 0 points (TR); Match No. 7: Braidford 4 points (TR); Holloway 4 points (TR); Match No. 8: Thompson 4 points (TR); Braidford 2 points (TR); Match No. 12: Holloway 6 points (TR); Warwick 4 points (TR); Frampton 0 points (TS); Match No. 14: Holloway 6 points (TR); Warwick 2 points (TR); Match No. 15: Johnson 2 points (TR); Holloway 0 points (TR); Match No. 19: Johnson 4 points (TR); Warwick 2 points (TR); Match No. 22: T. Harding 4 points (TS); Match No. 23: Walker 6 points (TR); Carter 4 points (TR); Match No. 24: Warwick 6 points (TR); Carter 0 points (TR).

CONFERENCE LEAGUE AVERAGES

Rider	Mts	Rds	Pts	Bon	Tot	Avge	Max
Trevor Harding	4	20	53	2	55	11.00	1 Full; 1 Paid
Simon Walker	13	54	115	6	121	8.96	2 Paid
Malcolm Holloway	21	102	217	8	225	8.82	1 Paid
Jason Prynne	1	4	7	1	8	8.00	–
Chris Johnson	17	79	140	17	157	7.95	1 Full; 2 Paid
Mark Thompson	9	38	68	3	71	7.47	2 Full
Danny Warwick	24	110	156	25	181	6.58	1 Paid
Wayne Carter	2	9	12	1	13	5.78	–
Jamie Courtney	4	21	29	1	30	5.71	–
Nathan Irwin	22	109	129	26	155	5.69	1 Paid
John Morrison	1	3	3	0	3	4.00	–
James Purchase	11	43	34	6	40	3.72	–
Steve Braidford	3	9	8	0	8	3.56	–
Daniel Harding	14	57	27	10	37	2.60	–

SWINDON: back row, left to right: Simon Walker, Marc Andrews, James Purchase, Jamie Courtney, Danny Warwick, Nathan Irwin, Martin Satchell (Team Manager). Front, kneeling: Daniel Harding, Chris Johnson. On bike: Malcolm Holloway.

Rider	Mts	Rds	Pts	Bon	Tot	Avge	Max
Marc Andrews	3	6	2	1	3	2.00	–
Jordan Frampton	13	51	19	5	24	1.88	–
Danny Betson	1	2	0	0	0	0.00	–
Martin Elliott	1	3	0	0	0	0.00	–
Cal McDade	1	1	0	0	0	0.00	–

OTHER MEETINGS

19 March: Conference Challenge

Weymouth 47 Swindon 46 (Steve Braidford 14+1; Malcolm Holloway 9; Chris Johnson 8; Daniel Harding 7+2; James Purchase 5+2; Marc Andrews 2+1; Jordan Frampton 1+1).

4 July: Festival of Speed (staged at Sittingbourne)

FIRST SEMI-FINAL: Wimbledon 24, Weymouth 19, Coventry 11. SECOND SEMI-FINAL: Swindon 24 (Chris Johnson 8; Danny Warwick 6+1; Nathan Irwin 5+3; Steve Braidford 5+2), Armadale 16, Sittingbourne 14. FINAL: Wimbledon 21, Weymouth 20, Swindon 13 (Chris Johnson 6; Danny Warwick 5; Jordan Frampton 1+1; Nathan Irwin 1+1).

WEYMOUTH HAVEN WILDCATS

ADDRESS: Wessex Stadium (2), Radipole Lane, Weymouth, Dorset, DT4 9XJ.
CLUB CHAIRMAN: Brian White.
TRACK LENGTH: 223 metres.
TRACK RECORD: 53.5 seconds – Paul Lee (14/05/04).
FIRST MEETING: 15 August 2003.
YEARS OF OPERATION: 2003 Open; 2004 Conference League.

PREVIOUS VENUE: Wessex Stadium (1), Radipole Lane, Weymouth, Dorset.
YEARS OF OPERATION: 1954 Open; 1955 National League Division Two; 1962-63 Open; 1964 Metropolitan League; 1965 Open; 1966-67 Training; 1968 British League Division 2; 1969-70 Training; 1971-73 Open & Training; 1974 British League Division Two; 1975-84 National League; 1985 Open & Training.

CLUB HONOURS

PAIRS CHAMPIONS: 1982, 1983.

RIDER ROSTER 2004

Wayne BARRETT; Matt BATES; Chris COURAGE; Chris FERGUSON; Daniel GIFFARD; Jack GLEDHILL; David MASON; Jason PRYNNE; Mark THOMPSON; Carl WARWICK.

OTHER APPEARANCES/GUESTS (official matches only):

Andrew BLACKBURN; Corey BLACKMAN; Paul CANDY; Scott CHESTER; Clayton CHUBB; Justin ELKINS; Martin ELLIOTT; Grant HAYES; Thomas HILL; Shane HOOPER; Sam HURST; Nathan IRWIN; Billy LEGG; Keith MABEN; Wayne PARKER; Mark RICHARDSON; Nick SIMMONS; Danny WARWICK; Rhys WILDING; Dean WILSON.

CONFERENCE LEAGUE

No	DATE	OPPONENTS	H/A	RESULT	MASON	THOMPSON	D. WARWICK	COURAGE	GLEDHILL	HOOPER	C. WARWICK	PRYNNE	BARRETT	GIFFARD	FERGUSON	OTHERS
1	21/3	Newport	A	D45-45	–	R/R	5+2 (4)	13 (6)	5+2 (4)	1 (1)	–	–	–	–	–	21+2 (15)
2	2/4	Carmarthen	H	L42-48	14+1 (6)	R/R	5 (5)	11 (6)	9 (5)	–	–	–	–	–	–	3 (8)
3	17/4	Armadale†	A	L21-53	R/R	0 (2)	4 (5)	–	4 (5)	–	2+1 (5)	–	–	–	–	11 (7)
4	2/5	Mildenhall	A	L32-60	9+1 (5)	2 (4)	–	13+1 (5)	3+1 (5)	–	1 (4)	2 (4)	–	–	–	2 (3)
5	3/5	Wimbledon	H	L45-47	17 (5)	3+2 (4)	–	11+2 (5)	11+1 (7)	0 (3)	3+2 (5)	0 (1)	–	–	–	–
6	7/5	Buxton	H	W47-42	12+1 (5)	3+1 (4)	–	7 (5)	5+1 (4)	0 (3)	10 (5)	10 (4)	–	–	–	–
7	21/5	Newport	H	W55-37*	14+1 (5)	–	–	9 (4)	12+2 (6)	3 (3)	4+1 (5)	8+2 (4)	5 (3)	–	–	–
8	23/5	Newcastle	A	L44-45	10 (5)	–	–	5+1 (4)	–	1+1 (3)	10+3 (6)	6+2 (4)	11 (5)	–	–	1 (3)
9	28/5	Newcastle	H	W51-44*	13+1 (5)	4 (4)	–	11 (5)	5 (3)	–	5+2 (5)	7+2 (4)	6 (1)	–	–	–
10	4/6	Swindon	H	W48-47	8+1 (5)	–	–	3+1 (4)	6+1 (4)	–	4+1 (4)	9 (4)	6+2 (4)	12+1 (5)	–	–
11	13/6	Rye House	A	L30-61	12+1 (5)	–	–	6 (5)	2 (6)	–	–	0 (1)	3 (2)	2 (4)	5+2 (7)	–
12	16/6	Wimbledon	A	W47-43*	6+2 (4)	–	–	6 (4)	1 (3)	–	2 (4)	–	12 (5)	15 (5)	5+1 (5)	–
13	18/6	Rye House	H	W59-34	7+1 (4)	–	–	13 (5)	8+3 (4)	–	6+4 (4)	–	9 (5)	9+2 (4)	7+2 (4)	–
14	2/7	Stoke	H	W57-36	11 (4)	–	–	8+1 (4)	10+1 (6)	–	3+1 (4)	–	9+1 (4)	11+1 (5)	5+1 (3)	–
15	20/7	Armadale	H	W46-45	12 (5)	–	–	5 (4)	4+2 (4)	–	3+2 (3)	–	7 (5)	8+2 (4)	7+2 (5)	–
16	13/8	Mildenhall	H	L35-58	R/R	–	–	9 (6)	3 (6)	–	–	–	5 (6)	11 (5)	6+2 (4)	1 (3)
17	15/8	Buxton	A	L33-59	R/R	–	–	15 (6)	0 (3)	–	7+1 (7)	–	4+1 (4)	7+1 (6)	–	0 (4)
18	20/8	Oxford	A	L39-54	11+2 (6)	–	–	5+1 (5)	0 (3)	–	–	–	11 (6)	6 (5)	6+2 (5)	R/R
19	24/8	Oxford	H	L45-48	10+1 (5)	–	–	8 (5)	–	–	3+1 (4)	–	6+2 (4)	9 (4)	3+1 (4)	6+1 (4)
20	30/8	Boston	H	W55-40	14+1 (5)	–	–	11 (5)	6+2 (4)	–	9+1 (6)	–	13+2 (5)	R/R	2+1 (5)	–
21	19/9	Carmarthen	A	W48-42	14+1 (6)	–	–	10+2 (5)	5+1 (6)	–	–	–	R/R	14 (6)	5 (4)	0 (3)
22	23/9	Swindon	A	L39-55	6 (4)	–	–	8 (4)	4+2 (5)	–	–	–	10+2 (5)	9+1 (4)	2+1 (4)	0 (4)
23	11/10	Boston	A	L44-50*	13 (6)	–	–	–	8+1 (6)	–	–	–	10 (4)	12+1 (5)	1 (3)	0 (6)
24	16/10	Stoke	A	L40-50*	R/R	–	–	10 (6)	8 (6)	–	–	–	–	14 (5)	6+4 (6)	2 (7)

*Denotes bonus-point victory

†Meeting abandoned after heat twelve, with the result permitted to stand.

DETAILS OF OTHER RIDERS:

Match No. 1: Paul Candy 9+1 (6); Nathan Irwin 7+1 (4); Justin Elkins 5 (5); Match No. 2: Paul Candy 3 (5); Nathan Irwin 0 (3); Match No. 3: Corey Blackman 9 (4); Keith Maben 2 (3); Match No. 4: Rhys Wilding 2 (3); Match No. 8: Andrew Blackburn 1 (3); Match No. 16: Matt Bates 1 (3); Match No. 17: Matt Bates 0 (4); Match No. 18: Corey Blackman R/R; Match No. 19: Nick Simmons 6+1 (4);

Match No. 21: Matt Bates 0 (3); Match No. 22: Billy Legg 0 (4); Match No. 23: Mark Richardson 0 (3); Matt Bates 0 (3); Match No. 24: Andrew Blackburn 1 (3); Grant Hayes 1 (4).

TACTICAL SUBSTITUTE AND TACTICAL RIDES, AS INCLUDED IN THE SCORES GRID:

Match No. 3: Blackman 4 points (TR); Match No. 4: Courage 4 points (TR); Mason 2 points (TR); Match No. 5: Mason 6 points (TR); Match No. 10: Giffard 6 points (TR); Match No. 11: Mason 6 points (TR); Barrett 2 points (TR); Match No. 16: Giffard 6 points (TR); Barrett 0 points (TR); Match No. 17: Courage 6 points (TR); Giffard 0 points (TR); Match No. 18: Mason 6 points (TR); Match No. 22: Giffard 4 points (TR); Barrett 4 points (TR); Match No. 23: Giffard 6 points (TR); Mason 2 points (TS).

CONFERENCE LEAGUE AVERAGES

Rider	Mts	Rds	Pts	Bon	Tot	Avge	Max
David Mason	19	95	202	15	217	9.14	2 paid
Daniel Giffard	14	67	128	9	137	8.18	1 full
Wayne Barrett	16	71	124	10	134	7.55	1 paid
Chris Courage	22	108	192	9	201	7.44	–
Jason Prynne	8	26	42	6	48	7.38	–
Corey Blackman	1	4	7	0	7	7.00	–
Nick Simmons	1	4	6	1	7	7.00	–
Chris Ferguson	13	59	60	19	79	5.36	–
Jack Gledhill	22	105	119	20	139	5.30	–
Carl Warwick	15	71	72	20	92	5.18	–
Paul Candy	2	11	12	1	13	4.73	–
Nathan Irwin	2	7	7	1	8	4.57	–
Danny Warwick	3	14	14	2	16	4.57	–
Justin Elkins	1	5	5	0	5	4.00	–
Mark Thompson	5	18	12	3	15	3.33	–
Keith Maben	1	3	2	0	2	2.67	–
Rhys Wilding	1	3	2	0	2	2.67	–
Shane Hooper	5	13	5	1	6	1.85	–
Andrew Blackburn	2	6	2	0	2	1.33	–
Grant Hayes	1	4	1	0	1	1.00	–
Matt Bates	4	13	1	0	1	0.31	–
Billy Legg	1	4	0	0	0	0.00	–
Mark Richardson	1	3	0	0	0	0.00	–

CONFERENCE TROPHY

No	DATE	OPPONENTS	H/A	RESULT	MASON	THOMPSON	BARRETT	COURAGE	C. WARWICK	GLEDHILL	BLACKMAN	GIFFARD	FERGUSON	BATES	OTHERS
1	14/5	Mildenhall	H	L43-52	11+2 (5)	3 (4)	8+1 (4)	15 (5)	3+2 (4)	3 (5)	–	–	–	–	0 (3)
2	17/5	Sheffield	A	L34-60	10 (5)	7+1 (5)	9 (5)	4 (4)	1 (5)	2 (2)	–	–	–	–	1 (3)
3	23/7	Wimbledon	H	W48-45	11 (5)	–	7+1 (4)	9 (5)	–	7+2 (4)	3 (4)	7 (4)	4+2 (4)	–	–
4	30/7	Coventry	H	W64-29	10+2 (4)	–	10+1 (4)	9+1 (4)	–	7+2 (4)	10+3 (5)	9+1 (4)	9+3 (5)	–	–
5	22/8	Mildenhall	A	L42-53	11+2 (6)	–	2+1 (4)	6 (5)	3+1 (5)	–	R/R	18 (6)	2 (4)	–	–
6	25/8	Wimbledon†	A	D42-42*	8 (4)	–	10+1 (4)	6 (4)	4 (4)	3+1 (4)	–	0 (1)	11+1 (7)	–	–

WEYMOUTH: back row, left to right: Mike Vernam (Team Manager), Shane Hooper, Danny Warwick, Jack Gledhill, Brian White (Chairman). Front row: Paul Candy, Chris Courage, Nathan Irwin, Justin Elkins.

CONFERENCE TROPHY continued

No	DATE	OPPONENTS	H/A	RESULT	MASON	THOMPSON	BARRETT	COURAGE	C. WARWICK	GLEDHILL	BLACKMAN	GIFFARD	FERGUSON	BATES	OTHERS
7	18/9	King's Lynn	A	W47-43	9+1 (5)	–	11 (5)	3+1 (4)	–	9+1 (4)	–	8+1 (4)	7+3 (5)	–	0 (3)
8	24/9	Buxton	H	W52-43	13 (5)	–	6+1 (4)	7+1 (4)	–	12+2 (6)	–	9 (5)	4+1 (3)	1+1 (3)	–
9	26/9	Buxton	A	L39-53	8+1 (5)	–	3 (4)	5 (4)	–	0 (3)	–	14 (5)	8+1 (6)	–	1 (3)
10	27/9	Coventry	A	W47-46*	8 (4)	–	7+1 (4)	9+1 (5)	–	9+1 (5)	–	10+1 (5)	4+3 (4)	–	0 (3)
11	24/10	Sheffield	H	W56-39	14+1 (5)	–	R/R	11 (4)	–	–	–	13+1 (5)	–	8+1 (6)	10+3 (7)
12	31/10	King's Lynn	H	W62-31*	11+1 (4)	–	R/R	12 (4)	–	16+3 (7)	–	12 (4)	–	6+1 (7)	5+2 (4)

*Denotes bonus-point victory

†Meeting abandoned after heat fourteen, with the result permitted to stand.

DETAILS OF OTHER RIDERS:

Match No. 1: Clayton Chubb 0 (3); Match No. 2: Andrew Blackburn 1 (3); Match No. 7: Dean Wilson 0 (3); Match No. 9: Thomas Hill 1 (3); Match No. 10: Scott Chester 0 (3); Match No. 11: Sam Hurst 10+3 (7); Match No. 12: Wayne Parker 5+2 (4).

TACTICAL SUBSTITUTE AND TACTICAL RIDES, AS INCLUDED IN THE SCORES GRID:

Match No. 1: Courage 6 points (TR); Mason 4 points (TR); Match No. 2: Barrett 6 points (TR); Mason 2 points (TR); Thompson 0 points (TS); Match No. 5: Giffard 6 points (TR); Mason 4 points (TR); Match No. 9: Giffard 4 points (TR); Mason 2 points (TR).

CONFERENCE TROPHY AVERAGES

Rider	Mts	Rds	Pts	Bon	Tot	Avge	Max
Daniel Giffard	10	43	95	4	99	9.21	1 full
David Mason	12	57	118	10	128	8.98	3 paid
Chris Courage	12	52	93	4	97	7.46	1 full
Sam Hurst	1	7	10	3	13	7.43	–
Wayne Barrett	10	42	70	7	77	7.33	–
Jack Gledhill	10	44	68	12	80	7.27	–
Corey Blackman	2	9	13	3	16	7.11	–
Wayne Parker	1	4	5	2	7	7.00	–
Chris Ferguson	8	38	49	14	63	6.63	–
Mark Thompson	2	9	10	1	11	4.89	–
Matt Bates	3	16	15	3	18	4.50	–
Carl Warwick	4	18	11	3	14	3.11	–
Andrew Blackburn	1	3	1	0	1	1.33	–
Thomas Hill	1	3	1	0	1	1.33	–
Scott Chester	1	3	0	0	0	0.00	–
Clayton Chubb	1	3	0	0	0	0.00	–
Dean Wilson	1	3	0	0	0	0.00	–

KNOCK-OUT CUP

No	DATE	OPPONENTS	H/A	RESULT	MASON	D. WARWICK	THOMPSON	PRYNNE	COURAGE	C. WARWICK	GLEDHILL	BARRETT	GIFFARD	FERGUSON	OTHERS
1	9/4	Stoke	H	W53-41	11 (6)	6+1 (5)	R/R	11+2 (5)	13+1 (6)	2+2 (3)	10+2 (5)	–	–	–	–
2	12/5	Stoke	A	W47-42*	14 (5)	–	2 (4)	–	10+2 (4)	0 (4)	9+1 (7)	12 (4)	–	–	0 (3)
3	25/6	Wimbledon	H	L47-48	9+1 (5)	–	–	–	8 (4)	4+2 (4)	7+1 (4)	11 (5)	7+2 (4)	1 (4)	–
4	21/7	Wimbledon	A	L38-56	12+1 (5)	–	–	–	1 (5)	–	1 (3)	12+1 (5)	7+2 (4)	5 (5)	0 (3)

*Denotes aggregate victory

NOTE: Chris Courage is not credited with a paid maximum in the match at Stoke, as he missed his second programmed ride (heat six) through a two-minute exclusion.

DETAILS OF OTHER RIDERS:

Match No. 2: Andrew Blackburn 0 (3); Match No. 4: Martin Elliott 0 (3).

TACTICAL SUBSTITUTE AND TACTICAL RIDES, AS INCLUDED IN THE SCORES GRID:

Match No. 4: Barrett 4 points (TR); Mason 4 points (TR); Courage 0 points (TS).

OTHER MEETINGS

19 March: Conference Challenge

Weymouth 47 (Chris Courage 11+1; Justin Elkins 9; Mark Thompson 8; Jack Gledhill 8; Danny Warwick 5+1; Paul Candy 4; Nathan Irwin 2) Swindon 46.

16 April: Conference League

Weymouth 24 (David Mason 9; Jack Gledhill 6; Chris Courage 5; Danny Warwick 4; Jason Prynne 0; Carl Warwick 0; Mark Thompson R/R) Boston 30 – meeting abandoned after heat nine.

11 June: Vic Harding Memorial Three-Team Tournament

Weymouth 20 (Chris Courage 10; Jack Gledhill 9; Shane Hooper (Res) 1+1; David Mason DNR; Daniel Giffard DNR), Hackney 25 (Ben Powell 11; Lee Smart 9; James Purchase 4+3; Sam Hurst 1), Sunderland 25 (Chris Ferguson 9; Karlis Ezergailis 8; Carl Warwick 4; Marc Andrews (Res) 4; Paul Candy DNR). VIC HARDING MEMORIAL TROPHY FINAL: 1st Gledhill; 2nd Smart; 3rd Ferguson; 4th Powell. Note: Mason, Giffard and Candy were all severely delayed by traffic congestion.

4 July: Festival of Speed (Staged at Sittingbourne)

FIRST SEMI-FINAL: Wimbledon 24, Weymouth 19 (David Mason 9; Chris Courage 5; Chris Ferguson 3+1; Daniel Giffard 2+1), Coventry 11. SECOND SEMI-FINAL: Swindon 24, Armadale 16, Sittingbourne 14. FINAL: Wimbledon 21, Weymouth 20 (David Mason 8; Chris Courage 6; Daniel Giffard 3+1; Chris Ferguson 3), Swindon 13.

10 September: Conference Trophy

Weymouth 5 (David Mason 3; Nick Simmons 2+1; Daniel Giffard DNR; Wayne Barrett DNR; Chris Courage DNR; Jack Gledhill DNR; Carl Warwick DNR) Sheffield 1 – meeting abandoned after heat one.

9 October: 50th Anniversary Meeting

Great Britain Under-21 54 (Ritchie Hawkins 12; Chris Schramm 10+2; Richard Hall 8; Daniel Giffard 7+1; Ben Barker 6+2; Lee Smart 6+1; Jack Gledhill 5+4) Rest of the World 39 (Karlis Ezergailis 14; Tom Brown 13; Chris Ferguson 4; Justin Elkins 4; Troy Batchelor 2; Matt Bates 2; Daniel Harding R/R).

INDIVIDUAL MEETINGS

26 March: Wessex Rosebowl

1st Chris Courage 14; 2nd Jason Prynne 13; =3rd Wayne Barrett, Ben Barker 11; Danny Warwick 10; James Purchase 7; Dean Felton 7; Nathan Irwin 5; Matthew Wright 4; Carl Warwick (Res) 4; Shane Hooper 2; Jack Gledhill 1; Paul Candy 1.

3 May: British Under-15 Championship (First Round)

1st Josh Auty 15; 2nd Shane Waldron 14; 3rd Scott Campos 12; Simon Lambert 11; James Humby 10; Gary Cottham 9; Matt Bates 9; Kyle Hughes 8; Sam Hurst 6; George Piper 6; Aaron Baseby 5; Ben Hopwood 5; Joe Reynolds 4; Lewis Bridger (Res) 3; Trevor Heath 2; Tim Webster 0; Ben Hannon 0; Andy Braithwaite (Res) DNR. SERIES POINTS: 1st Auty 17; 2nd Waldron 15; 3rd Campos 14; Lambert 13; Humby 12; Cottham 11; Bates 11; Hughes 9; Hurst 8; Piper 8; Baseby 6; Hopwood 6; Reynolds 4; Bridger 3; Heath 2; Webster 1; Hannon 1; Braithwaite 1.

6 August: Weymouth Open Championship

1st David Mason 15; 2nd Justin Elkins 14; 3rd Lee Smart 13; Chris Johnson 12; Jack Gledhill 9; Ben Barker 9; Chris Courage 9; Andre Cross 7; Carl Warwick 6; Karlis Ezergailis 6; Chris Ferguson 5; Matt Bates 5; David Hooper (Res) 3; Paul Candy 2; Sam Martin 1; Sam Hurst 0; Kyle Hughes 0.

WIMBLEDON GMB DONS

ADDRESS: Wimbledon Stadium, Plough Lane, London, SW17 0BL.
CLUB CHAIRMEN: Ian Perkin & David Croucher.
TRACK LENGTH: 250 metres.
TRACK RECORD: 59.5 seconds – Wayne Barrett (18/07/02).
FIRST MEETING: 28 May 1928.
YEARS OF OPERATION: 1928 Open; 1929-31 Southern League; 1932-33 National League; 1934 National League & Reserve League; 1935-36 National League; 1937-39 National League Division One; 1946 National League; 1947-56 National League Division One; 1957-64 National League; 1965-67 British League; 1968-74 British League Division One; 1975-84 British League; 1985-90 National League; 1991 British League Division One; 2002-04 Conference League.

CLUB HONOURS

NATIONAL TROPHY WINNERS: 1938, 1950, 1951, 1953, 1956, 1959, 1960, 1962.
RAC CUP WINNERS: 1954.
LEAGUE CHAMPIONS: 1954, 1955, 1956, 1958, 1959, 1960, 1961.
BRITANNIA SHIELD WINNERS: 1959.
KNOCK-OUT CUP WINNERS: 1962, 1968, 1969, 1970.
PAIRS CHAMPIONS: 2004.

RIDER ROSTER 2004

Wayne BROADHURST; Mark BURROWS; James CLEMENT; Peter COLLYER; Andre CROSS; Barrie EVANS; Gavin HEDGE; Marc NORRIS; James THEOBALD; Matthew WRIGHT.

OTHER APPEARANCES/GUESTS (official matches only):
Wayne BARRETT; Peter BOAST; James HUMBY; Jon STEVENS.

CONFERENCE LEAGUE

No	DATE	OPPONENTS	H/A	RESULT	EVANS	WRIGHT	BROADHURST	HEDGE	BURROWS	CROSS	CLEMENT	NORRIS	THEOBALD	COLLYER	OTHERS
1	31/3	Mildenhall	H	L45-48	10 (5)	4 (4)	–	6+1 (4)	5+1 (4)	6 (4)	3+2 (4)	–	–	–	11+2 (5)
2	11/4	Boston	A	L43-52	13+2 (6)	4+1 (4)	8 (4)	1+1 (4)	14 (5)	2 (4)	1+1 (3)	–	–	–	–
3	14/4	Carmarthen	H	W54-40	8+2 (4)	8 (4)	11+3 (5)	9 (4)	14 (5)	0 (3)	4 (5)	–	–	–	–
4	25/4	Mildenhall	A	L36-59	3 (4)	2+1 (4)	8+1 (5)	3+1 (4)	15 (5)	5+1 (5)	0 (3)	–	–	–	–
5	3/5	Weymouth	A	W47-45	9 (5)	6+2 (4)	12 (5)	6+2 (4)	6 (4)	6+1 (5)	2+1 (3)	–	–	–	–
6	26/5	Newcastle	H	W55-43	10 (6)	7+3 (5)	R/R	5+1 (4)	18 (6)	4+2 (4)	11 (5)	–	–	–	–
7	31/5	Rye House	A	L41-52	15+1 (6)	5+1 (5)	R/R	3+1 (4)	12 (6)	5 (5)	1+1 (4)	–	–	–	–
8	5/6	Armadale	A	L37-58	10 (5)	2 (4)	4 (4)	5+1 (4)	12 (5)	2 (4)	2+1 (4)	–	–	–	–
9	6/6	Newcastle†	A	W41-31*	R/R	3+1 (4)	6+2 (4)	10 (4)	10 (4)	10+2 (5)	2+1 (3)	–	–	–	–
10	9/6	Oxford	H	L47-48	R/R	2+1 (4)	8+3 (6)	8 (5)	17 (6)	3+1 (3)	9 (6)	–	–	–	–
11	16/6	Weymouth	H	L43-47	10 (5)	2+1 (3)	5+3 (4)	4 (4)	9+1 (5)	–	12+1 (6)	–	1 (3)	–	–

CONFERENCE LEAGUE continued

No	DATE	OPPONENTS	H/A	RESULT	EVANS	WRIGHT	BROADHURST	HEDGE	BURROWS	CROSS	CLEMENT	NORRIS	THEOBALD	COLLYER	OTHERS
12	14/7	Newport	H	W65-25	14+1 (5)	9+3 (4)	10+1 (4)	9+2 (4)	11+1 (4)	4+1 (4)	8+2 (5)	–	–	–	–
13	18/7	Swindon	A	L41-53	R/R	5+2 (4)	7 (5)	2+2 (4)	11 (6)	5+1 (4)	11+2 (7)	–	–	–	–
14	26/7	Swindon	H	W57-38*	R/R	7+2 (5)	10+1 (5)	–	16 (6)	5 (4)	11+3 (6)	8+1 (4)	–	–	–
15	4/8	Boston	H	W47-46	12+2 (5)	3+1 (4)	7+1 (4)	–	14 (5)	2+1 (3)	5+2 (5)	4+1 (4)	–	–	–
16	9/8	Armadale	H	W59-37*	12+2 (5)	5 (4)	7+2 (4)	–	15 (5)	5 (4)	8+2 (5)	7+2 (4)	–	–	–
17	22/8	Carmarthen	A	W55-38*	12 (4)	4+2 (4)	11+1 (5)	–	12+1 (5)	2 (1)	7+3 (7)	7+1 (4)	–	–	–
18	4/9	Stoke	A	L42-51	14 (6)	1+1 (4)	16 (6)	–	R/R	–	6+1 (6)	–	4 (5)	–	1+1 (3)
19	5/9	Newport	A	L43-47*	12 (6)	8 (5)	11 (6)	–	R/R	–	5+2 (4)	–	6+2 (6)	–	1+1 (3)
20	15/9	Buxton	H	W51-44	8 (4)	9+2 (5)	6+2 (4)	–	12 (5)	–	9 (5)	–	1 (3)	6+4 (4)	–
21	29/9	Stoke	H	W62-32*	12 (4)	7+2 (4)	9+1 (4)	–	11+1 (4)	–	9+1 (5)	–	9+1 (5)	5+1 (4)	–
22	1/10	Oxford	A	L43-45	11+1 (5)	4+4 (4)	8 (4)	–	10 (5)	–	4+1 (5)	–	6+1 (4)	–	0 (3)
23	23/10	Buxton	A	L41-48	7 (4)	8+2 (4)	11 (5)	–	11 (5)	–	4 (5)	–	0 (0)	0 (0)	–
24	24/10	Rye House	H®	L43-53	11 (5)	7+2 (4)	7+1 (4)	–	13+1 (6)	–	1 (4)	–	1 (3)	3+1 (4)	–

*Denotes bonus-point victory

†Meeting abandoned after heat twelve, with the result permitted to stand.

®Match raced at Rye House.

DETAILS OF OTHER RIDERS:

Match No. 1: Wayne Barrett 11+2 (5); Match No. 18: Jon Stevens 1+1 (3); Match No. 19: James Humby 1+1 (3); Match No. 22: James Humby 0 (3).

TACTICAL SUBSTITUTE AND TACTICAL RIDES, AS INCLUDED IN THE SCORES GRID:

Match No. 1: Barrett 6 points (TR); Burrows 0 points (TR); Match No. 2: Burrows 4 points (TR); Broadhurst 4 points (TR); Evans 4 points (TS); Match No. 4: Burrows 6 points (TR); Broadhurst 4 points (TR); Match No. 7: Burrows 6 points (TR); Evans 2 points (TR); Match No. 8: Burrows 6 points (TR); Evans 4 points (TR); Match No. 13: Burrows 4 points (TR); Clement 4 points (TR); Match No. 15: Evans 6 points (TR); Match No. 18: Broadhurst 6 points (TR); Match No. 23: Wright 4 points (TR); Burrows 0 points (TR); Match No. 24: Broadhurst 4 points (TR); Evans 4 points (TR); Burrows 4 points (TS).

CONFERENCE LEAGUE AVERAGES

Rider	Mts	Rds	Pts	Bon	Tot	Avge	Max
Mark Burrows	22	111	253	6	259	9.33	2 Full; 2 Paid
Barrie Evans	20	99	203	11	214	8.65	2 Full; 1 Paid
Wayne Broadhurst	21	97	173	22	195	8.04	–
Wayne Barrett	1	5	8	2	10	8.00	–
Marc Norris	4	16	26	5	31	7.75	–
Peter Collyer	4	12	14	6	20	6.67	–
Gavin Hedge	13	53	71	12	83	6.26	–
Matthew Wright	24	100	120	34	154	6.16	1 Paid
James Clement	24	115	133	27	160	5.57	–
Andre Cross	16	62	66	10	76	4.90	–
James Theobald	8	29	28	4	32	4.41	–
Jon Stevens	1	3	1	1	2	2.67	–
James Humby	2	6	1	1	2	1.33	–

WIMBLEDON: back row, left to right: Gavin Hedge, Matthew Wright, Jamie Courtney, Barrie Evans, James Clement, Mark Burrows. Front row: James Theobald, Gareth Hickmott, Matt Burrows (Mascot). On bike: Wayne Broadhurst.

CONFERENCE TROPHY

No	DATE	OPPONENTS	H/A	RESULT	EVANS	WRIGHT	BROADHURST	HEDGE	BURROWS	CROSS	CLEMENT	NORRIS	THEOBALD	COLLYER	OTHERS
1	7/4	Buxton	H	W57-38	9 (4)	7+2 (4)	7+2 (4)	9+1 (5)	13+1 (5)	6+1 (4)	6+1 (4)	–	–	–	–
2	19/4	Coventry	A	W51-40	12+3 (5)	7 (4)	15 (5)	5 (4)	9 (4)	3 (5)	0 (3)	–	–	–	–
3	17/5	Sheffield	A	L36-58	7 (5)	2 (4)	4 (2)	5+1 (4)	12 (5)	5+1 (6)	1+1 (4)	–	–	–	–
4	30/6	Coventry	H	W55-39*	14 (5)	5+2 (4)	6+1 (4)	6+1 (4)	13+2 (5)	–	7+1 (4)	–	4+2 (4)	–	–
5	11/7	Mildenhall	A	L43-52	–	4 (4)	9 (4)	4+2 (4)	15 (5)	1 (3)	8+2 (7)	–	–	–	2+1 (3)
6	23/7	Weymouth	A	L45-48	14 (5)	3 (4)	6+1 (4)	–	13+2 (5)	4+1 (4)	1+1 (4)	4 (4)	–	–	–
7	28/7	King's Lynn	H	W53-41	8+1 (4)	2 (3)	11+1 (5)	–	11 (4)	3+2 (4)	8+1 (5)	10+1 (5)	–	–	–
8	11/8	Sheffield	H	W51-45	14 (6)	7+3 (5)	10+1 (6)	–	R/R	10+2 (4)	5 (4)	5+1 (5)	–	–	–
9	25/8	Weymouth†	H	D42-42	11+1 (4)	5+1 (4)	5 (4)	–	9 (4)	–	5+1 (5)	6+2 (4)	1 (3)	–	–
10	29/8	Buxton	A	L39-55*	9+1 (5)	2+2 (4)	15 (5)	–	2 (1)	–	8+1 (7)	–	1+1 (4)	2+1 (4)	–
11	18/9	King's Lynn	A	W55-41*	14 (5)	11+1 (5)	8+2 (4)	–	7+1 (4)	–	6 (4)	–	6+2 (4)	3+1 (4)	–
12	22/9	Mildenhall	H	W48-45	12+2 (5)	7 (4)	4+2 (4)	–	15 (5)	–	8+1 (5)	–	1 (3)	1 (4)	–

*Denotes bonus-point victory

†Meeting abandoned after heat fourteen, with the result permitted to stand.

DETAILS OF OTHER RIDER:

Match No. 5: Peter Boast 2+1 (3).

TACTICAL RIDES, AS INCLUDED IN THE SCORES GRID:

Match No. 3: Burrows 6 points (TR); Evans 2 points (TR); Match No. 5: Burrows 6 points (TR); Broadhurst 4 points (TR); Match No. 6: Burrows 6 points (TR); Match No. 10: Broadhurst 6 points (TR); Evans 2 points (TR).

CONFERENCE TROPHY AVERAGES

Rider	Mts	Rds	Pts	Bon	Tot	Avge	Max
Mark Burrows	11	47	110	6	116	9.87	1 Full; 1 Paid
Barrie Evans	11	53	122	8	130	9.81	2 Paid
Wayne Broadhurst	12	51	95	10	105	8.24	1 Full
Gavin Hedge	5	21	29	5	34	6.48	–
Marc Norris	4	18	25	4	29	6.44	–
Matthew Wright	12	49	62	11	73	5.96	–
James Clement	12	56	63	10	73	5.21	–
Andre Cross	7	30	32	7	39	5.20	1 Paid
Peter Boast	1	3	2	1	3	4.00	–
James Theobald	5	18	13	5	18	4.00	–
Peter Collyer	3	12	6	2	8	2.67	–

KNOCK-OUT CUP

No	DATE	OPPONENTS	H/A	RESULT	EVANS	WRIGHT	BROADHURST	HEDGE	BURROWS	CLEMENT	CROSS	NORRIS	THEOBALD	COLLYER
1	16/5	Sittingbourne	A	W53-40	13 (5)	7+1 (4)	10 (4)	2 (4)	13+1 (5)	2+1 (4)	6+2 (4)	-	-	-
2	19/5	Sittingbourne	H	W55-38*	15+1 (6)	7+4 (5)	R/R	14 (6)	7+1 (5)	6+1 (4)	6 (4)	-	-	-
3	25/6	Weymouth	A	W48-47	15 (5)	2 (4)	8+1 (4)	1+1 (3)	12+2 (6)	2+1 (3)	8 (5)	-	-	-
4	21/7	Weymouth	H	W56-38*	6 (4)	9+2 (4)	6+1 (4)	-	14+1 (5)	11+1 (5)	4+1 (4)	6 (4)	-	-
5	1/9	Boston	H	L38-56	14 (6)	4+1 (4)	7 (5)	-	R/R	7+2 (7)	-	0 (1)	6 (5)	-
6	24/9	Boston	A	L43-54	13+2 (6)	7+1 (4)	4+1 (4)	-	15 (5)	1 (3)	-	-	2+1 (4)	1 (4)

*Denotes aggregate victory

TACTICAL SUBSTITUTE AND TACTICAL RIDES, AS INCLUDED IN THE SCORES GRID:

Match No. 3: Evans 4 points (TR); Burrows 4 points (TS); Broadhurst 2 points (TR); Match No. 5: Broadhurst 4 points (TR); Evans 4 points (TR); Match No. 6: Burrows 6 points (TR); Wright 4 points (TR); Evans 4 points (TS).

OTHER MEETINGS

12 May: Challenge

Wimbledon 33 (Mark Burrows 12; Wayne Broadhurst 9+1; Gavin Hedge 4+1; Barrie Evans 4; Andre Cross 2; Matthew Wright 1+1; James Clement 1) Great Britain Under-21 61 (James Wright 14; Chris Schramm 12+2; Ritchie Hawkins 10+1; Steve Boxall 9+1; William Lawson 7; Jason King 6+3; Ben Barker 3+1).

4 July: Festival of Speed (staged at Sittingbourne)

FIRST SEMI-FINAL: Wimbledon 24 (Barrie Evans 8; James Clement 7+1; Wayne Broadhurst 6+2; Matthew Wright 3+2), Weymouth 19, Coventry 11. SECOND SEMI-FINAL: Swindon 24, Armadale 16, Sittingbourne 14. FINAL: Wimbledon 21 (Barrie Evans 9; Wayne Broadhurst 8; James Clement 2; Matthew Wright 2), Weymouth 20, Swindon 13.

8 September: Conference League

Wimbledon 31 (Barrie Evans 7+1; James Clement 6+1; Matthew Wright 5; James Theobald 5+1; Wayne Broadhurst 5; Peter Collyer 2+2; Mark Burrows R/R) Rye House 35 – meeting abandoned after heat eleven.

6 October: Conference League

Wimbledon 8 (James Theobald 3; James Clement 2+1; Barrie Evans 2; Peter Collyer 1+1; Matthew Wright DNR; Wayne Broadhurst DNR; Mark Burrows DNR) Rye House 3 – meeting abandoned after heat two.

MAJOR BRITISH MEETINGS 2004

SUZUKI ELITE LEAGUE PAIRS CHAMPIONSHIP
SUPPORTED BY PEBLEY BEACH SUZUKI
11 APRIL, SWINDON

1st	SWINDON
2nd	BELLE VUE
3rd	EASTBOURNE
4th	PETERBOROUGH

GROUP A	QUALIFYING SCORES				TOTALS
BELLE VUE 25					
Jason Crump	3*	3*	2*	4	12 (3)
Joe Screen	4	4	3	2	13
POOLE 14					
Tony Rickardsson	2	4	4	X	10
Jason Lyons	0	0	2	2	4
COVENTRY 11					
Andreas Jonsson	2	2	3	4	11
Billy Janniro	0	0	0	R	0
SWINDON 25					
Leigh Adams	3*	4	4	4	15 (1)
Charlie Gjedde	4	3*	0	3*	10 (2)
OXFORD 15					
Travis McGowan	2*	0	2*	0	4 (2)
Sebastian Ulamek	3	2	3	3	11

GROUP B	QUALIFYING SCORES				TOTALS
WOLVERHAMPTON 16					
Mikael Max	3	4	3	4	14
David Howe	R	2	0	0	2
PETERBOROUGH 22					
Lee Richardson	2	3*	4	2	11 (1)
Lukas Dryml	4	4	3*	0	11 (1)
ARENA-ESSEX 10					
Mark Loram	2	R	0	3	5
Dean Barker	0	3	2	0	5
EASTBOURNE 26					
Nicki Pedersen	3*	4	4	4	15 (1)
Adam Shields	4	2	2	3*	11 (1)
IPSWICH 16					
Scott Nicholls	R	F	4	2*	6 (1)
Hans N. Andersen	2	3	2	3	10

RACE DETAILS

HEAT ONE:	Joe Screen, Jason Crump, Tony Rickardsson, Jason Lyons.
HEAT TWO:	Lukas Dryml, Mikael Max, Lee Richardson, David Howe (ret).
HEAT THREE:	Charlie Gjedde, Leigh Adams, Andreas Jonsson, Billy Janniro.
HEAT FOUR:	Adam Shields, Nicki Pedersen, Mark Loram, Dean Barker.
HEAT FIVE:	Tony Rickardsson, Sebastian Ulamek, Travis McGowan, Jason Lyons.
HEAT SIX:	Lukas Dryml, Lee Richardson, Hans N. Andersen, Scott Nicholls (ret).
HEAT SEVEN:	Joe Screen, Jason Crump, Andreas Jonsson, Billy Janniro.
HEAT EIGHT:	Mikael Max, Dean Barker, David Howe, Mark Loram (ret).
HEAT NINE:	Leigh Adams, Charlie Gjedde, Sebastian Ulamek, Travis McGowan.
HEAT TEN:	Nicki Pedersen, Hans N. Andersen, Adam Shields, Scott Nicholls (ret).
HEAT ELEVEN:	Tony Rickardsson, Andreas Jonsson, Jason Lyons, Billy Janniro.
HEAT TWELVE:	Lee Richardson, Lukas Dryml, Dean Barker, Mark Loram.
HEAT THIRTEEN:	Leigh Adams, Joe Screen, Jason Crump, Charlie Gjedde.
HEAT FOURTEEN:	Nicki Pedersen, Mikael Max, Adam Shields, David Howe.
HEAT FIFTEEN:	Andreas Jonsson, Sebastian Ulamek, Travis McGowan, Billy Janniro (ret).
HEAT SIXTEEN:	Scott Nicholls, Mark Loram, Hans N. Andersen, Dean Barker.
HEAT SEVENTEEN:	(Rerun twice) Leigh Adams, Charlie Gjedde, Jason Lyons, Tony Rickardsson (f, ex).
HEAT EIGHTEEN:	Nicki Pedersen, Adam Shields, Lee Richardson, Lukas Dryml.
HEAT NINETEEN:	Jason Crump, Sebastian Ulamek, Joe Screen, Travis McGowan.
HEAT TWENTY:	Mikael Max, Hans N. Andersen, Scott Nicholls, David Howe.
FIRST SEMI-FINAL:	Jason Crump, Joe Screen, Lukas Dryml, Lee Richardson.
SECOND SEMI-FINAL:	Leigh Adams, Charlie Gjedde, Nicki Pedersen, Adam Shields.
CONSOLATION FINAL:	Nicki Pedersen, Adam Shields, Lee Richardson, Lukas Dryml.
GRAND FINAL:	Jason Crump, Leigh Adams, Charlie Gjedde, Joe Screen.

ROLL OF HONOUR

NOTE: Known as the British League Pairs Championship from 1976-78 and the British Open Pairs Championship from 1984-87.

YEAR	FIRST	SECOND
1976	Ipswich (John Louis & Billy Sanders)	Coventry (Ole Olsen & Mitch Shirra)
1977	Ipswich (Billy Sanders & John Louis)	King's Lynn (Michael Lee & David Gagen)
1978	Cradley Heath (Steve Bastable & Bruce Penhall) & Coventry (Ole Olsen & Mitch Shirra) [shared]	
1979-83	Not staged	
1984	Belle Vue (Peter Collins & Chris Morton)	Reading (Mitch Shirra & Tim Hunt)
1985	Oxford (Hans Nielsen & Simon Wigg)	Reading (John Davis & Mitch Shirra)
1986	Oxford (Simon Wigg & Hans Nielsen)	Coventry (Kelvin Tatum & John Jorgensen)
1987	Oxford (Hans Nielsen & Andy Grahame)	Swindon (Mitch Shirra & Jimmy Nilsen)
1988-2003	Not staged	
2004	Swindon (Leigh Adams & Charlie Gjedde)	Belle Vue (Jason Crump & Joe Screen)

BRITISH UNDER-21 CHAMPIONSHIP FINAL

1 MAY, RYE HOUSE

1st RITCHIE HAWKINS
2nd STEVE BOXALL
3rd EDWARD KENNETT
4th JAMIE SMITH

	QUALIFYING SCORES					TOTAL
Jamie Smith	3	3	3	2	2	13
Edward Kennett	3	2	2	3	3	13
Steve Boxall	3	2	X	2	3	10
Ritchie Hawkins	2	3	1	3	1	10
Ben Wilson	1	0	3	3	2	9
Jason King	1	3	R	2	3	9
Daniel King	3	2	R	0	3	8
Jamie Robertson	1	1	3	3	0	8
James Wright	2	1	3	X	2	8
Rob Grant jr	0	3	2	1	1	7
William Lawson	1	2	2	1	1	7
Darren Mallett	0	0	1	2	2	5
Richard Hall	2	0	2	X	R	4
Adam Allott	2	1	1	R	0	4
James Brundle	0	1	1	1	0	3
Lee Smart	0	0	0	0	1	1

RACE DETAILS

HEAT ONE: Edward Kennett, James Wright, William Lawson, Lee Smart.
HEAT TWO: Steve Boxall, Ritchie Hawkins, Ben Wilson, Darren Mallett (f, rem).
HEAT THREE: Daniel King, Richard Hall, Jason King, Rob Grant jr (ret).
HEAT FOUR: Jamie Smith, Adam Allott, Jamie Robertson, James Brundle.
HEAT FIVE: Jason King, Steve Boxall, Jamie Robertson, Lee Smart.
HEAT SIX: Jamie Smith, Daniel King, James Wright, Ben Wilson.
HEAT SEVEN: (Rerun) Ritchie Hawkins, Edward Kennett, Adam Allott, Richard Hal (f, rem).
HEAT EIGHT: Rob Grant jr, William Lawson, James Brundle, Darren Mallett.
HEAT NINE: Ben Wilson, Richard Hall, James Brundle, Lee Smart.
HEAT TEN: (Rerun) James Wright, Rob Grant jr, Adam Allott, Steve Boxall (f, ex).
HEAT ELEVEN: Jamie Smith, Edward Kennett, Darren Mallett, Jason King (ret).
HEAT TWELVE: Jamie Robertson, William Lawson, Ritchie Hawkins, Daniel King (ret).
HEAT THIRTEEN: Ritchie Hawkins, Jamie Smith, Rob Grant jr, Lee Smart.
HEAT FOURTEEN: (Rerun – awarded) Jamie Robertson, Darren Mallett, Richard Hall (f, ex), James Wright (f, ex).
HEAT FIFTEEN: Edward Kennett, Steve Boxall, James Brundle, Daniel King.
HEAT SIXTEEN: Ben Wilson, Jason King, William Lawson, Adam Allott (ret).
HEAT SEVENTEEN: Daniel King, Darren Mallett, Lee Smart, Adam Allott.
HEAT EIGHTEEN: Jason King, James Wright, Ritchie Hawkins, James Brundle.
HEAT NINETEEN: Edward Kennett, Ben Wilson, Rob Grant jr, Jamie Robertson.

HEAT TWENTY: Steve Boxall, Jamie Smith, William Lawson, Richard Hall (ret).
SEMI-FINAL: Steve Boxall, Ritchie Hawkins, Jason King, Ben Wilson.
FINAL: Ritchie Hawkins, Steve Boxall, Edward Kennett, Jamie Smith.

ROLL OF HONOUR

NOTE: Became known as the British Under-21 Championship in 1987, having previously been called the Junior Championship of Great Britain.

YEAR	FIRST	SECOND	THIRD
1969	Graham Plant	Geoff Ambrose	Mick Bell
1970	Barry Thomas	Dave Jessup	Mick Bell
1971	Ian Turner	Dave Jessup	Peter Ingram
1972	Allen Emmett	Gordon Kennett	Tony Davey
1973	Peter Collins	Barney Kennett	David Gagen
1974	Chris Morton	Steve Bastable	Neil Middleditch
1975	Neil Middleditch	Steve Weatherley	Joe Owen
1976	Michael Lee	Steve Weatherley	Colin Richardson
1977	Les Collins	Phil Collins	Colin Richardson
1978	Phil Collins	Ian Gledhill	Bob Garrad
1979	Kenny Carter	Nigel Flatman	Mel Taylor
1980	Mark Courtney	Kevin Smith	John Barker
1981	Rob Lightfoot	Peter Carr	Neil Evitts
1982	Peter Carr	Martin Hagon	Simon Cross
1983	Keith Millard	Simon Cross	Kenny McKinna
1984	Marvyn Cox	Simon Cross	Andy Smith
1985	Carl Blackbird	David Mullett	Andy Smith
1986	Gary Havelock	Andrew Silver	Daz Sumner
1987	Daz Sumner	David Biles	Mark Loram
1988	Mark Loram	Andy Phillips	Martin Dugard
1989	Martin Dugard	Chris Louis	Dean Barker
1990	Joe Screen	Mark Loram	Chris Louis
1991	Not Staged		
1992	Scott Smith	Mark Loram	Joe Screen
1993	Joe Screen	Carl Stonehewer	David Norris
1994	Paul Hurry	Ben Howe	James Grieves
1995	Ben Howe	Paul Hurry	Savalas Clouting
1996	Savalas Clouting	Scott Nicholls	Paul Hurry
1997	Leigh Lanham	Lee Richardson	Scott Nicholls
1998	Scott Nicholls	Lee Richardson	Paul Lee
1999	Scott Nicholls	Lee Richardson	David Howe
2000	David Howe	Lee Richardson	Paul Lee
2001	Simon Stead	David Howe	Paul Lee
2002	Simon Stead	Ross Brady	Olly Allen
2003	Simon Stead	Olly Allen	Edward Kennett
2004	Ritchie Hawkins	Steve Boxall	Edward Kennett

CONFERENCE LEAGUE PAIRS CHAMPIONSHIP

2 JUNE, WIMBLEDON

1st	WIMBLEDON
2nd	MILDENHALL
3rd	RYE HOUSE
4th	BUXTON

WIMBLEDON 25	RACE SCORES						TOTALS
Mark Burrows	2	1*	2*	2*	3	3	13 (3)
Barrie Evans	R	2	3	3	2*	2*	12 (2)
MILDENHALL 22							
Ritchie Hawkins	2*	1*	2*	3	2*	1	11 (4)
Jon Armstrong	3	2	3	0	3	R	11
RYE HOUSE 21							
Steve Boxall	3	3	3	1*	3	3	16 (1)
Tommy Allen	1	F	0	2	0	2*	5 (1)
BUXTON 19							
James Wright	3	3	2	2	3	3	16
Jonathon Bethell	1	0	1*	1*	0	0	3 (2)
BOSTON 18							
Richard Hall	2*	2*	R	3	1	1*	9 (3)
David McAllan	3	3	1	0	0	2	9
WEYMOUTH 13							
David Mason	1	2	3	1	1*	0	8 (1)
Wayne Barrett	0	0	2*	0	2	1	5 (1)
CARMARTHEN 8							
Chris Hunt	1	0	1	0	1*	0	3 (1)
Dean Felton	R	1	0	1	2	1	5

RACE DETAILS

HEAT ONE:	David McAllan, Richard Hall, David Mason, Wayne Barrett.
HEAT TWO:	Jon Armstrong, Ritchie Hawkins, Chris Hunt, Dean Felton (ret).
HEAT THREE:	(Rerun) Steve Boxall, Mark Burrows, Tommy Allen, Barrie Evans (ret).
HEAT FOUR:	James Wright, David Mason, Jonathon Bethell, Wayne Barrett.
HEAT FIVE:	David McAllan, Richard Hall, Dean Felton, Chris Hunt.
HEAT SIX:	Steve Boxall, Jon Armstrong, Ritchie Hawkins, Tommy Allen (fell).
HEAT SEVEN:	James Wright, Barrie Evans, Mark Burrows, Jonathon Bethell.
HEAT EIGHT:	David Mason, Wayne Barrett, Chris Hunt, Dean Felton.

HEAT NINE:	Jon Armstrong, Ritchie Hawkins, David McAllan, Richard Hall (ret).
HEAT TEN:	(Rerun) Steve Boxall, James Wright, Jonathon Bethell, Tommy Allen (f, rem).
HEAT ELEVEN:	Barrie Evans, Mark Burrows, David Mason, Wayne Barrett.
HEAT TWELVE:	Richard Hall, Tommy Allen, Steve Boxall, David McAllan.
HEAT THIRTEEN:	Barrie Evans, Mark Burrows, Dean Felton, Chris Hunt.
HEAT FOURTEEN:	Ritchie Hawkins, James Wright, Jonathon Bethell, Jon Armstrong.
HEAT FIFTEEN:	Steve Boxall, Wayne Barrett, David Mason, Tommy Allen.
HEAT SIXTEEN:	Mark Burrows, Barrie Evans, Richard Hall, David McAllan.
HEAT SEVENTEEN:	James Wright, Dean Felton, Chris Hunt, Jonathon Bethell (f, rem).
HEAT EIGHTEEN:	Jon Armstrong, Ritchie Hawkins, Wayne Barrett, David Mason.
HEAT NINETEEN:	James Wright, David McAllan, Richard Hall, Jonathon Bethell.
HEAT TWENTY:	Steve Boxall, Tommy Allen, Dean Felton, Chris Hunt.
HEAT TWENTY-ONE:	(Rerun) Mark Burrows, Barrie Evans, Ritchie Hawkins, Jon Armstrong (ret).

ROLL OF HONOUR

YEAR	FIRST	SECOND
2004	Wimbledon (Mark Burrows & Barrie Evans)	Mildenhall (Ritchie Hawkins & Jon Armstrong)

PREMIER LEAGUE PAIRS CHAMPIONSHIP

20 JUNE, READING

1st	READING
2nd	STOKE
3rd	RYE HOUSE
4th	GLASGOW

GROUP A	QUALIFYING SCORES				TOTALS
RYE HOUSE 24					
Chris Neath	4	2*	4	4	14 (1)
Scott Robson	2	3	2	3*	10 (1)
GLASGOW 22					
Shane Parker	3	2*	3*	4	12 (2)
George Stancl	R	3	4	3*	10 (1)
BERWICK 18					
Claus Kristensen	4	3*	3	2	12 (1)
Josef Franc	0	4	2*	0	6 (1)
WORKINGTON 17					
Carl Stonehewer	4	4	3	4	15
Aidan Collins	2	0	0	0	2
EXETER 9					
Seemond Stephens	0	0	0	2	2
Mark Simmonds	3	2	2	0	7

GROUP B	QUALIFYING SCORES				TOTALS
READING 24					
Danny Bird	4	4	0	4	12
Phil Morris	3*	3*	4	2	12 (2)
STOKE 19					
Paul Pickering	0	3*	4	F	7
Alan Mogridge	2	4	3*	3	12 (1)
ISLE OF WIGHT 18					
Craig Boyce	2	3*	2	3	10 (1)
Jason Bunyan	0	4	4	X	8
SHEFFIELD 17					
Ricky Ashworth	4	2	2*	4	12 (1)
Andre Compton	X	0	3	2	5
SOMERSET 12					
Paul Fry	3	0	0	0	3
Glenn Cunningham	2*	2	3	2	9 (1)

RACE DETAILS

HEAT ONE:	Chris Neath, Shane Parker, Scott Robson, George Stancl (ret).
HEAT TWO:	Danny Bird, Phil Morris, Craig Boyce, Jason Bunyan.
HEAT THREE:	Carl Stonehewer, Mark Simmonds, Aidan Collins, Seemond Stephens.
HEAT FOUR:	(Rerun) Ricky Ashworth, Paul Fry, Glenn Cunningham, Andre Compton (f, ex).
HEAT FIVE:	Claus Kristensen, Scott Robson, Chris Neath, Josef Franc.
HEAT SIX:	Jason Bunyan, Craig Boyce, Alan Mogridge, Paul Pickering.
HEAT SEVEN:	Carl Stonehewer, George Stancl, Shane Parker, Aidan Collins.
HEAT EIGHT:	Danny Bird, Phil Morris, Glenn Cunningham, Paul Fry.
HEAT NINE:	Josef Franc, Claus Kristensen, Mark Simmonds, Seemond Stephens.
HEAT TEN:	Alan Mogridge, Paul Pickering, Ricky Ashworth, Andre Compton.
HEAT ELEVEN:	Chris Neath, Carl Stonehewer, Scott Robson, Aidan Collins.
HEAT TWELVE:	Jason Bunyan, Glenn Cunningham, Craig Boyce, Paul Fry.
HEAT THIRTEEN:	George Stancl, Shane Parker, Mark Simmonds, Seemond Stephens.
HEAT FOURTEEN:	Phil Morris, Andre Compton, Ricky Ashworth, Danny Bird.
HEAT FIFTEEN:	Carl Stonehewer, Claus Kristensen, Josef Franc, Aidan Collins.
HEAT SIXTEEN:	Paul Pickering, Alan Mogridge, Glenn Cunningham, Paul Fry.
HEAT SEVENTEEN:	Chris Neath, Scott Robson, Seemond Stephens, Mark Simmonds.
HEAT EIGHTEEN:	Ricky Ashworth, Craig Boyce, Andre Compton, Jason Bunyan (fell).
HEAT NINETEEN:	Shane Parker, George Stancl, Claus Kristensen, Josef Franc.
HEAT TWENTY:	Danny Bird, Alan Mogridge, Phil Morris, Paul Pickering.
FIRST SEMI-FINAL:	Chris Neath, Paul Pickering, Alan Mogridge, Scott Robson.
SECOND SEMI-FINAL:	Danny Bird, Shane Parker, Phil Morris, George Stancl.
CONSOLATION FINAL:	Shane Parker, Chris Neath, Scott Robson, George Stancl.
GRAND FINAL:	Danny Bird, Phil Morris, Paul Pickering, Alan Mogridge.

ROLL OF HONOUR

NOTE: Became known as the Premier League Pairs Championship in 1997, having previously been known as the National League Pairs Championship (1975-90) and Division Two Pairs Championship (1994).

YEAR	FIRST	SECOND
1975	Newcastle (Tom Owen & Brian Havelock)	Ellesmere Port (John Jackson & Colin Goad)
1976	Ellesmere Port (John Jackson & Chris Turner)	Newcastle (Joe Owen & Tom Owen)
1977	Boston (Robert Hollingworth & Colin Cook)	Newport (Jim Brett & Brian Woodward)
1978	Ellesmere Port (John Jackson & Steve Finch)	Newcastle (Tom Owen & Robbie Blackadder)
1979	Milton Keynes (Andy Grahame & Bob Humphreys)	Ellesmere Port (John Jackson & Steve Finch)
1980	Middlesbrough (Mark Courtney & Steve Wilcock)	Boston (Robert Hollingworth & Gary Guglielmi)
1981	Canterbury (Mike Ferreira & Denzil Kent)	Berwick (Wayne Brown & Steve McDermott)
1982	Weymouth (Martin Yeates & Simon Wigg)	Long Eaton (Alan Molyneux & Dave Perks)
1983	Weymouth (Martin Yeates & Simon Cross)	Glasgow (Jim McMillan & Steve Lawson)
1984	Stoke (Nigel Crabtree & Tom Owen)	Berwick (Bruce Cribb & Steve McDermott)
1985	Ellesmere Port (Joe Owen & Louis Carr)	Poole (Martin Yeates & Stan Bear)

YEAR	FIRST	SECOND
1986	Edinburgh (Les Collins & Doug Wyer)	Hackney (Barry Thomas & Andy Galvin)
1987	Mildenhall (Dave Jessup & Mel Taylor)	Peterborough (Ian Barney & Kevin Hawkins)
1988	Stoke (Graham Jones & Steve Bastable)	Poole (Steve Schofield & David Biles)
1989	Stoke (Nigel Crabtree & Eric Monaghan)	Mildenhall (Preben Eriksen & Peter Glanz)
1990	Hackney (Steve Schofield & Andy Galvin)	Exeter (Steve Regeling & Peter Jeffery)
1991-93	Not Staged	
1994	Swindon (Tony Olsson & Tony Langdon)	Glasgow (Nigel Crabtree & David Walsh)
1995-96	Not Staged	
1997	Long Eaton (Martin Dixon & Carl Stonehewer)	Reading (David Mullett & Lee Richardson)
1998	Peterborough (Glenn Cunningham & Brett Woodifield)	Exeter (Frank Smart & Michael Coles)
1999	Workington (Carl Stonehewer & Brent Werner)	Arena-Essex (Colin White & Leigh Lanham)
2000	Workington (Carl Stonehewer & Mick Powell)	Isle of Wight (Ray Morton & Danny Bird)
2001	Workington (Carl Stonehewer & Peter I. Karlsson)	Newcastle (Bjarne Pedersen & Jesper Olsen)
2002	Isle of Wight (Adam Shields & Danny Bird)	Newport (Frank Smart & Craig Watson)
2003	Workington (Carl Stonehewer & Simon Stead)	Newport (Frank Smart & Niels-Kristian Iversen)
2004	Reading (Danny Bird & Phil Morris)	Stoke (Paul Pickering & Alan Mogridge)

CHAMPIONSHIP OF GREAT BRITAIN FINAL

9 JULY, OXFORD

1st JOE SCREEN
2nd DAVID NORRIS
3rd MARK LORAM
4th SCOTT NICHOLLS

	QUALIFYING SCORES					TOTAL
Scott Nicholls	3	3	3	3	3	15
David Norris	3	2	3	3	3	14
Mark Loram	R	3	3	3	1	10
Joe Screen	3	0	1	3	3	10
Chris Neath	2	3	1	2	2	10
Carl Stonehewer	1	3	0	2	3	9
David Howe	3	0	2	2	2	9
Danny Bird	1	2	3	1	1	8
Andrew Moore	0	2	1	2	2	7
Dean Barker	2	1	2	1	1	7
Andre Compton	1	1	2	1	2	7
Chris Harris	2	2	1	1	0	6
Michael Coles	0	1	2	0	1	4
Gary Havelock	2	1	X	–	–	3
Seemond Stephens	1	0	0	0	0	1
Stuart Robson	0	R	F	F	0	0
Chris Mills (Res)	X	–	–	–	–	0
Craig Branney (Res)	0	–	–	–	–	0

RACE DETAILS

HEAT ONE:	David Norris, Chris Neath, Danny Bird, Mark Loram (ret).
HEAT TWO:	Joe Screen, Dean Barker, Andre Compton, Michael Coles.
HEAT THREE:	Scott Nicholls, Chris Harris, Carl Stonehewer, Andrew Moore.
HEAT FOUR:	David Howe, Gary Havelock, Seemond Stephens, Stuart Robson (f, rem).
HEAT FIVE:	Scott Nicholls, David Norris, Gary Havelock, Joe Screen.
HEAT SIX:	Mark Loram, Chris Harris, Michael Coles, Seemond Stephens.
HEAT SEVEN:	Chris Neath, Andrew Moore, Andre Compton, David Howe.
HEAT EIGHT:	Carl Stonehewer, Danny Bird, Dean Barker, Stuart Robson (f, rem, ret).
HEAT NINE:	David Norris, Michael Coles, Andrew Moore, Stuart Robson (fell).
HEAT TEN:	Mark Loram, David Howe, Joe Screen, Carl Stonehewer.
HEAT ELEVEN:	Scott Nicholls, Dean Barker, Chris Neath, Seemond Stephens.
HEAT TWELVE:	(Rerun) Danny Bird, Andre Compton, Chris Harris, Gary Havelock (f, ex).
HEAT THIRTEEN:	David Norris, Carl Stonehewer, Andre Compton, Seemond Stephens.
HEAT FOURTEEN:	(Rerun) Mark Loram, Andrew Moore, Dean Barker, Chris Mills (f, ex).
HEAT FIFTEEN:	Joe Screen, Chris Neath, Chris Harris, Stuart Robson (fell).

HEAT SIXTEEN:	Scott Nicholls, David Howe, Danny Bird, Michael Coles.
HEAT SEVENTEEN:	David Norris, David Howe, Dean Barker, Chris Harris.
HEAT EIGHTEEN:	Scott Nicholls, Andre Compton, Mark Loram, Stuart Robson.
HEAT NINETEEN:	Carl Stonehewer, Chris Neath, Michael Coles, Craig Branney.
HEAT TWENTY:	Joe Screen, Andrew Moore, Danny Bird, Seemond Stephens.
FINAL:	Joe Screen, David Norris (fell), Mark Loram (ret), Scott Nicholls (ret).

ROLL OF HONOUR

NOTE: Became known as the Championship of Great Britain in 2002, having previously been called the British Final.

YEAR	FIRST	SECOND	THIRD
1961	Barry Briggs	Peter Craven	Ronnie Moore
1962	Peter Craven	Barry Briggs	Ronnie Moore
1963	Peter Craven	Barry Briggs	Leo McAuliffe
1964	Barry Briggs	Ken McKinlay	Ron How
1965	Barry Briggs	Nigel Boocock	Ken McKinlay
1966	Barry Briggs	Ivan Mauger	Colin Pratt
1967	Barry Briggs	Ivan Mauger	Eric Boocock
1968	Ivan Mauger	Barry Briggs	Eric Boocock
1969	Barry Briggs	Nigel Boocock	Ronnie Moore
1970	Ivan Mauger	Ronnie Moore	Roy Trigg
1971	Ivan Mauger	Barry Briggs	Tony Lomas
1972	Ivan Mauger	Nigel Boocock	Barry Briggs
1973	Ray Wilson	Bob Valentine	Peter Collins
1974	Eric Boocock	Terry Betts	Dave Jessup
1975	John Louis	Peter Collins	Malcolm Simmons
1976	Malcolm Simmons	Chris Morton	Doug Wyer
1977	Michael Lee	Dave Jessup	Doug Wyer
1978	Michael Lee	Dave Jessup	Malcolm Simmons
1979	Peter Collins	Michael Lee	Dave Jessup
1980	Dave Jessup	Michael Lee	Phil Collins
1981	Steve Bastable	Kenny Carter	John Louis
1982	Andy Grahame	Alan Grahame	Kenny Carter
1983	Chris Morton	Michael Lee	Andy Grahame
1984	Kenny Carter	Andy Grahame	Dave Jessup
1985	Kenny Carter	John Davis	Kelvin Tatum
1986	Neil Evitts	Phil Collins	Jeremy Doncaster
1987	Kelvin Tatum	Neil Evitts	Simon Wigg
1988	Simon Wigg	Kelvin Tatum	Chris Morton
1989	Simon Wigg	Kelvin Tatum	Alan Grahame
1990	Kelvin Tatum	Simon Cross	Jeremy Doncaster
1991	Gary Havelock	Kelvin Tatum	Chris Louis
1992	Gary Havelock	Martin Dugard	Andy Smith
1993	Andy Smith	Joe Screen	Gary Havelock

	FIRST	SECOND	THIRD
1994	Andy Smith	Joe Screen	Steve Schofield
1995	Andy Smith	Joe Screen	Dean Barker
1996	Joe Screen	Chris Louis	Carl Stonehewer
1997	Mark Loram	Chris Louis	Sean Wilson
1998	Chris Louis	Joe Screen	Paul Hurry
1999	Mark Loram	Joe Screen	Chris Louis
2000	Chris Louis	Paul Hurry	Martin Dugard
2001	Mark Loram	Stuart Robson	Martin Dugard
2002	Scott Nicholls	Lee Richardson	David Howe
2003	Scott Nicholls	Dean Barker	David Norris
2004	Joe Screen	David Norris	Mark Loram

CORBETT BOOKMAKERS CONFERENCE LEAGUE FOUR-TEAM CHAMPIONSHIP

10 JULY, STOKE

1st	MILDENHALL
=2nd	NEWCASTLE
=2nd	WIMBLEDON
4th	STOKE

FIRST SEMI-FINAL

STOKE 17	QUALIFYING SCORES		TOTAL
Justin Elkins	3	0	3
Luke Priest	2	2	4
Tom Brown	2	2	4
Rob Grant jr	3	3	6
MILDENHALL 12			
Jon Armstrong	3	3	6
Jason King	2	1	3
Gary Phelps	1	1	2
Tony Dart	R	1	1
CARMARTHEN 11			
Dean Felton	R	1	1
Steven Jones	0	0	0
Steve Bishop	3	3	6
Darren Pugh	1	3	4
BOSTON 7			
David McAllan	R	2	2
Richie Dennis	R	2	2
James Cockle	1	0	1
Robert Hollingworth	2	0	2

RACE DETAILS

HEAT ONE:	Justin Elkins, Robert Hollingworth, Gary Phelps, Steven Jones.
HEAT TWO:	Steve Bishop, Luke Priest, Tony Dart (ret), David McAllan (ret).
HEAT THREE:	Jon Armstrong, Tom Brown, Darren Pugh, Richie Dennis (f, rem).
HEAT FOUR:	Rob Grant jr, Jason King, James Cockle, Dean Felton (ret).
HEAT FIVE:	Jon Armstrong, David McAllan, Dean Felton, Justin Elkins.
HEAT SIX:	Rob Grant jr, Richie Dennis, Tony Dart, Steven Jones.
HEAT SEVEN:	Steve Bishop, Tom Brown, Gary Phelps, James Cockle (f, rem).
HEAT EIGHT:	Darren Pugh, Luke Priest, Jason King, Robert Hollingworth.

SECOND SEMI-FINAL

NEWCASTLE 15	QUALIFYING SCORES		TOTAL
Lee Dicken	3	3	6
Jamie Robertson	3	1	4
John Branney	R	2	2
Paul Sharples	0	–	–
Michael Pickering (Res)	3	–	3
WIMBLEDON 15			
Barrie Evans	2	2	4
Gavin Hedge	1	1	2
Wayne Broadhurst	2	3	5
Mark Burrows	2	2	4
BUXTON 9			
Jonathon Bethell	1	1	2
Benji Compton	1	2	3
Alan Brown	1	0	1
Carl Belfield	3	0	3
WEYMOUTH 9			
David Mason	2	0	2
Wayne Barrett	3	3	6
Daniel Giffard	0	1	1
Jack Gledhill	X	0	0

RACE DETAILS

HEAT ONE:	Lee Dicken, Mark Burrows, Benji Compton, Daniel Giffard.
HEAT TWO:	(Rerun) Jamie Robertson, Barrie Evans, Alan Brown, Jack Gledhill (ex, foul riding).
HEAT THREE:	(Rerun) Carl Belfield, David Mason, Gavin Hedge (15 met), John Branney (ret).
HEAT FOUR:	Wayne Barrett, Wayne Broadhurst, Jonathon Bethell, Paul Sharples.
HEAT FIVE:	Lee Dicken, Barrie Evans, Jonathon Bethell, David Mason.
HEAT SIX:	Michael Pickering, Benji Compton, Gavin Hedge, Jack Gledhill (f, rem).
HEAT SEVEN:	Wayne Broadhurst, John Branney, Daniel Giffard, Alan Brown (f, rem).
HEAT EIGHT:	Wayne Barrett, Mark Burrows, Jamie Robertson, Carl Belfield.

FINAL

MILDENHALL 16	RACE SCORES		TOTAL
Jon Armstrong	3	2	5
Jason King	2	3	5
Gary Phelps	1	1	2
Tony Dart	2	2	4
NEWCASTLE 13			
Lee Dicken	3	3	6
Jamie Robertson	2	3	5
John Branney	1	F	1
Paul Sharples	1	–	1
Michael Pickering (Res)	0	–	0
WIMBLEDON 13			
Barrie Evans	3	R	3
Gavin Hedge	0	2	2
Wayne Broadhurst	1	3	4
Mark Burrows	3	1	4
STOKE 6			
Justin Elkins	0	1	1
Luke Priest	2	0	2
Tom Brown	1	2	3
Rob Grant jr	R	R	0

RACE DETAILS

HEAT ONE: Mark Burrows, Jason King, John Branney, Justin Elkins.
HEAT TWO: Barrie Evans, Luke Priest, Gary Phelps, Michael Pickering.
HEAT THREE: Lee Dicken, Tony Dart, Tom Brown, Gavin Hedge.
HEAT FOUR: Jon Armstrong, Jamie Robertson, Wayne Broadhurst, Rob Grant jr (ret).
HEAT FIVE: (Rerun) Lee Dicken, Jon Armstrong, Justin Elkins, Barrie Evans (ret).
HEAT SIX: Jason King, Gavin Hedge, Paul Sharples, Rob Grant jr (ret).
HEAT SEVEN: (Rerun) Wayne Broadhurst, Tom Brown, Gary Phelps, John Branney (fell).
HEAT EIGHT: Jamie Robertson, Tony Dart, Mark Burrows, Luke Priest.

ROLL OF HONOUR

YEAR	FIRST	SECOND	THIRD	FOURTH
2003	Rye House	Mildenhall	Peterborough	Boston
2004	Mildenhall	Newcastle/Wimbledon (shared)	–	Stoke

PREMIER LEAGUE FOUR-TEAM CHAMPIONSHIP

21 AUGUST, WORKINGTON

1st	WORKINGTON
2nd	STOKE
3rd	GLASGOW
4th	RYE HOUSE

FIRST SEMI-FINAL

WORKINGTON 17	QUALIFYING SCORES		TOTAL
Carl Stonehewer	2	3	5
Simon Stead	3	3	6
Kauko Nieminen	3	1	4
Aidan Collins	1	–	1
Rusty Harrison (Res)	1	–	1
STOKE 13			
Paul Pickering	2	1	3
Jan Staechmann	2	2	4
Alan Mogridge	3	3	6
Robbie Kessler	0	0	0
READING 12			
Matej Zagar	2	2	4
Phil Morris	1	3	4
Andrew Appleton	0	2	2
Chris Schramm	1	1	2
BERWICK 6			
Adrian Rymel	3	0	3
Claus Kristensen	0	2	2
Josef Franc	1	0	1
Adam Pietraszko	R	R	0

RACE DETAILS

HEAT ONE:	Adrian Rymel, Jan Staechmann, Aidan Collins, Andrew Appleton.
HEAT TWO:	Alan Mogridge, Carl Stonehewer, Chris Schramm, Claus Kristensen.
HEAT THREE:	Simon Stead, Matej Zagar, Josef Franc, Robbie Kessler.
HEAT FOUR:	Kauko Nieminen, Paul Pickering, Phil Morris, Adam Pietraszko (ret).
HEAT FIVE:	Carl Stonehewer, Matej Zagar, Paul Pickering, Adrian Rymel.
HEAT SIX:	Simon Stead, Jan Staechmann, Chris Schramm, Adam Pietraszko (ret).
HEAT SEVEN:	Alan Mogridge, Andrew Appleton, Kauko Nieminen, Josef Franc.
HEAT EIGHT:	Phil Morris, Claus Kristensen, Rusty Harrison, Robbie Kessler.

SECOND SEMI-FINAL

GLASGOW 15	QUALIFYING SCORES		TOTAL
James Grieves	3	2	5
Paul Bentley	0	3	3
Shane Parker	3	1	4
George Stancl	2	1	3
RYE HOUSE 14			
Brent Werner	2	1	3
Chris Neath	0	2	2
Davey Watt	2	2	4
Scott Robson	2	3	5
HULL 12			
Magnus Karlsson	3	3	6
Ross Brady	1	2	3
Garry Stead	1	0	1
Emil Kramer	1	–	1
Paul Thorp (Res)	1	–	1
EDINBURGH 7			
Frede Schott	3	R	3
Cameron Woodward	0	0	0
Rory Schlein	1	3	4
Matthew Wethers	0	0	0

RACE DETAILS

HEAT ONE:	Frede Schott, Scott Robson, Garry Stead, Paul Bentley.
HEAT TWO:	Shane Parker, Brent Werner, Paul Thorp, Cameron Woodward.
HEAT THREE:	Magnus Karlsson, George Stancl, Rory Schlein, Chris Neath.
HEAT FOUR:	James Grieves, Davey Watt, Ross Brady, Matthew Wethers.
HEAT FIVE:	Magnus Karlsson, James Grieves, Brent Werner, Frede Schott (f, rem, ret).
HEAT SIX:	Paul Bentley, Chris Neath, Emil Kramer, Matthew Wethers.
HEAT SEVEN:	Rory Schlein, Davey Watt, Shane Parker, Garry Stead.
HEAT EIGHT:	Scott Robson, Ross Brady, George Stancl, Cameron Woodward

FINAL

WORKINGTON 29	RACE SCORES			TOTAL
Carl Stonehewer	3	3	2	8
Simon Stead	3	3	3	9
Kauko Nieminen	2	3	1	6
Aidan Collins	–	–	–	–
Rusty Harrison (Res)	2	1	3	6

STOKE 20				TOTAL
Paul Pickering	1	2	0	3
Jan Staechmann	3	2	2	7
Alan Mogridge	2	2	3	7
Robbie Kessler	1	X	–	1
Trent Leverington (Res)	2	–	–	2
GLASGOW 12				
James Grieves	0	0	–	0
Paul Bentley	0	2	3	5
Shane Parker	2	0	1	3
George Stancl	3	0	1	4
Eric Carrillo (Res)	F	–	–	0
RYE HOUSE 11				
Brent Werner	0	1	1	2
Chris Neath	0	3	R	3
Davey Watt	1	1	0	2
Scott Robson	1	1	2	4

RACE DETAILS

HEAT ONE:	Carl Stonehewer, Alan Mogridge, Scott Robson, Paul Bentley.
HEAT TWO:	Simon Stead, Shane Parker, Robbie Kessler, Brent Werner.
HEAT THREE:	George Stancl, Kauko Nieminen, Paul Pickering, Chris Neath.
HEAT FOUR:	Jan Staechmann, Rusty Harrison, Davey Watt, James Grieves.
HEAT FIVE:	Carl Stonehewer, Paul Pickering, Brent Werner, James Grieves.
HEAT SIX:	(Rerun) Chris Neath, Paul Bentley, Rusty Harrison, Robbie Kessler (f, ex).
HEAT SEVEN:	Kauko Nieminen, Alan Mogridge, Davey Watt, Shane Parker.
HEAT EIGHT:	Simon Stead, Jan Staechmann, Scott Robson, George Stancl.
HEAT NINE:	Rusty Harrison, Trent Leverington, Brent Werner, Eric Carrillo (fell).
HEAT TEN:	Paul Bentley, Scott Robson, Kauko Nieminen, Paul Pickering.
HEAT ELEVEN:	Alan Mogridge, Carl Stonehewer, Shane Parker, Davey Watt.
HEAT TWELVE:	Simon Stead, Jan Staechmann, George Stancl, Chris Neath (ret).

ROLL OF HONOUR

NOTE: Became known as the Premier League Four-Team Championship in 1997, having previously been known as the National League Four-Team Championship (1976-90) and the Division Two Four-Team Championship (1991-94).

YEAR	FIRST	SECOND	THIRD	FOURTH
1976	Newcastle	Eastbourne	Ellesmere Port	Workington
1977	Peterborough	Canterbury	Eastbourne	Stoke
1978	Peterborough	Stoke	Canterbury	Ellesmere Port

YEAR	FIRST	SECOND	THIRD	FOURTH
1979	Ellesmere Port	Mildenhall	Peterborough	Berwick
1980	Crayford	Rye House	Ellesmere Port	Stoke
1981	Edinburgh	Newcastle	Middlesbrough	Wolverhampton
1982	Newcastle	Mildenhall	Middlesbrough	Rye House
1983	Newcastle	Mildenhall	Milton Keynes	Long Eaton
1984	Mildenhall	Stoke	Milton Keynes	Boston
1985	Middlesbrough	Peterborough	Hackney	Stoke
1986	Middlesbrough	Arena-Essex	Hackney	Mildenhall
1987	Mildenhall	Arena-Essex	Eastbourne	Wimbledon
1988	Peterborough	Mildenhall	Eastbourne	Poole
1989	Peterborough	Stoke	Exeter	Eastbourne
1990	Stoke	Poole	Hackney	Ipswich
1991	Arena-Essex	Long Eaton	Edinburgh	Milton Keynes
1992	Peterborough	Edinburgh	Rye House	Glasgow
1993	Edinburgh	Swindon	Long Eaton	Rye House
1994	Oxford	Long Eaton	Peterborough	Edinburgh
1995-96		Not Staged		
1997	Long Eaton	Edinburgh	Oxford	Berwick
1998	Peterborough	Edinburgh	Hull	Reading
1999	Sheffield	Newport	Isle of Wight	Arena-Essex
2000	Sheffield	Isle of Wight	Swindon	Berwick
2001	Workington	Newcastle	Sheffield	Isle of Wight
2002	Berwick	Arena-Essex	Newport	Hull
2003	Swindon	Trelawny	Newport	Glasgow
2004	Workington	Stoke	Glasgow	Rye House

SAUNDERS SURFACING CONFERENCE LEAGUE RIDERS' CHAMPIONSHIP

28 AUGUST, RYE HOUSE

1st JAMES WRIGHT
2nd MARK BURROWS
3rd RICHARD HALL
4th MATTHEW WETHERS

RIDER	RACE SCORES					TOTAL
James Wright	3	3	3	3	2	14
Mark Burrows	2	3	3	2	2	12
Richard Hall	2	3	2	2	3	12
Matthew Wethers	R	2	3	3	3	11
Steve Boxall	3	1	X	3	3	10
Chris Schramm	3	3	2	F	2	10
David Mason	1	2	2	2	3	10
Barrie Evans	2	2	1	1	2	8
Malcolm Holloway	1	2	3	0	X	6
Dean Felton	2	0	2	1	1	6
Jamie Westacott	0	0	1	3	1	5
Ritchie Hawkins	1	1	1	1	1	5
Justin Elkins	3	X	–	–	–	3
Jamie Robertson	1	1	R	1	0	3
Lee Smart	0	0	0	2	0	2
Joel Parsons	X	1	–	–	–	1
Karl Mason (Res)	X	0	1	–	–	1
Jack Hargreaves (Res)	0	F	0	–	–	0

RACE DETAILS

HEAT ONE: Chris Schramm, Richard Hall, David Mason, Jamie Westacott.
HEAT TWO: (Rerun) James Wright, Mark Burrows, Malcolm Holloway, Matthew Wethers (ret).
HEAT THREE: (Awarded) Steve Boxall, Barrie Evans, Ritchie Hawkins, Joel Parsons (ex, foul riding).
HEAT FOUR: Justin Elkins, Dean Felton, Jamie Robertson, Lee Smart.
HEAT FIVE: Richard Hall, Matthew Wethers, Steve Boxall, Lee Smart.
HEAT SIX: Mark Burrows, Barrie Evans, Jamie Robertson, Jamie Westacott.
HEAT SEVEN: James Wright, David Mason, Ritchie Hawkins, Dean Felton.
HEAT EIGHT: (Rerun) Chris Schramm, Malcolm Holloway, Joel Parsons, Justin Elkins (f, ex).
HEAT NINE: Mark Burrows, Richard Hall, Ritchie Hawkins, Jack Hargreaves.
HEAT TEN: (Rerun) Matthew Wethers, Dean Felton, Jamie Westacott, Karl Mason (ex, foul riding).
HEAT ELEVEN: (Rerun) Malcolm Holloway, David Mason, Jamie Robertson (ret), Steve Boxall (ex, foul riding).
HEAT TWELVE: James Wright, Chris Schramm, Barrie Evans, Lee Smart.

HEAT THIRTEEN: James Wright, Richard Hall, Jamie Robertson, Karl Mason.
HEAT FOURTEEN: Jamie Westacott, Lee Smart, Ritchie Hawkins, Malcolm Holloway (f, rem).
HEAT FIFTEEN: Matthew Wethers, David Mason, Barrie Evans (f, rem), Jack Hargreaves (fell).
HEAT SIXTEEN: Steve Boxall, Mark Burrows, Dean Felton, Chris Schramm (fell).
HEAT SEVENTEEN: (Rerun) Richard Hall, Barrie Evans, Dean Felton, Malcolm Holloway (f, ex).
HEAT EIGHTEEN: Steve Boxall, James Wright, Jamie Westacott, Jack Hargreaves.
HEAT NINETEEN: David Mason, Mark Burrows, Karl Mason, Lee Smart.
HEAT TWENTY: Matthew Wethers, Chris Schramm, Ritchie Hawkins, Jamie Robertson.
SECOND-PLACE RUN-OFF: Mark Burrows, Richard Hall (f, rem).

ROLL OF HONOUR

NOTE: Previously known as Division Three Riders' Championship (1994), Academy League Riders' Championship (1995) and Amateur League Riders' Championship (1997).

YEAR	FIRST	SECOND	THIRD
1994	Andy Howe	Kevin Little	Colin Earl
1995	Kevin Little	Chris Cobby	Andre Compton
1996	Mike Hampson	Justin Elkins	Graeme Gordon
1997	Jon Armstrong	Bobby Eldridge	David Howe
1998	Steve Bishop	Andrew Appleton	Seemond Stephens
1999	Jonathan Swales	Steve Camden	Scott Courtney
2000	Scott Pegler	Steve Bishop	Adam Allott
2001	David Mason	Scott Pegler	Simon Wolstenholme
2002	James Birkinshaw	Edward Kennett	Jamie Robertson
2003	Barrie Evans	Jamie Robertson	Trevor Harding
2004	James Wright	Mark Burrows	Richard Hall

PREMIER LEAGUE RIDERS' CHAMPIONSHIP

19 SEPTEMBER, SHEFFIELD

1st	ANDRE COMPTON
2nd	MARK LEMON
3rd	SIMON STEAD
4th	CRAIG BOYCE

RIDER	QUALIFYING SCORES					TOTAL
Simon Stead	3	3	3	3	3	15
Craig Boyce	2	1	3	3	2	11
Mark Lemon	2	2	2	2	3	11
Craig Watson	3	3	2	R	2	10
Andre Compton	2	3	3	2	0	10
Danny Bird	2	X	3	1	3	9
Carl Stonehewer	3	2	1	3	R	9
Tomas Topinka	1	3	1	0	3	8
Adrian Rymel	0	2	2	3	0	7
Jan Staechmann	1	2	2	1	1	7
Rory Schlein	3	1	X	–	–	4
Shane Parker	1	R	R	1	2	4
Glenn Cunningham	1	1	1	F	1	4
Jason Lyons	R	1	0	R	2	3
Chris Neath	R	R	0	2	1	3
Luke Priest (Res)	2	1	–	–	–	3
Paul Cooper (Res)	1	0	–	–	–	1
Ross Brady	X	R	–	–	–	0

RACE DETAILS

HEAT ONE:	(Rerun) Craig Watson, Andre Compton, Glenn Cunningham, Ross Brady (f, ex).
HEAT TWO:	Carl Stonehewer, Mark Lemon, Tomas Topinka, Adrian Rymel.
HEAT THREE:	Rory Schlein, Danny Bird, Jan Staechmann, Chris Neath (ret).
HEAT FOUR:	Simon Stead, Craig Boyce, Shane Parker, Jason Lyons (ret).
HEAT FIVE:	(Awarded) Craig Watson, Mark Lemon, Jason Lyons, Danny Bird (f, ex).
HEAT SIX:	Tomas Topinka, Jan Staechmann, Glenn Cunningham, Shane Parker (ret).
HEAT SEVEN:	Simon Stead, Carl Stonehewer, Rory Schlein, Ross Brady (ret).
HEAT EIGHT:	Andre Compton, Adrian Rymel, Craig Boyce, Chris Neath (ret).
HEAT NINE:	(Rerun) Craig Boyce, Craig Watson, Tomas Topinka, Rory Schlein (f, ex).
HEAT TEN:	Simon Stead, Mark Lemon, Glenn Cunningham, Chris Neath.
HEAT ELEVEN:	Danny Bird, Adrian Rymel, Paul Cooper, Shane Parker (ret).
HEAT TWELVE:	Andre Compton, Jan Staechmann, Carl Stonehewer, Jason Lyons.
HEAT THIRTEEN:	Carl Stonehewer, Chris Neath, Shane Parker, Craig Watson (ret).
HEAT FOURTEEN:	Adrian Rymel, Luke Priest, Glenn Cunningham (fell), Jason Lyons (ret).

HEAT FIFTEEN:	Craig Boyce, Mark Lemon, Jan Staechmann, Paul Cooper.
HEAT SIXTEEN:	Simon Stead, Andre Compton, Danny Bird, Tomas Topinka.
HEAT SEVENTEEN:	Simon Stead, Craig Watson, Jan Staechmann, Adrian Rymel.
HEAT EIGHTEEN:	Danny Bird, Craig Boyce, Glenn Cunningham, Carl Stonehewer (ret).
HEAT NINETEEN:	Tomas Topinka, Jason Lyons, Chris Neath (three riders only).
HEAT TWENTY:	Mark Lemon, Shane Parker, Luke Priest, Andre Compton (f, rem).
SEMI-FINAL:	(Rerun) Andre Compton, Mark Lemon, Craig Watson (fell), Danny Bird (f, ex).
FINAL:	(Awarded) Andre Compton, Mark Lemon, Simon Stead (f, ex), Craig Boyce (ex, 2 mins).

ROLL OF HONOUR

NOTE: Became known as the Premier League Riders' Championship in 1997 having previously been known as the Division Two Riders' Championship (1968-74 and 1991-94) and National League Riders' Championship (1975-90).

YEAR	FIRST	SECOND	THIRD
1968	Graham Plant	Ken Eyre	Graeme Smith
1969	Geoff Ambrose	Mick Bell	Ross Gilbertson
1970	Dave Jessup	Barry Crowson	Gary Peterson
1971	John Louis	Malcolm Shakespeare	Hugh Saunders
1972	Phil Crump	Arthur Price	Bob Coles
1973	Arthur Price	Bobby McNeil	Lou Sansom
1974	Carl Glover	Ted Hubbard	Phil Herne
1975	Laurie Etheridge	Brian Collins	Arthur Browning
1976	Joe Owen	John Jackson	Ted Hubbard
1977	Colin Richardson	Martin Yeates	Tom Owen
1978	Steve Koppe	John Jackson	Ted Hubbard
1979	Ian Gledhill	Steve Wilcock	Andy Grahame
1980	Wayne Brown	Martin Yeates	Steve Finch
1981	Mike Ferreira	Simon Wigg	Bruce Cribb
1982	Joe Owen	Steve Lomas	Bob Garrad
1983	Steve McDermott	Richard Knight	Martin Yeates
1984	Ian Barney	Dave Perks	Martin Yeates
1985	Neil Middleditch	Kevin Hawkins	Trevor Banks
1986	Paul Thorp	Steve Schofield	Les Collins
1987	Andrew Silver	Nigel Crabtree	David Blackburn
1988	Troy Butler	Mark Loram	Kenny McKinna
1989	Mark Loram	Kenny McKinna	David Blackburn
1990	Andy Grahame	Chris Louis	Craig Boyce
1991	Jan Staechmann	David Bargh	Troy Butler
1992	Robert Nagy	Mick Poole	Richard Green
1993	Gary Allan	Mick Poole	Tony Langdon
1994	Paul Bentley	Tony Olsson	Tony Langdon
1995-96	Not Staged		

	FIRST	SECOND	THIRD
1997	Peter Carr	Glenn Cunningham	Robert Eriksson
1998	Glenn Cunningham	Carl Stonehewer	Peter Carr
1999	Sean Wilson	Jesper Olsen	Craig Watson
2000	Carl Stonehewer	Peter Carr	Paul Pickering
2001	Carl Stonehewer	Sean Wilson	Bjarne Pedersen
2002	Adam Shields	Craig Watson	Phil Morris
2003	Sean Wilson	Adam Shields	Carl Stonehewer
2004	Andre Compton	Mark Lemon	Simon Stead

ELITE LEAGUE RIDERS' CHAMPIONSHIP

17 OCTOBER, POOLE

1st	BJARNE PEDERSEN
2nd	RYAN SULLIVAN
3rd	HANS N. ANDERSEN
4th	RORY SCHLEIN

	QUALIFYING SCORES					TOTAL
Ryan Sullivan	3	3	3	3	2	14
Rory Schlein	3	3	2	1	3	12
Hans N. Andersen	1	3	2	3	3	12
Mikael Max	2	2	2	3	3	12
Matej Ferjan	2	3	3	3	0	11
Bjarne Pedersen	3	2	2	2	2	11
Leigh Adams	2	2	3	1	1	9
Scott Nicholls	3	1	1	0	3	8
Adam Shields	2	1	1	2	1	7
David Howe	0	0	3	1	2	6
Davey Watt	1	1	1	2	0	5
Gary Havelock	0	2	0	0	2	4
Rafal Dobrucki	1	0	0	2	0	3
Chris Harris	1	1	0	R	1	3
Josh Larsen	0	0	1	1	1	3
Sebastian Tresarrieu	0	0	R	0	0	0

RACE DETAILS

HEAT ONE:	Ryan Sullivan, Leigh Adams, Rafal Dobrucki, David Howe.
HEAT TWO:	Bjarne Pedersen, Matej Ferjan, Chris Harris, Sebastian Tresarrieu.
HEAT THREE:	Scott Nicholls, Adam Shields, Davey Watt, Josh Larsen.
HEAT FOUR:	Rory Schlein, Mikael Max, Hans N. Andersen, Gary Havelock.
HEAT FIVE:	Rory Schlein, Leigh Adams, Chris Harris, Josh Larsen.
HEAT SIX:	Ryan Sullivan, Gary Havelock, Davey Watt, Sebastian Tresarrieu.
HEAT SEVEN:	Matej Ferjan, Mikael Max, Scott Nicholls, David Howe.
HEAT EIGHT:	Hans N. Andersen, Bjarne Pedersen, Adam Shields, Rafal Dobrucki.
HEAT NINE:	Leigh Adams, Hans N. Andersen, Scott Nicholls, Sebastian Tresarrieu (ret).
HEAT TEN:	Ryan Sullivan, Mikael Max, Adam Shields, Chris Harris.
HEAT ELEVEN:	David Howe, Bjarne Pedersen, Josh Larsen, Gary Havelock.
HEAT TWELVE:	Matej Ferjan, Rory Schlein, Davey Watt, Rafal Dobrucki.
HEAT THIRTEEN:	Matej Ferjan, Adam Shields, Leigh Adams, Gary Havelock.
HEAT FOURTEEN:	Ryan Sullivan, Bjarne Pedersen, Rory Schlein, Scott Nicholls.
HEAT FIFTEEN:	Hans N. Andersen, Davey Watt, David Howe, Chris Harris (ret)

HEAT SIXTEEN:	Mikael Max, Rafal Dobrucki, Josh Larsen, Sebastian Tresarrieu.
HEAT SEVENTEEN:	Mikael Max, Bjarne Pedersen, Leigh Adams, Davey Watt.
HEAT EIGHTEEN:	Hans N. Andersen, Ryan Sullivan, Josh Larsen, Matej Ferjan.
HEAT NINETEEN:	Rory Schlein, David Howe, Adam Shields, Sebastian Tresarrieu.
HEAT TWENTY:	Scott Nicholls, Gary Havelock, Chris Harris, Rafal Dobrucki.
SEMI-FINAL:	Hans N. Andersen, Bjarne Pedersen, Matej Ferjan, Mikael Max.
FINAL:	(Rerun) Bjarne Pedersen, Ryan Sullivan, Hans N. Andersen, Rory Schlein.

ROLL OF HONOUR

NOTE: Became known as the Elite League Riders' Championship in 1997, having previously been known as British League Riders' Championship (1965-67 and 1975-90), Division One Riders' Championship (1968-74 and 1990-94) and Premier League Riders' Championship (1995-96).

YEAR	FIRST	SECOND	THIRD
1965	Barry Briggs	Jimmy Gooch	Cyril Maidment
1966	Barry Briggs	Olle Nygren	Norman Hunter
1967	Barry Briggs	Nigel Boocock	Ray Wilson
1968	Barry Briggs	Eric Boocock	Ivan Mauger
1969	Barry Briggs	Ivan Mauger	Jim Airey
1970	Barry Briggs	Anders Michanek	Eric Boocock
1971	Ivan Mauger	Barry Briggs	Jim McMillan
1972	Ole Olsen	Martin Ashby	Ronnie Moore
1973	Ivan Mauger	Ray Wilson	Anders Michanek
1974	Peter Collins	Ivan Mauger	Phil Crump
1975	Peter Collins	Phil Crump	Martin Ashby
1976	Ole Olsen	Peter Collins	John Louis
1977	Ole Olsen	Peter Collins	Michael Lee
1978	Ole Olsen	Peter Collins	Steve Bastable
1979	John Louis	Bruce Penhall	Michael Lee
1980	Les Collins	Bruce Penhall	Larry Ross
1981	Kenny Carter	Chris Morton	Shawn Moran
1982	Kenny Carter	Shawn Moran	Hans Nielsen
1983	Erik Gundersen	Michael Lee	Hans Nielsen
1984	Chris Morton	Hans Nielsen	Erik Gundersen
1985	Erik Gundersen	Peter Collins	Chris Morton
1986	Hans Nielsen	Erik Gundersen	Shawn Moran
1987	Hans Nielsen	Chris Morton	Kelly Moran
1988	Jan O. Pedersen	Erik Gundersen	Hans Nielsen
1989	Shawn Moran	Hans Nielsen	Brian Karger
1990	Hans Nielsen	Kelly Moran	Ronnie Correy
1991	Sam Ermolenko	Hans Nielsen	Joe Screen
1992	Joe Screen	Per Jonsson	Gary Havelock
1993	Per Jonsson	Henrik Gustafsson	Chris Louis

YEAR	FIRST	SECOND	THIRD
1994	Sam Ermolenko	Hans Nielsen	Martin Dugard
1995	Gary Havelock	Billy Hamill	Jason Crump
1996	Sam Ermolenko	Jason Crump	Leigh Adams
1997	Greg Hancock	Tony Rickardsson	Chris Louis
1998	Tony Rickardsson	Jason Crump	Joe Screen
1999	Jason Crump	Todd Wiltshire	Jason Lyons
2000	Ryan Sullivan	Greg Hancock	Nicki Pedersen
2001	Jason Crump	Scott Nicholls	Nicki Pedersen
2002	Tony Rickardsson	Nicki Pedersen	Jason Crump
2003	Lee Richardson	Andreas Jonsson	Scott Nicholls
2004	Bjarne Pedersen	Ryan Sullivan	Hans N. Andersen

GRAND PRIX 2004

GRAND PRIX 2004

	SWEDEN	CZECH REP.	EUROPE	BRITAIN	DENMARK	SCANDINAVIA	SLOVENIA	POLAND	NORWAY	TOTAL
JASON CRUMP	20	25	8	16	25	20	13	20	11	158
TONY RICKARDSSON	18	18	18	8	7	18	25	18	25	155
GREG HANCOCK	13	11	8	25	18	16	20	6	20	137
LEIGH ADAMS	25	13	11	20	11	11	11	13	16	131
NICKI PEDERSEN	13	8	13	13	16	13	13	11	13	113
TOMASZ GOLLOB	16	13	7	11	6	11	6	25	18	113
ANDREAS JONSSON	5	7	7	13	20	8	16	8	13	97
JAROSLAW HAMPEL	3	20	20	6	–	6	6	13	7	81
HANS N. ANDERSEN	4	6	3	3	7	25	18	8	6	80
BJARNE PEDERSEN	8	4	25	6	8	8	11	5	3	78
LEE RICHARDSON	11	11	5	18	5	7	7	7	5	76
SCOTT NICHOLLS	5	–	4	11	11	13	5	11	6	66
RYAN SULLIVAN	7	16	11	5	4	4	4	6	8	65
RUNE HOLTA	6	8	1	5	4	1	8	16	11	60
PIOTR PROTASIEWICZ	2	1	16	7	5	5	5	7	7	55
MIKAEL MAX	6	3	6	2	8	5	7	4	8	49
MARK LORAM	8	4	6	7	2	2	3	4	2	38
JESPER B. JENSEN	11	5	2	1	6	4	1	2	5	37
BOHUMIL BRHEL	7	7	5	4	2	3	2	1	1	32
KAJ LAUKKANEN	1	1	3	1	3	6	3	3	4	25
LUKAS DRYML	3	6	2	2	1	3	4	1	–	22
ALES DRYML	1	3	1	3	3	1	2	5	3	22
GRZEGORZ WALASEK	–	–	13	–	–	–	–	–	–	13
NIELS-KRISTIAN IVERSEN	–	–	–	–	13	–	–	–	–	13
KENNETH BJERRE	–	–	–	–	13	–	–	–	–	13
DAVID NORRIS	–	–	–	8	–	–	–	–	–	8
MATEJ ZAGAR	–	–	–	–	–	–	8	–	–	8
PETER KARLSSON	–	–	–	–	–	7	–	–	–	7
RAFAL DOBRUCKI	–	5	–	–	–	–	–	–	–	5
FREDRIK LINDGREN	4	–	–	–	–	–	–	–	–	4
WIESLAW JAGUS	–	–	4	–	–	–	–	–	–	4
CHRIS LOUIS	–	–	–	4	–	–	–	–	–	4
ARNT FORLAND	–	–	–	–	–	–	–	–	4	4
KRZYSZTOF KASPRZAK	–	–	–	–	–	–	–	3	–	3
PETER LJUNG	2	–	–	–	–	–	–	–	–	2
ROBERT BARTH	–	2	–	–	–	–	–	–	–	2
TONI SVAB	–	2	–	–	–	–	–	–	–	2
ANTONIO LINDBACK	–	–	–	–	–	2	–	–	–	2
TOMASZ CHRZANOWSKI	–	–	–	–	–	–	–	2	–	2
RUNE SOLA	–	–	–	–	–	–	–	–	2	2
SIMON STEAD	–	–	–	–	1	–	–	–	–	1
IZAK SANTEJ	–	–	–	–	–	–	1	–	–	1
JOONAS KYLMAKORPI	–	–	–	–	–	–	–	–	1	1

GRAND PRIX OF SWEDEN (ROUND ONE)

1 MAY, OLYMPIC STADIUM, STOCKHOLM

The cream of world speedway converged on Stockholm's Olympic Stadium for the start of the tenth Grand Prix series, and Leigh Adams gave notice that the superb start he had made to the Elite League campaign with Swindon wasn't just going to be restricted to domestic racing. Many times in the past referred to as a 'nearly man' of the sport, the super-smooth speedster gave an assured display, often coming from behind to land the third GP success of his career and put himself in pole position for the Championship. Adams first entered the fray in the ninth heat, when a poor getaway left him with work to do before overhauling Rune Holta for third place. That took him on to heat fourteen and, following another slow start, the Aussie remarkably carved his way through from fourth to first place inside the opening lap. It was plain sailing for the remainder of the race, with Adams taking the fluttering flag ahead of Jason Crump, Mark Loram and Lee Richardson.

Next up for the classy racer was a rerun twentieth heat and, once more, Swindon's leading light failed to leave the gate on level terms with his opponents. No matter though, for while Tony Rickardsson was romping away to victory, Adams calmly made his way past Nicki Pedersen and Greg Hancock to finish second. Having cruised into the semi-finals, Adams made his best start of the evening in heat twenty-three and never looked back as he strode home from Crump, Hancock and Lee Richardson. So to the final, when he came up against Crump, his great Australian adversary, for a third time, with multi-World Champion Rickardsson and the always-exciting Tomasz Gollob completing the line-up. Crump duly got the drop to lead into the first corner, but Adams took a speedy inside route entering the back straight and just took the field to the cleaners, winning with great style ahead of the three-times GP series runner-up and Rickardsson, with Gollob at the rear. Still, fourth place for the Pole could be regarded as a triumph for a rider known to have an aversion to the one-off, temporary circuits.

Indeed, Gollob's performance on the night was quite remarkable, since his opening couple of rides had resulted in third and fourth-place finishes respectively. Facing elimination in heat eighteen, Gollob kept himself alive by thundering to victory after passing Loram on the back straight, and then in heat twenty-two he produced one of his trademark party pieces. The sharper-starting Hancock initially led, only for TG to scream around the outside to lead off the fourth bend. With the Pole riding increasingly wider, Hancock hit back to sneak inside on the final lap, but Gollob just wouldn't be beaten and daringly took the extreme line around the American to win off the last bend. In a restarted second semi-final, Gollob trailed surprise-package Jesper B. Jensen for three laps, prior to successfully diving underneath on the first corner for another race win. Jensen came down as the Tarnow rider went through, but referee Tony Steele saw nothing amiss and it looked more like the chirpy Dane had simply been caught out by track conditions, rather than receiving any contact from the spirited Pole.

Other points of interest from an entertaining night were the battling performances of British boys Loram and Richardson, with the former looking back at his very best following an injury-ravaged 2003 campaign. Scott Nicholls was scheduled to be the third Englishman in the meeting, but he unfortunately had to withdraw due to the effects of a nasty tyre burn to the left leg, sustained the previous Saturday while riding for Ipswich in an Elite League fixture versus Swindon at Foxhall Heath. This meant three races going ahead with a rider short, but at least Nicholls was the recipient of five Grand Prix points.

One final observation was that the starting tapes appeared to be going up in a lop-sided fashion throughout the meeting, creating the unusual sight of riders looking to their right from the inside grids prior to the release of the gate.

RACE DETAILS

PRE-MAIN EVENT

HEAT ONE:	Ryan Sullivan, Lee Richardson, Hans N. Andersen, Fredrik Lindgren.
HEAT TWO:	Andreas Jonsson, Bohumil Brhel, Bjarne Pedersen, Peter Ljung.
HEAT THREE:	Jaroslaw Hampel, Mark Loram, Mikael Max, Kaj Laukkanen.
HEAT FOUR:	Jesper B. Jensen, Lukas Dryml, Piotr Protasiewicz, Ales Dryml.
HEAT FIVE:	Mikael Max, Hans N. Andersen, Peter Ljung, Ales Dryml.
HEAT SIX:	(Rerun) Bjarne Pedersen, Fredrik Lindgren, Piotr Protasiewicz (ret), Kaj Laukkanen (f, ex).
HEAT SEVEN:	Bohumil Brhel, Ryan Sullivan, Jaroslaw Hampel, Lukas Dryml.
HEAT EIGHT:	Mark Loram, Jesper B. Jensen, Andreas Jonsson, Lee Richardson.
HEAT NINE:	Nicki Pedersen, Greg Hancock, Leigh Adams, Rune Holta.
HEAT TEN:	(Rerun) Tony Rickardsson, Jason Crump, Tomasz Gollob, Scott Nicholls (ns).
HEAT ELEVEN:	Mikael Max, Lee Richardson, Fredrik Lindgren, Jaroslaw Hampel.
HEAT TWELVE:	Andreas Jonsson, Bjarne Pedersen, Hans N. Andersen, Lukas Dryml.

MAIN EVENT

HEAT THIRTEEN:	Bohumil Brhel, Nicki Pedersen, Bjarne Pedersen, Scott Nicholls (ns).
HEAT FOURTEEN:	Leigh Adams, Jason Crump, Mark Loram, Lee Richardson.
HEAT FIFTEEN:	Ryan Sullivan, Greg Hancock, Andreas Jonsson, Tomasz Gollob.
HEAT SIXTEEN:	(Rerun) Tony Rickardsson, Jesper B. Jensen, Mikael Max, Rune Holta (f, ex).
HEAT SEVENTEEN:	Lee Richardson, Bjarne Pedersen, Rune Holta, Andreas Jonsson.
HEAT EIGHTEEN:	Tomasz Gollob, Mark Loram, Mikael Max, Scott Nicholls (ns).
HEAT NINETEEN:	Jason Crump, Jesper B. Jensen, Ryan Sullivan, Bohumil Brhel.
HEAT TWENTY:	(Rerun) Tony Rickardsson, Leigh Adams, Greg Hancock, Nicki Pedersen (ret).
HEAT TWENTY-ONE:	Lee Richardson, Nicki Pedersen, Mark Loram, Ryan Sullivan.
HEAT TWENTY-TWO:	Tomasz Gollob, Greg Hancock, Bjarne Pedersen, Bohumil Brhel.

SEMI-FINALS

HEAT TWENTY-THREE:	Leigh Adams, Jason Crump, Greg Hancock, Lee Richardson.
HEAT TWENTY-FOUR:	(Rerun) Tomasz Gollob, Tony Rickardsson, Nicki Pedersen, Jesper B. Jensen (fell).

GRAND FINAL

HEAT TWENTY-FIVE:	Leigh Adams, Jason Crump, Tony Rickardsson, Tomasz Gollob.

NOTE: Eliminated riders are underlined throughout

GRAND PRIX OF THE CZECH REPUBLIC (ROUND TWO)

15 MAY, MARKETA STADIUM, PRAGUE

Beautiful Prague was the setting for the second Grand Prix of the series, although there was nothing desirable about the wet weather which caused the start to be held up by some two hours. The delay didn't dampen the spirits of the supporters though, particularly the huge Polish contingent, who simply burnt up the time by dancing away on the terraces and generally enjoying themselves! All the slush was eventually removed from the circuit by a large blade and with the wet stuff finally relenting, the Marketa circuit supplied an entertaining and incident-packed meeting for the patient fans to enjoy. With the unlucky Scott Nicholls ruled out through the leg injury he suffered at Ipswich on 24 April, Oxford's in-form Pole Rafal Dobrucki was brought into the line-up, along with wildcard entrants Robert Barth and Toni Svab.

The first few races were uneventful and gave no indication of the spectacle which would unfold, with victory in the event finally going the way of Jason Crump for a third successive year. The ultra-competitive Australian first came to the line in heat ten, but it was the slick-starting Tony Rickardsson who roared away to win, leaving the gritty Belle Vue star to pass Greg Hancock for second place towards the end of lap one. The Aussie moved on to heat fourteen, which was to provide the meeting's first flashpoint. Crump initially held off Nicki Pedersen, but it was Ryan Sullivan on a sweeping outside run who shot ahead entering the back straight. Meanwhile, Czech veteran Bohumil Brhel delighted the home fans by challenging Pedersen on the outside, only to come down following contact from the reigning World Champion, with referee Mick Posselwhite deeming the Dane at fault. At the second attempt, Sullivan streaked clear for a fine win, while Brhel thrilled the crowd by scorching past Crump in road-racing style behind. It's never that easy to beat Crump, however, and the world number two showed all his spirit to round the home crowd's favourite on lap four.

With the rain having returned, heat nineteen was the next one for Crump to negotiate, although he again had to settle for the runner-up position behind inspired World Under-21 Champion Jaroslaw Hampel. Third place went to Tomasz Gollob, while Swedish GP victor Leigh Adams surprisingly brought up the rear after a slow getaway. Amid pouring rain, Crump then reappeared for the second semi-final and he made a dream start to post his first win of a drawn-out evening with aplomb. Behind, Adams looked to have held off Sullivan for a final slot, but the Poole teamster had the determination to mount a last-lap challenge, which successfully took him around his fellow countryman on the apex of the first corner.

With conditions deteriorating rapidly, Crump's fast reactions catapulted him ahead in the final and there was no looking back as he defeated Hampel, with Rickardsson securing third spot from Sullivan. The result saw Crump assume top spot in the overall standings on 45 points, ahead of Adams (38), Rickardsson (36) and Gollob (29).

Aside from heat fourteen, there were a couple of other races worth recalling. Heat sixteen took three attempts to run, the first ending when Rune Holta came down on the second bend and was excluded. The restart was extraordinary and abruptly ended on the back straight when Rickardsson alarmingly came down. Prior to that, the five-times World Champion had raced side-by-side with Hans N. Andersen, only for Gollob to steam through the middle in typically full-blooded fashion. As he did so, Andersen moved out, causing Rickardsson's machine to hit the air safety barrier and send him wildly out of control. The Swede was thrown all over the place as if on a bucking bronco, eventually landing with his left hand caught up in the spokes of his front wheel. It was a difficult one to call and the meeting official probably made the fairest decision in allowing all three riders to participate in the second rerun. Remarkably, 'Ricko' showed no ill effects from his tumble to win the race comfortably, while Gollob saw off Andersen for second place.

Heat twenty-one provided the other real talking point, when, with Gollob leading the way, Nicki Pedersen stormed across the track on the back straight and into the path of the oncoming Hancock, with the American clipping the fence and coming to grief in a manner not dissimilar to Rickardsson in heat sixteen. Amazingly, Mick Posselwhite called for a rerun with all four riders and it was Pedersen who made the gate. The Dane's lead only lasted a lap, though, before Gollob thundered through on the inside and, later, Hancock showed his class when a hard but fair manoeuvre relegated Pedersen from further participation on the night. The American racer had certainly made his point – and in the best possible way too!

RACE DETAILS

PRE-MAIN EVENT

HEAT ONE:	Andreas Jonsson, Mark Loram, Hans N. Andersen, Toni Svab.
HEAT TWO:	Bjarne Pedersen, Lukas Dryml, Rafal Dobrucki, Robert Barth
HEAT THREE:	Jaroslaw Hampel, Ryan Sullivan, Ales Dryml, Mikael Max.
HEAT FOUR:	(Rerun) Rune Holta, Bohumil Brhel, Kaj Laukkanen, Piotr Protasiewicz.
HEAT FIVE:	Hans N. Andersen, Ales Dryml, Robert Barth, Piotr Protasiewicz (fell).
HEAT SIX:	Rafal Dobrucki, Mikael Max, Toni Svab, Kaj Laukkanen.
HEAT SEVEN:	(Rerun) Andreas Jonsson, Jaroslaw Hampel, Bohumil Brhel, Lukas Dryml.
HEAT EIGHT:	Ryan Sullivan, Rune Holta, Mark Loram, Bjarne Pedersen.
HEAT NINE:	Leigh Adams, Jesper B. Jensen, Nicki Pedersen, Tomasz Gollob.
HEAT TEN:	Tony Rickardsson, Jason Crump, Greg Hancock, Lee Richardson.
HEAT ELEVEN:	Hans N. Andersen, Bohumil Brhel, Bjarne Pedersen, Mikael Max.
HEAT TWELVE:	Rafal Dobrucki, Lukas Dryml, Mark Loram, Ales Dryml.

MAIN EVENT

HEAT THIRTEEN:	Leigh Adams, Lee Richardson, Lukas Dryml, Andreas Jonsson.
HEAT FOURTEEN:	(Rerun) Ryan Sullivan, Jason Crump, Bohumil Brhel, Nicki Pedersen (ex, foul riding).
HEAT FIFTEEN:	Jaroslaw Hampel, Greg Hancock, Jesper B. Jensen, Rafal Dobrucki.
HEAT SIXTEEN:	(Rerun twice) Tony Rickardsson, Tomasz Gollob, Hans N. Andersen, Rune Holta (f, ex).
HEAT SEVENTEEN:	Nicki Pedersen, Rune Holta, Lukas Dryml, Jesper B. Jensen (ret).
HEAT EIGHTEEN:	Bohumil Brhel, Andreas Jonsson, Hans N. Andersen, Rafal Dobrucki (ret).
HEAT NINETEEN:	Jaroslaw Hampel, Jason Crump, Tomasz Gollob, Leigh Adams.
HEAT TWENTY:	Ryan Sullivan, Tony Rickardsson, Lee Richardson, Greg Hancock.
HEAT TWENTY-ONE:	(Rerun) Tomasz Gollob, Greg Hancock, Nicki Pedersen, Andreas Jonsson.
HEAT TWENTY-TWO:	Leigh Adams, Lee Richardson, Rune Holta, Bohumil Brhel.

SEMI-FINALS

HEAT TWENTY-THREE:	Tony Rickardsson, Jaroslaw Hampel, Tomasz Gollob, Lee Richardson.
HEAT TWENTY-FOUR:	Jason Crump, Ryan Sullivan, Leigh Adams, Greg Hancock.

GRAND FINAL

HEAT TWENTY-FIVE :	Jason Crump, Jaroslaw Hampel, Tony Rickardsson, Ryan Sullivan.

NOTE: Eliminated riders are underlined throughout

GRAND PRIX OF EUROPE (ROUND THREE)

29 MAY, OLYMPIC STADIUM, WROCLAW, POLAND

Run in glorious sunshine, the brilliant Wroclaw racing strip served up a topsy-turvy meeting and it was simply impossible to predict the ultimate victor as events unfolded. Indeed, when Bjarne Pedersen posted an opening-heat victory from Mark Loram and 2003 World Champion Nicki Pedersen, little did anyone know that Poole's classy Dane would also go on and win the all-important last race of the evening. At one stage, it had even looked a possibility that Polish riders might take all four places in the final, such was the pace they were setting on the track.

Prior to the building excitement of the latter stages, Lukas Dryml and Rune Holta were the first riders to depart from the scene in heat five, with the Norwegian tumbling out after Hans N. Andersen had seemingly made contact when sliding through on the inside of the third bend. The next to go in the sixth heat were Lukas' brother, Ales, and Jesper B. Jensen, while up front, wildcard Pole Wieslaw Jagus impressively took victory from the returning Scott Nicholls. Regrettably though, the battling Brit went out at the next hurdle in heat eleven, with Kaj Laukkanen going the same way. Heat twelve then put paid to the chances of Andersen and Jagus, thereby reducing the field to sixteen remaining competitors.

The top eight from the previous round had entered the fray in heat nine, when Jason Crump charged to victory from Lee Richardson and Ryan Sullivan after Leigh Adams had unluckily pulled out through a broken throttle cable while placed second. Following on from his runner-up finish in Prague, Jaroslaw Hampel again looked good as he streaked clear in heat ten, but he reckoned without fellow countryman Tomasz Gollob, who revved his huge army of fans into a frenzy when a typically daring effort saw him fly around the outside exiting the fourth bend of lap one. While Gollob went on to collect a huge win, Hampel comfortably kept five-times World Champion Tony Rickardsson in third spot for the duration.

Another Pole, Grzegorz Walasek, surprised everyone in heat thirteen, when he blasted past Greg Hancock on the back straight and then powered inside Crump in front of the main grandstand. Hancock later retired on lap three with a puncture, but there was no stopping the speedy Pole, who had only been called into the meeting to replace injured wildcard Slawomir Drabik. The pumped-up partisan crowd had more to be enthralled by in heat fourteen, when Hampel and Piotr Protasiewicz easily filled the leading two positions from Mikael Max and Sullivan. After his first-race success, Bjarne Pedersen had run a second to Andreas Jonsson in heat seven, and he followed that up with a similar finish behind Rickardsson in heat fifteen – both speedsters cleverly working their way past Richardson, who had led the first couple of laps. Gollob had his fans drooling with another big win in the next heat, while behind, Adams had used his favoured inside line to take up second position, only for Nicki Pedersen to displace him later on the home straight.

It was the turn of four more riders to fall by the wayside over heats seventeen and eighteen, namely British lads Loram and Richardson in the former, followed by Max and the very unfortunate Bohumil Brhel, who was leading the latter when he shed a chain. The Poles continued to march on, however, with Walasek and Hampel notching successive victories ahead of the unrelated Pedersens, Nicki and Bjarne respectively, although the Arena-Essex ace gained his win at the expense of Rickardsson, who, after bustling his way into the lead, dramatically lifted on the second bend of the final lap and bit the dust after losing the back end of his steed.

Amid rapturous enthusiasm from the packed terraces, a clearly delighted Protasiewicz claimed a semi-final slot by winning heat twenty-one, with Adams joining him after surging through from fourth to second on the back straight, the gifted Aussie's inside manoeuvre spelling the end for Crump and Jonsson. The cheering momentarily died down in heat twenty-two, when Gollob was eliminated after suffering a mechanical failure on the first turn. That left Hancock in the fresh air, but he was brilliantly passed by Rickardsson in mid-race, with Sullivan's persistence finally paying off, when he also ousted the American on the last lap.

Bjarne Pedersen made the break in the first semi, but was quickly passed by a charging Protasiewicz, whose efforts immediately cheered the audience after their disappointment of the previous race. With 'Pepe' on his way, Walasek and Pedersen traded places, and the Dane required all his skill to eventually secure second place. With the noise level increasing further, a turbo-start off the outside gate took Hampel to the fore in the other semi, with the consistent Ricko making it three finals out of three in beating Nicki Pedersen and Adams for the vital second position.

All eyes were no doubt fixed on the Polish duo in the final, but it was Bjarne Pedersen all the way from the tapes who took the accolades for the first time at this high level, while Hampel could again be well satisfied with second spot. Meanwhile, battling to the end, Rickardsson found a way past Protasiewicz coming off the last bend: the third place giving him 18 GP points and first position overall on a total of 54. Having completed a third of the series, the leaders were tightly bunched with Crump (53), Adams (49) and the fast-rising Hampel (43) chomping at the bit just behind the Swedish great.

RACE DETAILS

PRE-MAIN EVENT

HEAT ONE:	Bjarne Pedersen, Mark Loram, Nicki Pedersen, Wieslaw Jagus.
HEAT TWO:	Mikael Max, Grzegorz Walasek, Jesper B. Jensen, Rune Holta.
HEAT THREE:	(Rerun) Andreas Jonsson, Kaj Laukkanen, Hans N. Andersen, Scott Nicholls (ret).
HEAT FOUR:	Bohumil Brhel, Piotr Protasiewicz, Ales Dryml, Lukas Dryml.
HEAT FIVE:	(Rerun) Nicki Pedersen, Hans N. Andersen, Lukas Dryml, Rune Holta (f, ex).
HEAT SIX:	Wieslaw Jagus, Scott Nicholls, Jesper B. Jensen, Ales Dryml.
HEAT SEVEN:	Andreas Jonsson, Bjarne Pedersen, Piotr Protasiewicz, Grzegorz Walasek.
HEAT EIGHT:	Mikael Max, Mark Loram, Bohumil Brhel, Kaj Laukkanen.
HEAT NINE:	Jason Crump, Lee Richardson, Ryan Sullivan, Leigh Adams (ret).
HEAT TEN:	Tomasz Gollob, Jaroslaw Hampel, Tony Rickardsson, Greg Hancock.
HEAT ELEVEN:	Nicki Pedersen, Piotr Protasiewicz, Scott Nicholls, Kaj Laukkanen.
HEAT TWELVE:	Bohumil Brhel, Grzegorz Walasek, Wieslaw Jagus, Hans N. Andersen.

MAIN EVENT

HEAT THIRTEEN:	Grzegorz Walasek, Jason Crump, Andreas Jonsson, Greg Hancock (ret).
HEAT FOURTEEN:	Jaroslaw Hampel, Piotr Protasiewicz, Mikael Max, Ryan Sullivan.
HEAT FIFTEEN:	Tony Rickardsson, Bjarne Pedersen, Lee Richardson, Bohumil Brhel.
HEAT SIXTEEN:	Tomasz Gollob, Nicki Pedersen, Leigh Adams, Mark Loram.
HEAT SEVENTEEN:	Andreas Jonsson, Ryan Sullivan, Mark Loram, Lee Richardson.
HEAT EIGHTEEN:	Greg Hancock, Leigh Adams, Mikael Max, Bohumil Brhel (ret).
HEAT NINETEEN:	Grzegorz Walasek, Nicki Pedersen, Piotr Protasiewicz, Tony Rickardsson (fell).

HEAT TWENTY:	Jaroslaw Hampel, Bjarne Pedersen, Tomasz Gollob, Jason Crump.
HEAT TWENTY-ONE:	Piotr Protasiewicz, Leigh Adams, Jason Crump, Andreas Jonsson.
HEAT TWENTY-TWO:	Tony Rickardsson, Ryan Sullivan, Greg Hancock, Tomasz Gollob (ret).

SEMI-FINALS

HEAT TWENTY-THREE:	Piotr Protasiewicz, Bjarne Pedersen, Grzegorz Walasek, Ryan Sullivan.
HEAT TWENTY-FOUR:	Jaroslaw Hampel, Tony Rickardsson, Nicki Pedersen, Leigh Adams.

GRAND FINAL

HEAT TWENTY-FIVE:	Bjarne Pedersen, Jaroslaw Hampel, Tony Rickardsson, Piotr Protasiewicz.

NOTE: Eliminated riders are underlined throughout

GRAND PRIX OF BRITAIN (ROUND FOUR)

12 JUNE, MILLENNIUM STADIUM, CARDIFF

Riders and fans alike made the now annual speedway pilgrimage to the wonderful Millennium Stadium for what was actually the sixty-fifth Grand Prix since the competition's inception in 1995. The home contingent was swelled to five riders, with Chris Louis and David Norris in the line-up as wildcards; the latter, deservedly included after producing such consistently good form at Elite League level for Eastbourne, captivated the large audience with a super showing. Indeed, he earned the tag of 'Mr Entertainer' and it was a shame that his wholehearted efforts yielded just eight GP points in the final analysis.

Victory on the night eventually went to American Greg Hancock, although silky smooth Australian Leigh Adams was only inches adrift at the end of a gripping finale. The last heat epitomized a brilliant night of racing, proving that it is possible to produce decent one-off circuits – all those responsible for its preparation could feel justly proud that so much has been learnt in a relatively short space of time.

Amazingly, like Bjarne Pedersen in the previous round at Wroclaw, Hancock set the Cardiff ball rolling with victory in the opening heat ahead of Scott Nicholls, before going on to claim a maximum 25 points. So honoured to have been called-up for the meeting, Norris first appeared in heat two and really set the crowd alight. Tomasz Gollob charged into an early lead from Bohumil Brhel, only for the Brit to take a fast outside route past the veteran Czech down the back straight of the initial lap. Then the East Sussex boy caught up with the Pole on lap two, beautifully sweeping through on the third turn. His subsequent victory was well received and it was clear to see just what it meant to Norris as he took the applause on the warm-down lap. Lee Richardson had to settle for second spot behind Andreas Jonsson in the next race, before the noise levels again went up a notch to herald Mark Loram's fourth-heat success over Rune Holta.

Having run a last in the meeting's opener, Louis was back out in the sixth-heat eliminator and, although Brhel was never headed from the gate, the influential Ipswich teamster showed his mettle to hold out Lukas Dryml for second place. Hancock returned to the fray in heat seven, but after making a good start he was relegated to the runner-up position when Jonsson swept by on the outside coming off the fourth bend of the initial lap. The qualification system threw up a battle of the Brits in the next race and, while Richardson was never headed from the tapes, the action behind was fast and furious. This saw Loram drive under Norris on lap two, only for the Eastbourne racer to reverse the positions a couple of bends later, with Nicholls also finding a route past England's last World Champion in the closing stages.

It was time for the leading protagonists to enter the contest in heats nine and ten, with respective victories posted by Nicki Pedersen and Leigh Adams. The second of the two races was the most interesting, with Adams rounding the faster-starting Tony Rickardsson on the back straight and holding on for the win, despite hitting a bump on the third bend and momentarily getting awkwardly out of shape. Heat twelve had to be restarted after Brhel and Andersen had taken a close inspection of the track on a fierce first turn. The rerun saw Nicholls lead from Brhel, while Andersen and Holta exchanged places in a ding-dong scrap. This culminated in Andersen forcefully diving under Holta on the first bend of the final lap, with the Norwegian falling heavily. The Dane was adjudged to have been at fault, and with Brhel failing to beat the designated time allowance, the second rerun ended up as a match race, which resulted in Holta claiming the win after cutting under Nicholls on the back straight.

Two races later, the crowd was in ecstasy when Loram dashed outside fellow countryman Richardson for victory, with five-times World Champion Rickardsson trailing in third spot, despite starting from the advantageous inside grid. Crump, having run a second in his previous outing, got back to winning ways in heat fifteen, with Hancock ousting Sullivan on the fourth bend for a good second. Adams just held sway from the inside grid to win heat sixteen, while Gollob repelled the pressing Norris behind. Nicholls and Piotr Protasiewicz marched on in the next race, the Pole producing a particularly good ride to send Bjarne Pedersen and Ryan Sullivan through the trapdoor.

Norris again livened up proceedings in heat eighteen, when, after completely missing the start, he took a sweet inside line around the opening corner, going from fourth to first in the process. With the positions set, the battling Englishman crossed the line ahead of Rickardsson, sending Jaroslaw Hampel and Holta home early. With Nicki Pedersen away, Richardson slid off on the first turn of heat nineteen and, although referee Marek Wojacek's decision to exclude the Brit was unpopular with the fans, replays proved the official to be correct. Gollob produced a trademark ride in the rerun, bravely squeezing through the smallest of gaps to pass Pedersen on the back straight. Pedersen came back to reclaim first place, but a later loss of control let the Pole through for the win, with Crump also coming by for second when the reigning World Champion caught a rut on the last bend. Heat twenty was a thriller, with Hancock initially to the fore. Behind, Jonsson eventually got the better of a terrific duel with Loram, prior to just getting up to grab the verdict on the line from Hancock. In a final flurry of activity, the last-placed but ever-challenging Adams found the speed to swap places with Loram.

With the stakes rising, Nicki Pedersen jumped from the trap in heat twenty-one, but the race was soon halted when a domino effect caused Rickardsson to tumble on the first turn. Pedersen was a clear victor from Nicholls at the second attempt, with Rickardsson heading out despite valiantly passing Loram in mid-race. Adams was a tapes-to-flag victor in the next eliminator, with Richardson joining him at the semi-final stage after edging out the gallant Norris. The first semi went the way of Hancock from Richardson, with Nicki Pedersen and Gollob the two to fall by the wayside. An Aussie 1-2 followed, with Crump taking command from the start, while Adams rounded Jonsson and Nicholls on the first corner to book a final place alongside his compatriot. The big showdown saw Hancock gate with Richardson, but the Oxford skipper just managed to show exiting the second bend. The pressing Adams powered under Richardson on the back straight next time around and set after the American, his final push only just failing on the line. With Crump bringing up the rear, it meant he and Adams had a share of top spot in the title chase, both having amassed 69 points, with Rickardsson (62) dropping back to third place ahead of Hancock (57).

RACE DETAILS

PRE-MAIN EVENT

HEAT ONE: Greg Hancock, Scott Nicholls, Hans N. Andersen, Chris Louis.
HEAT TWO: David Norris, Tomasz Gollob, Bohumil Brhel, Kaj Laukkanen.
HEAT THREE: Andreas Jonsson, Lee Richardson, Ales Dryml, Lukas Dryml.
HEAT FOUR: Mark Loram, Rune Holta, Jesper B. Jensen, Mikael Max.
HEAT FIVE: Ales Dryml, Hans N. Andersen, Mikael Max, Kaj Laukkanen.
HEAT SIX: Bohumil Brhel, Chris Louis, Lukas Dryml, Jesper B. Jensen.
HEAT SEVEN: Andreas Jonsson, Greg Hancock, Tomasz Gollob, Rune Holta.
HEAT EIGHT: Lee Richardson, David Norris, Scott Nicholls, Mark Loram.
HEAT NINE: Nicki Pedersen, Jason Crump, Bjarne Pedersen, Piotr Protasiewicz.
HEAT TEN: Leigh Adams, Tony Rickardsson, Ryan Sullivan, Jaroslaw Hampel.
HEAT ELEVEN: Tomasz Gollob, Mark Loram, Chris Louis, Ales Dryml (ret).
HEAT TWELVE: (Rerun twice) Rune Holta, Scott Nicholls, Bohumil Brhel (ex, two minutes), Hans N. Andersen (ex, foul riding).

MAIN EVENT

HEAT THIRTEEN: Nicki Pedersen, Andreas Jonsson, Scott Nicholls, Jaroslaw Hampel.
HEAT FOURTEEN: Mark Loram, Lee Richardson, Tony Rickardsson, Bjarne Pedersen.
HEAT FIFTEEN: Jason Crump, Greg Hancock, Ryan Sullivan, Rune Holta.
HEAT SIXTEEN: Leigh Adams, Tomasz Gollob, David Norris, Piotr Protasiewicz.
HEAT SEVENTEEN: Scott Nicholls, Piotr Protasiewicz, Bjarne Pedersen, Ryan Sullivan.
HEAT EIGHTEEN: David Norris, Tony Rickardsson, Jaroslaw Hampel, Rune Holta.
HEAT NINETEEN: (Rerun) Tomasz Gollob, Jason Crump, Nicki Pedersen, Lee Richardson (f, ex).
HEAT TWENTY: Andreas Jonsson, Greg Hancock, Leigh Adams, Mark Loram.
HEAT TWENTY-ONE: (Rerun) Nicki Pedersen, Scott Nicholls, Tony Rickardsson, Mark Loram.
HEAT TWENTY-TWO: Leigh Adams, Lee Richardson, David Norris, Piotr Protasiewicz.

SEMI-FINALS

HEAT TWENTY-THREE: Greg Hancock, Lee Richardson, Nicki Pedersen, Tomasz Gollob.
HEAT TWENTY-FOUR: Jason Crump, Leigh Adams, Andreas Jonsson, Scott Nicholls.

GRAND FINAL

HEAT TWENTY-FIVE: Greg Hancock, Leigh Adams, Lee Richardson, Jason Crump.

NOTE: Eliminated riders are underlined throughout

GRAND PRIX OF DENMARK (ROUND FIVE)

26 JUNE, PARKEN, COPENHAGEN

The Grand Prix series went past the halfway mark at the superbly appointed Parken Stadium in Copenhagen, with the Danish duo of Kenneth Bjerre and Niels-Kristian Iversen called up as wildcards for the event. Meanwhile, stylish Brit Simon Stead was a late replacement for Jaroslaw Hampel, who was unfortunately forced to withdraw through injury. Before a lively audience, two riders went into the round jointly holding first place, namely Jason Crump and Leigh Adams, but at the end of it all, one had taken a great stride forward. The specially prepared 275-metre circuit served up some incident-packed racing, with several riders caught out in particular by a rut that appeared on the fourth turn as the action unfurled towards the latter part of the proceedings.

Prior to that, the early exchanges saw Iversen and Bjerre excel in their first meeting at this level, both charging through to the Main Event in determined fashion. Two of the English contingent were among the first set of casualties, with Stead and Mark Loram joined in the changing room by the Czech pair of Bohumil Brhel and Lukas Dryml. The atmosphere went up a few degrees when Nicki Pedersen entered the action in heat nine and the reigning World Champion didn't disappoint the partisan home crowd. After initially holding sway from the gate, Pedersen was caught and passed on the inside by a quick-moving Greg Hancock on lap two, but the American's lead was only momentarily held on the back straight, as the Dane charged back around the outside for an impressive win. Behind, Crump had a steady if unspectacular opening ride, while Scott Nicholls brought up the rear.

The tenth heat saw Andreas Jonsson make the break ahead, with Adams beautifully cutting inside to lead off the first corner. The Swede wasn't to be denied though, with victory going his way after a burst of speed had taken him around the Swindon man entering the first bend of lap two. A rerun eleventh heat spelt the end of the night for Rune Holta and Ales Dryml, with Ryan Sullivan and Kaj Laukkanen following suit in the next race. Nicki Pedersen marched on with a huge win over Tony Rickardsson and Lee Richardson in heat thirteen, prior to Adams using the inside gate to great effect in posting victory over his rival-in-chief, Crump.

Heat sixteen was to prove eventful, with a clutch problem causing much activity in the Iversen camp. However, as the clock ticked down, his team showed they were really on the ball by quickly producing a second steed. When the tapes were released, Jonsson carried on where he had left off in heat ten, leading the charge from Iversen. The race was to end suddenly on lap three though, when Nicholls lifted alarmingly exiting the fourth bend and crashed down. With the Brit excluded, Jonsson produced a repeat performance to defeat Iversen, with the third-placed Mikael Max left to face an elimination heat.

Top Pole Tomasz Gollob had barely been noticeable in running two third places prior to heat seventeen, but with the dreaded exit door in sight he made a rapid start to lead from Richardson. Clearly there was a lot at stake and, with the crowd on his side, Bjerre hurtled under Richardson entering the first bend of lap two, forcing the Peterborough racer to adjust his position in a split second. Inevitably, Richardson lost control and fell, with the closely following Nicholls doing a superb job in laying his machine down, thereby sparing both men from injury. Referee Tony Steele saw no reason to penalize the Dane, so as the primary cause of the stoppage, it was Richardson who headed out. Gollob again gated ahead in the rerun, only to veer wide on the second bend and allow both Bjerre and Nicholls through. Although he chased hard, there was no way back for the Pole and he was somewhat unlucky to be heading out, having held a comfortable lead in the initial running. The next race signalled the end of the road for Jesper B. Jensen and Piotr Protasiewicz, with the action set to dramatically hot up in heat nineteen, when Nicki Pedersen faced Crump. Showing lightning reactions, it was Pedersen who popped away from the gate, but Crump built up a head of steam down the back straight and shaped for an outside challenge on the apex of the third/fourth corner. However, Pedersen moved across the track and closed the door, leaving Crump with no option other than to bale out. Despite protestations, Pedersen was excluded by the meeting official and it was Hancock who dashed home at the second attempt, with Crump in his slipstream.

There was more drama in heat twenty when, with Jonsson once again leading, fellow Swede Rickardsson dramatically lifted on the fourth turn of lap three and took a real purler into the air safety barrier. Jonsson headed Adams in the rerun, but the race only reached the third corner, when Hans N. Andersen fell heavily after his engine had suffered a malfunction. With just two speedsters remaining, Adams took command from the start of the second rerun and was never troubled as he headed into the semi-finals. The remarkable wildcard twosome of Iversen and Bjerre strode on in heat twenty-one, both punching the air with delight as they crossed the line to send Max and Rickardsson spiralling from the contest.

Andersen showed ahead from the tapes in heat twenty-two, but was soon passed by a charging Nicki Pedersen. Both men seemed set for berths in the last eight, but on the very last bend, the unfortunate Andersen suffered another blow-up and, although completely out of control, he careered across the finish line, but not before Nicholls and Bjarne Pedersen had relegated him to last place. The first semi-final saw Hancock and Nicholls dice on the opening lap, with the two actually making contact on the difficult fourth corner. While Hancock went on to win, the Brit amazingly came to grief yards from the chequered flag after again hitting the notorious fourth bend rut. Jonsson did quite brilliantly to avoid Nicholls' bucking machine and his efforts were rewarded with a place in the final.

The second semi-final wasn't quite so eventful, as Crump overturned any psychological advantage Adams might have gained from their earlier tussle by sweeping to victory after cutting across the pack from the inside gate. Nicki Pedersen followed him into the big showdown, while namesake Bjarne accompanied Adams through the exit door.

So to the final, and with Crump again leading after a jet-propelled getaway, the chasing Nicki Pedersen lifted badly on the fourth bend of lap two and parted company from his machine. His bike eventually came to rest some way down the home straight and, showing great concern for the remaining competitors, Pedersen ran down the track and hauled it out of harm's way. The race was stopped despite his well-intentioned efforts, with Crump and Jonsson breaking clear from Hancock in the rerun. It was the Aussie who took the initiative on the back straight, however, and went on to secure the tenth GP win of his career. More significantly for the three-times world number two, he opened up a 14-point lead in the title chase as the result took him on to 94 points, with Adams (80), Hancock (75), Rickardsson (69) and Nicki Pedersen (63) as his nearest challengers.

RACE DETAILS

PRE-MAIN EVENT

HEAT ONE:	Tony Rickardsson, Kenneth Bjerre, Bohumil Brhel, Hans N. Andersen (ret).
HEAT TWO:	Niels-Kristian Iversen, Ryan Sullivan, Mark Loram, Ales Dryml.
HEAT THREE:	Jesper B. Jensen, Rune Holta, Piotr Protasiewicz, Lukas Dryml.

HEAT FOUR:	Kaj Laukkanen, Bjarne Pedersen, Mikael Max, Simon Stead.
HEAT FIVE:	Ales Dryml, Piotr Protasiewicz, Bohumil Brhel, Simon Stead.
HEAT SIX:	(Rerun) Hans N. Andersen, Mikael Max, Mark Loram, Lukas Dryml.
HEAT SEVEN:	Tony Rickardsson, Bjarne Pedersen, Jesper B. Jensen, Ryan Sullivan.
HEAT EIGHT:	Kenneth Bjerre, Niels-Kristian Iversen, Kaj Laukkanen, Rune Holta.
HEAT NINE:	Nicki Pedersen, Greg Hancock, Jason Crump, Scott Nicholls.
HEAT TEN:	Andreas Jonsson, Leigh Adams, Tomasz Gollob, Lee Richardson.
HEAT ELEVEN:	(Rerun) Mikael Max, Jesper B. Jensen, Rune Holta, Ales Dryml.
HEAT TWELVE:	Hans N. Andersen, Piotr Protasiewicz, Ryan Sullivan, Kaj Laukkanen.

MAIN EVENT

HEAT THIRTEEN:	Nicki Pedersen, Tony Rickardsson, Lee Richardson, Piotr Protasiewicz.
HEAT FOURTEEN:	Leigh Adams, Jason Crump, Jesper B. Jensen, Kenneth Bjerre.
HEAT FIFTEEN:	Greg Hancock, Hans N. Andersen, Tomasz Gollob, Bjarne Pedersen.
HEAT SIXTEEN:	(Rerun) Andreas Jonsson, Niels-Kristian Iversen, Mikael Max, Scott Nicholls (f, ex).
HEAT SEVENTEEN:	(Rerun) Kenneth Bjerre, Scott Nicholls, Tomasz Gollob, Lee Richardson (f, ex).
HEAT EIGHTEEN:	Bjarne Pedersen, Mikael Max, Jesper B. Jensen, Piotr Protasiewicz.
HEAT NINETEEN:	(Rerun) Greg Hancock, Jason Crump, Niels-Kristian Iversen, Nicki Pedersen (ex, impeding opponent).
HEAT TWENTY:	(Rerun twice) Leigh Adams, Andreas Jonsson, Hans N. Andersen (f, ex), Tony Rickardsson (f, ex).
HEAT TWENTY-ONE:	Niels-Kristian Iversen, Kenneth Bjerre, Mikael Max, Tony Rickardsson.
HEAT TWENTY-TWO:	Nicki Pedersen, Scott Nicholls, Bjarne Pedersen, Hans N. Andersen.

SEMI-FINALS

HEAT TWENTY-THREE:	Greg Hancock, Andreas Jonsson, Niels-Kristian Iversen, Scott Nicholls (fell).
HEAT TWENTY-FOUR:	Jason Crump, Nicki Pedersen, Kenneth Bjerre, Leigh Adams.

GRAND FINAL

HEAT TWENTY-FIVE:	(Rerun) Jason Crump, Andreas Jonsson, Greg Hancock, Nicki Pedersen (f, ex).

NOTE: Eliminated riders are underlined throughout

GRAND PRIX OF SCANDINAVIA (ROUND SIX)

21 AUGUST, ULLEVI STADIUM, GOTHENBURG

Having been roundly vilified following the World Cup final at Poole two weeks previously, the Scandinavian Grand Prix turned into something of a fairytale for Hans N. Andersen. In front of 16,251 spectators, the Dane showed his undoubted class to reach the final, before leading home an excellent field from start to finish. Meanwhile, taking second place in the showdown was Jason Crump and, in so doing, the Australian opened up a commanding 23-point lead over his nearest rivals. After a break of almost two months, the GP series got going again and with the scheduled Friday practice abandoned due to heavy rainfall, Ole Olsen and his track team did a remarkable job in producing a suitable racing strip for the Saturday evening event. While the likes of Andersen, Tony Rickardsson and Tomasz Gollob comfortably negotiated the opening exchanges, notable early casualties included Mark Loram and wildcard Antonio Lindback in heats five and six respectively.

Andersen's first outing had occurred in heat three, when he took a neat inside line to pass the faster-starting Piotr Protasiewicz for a fine win. However, in heat seven, the Ipswich heat-leader was unable to improve on third place behind Rickardsson and Jaroslaw Hampel. That sent the Dane into an eleventh-heat eliminator, but, remaining calm, he sped away from the tapes to beat Peter Karlsson, with Ryan Sullivan surprisingly heading out in third position. Crump's initial outing had occurred two races earlier, when a forceful first turn (at one point with his front wheel over the inner kerb) provided the necessary advantage over his opponents. Behind, Leigh Adams, who entered the meeting as Crump's closest challenger in the GP standings, held second place briefly, but was relegated to the rear on the back straight and was unable to recover any ground on the unrelated Pedersens, Nicki and Bjarne.

Crump made his next appearance on the narrow circuit in heat thirteen, which had to be restarted after a clutch problem had dragged Mikael Max into the tapes; the Swede becoming the second rider to suffer such misfortune, following Ales Dryml's similar malfunction in heat six. The rerun saw Rickardsson surge into the lead, but Crump energetically hounded him down and, after taking the high line around the third and fourth turns, the Aussie decisively tore outside on the home straight as they began lap two. Gollob completed a hat-trick of wins when defeating Scott Nicholls in the next race, prior to Nicki Pedersen taking a rerun heat fifteen from Greg Hancock and Lee Richardson.

In heat sixteen, Adams was at his best, making no mistake to triumph over Andersen, as the meeting reached its crucial stage. Keeping the British flag flying, Richardson safely came through a 'trapdoor' race in heat seventeen, steaming past Karlsson on the back straight of the opening lap for a brilliant victory. There was plenty to talk about in heat nineteen, when Crump chased Nicki Pedersen into the first turn and could visibly be seen to kick the rear wheel of the Dane's machine! Pedersen was unaffected by the incident, but the Bristol-born racer lifted on the first corner and fell awkwardly for an exclusion.

The rerun had the crowd on the edge of their seats as Nicholls cut back to lead from Pedersen entering the back straight, only for the reigning World Champion to determinedly retake first spot shortly afterwards. Then, on the fourth bend, Andersen came from nowhere to sweep by for an excellent success. Adams held off Gollob at the start of heat twenty, but was unable to prevent Rickardsson from dashing past, with the Pole subsequently following suit, as the Elite League's main man appeared to be struggling for speed. Nicholls was victorious in heat twenty-one, after fellow Englishman Richardson had regrettably failed to leave the gate due to a mechanical gremlin. The battle for second place was intense, with Andreas Jonsson buzzing all over Hancock for the duration, prior to driving inside on the back straight of the final lap. That wasn't the end of the titanic tussle though, as the American took a daring line right out by the air barrier on the final corner and the momentum generated was sufficient for him to win the dash to the line.

Adams was an all-the-way victor in the next race, while Crump had a roller-coaster first lap, going from second to last, before powering past Bjarne Pedersen and Karlsson to regain the runner-up position. Andersen and Crump held the favourable positions through the first semi-final, thereby spelling the end of Nicholls' and Gollob's aspirations. The other semi-final resulted in a clear victory for Rickardsson, while Hancock again used the outside dirt line to good effect, eliminating Nicki Pedersen and Adams in the process.

So to the most important four laps of the evening and Crump appeared to be in the ascendancy from the start, but it was Andersen who raced through on a perfect inside line for the biggest race win of his life. Crump and Rickardsson were left to scrap away for second place, but it was the Aussie who held on to take his overall tally to 114 points at the head of the leaderboard. Hancock's fourth-place finish in the final took him level with Adams on 91 points, while Rickardsson moved his total to 87. Glory for Hans N. Andersen made him the fifteenth rider to win a GP and he joined an illustrious list of five previous Danish victors: Tommy Knudsen, Hans Nielsen, Brian Andersen, Nicki Pedersen and Bjarne Pedersen.

RACE DETAILS

PRE-MAIN EVENT

HEAT ONE:	Tony Rickardsson, Ryan Sullivan, Rune Holta, Antonio Lindback.
HEAT TWO:	Kaj Laukkanen, Jaroslaw Hampel, Lee Richardson, Peter Karlsson.
HEAT THREE:	Hans N. Andersen, Piotr Protasiewicz, Lukas Dryml, Ales Dryml.
HEAT FOUR:	Tomasz Gollob, Jesper B. Jensen, Bohumil Brhel, Mark Loram (ret).
HEAT FIVE:	Peter Karlsson, Lukas Dryml, Mark Loram, Rune Holta.
HEAT SIX:	(Rerun twice) Lee Richardson, Bohumil Brhel, Antonio Lindback Ales Dryml (ex, tapes).
HEAT SEVEN:	Tony Rickardsson, Jaroslaw Hampel, Hans N. Andersen, Jesper B. Jensen (fell).
HEAT EIGHT:	(Rerun) Tomasz Gollob, Piotr Protasiewicz, Kaj Laukkanen, Ryan Sullivan (f, ex).
HEAT NINE:	Jason Crump, Nicki Pedersen, Bjarne Pedersen, Leigh Adams.
HEAT TEN:	Andreas Jonsson, Scott Nicholls, Greg Hancock, Mikael Max.
HEAT ELEVEN:	Hans N. Andersen, Peter Karlsson, Ryan Sullivan, Bohumil Brhel.
HEAT TWELVE:	Lee Richardson, Kaj Laukkanen, Jesper B. Jensen, Lukas Dryml.

MAIN EVENT

HEAT THIRTEEN:	(Rerun) Jason Crump, Tony Rickardsson, Kaj Laukkanen, Mikael Max (ex, tapes).
HEAT FOURTEEN:	Tomasz Gollob, Scott Nicholls, Bjarne Pedersen, Peter Karlsson.
HEAT FIFTEEN:	(Rerun) Nicki Pedersen, Greg Hancock, Lee Richardson, Jaroslaw Hampel.
HEAT SIXTEEN:	Leigh Adams, Hans N. Andersen, Andreas Jonsson, Piotr Protasiewicz.
HEAT SEVENTEEN:	Lee Richardson, Peter Karlsson, Kaj Laukkanen, Piotr Protasiewicz.
HEAT EIGHTEEN:	Bjarne Pedersen, Andreas Jonsson, Jaroslaw Hampel, Mikael Max.
HEAT NINETEEN:	(Rerun) Hans N. Andersen, Nicki Pedersen, Scott Nicholls, Jason Crump (f, ex).
HEAT TWENTY:	Tony Rickardsson, Tomasz Gollob, Leigh Adams, Greg Hancock.
HEAT TWENTY-ONE:	Scott Nicholls, Greg Hancock, Andreas Jonsson, Lee Richardson (ret).
HEAT TWENTY-TWO:	Leigh Adams, Jason Crump, Bjarne Pedersen, Peter Karlsson

SEMI-FINALS

HEAT TWENTY-THREE:	Hans N. Andersen, Jason Crump, Scott Nicholls, Tomasz Gollob.
HEAT TWENTY-FOUR:	Tony Rickardsson, Greg Hancock, Nicki Pedersen, Leigh Adams.

GRAND FINAL

HEAT TWENTY-FIVE:	Hans N. Andersen, Jason Crump, Tony Rickardsson, Greg Hancock.

NOTE: Eliminated riders are underlined throughout

GRAND PRIX OF SLOVENIA (ROUND SEVEN)

4 SEPTEMBER, MATIJE GUBCA STADIUM, KRSKO

Jason Crump edged a little nearer to the World Championship at the Matije Gubca Stadium, but at the end of a speedway fest on the wide and sweeping 388-metre circuit, he had former title-holders Tony Rickardsson and Greg Hancock breathing down his neck. While the high-quality field no doubt weighed up the track, the first four heats were won from the inside gate. The sequence was broken in heat five, when Jaroslaw Hampel cut across from the outside grid to take victory from Mikael Max. That accounted for Ales Dryml and Jesper B. Jensen, with Bohumil Brhel and home nation wildcard Izak Santej heading out in the next race. Up front, meanwhile, a super race ended with Mark Loram taking victory after roaring inside Lukas Dryml on the last bend.

Hancock first appeared in heat nine, but could only run a third place behind a galloping Tomasz Gollob and the fast-rising Hans N. Andersen. Even more surprising, perhaps, was the sight of reigning World Champion Nicki Pedersen bringing up the rear. Rickardsson won heat ten at a canter, while Crump saw off fellow Aussie Leigh Adams for second spot. Heat eleven put paid to the chances of Lukas Dryml and Kaj Laukkanen, while Hampel beat off a mid-race challenge from Jonsson for victory, having previously driven inside the Swede on the fourth bend of the opening lap.

Max was an all-the-way victor in heat twelve, but the action was fast and furious behind. Ryan Sullivan flew past Slovenian wildcard Matej Zagar on the third lap, only for the brilliant Reading speedster to produce a ruthless last bend, moving 'Sully' off line and out of the meeting. Interest also unfortunately ended for battling Brit Loram, who just couldn't improve on fourth position, despite his usual level of full-blooded commitment. Zagar was immediately back on track in heat thirteen, when he again used the inside line around the fourth bend to good effect, passing Gollob on the first lap for a fine success. The Pole was later relegated to third place, when Norwegian Rune Holta found the required drive to speed ahead. Crump survived a dodgy moment to win the next heat from Jonsson and Hancock, after hitting a hole and lifting on the third bend of lap one.

Heat fifteen saw Andersen jump ahead from the gate, only for Adams to cruise by on a faster outside line going down the back straight. The Dane attempted to come back in the same place on lap two, but the smooth-riding Australian repelled his challenge, before going on to take the fluttering victor's flag. Rickardsson posted a second conclusive win in heat sixteen and certainly looked to be at his brilliant best, as he left Nicki Pedersen trailing. With Max and Bjarne Pedersen filling the all-important first two places in the subsequent race, it meant farewell to the Polish pair of Gollob and Piotr Protasiewicz. Despite interchanging positions with Pedersen during the race, Gollob was eventually outpaced by the clever Dane, as he failed to reach the semi-finals. Lee Richardson kept the British fans happy with a win over Hancock in heat eighteen, but it was curtains for Hampel and the other remaining English Lion, Scott Nicholls.

In heat nineteen, Adams dashed to the fore and had the track to himself for much of the race. Behind, a late bid took Jonsson steaming inside Nicki Pedersen on the back straight last time around and the thrilling Swede was extremely close to Adams at the finish. A pumped-up Rickardsson ripped through the pack to triumph in heat twenty, leaving the rest of the field to knock chunks out of each other. Andersen it was who eventually came home second, while Crump had to settle for third place. Nicki Pedersen led the charge in heat twenty-one, but it was an inspired Hancock who took victory after storming inside the Eastbourne racer on the fourth bend. Holta and Max were the unlucky duo to head out, with local hero Zagar and

Richardson joining them in the dressing room following heat twenty-two. Up front, Bjarne Pedersen crossed the line ahead after taking the lead on the back straight of lap one, with Crump safely joining him in the last eight.

Andersen blasted clear to take victory in the first semi-final, while Crump looked set to join him in the meeting's major race. However, a determined Hancock had other ideas and, after surviving the effects of a rut, the American, not for the first time, burst through on the fourth bend of lap three. Rickardsson was again untroubled on his way to another win in the other semi-final and Jonsson deservedly joined him in the big showdown after holding Nicki Pedersen at bay. Hancock sped from the tapes in the final, but he had no answer when Rickardsson drilled through for his fifth straight success on the much-used inside line coming off the fourth bend of lap one. At the back, Jonsson shadowed Andersen and shaped to make his move just prior to the third bend on the final lap. Dramatically though, Andersen slowed and the Swede ran into his rear wheel, before falling.

Crump had taken a 23-point lead into the meeting, but Rickardsson's thirteenth GP victory had shaved 8 points off that advantage, with Hancock also ready to pounce, just a single point adrift of the Swede. In summary, with two rounds remaining, Crump had 127 points, with Rickardsson (112) and Hancock (111) right on his heels. Adams, meanwhile, dropped down to fourth position overall (102), having failed to make any impression at the back in the first semi-final.

RACE DETAILS

PRE-MAIN EVENT

HEAT ONE:	Andreas Jonsson, Ryan Sullivan, Jesper B. Jensen, Izak Santej.
HEAT TWO:	Bjarne Pedersen, Matej Zagar, Lukas Dryml, Mikael Max.
HEAT THREE:	Lee Richardson, Piotr Protasiewicz, Ales Dryml, Bohumil Brhel.
HEAT FOUR:	Kaj Laukkanen, Rune Holta, Mark Loram, Jaroslaw Hampel.
HEAT FIVE:	Jaroslaw Hampel, Mikael Max, <u>Ales Dryml</u>, <u>Jesper B. Jensen</u>.
HEAT SIX:	Mark Loram, Lukas Dryml, <u>Bohumil Brhel</u>, <u>Izak Santej</u>.
HEAT SEVEN:	Rune Holta, Lee Richardson, Andreas Jonsson, Matej Zagar.
HEAT EIGHT:	Bjarne Pedersen, Piotr Protasiewicz, Ryan Sullivan, Kaj Laukkanen.
HEAT NINE:	Tomasz Gollob, Hans N. Andersen, Greg Hancock, Nicki Pedersen.
HEAT TEN:	Tony Rickardsson, Jason Crump, Leigh Adams, Scott Nicholls.
HEAT ELEVEN:	Jaroslaw Hampel, Andreas Jonsson, <u>Lukas Dryml</u>, <u>Kaj Laukkanen</u>.
HEAT TWELVE:	Mikael Max, Matej Zagar, <u>Ryan Sullivan</u>, <u>Mark Loram</u>.

MAIN EVENT

HEAT THIRTEEN:	Matej Zagar, Rune Holta, Tomasz Gollob, Scott Nicholls.
HEAT FOURTEEN:	Jason Crump, Andreas Jonsson, Greg Hancock, Bjarne Pedersen.
HEAT FIFTEEN:	Leigh Adams, Hans N. Andersen, Mikael Max, Lee Richardson.
HEAT SIXTEEN:	Tony Rickardsson, Nicki Pedersen, Jaroslaw Hampel, Piotr Protasiewicz.
HEAT SEVENTEEN:	Mikael Max, Bjarne Pedersen, <u>Tomasz Gollob</u>, <u>Piotr Protasiewicz</u>.
HEAT EIGHTEEN:	Lee Richardson, Greg Hancock, <u>Jaroslaw Hampel</u>, <u>Scott Nicholls</u>.
HEAT NINETEEN:	Leigh Adams, Andreas Jonsson, Nicki Pedersen, Matej Zagar.
HEAT TWENTY:	Tony Rickardsson, Hans N. Andersen, Jason Crump, Rune Holta.
HEAT TWENTY-ONE:	Greg Hancock, Nicki Pedersen, <u>Rune Holta</u>, <u>Mikael Max</u>.
HEAT TWENTY-TWO:	Bjarne Pedersen, Jason Crump, <u>Matej Zagar</u>, <u>Lee Richardson</u>.

SEMI-FINALS

HEAT TWENTY-THREE: Hans N. Andersen, Greg Hancock, Jason Crump, Leigh Adams.

HEAT TWENTY-FOUR: Tony Rickardsson, Andreas Jonsson, Nicki Pedersen, Bjarne Pedersen.

GRAND FINAL

HEAT TWENTY-FIVE: Tony Rickardsson, Greg Hancock, Hans N. Andersen, Andreas Jonsson (fell).

NOTE: Eliminated riders are underlined throughout

GRAND PRIX OF POLAND (ROUND EIGHT)

18 SEPTEMBER, POLONIA STADIUM, BYDGOSZCZ

Super Aussie Jason Crump produced a rock-steady performance to move within touching distance of his first World Championship title, although in truth, he was somewhat overshadowed by the 'King of Bydgoszcz' himself, namely the one and only Tomasz Gollob. Indeed, Atomic 'Tomek' ripped up the 348-metre raceway to scoop the Polish GP for a third successive year, while also taking his tally of Grand Prix wins to nine. In front of a full house of some 25,000 fans, the country's most famous sportsman whipped his supporters into a frenzy with an assured display, before milking their applause amid wonderful celebratory scenes at the end of a superb evening.

Prior to the meeting, the field was reduced to twenty-three competitors, when the doctor ruled Peterborough's Lukas Dryml unfit to race after crashing in an Elite League match at Ipswich just two nights previously. Polish wildcard Krzysztof Kasprzak stirred the fans in the opening heat, winning his debut Grand Prix ride in assured fashion after shooting across from the outside grid. A great reception greeted Gollob's first appearance in heat four and the hometown man initially appeared to have held off Ales Dryml on a tight first corner. The Czech, however, had the legs to pull ahead on the back straight, but with TG in hot pursuit, everyone held their breath in expectation of a big dive into the third turn. Gollob didn't disappoint and charged through, in the process opening the door for Jaroslaw Hampel to make it a Polish 1-2.

There were no surprises among the early departees and Gollob simply strode on in heat eight, winning comfortably from Rune Holta and Scott Nicholls – the Englishman bravely rounding Mikael Max on the third bend of lap three. It was the turn of the top eight from Slovenia to enter the fray in heat nine and Tony Rickardsson looked to be on a mission as he sped home by some margin from Andreas Jonsson. The fast-starting Hans N. Andersen was never troubled in the next heat, while Crump finished second after passing Greg Hancock on the back straight of lap one, with Leigh Adams later also ousting the American for a battling third.

After Messrs Max and Kasprzak, together with Mark Loram and Kaj Laukkanen, had failed to progress past the second batch of elimination races, Rickardsson cantered to another win ahead of Hampel. The mighty Swede did survive a mini-scare on his way to the flag though, for such was the speed he had generated, he actually clipped the air safety barrier at one point. Crump got away well in heat fourteen, but the race was stopped on lap two, when Bjarne Pedersen came down on the second bend as a charging Gollob swept through. Replays of the incident showed no contact and referee Tony Steele made the only decision he really could and that was to exclude the Dane. In the rerun, both Crump and Gollob went out wide in the search for drive, with Ryan Sullivan taking advantage to nip ahead on a less extravagant inside line around the first corner. 'Sully' was quickly outpaced, however, as Crump surged on to win, with Gollob pressing him all the way.

Adams catapulted away from the tapes for a fine victory in heat fifteen, with Nicki Pedersen following suit in the next race. After Hancock had lifted from the gate, Lee Richardson raised the British spirits by racing to an excellent success from Andersen in the heat seventeen eliminator. Meanwhile, back in fourth position and accompanying the fan-friendly American through the trapdoor was Bjarne Pedersen. The heat that followed meant the end for two more competitors and it saw Piotr Protasiewicz pass Nicholls in mid-race for victory, leaving Sullivan and Ales Dryml to load their vans for the journey home. Holta took the outside route to lead heat nineteen from Adams, with Rickardsson and Gollob surprisingly holding the minor placings. As Holta lapped up the fresh air, Adams had the misfortune to shed a primary chain at the start of lap three, allowing 'Ricko' and Gollob to upgrade their positions. Crump continued to enhance his ambition in heat twenty, winning all the way from Nicki Pedersen and Hampel, while Jonsson brought up the rear after almost running into the 2003 World Champion on the back straight of the opening lap.

With the tension rising, Gollob was back at his best in heat twenty-one, sprinting away to triumph over Nicholls, while Jonsson had a hair-raising ride in third spot. The Swede's efforts were to no avail sadly and, along with Richardson, both went out. Hampel led the charge in the last elimination race of the evening, while Adams cleverly took up second place after sneaking inside on the first corner. Andersen gave chase, but a mistake on the back straight of lap three put paid to his chances and he joined back-marker Protasiewicz in the dressing room.

Having maintained his 100 per cent record of semi-final appearances in the series, Swindon's number one got the drop to lead the vital race, albeit only to the first corner. Behind, Gollob and Holta tangled, with the Norwegian falling heavily. Up in the box, Mr Steele again made the correct decision, sanctioning an 'all-four' restart. The second attempt saw Adams emerge from the first bend shake-up, only for Holta to move sweetly by and into the lead. All eyes were firmly fixed on Gollob though, since, having gone wide on the second bend, he went full tilt down the back straight to blast ahead. That was that, as TG thundered into the final, along with Holta.

The second semi-final went the way of Crump, while Rickardsson had to draw upon his vast experience to find a route around Hampel halfway through the race. So to the final, the initial running of which saw Holta and Gollob again clash, with the Pole sent sprawling into the air safety barrier. Simultaneously, Rickardsson spun and fell on the first bend, with the meeting official permitting a full quota of riders to contest the rerun. An electric start from gate four then ensured Gollob stayed out of any bother and, after cruising into the lead up the back straight, he kept a frantic Crump at bay to win amid a carnival-like atmosphere. With Rickardsson filling third place, it meant he was the only rider who could possibly stop Crump from lifting the world crown in the final round at the Viking Ship Stadium in Hamar, Norway, the Aussie having accumulated 147 points compared to Rickardsson's tally of 130.

RACE DETAILS

PRE-MAIN EVENT

HEAT ONE:	Krzysztof Kasprzak, Rune Holta, Ryan Sullivan, Lukas Dryml (ns).
HEAT TWO:	Mikael Max, Mark Loram, Piotr Protasiewicz, Tomasz Chrzanowski.
HEAT THREE:	Lee Richardson, Scott Nicholls, Kaj Laukkanen, Jesper B. Jensen.

HEAT FOUR:	Tomasz Gollob, Jaroslaw Hampel, Ales Dryml, Bohumil Brhel.
HEAT FIVE:	Ryan Sullivan, Kaj Laukkanen, Tomasz Chrzanowski, Bohumil Brhel.
HEAT SIX:	Piotr Protasiewicz, Ales Dryml, Jesper B. Jensen, Lukas Dryml (ns).
HEAT SEVEN:	Jaroslaw Hampel, Lee Richardson, Krzysztof Kasprzak, Mark Loram.
HEAT EIGHT:	Tomasz Gollob, Rune Holta, Scott Nicholls, Mikael Max.
HEAT NINE:	Tony Rickardsson, Andreas Jonsson, Bjarne Pedersen, Nicki Pedersen.
HEAT TEN:	Hans N. Andersen, Jason Crump, Leigh Adams, Greg Hancock.
HEAT ELEVEN:	Ales Dryml, Ryan Sullivan, Mikael Max, Krzysztof Kasprzak.
HEAT TWELVE:	Scott Nicholls, Piotr Protasiewicz, Mark Loram, Kaj Laukkanen.

MAIN EVENT

HEAT THIRTEEN:	Tony Rickardsson, Jaroslaw Hampel, Greg Hancock, Piotr Protasiewicz.
HEAT FOURTEEN:	(Rerun) Jason Crump, Tomasz Gollob, Ryan Sullivan, Bjarne Pedersen (f, ex).
HEAT FIFTEEN:	Leigh Adams, Andreas Jonsson, Lee Richardson, Scott Nicholls.
HEAT SIXTEEN:	Nicki Pedersen, Rune Holta, Ales Dryml, Hans N. Andersen.
HEAT SEVENTEEN:	Lee Richardson, Hans N. Andersen, Greg Hancock, Bjarne Pedersen.
HEAT EIGHTEEN:	Piotr Protasiewicz, Scott Nicholls, Ryan Sullivan, Ales Dryml.
HEAT NINETEEN:	Rune Holta, Tony Rickardsson, Tomasz Gollob, Leigh Adams (ret).
HEAT TWENTY:	Jason Crump, Nicki Pedersen, Jaroslaw Hampel, Andreas Jonsson.
HEAT TWENTY-ONE:	Tomasz Gollob, Scott Nicholls, Andreas Jonsson, Lee Richardson.
HEAT TWENTY-TWO:	Jaroslaw Hampel, Leigh Adams, Hans N. Andersen, Piotr Protasiewicz.

SEMI-FINALS

HEAT TWENTY-THREE:	(Rerun) Tomasz Gollob, Rune Holta, Leigh Adams, Nicki Pedersen.
HEAT TWENTY-FOUR:	Jason Crump, Tony Rickardsson, Jaroslaw Hampel, Scott Nicholls.

GRAND FINAL

HEAT TWENTY-FIVE:	(Rerun) Tomasz Gollob, Jason Crump, Tony Rickardsson, Rune Holta.

NOTE: Eliminated riders are underlined throughout

GRAND PRIX OF NORWAY (ROUND NINE)

2 OCTOBER, VIKING SHIP STADIUM, HAMAR

A chilly Norwegian evening saw the long and winding Grand Prix road reach its conclusion and, on a particularly dry temporary circuit, Jason Crump finally realized his dream of being crowned World Champion. Having been on the cusp of glory going into the meeting, the three-times runner-up eventually scooped the sport's major prize in a bizarre heat nineteen, which took four attempts to complete. Initially, Crump, Nicki Pedersen and Ryan Sullivan all came down after the short run to the first turn. Slow motion replays showed that the strap on Pedersen's steel shoe had actually wrapped itself around Crump's footrest and the two dragged each other into the air safety barrier, with Sullivan also ending up in the resultant melee. Pedersen was particularly lucky to walk away unscathed, while 'Sully' wasn't so fortunate and took a nasty knock to the hand. Referee Tony Steele deemed no one at fault, but there was further drama when home favourite Rune Holta pulled back from the line in the rerun and was rightly excluded for delaying the start. After running out of room, the brave Sullivan came down on the first corner at the third time of asking and, after his exclusion light had been illuminated, it suddenly dawned on Crump that there were only two competitors left in the race and, as such, he had made it to the semi-finals and was therefore guaranteed sufficient points not to be overhauled at the head of the leaderboard. In his delight, he rode back to the pits with arms raised aloft and promptly fell from his bike! The first to reach him was proud father, Phil, who lifted him from the ground and the embrace that followed showed just what it meant to both of them. With mechanics and fellow riders joining in the celebrations, the little matter of another rerun seemed momentarily forgotten. However, order was soon restored and, although Crump made a crisp getaway, Pedersen charged past on the back straight, leaving the jubilant Aussie to pull celebratory wheelies as he ironically followed the outgoing World Champion home.

The earlier races had failed to ignite the crowd, with gating of paramount importance. Joonas Kylmakorpi and home wildcard Rune Sola were the first to fall by the wayside, closely followed by disappointed 2000 World Champion Mark Loram and veteran Czech Bohumil Brhel. Heat nine provided some cheer for the Norwegians, as Holta took victory after a fast start, while Leigh Adams sped outside Tomasz Gollob for second place on the back straight of the initial lap. There was dismay for Scott Nicholls, however, the Englishman dropping out of the race through a carburettor problem.

Crump came to the line for his opening outing in the next race and the Aussie was amazingly relegated to last position following a tight old first turn. Then he nearly came off on the back straight after almost clipping the rear wheel of Jaroslaw Hampel's machine. Up front, Tony Rickardsson went about the business of smoothly defeating Nicki Pedersen, leaving Crump to chase down the Pole. After working extremely hard, the Belle Vue linchpin's efforts were rewarded when he cut inside Hampel on the first bend of lap four, his third place taking him on to heat fifteen. Prior to that, the next brace of eliminators saw the end of the other home wildcard, Arnt Forland, together with Ales Dryml and Kaj Laukkanen, plus, surprisingly, Bjarne Pedersen – who thereby relinquished eighth place overall in the standings and with it a guaranteed place in the revamped 2005 series. Tailing Jesper B. Jensen, Poole's popular Dane lost out in a battle for second position with a third compatriot, Hans N. Andersen, at the start of lap two, before a mistake entering the back straight allowed Laukkanen by. Holta edged clear off the second bend to defeat Andreas Jonsson in heat thirteen, with Gollob winning the next race after a forceful first turn.

So to heat fifteen, and Crump showed his mettle, making a crisp getaway to win from Adams, with Brit Lee Richardson beating Jensen for third position. Heat sixteen was brought back after Nicholls had spun around and fallen on the second bend, with Mikael Max unable to avoid sideswiping the stricken rider. The stoppage was a shame, since it was shaping into a great race, as Rickardsson fought to hold off a charging Sullivan on the back straight. The super Swede had it all his own way in the rerun though and simply swept Sullivan away. Hampel appeared to have done enough to ward off Greg Hancock in heat seventeen, but the American was having none of it and was to post a super success after driving inside the former World Under-21 Champion exiting the fourth bend of the opening lap.

In the minor positions, regrettably it was the end of the 2004 journey for the English pair of Nicholls and Richardson. In heat eighteen, Max and Piotr Protasiewicz combined to squeeze out Ipswich's Danish duo of Andersen and Jensen; for the former of the two it ended any hopes of a top-eight place in the final results grid for the series, with Hampel confirmed as the last automatic qualifier for 2005.

Following Crump's eventual moment of glory in heat nineteen, the scrap for victory on the night hotted up, not to mention the battle between Hancock and Adams for third place overall. Slipping out in the final two eliminators were Sullivan, Protasiewicz, Max and Hampel, with the first semi-final subsequently ending on the first turn after a bunching incident had caused Holta to accidentally knock Gollob from his steed. Rickardsson was to take the rerun, while Gollob rode a back straight like only he possibly could, storming inside both Holta and Nicki Pedersen, before almost drawing level with the former Poole rider on the third bend. With 'Ricko' and the galloping Gollob safely though, Adams and Hancock took their personal duel into the 225th race of the series, the Aussie jetting swiftly from the outside, prior to ousting Hancock at the end of the back straight to triumph in the other semi-final.

The grand finale resulted in a clear-cut win for Rickardsson, it being the fourteenth GP success of his outstanding career. Meanwhile, Hancock raced around Gollob for second place and there was nothing Adams could do after getting boxed-in on the run to the first corner. That gave the American third place on the World Championship rostrum, while Adams was left frustratingly devoid of a medal in fourth place for a third year on the bounce. With the curtain brought down on the 70th Grand Prix since the inaugural round at Wroclaw, Poland on 20 May 1995, two riders remarkably remained as having appeared in each and every one, namely Messrs Rickardsson and Hancock.

RACE DETAILS

PRE-MAIN EVENT

HEAT ONE:	Andreas Jonsson, Ales Dryml, Rune Sola, Mark Loram.
HEAT TWO:	Mikael Max, Bjarne Pedersen, Arnt Forland, Hans N. Andersen.
HEAT THREE:	Piotr Protasiewicz, Kaj Laukkanen, Ryan Sullivan, Bohumil Brhel (fell).
HEAT FOUR:	Greg Hancock, Lee Richardson, Jesper B. Jensen, Joonas Kylmakorpi.
HEAT FIVE:	Ryan Sullivan, Hans N. Andersen, <u>Rune Sola</u>, <u>Joonas Kylmakorpi</u>.
HEAT SIX:	Jesper B. Jensen, Arnt Forland, <u>Mark Loram</u>, <u>Bohumil Brhel</u>.
HEAT SEVEN:	Andreas Jonsson, Lee Richardson, Piotr Protasiewicz, Bjarne Pedersen.
HEAT EIGHT:	Greg Hancock, Mikael Max, Kaj Laukkanen, Ales Dryml.
HEAT NINE:	Rune Holta, Leigh Adams, Tomasz Gollob, Scott Nicholls (ret).
HEAT TEN:	Tony Rickardsson, Nicki Pedersen, Jason Crump, Jaroslaw Hampel.
HEAT ELEVEN:	Ryan Sullivan, Piotr Protasiewicz, <u>Arnt Forland</u>, <u>Ales Dryml</u>.
HEAT TWELVE:	Jesper B. Jensen, Hans N. Andersen, <u>Kaj Laukkanen</u>, <u>Bjarne Pedersen</u>.

MAIN EVENT

HEAT THIRTEEN:	Rune Holta, Andreas Jonsson, Jaroslaw Hampel, Hans N. Andersen.
HEAT FOURTEEN:	Tomasz Gollob, Nicki Pedersen, Piotr Protasiewicz, Greg Hancock.
HEAT FIFTEEN:	Jason Crump, Leigh Adams, Lee Richardson, Jesper B. Jensen.
HEAT SIXTEEN:	(Rerun) Tony Rickardsson, Ryan Sullivan, Mikael Max, Scott Nicholls (f, ex).
HEAT SEVENTEEN:	Greg Hancock, Jaroslaw Hampel, <u>Scott Nicholls</u>, <u>Lee Richardson</u>.
HEAT EIGHTEEN:	Mikael Max, Piotr Protasiewicz, <u>Hans N. Andersen</u>, <u>Jesper B. Jensen</u>.

HEAT NINETEEN: (Rerun three times) Nicki Pedersen, Jason Crump, Ryan Sullivan (f, ex), Rune Holta (ex, delaying start).

HEAT TWENTY: Andreas Jonsson, Tomasz Gollob, Leigh Adams, Tony Rickardsson.

HEAT TWENTY-ONE: Tony Rickardsson, Greg Hancock, Ryan Sullivan, Piotr Protasiewicz.

HEAT TWENTY-TWO: Leigh Adams, Rune Holta, Mikael Max, Jaroslaw Hampel.

SEMI-FINALS

HEAT TWENTY-THREE: (Rerun) Tony Rickardsson, Tomasz Gollob, Nicki Pedersen, Rune Holta.

HEAT TWENTY-FOUR: Leigh Adams, Greg Hancock, Andreas Jonsson, Jason Crump.

GRAND FINAL

HEAT TWENTY-FIVE: Tony Rickardsson, Greg Hancock, Tomasz Gollob, Leigh Adams.

NOTE: Eliminated riders are underlined throughout

WORLD CHAMPIONSHIP ROLL OF HONOUR

NOTE: Run as a one-off World Final from 1936-94 and as the Grand Prix from 1995-04

YEAR	FIRST	SECOND	THIRD
1936	Lionel Van Praag	Eric Langton	Bluey Wilkinson
1937	Jack Milne	Wilbur Lamoreaux	Cordy Milne
1938	Bluey Wilkinson	Jack Milne	Wilbur Lamoreaux
1939-48	Not Staged		
1949	Tommy Price	Jack Parker	Louis Lawson
1950	Freddie Williams	Wally Green	Graham Warren
1951	Jack Young	Split Waterman	Jack Biggs
1952	Jack Young	Freddie Williams	Bob Oakley
1953	Freddie Williams	Split Waterman	Geoff Mardon
1954	Ronnie Moore	Brian Crutcher	Olle Nygren
1955	Peter Craven	Ronnie Moore	Barry Briggs
1956	Ove Fundin	Ronnie Moore	Arthur Forrest
1957	Barry Briggs	Ove Fundin	Peter Craven
1958	Barry Briggs	Ove Fundin	Aub Lawson
1959	Ronnie Moore	Ove Fundin	Barry Briggs
1960	Ove Fundin	Ronnie Moore	Peter Craven
1961	Ove Fundin	Bjorn Knutsson	Gote Nordin
1962	Peter Craven	Barry Briggs	Ove Fundin
1963	Ove Fundin	Bjorn Knutsson	Barry Briggs
1964	Barry Briggs	Igor Plechanov	Ove Fundin
1965	Bjorn Knutsson	Igor Plechanov	Ove Fundin
1966	Barry Briggs	Sverre Harrfeldt	Antoni Woryna
1967	Ove Fundin	Bengt Jansson	Ivan Mauger
1968	Ivan Mauger	Barry Briggs	Edward Jancarz
1969	Ivan Mauger	Barry Briggs	Soren Sjosten
1970	Ivan Mauger	Pawel Waloszek	Antoni Woryna
1971	Ole Olsen	Ivan Mauger	Bengt Jansson
1972	Ivan Mauger	Bernt Persson	Ole Olsen
1973	Jerzy Szczakiel	Ivan Mauger	Zenon Plech
1974	Anders Michanek	Ivan Mauger	Soren Sjosten
1975	Ole Olsen	Anders Michanek	John Louis
1976	Peter Collins	Malcolm Simmons	Phil Crump
1977	Ivan Mauger	Peter Collins	Ole Olsen
1978	Ole Olsen	Gordon Kennett	Scott Autrey
1979	Ivan Mauger	Zenon Plech	Michael Lee
1980	Michael Lee	Dave Jessup	Billy Sanders
1981	Bruce Penhall	Ole Olsen	Tommy Knudsen
1982	Bruce Penhall	Les Collins	Dennis Sigalos
1983	Egon Muller	Billy Sanders	Michael Lee
1984	Erik Gundersen	Hans Nielsen	Lance King
1985	Erik Gundersen	Hans Nielsen	Sam Ermolenko

YEAR	FIRST	SECOND	THIRD
1986	Hans Nielsen	Jan O. Pedersen	Kelvin Tatum
1987	Hans Nielsen	Erik Gundersen	Sam Ermolenko
1988	Erik Gundersen	Hans Nielsen	Jan O. Pedersen
1989	Hans Nielsen	Simon Wigg	Jeremy Doncaster
1990	Per Jonsson	Shawn Moran	Todd Wiltshire
1991	Jan O. Pedersen	Tony Rickardsson	Hans Nielsen
1992	Gary Havelock	Per Jonsson	Gert Handberg
1993	Sam Ermolenko	Hans Nielsen	Chris Louis
1994	Tony Rickardsson	Hans Nielsen	Craig Boyce
1995	Hans Nielsen	Tony Rickardsson	Sam Ermolenko
1996	Billy Hamill	Hans Nielsen	Greg Hancock
1997	Greg Hancock	Billy Hamill	Tomasz Gollob
1998	Tony Rickardsson	Jimmy Nilsen	Tomasz Gollob
1999	Tony Rickardsson	Tomasz Gollob	Hans Nielsen
2000	Mark Loram	Billy Hamill	Tony Rickardsson
2001	Tony Rickardsson	Jason Crump	Tomasz Gollob
2002	Tony Rickardsson	Jason Crump	Ryan Sullivan
2003	Nicki Pedersen	Jason Crump	Tony Rickardsson
2004	Jason Crump	Tony Rickardsson	Greg Hancock

NOTE: In 1990, Shawn Moran was subsequently stripped of second place, having tested positive in a drugs test at the Overseas Final.

WORLD CHAMPIONSHIP QUALIFYING

(FOR THE 2005 GRAND PRIX SERIES)

ROUND ONE: 8 May, Krsko, Slovenia

QUALIFYING SCORES: Matej Zagar 15; David Ruud 11; Matej Ferjan 11; Chris Neath 11; Izak Santej 11; Niklas Klingberg 11; Peter Ljung 10; Theo Pijper 7; Ryan Fisher 7; Denis Stojs 6; Henrik Moller 5; Olly Allen 3; Ivan Vargek 2; Thomas Stange 2; Brian Lyngso 2; Primoz Legan (Res) 2; Christophe Martin 1. FIRST SEMI-FINAL: 1st Klingberg; 2nd Zagar; 3rd Ferjan; 4th Ljung. SECOND SEMI-FINAL: 1st Ruud; 2nd Pijper; 3rd Neath; 4th Santej. FINAL: 1st Zagar; 2nd Klingberg; 3rd Ruud; 4th Pijper.

ROUND TWO: 8 May, Terenzano, Italy

QUALIFYING SCORES: Sebastian Ulamek 15; Niels-Kristian Iversen 13; Lukas Dryml 10; Wieslaw Jagus 10; Ales Dryml 9; David Norris 9; Stuart Robson 9; Ronni Pedersen 8; Simone Terenzani 6; Chris Slabon 5; Jernej Kolenko 5; Tomi Reima 5; Kaj Laukkanen 4; Christian Hefenbrock 2; Mirko Wolter 2; Paolo Salvatelli 1. FIRST SEMI-FINAL: 1st Ulamek; 2nd Norris; 3rd Robson; 4th L. Dryml. SECOND SEMI-FINAL: 1st Jagus; 2nd Iversen; 3rd Pedersen; 4th A. Dryml. FINAL: 1st Jagus; 2nd Ulamek; 3rd Iversen; 4th Norris.

ROUND THREE: 9 May, Zielona Gora, Poland

QUALIFYING SCORES: Jacek Rempala 12; Hans N. Andersen 12; Jaroslaw Hampel 12; Janusz Kolodziej 11; Stefan Andersson 10; Sergei Darkin 10; Antonio Lindback 9; Damian Balinski 8;

Mark Lemon 8; Rinat Gafurov 8; Leigh Lanham 7; Henning Bager 6; Chris Harris 3; Kastas Poudzhuks 2; Rune Sola 2; Jan Mikke Bjerk 0. FIRST SEMI-FINAL: 1st Lindback; 2nd Kolodziej; 3rd Darkin; 4th Rempala. SECOND SEMI-FINAL: 1st Andersson; 2nd Hampel; 3rd Andersen; 4th Balinski. FINAL: 1st Hampel; 2nd Lindback; 3rd Kolodziej; 4th Andersson.

ROUND FOUR: 22 May, Slany, Czech Republic

QUALIFYING SCORES: Tomasz Chrzanowski 14; Craig Watson 13; Matthias Schultz 12; Stefan Danno 11; Toni Svab 9; Tomas Topinka 9; Josef Franc 9; Laszlo Svatmari 8; Slawomir Drabik 7; Fritz Wallner 7; Joachim Kugelmann 6; Tomas Suchanek 5; Niklas Aspgren 4; Pavel Ondrasik 3; Manuel Hautzinger 1; Zsolt Bence 1; Eddie Turksema (Res) 0. FIRST SEMI-FINAL: 1st Chrzanowski; 2nd Danno; 3rd Franc; 4th Topinka. SECOND SEMI-FINAL: 1st Svab; 2nd Svatmari; 3rd Schultz; 4th Watson. FINAL: 1st Svab; 2nd Chrzanowski; 3rd Danno; 4th Svatmari.

FIRST SEMI-FINAL: 5 June, Lonigo, Italy

QUALIFYING SCORES: Wieslaw Jagus 13; Hans N. Andersen 12; Antonio Lindback 12; Tomasz Chrzanowski 11; Niels-Kristian Iversen 11; Marcin Rempala 10; Bohumil Brhel 9; Roman Povazhny 7; Stuart Robson 7; Jacek Rempala 7; Laszlo Szatmari 6; Andrea Maida 5; Izak Santej 3; David Ruud 3; Chris Neath 3; Josef Franc 1. Due to torrential rain, the meeting was abandoned prior to the semi-finals and final, with the eight qualifiers being: Jagus, Andersen, Lindback, Chrzanowski, Iversen, M. Rempala, Brhel and Povazhny – the lattermost going through on the countback ruling.

SECOND SEMI-FINAL: 20 June, Heusden-Zolder, Belgium

QUALIFYING SCORES: Craig Watson 12; Sebastian Ulamek 12; Peter Karlsson 11; Damian Balinksi 10; Kenneth Bjerre 10; David Norris 9; Ronni Pedersen 8; Stefan Andersson 8; Niklas Klingberg 8; David Howe 7; Stefan Danno 7; Matej Ferjan 6; Lukas Dryml 5; Janusz Kolodziej 5; Theo Pijper 2; Matthias Schultz 0. FIRST SEMI-FINAL: 1st Balinski; 2nd Pedersen; 3rd Norris; 4th Watson. SECOND SEMI-FINAL: 1st Ulamek; 2nd Karlsson; 3rd Bjerre; 4th Andersson. FINAL: 1st Karlsson; 2nd Ulamek; 3rd Pedersen; 4th Balinski.

FINAL

14 AUGUST, VOJENS, DENMARK

1st	ANTONIO LINDBACK
2nd	TOMASZ CHRZANOWSKI
3rd	KENNETH BJERRE
4th	HANS N. ANDERSEN

	QUALIFYING SCORES					TOTAL
Hans N. Andersen	3	2	3	3	3	14
Antonio Lindback	2	3	3	2	2	12
Roman Povazhny	3	3	2	X	2	10
Damian Balinski	2	1	3	2	2	10
Peter Karlsson	3	F	0	3	3	9
Tomasz Chrzanowski	1	2	1	3	2	9

	QUALIFYING SCORES					TOTAL
Stefan Andersson	0	2	2	1	3	8
Kenneth Bjerre	3	0	1	0	3	7
Bohumil Brhel	1	1	2	3	0	7
Marcin Rempala	0	3	1	2	1	7
David Norris	2	1	3	X	1	7
Niels-Kristian Iversen	1	3	0	1	1	6
Niklas Klingberg	0	2	1	2	1	6
Wieslaw Jagus	2	X	2	0	R	4
Ronni Pedersen	1	1	0	1	0	3
Craig Watson	0	0	R	–	–	0

RACE DETAILS

HEAT ONE: Hans N. Andersen, David Norris, Ronni Pedersen, Stefan Andersson.
HEAT TWO: Peter Karlsson, Damian Balinski, Tomasz Chrzanowski, Marcin Rempala.
HEAT THREE: (Rerun) Kenneth Bjerre, Wieslaw Jagus, Bohumil Brhel, Craig Watson.
HEAT FOUR: Roman Povazhny, Antonio Lindback, Niels-Kristian Iversen, Niklas Klingberg.
HEAT FIVE: Roman Povazhny, Tomasz Chrzanowski, Ronni Pedersen, Craig Watson.
HEAT SIX: Marcin Rempala, Niklas Klingberg, David Norris, Kenneth Bjerre.
HEAT SEVEN: Niels-Kristian Iversen, Stefan Andersson, Bohumil Brhel, Peter Karlsson (fell).
HEAT EIGHT: (Rerun) Antonio Lindback, Hans N. Andersen, Damian Balinski, Wieslaw Jagus (f, ex).
HEAT NINE: Antonio Lindback, Bohumil Brhel, Marcin Rempala, Ronni Pedersen.
HEAT TEN: (Rerun) David Norris, Wieslaw Jagus, Tomasz Chrzanowski, Niels-Kristian Iversen.
HEAT ELEVEN: Damian Balinski, Stefan Andersson, Niklas Klingberg, Craig Watson (ret).
HEAT TWELVE: Hans N. Andersen, Roman Povazhny, Kenneth Bjerre, Peter Karlsson.
HEAT THIRTEEN: Peter Karlsson, Niklas Klingberg, Ronni Pedersen, Wieslaw Jagus.
HEAT FOURTEEN: (Rerun twice) Bohumil Brhel, Damian Balinski, Roman Povazhny (f, ex), David Norris (f, ex).
HEAT FIFTEEN: Tomasz Chrzanowski, Antonio Lindback, Stefan Andersson, Kenneth Bjerre.
HEAT SIXTEEN: Hans N. Andersen, Marcin Rempala, Niels-Kristian Iversen, Craig Watson (ns).
HEAT SEVENTEEN: Kenneth Bjerre, Damian Balinski, Niels-Kristian Iversen, Ronni Pedersen.
HEAT EIGHTEEN: Peter Karlsson, Antonio Lindback, David Norris, Craig Watson (ns).
HEAT NINETEEN: Stefan Andersson, Roman Povazhny, Marcin Rempala, Wieslaw Jagus (ret).
HEAT TWENTY: Hans N. Andersen, Tomasz Chrzanowski, Niklas Klingberg, Bohumil Brhel.
FIRST SEMI-FINAL: Tomasz Chrzanowski, Hans N. Andersen, Stefan Andersson, Damian Balinski (ret).
SECOND SEMI-FINAL: Antonio Lindback, Kenneth Bjerre, Peter Karlsson, Roman Povazhny (ex, foul riding).
FINAL: Antonio Lindback, Tomasz Chrzanowski, Kenneth Bjerre, Hans N. Andersen (ret).

NOTE: Antonio Lindback and Tomasz Chrzanowski qualified for the 2005 GP series.

MAJOR INTERNATIONAL MEETINGS 2004

MAJOR INTERNATIONAL MEETINGS 2004

WORLD CUP

NOTE: Formerly known as the World Team Cup (1960-2000)

QUALIFYING ROUND ONE

3 JULY, LONIGO, ITALY

ITALY 54 (Emiliano Sanchez 12; Paolo Salvatelli 11; Armando Castagna 11; Simone Terenzani 11; Andrea Maida 9).

GERMANY 47 (Martin Smolinksi 14; Mirko Wolter 10; Matthias Schultz 9; Christian Hefenbrock 9; Thomas Stange 5).

FINLAND 31 (Kaj Laukkanen 15; Kauko Nieminen 7; Tero Aarnio 5; Tomi Reima 2; Juha Hautamaki 2).

LATVIA 18 (Andrey Korolev 6; Kjastes Puodzhuks 5; Nikolai Kokin 5; Leonid Paura 1; Alexander Biznya 1).

QUALIFYING ROUND TWO

10 JULY, GYULA, HUNGARY

HUNGARY 51 (Sandor Tihanyi 14; Norbert Magosi 13; Attila Stefani 10; Laszlo Szatmari 10; Szabolcs Vida 4).

SLOVENIA 47 (Matej Zagar 18; Izak Santej 13; Jernej Kolenko 10; Primoz Legan 3; Ales Kraljic 3).

RUSSIA 42 (Ilya Bondarenko 14; Roman Ivanov 10; Sergei Eroshin 10; Denis Saifutdinov 5; Viktor Golubovsky 3).

AUSTRIA 10 (Manuel Hauzinger 6; Fritz Wallner 4; Norbert Grogler 0; Mario Ozelt 0; Oliver Ozelt 0).

EVENT ONE

2 AUGUST, EASTBOURNE

Amid a carnival atmosphere, the British-staged World Cup finals kicked off at Eastbourne and, on a well-prepared circuit, Team Great Britain gave an assured performance to qualify straight through to the final. Mark Loram led the way with a fabulous five-ride maximum and, while the Arena-Essex ace is more renowned for battling through from the back, he did it after making clean starts in every race. This was a team performance in every sense of the word though, fully vindicating manager Neil Middleditch's choice of line-up. Lee Richardson and skipper Scott Nicholls produced solid showings, while David Norris recovered from a second-race fall to reel off a hat-trick of excellent wins on his home track. Backing their efforts was Joe Screen and, although the Belle Vue man did not manage to post any victories, he put in a superhuman effort to collect all his points. The early stages saw the Brits vying for top spot with both Sweden and Poland, but there was daylight from the point when Richardson rounded the field to take heat ten. While the Polish lads faded in the latter stages, the Swedes were always a threat and never stopped trying, with Great Britain having to wait until heat twenty-three until they mathematically assured their final spot. Hungary was the meeting's other competing nation, but with their riders more used to the larger Continental tracks, they were totally outclassed and only really made up the numbers.

All in all, this was a great night of speedway, played out in front of a packed Arlington audience. Among the many highlights was a superb heat three, which saw Grzegorz Walasek triumph after forcing his way to the fore on the first corner. Behind, Mikael Max and the 'Screen Machine' engaged in a terrific dust-up, with the Chesterfield-born racer just coming through to shade the verdict on the line. No meeting at this level would be complete without the presence of Tomasz Gollob and the Pole was at his best in blocking Nicholls for the duration to win a rerun heat nine. This followed an exclusion for Tony Rickardsson, after the five-times World Champion had been punished for delaying the start; the first of three such decisions by referee Wojciech Grodzki. After collecting unwanted drive and falling in his chase of Antonio Lindback in heat seven, Norris regained his composure to beautifully cut under Peter Karlsson on his way to the fluttering flag in a rerun twelfth race. Screen again gave his all in a twice restarted heat thirteen, but was eventually beaten by Gollob, whose six points as a tactical joker temporarily gave Poland second place ahead of Sweden.

Loram made a quick getaway in heat sixteen, only for Jaroslaw Hampel to fly outside on the back straight. The Englishman reacted almost immediately to dive through on the third and fourth bends, before ripping around the 275-metre raceway to record a comprehensive success. Perhaps the best race of the night occurred in heat twenty-two, when Norris ousted Mikael Max and set off in pursuit of Gollob. Despite clawing back a huge deficit, it looked as if the speedy Pole would hold on for the victory; however, a quite fantastic inside line around the last turn gave Norris the edge and he completed the job by narrowly winning the race to the line. Having done so much to rejuvenate his career in 2004, this most passionate of British riders then demonstrated exactly what the victory meant to him as he accepted joyous applause from the crowd on his lap of honour. Screen served up one last thrill in the very next race, when he went right out in the dirt to daringly pass Hampel on the fourth bend of lap three, prior to following Karlsson home, his hard-earned 2 points giving Team Great Britain their final slot, while leaving Sweden and Poland to face a very difficult Race-Off meeting.

TEAM GREAT BRITAIN 58	RACE SCORES						TOTAL
Mark Loram	3	3	3	3	3	–	15
David Norris	2	X	3	3	3	–	11
Joe Screen	2	2	2	1	2	–	9
Scott Nicholls	2	2	3	3	3	–	13
Lee Richardson	2	3	2	1	2	–	10

SWEDEN 50	RACE SCORES						TOTAL
Andreas Jonsson	2	3	4	2	3	–	14
Tony Rickardsson	3	X	3	3	2	–	11
Mikael Max	1	1	2	2	1	–	7
Peter Karlsson	3	2	2	3	3	–	13
Antonio Lindback	T	3	X	R	2	–	5
POLAND 39							
Tomasz Gollob	1	3	6	2	2	–	14
Jaroslaw Hampel	1	2	1	2	2	1	9
Grzegorz Walasek	3	1	1	T	1	–	6
Janusz Kolodziej	1	2	1	1	–	–	5
Krzysztof Kasprzak	3	1	X	1	X	–	5
HUNGARY 6							
Norbert Magosi	0	1	X	0	0	–	1
Sandor Tihanyi	F	0	0	0	0	–	0
Attila Stefani	0	1	1	0	–	–	2
Laszlo Szatmari	0	0	X	1	1	X	2
Szabolcs Vida	1	F	0	0	0	–	1

RACE DETAILS

HEAT ONE: Mark Loram, Andreas Jonsson, Tomasz Gollob, Norbert Magosi.

HEAT TWO: Tony Rickardsson, David Norris, Jaroslaw Hampel, Sandor Tihanyi (fell).

HEAT THREE: Grzegorz Walasek, Joe Screen, Mikael Max, Attila Stefani.

HEAT FOUR: Peter Karlsson, Scott Nicholls, Janusz Kolodziej, Laszlo Szatmari.

HEAT FIVE: (Rerun twice) Krzysztof Kasprzak, Lee Richardson, Szabolcs Vida, Antonio Lindback (ex, tapes).

HEAT SIX: Mark Loram, Peter Karlsson, Grzegorz Walasek, Szabolcs Vida (fell).

HEAT SEVEN: (Rerun) Antonio Lindback, Janusz Kolodziej, Norbert Magosi, David Norris (f, ex).

HEAT EIGHT: Andreas Jonsson, Joe Screen, Krzysztof Kasprzak, Sandor Tihanyi.

HEAT NINE: (Rerun) Tomasz Gollob, Scott Nicholls, Attila Stefani, Tony Rickardsson (ex, delaying start).

HEAT TEN: Lee Richardson, Jaroslaw Hampel, Mikael Max, Laszlo Szatmari.

HEAT ELEVEN: Mark Loram, Mikael Max, Janusz Kolodziej, Sandor Tihanyi.

HEAT TWELVE: (Rerun) David Norris, Peter Karlsson, Attila Stefani, Krzysztof Kasprzak (f, ex).

HEAT THIRTEEN: (Rerun twice) Tomasz Gollob (tactical joker), Joe Screen, Antonio Lindback (f, ex), Laszlo Szatmari (f, ex).

HEAT FOURTEEN: Scott Nicholls, Andreas Jonsson (tactical joker), Jaroslaw Hampel, Szabolcs Vida.

HEAT FIFTEEN: (Rerun) Tony Rickardsson, Lee Richardson, Grzegorz Walasek, Norbert Magosi (ex, delaying start).

HEAT SIXTEEN: Mark Loram, Jaroslaw Hampel, Laszlo Szatmari, Antonio Lindback (ret).

HEAT SEVENTEEN: (Rerun) David Norris, Andreas Jonsson, Laszlo Szatmari, Grzegorz Walasek (ex, tapes).

HEAT EIGHTEEN: Tony Rickardsson, Jaroslaw Hampel, Joe Screen, Szabolcs Vida.

HEAT NINETEEN: Scott Nicholls, Mikael Max, Krzysztof Kasprzak, Norbert Magosi (tactical joker).

HEAT TWENTY: Peter Karlsson, Tomasz Gollob, Lee Richardson, Sandor Tihanyi.

HEAT TWENTY-ONE: (Rerun twice) Mark Loram, Tony Rickardsson, Laszlo Szatmari (f, ex), Krzysztof Kasprzak (ex, delaying start).

HEAT TWENTY-TWO: David Norris, Tomasz Gollob, Mikael Max, Szabolcs Vida.

HEAT TWENTY-THREE: (Rerun) Peter Karlsson, Joe Screen, Jaroslaw Hampel, Norbert Magosi.

HEAT TWENTY-FOUR: Scott Nicholls, Antonio Lindback, Grzegorz Walasek, Sandor Tihanyi.

HEAT TWENTY-FIVE: Andreas Jonsson, Lee Richardson, Janusz Kolodziej, Attila Stefani.

EVENT TWO

3 AUGUST, EASTBOURNE

Round two of the Speedway World Cup served up plenty of thrills, with Denmark and Australia going head-to-head for a place in the final alongside the already qualified Team Great Britain. A competitive Czech Republic quintet kept the big two on their toes, while Italy gave a much better account than the Hungarians had the previous evening. Although Australia drew level on a couple of occasions, the Danes were never headed and appeared to ride with greater desire, no doubt generated by a superb team spirit and the high level of input from team boss Jacob Olsen. The Scandinavians were in the ascendancy from the off, as Hans N. Andersen and reigning World Champion Nicki Pedersen posted successive victories. Kenneth Bjerre looked set to make it three in a row, but the diminutive Belle Vue racer was eventually taken apart in breathtaking fashion by Leigh Adams. After trying the inside line on several occasions, the Swindon ace found the drive to go around the outside on the first corner of the last lap for a scintillating success.

Wins followed for Jason Crump and Adam Shields, to leave the meeting's two major forces locked together on twelve points apiece at the head of the leaderboard – Shields doing particularly well to get out in the dirt and block Bjarne Pedersen's run in the latter. The Danes were quickly back in front though, when Niels-Kristian Iversen produced an excellent effort to get the better of Adams in heat six. Crump's second victory in the next race once more levelled the scores, only for the highly motivated Danes to pull away again, courtesy of a brace of wins from Andersen and Nicki Pedersen respectively. Denmark's charge was derailed temporarily in heat ten, however, when Bjerre was excluded after piling into the air safety barrier, having collected some unwanted drive exiting the second bend. Following a long delay while the damaged barrier was repaired, the rerun saw Steve Johnston take advantage of the opportunity to bring the Australians back within a point, but only after a full-throttle duel with the Czech Republic's Tomas Topinka. After leading from the gate, 'Johno' went a little too wide and this allowed the Czech to nip inside and lead up the back straight. Topinka appeared to have the race under control, but was unprepared for a wonderful outside burst off the fourth turn of lap three which took the all-action Aussie ahead.

That proved a minor hiccup for the Danes, and indeed Bjerre, who recovered his composure brilliantly to win from Crump in heat eleven. Amazingly, there was a Danish triumph in each of the five races that followed to leave them perched on 41 points, with Australia trailing on 34. Team manager Neil Street gave Adams the nod for a tactical joker ride in heat seventeen and the 'Armchair Thriller' did all that was required to net 6 points. The possibility of an added bonus was on the cards for the Australians when Topinka slotted into second place, but

Andersen was to limit the damage when he shot past the Czech on the back straight of lap two. Crump further reduced the deficit in heat eighteen by comfortably defeating Nicki Pedersen – thus leaving the scores at Denmark 45, Australia 43, Czech Republic 19, Italy 4. Bjerre then outpaced the field from the gate in heat nineteen and there was disaster for Shields on the last lap, when he drifted out on the pits bend and hit the deck. Respite for Antipodeans followed in a classic heat twenty, which gave Ryan Sullivan his first win of the night. He initially made the start, only for Iversen to steam outside off the second turn in road racing style. 'Flyin' Ryan' lived up to his nickname on the final lap, however, finding a tremendous amount of drive to blast through on the inside going down the back straight.

There was more super stuff in heat twenty-one, when, with his front wheel in the air, Shields bounced off the air barrier in his pursuit of Nicki Pedersen. Having regained control of his steed, the Australian cut inside Topinka entering the third bend of lap two and again set after Pedersen. For a fantastic end to the race, Topinka came right back into the picture and, in a blanket finish, all three riders darted across the line almost in unison, with Pedersen just getting the verdict from Shields. Drama followed in heat twenty-two, when the home straight was plunged into darkness with Sullivan holding the lead. The riders' safety was clearly of paramount importance, but Polish official Wojciech Grodzki was unable to stop the race due to the red lights being on the same power circuit as the floodlighting. Finally the race was halted after three laps and, shortly afterwards, the whole stadium was bereft of lighting. A delay of almost half-an-hour ensued while the situation was rectified and the eventual rerun saw Sullivan lock the door on Bjerre exiting the second bend, with Paolo Salvatelli and Josef Franc relegating the Dane to last spot. Bjerre subsequently managed to oust Franc, but was unable to catch the Italian, as Australia closed to within three points of the Danes.

After bucking and rearing, Johnston came to grief on the second bend of heat twenty-three, earning an exclusion for his troubles. Tactical joker Ales Dryml dashed to victory in the restart, while Emiliano Sanchez opened his account after impressively racing around Iversen entering the back straight. It was indeed a rare sight to see Adams tumble in the penultimate race; the usually totally controlled speedster made the start and went out to find the racing line, only to pick up too much traction and lift, before running out of track and colliding with the air barrier next to the pits entrance. That left Denmark holding an unassailable lead and Bjarne Pedersen celebrated by winning the rerun, while Sanchez collected 4 points from a tactical joker outing in second position.

Incident-packed throughout, the meeting ended notably, with Lukas Dryml firstly passing Andersen and then charging inside Crump on the back straight of the final lap for a great victory. The result left Australia and the Czech Republic to meet Sweden and Poland in the Race-Off at Poole in order to determine the last two places in the final.

DENMARK 60	RACE SCORES						TOTAL
Hans N. Andersen	3	3	3	2	2	–	13
Nicki Pedersen	3	3	3	2	3	–	14
Kenneth Bjerre	2	X	3	3	1	–	9
Niels-Kristian Iversen	2	3	3	2	1	–	11
Bjarne Pedersen	2	2	3	3	3	–	13

AUSTRALIA 52	RACE SCORES						TOTAL
Ryan Sullivan	1	1	2	3	3	–	10
Steve Johnston	2	3	2	2	X	–	9
Leigh Adams	3	2	2	6	X	–	13
Jason Crump	3	3	2	3	1	–	12
Adam Shields	3	1	2	F	2	–	8
CZECH REPUBLIC 32							
Ales Dryml	2	1	1	2	6	–	12
Bohumil Brhel	1	2	1	0	1	–	5
Lukas Dryml	1	2	R	F	3	–	6
Tomas Topinka	1	1	2	1	1	1	7
Josef Franc	0	1	1	0	–	–	2
ITALY 14							
Andrea Maida	0	0	0	1	0	–	1
Paolo Salvatelli	F	0	1	0	2	–	3
Emiliano Sanchez	0	0	0	0	2	4	6
Daniele Tessari	0	0	0	–	–	–	0
Simone Terenzani	1	1	0	1	1	0	4

RACE DETAILS

HEAT ONE: Hans N. Andersen, Ales Dryml, Ryan Sullivan, Andrea Maida.
HEAT TWO: Nicki Pedersen, Steve Johnston, Bohumil Brhel, Paolo Salvatelli (fell).
HEAT THREE: Leigh Adams, Kenneth Bjerre, Lukas Dryml, Emiliano Sanchez.
HEAT FOUR: Jason Crump, Niels-Kristian Iversen, Tomas Topinka, Daniele Tessari.
HEAT FIVE: Adam Shields, Bjarne Pedersen, Simone Terenzani, Josef Franc.
HEAT SIX: Niels-Kristian Iversen, Leigh Adams, Tomas Topinka, Andrea Maida.
HEAT SEVEN: Jason Crump, Bjarne Pedersen, Ales Dryml, Paolo Salvatelli.
HEAT EIGHT: Hans N. Andersen, Bohumil Brhel, Adam Shields, Emiliano Sanchez.
HEAT NINE: Nicki Pedersen, Lukas Dryml, Ryan Sullivan, Daniele Tessari.
HEAT TEN: (Rerun) Steve Johnston, Tomas Topinka, Simone Terenzani, Kenneth Bjerre (f, ex).
HEAT ELEVEN: Kenneth Bjerre, Jason Crump, Bohumil Brhel, Andrea Maida.
HEAT TWELVE: Niels-Kristian Iversen, Adam Shields, Paolo Salvatelli, Lukas Dryml (ret).
HEAT THIRTEEN: Bjarne Pedersen, Ryan Sullivan, Tomas Topinka, Emiliano Sanchez.
HEAT FOURTEEN: Hans N. Andersen, Steve Johnston, Josef Franc, Daniele Tessari (f, rem).
HEAT FIFTEEN: Nicki Pedersen, Leigh Adams, Ales Dryml, Simone Terenzani.
HEAT SIXTEEN: (Rerun) Bjarne Pedersen, Steve Johnston, Andrea Maida, Lukas Dryml (fell).
HEAT SEVENTEEN: Leigh Adams (tactical joker), Hans N. Andersen, Tomas Topinka, Paolo Salvatelli.
HEAT EIGHTEEN: Jason Crump, Nicki Pedersen, Josef Franc, Emiliano Sanchez.
HEAT NINETEEN: Kenneth Bjerre, Ales Dryml, Simone Terenzani, Adam Shields (fell).
HEAT TWENTY: Ryan Sullivan, Niels-Kristian Iversen, Simone Terenzani, Bohumil Brhel.
HEAT TWENTY-ONE: Nicki Pedersen, Adam Shields, Tomas Topinka, Andrea Maida.
HEAT TWENTY-TWO: (Rerun) Ryan Sullivan, Paolo Salvatelli, Kenneth Bjerre, Josef Franc.

HEAT TWENTY-THREE: (Rerun) Ales Dryml (tactical joker), Emiliano Sanchez, Niels-Kristian Iversen, Steve Johnston (f, ex).

HEAT TWENTY-FOUR: (Rerun) Bjarne Pedersen, Emiliano Sanchez (tactical joker), Bohumil Brhel, Leigh Adams (f, ex).

HEAT TWENTY-FIVE: Lukas Dryml, Hans N. Andersen, Jason Crump, Simon Terenzani.

RACE-OFF

5 AUGUST, POOLE

Widely referred to as the 'Group of Death', this meeting went right down to the wire and produced more twists than Chubby Checker in his heyday. With two places in the World Cup final up for grabs, three of the sport's major forces traded blow-for-blow throughout, while the Czech Republic played nothing more than a bit part in the drama that unfolded. Australia and Sweden had been expected to ease through, but with Poland in the mix it was never likely to be a formality.

So it was to prove, as the Poles set out their stall from the off. Grzegorz Walasek was a convincing winner of the opening heat and, if that came as a surprise, then it was positively a shock to see Ryan Sullivan trail home last, behind Tomas Topinka and Mikael Max, on his home circuit. More of the same followed in heat two, when 2003 World Under-21 Champion Jaroslaw Hampel was a comprehensive victor, with Steve Johnston collecting Australia's first points after a ferocious inside move on Tony Rickardsson entering the first bend of lap two. Following an even break to the third race, Antonio Lindback attempted to speed through on the inside line, but lifted off the second bend and clattered into the side of Leigh Adams. The impact brought both men down untidily and referee Mick Bates was left with no option other than to exclude the over-anxious nineteen-year-old Brazilian-born Swede. Adams remained completely unfazed by the incident as he headed off Tomasz Gollob on the first corner and eased away to win the rerun with typically stylish assurance.

Jason Crump hauled Australia back into contention by taking heat four from Andreas Jonsson, the Swede producing the first of several thrilling efforts in steaming outside Lukas Dryml on the back straight of the initial lap. Australia had elected to replace Adam Shields with Craig Boyce going into the meeting – no doubt thinking the veteran's greater knowledge of the Wimborne Road raceway would be advantageous. However, in heat five, the Aussie, who holds all the records in terms of points scoring for Poole, ran a last. Meanwhile, Peter Karlsson was an all-the-way winner from the gate, while Krzystzof Kasprzak and Josef Franc relegated Boyce to the rear inside the first half-lap.

After each rider had taken their opening outing, the scores stood at: Poland 11, Australia 8, Sweden 7, Czech Republic 4. Successive wins from Adams and Crump then put the Aussies in the ascendancy, prior to an eventful heat eight. This saw Lindback lead from the gate, but in negotiating the first corner he moved across the track and, having squeezed Boyce up by the fence on the second bend, the Swede lifted and caused the experienced Australian to fall. With Lindback excluded, Boyce sped away from the tapes in the rerun, only to run wide on the back straight. Firstly, Topinka dashed by on his way to an impressive victory and then Hampel surged through to keep the Poles in the reckoning. While Gollob was winning the ninth heat, Sullivan and Jonsson engaged in a thrilling tussle behind. Having seen off Sullivan, the race culminated in the Swede superbly cutting back off the last bend to seize second place from Ales Dryml on the line. That put Poland in front again and they further extended their advantage through the next two races, prior to Gollob returning to the fray in heat twelve. However, it was Rickardsson who shot away for the win, leaving Gollob to thunder inside Lukas Dryml on the home straight of lap two in familiar no-holds-barred fashion.

Heat thirteen ended curtly on the first bend when Lindback caught Kolodziej's leg, causing the Pole to fall. Surprisingly, an 'all-four' restart was called and Lindback made the most of his reprieve to dash inside the faster-starting Sullivan and lead up the back straight. Although 'Sully' hit back on a speedier outside line around the fourth turn, Lindback wouldn't be denied as he decisively steamed inside the Australian in front of the well-appointed glass-fronted grandstand on lap two. A fast trap took Kasprzak to victory in the next race, though all eyes were focussed on Jonsson, wondering just what the thrillmaker-in-chief would get up to after failing to gate on level terms. The Swede didn't let the expectant crowd down either, bravely going from fourth to second through the smallest of gaps between Topinka and Johnston on the back straight of lap two.

The action continued unabated when Adams defeated Karlsson in heat fifteen, with Ales Dryml beautifully riding the white line off the last bend to oust Walasek for the odd point. Australia had gone into the race eight points adrift of Poland, but remarkably they didn't play the joker. It was a decision they were to rue in the final analysis. The tension rose in heat sixteen, when, with Gollob a clear winner, Max was excluded after Johnston had fallen on the third bend of the final lap. Television replays clearly revealed that Max had taken the Australian's leg away as they jostled for position. Respective wins for Adams and Crump kept the meeting at boiling point, with only three points separating the leaders after eighteen heats: Poland 33, Australia 31, Sweden 30, Czech Republic 14.

The first running of heat nineteen ended on the third bend, when Bohumil Brhel challenged Boyce and, after his leg had touched the real wheel of his opponent, the Czech lost control before virtually disappearing under the air safety barrier. Jonsson was up to his daredevil antics in the restart, although he seemed out of contention after initially clashing with Walasek on the back straight. The spectacular Swede simply wound on the throttle though, and a flying outside line took him past race-leader Boyce on the back straight of lap three. Despite being in fresh air, he continued to go at a terrific rate and over-cooked the second bend of the final lap, with his back end swinging around wildly and actually clipping the fence. Somehow, after lifting, he managed to regain control and cantered on for a win that had many folk shaking their heads in disbelief.

Sullivan came good with a twentieth-heat win, bringing the three leading sides to within a single point of each other in the process. An amazing heat twenty-one followed, with Ales Dryml seemingly getting the better of a determined Kolodziej, after surging outside on the back straight of lap two. However, the Pole didn't throw in the towel and a storming outside effort on the last bend carried him to victory by a matter of inches. With Boyce at the back and Sullivan only managing a third place in heat twenty-two, the Aussies had it all to do as Poland and Sweden jointly held sway on 40 points apiece. Lindback showed nerves of steel, riding right out by the back-straight fence in heat twenty-three, prior to sweeping around turns three and four for a super success over Lukas Dryml. Sweden duly made sure of a final slot in the penultimate race, when Jonsson held off Adams and Hampel for his second win of the night.

Going into the last heat, the scores stood at Sweden 46, Poland 41, Australia 40, Czech Republic 17 and the Aussies at last took the opportunity of utilizing the tactical joker. Crump was their man and it seemed inconceivable that they could possibly fail to join the Swedes in the final. While Karlsson wrapped up a good evening for himself and his country by leading from tapes to flag, a crucial battle went on behind. Fittingly, two of the world's greatest speedway exponents, Messrs Crump and Gollob, were involved – and what a scrap they produced. Crump took up second position behind Karlsson from the gate, with Gollob subsequently getting the drive to dash past on the back straight of lap two. Next time around, the Pole made a slight mistake on the pits bend, allowing Crump to pass again. In a final throw of the dice, Gollob got on the faster outside line and gained sufficient momentum to whip ahead of Crump on the home straight as they entered lap three. There was no way back for Crump and even though his solitary point was doubled, it was Poland who grabbed the one remaining final spot. No two ways about it, this meeting was a terrific advertisement for speedway and certainly one that will be talked about for many years.

SWEDEN 49	RACE SCORES						TOTAL
Mikael Max	1	1	2	X	2	–	6
Tony Rickardsson	1	2	3	1	3	–	10
Antonio Lindback	X	X	3	2	3	–	8
Andreas Jonsson	2	2	2	3	3	–	12
Peter Karlsson	3	3	2	2	3	–	13
POLAND 43							
Grzegorz Walasek	3	1	0	1	0	–	5
Jaroslaw Hampel	3	2	3	1	1	–	10
Tomasz Gollob	2	3	2	3	2	–	12
Janusz Kolodziej	1	2	1	2	3	–	9
Krzysztof Kasprzak	2	0	3	0	2	–	7
AUSTRALIA 42							
Ryan Sullivan	0	0	2	3	1	–	6
Steve Johnston	2	1	1	2	1	–	7
Leigh Adams	3	3	3	3	2	–	14
Jason Crump	3	3	1	3	2	–	12
Craig Boyce	0	1	0	2	0	–	3
CZECH REPUBLIC 17							
Tomas Topinka	2	3	0	0	0	0	5
Ales Dryml	0	1	1	1	1	–	4
Bohumil Brhel	1	0	0	X	0	–	1
Lukas Dryml	F	2	1	0	2	–	5
Josef Franc	1	0	1	0	–	–	2

RACE DETAILS

HEAT ONE: Grzegorz Walasek, Tomas Topinka, Mikael Max, Ryan Sullivan.

HEAT TWO: Jaroslaw Hampel, Steve Johnston, Tony Rickardsson, Ales Dryml.

HEAT THREE: (Rerun) Leigh Adams, Tomasz Gollob, Bohumil Brhel, Antonio Lindback (f, ex).

HEAT FOUR:	Jason Crump, Andreas Jonsson, Janusz Kolodziej, Lukas Dryml (fell).
HEAT FIVE:	Peter Karlsson, Krzysztof Kasprzak, Josef Franc, Craig Boyce.
HEAT SIX:	Leigh Adams, Lukas Dryml, Mikael Max, Krzysztof Kasprzak.
HEAT SEVEN:	Jason Crump, Tony Rickardsson, Grzegorz Walasek, Josef Franc.
HEAT EIGHT:	(Rerun) Tomas Topinka, Jaroslaw Hampel, Craig Boyce, Antonio Lindback (ex, foul riding).
HEAT NINE:	Tomasz Gollob, Andreas Jonsson, Ales Dryml, Ryan Sullivan.
HEAT TEN:	Peter Karlsson, Janusz Kolodziej, Steve Johnston, Bohumil Brhel.
HEAT ELEVEN:	Jaroslaw Hampel, Mikael Max, Jason Crump, Bohumil Brhel.
HEAT TWELVE:	Tony Rickardsson, Tomasz Gollob, Lukas Dryml, Craig Boyce.
HEAT THIRTEEN:	(Rerun) Antonio Lindback, Ryan Sullivan, Janusz Kolodziej, Tomas Topinka (tactical joker).
HEAT FOURTEEN:	Krzysztof Kasprzak, Andreas Jonsson, Steve Johnston, Tomas Topinka.
HEAT FIFTEEN:	Leigh Adams, Peter Karlsson, Ales Dryml, Grzegorz Walasek.
HEAT SIXTEEN:	Tomasz Gollob, Steve Johnston, Josef Franc, Mikael Max (ex, foul riding).
HEAT SEVENTEEN:	Leigh Adams, Janusz Kolodziej, Tony Rickardsson, Tomas Topinka.
HEAT EIGHTEEN:	Jason Crump, Antonio Lindback, Ales Dryml, Krzysztof Kasprzak.
HEAT NINETEEN:	(Rerun) Andreas Jonsson, Craig Boyce, Grzegorz Walasek, Bohumil Brhel (f, ex).
HEAT TWENTY:	Ryan Sullivan, Peter Karlsson, Jaroslaw Hampel, Lukas Dryml.
HEAT TWENTY-ONE:	Janusz Kolodziej, Mikael Max, Ales Dryml, Craig Boyce.
HEAT TWENTY-TWO:	Tony Rickardsson, Krzysztof Kasprzak, Ryan Sullivan, Bohumil Brhel.
HEAT TWENTY-THREE:	Antonio Lindback, Lukas Dryml, Steve Johnston, Grzegorz Walasek.
HEAT TWENTY-FOUR:	Andreas Jonsson, Leigh Adams, Jaroslaw Hampel, Josef Franc.
HEAT TWENTY-FIVE:	Peter Karlsson, Tomasz Gollob, Jason Crump (tactical joker), Tomas Topinka.

FINAL

7 AUGUST, POOLE

With temporary stands full to the brim, a packed Wimborne Road played host to a World Cup final which, given the previous qualifying rounds, was nigh on impossible to predict. As things turned out, Team Great Britain performed heroically and led for much of the way, but it was Sweden who snatched victory at the death to repeat their success of 2003. For the British lads, their heartache at losing by a single point was compounded by a couple of controversial incidents, which were the cause of much debate. The first occurred in heat eighteen, when GB went into the race on 36 points, with the Swedes lying second on 30. Scott Nicholls was holding third position when he put his arm up and stopped after seeing a red light when exiting the fourth bend of lap three. Unfortunately, the light had not come via referee Mick Bates and the race carried on. The odd point would no doubt have proved crucial in the final analysis, but despite protestations after the race, there was little the meeting official could do about the situation and Great Britain's lead had been cut from six to three points at one fell swoop. The general consensus of opinion was that the mysterious red light had come from a camera in the crowd, but that was of little consolation to anyone in the home camp.

Dramatically, the outcome of the World Cup was to go to the final heat, with both Great Britain and Sweden entering the race level on 46 points apiece. Ironically, Nicholls was again Great Britain's representative, while Peter Karlsson was the man Sweden looked to for victory.

As the tapes rose, it was Dane Hans N. Andersen who made the break to lead, with Karlsson holding second spot from Nicholls. As they went down the back straight, Andersen looked over his right shoulder and then appeared to ease off the gas, with Karlsson sweeping past on the outside. Nicholls later managed to displace Andersen, but there was no catching the phlegmatic Karlsson as he made sure of Sweden's second successive triumph. With fingers being pointed, Andersen eventually trundled home at the rear, as Tomasz Gollob surprisingly collected his only point of the meeting, having been so outstanding in the Race-Off.

Sweden took the glory and the splendid Ove Fundin Trophy, but the British boys could be justly proud of a lionhearted performance that propelled them to the verge of greatness. Although the meeting never quite lived up to the excitement generated by the Race-Off, there was still plenty to enthuse over and, with Great Britain doing well throughout, the tension level was always locked on a high notch. Strangely, Poland never got going after their brilliance in the Race-Off and, while Gollob epitomized his side's disappointing performance, there were bright showings from Janusz Kolodziej and, to a lesser extent, Marcin Rempala, who came into the side at the expense of Grzegorz Walasek.

Meanwhile, Denmark, renowned for their tremendous team spirit, faded in the latter stages and it was a major shock to see Nicki Pedersen collect just four points. The Danes had started brightly, with Andersen recovering from a first-bend fall to take victory from Mikael Max and David Norris in a rerun opening heat. Three races later, Great Britain had taken the lead after Nicholls put together a textbook ride to defeat Kolodziej – the thrilling Pole having traded places with Andreas Jonsson to secure second spot. Gary Havelock, brought into the British quintet in place of Joe Screen because of his greater knowledge of the Poole circuit, then overhauled the lively Rempala to win a restarted fifth heat (and in the process fully justify his call-up).

Despite not winning races, the English boys managed to stay in front by filling scoring positions throughout the next three heats. Then, after Gollob had tumbled at the start of heat nine, Norris produced a super effort to triumph from his Eastbourne teammate Pedersen. For the many home supporters in the audience, the scoreboard certainly made for pleasant reading after that, since Great Britain led on 18 points, with Sweden and Denmark locked together on 15 apiece, while Poland trailed on 6. Successive victories for Karlsson, Max and Tony Rickardsson put Sweden in the ascendancy, before Norris again sparkled in a rerun heat thirteen; his win from the all-action Kolodziej restoring Great Britain's advantage, albeit by just a point over the Swedes. Lee Richardson came to life in the next race, bursting through the pack on the back straight of the opening lap to lead from Andreas Jonsson. The Swede hit back to pass entering the third bend of lap three, only for Richardson to cleverly turn back underneath off the fourth bend on his way to the flag.

Karlsson took heat fifteen, before successive wins from Richardson and Mark Loram put the Brits six points ahead of Sweden. Uncharacteristically, Rickardsson brought up the rear in the latter, his only blemish in an otherwise brilliant performance, but despite the deficit there was no tactical joker played in the previously mentioned heat eighteen.

The tension had become almost unbearable at this point, but it didn't prevent heat nineteen from turning into a speedway classic. Havelock initially led from the tapes, but was passed on the inside of bend three by Andersen. While the Dane cantered on to his second success of the evening, it left 'Havvy' and Rempala to trade places for the rest of the race, with the former World Champion just having the legs to come out on top. All of a sudden, with Jonsson at the back, the British lead was back to five points, but the picture changed again in heat twenty. This saw Karlsson claim his third straight success, while Jaroslaw Hampel relegated Norris to third place after a sweet inside pass on lap two. Havelock missed the start in heat twenty-one, but cut back beautifully on the first corner to lead up the back straight. However, the race was stopped when Nicki Pedersen got out of shape and inadvertently took Max clean out on the second bend. With the Dane excluded, Max sped from the gate in the rerun, but it was Kolodziej who posted a fine win after bravely going around the Swede on turns three and four.

Meanwhile, Havelock collected the remaining point and the total for GB crept up to 40 points, with Sweden lurking just behind on 38. That lead was completely wiped out in the next race, when Rickardsson emphatically returned to winning ways ahead of Rempala, while Norris was unable to improve on third place. Antonio Lindback led the charge in heat twenty-three, with Kolodziej, taking a tactical joker outing, holding second from Richardson. Dramatically, the Pole had the misfortune to shed a chain on the fourth corner and straightened up as a result, causing Richardson to swerve in order to avoid a collision. Mick Bates immediately stopped the race and excluded Kolodziej for impeding an opponent and the Brit made the most of his second chance, flying from the traps to defeat Lindback and give his side the slenderest of leads.

In the penultimate heat, Jonsson, who had been strangely subdued, suddenly came good and his best ride of the evening was sufficient to beat a typically pressing Loram and tie things up going into the last race. As things transpired, it wasn't to be for Great Britain, but nobody could fault their efforts and it had indeed been a joy to witness plenty of old-fashioned bulldog determination.

SWEDEN 49	RACE SCORES						TOTAL
Mikael Max	2	1	3	1	2	–	9
Tony Rickardsson	3	3	3	0	3	–	12
Antonio Lindback	1	3	0	3	2	–	9
Andreas Jonsson	1	1	2	0	3	–	7
Peter Karlsson	X	3	3	3	3	–	12
TEAM GREAT BRITAIN 48							
David Norris	1	3	3	1	1	–	9
Lee Richardson	1	0	3	3	3	–	10
Mark Loram	3	2	2	3	2	–	12
Scott Nicholls	3	1	2	R	2	–	8
Gary Havelock	3	1	2	2	1	–	9
DENMARK 32							
Hans N. Andersen	3	2	1	2	3	0	11
Nicki Pedersen	0	2	1	1	X	–	4
Kenneth Bjerre	2	1	1	0	–	–	4
Niels-Kristian Iversen	F	3	1	0	1	–	5
Bjarne Pedersen	1	2	2	2	1	–	8
POLAND 22							
Krzysztof Kasprzak	0	0	0	–	–	–	0
Jaroslaw Hampel	2	0	0	2	0	–	4
Tomasz Gollob	0	F	0	0	1	–	1
Janusz Kolodziej	2	2	2	1	3	X	10
Marcin Rempala	2	0	0	2	1	2	7

RACE DETAILS

HEAT ONE:	(Rerun) Hans N. Andersen, Mikael Max, David Norris, Krzysztof Kasprzak.
HEAT TWO:	Tony Rickardsson, Jaroslaw Hampel, Lee Richardson, Nicki Pedersen.
HEAT THREE:	Mark Loram, Kenneth Bjerre, Antonio Lindback, Tomasz Gollob.
HEAT FOUR:	Scott Nicholls, Janusz Kolodziej, Andreas Jonsson, Niels-Kristian Iversen (fell).
HEAT FIVE:	(Rerun) Gary Havelock, Marcin Rempala, Bjarne Pedersen, Peter Karlsson (f, ex).
HEAT SIX:	Niels-Kristian Iversen, Mark Loram, Mikael Max, Marcin Rempala.
HEAT SEVEN:	(Rerun) Tony Rickardsson, Bjarne Pedersen, Scott Nicholls, Krzysztof Kasprzak.
HEAT EIGHT:	Antonio Lindback, Hans N. Andersen, Gary Havelock, Jaroslaw Hampel.
HEAT NINE:	(Rerun) David Norris, Nicki Pedersen, Andreas Jonsson, Tomasz Gollob (fell).
HEAT TEN:	(Rerun) Peter Karlsson, Janusz Kolodziej, Kenneth Bjerre, Lee Richardson.
HEAT ELEVEN:	Mikael Max, Scott Nicholls, Kenneth Bjerre, Jaroslaw Hampel.
HEAT TWELVE:	Tony Rickardsson, Gary Havelock, Niels-Kristian Iversen, Tomasz Gollob.
HEAT THIRTEEN:	(Rerun) David Norris, Janusz Kolodziej, Bjarne Pedersen (tactical joker), Antonio Lindback.
HEAT FOURTEEN:	Lee Richardson, Andreas Jonsson, Hans N. Andersen, Marcin Rempala.
HEAT FIFTEEN:	Peter Karlsson, Mark Loram, Nicki Pedersen, Krzysztof Kasprzak.
HEAT SIXTEEN:	Lee Richardson, Bjarne Pedersen, Mikael Max, Tomasz Gollob.
HEAT SEVENTEEN:	Mark Loram, Hans N. Andersen, Janusz Kolodziej, Tony Rickardsson.
HEAT EIGHTEEN:	Antonio Lindback, Marcin Rempala, Nicki Pedersen, Scott Nicholls (ret).
HEAT NINETEEN:	Hans N. Andersen, Gary Havelock, Marcin Rempala, Andreas Jonsson.
HEAT TWENTY:	Peter Karlsson, Jaroslaw Hampel, David Norris, Niels-Kristian Iversen.
HEAT TWENTY-ONE:	(Rerun) Janusz Kolodziej, Mikael Max, Gary Havelock, Nicki Pedersen (f, ex).
HEAT TWENTY-TWO:	Tony Rickardsson, Marcin Rempala, David Norris, Kenneth Bjerre.
HEAT TWENTY-THREE:	(Rerun) Lee Richardson, Antonio Lindback, Niels-Kristian Iversen, Janusz Kolodziej (tactical joker; ex, impeding opponent).
HEAT TWENTY-FOUR:	Andreas Jonsson, Mark Loram, Bjarne Pedersen, Jaroslaw Hampel.
HEAT TWENTY-FIVE:	Peter Karlsson, Scott Nicholls, Tomasz Gollob, Hans N. Andersen.

ROLL OF HONOUR

YEAR	FIRST	SECOND	THIRD	FOURTH
1960	Sweden	Great Britain	Czechoslovakia	Poland
1961	Poland	Sweden	Great Britain	Czechoslovakia
1962	Sweden	Great Britain	Poland	Czechoslovakia
1963	Sweden	Czechoslovakia	Great Britain	Poland
1964	Sweden	Soviet Union	Great Britain	Poland
1965	Poland	Sweden	Great Britain	Soviet Union
1966	Poland	Soviet Union	Sweden	Great Britain
1967	Sweden	Poland	Great Britain/Soviet Union	–
1968	Great Britain	Sweden	Poland	Czechoslovakia
1969	Poland	Great Britain	Soviet Union	Sweden
1970	Sweden	Great Britain	Poland	Czechoslovakia

YEAR	FIRST	SECOND	THIRD	FOURTH
1971	Great Britain	Soviet Union	Poland	Sweden
1972	Great Britain	Soviet Union	Poland	Sweden
1973	Great Britain	Sweden	Soviet Union	Poland
1974	England	Sweden	Poland	Soviet Union
1975	England	Soviet Union	Sweden	Poland
1976	Australia	Poland	Sweden	Soviet Union
1977	England	Poland	Czechoslovakia	Sweden
1978	Denmark	England	Poland	Czechoslovakia
1979	New Zealand	Denmark	Czechoslovakia	Poland
1980	England	USA	Poland	Czechoslovakia
1981	Denmark	England	West Germany	Soviet Union
1982	USA	Denmark	West Germany	Czechoslovakia
1983	Denmark	England	USA	Czechoslovakia
1984	Denmark	England	USA	Poland
1985	Denmark	USA	England	Sweden
1986	Denmark	USA	England	Sweden
1987	Denmark	England	USA	Czechoslovakia
1988	Denmark	USA	Sweden	England
1989	England	Denmark	Sweden	USA
1990	USA	England	Denmark	Czechoslovakia
1991	Denmark	Sweden	USA	England
1992	USA	Sweden	England	Denmark
1993	USA	Denmark	Sweden	England
1994	Sweden	Poland	Denmark	Australia
1995	Denmark	England	USA	Sweden
1996	Poland	Russia	Denmark	Germany
1997	Denmark	Poland	Sweden	Germany
1998	USA	Sweden	Denmark	Poland
1999	Australia	Czech Republic	USA	England
2000	Sweden	England	USA	Australia
2001	Australia	Poland	Sweden	Denmark
2002	Australia	Denmark	Sweden	Poland
2003	Sweden	Australia	Denmark	Poland
2004	Sweden	Great Britain	Denmark	Poland

WORLD UNDER-21 CHAMPIONSHIP

NOTE: Formerly known as the European Junior Championship (1977-87)

QUALIFYING ROUNDS

ROUND ONE; 23 May, Rawicz, Poland

QUALIFYING SCORES: Robert Miskowiak 13; Pawl Hlib 13; Piotr Swiderski 12; Rory Schlein 11; Kyle Legault 11; Jamie Smith 9; Tomas Suchanek 9; Szabolcs Vida 8; Miroslaw Fencl 7; Ben Wilson 6; Eric Carrillo 5; Byron Bekker 5; Marcin Rempala (Res) 3; Ben Powell 3; Zbigniew Suchecki (Res) 2; Tamas Sike 2; Manuel Novotny 0; Jan Halabrin 0. FIRST SEMI-FINAL: 1st Miskowiak; 2nd Schlein; 3rd Suchanek; 4th Smith. SECOND SEMI-FINAL: 1st Swiderski; 2nd Hlib; 3rd Vida; 4th Legault. FINAL: 1st Miskowiak; 2nd Swiderski; 3rd Schlein; 4th Hlib.

ROUND TWO; 23 May, Daugavpils, Latvia

QUALIFYING SCORES: Denis Gizatulin 14; Adrian Miedzinski 14; Christian Hefenbrock 12; Janusz Kolodziej 12; Miroslaw Jablonski 10; Maxim Kalimulin 9; Daniel King 9; Andrej Karpov 7; Trevor Harding 6; Kjastas Puodzuks 6; Jason King 5; Leonid Paura 4; Tobias Busch 4; Roman Ivanov 3; Ivan Vargek 1; Aleksandrs Dovzenko 0. FIRST SEMI-FINAL: 1st Kolodziej; 2nd D. King; 3rd Kalimulin; 4th Gizatulin. SECOND SEMI-FINAL: 1st Miedzinski; 2nd Jablonski; 3rd Hefenbrock; 4th Karpov. FINAL: 1st Miedzinski; 2nd Kolodziej; 3rd Jablonski; 4th D. King.

ROUND THREE; 31 May, Abensberg, Germany

QUALIFYING SCORES: Matej Zagar 14; Tobias Kroner 12; Martin Smolinski 12; Steve Boxall 10; Patrick Linhart 9; Rene Schafer 9; Daniele Tessari 9; Edward Kennett 8; Ryan Fisher 8; Jannick De Jong 7; Bryan Yarrow 6; Zdenek Simota 5; Hans-Jorg Muller 5; Mattia Carpanese 3; Primoz Legan 2; Jerome Lespinasse 1. FIRST SEMI-FINAL: 1st Boxall; 2nd Tessari; 3rd Zagar; 4th Schafer. SECOND SEMI-FINAL: 1st Smolinski; 2nd Kroner; 3rd Kennett; 4th Linhart. FINAL: 1st Smolinski; 2nd Boxall; 3rd Kroner; 4th Tessari.

ROUND FOUR; 6 June, Vargaus, Finland

QUALIFYING SCORES: Fredrik Lindgren 14; Morten Risager 14; Jonas Davidsson 13; Mads Korneliussen 11; Henrik Moller 10; Eric Andersson 10; Tobias Messing 9; Tero Aarnio 8; Niklas Fridell 8; Rene Lehtinen 6; Rune Sola 5; Rune Knudsen 5; Lars Hansen 4; Petri Koskela 2; Joni Keskinen 1; Aarni Heikkila 0; Joni Kitala 0. FIRST SEMI-FINAL: 1st Lindgren; 2nd Korneliussen; 3rd Andersson; 4th Messing. SECOND SEMI-FINAL: 1st Davidsson; 2nd Risager; 3rd Moller; 4th Aarnio. FINAL: 1st Lindgren; 2nd Korneliussen; 3rd Risager; 4th Davidsson.

FIRST SEMI-FINAL: 24 July, Wiener Neustadt, Austria

QUALIFYING SCORES: Janusz Kolodziej 15; Antonio Lindback 11; Martin Smolinski 11; Robert Miskowiak 11; Jonas Davidsson 9; Piotr Swiderski 9; Mads Korneliussen 8; Rory Schlein 7; Denis Gizatulin 7; Ritchie Hawkins 6; Daniel King 6; Jan Jaros 5; Daniele Tessari 5; Tobias Kroner 4; Ales Kraljic 3; Szabolcs Vida 2; Rene Schafer 0. FIRST SEMI-FINAL: 1st Miskowiak; 2nd Swiderski; 3rd Korneliussen; 4th Kolodziej. SECOND SEMI-FINAL: 1st Lindback; 2nd Smolinski; 3rd Davidsson; 4th Schlein. FINAL: 1st Miskowiak; 2nd Smolinksi; 3rd Lindback; 4th Swiderski.

SECOND SEMI-FINAL: 24 July, Vetlanda, Sweden

QUALIFYING SCORES: Matej Zagar 13; Krzysztof Kasprzak 13; Adrian Miedzinski 12; Fredrik Lindgren 11; Kenneth Bjerre 10; Daniel Davidsson 10; Christian Hefenbrock 8; Eric Andersson 8; Pavel Hlib 8; Tomas Suchanek 7; Morten Risager 7; Miroslaw Jablonski 4; Henrik Moller 4; Edward Kennett 3; Steve Boxall 2; Mathias Schultz 0. FIRST SEMI-FINAL: 1st Zagar; 2nd Lindgren; 3rd Davidsson; 4th Hefenbrock. SECOND SEMI-FINAL: 1st Bjerre; 2nd Andersson; 3rd Kasprzak; 4th Miedzinski. FINAL: 1st Bjerre; 2nd Lindgren; 3rd Zagar; 4th Andersson.

WORLD UNDER-21 CHAMPIONSHIP FINAL

11 SEPTEMBER, WROCLAW, POLAND

1st	ROBERT MISKOWIAK
2nd	KENNETH BJERRE
3rd	MATEJ ZAGAR
4th	RORY SCHLEIN

	QUALIFYING SCORES					TOTAL
Adrian Miedzinski	3	3	2	3	2	13
Robert Miskowiak	3	3	3	1	2	12
Antonio Lindback	3	2	3	2	2	12
Piotr Swiderski	0	1	3	2	3	9
Martin Smolinski	2	3	1	2	1	9
Matej Zagar	X	0	3	3	2	8
Kenneth Bjerre	2	X	2	1	3	8
Rory Schlein	2	1	2	0	3	8
Krzysztof Kasprzak	1	1	2	3	1	8
Fredrik Lindgren	1	2	1	1	3	8
Mads Korneliussen	2	2	1	2	0	7
Jonas Davidsson	0	2	0	3	1	6
Eric Andersson	3	1	1	0	R	5
Denis Gizatulin	0	3	0	0	1	4
Christian Hefenbrock	1	0	0	1	0	2
Daniel Davidsson	1	0	0	0	R	1

RACE DETAILS

HEAT ONE:	Eric Andersson, Rory Schlein, Christian Hefenbrock, Denis Gizatulin.
HEAT TWO:	Robert Miskowiak, Kenneth Bjerre, Krzysztof Kasprzak, Jonas Davidsson.
HEAT THREE:	(Rerun) Adrian Miedzinski, Martin Smolinski, Daniel Davidsson, Matej Zagar (f, ex).
HEAT FOUR:	Antonio Lindback, Mads Korneliussen, Fredrik Lindgren, Piotr Swiderski.
HEAT FIVE:	Robert Miskowiak, Fredrik Lindgren, Rory Schlein, Daniel Davidsson.

HEAT SIX:	Denis Gizatulin, Jonas Davidsson, Piotr Swiderski, Matej Zagar.
HEAT SEVEN:	(Rerun) Martin Smolinski, Mads Korneliussen, Eric Andersson, Kenneth Bjerre (ex, not under power).
HEAT EIGHT:	Adrian Miedzinski, Antonio Lindback, Krzysztof Kasprzak, Christian Hefenbrock.
HEAT NINE:	Antonio Lindback, Rory Schlein, Martin Smolinski, Jonas Davidsson.
HEAT TEN:	Robert Miskowiak, Adrian Miedzinski, Mads Korneliussen, Denis Gizatulin.
HEAT ELEVEN:	Piotr Swiderski, Krzysztof Kasprzak, Eric Andersson, Daniel Davidsson.
HEAT TWELVE:	Matej Zagar, Kenneth Bjerre, Fredrik Lindgren, Christian Hefenbrock.
HEAT THIRTEEN:	Adrian Miedzinski, Piotr Swiderski, Kenneth Bjerre, Rory Schlein.
HEAT FOURTEEN:	Krzysztof Kasprzak, Martin Smolinski, Fredrik Lindgren, Denis Gizatulin.
HEAT FIFTEEN:	Matej Zagar, Antonio Lindback, Robert Miskowiak, Eric Andersson.
HEAT SIXTEEN:	Jonas Davidsson, Mads Korneliussen, Christian Hefenbrock, Daniel Davidsson.
HEAT SEVENTEEN:	Rory Schlein, Matej Zagar, Krzysztof Kasprzak, Mads Korneliussen.
HEAT EIGHTEEN:	Kenneth Bjerre, Antonio Lindback, Denis Gizatulin, Daniel Davidsson (ret).
HEAT NINETEEN:	Fredrik Lindgren, Adrian Miedzinski, Jonas Davidsson, Eric Andersson (ret).
HEAT TWENTY:	Piotr Swiderski, Robert Miskowiak, Martin Smolinski, Christian Hefenbrock.
FIRST SEMI-FINAL:	Rory Schlein, Matej Zagar, Piotr Swiderski, Adrian Miedzinski (ret).
SECOND SEMI-FINAL:	(Rerun twice) Kenneth Bjerre, Robert Miskowiak, Martin Smolinski (f, ex), Antonio Lindback (f, ex).
FINAL:	(Rerun) Robert Miskowiak, Kenneth Bjerre, Matej Zagar, Rory Schlein (f, ex).

ROLL OF HONOUR

YEAR	FIRST	SECOND	THIRD
1977	Alf Busk	Joe Owen	Les Collins
1978	Finn Jensen	Kevin Jolly	Neil Middleditch
1979	Ron Preston	Airat Faljzulin	Ari Koponen
1980	Tommy Knudsen	Tony Briggs	Dennis Sigalos
1981	Shawn Moran	Toni Kasper	Jiri Hnidak
1982	Toni Kasper	Mark Courtney	Peter Ravn
1983	Steve Baker	David Bargh	Marvyn Cox
1984	Marvyn Cox	Neil Evitts	Steve Lucero
1985	Per Jonsson	Jimmy Nilsen	Ole Hansen
1986	Igor Marko	Tony Olsson	Brian Karger
1987	Gary Havelock	Piotr Swist	Sean Wilson
1988	Peter Nahlin	Henrik Gustafsson	Brian Karger
1989	Gert Handberg	Chris Louis	Niklas Karlsson
1990	Chris Louis	Rene Aas	Tony Rickardsson
1991	Brian Andersen	Morten Andersen	Jason Lyons
1992	Leigh Adams	Mark Loram	Joe Screen
1993	Joe Screen	Mikael Karlsson	Rune Holta
1994	Mikael Karlsson	Rune Holta	Jason Crump
1995	Jason Crump	Dalle Anderson	Ryan Sullivan
1996	Piotr Protasiewicz	Ryan Sullivan	Jesper B. Jensen
1997	Jesper B. Jensen	Rafal Dobrucki	Scott Nicholls

YEAR	FIRST	SECOND	THIRD
1998	Robert Dados	Krzysztof Jablonski	Matej Ferjan
1999	Lee Richardson	Ales Dryml	Nigel Sadler
2000	Andreas Jonsson	Krzysztof Cegielski	Jaroslaw Hampel
2001	David Kujawa	Lukas Dryml	Rafal Okoniewski
2002	Lukas Dryml	Krzysztof Kasprzak	David Howe
2003	Jaroslaw Hampel	Chris Harris	Rafal Szombierski
2004	Robert Miskowiak	Kenneth Bjerre	Matej Zagar

EUROPEAN CHAMPIONSHIP

QUALIFYING ROUNDS

FIRST SEMI-FINAL; 27 June, Lendava, Slovenia

1st Matej Ferjan 15; 2nd Andrzej Huszcza 14; 3rd Jacek Krzyzaniak (after run-off) 11; Izak Santej 11; Matej Zagar 10; Fritz Wallner 9; Laszlo Szatmari 8; Adrian Rymel 8; Simone Terenzani 8; Jernej Kolenko 6; Andrea Maida 5; Primoz Legan 4; Sandor Tihanyi 4; Ivan Vargek 3; Henry van der Steen 2; Arjan Borgers 0; Tomasz Rempala (Res) 0.

SECOND SEMI-FINAL; 3 July, Straslund, Germany

1st Janusz Kolodziej 13; 2nd Renat Gafurov 12; 3rd Richard Wolff (after run-off) 11; Joachim Kugelmann 11; Krzysztof Jablonski 10; Marcin Rempala 9; Josef Franc 9; Tomas Suchanek 9; Zbigniew Czerwinski 9; Roberto Haupt 8; Miroslav Fencl 7; Ilya Bondarenko 4; Bohumil Brhel 3; Pavel Ondrasik 3; Vladimir Visvader 1; Mircea Agrisan 1.

EUROPEAN CHAMPIONSHIP FINAL

29 AUGUST, HOLSTED, DENMARK

1st	MATEJ ZAGAR
2nd	MATEJ FERJAN
3rd	HANS N. ANDERSEN
4th	NIELS-KRISTIAN IVERSEN

	RACE SCORES					TOTAL
Matej Zagar	3	3	2	2	3	14
Matej Ferjan	3	3	3	2	3	14
Hans N. Andersen	2	1	3	3	3	12
Niels-Kristian Iversen	3	2	2	2	2	11
Jacek Krzyzaniak	1	3	1	3	2	10
Krzysztof Jablonski	2	2	3	1	1	9
Renat Gafurov	2	X	1	2	3	8
Janusz Kolodziej	2	3	2	X	–	7
Niklas Klingberg	3	R	0	3	0	6
Freddie Eriksson	1	0	1	2	2	6
David Ruud	0	2	1	1	2	6
Andrzej Huszcza	1	R	3	1	0	5
Morten Risager	0	1	2	1	0	4
Izak Santej	0	2	0	0	1	3
Richard Wolff	0	1	0	0	1	2
Joachim Kugelmann	1	X	0	0	–	1
Marcin Rempala (Res)	1	–	–	–	–	1

RACE DETAILS

HEAT ONE:	Matej Ferjan, Krzysztof Jablonski, Freddie Eriksson, Izak Santej.
HEAT TWO:	Niklas Klingberg, Hans N. Andersen, Joachim Kugelmann, David Ruud.
HEAT THREE:	Matej Zagar, Janusz Kolodziej, Andrzej Huszcza, Richard Wolff.
HEAT FOUR:	Niels-Kristian Iversen, Renat Gafurov, Jacek Krzyzaniak, Morten Risager.
HEAT FIVE:	(Rerun) Jacek Krzyzaniak, Izak Santej, Richard Wolff, Joachim Kugelmann (f, ex).
HEAT SIX:	Matej Zagar, Niels-Kristian Iversen, Hans N. Andersen, Freddie Eriksson.
HEAT SEVEN:	Janusz Kolodziej, Krzysztof Jablonski, Morten Risager, Niklas Klingberg (ret).
HEAT EIGHT:	(Rerun) Matej Ferjan, David Ruud, Andrzej Huszcza (ret), Renat Gafurov (f, ex).
HEAT NINE:	Hans N. Andersen, Janusz Kolodziej, Renat Gafurov, Izak Santej.
HEAT TEN:	Andrzej Huszcza, Morten Risager, Freddie Eriksson, Joachim Kugelmann.
HEAT ELEVEN:	Krzysztof Jablonski, Niels-Kristian Iversen, David Ruud, Richard Wolff.
HEAT TWELVE:	Matej Ferjan, Matej Zagar, Jacek Krzyzaniak, Niklas Klingberg.
HEAT THIRTEEN:	Niklas Klingberg, Niels-Kristian Iversen, Andrzej Huszcza, Izak Santej.
HEAT FOURTEEN:	(Rerun) Jacek Krzyzaniak, Freddie Eriksson, David Ruud, Janusz Kolodziej (f, ex).
HEAT FIFTEEN:	Matej Zagar, Renat Gafurov, Krzysztof Jablonski, Joachim Kugelmann.
HEAT SIXTEEN:	Hans N. Andersen, Matej Ferjan, Morten Risager, Richard Wolff.
HEAT SEVENTEEN:	Matej Zagar, David Ruud, Izak Santej, Morten Risager.
HEAT EIGHTEEN:	Renat Gafurov, Freddie Eriksson, Richard Wolff, Niklas Klingberg.
HEAT NINETEEN:	Hans N. Andersen, Jacek Krzyzaniak, Krzysztof Jablonski, Andrzej Huszcza.
HEAT TWENTY:	Matej Ferjan, Niels-Kristian Iversen, Marcin Rempala, Joachim Kugelmann (ns).
FIRST PLACE RUN-OFF:	Matej Zagar, Matej Ferjan.

ROLL OF HONOUR

YEAR	FIRST	SECOND	THIRD
2001	Bohumil Brhel	Mariusz Staszewski	Krzysztof Cegielski
2002	Magnus Zetterstrom	Krzysztof Kasprzak	Rafal Szombierski
2003	Krzysztof Kasprzak	Slawomir Drabik	Magnus Zetterstrom
2004	Matej Zagar	Matej Ferjan	Hans N. Andersen

EUROPEAN UNDER-19 CHAMPIONSHIP FINAL

28 AUGUST, RYBNIK, POLAND

1st	ANTONIO LINDBACK
2nd	KAROL ZABIK
3rd	MORTEN RISAGER
4th	FREDRIK LINDGREN

	RACE SCORES					TOTAL
Antonio Lindback	3	3	3	3	3	15
Karol Zabik	3	1	3	3	2	12
Morten Risager	3	3	2	3	1	12
Fredrik Lindgren	2	3	3	R	3	11
Kjastas Poudzhuks	2	1	2	3	2	10
Henrik Moller	2	0	2	1	3	8
Pawel Hlib	1	2	3	2	R	8
Christian Hefenbrock	1	3	1	1	0	6
Krzysztof Buczkowski	0	2	2	2	0	6
Zdenek Simota	0	1	1	2	2	6
Lubos Tomicek	1	1	1	2	1	6
Filip Sitera	0	2	0	0	3	5
Adrian Miedzinski	3	2	R	X	–	5
Tobias Messing	1	0	0	1	2	4
Miroslaw Jablonski	2	R	1	R	1	4
Mathieu Tresarrieu	0	0	0	1	R	1
Alexander Lischke (Res)	1	–	–	–	–	1

RACE DETAILS

HEAT ONE:	Antonio Lindback, Fredrik Lindgren, Lubos Tomicek, Filip Sitera.
HEAT TWO:	Morten Risager, Henrik Moller, Christian Hefenbrock, Mathieu Tresarrieu.
HEAT THREE:	Karol Zabik, Kjastas Poudzhuks, Tobias Messing, Zdenek Simota.
HEAT FOUR:	Adrian Miedzinski, Miroslaw Jablonski, Pawel Hlib, Krzysztof Buczkowski.
HEAT FIVE:	Fredrik Lindgren, Adrian Miedzinski, Kjastas Poudzhuks, Henrik Moller.
HEAT SIX:	Antonio Lindback, Pawel Hlib, Karol Zabik, Mathieu Tresarrieu.
HEAT SEVEN:	Morten Risager, Filip Sitera, Zdenek Simota, Miroslaw Jablonski (ret).
HEAT EIGHT:	Christian Hefenbrock, Krzysztof Buczkowski, Lubos Tomicek, Tobias Messing.
HEAT NINE:	Fredrik Lindgren, Krzysztof Buczkowski, Zdenek Simota, Mathieu Tresarrieu.
HEAT TEN:	Antonio Lindback, Henrik Moller, Miroslaw Jablonski, Tobias Messing.
HEAT ELEVEN:	Pawel Hlib, Kjastas Poudzhuks, Christian Hefenbrock, Filip Sitera.
HEAT TWELVE:	Karol Zabik, Morten Risager, Lubos Tomicek, Adrian Miedzinski (ret).
HEAT THIRTEEN:	Morten Risager, Pawel Hlib, Tobias Messing, Fredrik Lindgren (ret).
HEAT FOURTEEN:	(Rerun) Antonio Lindback, Zdenek Simota, Christian Hefenbrock, Adrian Miedzinski (f, ex).

HEAT FIFTEEN: Karol Zabik, Krzysztof Buczkowski, Henrik Moller, Filip Sitera.
HEAT SIXTEEN: Kjastas Poudzhuks, Lubos Tomicek, Mathieu Tresarrieu, Miroslaw Jablonski (ret).
HEAT SEVENTEEN: Fredrik Lindgren, Karol Zabik, Miroslaw Jablonski, Christian Hefenbrock.
HEAT EIGHTEEN: Antonio Lindback, Kjastas Poudzhuks, Morten Risager, Krzysztof Buczkowski.
HEAT NINETEEN: Filip Sitera, Tobias Messing, Alexander Lischke, Mathieu Tresarrieu (ret).
HEAT TWENTY: Henrik Moller, Zdenek Simota, Lubos Tomicek, Pawel Hlib (ret).
SECOND PLACE RUN-OFF: Karol Zabik, Morten Risager.

ROLL OF HONOUR

YEAR	FIRST	SECOND	THIRD
1998	Rafal Okoniewski	Ales Dryml	Hans N. Andersen
1999	Rafal Okoniewski	Karol Malecha	Jaroslaw Hampel
2000	Lukas Dryml	Niels-Kristian Iversen	Zbigniew Czerwinski
2001	Lukasz Romanek	Daniel Davidsson	Rafal Kurmanski
2002	Matej Zagar	Kenneth Bjerre	Fredrik Lindgren
2003	Kenneth Bjerre	Janusz Kolodziej	Antonio Lindback
2004	Antonio Lindback	Karol Zabik	Morten Risager

RIDER INDEX 2004

RIDER INDEX 2004

The following is an A-Z list of riders who appeared in British racing in 2004, and includes all meetings in the Elite League (and Knock-Out Cup), Premier League (and Knock-Out Cup) and Conference League (and Knock-Out Cup & Conference Trophy).

ADAMS, Leigh *b. 28 April 1971, Mildura, Victoria, Australia.*
BRITISH CAREER: (1989) Poole; (1990-92) Swindon; (1993-95) Arena-Essex; (1996) London; (1997-98) Swindon; (1999-00) King's Lynn; (2001-02) Oxford; (2003) Poole; (2004) Swindon.

ALLEN, Olly *b. 27 May 1982, Norwich, Norfolk.*
BRITISH CAREER: (1997) Peterborough (AL); (1998) Mildenhall, Norfolk, Peterborough, Arena-Essex; (1999-01) Swindon; (2002) Swindon, Peterborough; (2003) Swindon, Wolverhampton; (2004) Swindon.

ALLEN, Tommy *b. 4 September 1984, Norwich, Norfolk.*
BRITISH CAREER: (2002) Swindon (CT & PL), Mildenhall; (2003) Swindon (PL & CL); (2004) Rye House (PL & CL).

ALLOTT, Adam *b. 19 March 1983, Stockport, Cheshire.*
BRITISH CAREER: (1998) Norfolk, Buxton; (1999) Buxton, Sheffield; (2000) Sheffield, Owlerton; (2001) Sheffield; (2002) Sheffield (CL), Swindon, Somerset; (2003) Buxton, Stoke (BLC), King's Lynn; (2004) King's Lynn.

ANDERSEN, Hans N. *b. 3 November 1980, Odense, Denmark.*
BRITISH CAREER: (2001-02) Poole; (2003) Peterborough; (2004) Ipswich.

ANDREWS, Darren *b. 19 January 1977, Banbury, Oxfordshire.*
BRITISH CAREER: (1993) Coventry, Oxford; (1994) Coventry, Oxford, Mildenhall; (1995) Sittingbourne; (1996) Reading (CL); (1997) Berwick, Hull, Long Eaton, Oxford (PL & AL), Isle of Wight; (2000) St Austell; (2001) Rye House; (2002) Mildenhall, Hull; (2003) Oxford (CL & BLC), Carmarthen (CT); (2004) Wolverhampton, Stoke (CL), Coventry (CT).

ANDREWS, Marc *b. 23 November 1986, Poole, Dorset.*
BRITISH CAREER: (2004) Stoke (CL), Swindon (CL), King's Lynn (CT).

APPLETON, Andrew *b. 18 June 1982, Reading, Berkshire.*
BRITISH CAREER: (1997) Oxford (AL); (1998) Newport (CL & PL), Arena-Essex, Edinburgh; (1999) Newport (PL & CL); (2000) Newport; (2001) Oxford; (2002) Oxford, Reading; (2003) Reading; (2004) Reading, Peterborough.

ARMSTRONG, Jon *b. 1 August 1974, Manchester, Greater Manchester.*
BRITISH CAREER: (1992-93) Belle Vue; (1994) Coventry; (1996) Buxton, Sheffield; (1997) Buxton, Belle Vue (AL), Swindon, Stoke; (1998) Newport (CL & PL); (1999) Belle Vue, Stoke; (2000) Newport (PL); (2001) Stoke; (2002) Buxton, Stoke; (2003) Stoke (2004) Belle Vue, Mildenhall, Newcastle (PL).

ASHWORTH, Ricky *b. 17 August 1982, Salford, Greater Manchester.*
BRITISH CAREER: (2001) Sheffield (CL); (2002) Sheffield (PL & CL); (2003) Sheffield (PL), Poole (BLC); (2004) Sheffield (PL), Peterborough.

ATKIN, Tony *b. 8 April 1966, Wrexham, North Wales.*
BRITISH CAREER: (1986) Stoke; (1994) Wolverhampton; (1995) Bradford; (1996) Sheffield, Wolverhampton, Buxton; (1997) Stoke; (1999-02) Stoke; (2003-04) Newport.

BAGER, Henning *b. 18 February 1981, Esbjerg, Denmark.*
BRITISH CAREER: (2001) Glasgow; (2002) Peterborough, Isle of Wight; (2003) Arena-Essex; (2004) Peterborough.

BALDWIN, Carl *b. 4 July 1964, Ipswich, Suffolk.*
BRITISH CAREER: (1980) Mildenhall, Hull; (1981) Mildenhall; (1982-84) Mildenhall, Ipswich; (1985) Mildenhall; (1986) Peterborough, King's Lynn; (1987) Peterborough, Boston; (1988-89) Milton Keynes; (2002) Ipswich, Arena-Essex, Mildenhall; (2003) Mildenhall, Ipswich (BLC); (2004) Mildenhall.

BARKER, Ben *b. 10 March 1988, Truro, Cornwall.*
BRITISH CAREER: (2003) Oxford (CL), Trelawny (CT); (2004) Oxford (CL), Isle of Wight (PT), Coventry (CT), Edinburgh.

BARKER, Dean *b. 2 August 1970, Isleworth, Middlesex.*
BRITISH CAREER: (1986) Eastbourne; (1987-88) Eastbourne, Cradley Heath; (1989) Eastbourne; (1990-92) Oxford; (1993-95) Eastbourne; (1997) Eastbourne; (1999-03) Eastbourne; (2004) Arena-Essex.

BARNETT, Russell *b. 26 May 1987, Newport, South Wales.*
BRITISH CAREER: (2003) Mildenhall (CT), Rye House (CL), Newport (CL), Oxford (CL); (2004) Newport (CL).

BARRETT, Wayne *b. 22 March 1968, Redruth, Cornwall.*
BRITISH CAREER: (1984) Weymouth; (1986-87) Poole; (1997) St Austell, Newport; (1998) St Austell; (1999-00) St Austell, Exeter; (2001) Trelawny, Boston; (2002) Boston, Wimbledon, Trelawny; (2003) Wimbledon, Eastbourne (BLC); (2004) Wimbledon, Oxford (CL), Weymouth.

BASEBY, Mark *b. 28 February 1988, Pembury, Kent.*
BRITISH CAREER: (2003) Stoke (CT), Swindon (CL); (2004) Rye House (CL), Sittingbourne (KOC).

BATES, Matt *b. 26 July 1989, Exeter, Devon.*
BRITISH CAREER: (2004) Coventry (CT), Weymouth.

BEATON, Gary *b. 20 August 1986, Glasgow, Scotland.*
BRITISH CAREER: (2002) Newport (CL), Newcastle (CL); (2003) Wolverhampton (CL), Armadale (CT), Newcastle (CL), Glasgow; (2004) Armadale, Hull (PT), Edinburgh (PT), Glasgow.

BEKKER, Byron *b. 2 July 1987, Johannesburg, South Africa.*
BRITISH CAREER: (2004) Newcastle (CL).

BELFIELD, Carl *b. 1 September 1977, Stockport, Cheshire.*
BRITISH CAREER: (2002) Buxton; (2004) Buxton.

BENTLEY, Paul *b. 18 January 1968, Newcastle-upon-Tyne, Tyne and Wear.*
BRITISH CAREER: (1987) Newcastle; (1988-91) Middlesbrough; (1992) Coventry; (1993) Bradford; (1994) Middlesbrough; (1995-96) Coventry; (1997) Newcastle; (1998) Hull; (1999) Glasgow; (2000) Berwick; (2001) Hull; (2002-03) Berwick; (2004) Glasgow.

BETHELL, Jonathon *b. 18 March 1973, Kendal, Cumbria.*
BRITISH CAREER: (2003) Oxford (CL), Buxton; (2004) Buxton.

BETSON, Danny *b. 11 January 1988, Eastbourne, East Sussex.*
BRITISH CAREER: (2004) Mildenhall, Swindon (CL).

BIRD, Danny *b. 16 November 1979, Guildford, Surrey.*
BRITISH CAREER: (1998-01) Isle of Wight; (2002-03) Isle of Wight, Ipswich; (2004) Reading, Ipswich.

BIRKINSHAW, James *b. 6 March 1980, Sheffield, South Yorkshire.*
BRITISH CAREER: (1996) Owlerton, Sheffield, Hull; (1997) Sheffield, Belle Vue (AL), Newcastle; (1998) Newcastle, St Austell; (1999) Workington, Edinburgh, Linlithgow, Berwick, Sheffield, Stoke; (2000) Sheffield (PL & CL), Glasgow; (2001) Newcastle, Sheffield (CL), Isle of Wight; (2002) Sheffield (PL), Boston, Wolverhampton (CT); (2003) Sheffield (PL); (2004) Sheffield (PL) & Buxton.

BISHOP, Steve *b. 28 November 1963, Bristol, Avon.*
BRITISH CAREER: (1981) Swindon, Canterbury; (1982-83) Swindon, Exeter; (1984) Stoke, Exeter; (1985) Exeter; (1986) Exeter, Swindon; (1987) Arena-Essex; (1988) Poole, Long Eaton; (1989) Long Eaton, Exeter; (1990) Exeter; (1995) Oxford; (1997-98) St Austell; (1999) Swindon; (2000-02) Somerset; (2003) Somerset, Hull; (2004) Carmarthen, Somerset.

BJERRE, Kenneth *b. 24 May 1984, Esbjerg, Denmark.*
BRITISH CAREER: (2002) Newcastle; (2003) Newcastle, Peterborough; (2004) Belle Vue.

BLACKBURN, Andrew *b. 20 March 1985, Sheffield, South Yorkshire.*
BRITISH CAREER: (2004) Stoke (CL), Weymouth.

BLACKMAN, Corey *b. 30 April 1977, Perth, Western Australia.*
BRITISH CAREER: (2002) Carmarthen, Reading, Edinburgh, Glasgow, Exeter, Wolverhampton (CT), Sheffield (CL), Trelawny; (2003) Exeter, Carmarthen; (2004) Glasgow, Weymouth, Newcastle (CL).

BLAKE, Daniel *b. 7 August 1988, Harlow, Essex.*
BRITISH CAREER: (2004) Mildenhall.

BOAST, Peter *b. 11 April 1964, Louth, Lincolnshire.*
BRITISH CAREER: (1994) Mildenhall; (1995) Mildenhall, Sheffield, Wolverhampton, Swindon; (1996) Mildenhall, Sheffield; (1997) Sheffield; (1998) Skegness, Norfolk, Sheffield; (1999) Sheffield, King's Lynn (CL); (2000-02) Boston; (2003) Boston, Coventry (BLC), Hull; (2004) Sittingbourne (KOC), Wimbledon (CT).

BOWEN, Luke *b. 26 January 1986, Harlow, Essex.*
BRITISH CAREER: (2002) Rye House (CL), Carmarthen; (2003) Rye House (CL & PL); (2004) Rye House (CL & PL), King's Lynn (CLKOC).

BOXALL, Steve *b. 16 May 1987, Canterbury, Kent.*
BRITISH CAREER: (2002) Rye House (CL); (2003) Rye House (CL), Ipswich (BLC), Reading (BLC), King's Lynn; (2004) Rye House (PL & CL).

BOYCE, Craig *b. 2 August 1967, Sydney, New South Wales, Australia.*
BRITISH CAREER: (1988-90) Poole; (1991) Oxford; (1992-94) Poole; (1995) Swindon; (1996-98) Poole; (1999) Oxford; (2000) King's Lynn; (2001-02) Ipswich; (2003) Poole (BLC), Oxford, Ipswich; (2004) Isle of Wight.

BRADY, Ross *b. 17 February 1981, Winchburgh, Broxburn, Scotland.*
BRITISH CAREER: (1997) Lathallan, Peterborough (AL); (1998) Mildenhall, Peterborough (PL), Berwick; (1999-00) Edinburgh; (2001) King's Lynn, Hull; (2002) Hull; (2003) Glasgow, Sheffield (CL & PL); (2004) Hull.

BRAIDFORD, Steve *b. 31 December 1985, Maidstone, Kent.*
BRITISH CAREER: (2002) Wolverhampton (CT), Isle of Wight, Wimbledon; (2003) Wolverhampton (CL & BLC), King's Lynn (BLC); (2004) Reading, Swindon (CL).

BRANNEY, Craig *b. 31 July 1982, Whitehaven, Cumbria.*
BRITISH CAREER: (2000) Ashfield; (2001) Workington, Buxton, Isle of Wight, Newport (PL); (2002) Newcastle (CL), Hull; (2003) Newcastle (PL & CL), Armadale (CT), Workington,

Swindon (PL), Hull, Reading, Edinburgh, Somerset; (2004) Oxford (CL), Newport (PT), King's Lynn (CT & PL), Berwick.

BRANNEY, John *b. 7 November 1985, Whitehaven, Cumbria.*

BRITISH CAREER: (2002) Rye House (CL), Newcastle (CL); (2003) Newcastle (CL), Wimbledon (CT), Mildenhall (CT), King's Lynn, Exeter, Newport (PL), Buxton (CT); (2004) Newcastle (CL), King's Lynn (CT).

BROADHURST, Wayne *b. 28 February 1967, Minsterley, Shropshire.*

BRITISH CAREER: (1987) Coventry; (1988) Coventry, Stoke; (1989) Coventry; (1999) Stoke, Workington; (2000) Stoke; (2001) Wolverhampton, Stoke; (2002) Mildenhall; (2003) Mildenhall, Wolverhampton, Poole (BLC), Belle Vue (BLC); (2004) Wimbledon.

BROWN, Alan *b. 19 February 1959, Stoke-on-Trent, Staffordshire.*

BRITISH CAREER: (2002) Buxton; (2003) Oxford (CL), Buxton, Newport (CL), Trelawny (CT); (2004) Buxton.

BROWN, Tom *b. 19 June 1984, Panteg, Pontypool, Wales.*

BRITISH CAREER: (2000) Peterborough (CL), Newport (CL); (2001) Newport (CL & PL), Isle of Wight, Exeter; (2002) Workington, Newport (CL), Swindon (CT & PL), Isle of Wight, Edinburgh, Trelawny; (2003) Trelawny (PL & CT), Newport (CL); (2004) Berwick, Stoke (CL & PL), Coventry (CT), Newport (KOC), Glasgow, Exeter (PT), Ipswich.

BRUNDLE, James *b. 15 December 1986, King's Lynn, Norfolk.*

BRITISH CAREER: (2002) King's Lynn (CL), Mildenhall; (2003) King's Lynn (PL), Mildenhall; (2004) King's Lynn, Mildenhall.

BUNYAN, Jason *b. 9 March 1979, Milton Keynes, Buckinghamshire.*

BRITISH CAREER: (1995) Poole; (1996) Eastbourne (CL); (1997) Oxford, Isle of Wight, Peterborough (AL); (1998) Isle of Wight; (1999-01) Ipswich; (2002) Reading; (2003) Coventry, Stoke (BLC); (2004) Isle of Wight, Coventry.

BURCHATT, Barry *b. 25 October 1987, Farnborough, Kent.*

BRITISH CAREER: (2003) Newport (CL), Rye House (CL), Wimbledon; (2004) Rye House (CL).

BURNETT, Paul *b. 24 October 1981, Bradford, West Yorkshire.*

BRITISH CAREER: (1997) Buxton, Belle Vue (AL), Western Warriors; (1998-04) Buxton.

BURROWS, Mark *b. 6 June 1964, Sheffield, South Yorkshire.*

BRITISH CAREER: (1984) Scunthorpe, Sheffield; (1985) Scunthorpe, Edinburgh; (1986) Edinburgh; (1987) Middlesbrough; (1992) Glasgow, Middlesbrough; (1993) Middlesbrough; (1994) Buxton, Cleveland, Middlesbrough, Belle Vue, Coventry; (1995) Buxton, Long Eaton, Middlesbrough, Hull; (1996) Buxton; (1997-01) Stoke; (2002) Stoke, Belle Vue; (2003) Stoke (CT), Wimbledon, Coventry (BLC), Wolverhampton (BLC), Eastbourne (BLC), Belle Vue (BLC); (2004) Wimbledon.

CAMPBELL, Barry *b. 26 August 1979, Glasgow, Scotland.*

BRITISH CAREER: (1995) Linlithgow, Swindon; (1996) Linlithgow, Edinburgh; (1997) Edinburgh, Lathallan; (1998) Edinburgh; (1999) Belle Vue, Workington; (2000-01) Workington; (2003) Edinburgh, Armadale (CT), Reading, Swindon (CL), Belle Vue (BLC); (2004) Glasgow, Armadale, Edinburgh.

CAMPOS, Scott *b. 1 May 1989, Ipswich, Suffolk.*

BRITISH CAREER: (2004) Mildenhall, Rye House (CL).

CANDY, Paul *b. 4 February 1980, Basingstoke, Hampshire.*

BRITISH CAREER: (2003) Carmarthen, Somerset, Exeter; (2004) Weymouth, Newport (CL), Exeter.

CARRILLO, Eric *b. 25 June 1984, Haywood, California, USA.*
BRITISH CAREER: (2004) Wolverhampton, Glasgow.

CARR, Peter *b. 22 January 1963, Preston, Lancashire.*
BRITISH CAREER: (1979) Ellesmere Port, Hackney; (1980) Ellesmere Port, Belle Vue, Birmingham, Hull; (1981) Ellesmere Port, Belle Vue; (1982-84) Belle Vue; (1985-88) Sheffield; (1989-90) Newcastle; (1991-93) Sheffield; (1994-95) Belle Vue; (1997-04) Edinburgh.

CARTER, Wayne *b. 19 December 1970, Halifax, West Yorkshire.*
BRITISH CAREER: (1989) Mildenhall, Wolverhampton; (1990) Wolverhampton; (1991) Wolverhampton, Middlesbrough; (1992) Wolverhampton; (1993) Middlesbrough; (1994-95) Wolverhampton; (1996) Belle Vue, Middlesbrough; (1997) Skegness, Isle of Wight, Peterborough, Belle Vue, Wolverhampton, Bradford; (1998-99) Isle of Wight; (2000) Wolverhampton; (2001) Belle Vue, Berwick; (2002) Coventry, Newcastle; (2003) Wolverhampton (BLC), Edinburgh; (2004) Sheffield (CT), Swindon (CL)

CARTWRIGHT, Simon *b. 2 November 1978, Northallerton, North Yorkshire.*
BRITISH CAREER: (1996) Owlerton; (1997) Belle Vue (AL & EL); (1998) Hull, Norfolk; (1999-00) Sheffield; (2001) Stoke, Glasgow; (2002) Berwick; (2003) Hull; (2004) Berwick.

CHESTER, Scott *b. 6 January 1982, Leicester, Leicestershire.*
BRITISH CAREER: (2004) Buxton, King's Lynn (CT), Weymouth (CT).

CHUBB, Clayton *b. 29 October 1987, Yeovil, Somerset.*
BRITISH CAREER: (2004) Stoke (CLKOC), Weymouth (CT).

CLEMENT, James *b. 29 August 1985, Crawley, West Sussex.*
BRITISH CAREER: (2003) Wimbledon, Arena-Essex (BLC); (2004) Wimbledon, Isle of Wight (PT).

CLEWS, Paul *b. 19 July 1979, Coventry, Warwickshire.*
BRITISH CAREER: (1995) Coventry; (1996) Peterborough (CL & PL), Coventry, Oxford, Anglian Angels; (1997) Skegness, Isle of Wight, Peterborough (AL), Coventry; (1998) Peterborough; (1999-03) Reading; (2004) Stoke.

CLIFTON, Luke *b. 29 March 1982, Canterbury, Kent.*
BRITISH CAREER: (1997) Anglian Angels; (1998) Skegness, Norfolk, King's Lynn (EL); (1999) King's Lynn (CL); (2000) Boston, Edinburgh, Arena-Essex; (2001) Arena-Essex, Boston; (2003) Boston; (2004) Boston, Rye House (CL).

COCKLE, James *b. 26 May 1986, Enfield, Middlesex.*
BRITISH CAREER: (2001) Rye House; (2002) Rye House (CL & PL); (2003) Rye House (CL); (2004) Reading, Boston, Sheffield (CT), Edinburgh, Glasgow.

COLES, Michael *b. 11 August 1965, Exeter, Devon.*
BRITISH CAREER: (1982-83) Exeter; (1984) Exeter, Weymouth; (1985-87) Exeter; (1988) Mildenhall; (1989-93) Edinburgh; (1994) Belle Vue; (1995) Oxford; (1996) Exeter; (1997) Exeter, King's Lynn; (1998-04) Exeter.

COLLINS, Aidan *b. 21 April 1982, Stockport, Greater Manchester.*
BRITISH CAREER: (1998) Newport (CL); (1999) Buxton, Edinburgh; (2000) Glasgow, Ashfield; (2001) Glasgow; (2002) Buxton, Swindon, Edinburgh; (2003-04) Workington.

COLLINS, Chris *b. 18 July 1982, Manchester, Greater Manchester.*
BRITISH CAREER: (2001) Buxton, Newcastle, Stoke; (2002) Buxton, Newport (PL), Workington; (2003) Workington, Buxton; (2004) Mildenhall.

COLLINS, Neil *b. 15 October 1961, Partington, Greater Manchester.*
BRITISH CAREER: (1978) Ellesmere Port; (1979) Nottingham, Workington, Sheffield; (1980) Edinburgh, Sheffield; (1981) Edinburgh, Cradley Heath, Belle Vue; (1982-83) Leicester;

(1984-88) Sheffield; (1989-90) Wolverhampton; (1991) Belle Vue; (1992) Glasgow; (1993-94) Long Eaton; (1995) Sheffield; (1996) Belle Vue; (1997) Glasgow; (1998) Stoke; (1999-00) Swindon; (2001) Belle Vue, Workington; (2002) Somerset; (2003) Hull, Peterborough (BLC & CL 4-Team Championships), Belle Vue; (2004) Somerset.

COLLYER, Peter *b. 2 December 1981, Frimley Green, Camberley, Surrey.*
BRITISH CAREER: (1999) Reading, Glasgow, Rye House, Newcastle; (2002) Wimbledon, Carmarthen, Reading; (2003) Wimbledon, Reading (BLC); (2004) Wimbledon.

COLVIN, Shane *b. 4 February 1982, Hastings, East Sussex.*
BRITISH CAREER: (1997) Oxford (AL), Ryde, M4 Raven Sprockets; (1998) Newport (CL); (1999) Reading, Mildenhall; (2000) Reading, Mildenhall, Ashfield; (2001) Reading, Newport (CL), Trelawny; (2002) Carmarthen, Wolverhampton (CLKOC), Workington, Reading; (2003) Reading; (2004) Carmarthen, Sittingbourne (KOC), Sheffield.

COMPTON, Andre *b. 15 May 1977, Dewsbury, West Yorkshire.*
BRITISH CAREER: (1993) Bradford, Newcastle; (1994) Stoke, Newcastle, Buxton; (1995) Hull, Buxton; (1996) Buxton; (1997) Newcastle, Berwick; (1998-99) Sheffield; (2000) Peterborough, Newcastle; (2001) Newcastle; (2002) Newcastle, Poole; (2003) Sheffield, Poole; (2004) Sheffield, Poole, Belle Vue.

COMPTON, Benji *b. 17 September 1986, Tenerife, Spain.*
BRITISH CAREER: (2002) Newcastle (CL); (2003) Sheffield (CL & PL), Swindon (PL), Hull (BLC), Mildenhall (KOC), Exeter; (2004) Buxton, Edinburgh, Exeter (KOC), Sheffield (PL).

COOK, Harland *b. 6 August 1988, Watford, Hertfordshire.*
BRITISH CAREER: (2003) Rye House (CL); (2004) Rye House (CL), Coventry (CT).

COOPER, Paul *b. 7 June 1982, York, North Yorkshire.*
BRITISH CAREER: (2003) Sheffield (CL); (2004) Workington (PT), Berwick, Sheffield (CT), Oxford (CL).

CORREY, Ronnie *b. 8 November 1966, Bellflower, California, USA.*
BRITISH CAREER: (1987-93) Wolverhampton; (1995) Long Eaton; (1996-97) Wolverhampton; (1998-99) Belle Vue; (2000) Wolverhampton; (2004) Belle Vue.

COTTHAM, Gary *b.* 13 September 1989, Eastbourne, East Sussex.
BRITISH CAREER: (2004) Rye House (CL).

COURAGE, Chris *b. 23 May 1982, Poole, Dorset.*
BRITISH CAREER: (1997) Western Warriors, Anglian Angels; (1998) Newport (CL & PL), Isle of Wight, Exeter; (1999) Exeter, Isle of Wight, Newport (CL); (2000) Newport (CL & PL), Arena-Essex; (2001) Rye House, Arena-Essex; (2002) Rye House (PL & CL); (2004) Weymouth, Newport (PT), Isle of Wight.

COURTNEY, Jamie *b. 22 April 1988, Ashington, Northumberland.*
BRITISH CAREER: (2003) Rye House (CL), Trelawny (CT); (2004) Swindon (CL), Isle of Wight, Oxford (CL).

CROSS, Andre *b. 12 June 1967, Norwich, Norfolk.*
BRITISH CAREER: (2002-04) Wimbledon.

CRUMP, Jason *b. 6 August 1975, Bristol, Avon.*
BRITISH CAREER: (1991) Poole; (1992) Peterborough; (1993) Swindon; (1994-95) Poole; (1996-97) Peterborough; (1998) Oxford; (1999) Peterborough; (2000-01) King's Lynn; (2002-04) Belle Vue.

CUNNINGHAM, Glenn *b. 10 June 1975, Bristol, Avon.*
BRITISH CAREER: (1991-92) Oxford; (1993-96) Swindon; (1997) Reading; (1998) Peterborough;

(1999) Swindon; (2000) Peterborough, Belle Vue; (2001) Newport; (2002) Somerset; (2003) Somerset, Eastbourne; (2004) Somerset, Swindon.

DALLAWAY, Lewis *b. 26 February 1986, Walsall, West Midlands.*
BRITISH CAREER: (2004) King's Lynn (CT).

DARKIN, Sergei *b. 18 June, 1973, Fergana, Uzbekistan.*
BRITISH CAREER: (2001) Eastbourne; (2004) Coventry.

DART, Tony *b. 2 September 1979, Ashford, Kent.*
BRITISH CAREER: (2003) Mildenhall, King's Lynn, Workington, Peterborough (BLC), Isle of Wight (KOC); (2004) Isle of Wight (PT), Mildenhall.

DAVIDSSON, Daniel *b. 17 March 1983, Motala, Sweden.*
BRITISH CAREER: (2003) Poole (BLC); (2004) Poole.

DAVIDSSON, Jonas *b. 7 August 1984, Motala, Sweden.*
BRITISH CAREER: (2003) Reading; (2004) Oxford.

DENNIS, Richie *b. 16 April 1988, Boston, Lincolnshire.*
BRITISH CAREER: (2003) Peterborough (CL); (2004) Boston, King's Lynn (CT).

DERBYSHIRE, Lee *b. 3 December 1981, Stockport, Greater Manchester.*
BRITISH CAREER: (2002) Buxton; (2003) Buxton, Hull, King's Lynn, Belle Vue (BLC); (2004) Buxton.

DICKEN, Lee *b. 25 August 1978, Hull, East Yorkshire.*
BRITISH CAREER: (1994) Buxton; (1995) Hull, Stoke, Peterborough; (1996) Hull, Owlerton, Sheffield; (1997-98) Hull; (1999) Hull, Exeter; (2000) Hull; (2001) Hull, Arena-Essex; (2002) Newport, Wolverhampton; (2003) Hull, Newcastle; (2004) Newcastle (CL & PL), Glasgow.

DOBRUCKI, Rafal *b. 27 December 1976, Leszno, Poland.*
BRITISH CAREER: (2004) Oxford.

DOHERTY, John *b. 15 April 1989, Wales.*
BRITISH CAREER: (2004) Mildenhall.

DOOLAN, Kevin *b. 30 November 1980, Shepparton, Victoria, Australia.*
BRITISH CAREER: (1999-00) Belle Vue; (2002) Berwick; (2003) Glasgow; (2004) King's Lynn.

DOWNS, Carl *b. 13 November 1983, Coventry, Warwickshire.*
BRITISH CAREER: (1999) King's Lynn (CL); (2000) Boston, Peterborough (CL), Sheffield (CL); (2001) Newport (CL), Mildenhall; (2002) King's Lynn (CL); (2003) Oxford (CL & BLC), Coventry (BLC), Stoke (CT), Isle of Wight; (2004) Coventry (CT), Sittingbourne (KOC), Oxford (CL), Newcastle (CL & PL).

DRYML, Ales *b. 19 October 1979, Pardubice, Czech Republic.*
BRITISH CAREER: (2000-02) Oxford; (2003) Belle Vue, Poole; (2004) Peterborough.

DRYML, Lukas *b. 16 April 1981, Pardubice, Czech Republic.*
BRITISH CAREER: (2000-02) Oxford; (2003) Poole; (2004) Peterborough.

DUNWORTH, Wayne *b. 20 January 1967, Nottingham, Nottinghamshire.*
BRITISH CAREER: (1984) Boston; (1986) Mildenhall; (1987) Boston; (2002) Boston, Carmarthen; (2003) Trelawny (CT), Boston, Peterborough (CL), Armadale (CT); (2004) Boston, King's Lynn (CT).

ELKINS, Justin *b. 27 August 1974, Salisbury, Wiltshire.*
BRITISH CAREER: (1990) Poole; (1991) Rye House, Exeter; (1992) Swindon; (1993) Poole; (1994) Poole, Reading, Coventry, Exeter; (1995) Peterborough, Poole; (1996) Ryde, Eastbourne (PL & CL); (1997) Long Eaton; (1998) Reading; (1999) Reading, Edinburgh;

(2000) Poole, Arena-Essex; (2001) Hull, Workington, Exeter; (2002) Isle of Wight, Wimbledon, Newport (PL); (2003) Poole (BLC); (2004) Weymouth, Stoke (CL & PL).

ELLIOTT, Martin *b. 30 September 1970, Glasgow, Scotland.*

BRITISH CAREER: (2004) Weymouth (KOC), Swindon (CL).

ERMOLENKO, Sam *b. 23 November 1960, Maywood, California, USA.*

BRITISH CAREER: (1983-84) Poole; (1986-95) Wolverhampton; (1996) Sheffield; (1997) Belle Vue; (1998) Wolverhampton; (1999) Hull; (2000-01) Wolverhampton; (2002) Belle Vue; (2003-04) Wolverhampton.

EVANS, Barrie *b. 16 April 1984, King's Lynn, Norfolk.*

BRITISH CAREER: (1999) Mildenhall; (2000) Arena-Essex, Mildenhall; (2001) Arena-Essex, Mildenhall, Exeter; (2002) Newport, Rye House (CL); (2003) Hull, Rye House (CL); (2004) Wimbledon, Newport (PL).

EZERGAILIS, Karlis *b. 8 April 1985, Melbourne, Victoria, Australia.*

BRITISH CAREER: (2004) Newport (CL & PL), Isle of Wight, Coventry (CT), Reading, Rye House (PL).

FELTON, Dean *b. 18 August 1969, Wolverhampton, West Midlands.*

BRITISH CAREER: (1994) Buxton, Oxford, Ipswich; (1995-96) Buxton; (1997) Buxton, Stoke, Edinburgh, Skegness, Long Eaton, Shuttle Cubs; (1998) Stoke; (1999) Berwick, Glasgow; (2000) Buxton, Berwick; (2001) Stoke, Buxton, Edinburgh, Berwick; (2002) Carmarthen; (2003) Carmarthen, Belle Vue (BLC), Poole (BLC), Eastbourne (BLC), Wolverhampton (BLC); (2004) Carmarthen, King's Lynn (CT).

FERGUSON, Chris *b. 10 July 1981, Mildura, Victoria, Australia.*

BRITISH CAREER: (2004) Weymouth.

FERJAN, Matej *b. 5 January 1977, Ljubljana, Slovenia.*

BRITISH CAREER: (1998) Belle Vue; (1999) Poole; (2000) Ipswich; (2001) Peterborough, Belle Vue; (2002) Belle Vue; (2003) Oxford; (2004) Poole.

FERROW, Alan *b. 28 April 1982, Ashington, Northumberland.*

BRITISH CAREER: (2003) Trelawny (CT), Arena-Essex, Newport (PL); (2004) Rye House (CL).

FISHER, Ryan *b. 7 September 1983, Norco, California, USA.*

BRITISH CAREER: (2002-03) Coventry; (2004) Oxford.

FLINT, Gary *b. 5 May 1982, Ashington, Durham.*

BRITISH CAREER: (1999) Berwick, Linlithgow, St Austell; (2000) Ashfield, Berwick; (2001) Buxton, Newcastle, Exeter, Sheffield (PL), Berwick; (2002) Newcastle (CL), Somerset, Rye House (PL), Isle of Wight, Glasgow; (2003) Buxton, Sheffield (CL), Reading, Stoke (CT); (2004) Sheffield (CT), Stoke (CL), Oxford (CL).

FRAMPTON, Jordan *b. 8 March 1985, Poole, Dorset.*

BRITISH CAREER: (2004) Swindon (CL), Sheffield (CT), King's Lynn (CT).

FRANC, Josef *b. 18 January 1979, Kutna Hora, Czech Republic.*

BRITISH CAREER: (2001) Berwick; (2003-04) Berwick.

FRY, Paul *b. 25 October 1964, Ledbury, Worcestershire.*

BRITISH CAREER: (1984) Newcastle, Cradley Heath, Arena-Essex; (1986-87) Cradley Heath; (1988) Stoke; (1989-90) Long Eaton; (1991) King's Lynn; (1992-96) Exeter; (1997-98) Newport; (1999) Stoke; (2000-02) Swindon; (2003) Swindon, Peterborough; (2004) Somerset, Belle Vue.

GARROD, Dean *b. 11 October 1975, Norwich, Norfolk.*

BRITISH CAREER: (1993) Middlesbrough; (1994) Mildenhall; (1995-96) Mildenhall, Poole; (1997)

Mildenhall, Newport; (1998) Mildenhall, Arena-Essex, Sheffield; (1999) Mildenhall, Buxton; (2000-03) Boston; (2004) Sittingbourne (KOC), King's Lynn (CT), Boston.

GEER, Chris *b. 19 February 1985, Eastbourne, East Sussex.*

BRITISH CAREER: (2001) Mildenhall; (2002) Wimbledon, Reading; (2004) Sittingbourne (KOC).

GIFFARD, Daniel *b. 10 November 1984, Eastbourne, East Sussex.*

BRITISH CAREER: (2000) Rye House; (2001) Rye House, Reading, Berwick, Newport; (2002) Isle of Wight, Rye House (CL & PL), Edinburgh; (2003) Wimbledon, Eastbourne (BLC), Somerset, Stoke; (2004) Stoke (PL & CL), Weymouth.

GJEDDE, Charlie *b. 28 December 1979, Holstebro, Denmark.*

BRITISH CAREER: (1998) Swindon; (1999) Coventry, Wolverhampton; (2001) Reading; (2002) Swindon; (2003) Swindon, Oxford; (2004) Swindon.

GLEDHILL, Jack *b. 25 June 1986, Leamington Spa, Warwickshire.*

BRITISH CAREER: (2002) Swindon (CT), Newport (CL); (2003) Swindon (CL); (2004) Weymouth.

GORDON, Graeme *b. 16 June 1976, Wallington, Surrey.*

BRITISH CAREER: (1993) Exeter; (1994) Swindon; (1995) Devon, Exeter; (1996) Devon, Buxton, Exeter; (1997-00) Exeter; (2001) Trelawny; (2002) Wimbledon, Somerset; (2003) Somerset; (2004) Exeter.

GOUGH, David *b. 11 January 1986, Newport, South Wales.*

BRITISH CAREER: (2001) Newport (CL); (2002) Carmarthen; (2003) Carmarthen, Somerset (BLC), Newport (CL); (2004) Newport (CL).

GRANT, Rob (sr) *b. 17 February 1959, Throckley, Tyne and Wear.*

BRITISH CAREER: (1978-83) Berwick; (1984) Edinburgh, Berwick; (1985-91) Berwick; (2002) Berwick; (2004) Stoke (CL).

GRANT, Rob (jr) *b. 10 June 1984, Newcastle-upon-Tyne, Tyne and Wear.*

BRITISH CAREER: (1999) Linlithgow; (2000) Ashfield, Newcastle; (2001) Newcastle; (2002) Newcastle, Boston, Stoke; (2003) Berwick, Sheffield (CL), Stoke; (2004) Stoke (PL & CL).

GRIEVES, James *b. 28 September 1974, Paisley, Scotland.*

BRITISH CAREER: (1991-95) Glasgow; (1996-97) Wolverhampton; (1998) Wolverhampton, Berwick; (1999) Edinburgh; (2000-02) Glasgow; (2003-04) Glasgow, Wolverhampton.

HAIGH, David *b. 12 December 1984, Whitehaven, Cumbria.*

BRITISH CAREER: (2002) Newcastle (CL); (2003) Wimbledon, Newcastle (CL), Peterborough (CL); (2004) Newcastle (CL), Stoke (CL).

HALL, Richard *b. 23 August 1984, Northallerton, North Yorkshire.*

BRITISH CAREER: (2001) Newcastle; (2002) Newcastle (PL & CL), Trelawny, Glasgow; (2003) Sheffield (CL & PL), Stoke (PL), Coventry (BLC), Berwick (KOC), Hull, Newport (PL), Boston (KOC & CT), Exeter, Reading, Workington, Somerset; (2004) Sheffield (PL & CT), Boston.

HANCOCK, Greg *b. 3 June 1970, Whittier, California, USA.*

BRITISH CAREER: (1989-95) Cradley Heath; (1996) Cradley Heath + Stoke; (1997-01) Coventry; (2003-04) Oxford.

HARDING, Daniel *b. 2 July 1988, Perth, Western Australia.*

BRITISH CAREER: (2004) Swindon (CL), King's Lynn (CT).

HARDING, Trevor *b. 1 November 1986, Perth, Western Australia.*

BRITISH CAREER: (2002) Sheffield (CL), Carmarthen; (2003) King's Lynn Boston; (2004) King's Lynn (PL & CT), Ipswich, Swindon (CL).

HARGREAVES, Jack *b. 28 May 1988, Shrewsbury, Shropshire.*
BRITISH CAREER: (2003) Wolverhampton (CL); (2004) Stoke (CL & PT).

HARRIS, Chris *b. 28 November 1982, Truro, Cornwall.*
BRITISH CAREER: (1998) St Austell; (1999-00) Exeter; (2001) Trelawny; (2002-03) Trelawny, Peterborough; (2004) Coventry.

HARRISON, Rusty *b. 11 October 1981, Adelaide, South Australia, Australia.*
BRITISH CAREER: (2000) Glasgow; (2001-04) Workington.

HATTON, Darren *b. 31 March 1982, Cardiff, South Glamorgan, Wales.*
BRITISH CAREER: (1999) King's Lynn (CL), Newport (CL); (2000) Rye House, Ashfield; (2002-04) Carmarthen.

HAVELOCK, Gary *b. 4 November 1968, Yarm, Cleveland.*
BRITISH CAREER: (1985) Middlesbrough, King's Lynn, Wolverhampton; (1986) Middlesbrough, Bradford; (1987-88) Bradford; (1990-97) Bradford; (1998) Eastbourne, Poole; (1999-02) Poole; (2003-04) Peterborough.

HAWKINS, Ritchie *b. 9 November 1983, Peterborough, Cambridgeshire.*
BRITISH CAREER: (2000) Sheffield (CL); (2001) Swindon, Sheffield (CL); (2002) Swindon (PL & CT); (2003) Swindon (PL & CL), Peterborough (BLC); (2004) Mildenhall, Berwick, Coventry.

HAYES, Grant *b. 24 January 1989, Halifax, West Yorkshire.*
BRITISH CAREER: (2004) Weymouth, Sheffield (CT).

HEATH, Trevor *b. 21 March 1989, Cuckfield, West Sussex.*
BRITISH CAREER: (2004) Sheffield (CT).

HEDGE, Gavin *b. 30 January 1971, Norwich, Norfolk.*
BRITISH CAREER: (1996) Peterborough (CL); (1997) Peterborough (AL), Ryde, Mildenhall, Skegness, Isle of Wight, Oxford; (1998) Skegness, Norfolk, Arena-Essex, Peterborough; (1999) Mildenhall, Glasgow; (2000-01) Mildenhall; (2002) Mildenhall, Reading, Wimbledon; (2003-04) Wimbledon.

HILL, Thomas *b. 16 September 1986, Sheffield, South Yorkshire.*
BRITISH CAREER: (2003) Peterborough (CL), Wolverhampton (CL); (2004) Buxton, Newport (CL), Weymouth.

HODGSON, Daniel *b. 21 January 1982, Bradford, West Yorkshire.*
BRITISH CAREER: (1998) Buxton; (1999) King's Lynn (CL); (2000) Buxton, Hull; (2001) Somerset, Sheffield (PL), Newport (CL); (2003) Carmarthen, King's Lynn (BLC); (2004) King's Lynn (CT).

HODGSON, Lee *b. 19 February 1985, Preston, Lancashire.*
BRITISH CAREER: (2000) Sheffield (CL); (2001) Sheffield (PL & CL), Arena-Essex, Swindon; (2002) Stoke, Workington, Mildenhall; (2003) Mildenhall, Somerset, Workington; (2004) Stoke (CL).

HOLLINGWORTH, Robert *b. 31 December 1955, Boston, Lincolnshire.*
BRITISH CAREER: (1973) Berwick; (1974) Boston; (1975) Boston, Hull, King's Lynn, Poole, Wolverhampton; (1976) Boston, Wolverhampton, White City; (1977) Boston, Wolverhampton; (1978) Edinburgh, Wolverhampton; (1979) Boston, King's Lynn; (1980-81) Boston, Coventry; (1982) Boston, King's Lynn; (1983) Scunthorpe; (1984) Boston; (1985) Mildenhall; (1986) Boston; (1999) King's Lynn (CL); (2000-02) Boston; (2003) Boston, Belle Vue (BLC), Poole (BLC); (2004) Boston.

HOLLOWAY, Malcolm *b. 22 December 1956, Stratton St. Margaret, Wiltshire.*
BRITISH CAREER: (1977) Swindon, Oxford; (1978-79) Milton Keynes, Swindon; (1980-83) Swindon; (1984-88) Reading; (1989) Mildenhall, Reading; (1996) Swindon (CL); (2000)

Somerset, Reading; (2001) Somerset; (2002) Somerset, Swindon (CT), Mildenhall (CL); (2003) Swindon (CL), Trelawny (CT & PL), Coventry (BLC); (2004) Swindon (CL), Sittingbourne (KOC), Reading.

HOOPER, Shane *b. 18 January 1988, Poole, Dorset.*
BRITISH CAREER: (2004) Weymouth.

HOWE, David *b. 1 March 1982, Leicester, Leicestershire.*
BRITISH CAREER: (1997) Peterborough (AL); (1998) Peterborough, Norfolk; (1999-01) Peterborough; (2002-04) Wolverhampton.

HUGHES, Danny *b. 2 September 1983, Manchester, Greater Manchester.*
BRITISH CAREER: (1999) Workington; (2000) Buxton, Belle Vue; (2001) Buxton, Newport (CL); (2002) Newport (CL), Stoke, Workington, Edinburgh; (2003) Newport (CL & PL), Belle Vue (BLC), Stoke (CT); (2004) Newcastle (PL & CL), Coventry (CT), Somerset.

HUGHES, Kyle *b. 15 June 1989, Bath, Somerset.*
BRITISH CAREER: (2004) Mildenhall.

HUMBY, James *b. 12 June 1989, Romsey, Hampshire.*
BRITISH CAREER: (2004) Stoke (CL), Wimbledon, Oxford (CL).

HUNT, Chris *b. 15 February 1964, Wallingford, Oxfordshire.*
BRITISH CAREER: (1980) Exeter; (1981) Swindon; (1982) Exeter, Milton Keynes; (1983) Milton Keynes, Glasgow; (1984) Milton Keynes; (2001) Isle of Wight, Newport (CL); (2002-03) Wimbledon; (2004) Carmarthen.

HURRY, Paul *b. 9 April 1975, Canterbury, Kent.*
BRITISH CAREER: (1991) Arena-Essex; (1992-93) Peterborough; (1994-95) Arena-Essex; (1996) London; (1997) King's Lynn; (1998-99) Oxford; (2000) Eastbourne; (2001-02) Wolverhampton; (2003) Ipswich; (2004) Arena-Essex.

HURST, Sam *b. 28 April 1989, Southampton, Hampshire.*
BRITISH CAREER: (2004) Newport (CL), Weymouth (CT), King's Lynn (CT).

IRVING, Kriss *b. 3 April 1987, Whitehaven, Cumbria.*
BRITISH CAREER: (2003) Newcastle (CL); (2004) Newcastle (CL), Stoke (CL).

IRWIN, Nathan *b. 28 March 1983, Cuckfield, Sussex.*
BRITISH CAREER: (1999) King's Lynn (CL); (2000) Peterborough (CL); (2002) Wimbledon; (2004) Weymouth, Swindon (CL).

IVERSEN, Niels-Kristian *b. 20 June 1982, Esbjerg, Denmark.*
BRITISH CAREER: (2001) King's Lynn; (2002) King's Lynn (Challenge only); (2003) Newport, Oxford; (2004) Oxford.

JACKSON, Andrew *b. 12 July 1975, Manchester, Greater Manchester.*
BRITISH CAREER: (2002) Wolverhampton (CT), Carmarthen, Newport (CL); (2003) Wolverhampton (CL), Sheffield (CL), Mildenhall (CT), Belle Vue (BLC), Swindon (CL), Trelawny (CT), Newcastle (CL); (2004) Carmarthen, Stoke (CL).

JANNIRO, Billy *b. 30 July 1980, Vallejo, California, USA.*
BRITISH CAREER: (2001-04) Coventry.

JANSSON, Kim *b. 30 October 1981, Gothenburg, Sweden.*
BRITISH CAREER: (2002) Ipswich; (2003-04) Ipswich.

JAROS, Jan *b. 11 November 1984, Prague, Czech Republic.*
BRITISH CAREER: (2003) King's Lynn (BLC); (2004) Belle Vue.

JEDRZEJAK, Tomasz *b. 14 July 1979, Ostrow, Poland.*
BRITISH CAREER: (2001-02) Belle Vue; (2004) Belle Vue.

JENSEN, Jesper B. *b. 14 October 1977, Esbjerg, Denmark.*
BRITISH CAREER: (1997-03) Wolverhampton; (2004) Ipswich.

JENSEN, Steen *b. 17 November 1984, Brovst, Denmark.*
BRITISH CAREER: (2004) Eastbourne.

JIROUT, Mario *b. 21 July 1976, Pardubice, Czech Republic.*
BRITISH CAREER: (1995-97) Peterborough; (1999) Peterborough; (2001) Peterborough; (2002-03) Somerset; (2004) Newcastle (PT).

JOHANSSON, Tobias *b. 15 September 1977, Vaxjo, Sweden.*
BRITISH CAREER: (2004) Belle Vue, Edinburgh.

JOHNSON, Ashley *b. 29 September 1984, Middlesbrough, Cleveland.*
BRITISH CAREER: (2004) Newcastle (CL).

JOHNSON, Chris *b. 13 October 1987, Chichester, Sussex.*
BRITISH CAREER: (2003) Oxford (CL), Trelawny (CT), Isle of Wight; (2004) Isle of Wight, Swindon (CL), Somerset, Reading, King's Lynn (CT).

JOHNSTON, Steve *b. 12 October 1971, Kalgoorlie, Western Australia.*
BRITISH CAREER: (1992) Sheffield; (1993) Sheffield, Long Eaton; (1994-96) Long Eaton; (1997) Ipswich; (1998-02) Oxford; (2003) Belle Vue; (2004) Swindon.

JONES, Graham *b. 5 May 1963, Oswestry, Shropshire.*
BRITISH CAREER: (1984-87) Stoke; (1988) Stoke, Belle Vue, Reading, Sheffield, Wolverhampton, King's Lynn, Ipswich; (1989-93) Wolverhampton; (1994) Middlesbrough; (1995) Hull; (1996) Hull, Middlesbrough; (2003) Wolverhampton (CL & BLC), Stoke (CT), Coventry (BLC), Belle Vue (BLC), Eastbourne (BLC), Poole (BLC); (2004) Glasgow.

JONES, Steven *b. 27 September 1979, Gateshead, Tyne and Wear.*
BRITISH CAREER: (1997) Lathallan; (1998) Edinburgh, Newcastle; (1999) Newcastle, Linlithgow; (2002-03) Newcastle (CL); (2004) Carmarthen.

JONSSON, Andreas *b. 3 September 1980, Hallstavik, Sweden.*
BRITISH CAREER: (1998-99) Coventry; (2001-04) Coventry.

JORGENSEN, John *b. 18 July 1962, Middelfart, Denmark.*
BRITISH CAREER: (1982-83) Birmingham; (1984-95) Coventry; (1996) Swindon; (1997) Coventry; (1998) Swindon; (1999) Wolverhampton; (2000) Belle Vue, Coventry; (2001) Peterborough; (2004) Somerset, Coventry.

JUUL, Richard *b. 30 October 1970, Copenhagen, Denmark.*
BRITISH CAREER: (1991-94) Newcastle; (1995) Wolverhampton; (1997) Newcastle, Berwick; (1998) Stoke; (1999) Wolverhampton; (2000) Glasgow, Isle of Wight; (2001-04) Newcastle.

KARLSSON, Magnus *b. 28 December 1981, Gullspang, Sweden.*
BRITISH CAREER: (2002) Edinburgh; (2003) Edinburgh, Wolverhampton; (2004) Hull, Wolverhampton.

KASPRZAK, Krzysztof *b. 18 July 1984, Leszno, Poland.*
BRITISH CAREER: (2003) Poole; (2004) Swindon (Challenge only), Poole.

KENNETT, Edward *b. 28 August 1986, Hastings, Sussex.*
BRITISH CAREER: (2001) Rye House, Mildenhall; (2002-03) Rye House (CL & PL), Eastbourne; (2004) Eastbourne.

KESSLER, Robbie *b. 5 April 1973, Neuwied, Germany.*
BRITISH CAREER: (1994) Sheffield; (1996-97) Sheffield; (1999) King's Lynn; (2000-01) Sheffield; (2002) Hull; (2003) Stoke; (2004) Stoke, Peterborough.

KING, Daniel *b. 14 August 1986, Maidstone, Kent.*
BRITISH CAREER: (2001) Peterborough (CL); (2002) Peterborough (CL), Swindon (CT); (2003) Peterborough (CL), Ipswich (BLC), Reading, Mildenhall, Arena-Essex; (2004) Ipswich, Mildenhall.

KING, Jason *b. 13 April 1985, Maidstone, Kent.*
BRITISH CAREER: (2000) Peterborough (CL); (2001) Peterborough (CL), Newport (PL), Newcastle; (2002) Swindon (PL & CT), Peterborough (CL & ELKOC); (2003) Arena-Essex, Peterborough (CL); (2004) Mildenhall, Peterborough (EL), Rye House.

KNOTT, Paul *b. 25 January 1980, Maidstone, Kent.*
BRITISH CAREER: (2004) King's Lynn (CT).

KORNELIUSSEN, Mads *b. 15 June 1983, Aalborg, Denmark.*
BRITISH CAREER: (2003-04) Newport.

KRAMER, Emil *b. 14 November 1979, Mariestad, Sweden.*
BRITISH CAREER: (2002) King's Lynn, Hull; (2003) Oxford (BLC), Hull; (2004) Hull, Oxford.

KRISTENSEN, Claus *b. 11 June 1977, Holstebro, Denmark.*
BRITISH CAREER: (1999) Berwick; (2000-01) Swindon; (2002-03) Berwick; (2004) Berwick, Swindon.

KUJAWA, Dawid *b. 13 April 1981, Zielona Gora, Poland.*
BRITISH CAREER: (2004) Newport (Challenge only).

KURMANSKI, Rafal *b. 22 August 1982, Zielona Gora, Poland.*
BRITISH CAREER: (2004) Swindon.

KYLMAKORPI, Joonas *b. 14 February 1980, Seinajoki, Finland.*
BRITISH CAREER: (2001) Eastbourne; (2002) Ipswich; (2003) Arena-Essex, Eastbourne; (2004) Eastbourne.

LAMBERT, Simon *b. 21 February 1989, Boston, Lincolnshire.*
BRITISH CAREER: (2004) Boston, King's Lynn (CT).

LANGLEY, Karl *b. 2 June 1981, Whitehaven, Cumbria.*
BRITISH CAREER: (2002) Workington; (2003) Newcastle (CL), Armadale (CLKOC), Mildenhall, Poole (BLC); (2004) Newcastle (CL), Sheffield (CT).

LANHAM, Leigh *b. 15 August 1977, Ipswich, Suffolk.*
BRITISH CAREER: (1993) Ipswich, Arena-Essex; (1994-96) Ipswich; (1997) Exeter, Bradford, King's Lynn; (1998-99) Arena-Essex; (2001) Arena-Essex; (2002-03) Arena-Essex, Ipswich; (2004) Arena-Essex.

LARSEN, Josh *b. 12 May 1972, Anaheim, California, USA.*
BRITISH CAREER: (1992-93) Arena-Essex; (1995) Arena-Essex; (1996) London; (1997) Bradford; (1999) Eastbourne; (2003) Belle Vue; (2004) Arena-Essex.

LAUKKANEN, Kaj *b. 8 April 1975, Seinajoki, Finland.*
BRITISH CAREER: (1995-96) Long Eaton; (1998) Glasgow; (1999-02) Belle Vue; (2003) Oxford; (2004) Belle Vue.

LAWSON, William *b. 27 February 1987, Auchterarder, Perthshire, Scotland.*
BRITISH CAREER: (2002) Newcastle (CL); (2003) Newcastle (PL & CL), Belle Vue (BLC); (2004) Newcastle (PL & CL).

LEE, Paul *b. 21 March 1981, Nottingham, Nottinghamshire.*
BRITISH CAREER: (1996) Peterborough (CL); (1997) Long Eaton, Shuttle Cubs, Peterborough (EL), Coventry; (1998) Hull; (1999-00) Sheffield; (2001) Coventry; (2002) Swindon; (2003) Mildenhall; (2004) Mildenhall, King's Lynn.

LEGG, Billy *b. 6 September 1988, Swindon, Wiltshire.*
BRITISH CAREER: (2003) Swindon (CL); (2004) Newport (CL), Mildenhall, Weymouth.

LEMON, Mark *b. 12 February 1973, Brainsdale, Victoria, Australia.*
BRITISH CAREER: (1990) Poole; (1991) Poole, Middlesbrough; (1992) Long Eaton, Middlesbrough; (1996) Oxford; (1997-98) Poole; (1999) Eastbourne, Hull; (2000) Oxford; (2002) Oxford; (2003) Somerset, Belle Vue; (2004) Exeter, Poole.

LEVERINGTON, Trent *b. 13 May 1980, Brisbane, Queensland, Australia.*
BRITISH CAREER: (2003) Glasgow, Armadale, Wolverhampton (CL); (2004) Buxton, Stoke (CLKOC & PL).

LINDBACK, Antonio *b. 5 May 1985, Rio de Janeiro, Brazil.*
BRITISH CAREER: (2003-04) Poole.

LINDGREN, Fredrik *b. 15 September 1985, Orebro, Sweden.*
BRITISH CAREER: (2003-04) Wolverhampton.

LITTLE, Kevin *b. 24 September 1972, Edinburgh, Scotland.*
BRITISH CAREER: (1989) Glasgow, Berwick; (1990-91) Berwick; (1992) Bradford; (1993) Edinburgh; (1994) Edinburgh, Berwick; (1995) Berwick, Belle Vue, Edinburgh, Coventry; (1996) Coventry; (1997) Berwick; (1998-00) Edinburgh; (2001-04) Newcastle.

LJUNG, Peter *b. 30 October 1982, Vaxjo, Sweden.*
BRITISH CAREER: (2003) Eastbourne, Reading; (2004) Eastbourne, Swindon.

LOBB, Roger *b. 20 April 1978, Shepton Mallet, Somerset.*
BRITISH CAREER: (1995) Devon; (1996) Devon, Reading (CL), Exeter; (1997) Western Warriors, Reading, Newport (PL), Exeter; (1998) St Austell, Newport (CL), Exeter; (1999) Arena-Essex; (2000) Exeter; (2002-04) Exeter.

LORAM, Mark *b. 12 January 1971, Mtarfa, Malta.*
BRITISH CAREER: (1987) Hackney; (1988) Hackney, King's Lynn, Belle Vue, Reading, Swindon; (1989) Ipswich; (1990-94) King's Lynn; (1995-96) Exeter; (1997) Bradford; (1998) Wolverhampton; (1999-00) Poole; (2001) Peterborough; (2002-03) Eastbourne; (2004) Arena-Essex.

LOUIS, Chris *b. 9 July 1969, Ipswich, Suffolk.*
BRITISH CAREER: (1988) Hackney, Wolverhampton, King's Lynn, Ipswich; (1989-02) Ipswich; (2004) Ipswich.

LUND, Kristian *b. 8 August 1984, Outrup, Denmark.*
BRITISH CAREER: (2003) Newcastle; (2004) Newcastle, Newport.

LYONS, Jason *b. 15 June 1970, Mildura, Victoria, Australia.*
BRITISH CAREER: (1990-91) Glasgow; (1992-03) Belle Vue; (2004) Poole, Newcastle.

MacPHAIL, John *b. 13 April 1988, Edinburgh, Scotland.*
BRITISH CAREER: (2003) Stoke (CT); (2004) Armadale, Newcastle (CL), Stoke (CL).

McALLAN, David *b. 20 June 1980, Edinburgh, Scotland.*
BRITISH CAREER: (1996) Berwick; (1997) Berwick (PL & AL), Sheffield; (1998) Berwick, Newcastle; (1999) Edinburgh, Linlithgow; (2000) Ashfield, Stoke; (2001) Berwick, Boston, Stoke, Workington, Glasgow, Edinburgh, Newcastle; (2002) Glasgow, Sheffield (CL); (2003-04) Glasgow, Boston.

McALLISTER, Steven *b. 31 December 1981, Glasgow, Scotland.*
BRITISH CAREER: (1997) Lathallan; (1999) Linlithgow, Stoke; (2000) Berwick, Ashfield, Reading, Stoke; (2004) Armadale.

McBAIN, James *b. 14 December 1988, Glasgow, Scotland.*
BRITISH CAREER: (2004) Armadale.

McDADE, Cal *b. 25 April 1987, Glasgow, Scotland.*
BRITISH CAREER: (2004) Swindon (CL).

McGOWAN, Travis *b. 13 January 1981, Mildura, Victoria, Australia.*
BRITISH CAREER: (1999-00) King's Lynn; (2002) King's Lynn; (2003-04) Oxford.

McKINNA, Adam *b. 17 August 1986, Preston, Lancashire.*
BRITISH CAREER: (2004) Armadale

MABEN, Keith *b. 24 December 1982, Edinburgh, Scotland.*
BRITISH CAREER: (2003) Armadale, Mildenhall (CT), Stoke (KOC); (2004) Armadale, Weymouth, Mildenhall.

MADSEN, Tom P. *b. 24 November 1977, Esbjerg, Denmark.*
BRITISH CAREER: (1999) Berwick; (2000-02) King's Lynn; (2003) Ipswich, King's Lynn; (2004) King's Lynn, Oxford, Berwick.

MAGOSI, Norbert *b. 10 April 1975, Debrecen, Hungary.*
BRITISH CAREER: (2004) Peterborough.

MAKOVSKY, Michal *b. 6 April 1976, Hradec Kralove, Czech Republic.*
BRITISH CAREER: (2001-04) Berwick.

MALLETT, Darren *b. 25 May 1986, Boston, Lincolnshire.*
BRITISH CAREER: (2001) Somerset, Boston; (2002) Boston; (2003) Boston, King's Lynn; (2004) King's Lynn (PL & CT), Boston.

MALLETT, Nick *b. 12 May 1987, Newport, South Wales.*
BRITISH CAREER: (2002) Swindon (CT); (2003) Newport (CL), Peterborough (CL); (2004) Newport (CL).

MANN, James *b. 25 October 1983, Bolton, Greater Manchester.*
BRITISH CAREER: (1999) Buxton; (2000) Buxton, Workington, Stoke, Ipswich; (2001) Workington, Buxton; (2002) Workington, Buxton; (2003) Somerset, Mildenhall; (2004) Mildenhall.

MARKHAM, John *b. 4 April 1982, Leamington Spa, Warwickshire.*
BRITISH CAREER: (2004) Oxford (CL).

MARSH, Krister *b. 23 March 1976, Hereford, Hereford & Worcester.*
BRITISH CAREER: (1995) Devon; (1996) Swindon (CL & PL), Sheffield, London; (1997) Oxford (AL & PL), Reading; (1998) Reading; (1999) Swindon; (2000) Reading, Newcastle; (2001) Newport, Swindon, Exeter; (2002-03) Exeter; (2004) Isle of Wight.

MARTIN, Sam *b. 8 February 1989, Adelaide, South Australia.*
BRITISH CAREER: (2004) Oxford (CL).

MASON, David *b. 20 December 1976, Crawley, West Sussex.*
BRITISH CAREER: (1995) Sittingbourne, Reading, Arena-Essex, Swindon, Poole, Oxford; (1996) Sittingbourne, London, Reading; (1997) Arena-Essex; (1998) Newport, Stoke, Arena-Essex, Mildenhall; (1999) Swindon, Rye House; (2000) Rye House, Arena-Essex, Poole; (2001-03) Rye House; (2004) Weymouth.

MASON, Karl *b. 4 March 1986, Hillingdon, London.*
BRITISH CAREER: (2001) Buxton, Mildenhall, Somerset; (2002) Newport (CL), Reading; (2003) Newport (CL & PL), Exeter (BLC); (2004) Newport (PL & CL), Coventry (CT).

MASTERS, Steve *b. 6 December 1970, Eastbourne, East Sussex.*
BRITISH CAREER: (1989-91) Eastbourne; (1992-93) Swindon; (1994) Swindon (KOC), Cradley

Heath, Reading, Poole; (1995) Poole; (1996-97) Swindon; (1998) Swindon, Isle of Wight; (1999) Swindon; (2000) King's Lynn; (2001) Newport; (2002) Trelawny; (2003) Trelawny, Oxford; (2004) Rye House, Swindon.

MAX, Mikael (formerly Mikael Karlsson) *b. 21 August 1973, Gullspang, Sweden.*
BRITISH CAREER: (1993-94) Wolverhampton; (1996-99) Wolverhampton; (2001-04) Wolverhampton.

MEAKINS, Gordon *b. 18 March 1974, Aylesbury, Buckinghamshire.*
BRITISH CAREER: (1999) King's Lynn (CL); (2000) Peterborough (CL); (2001) Buxton; (2002) Carmarthen; (2003) Carmarthen, Somerset (BLC); (2004) Carmarthen.

MEAR, Robert *b. 12 January 1989, Welwyn Garden City, Hertfordshire.*
BRITISH CAREER: (2004) Rye House (CL).

MELDRUM, David *b. 6 October 1977, Berwick-upon-Tweed, Northumberland.*
BRITISH CAREER: (1994-95) Berwick; (1996) Berwick, Eastbourne (CL); (1997) Berwick (PL & AL); (1998) Berwick, Buxton; (1999-01) Berwick; (2002) Somerset, Wimbledon, Edinburgh; (2003) Berwick; (2004) Berwick, Newcastle (PL & CL).

MIEDZINSKI, Adrian *b. 20 August 1985, Torun, Poland.*
BRITISH CAREER: (2004) Eastbourne.

MILLS, Chris *b. 29 March 1983, Chelmsford, Essex.*
BRITISH CAREER: (2001) Arena-Essex; (2002) King's Lynn (CL), Wimbledon; (2003) Isle of Wight, Oxford (CL); (2004) Reading, Oxford (CL).

MINALL, David *b. 30 March 1987, Walsall, West Midlands.*
BRITISH CAREER: (2003-04) Newport (CL).

MITCHELL, Michael *b. 21 April 1984, Halifax, West Yorkshire.*
BRITISH CAREER: (2000) Peterborough (CL), Newport (CL); (2001) Sheffield (CL), Newport (CL); (2002) Mildenhall, Sheffield (CL), Buxton; (2003) Sheffield (CL), Stoke (CT), Rye House (CL); (2004) Stoke (CL), Sheffield (CT).

MOGRIDGE, Alan *b. 6 November 1963, Westminster, London.*
BRITISH CAREER: (1981) Wimbledon; (1982-83) Crayford, Wimbledon; (1984) Canterbury, Wolverhampton; (1985) Hackney; (1986) Canterbury, Rye House, Ipswich, Hackney; (1987) Hackney; (1988) Hackney, Sheffield, Bradford; (1989-90) Ipswich; (1991-92) Arena-Essex; (1993) Peterborough; (1994) Middlesbrough, Sheffield; (1995) Arena-Essex; (1996) London, Eastbourne; (1997) Eastbourne; (1999-00) Berwick; (2001) Swindon; (2002-04) Stoke.

MOLLER, Henrik *b. 3 September 1985, Fredericia, Denmark.*
BRITISH CAREER: (2004) Peterborough.

MOORE, Andrew *b. 6 October 1982, Lincoln, Lincolnshire.*
BRITISH CAREER: (1998) Skegness, Norfolk; (1999) Mildenhall, Sheffield (PL), Arena-Essex; (2000) Sheffield (CL & PL), Berwick; (2001) Sheffield (CL & PL); (2002-03) Sheffield (PL); (2004) Sheffield (PL), Swindon, Eastbourne.

MORRIS, Phil *b. 10 September 1975, Newport, Gwent, Wales.*
BRITISH CAREER: (1991-96) Reading; (1997) Stoke; (1998-03) Reading; (2004) Reading, Poole.

MORRISON, John *b. 14 January 1988, Ashington, Northumberland.*
BRITISH CAREER: (2004) Berwick (PT), Isle of Wight, Swindon (CL), Newcastle (CL).

MORTON, Ray *b. 19 June 1968, Peckham, London.*
BRITISH CAREER: (1985-87) King's Lynn; (1988) Wimbledon, King's Lynn; (1989-90) Wimbledon; (1991-92) Reading; (1993) Poole; (1994-95) Reading; (1996) Reading, Hull; (1998) Isle of Wight; (1999) Hull; (2000-03) Isle of Wight; (2004) Isle of Wight, Arena-Essex.

NEATH, Chris *b. 29 January 1982, Worcester, Hereford & Worcester.*
BRITISH CAREER: (1998-99) Newport (CL & PL); (2000-01) Newport; (2002-03) Swindon, Wolverhampton; (2004) Rye House, Wolverhampton.

NEEDS, Lawrence *b. 1 December 1986, Shrewsbury, Shropshire.*
BRITISH CAREER: (2002) Wolverhampton (CT); (2003) Wolverhampton (CL), Mildenhall; (2004) Coventry (CT).

NERMARK, Daniel *b. 30 July 1977, Karlstad, Sweden.*
BRITISH CAREER: (2001-02) Wolverhampton; (2003) Ipswich; (2004) Wolverhampton.

NETTLESHIP, Scott *b. 16 May 1984, Newcastle, Tyne and Wear.*
BRITISH CAREER: (2003) Newcastle (CL), Mildenhall, Swindon (CL), Carmarthen, Peterborough (CL); (2004) Newcastle (CL).

NEWITT, Jason *b. 13 January 1978, Oxford, Oxfordshire.*
BRITISH CAREER: (1996) Peterborough (CL); (1997) Peterborough (AL), Oxford (AL & PL); (2000) Somerset; (2003) Oxford (CL), Mildenhall; (2004) Oxford (CL).

NICHOLLS, Scott *b. 16 May 1978, Ipswich, Suffolk.*
BRITISH CAREER: (1994) Peterborough; (1995-98) Ipswich; (1999-00) Poole; (2001-04) Ipswich.

NICOL, Jamie *b. 10 September 1986, Stoke-on-Trent, Staffordshire.*
BRITISH CAREER: (2003) Stoke (CT); (2004) Stoke (CL).

NIEMINEN, Kauko *b. 29 August 1979, Seinajoki, Finland.*
BRITISH CAREER: (2002-04) Workington.

NORRIS, David *b. 20 August 1972, Eastbourne, East Sussex.*
BRITISH CAREER: (1988-89) Eastbourne; (1990-92) Ipswich; (1993) Ipswich, Eastbourne; (1994) Eastbourne; (1995) Reading; (1996-04) Eastbourne.

NORRIS, Marc *b. 3 April 1983, Eastbourne, East Sussex.*
BRITISH CAREER: (1999-00) Reading; (2004) Wimbledon.

NORTON, Danny *b. 27 August 1986, Hull, East Yorkshire.*
BRITISH CAREER: (2001-02) Peterborough (CL); (2003) Peterborough (CL & BLC), Armadale (CT), Swindon (PL), Reading, Mildenhall (KOC & CT), Poole (BLC), Oxford (BLC); (2004) Hull, Oxford (CL), Reading.

OLIVER, John *b. 22 July 1987, Melbourne, Victoria, Australia.*
BRITISH CAREER: (2003) Carmarthen (CL), Buxton, King's Lynn; (2004) King's Lynn (PT & CT), Boston, Somerset (KOC), Newport (PT), Coventry (CT).

OLSEN, Jesper *b. 10 February 1967, Valby, Denmark.*
BRITISH CAREER: (1991) Eastbourne; (1992) Mildenhall, Glasgow; (1993-95) Glasgow; (1996) Middlesbrough; (1997-02) Newcastle; (2003) Belle Vue; (2004) Newcastle.

ONDRASIK, Pavel *b. 10 December 1975, Prague, Czech Republic.*
BRITISH CAREER: (2001-03) Trelawny; (2004) Newport.

OSTERGAARD, Ulrich *b. 19 April 1981, Odense, Denmark.*
BRITISH CAREER: (2003) Eastbourne (BLC); (2004) Eastbourne, Isle of Wight.

PARKER, Ross *b. 11 December 1988, Manchester, Greater Manchester.*
BRITISH CAREER: (2004) Buxton.

PARKER, Shane *b. 29 April 1970, Adelaide, South Australia, Australia.*
BRITISH CAREER: (1990-94) Ipswich; (1995-96) Middlesbrough; (1997-98) King's Lynn; (1999) Hull; (2000) King's Lynn, Belle Vue; (2001-02) Peterborough; (2003) King's Lynn, Peterborough; (2004) Glasgow.

PARKER, Wayne *b. 26 March 1971, Swindon, Wiltshire.*
BRITISH CAREER: (1990) Oxford; (1993) Oxford; (2004) Weymouth.

PARSONS, Joel *b. 24 July 1985, Broken Hill, New South Wales, Australia.*
BRITISH CAREER: (2003) Reading, Eastbourne (BLC), Rye House (CL & PL), Newport (PL), Wimbledon (CT), Arena-Essex, Peterborough (BLC), Hull, King's Lynn; (2004) Rye House (CL & PT), Hull, Reading (KOC), King's Lynn (CT).

PEDERSEN, Bjarne *b. 12 July 1978, Ryrde, Denmark.*
BRITISH CAREER: (2000-01) Newcastle; (2002) Poole; (2003) Poole, Newcastle; (2004) Poole.

PEDERSEN, Nicki *b. 2 April 1977, Odense, Denmark.*
BRITISH CAREER: (1998) Newcastle; (1999-00) Wolverhampton; (2001-02) King's Lynn; (2003) Oxford, Eastbourne; (2004) Eastbourne.

PEDERSEN, Ronni *b. 6 October 1974, Middelfart, Denmark.*
BRITISH CAREER: (1993-95) Peterborough; (1997-98) Peterborough; (2001-02) King's Lynn; (2004) Arena-Essex.

PEGLER, Scott *b. 3 August 1973, Exeter, Devon.*
BRITISH CAREER: (1989-90) Exeter; (1992-94) Exeter; (1995) Exeter, Devon; (1996) Swindon (PL & CL); (1997) Newport (PL); (1998) Newport (PL & CL); (1999) Newport (PL); (2000-02) Newport (CL); (2003) Newport (CL), Poole (BLC); (2004) Newport (CL).

PESTELL, Jeremy *b. 18 October 1984, Northampton, Northamptonshire.*
BRITISH CAREER: (2001) Rye House; (2002) Rye House (CL), Wimbledon; (2003) Wolverhampton (CL); (2004) Coventry (CT), Newport.

PHELPS, Gary *b. 30 March 1977, Swindon, Wiltshire.*
BRITISH CAREER: (1996) Swindon (CL); (1997) M4 Raven Sprockets & Swindon; (1998) Norfolk, Isle of Wight; (1999) Workington, Berwick, King's Lynn (CL), St Austell, Edinburgh, Newcastle, Isle of Wight; (2000) Arena-Essex, St Austell, Isle of Wight, Workington; (2001) Trelawny, Somerset; (2002) Somerset, Isle of Wight; (2003) Isle of Wight; (2004) Edinburgh, Armadale, Mildenhall, Exeter.

PHILLIPS, Glen *b. 22 November 1982, Farnborough, Kent.*
BRITISH CAREER: (1999) Exeter, King's Lynn (CL); (2000) Isle of Wight, Somerset; (2001) Isle of Wight; (2002) Wimbledon, Reading; (2003-04) Isle of Wight.

PICKERING, Michael *b. 28 October 1982, Hull, East Yorkshire.*
BRITISH CAREER: (1998) Buxton; (2000) Buxton; (2002) Newport (CL); (2003) Hull, Newcastle (CL); (2004) Newcastle (CL & PT), Hull (PT), Berwick, Newport (PL), Edinburgh, King's Lynn (CLKOC).

PICKERING, Paul *b. 15 February 1966, Hartlepool, Cleveland.*
BRITISH CAREER: (1992) Middlesbrough; (1993) Middlesbrough, Bradford; (1994-96) Bradford; (1997) Reading; (1998-03) Stoke; (2004) Stoke, Ipswich.

PICKERING, Phil *b. 25 October 1963, Hull, East Yorkshire.*
BRITISH CAREER: (1996) Peterborough (CL), Sheffield (CL); (1998) Buxton; (1999) Berwick, Buxton; (2000) Buxton, Newcastle, Berwick, Hull; (2001) Berwick, Boston, Newport (PL), Trelawny; (2003) Buxton; (2004) Newcastle (CL).

PIETRASZKO, Adam *b. 18 August 1982, Czestochowa, Poland.*
BRITISH CAREER: (2004) Berwick, Peterborough.

PIJPER, Theo *b. 11 February 1980, Rinsumageest, Holland.*
BRITISH CAREER: (2002-04) Edinburgh.

PISZCZ, Tomasz *b. 8 June 1977, Gdansk, Poland.*
BRITISH CAREER: (2004) Peterborough, Coventry.

POVAZHNY, Roman *b. 23 October 1976, Togliatti, Russia.*
BRITISH CAREER: (1999) Eastbourne; (2000) Oxford, Wolverhampton; (2001) Eastbourne; (2002) King's Lynn; (2004) Eastbourne, Arena-Essex.

POWELL, Ben *b. 29 November 1984, Helensvale, Gold Coast, Queensland, Australia.*
BRITISH CAREER: (2002) Sheffield (CL), Edinburgh, Trelawny, Glasgow; (2003) Carmarthen, Exeter; (2004) Carmarthen, Coventry (CT), Boston.

PRIEST, Luke *b. 18 June 1985, Birmingham, West Midlands.*
BRITISH CAREER: (2000) Ashfield, Owlerton; (2001) Sheffield (CL), Boston (2002) Sheffield (CL), Wolverhampton (CT); (2003) Sheffield (CL & PL), Stoke (CT & PL), Workington, Exeter, Newport (BLC), Arena-Essex, Wolverhampton (BLC), Belle Vue (BLC); (2004) Newport (PL), Stoke (CL & PL), Edinburgh.

PRYER, Adam *b. 14 April 1983, King's Lynn, Norfolk.*
BRITISH CAREER: (1999) King's Lynn (CL); (2000) Peterborough (CL), Berwick; (2001) Peterborough (EL & CL); (2002) Peterborough (CL), Rye House (PL); (2003) Somerset, Peterborough (CL).

PRYNNE, Jason *b. 27 April 1974, Truro, Cornwall.*
BRITISH CAREER: (1997-99) St Austell; (2000) St Austell, Exeter; (2001) Exeter; (2002) Wimbledon, Exeter, Trelawny; (2003) Wimbledon, Trelawny; (2004) Weymouth, Swindon (CL).

PUGH, Darren *b. 7 June 1974, Shrewsbury, Shropshire.*
BRITISH CAREER: (2002) Carmarthen; (2004) Carmarthen.

PURCHASE, James *b. 21 October 1987, Southampton, Hampshire.*
BRITISH CAREER: (2003) Oxford (CL), Peterborough (CL & BLC); (2004) Swindon (CL), King's Lynn (CT).

READ, Matt *b. 5 August 1981, Maidstone, Kent.*
BRITISH CAREER: (1997) Anglian Angels, King's Lynn; (1998-99) Arena-Essex; (2000) Arena-Essex, Reading; (2002) Isle of Wight; (2003) Eastbourne (BLC), Somerset; (2004) Somerset, Eastbourne.

REYNOLDS, Joe *b. 20 March 1989, Wordsley, West Midlands.*
BRITISH CAREER: (2004) Buxton.

RICHARDSON, Lee *b. 25 April 1979, Hastings, Sussex.*
BRITISH CAREER: (1995) Reading; (1996) Reading (CL), Poole; (1997-98) Reading; (1999) Poole; (2000-03) Coventry; (2004) Peterborough.

RICHARDSON, Mark *b. 21 June 1988.*
BRITISH CAREER: (2004) Boston, Sheffield (CT), Weymouth.

RICKARDSSON, Tony *b. 17 August 1970, Grytas, Sweden.*
BRITISH CAREER: (1991-94) Ipswich; (1997-98) Ipswich; (1999) King's Lynn; (2001-04) Poole.

RISAGER, Morten *b. 30 September 1987, Arhus, Denmark.*
BRITISH CAREER: (2004) Coventry.

ROBERTSON, Jamie *b. 8 October 1986, Berwick-upon-Tweed, Northumberland.*
BRITISH CAREER: (2002) Newcastle (CL); (2003) Newcastle (PL & CL), Glasgow; (2004) Newcastle (PL & CL).

ROBSON, Scott *b. 15 August 1971, Sunderland, Tyne & Wear.*
BRITISH CAREER: (1987-92) Berwick; (1993-94) Newcastle; (1995-96) Middlesbrough; (1997)

Hull; (1998) Eastbourne, Berwick; (1999-00) Coventry; (2001) Berwick; (2002) Rye House; (2003) Rye House, Eastbourne; (2004) Rye House, Belle Vue.

ROBSON, Stuart *b. 8 November 1976, Sunderland, Tyne and Wear.*

BRITISH CAREER: (1993) Newcastle; (1994) Newcastle, Edinburgh; (1995) Coventry; (1996) Coventry, Middlesbrough; (1997) Hull; (1998-02) Coventry; (2003) Coventry, Newcastle; (2004) Coventry.

ROLPH, Darren *b. 17 May 1982, Braintree, Essex.*

BRITISH CAREER: (2003) Boston, King's Lynn; (2004) King's Lynn (CT & PL), Boston, Glasgow, Coventry (CT).

ROYNON, Adam *b. 30 August 1988, Barrow-in-Furness, Cumbria.*

BRITISH CAREER: (2003) Swindon (CL), Armadale (CT); (2004) Newcastle (CL), Mildenhall.

RUUD, David *b. 21 January 1980, Gislaved, Sweden.*

BRITISH CAREER: (2001) Poole; (2003) Poole, Arena-Essex; (2004) Swindon.

RYMEL, Adrian *b. 30 October 1975, Koprivnice, Czech Republic.*

BRITISH CAREER: (2001-03) Berwick; (2004) Berwick, Peterborough.

SANCHEZ, Emiliano *b. 9 December 1977, Buenos Aires, Argentina.*

BRITISH CAREER: (1999-01) Glasgow; (2002-03) Trelawny; (2004) Hull, Peterborough.

SCARBORO, Ricky *b. 31 July 1966, Grunby, Lincolnshire.*

BRITISH CAREER: (1999) Mildenhall, King's Lynn (CL); (2000) Boston; (2001) Boston, Newport (PL); (2002) Boston, King's Lynn (CL); (2003) Oxford (CL & BLC), Stoke (CT), Newport (PL); (2004) Oxford (CL), Coventry (CT).

SCHLEIN, Rory *b. 1 September 1984, Darwin, Northern Territory, Australia.*

BRITISH CAREER: (2001) Edinburgh, Berwick, Glasgow, Newport, Sheffield (CL & PL), Trelawny, Newcastle; (2002) Edinburgh, Sheffield (CL); (2003-04) Edinburgh, Belle Vue.

SCHOTT, Frede *b. 28 December 1970, Kolding, Denmark.*

BRITISH CAREER: (1990) Edinburgh; (1991) Edinburgh, Berwick; (1992-96) Belle Vue; (2002-04) Edinburgh.

SCHRAMM, Chris *b. 30 May 1984, Maldon, Essex.*

BRITISH CAREER: (2000) Peterborough (CL), Berwick, Arena-Essex; (2001) Peterborough (EL & CL), Isle of Wight, Reading; (2002) Reading, Peterborough (CL); (2003) Newport (PL), Wimbledon (CT), Peterborough (CL), Oxford (CL); (2004) Reading, Oxford (CL).

SCOTT, Blair *b. 14 May 1980, Edinburgh, Scotland.*

BRITISH CAREER: (1996) Linlithgow, Scottish Monarchs; (1997) Edinburgh, Lathallan; (1998-01) Edinburgh; (2002) Edinburgh, Belle Vue, Workington; (2003) Workington; (2004) Armadale, Berwick.

SCREEN, Joe *b. 27 November 1972, Chesterfield, Derbyshire.*

BRITISH CAREER: (1989-93) Belle Vue; (1994-97) Bradford; (1998) Belle Vue; (1999) Hull; (2000-02) Eastbourne; (2003) Eastbourne, Belle Vue; (2004) Belle Vue.

SHARPLES, Paul *b. 25 April 1974, Manchester, Greater Manchester.*

BRITISH CAREER: (2002) Belle Vue; (2003) Buxton; (2004) Buxton, Newcastle (CL).

SHIELD, Carl *b. 27 June 1979, Bishop Auckland, County Durham.*

BRITISH CAREER: (2002) Newcastle (CL), Sheffield (PLKOC); (2003) Berwick, Newcastle (CL), Armadale (CT), Edinburgh; (2004) Berwick (PT), Edinburgh (PT), Armadale, Sheffield (CT).

SHIELDS, Adam *b. 8 February 1977, Kurri-Kurri, New South Wales, Australia.*

BRITISH CAREER: (2000-02) Isle of Wight; (2003) Isle of Wight, Eastbourne; (2004) Eastbourne.

SIMMONS, Nick *b. 24 July 1981, Leamington Spa, Warwickshire.*

BRITISH CAREER: (1997) Shuttle Cubs, Ryde; (1998) Newport (CL & PL), Isle of Wight, Exeter; (1999) Isle of Wight, Stoke, Newport (CL); (2000) Arena-Essex; (2001) Newport (PL & CL), Somerset; (2002) Isle of Wight; (2003) Stoke, Reading, Mildenhall, Workington, King's Lynn, Exeter; (2004) Exeter, Weymouth.

SIMMONDS, Mark *b. 10 May 1971, Truro, Cornwall.*

BRITISH CAREER: (1989-96) Exeter; (1997) Isle of Wight; (1998-04) Exeter.

SKORNICKI, Adam *b. 22 October 1976, Wolsztyn, Poland.*

BRITISH CAREER: (2000-04) Wolverhampton.

SLEDZ, Dariusz *b. 15 September 1969, Lublin, Poland.*

BRITISH CAREER: (2004) Peterborough.

SMART, Lee *b. 5 April 1988, Swindon, Wiltshire.*

BRITISH CAREER: (2003) Swindon (CL), Stoke (CT); (2004) Mildenhall, Somerset.

SMETHILLS, Lee *b. 30 March 1982, Bolton, Greater Manchester.*

BRITISH CAREER: (1998) Mildenhall; (1999) Workington, Rye House, Buxton, Belle Vue, Newcastle; (2000) Workington, Buxton; (2001) Workington; (2002) Hull, Belle Vue; (2003) Exeter; (2004) Newcastle, Berwick.

SMITH, Andy *b. 25 May 1966, York, North Yorkshire.*

BRITISH CAREER: (1982-88) Belle Vue; (1989-90) Bradford; (1991) Swindon; (1992-95) Coventry; (1996) Bradford; (1997) Coventry; (1998) Belle Vue, Swindon; (1999-01) Belle Vue; (2003) Oxford (EL & CL); (2004) Swindon.

SMITH, Darren *b. 19 May 1981, Peterborough, Cambridgeshire.*

BRITISH CAREER: (1996) Mildenhall; (1997) Peterborough (AL); (1998) Skegness, Norfolk; (1999) Newcastle, Glasgow, Peterborough; (2001) Somerset, Boston; (2002) Boston, Wolverhampton (CL); (2003) Swindon (CL); (2004) Mildenhall.

SMITH, Jamie *b. 20 July 1983, Peterborough, Cambridgeshire.*

BRITISH CAREER: (1998) Norfolk; (1999) Eastbourne, Glasgow; (2000) Newcastle, Peterborough (CL), Hull, Somerset; (2001) Hull, Somerset; (2002) Hull; (2003) Swindon; (2004) Somerset, Coventry.

SMITH, Rob *b. 18 February 1988.*

BRITISH CAREER: (2004) Mildenhall.

SMITH, Scott *b. 4 February 1980, Brisbane, Queensland, Australia.*

BRITISH CAREER: (2001-02) Newport; (2003) Reading, Stoke; (2004) Newcastle.

SMOLINSKI, Martin *b. 6 December 1984, Grafelfing, Germany.*

BRITISH CAREER: (2004) Coventry.

SNEDDON, Derek *b. 27 July 1982, Falkirk, Scotland.*

BRITISH CAREER: (1998) Hull; (1999) Linlithgow, Isle of Wight; (2000) Ashfield, Edinburgh; (2001) Edinburgh, Glasgow; (2002) Newcastle; (2003) Edinburgh; (2004) Armadale.

SPEIGHT, David *b. 21 March 1980, Bradford, West Yorkshire.*

BRITISH CAREER: (2000) Owlerton; (2001) Sheffield (CL), Exeter, Stoke; (2002) Hull, Sheffield (CL), Wolverhampton (CT); (2003) Sheffield (CL), Coventry (BLC); (2004) Newcastle (CL), Sheffield (CT), Exeter (KOC), Stoke (CL).

STAECHMANN, Jan *b. 5 June 1966, Kolding, Denmark.*

BRITISH CAREER: (1985-90) Wolverhampton; (1991-94) Long Eaton; (1995-96) Hull; (1997) Peterborough; (1998-99) Oxford; (2000) Oxford, Belle Vue; (2001-02) Stoke; (2003) Stoke, Oxford; (2004) Stoke.

STANCL, George *b. 19 August 1975, Prague, Czech Republic.*
BRITISH CAREER: (1994-95) Sheffield; (1996-99) Wolverhampton; (2000) Coventry; (2002-04) Glasgow.

STEAD, Garry *b. 5 January 1972, Holmfirth, West Yorkshire.*
BRITISH CAREER: (1990-92) Stoke; (1993) Newcastle; (1994) Newcastle, Bradford; (1995) Bradford; (1996) Sheffield; (1997) Bradford; (1998) Wolverhampton; (1999-02) Hull; (2003) Hull, Eastbourne; (2004) Hull.

STEAD, Simon *b. 25 April 1982, Sheffield, South Yorkshire.*
BRITISH CAREER: (1997) Peterborough (AL); (1998) Peterborough (PL), Buxton; (1999-01) Sheffield; (2002) Sheffield, Peterborough; (2003-04) Workington, Wolverhampton.

STEPHENS, Seemond *b. 9 August 1967, St Austell, Cornwall.*
BRITISH CAREER: (1998) St Austell, Exeter, Sheffield, Swindon; (1999) Eastbourne, Swindon, St Austell; (2000-01) Exeter; (2002) Trelawny, Exeter; (2003) Exeter, Eastbourne; (2004) Exeter.

STEVENS, Jon *b. 3 January 1983, Croydon, Surrey.*
BRITISH CAREER: (2000) Rye House; (2001) Sheffield (CL); (2002) Wimbledon, Carmarthen; (2003-04) Wimbledon.

STODDART, Sean *b. 20 January 1987, Edinburgh, Scotland.*
BRITISH CAREER: (2003) Armadale, Trelawny (CT), Carmarthen (CT), Newcastle (CL); (2004) Armadale, Edinburgh.

STONEHEWER, Carl *b. 16 May 1972, Manchester, Greater Manchester.*
BRITISH CAREER: (1988-89) Belle Vue; (1990) Wolverhampton; (1991-93) Belle Vue; (1994) Peterborough; (1995-96) Long Eaton; (1997) Long Eaton, King's Lynn, Peterborough, Coventry, Eastbourne; (1998) Sheffield; (1999-02) Workington; (2003) Workington, Belle Vue; (2004) Workington.

SULLIVAN, Ryan *b. 20 January 1975, Melbourne, Victoria, Australia.*
BRITISH CAREER: (1994-97) Peterborough; (1998) Poole; (1999-03) Peterborough; (2004) Poole.

SVAB, Toni *b. 9 June 1974, Vlasim, Czech Republic.*
BRITISH CAREER: (1994-95) Exeter; (1996) Middlesbrough; (1997-00) Ipswich; (2001-02) Eastbourne; (2004) Belle Vue.

TACEY, Shaun *b. 27 November 1974, Norwich, Norfolk.*
BRITISH CAREER: (1992) Ipswich; (1993) Ipswich, Arena-Essex; (1994-96) Coventry; (1997) King's Lynn, Isle of Wight, Bradford, Coventry; (1998-00) Coventry; (2001-02) Arena-Essex; (2003) Hull; (2004) King's Lynn, Coventry.

TATUM, Kelvin MBE *b. 8 February 1964, Epsom, Surrey.*
BRITISH CAREER: (1983-84) Wimbledon; (1985-90) Coventry; (1991) Berwick; (1992-93) Bradford; (1994) Arena-Essex; (1995) Poole, Eastbourne; (1996) London; (1997) Belle Vue, Peterborough; (1998) Poole; (1999) Eastbourne; (2002-04) Arena-Essex.

THEOBALD, James *b. 31 December 1985, Ashford, Kent.*
BRITISH CAREER: (2002) Rye House (CL), Carmarthen; (2003) Rye House (CL), Mildenhall, Sheffield (CL), Newport (CL), Peterborough (CL); (2004) Sittingbourne (KOC), Wimbledon, King's Lynn (CLKOC).

THOMPSON, Mark *b. 8 July 1979, Orsett, Essex.*
BRITISH CAREER: (1996) Sittingbourne, Linlithgow, Mildenhall, Eastbourne (CL); (1997) Anglian Angels; (1998) Mildenhall, Newport, Stoke; (1999) King's Lynn (CL), Mildenhall, Newport (CL); (2000) St Austell; (2001) Peterborough (CL) & Exeter; (2002) King's Lynn (CL), Mildenhall, Arena-Essex, Workington, Stoke; (2003) Boston, Stoke (PL), Newport (BLC),

Somerset, Peterborough (BLC), Coventry (BLC), King's Lynn, Arena-Essex; (2004) Weymouth, Hull (PT), Swindon (CL), King's Lynn (CT), Sheffield (PL), Glasgow.

THORP, Paul *b. 9 September 1964, Macclesfield, Cheshire.*
BRITISH CAREER: (1980) Birmingham; (1981) Birmingham, Scunthorpe, Workington; (1982-83) Berwick, Birmingham; (1984-85) Stoke, Wolverhampton; (1986) Stoke, Sheffield, Belle Vue; (1987-88) Belle Vue; (1989-92) Bradford; (1993) Newcastle; (1994) Bradford; (1995-96) Hull; (1997) Belle Vue; (1998) Hull; (1999) Hull, Stoke; (2000-03) Hull; (2004) Hull, Belle Vue.

TOMICEK, Lubos *b. 14 March 1986, Prague, Czech Republic.*
BRITISH CAREER: (2003) Oxford (BLC); (2004) Newcastle.

TOPINKA, Tomas *b. 5 June 1974, Prague, Czech Republic.*
BRITISH CAREER: (1993-95) King's Lynn; (1996) Oxford; (1997-98) King's Lynn; (1999) Ipswich; (2001) Belle Vue; (2002) Coventry; (2003-04) King's Lynn.

TRESARRIEU, Sebastian *b. 10 January 1981, Cenon, France.*
BRITISH CAREER: (2001-03) Isle of Wight; (2004) Isle of Wight, Eastbourne.

TULLY, Andrew *b. 26 May 1987, Douglas, Isle of Man.*
BRITISH CAREER: (2003) Armadale (CT); (2004) Armadale, Edinburgh.

TUTTON, Matt *b. 19 June 1982, Newport, South Wales.*
BRITISH CAREER: (2000) Rye House; (2002) Swindon (CT), Wimbledon; (2003) Mildenhall, Buxton, Carmarthen (CT), Newport (CL); (2004) Newport (CL).

ULAMEK, Sebastian *b. 20 November 1975, Czestochowa, Poland.*
BRITISH CAREER: (2000) Wolverhampton; (2002) King's Lynn; (2003-04) Oxford.

WALASEK, Grzegorz *b. 29 August 1976, Krosno, Poland.*
BRITISH CAREER: (2000-02) Poole; (2004) Arena-Essex.

WALKER, Simon *b. 19 February 1980, Bristol, Avon.*
BRITISH CAREER: (2001) Newport (CL); (2002) Newport (CL), Arena-Essex, Swindon (CT), Trelawny; (2003) Swindon (CL), Trelawny (CT), Reading, Somerset, Poole (BLC), Exeter (BLC), Newport; (2004) Somerset, Swindon (CL), King's Lynn (CT).

WARWICK, Carl *b. 7 October 1981, Poole, Dorset.*
BRITISH CAREER: (2002-03) Newport (CL); (2004) Weymouth.

WARWICK, Danny *b. 21 November 1983, Poole, Dorset.*
BRITISH CAREER: (2002) Newport (CL), Reading; (2003) Newport (CL & PL), Poole (BLC), Exeter; (2004) Weymouth, Swindon (CL), King's Lynn (CT).

WATSON, Craig *b. 6 August 1976, Sydney, New South Wales, Australia.*
BRITISH CAREER: (1997-99) Newport; (2000-01) Poole; (2002) Newport; (2003) Newport, Belle Vue; (2004) Newport.

WATT, Davey *b. 6 January 1978, Townsville, Queensland, Australia.*
BRITISH CAREER: (2001) Isle of Wight; (2002) Newcastle; (2003) King's Lynn, Poole; (2004) Rye House, Poole, Eastbourne.

WEBSTER, Tim *b. 26 May 1989, Walsall, West Midlands.*
BRITISH CAREER: (2004) King's Lynn (CT).

WERNER, Brent *b. 15 April 1974, Los Angeles, California, USA.*
BRITISH CAREER: (1995-97) Long Eaton; (1998) Newcastle; (1999-00) Workington; (2001) Eastbourne; (2002) Rye House; (2003) Rye House, Peterborough; (2004) Rye House.

WESTACOTT, Jamie *b. 9 April 1988, Newport, South Wales.*
BRITISH CAREER: (2003) Newport (CL); (2004) Newport (CL), Isle of Wight (PT), Reading.

WETHERS, Matthew *b. 30 May 1985, Modbury, South Australia.*
BRITISH CAREER: (2003) Armadale (CT), Wolverhampton (CL), Edinburgh; (2004) Edinburgh, Armadale.

WHITE, Karl *b. 1 December 1987, Thurrock, Essex.*
BRITISH CAREER: (2004) Rye House (CL).

WILDING, Rhys *b. 6 July 1982, Ipswich, Suffolk.*
BRITISH CAREER: (2003) Armadale (CT), Mildenhall; (2004) Weymouth.

WILKINSON, Carl *b. 16 May 1981, Boston, Lincolnshire.*
BRITISH CAREER: (1997) Peterborough (AL); (1998) Norfolk; (1999) King's Lynn (CL); (2000) Boston, Newcastle, Glasgow; (2001) Boston, Newport (PL); (2002-03) Newport (PL & CL); (2004) Newport.

WILSON, Ben *b. 15 March 1986, Sheffield, South Yorkshire.*
BRITISH CAREER: (2001) Sheffield (CL); (2002) Sheffield (CL & PL), Glasgow; (2003) Sheffield (PL & CL) & Buxton (CT); (2004) Sheffield (PL & CT), Carmarthen (CL).

WILSON, Dean *b. 19 January 1988.*
BRITISH CAREER: (2004) Weymouth, King's Lynn (CT).

WILSON, Sean *b. 7 November 1969, York, North Yorkshire.*
BRITISH CAREER: (1986-88) Sheffield; (1989) Coventry; (1990) Coventry, King's Lynn; (1991-93) Bradford; (1995-96) Bradford; (1997) Coventry; (1998) Belle Vue; (1999-04) Sheffield.

WOODIFIELD, Brett *b. 15 March 1976, Gawler, South Australia.*
BRITISH CAREER: (1997) Skegness, Isle of Wight, Peterborough; (1998) Peterborough; (1999) Ipswich; (2000) Peterborough; (2001) Trelawny; (2003) Rye House; (2004) Workington.

WOODWARD, Cameron *b. 8 January 1985, Mildura, Victoria, Australia.*
BRITISH CAREER: (2003) Poole (BLC); (2004) Edinburgh.

WOODS, Mark *b. 30 January 1967, Melton, Woodbridge, Suffolk.*
BRITISH CAREER: (2004) Oxford (CL).

WRIGHT, Charles *b. 26 October 1988, Stockport, Cheshire.*
BRITISH CAREER: (2004) Buxton.

WRIGHT, James *b. 13 June 1986, Stockport, Cheshire.*
BRITISH CAREER: (2002) Buxton; (2003) Buxton, Belle Vue (BLC), Newcastle (PL), Stoke (PL), Workington, Hull, King's Lynn; (2004) Workington, Buxton.

WRIGHT, Matthew *b. 19 November 1985, Harlow, Essex.*
BRITISH CAREER: (2002) Boston, Mildenhall, Carmarthen, Wimbledon; (2003) Mildenhall, Ipswich (BLC), King's Lynn (KOC), Arena-Essex (BLC), Reading, Peterborough (BLC); (2004) Ipswich, Wimbledon.

YARROW, Bryan *b. 3 September 1984, Vallejo, California, USA.*
BRITISH CAREER: (2004) Coventry.

ZAGAR, Matej *b. 3 April 1983, Ljubljana, Slovenia.*
BRITISH CAREER: (2003) Trelawny; (2004) Reading.

ZETTERSTROM, Magnus *b. 9 December 1971, Eskilstuna, Sweden.*
BRITISH CAREER: (1996) Poole; (1998-99) Poole; (2000) Peterborough; (2001) Poole; (2002) Poole, Peterborough; (2003) Poole (BLC); (2004) Poole.

Other speedway titles published by Tempus

Homes of British Speedway

ROBERT BAMFORD & JOHN JARVIS

Having arrived in Britain in the late 1920s, dirt-track racing soon established itself as an incredibly popular sport. By the end of 1928 there were over fifty tracks in Britain and in the seven decades since then the sport has taken place at numerous locations throughout the country. Featuring over 300 venues, with statistical information and photographs, this comprehensive work is the definitive guide to the homes of British Speedway.

0 7524 2210 3

A History of the World Speedway Championship

ROBERT BAMFORD & GLYNN SHAILES

The definitive history of the major individual tournament in speedway. From the early days of the World Championship before the war to the modern Grand Prix, every race and all of the great riders are included.

0 7524 2402 5

No Bull The Authorised Biography of Billy Hamill

BRIAN BURFORD & BILLY HAMILL

When Billy Hamill embarked on a career in speedway as a wild junior, a future as an international star was a pipe dream. But in 1996, the man they call 'the Bullet' became the fourth American to win the sport's top individual prize. *No Bull* is his compelling biography, in which Billy gives his frank, honest and sometimes heart-breaking views of a career that saw him compete at the highest level for over a century.

0 7524 3219 2

Breaking the Limits Sam Ermolenko

BRIAN BURFORD & SAM ERMOLENKO

After a horrific road accident in his native California left him virtually unable to walk, it took Sam Ermolenko an awful lot of bravery and determination to make a recovery – let alone become Speedway World Champion! Despite a late start in the sport and a further series of severe injuries, Sam has overcome all the odds and reached the very top. This is his remarkable story.

0 7524 3225 7

If you are interested in purchasing other books published by Tempus, or in case you have difficulty finding any Tempus books in your local bookshop, you can also place orders directly through our website

www.tempus-publishing.com